Endorsement from:

Tom Owen
Archivist for Regional History Archives and Special Collections,
University of Louisville

"Letters writing both reveals and conceals. This extensive Rawert family correspondence between a Louisville Schnitzelburg family and a youthful soldier son headed to the European front during WWII is deceivingly chatty and routine about household, neighborhood and Army camp things. Between the lines however there's hand-wringing over the son's vulnerability to the horrors of the battlefield and the glossing of the mother's journey toward death. This lovingly prepared volume, part of a daughter's search for understanding of her troubled Father, is both a chronicle of Louisville in wartime and the story of war's effect on family members of German decent on opposite sides of the battlefield."

WW II Letters of Norbert A. Rawert,
US Army, and Family

As Always, Norb

Carol Rawert Trainer

Dear Roberto,
I'm so glad we became
kindred spirits via 'Be the
change' bookclub. Wishing
you lots of love + blessings!
♡ Carol
11-11-21

iUniverse®

AS ALWAYS, NORB
WW II LETTERS OF NORBERT A. RAWERT, US ARMY, AND FAMILY

iUniverse books may be ordered through booksellers or by contacting:

iUniverse
1663 Liberty Drive
Bloomington, IN 47403
www.iuniverse.com
1-800-Authors (1-800-288-4677)

ISBN: 978-1-5320-2299-9 (sc)
ISBN: 978-1-5320-2300-2 (e)

Library of Congress Control Number: 2017906794

Print information available on the last page.

iUniverse rev. date: 06/30/2017

Private Norbert A. Rawert, US Army, October 1942

Dedication

I dedicate this book to the memory of my father Norbert Anthony Rawert who enlisted in the US Army in 1941. His military service in WW II, specifically in the Battle of Normandy and on the Western Front, affected him the rest of his life. The memories of the war that my dad dealt with daily also affected my family and me.

I dedicate it to my mother Alma Lee (Pierce) who stood by my father as his girlfriend through the war years and as his wife from June 1946 until Norb's death in May 1988. As a child and young adult, I did not understand the difficulties she may have had in dealing with some of the lingering WW II caused issues that affected my father.

I dedicate it to my husband, Harold Trainer, who has been supportive of this at times overwhelming task. He encouraged me to continue and he has served as a reviewer and contributor. He helped plan memorial trips to France, Belgium and Germany to trace my dad's footsteps through those countries that he passed through during the war.

Lastly, I dedicate it to my family, especially my daughters Kristianne Trainer Welsh and Natasha Trainer Matt, and grandchildren Dillon Welsh, Aidon Welsh, Taya Matt and Makenzie Matt. I wrote it for them so that they will know about their heritage and the great sacrifice made by their grandfather and great-grandfather.

Contents

Foreword xi

Preface xv

Acknowledgment xvii

Introduction 1

    Rawert Family In Louisville, Kentucky, 1942-1945 1

    Norb's Family 4

    Duty Calls Norb 7

    Time Line of Norb's Assignments and Posts And HQ Co. 59th Signal

        Battalion Action in WW II 9

    The 59th Signal Battalion in WW II..13

    German Cousins Serve in Hitler's Third Reich..17

Chapter 1: 1942 19

Chapter 2: 1943 173

Chapter 3: 1944 375

Epilogue 465

Bibliography...471

Index 473

Photos and Images

Rawert Family at 1344 Texas Street... 5

Rawert Family, August 16, 1942 6

The Rawert Family Visits Fort Benjamin Harrison, Indiana, August 23, 1942............... 22

Norb on platform at Fort. Benjamin Harrison, IN, August 23, 1942 23

Southwestern Bell Certificate of Course Completion 167

Norb in overcoat at Camp Crowder, Missouri, January 1943............................183

Norb Playing 'Cool' at Ft. Jackson, June 18, 1943 285

Norb at home on furlough for his 23rd birthday, August 17, 1943 313

HDQ Company 59th Signal Battalion Class Photo, Camp Crowder, January 11, 1944 ... 382

Enlisted Record and Report of Separation, side A 467

Enlisted Record and Report of Separation, side A 468

Award of Disability or Pension Form 469

"Don't Quit" Poem 470

Resting Place at Zachery Taylor National Cemetery.......................................470

Carol and Harold Trainer at Normandy American Cemetery, FR, March 8, 2012 470

Foreword

By Harold A. Trainer, Maj., USAF, Retired

World War II produced the Greatest Generation. Many millions of Americans joined the war effort both as civilians and as members of the Armed Forces. Millions of the Armed Forces deployed to combat zones where they fought for our freedom against the Axis Powers of Germany, Japan and Italy in Africa, Europe and in the Pacific. So many of these young military men and women were casualties of the war. Some did not come back and they were buried in places like Normandy, France, The Netherlands, and the Philippines. Some went missing and were never to be found. Many came back without their health, hosting serious injuries - emotional, mental and physical. A lot of them became forever different from whom they were when they were young men and women civilians enjoying America. A large number of these Americans were of German heritage and fought in Europe against their own family relatives.

One young man, Norbert Anthony Rawert, twenty-two years old on the day he joined the Army, a St. X High School graduate and a fun filled person from the Schnitzelburg/ Germantown part of Louisville, Kentucky was a part of this Greatest Generation. After joining the Army in 1942, he was assigned to basic training and technical training as a Signal Corps telephone technician. He was then sent to Ft. Jackson, South Carolina and assigned to the 59th Signal Corps where he trained and prepared for the invasion of Europe and the fight to end the war. He landed in Normandy at Utah Beach shortly after D Day and became part of Operation Cobra, the allied effort to rid Europe of Hitler and his control of Europe.

In January 1944, he deployed with the HQ 59th Signal Battalion (BN) to England where he continued training and preparations for the invasion. The mission of the 59th Signal Corps was to provide communications support for the Army VIII Corps, communications that would allow command, control and air support for the movement of vast numbers of American military in ways that were critical to defeating the German forces in France, Belgium and Germany. Norb fought from the June landings at Utah Beach through France and into Belgium under very difficult and terrible conditions of war (little sleep, rain, cold, illness) and always facing enemy fire and danger, often witnessing horrific scenes of war.

The VIII Corps under Maj. General Troy Middleton was assigned to the First Army and moved west across the Cotentin Peninsula to face the German Line near St. Sauveur along the Douve River. The shelling here was intense and there was often close combat and many snipers. The stalemate here lasted until July 24. Some of First Army headed north to take Cherbourg a major German stronghold and port. On July 24, after Cherbourg fell, Norb and the 59th Signal Corps headed south towards Coutances as part of the Operation Cobra Breakthrough, a major and key battle. Ernie Pyle was in the area from which he wrote about the war and our soldiers. After the breakout through the German lines the VIII Corps and Norb's HQ 59th Signal Battalion continued to move south through Coutances, Granville and Avranches which is very close to the famous Mont Saint-Michel, a large and impressive castle that dates back to the Middle Ages.

Around August 1 and after the Operation Cobra Breakthrough, the VIII Corps transferred to the Third Army under Patton until on September 4 they transferred to the Ninth Army. The Ninth Army was split with some of it moving west to Brest where they lay siege to this important port until it fell in September. Sometime in September Norb's unit moved east and north to Belgium where some of the worst fighting of the war took place including the Hurtgen Forest and Battle of the Bulge. In October, somewhere on the Belgium Front, he became ill and was evacuated to France then England and then back to the US and finally to the Wakeman General and Convalescent Hospital at Camp Atterbury, Indiana, where he was honorably discharged in January 1945. He left as a combat veteran to face the many demands of war and the transition into civilian life.

Norb's family in Schnitzelburg had always been close to their German heritage and family. The family had originally emigrated from Germany in the mid-19th century for political, religious and economic reasons. Their family home was around Wessum, Germany, close to The Netherlands in northwest Germany. They were mostly farmers who worked and lived on farms. The German family were still suffering from the effects of WW I, i.e., hunger, unemployment and extreme difficulties. The Schnitzelburg family corresponded and sent care packages of food and clothing to the family in Germany. When America and its allies joined the war against Germany this family relationship made his involvement particularly emotional and significant for them.

Norb spent about two and a half years in the military, six months under difficult combat conditions. Thankfully, the letters of correspondence between Norb and his family were preserved for future generations. They give an interesting and revealing account of one soldier in the military during the war and during tough and deadly combat operations in Europe. They also provided an interesting account of his family and friends on the home front.

Norb, after honorable discharge and recognition as a veteran of WW II, made the difficult transition into civilian life. He married Alma Pierce and raised a family of three children. The eldest, Carol, who is a Viet Nam War era veteran, had been interested in her family's history and genealogy especially her dad's service during the war. Shortly after Norb's death in April 1988, Carol discovered that her brother, Norbert Rawert, Jr., was in possession of the WW II letters of Norbert Rawert and his family. She became determined to read these letters and to learn about her dad's service and write a documentary of her dad's war experiences. Her dad, as many combat veterans do, suffered from a form of

Post-Traumatic Stress Disorder (PTSD). It sometimes manifested itself in negative outcomes such as drinking, smoking, obesity, serious health problems, emotional and psychological challenges. It made life challenging for the family and Carol during her youth. However, her dad's natural kindness, progressiveness and willingness to make life good and happy for his family and himself helped to mitigate the problem. As time went on, her dad became an avid reader and student of history and the world and developed a formidable knowledge base and world view from which he could view his difficult combat experiences and understand his post traumatic syndrome disorder. He used this view to mitigate the potential of a challenging emotional war experience.

Carol used the letters and other genealogical and historical information to learn about her family history both in America and in Germany. She used this information to develop a relationship with her family's German family and in 2000, she and her husband Harold made a first trip to Ahaus, Germany the area from which her American family had emigrated and from which a number of them became members of the German Army during the war. One of these became especially close to Carol. His name was Josef Effkemann, a German soldier of WW II who fought throughout Europe and was wounded several times and captured by the British not in addition, far from where Norb fought. Through Josef and his family and a loyal distant cousin and local area historian, Alfons Effkemann, the American and German relationship flourished and matured and there have been half dozen trips to Germany over the years. On a recent visit we sat around the table and talked, laughed, drank beer and wondered about it all and who we are and why and how this all happened. A member of the family showed us a picture of himself when he was young laying flowers on the graves at the German Cemetery in Normandy. We were leaving for Normandy and the American Cemetery the next day. It was a truly meaningful and thoughtful time. World War II was probably necessary and the Normandy battlefield, cemeteries and our visits to Germany are a somber reminder of the costs of war on all sides including the experiences of Norbert Anthony Rawert from Schnitzelburg.

Preface

WW II affected everyone in the United States one way or the other. My father Norbert Rawert, Sr. served in the US Army as a Tech 5 in the HQ 59th Signal Battalion, which landed on the beach at Normandy about a week after the D Day Invasion on June 6, 1944. In addition to living through the war, the war lived through him for the rest of his life. His great sacrifice inspired me to compile a book of his and his family's saved correspondence during the years 1942 to 1945.

This has been a labor of love spanning fourteen years of research, book preparation, mastering ongoing technology changes in data processing software, printers and scanners and incessant technical problems. It is the story of a German-American family from Schnitzelburg in Louisville, Kentucky and of their love, faith and hope during a time of world war. The book offers a good understanding of what everyday life was like during the war, and how the war affected families. As I wrote the book, I felt the presence of my dad's family, now deceased, all around me and encouraging me to go on. I could envision being in the room with them as they wrote the original letters 74 years ago. They came to life again and I did not want this snapshot of history to be forgotten. The Rawert family were funny, sarcastic, strong minded and opinionated and very close. They were also faced with a war against their country of origin and some German family members with whom they remained in contact until the war began.

Age has stained, yellowed and cracked the letters. In addition to newspaper clippings inserted into the envelopes causing discoloration, the repeated sharing of the letters caused them much wear and tear. I present them as closely as possible to the way in which they were written, including some spelling and grammatical errors written on purpose for effect or as a joke. Many of the letter writers did not use correct punctuation, e.g., periods at the ends of sentences, so for the sake of readability I added periods and punctuation as needed for readability. I arranged the letters chronologically by dates that they were written, not by the dates they were received. To appreciate the letters, it helps to have an understanding of the personalities of the family members and their sarcastic and argumentative personalities, so occasionally, for clarity, I have added my comments within the letters in italics and square brackets, e.g., [*comments*]. In addition, the most often used names (Norb, Hermina, etc.) were not indexed on all occasions of appearance since it would lead to a very large and less than useful index.

Toward the end of 1944 and the beginning of 1945, the mail was often lost and sporadic. Such was the case with this family's correspondence. Postal delays or Norb's address changes oftentimes held up letter delivery, so at times it may seem the conversation does not flow evenly. The time between writing and mailing a letter and a person receiving it could be from three days to two months (late 1944) or more. During WW II, as in previous wars, unit officers censored the enlisted man's letters. The censors did not want the soldiers to say anything that would have been of value to the enemy, such as their location. They wanted to camouflage the troop strength. We have all heard the phrase, "Loose lips sink ships." The censoring officers were also trying to determine weakening of desire and morale among troops. In WW II, important information was actually cut out of the letters. Oftentimes the soldier would write that he couldn't say much or the censors would cut it out. Several lines were cut out of Norb's letters but I was never sure if it was from the censors or from his mother who did not appreciate his GI language. Early in WW II, the soldiers could not say where they were, even if they were in the Atlantic or Pacific Theaters. Later in the war as in Dad's case, he would write, "Somewhere in France," etc. This practice of censorship affected what the soldiers would write about so most of the letters were just about Mom and Pop stuff and did not give much detail about the war. They wanted to avoid the chance that their letters would be delayed or maybe not even delivered at all. Letters were kept mostly lighthearted so as not to demoralize Norb as he was serving. At times, I could tell what was going on by what he was not saying. In addition, towards the end of 1944, many letters were unfortunately missing and probably had to be left behind on the western Front when Norb was evacuated to a hospital.

It is through these letters to and from the small, predominately working class German neighborhood of Schnitzelburg came the names and places so familiar to the history of the most terrible war the world had known. They included Ardennes, Normandy; Utah Beach; Omaha Beach; Cotentin Peninsula; Bastogne; St. Lô; Bayeux; Caen; Cherbourg; Operation Overlord; Operation Cobra; Eisenhower; Patton; English Channel; Hitler; Brest; Paris; Belgium; President Roosevelt; Prime Minister Churchill; Battle of the Bulge; Schnee Eifel Forrest and more.

These names and places greatly affected the Rawert family and many others as they affected their sons and daughters in the armed forces fighting in defense of their country. These names and places were responsible for the concern, worry, deaths and wounding of young men and women fighting in Europe to protect their homeland from the ravages of Hitler and his Nazi Army. Some of these men and women never made it home, some would never be found, and most were changed forever mentally, emotionally and physically.

Carol Rawert Trainer

Acknowledgment

I would like to thank the following:

Earl Zortman (Lt. Col., US Army, retired 2013) for his research and writing of the history of the 59th Signal Battalion's role in WW II.

Josef Effkemann, my German 2nd cousin twice removed (a German veteran of WW II), for his efforts to contact the American branch of his family, the Effkemann/Heitkemper family. His memoire and family history *Die Effkemanns* was very helpful in putting together my family history.

Alfons Effkemann, a distant cousin and published local area historian from the Heek/Ahle area of Westphalia, Germany. I am so indebted to him and his dedicated research into my family heritage.

Norbert Rawert, Jr., my brother, for loaning me his letter collection for so many years. I kept thinking it would be done each year (and he never failed to remind me) but it has been a long process spanning over 14 years.

Panera Bread at Springhurst, especially Joanie Brenzel and Andrea May for their smiling and caring service and for keeping me nourished through this big adventure. Also a big thanks to Starbucks Coffee at the Paddocks where I frequented in the early days of the book.

And most of all, I want to thank my husband Harold Trainer. His ideas, input and encouragement to continue on to the finish helped me get the book to the publisher when at times it seemed like an impossible task. Without him, the book may not have happened.

It has been a labor of love.

Introduction

Rawert Family In Louisville, Kentucky, 1942-1945

Norb was born on August 17, 1920 to Herman ("Pop") and Catherine aka Wolskerman Rawert, both of German origin. He was the youngest of eight siblings. Because his mother was age 46 when he was born, he said he always felt like they were his grandparents instead of his parents. His older sisters doted on him and spoiled him. He was raised a happy and fun loving child, if not a bit spoiled and coddled by his older sisters.

Norb lived at 1137 Mulberry Street in the Schnitzelburg section of Louisville for the first 10 years of his life. Then around 1930, the family moved next door to a new home on the adjoining lot at 1344 Texas Street that Pop built for about $4,925. Their home was the center of family life and always lovingly referred to as "in home." Norb's dad and mom, his older unmarried sisters Margaret and Hermina all lived there. Norb's brother Joe and his wife Ann (Smith) lived at the old home at 1137 Mulberry at the time. His older sister Elizabeth lived a few blocks away at 834 Mulberry Street with her husband Leo J. Muth and their children: Shirley, Milton, Jimmy, Betsy, Katsy and Margie. His sister Joey was married to Lee Carter who was part American Indian and referred to as "Wahoo." He often made life miserable for Joey due to his alcoholism and fiery temper. Because of this, the family did not regard him well and some even feared him. Whenever the Muth kids would write to Norb, they would say they were "in home," or at "Mommy's," all referring to 1344 Texas Street. His brother John and wife Eleanor (Smith, Ann's sister), and family (Jack, Hilary, Vernon, Peggy and Norbert) lived in Plainview, on the outskirts of the city of Louisville at that time.

Norb's father was retired from Adler Piano Company where he was a craftsman of piano cabinets. In 1942 at age 71, he worked as a janitor and maintenance man for St. Brigid Catholic Church and School on Hepburn Avenue in Louisville. Herman, of strong German stock and work ethic, worked hard and long and watched his money carefully. He owned several properties and home rentals in Louisville.

Norb's mother Catherine was ill and battling diabetes, arthritis, cataracts and cancer among other illnesses. She was an extremely religious and devout Catholic and in most of her letters to Norb, she begged and reminded him to do his duty and go to the Sacraments. She was so fearful that he would be killed in the war without receiving the Sacraments. Norb mostly would ignore her questions. She loved her baby very much. Norb stayed out until early hours drinking, getting in arguments with his parents when he got home, sometimes in time for breakfast, which his mom made in the wee hours of the morning and referred to in letters as the second breakfast.

Many of the women family members worked as seamstresses in the drapery department at Hubbuch's Interiors of Louisville. Among them were Norb's sisters, Margaret (supervisor), Joey, and occasionally Hermina. In the evening and on weekends they also did work from their basement, which was set up for large-scale drapery production. One of the Hubbuch drivers would deliver the material to them and pick up the finished product. Norb's sister Elizabeth was a homemaker and her husband Leo J. (aka Moody).worked in the Muth's Candy Store owned by his brother Rudy. Norb's brother Joe was a painter and paperhanger for John Sabel Interiors and his wife Ann worked with Norb's sisters at Hubbuch Interiors. His brother John was a milk deliveryman for the local Plainview Dairy and his wife Eleanor was a homemaker.

Many letters refer to beer, in particularly Oertel's '92, a local brewery. The Rawert men, as were other men of the era and area, were heavy drinkers. Local taverns mentioned in the letter (Huelsman's) were only a short walk away using the alley that ran behind their house. Later in life, Norb always said that when he finally had to stop drinking beer due to serious health problems, that Oertel's went out of business. As a young child in the 1950's I remember holding my Poppy's hand and walking down the alley next to the house on our way to Huelsman's to fill his blue and white speckled porcelain pail with a growler of beer.

Norb attended grade school at St. Elizabeth of Hungary on Burnett Avenue, a short walk from home. A report card from the second grade showed him to be a good student with averages in all classes between 85-95 %. Norb attended St. Xavier (Saint X) High School in Louisville, where he worked his way through school by playing the clarinet. In 2015 Norb's great grandson Aidon Welsh, whom he never got to meet, took up the clarinet in honor of his great grandfather. Norb loved music throughout his life, especially music from the big band era. After he graduated in 1938, he worked at Park and Tilford Distillery (bourbon whiskey) in Louisville. He left work to enlist in the US Army on August 4, 1942 right before his 22nd birthday. He told his friend Randall Wise that he may have to go and kill some of his cousins in Germany. Little did he know that many years later I would meet these cousins face to face and learn of our family connection and involvement in WW II. As a young man, Norb was cocky but by the end of the war the cockiness had been knocked out of him, leaving him physically and mentally drained. His niece Shirley said that he was always so funny and happy before he left for the war. She asked her mom Elizabeth why he had changed so much and her mom told her that war does that to people. She also said that at some time while on the European front Norb was supposed to go on guard duty but a buddy filled in for him. While on guard duty, a German sniper killed him. This affected Norb greatly as did the brutality of the war itself and he often had nightmares.

Norb was very close to his family and mostly to his sister Hermina who dutifully wrote to him almost every day. His family was very concerned about him during the war. It was very hard on his elderly mother whose serious illness was kept secret from Norb for fear of disturbing him while he was at war. She held on to life always wanting to see her youngest child before she died. She got her wish and died a few days after Norb finally made it home to see her.

Before and after WW II, Norb's family had corresponded with their Effkemann family who changed their names to the Low Dutch or Plattdeutsch name of Heitkemper when they emigrated from Germany. Norb's maternal and paternal grandparents emigrated from the same small farming area of Heek/Ahle and Wessum, near Ahaus in Westphalia, Germany to Louisville. The small farming villages and towns were very close to each other and it is probable that the families knew each other before immigrating to Louisville.

Henry Gerhardt Rawert was Norb's paternal grandfather. He emigrated at age twenty-five with his sister and brother on the *Admiral* in 1867. They traveled from their home in Heek/Ahle, Germany to Bremen, and on to Castle Garden in New York City and on to Louisville by unknown means. He married Marianne Adelheid Viefhues in Louisville on July 5, 1870 at St. Martin of Tours Catholic Church. Marianne emigrated at age 36 in 1870 on the ship "Leipzig" which traveled from Bremen, Germany to Baltimore and then on to Louisville via Cincinnati. Marianne emigrated with her sister Franziska, who married Marianne's husband's brother, Herman Heinrich. She was 37 when she was married which was very soon after arriving in Louisville. Her first son Herman, Norb's father, was born about 8 months after her marriage.

John Herman Theodore Wolskerman was Norb's maternal grandfather. He emigrated in 1869 at age 27 from Ahaus/Heek area of Westphalia. He worked on the farms of the Haus Horst, which the author and her husband visited in 2000. He married Anna Margaretha Heitkemper (aka Effkemann) in Louisville on June 26 at St. Martin's Catholic Church. She left Germany with several brothers and sisters to make her way to new opportunity in America after her dad died and the oldest brother inherited the farm. She emigrated in 1864 at age 27. He was known to be a practicing Catholic and very religious man which affected the beliefs of Norb's mom.

In October 2000, during our first trip to Ahaus, Germany, my husband Harold and I met her large and gracious family, the Effkemanns. We stayed at the home of my second cousin twice-removed Josef Effkemann and his wife Josefa (now deceased). Josef had written to my 94-year-old cousin, Wilhelmina Heitkemper, trying to locate the family of his parents who had immigrated to the USA after Josef's grandfather died and left the farm to the oldest brother. Josef and a couple of his brothers also served in the German military in WW II. From the first hello and hug, it was as if we had always known each other. Over the ages, our hearts were still close together. It was a fairytale-like trip and the stuff of which dreams are made. Not only did we meet his family, but also he introduced us to a distant cousin Alfons Effkemann (published local area historian) and his wife Maria. The family treated us like royalty and they carefully planned each of the seven days for family research and enjoyment. It was an emotional time and amazing to reconnect with family after being separated for over 140 years. It was important to me to the testimonial of Cousin Josef Effkemann about his service and experience in WW II in order to get a view of the family on both sides of the war.

Norb's Family

Parents

Herman H. (aka Herm, Pop, Poppy) Rawert
Catherine (aka Katie, Kate, Mommy) Wolskerman Rawert

Siblings

1. Henry John, was born on June 18, 1898 and died on September 11, 1922 at age 24 in a motorcycle accident when Norb was two.
2. Margaret (Ma, Marge Marg), was born on September 8, 1899, unmarried; was Supervisor at Hubbuch Company's sewing room.
3. Josephine (Joey), was born Dec 7, 1901, She married Lee (Wahoo) Carter and had a stepson Dewey). She worked as a seamstress at Hubbuch's making custom order drapes and upholstery goods. She retired in the 1980's as a seamstress in the interior decorating department of Sears and Roebucks. She also worked from home making interior goods for local interior decorators.
4. John (Johnny, Johnny), was born on October 17, 1911. He married Eleanor Smith. Children were Jack, Hilary, Peggy, Vernon, Norbert (Norby) and Nancy (born after 1945). Worked as a deliveryman at Plainview Dairy.
5. Elizabeth, (Lip), was born on January 28, 1905. She married Leo (Moody, Muthy) Muth and their children were Shirley, Milton, Catherine (Katsy), Jim (Jimmy), Betsy (Bets) and Margie. They lived a few blocks away at 834 Mulberry Street.
6. Hermina (Meanie, Horse, Hog, H.R., Porky), was born on January 18, 1909. She had epilepsy, low thyroid problems and obesity problems. She was very intelligent, observant, and well read. Her letters to Norb make the bulk of this letter collection. She got the nickname of 'Horse" from her large laugh. She was always self deprecating about her size and beauty in these letters. She remained unmarried.
7. Joseph, was born December 16, 1913 and was married to Ann Smith). Their children were JoAnn, Kay and Bob. He worked as a painter and paperhanger for John Sabel Interiors.
8. Catherine (baby), was born on June 23, 1916. She died at age 2 ½ from Great Flu Epidemic of 1918.
9. Norb, was born on August 17, 1920, and married his girlfriend Alma Pierce in 1946. Their children were Carol Ann, born on March 22, 1947; Dolores, born on May 15, 1948; Norbert, Jr, born on May 11, 1950.

Rawert Family at 1344 Texas Street

August 16, 1942

Herman and Catherine
(Wolskerman) Rawert

The Rawert Family: L-R, Norbert, Josephine,
Joseph, Pop Herman, Margaret, Mommy
Catherine, Elizabeth, Hermina & John

Posing on front porch steps L-R:
Hermina Rawert, Joey (Carter),
Shirley Muth, Norb and Margaret

The Rawert Siblings. Top L-R: Joey
(Carter), John, Hermina, Margaret &
Norb. Bottom: Joe & Elizabeth.

Rawert Family, August 16, 1942

Rawert and Muth Cousins.
Row 1, L-R: Vernon, Hilary,
Peggy & Norb Rawert. Row
2: Betsy Katsy, Margie &
Shirley Muth. Row 3: Dewey
Carter, Milton & Jim Muth

Norb & Cousin Mary (or
Little Mary, Honeybunch)
Hollkamp, 8-16-42

The Leo J. and Elizabeth (Rawert) Muth Family:
Top row L-R: Jim, Shirley, Milton. Bottom: Katsy,
Leo (or Moody), Margie. Elizabeth & Betsy.

Duty Calls Norb

In 1942, Norbert Rawert most probably felt a call to duty in WW II as I, his daughter, did during the Vietnam War when I joined the USAF after high school in 1965. Randall Wise, a friend of Norb's, said that Norb left work at Park and Tilford Distillery in Louisville on August 4, 1942 and headed to the army recruiting station where he was inducted into the US Army on that day and entered active duty on August 18, 1942.

The first letter home from Norb was on August 20, 1942 from Co. F, Fort Harrison, Indiana. By August 25, Private First Class (1C) was in Company (Co.). E, 34th Battalion, SCRTC (possibly an acronym for South Central Rural Telephone Cooperative), Camp Crowder Missouri where he completed basic training on September 15.

He attended the Bell South Training School at the Mid-Western School at Camp Crowder, Missouri from September 23 to November 21, 1942 when he received a diploma for a 240-hour training course in Telephone Substation Installation and Maintenance at Southwestern Bell Telephone Company in Kansas City, Missouri. On November 23, Norb transferred from clerk duties to telephones. On November 24, Norb was assigned back to Headquarters Company (HQ. Co.), 59th Signal Battalion, Camp Crowder where he was a clerk in the 59th's motor depot where he tracked 126 Signal Corps trucks. He stated that he could have cross-trained to clerk if he wished. Later in the war, he did serve at times as clerk in the transportation section of HQ. Co. 59th Signal Battalion.

On February 4, 1943, Norb transferred to HQ Co. 59th Signal Battalion at Fort Jackson, South Carolina where he received a promotion to Corporal. On November 10, he earned an M-1 Sharpshooter award and medal. On November 10, after a month long maneuvers at Camp Forrest near Nashville, Tennessee, he also earned a Carbine Marksman medal. He was always a capable hunter.

According to his Enlistment Record and Report of Separation form and information from "1944 World War II Transportation Ship Crossings" as part of the 59th Signal Battalion Norb departed from New York, New York on January 29, 1944 on the British ship and troop transport, the RMS Aquitania. It was headed to nearby Glasgow, Scotland where they arrived on February 6, 1944, a nine-day trip across the Atlantic. The Aquitania was a British Shipping Company, Cunard Lines, ocean liner when upon its near retirement after 36 years of service it returned to military duty as a troop transport in both WW II and WW I.

Norb was based in England around four months and eight days waiting for and training for the 59th's participation in "Operation Overlord." The 59th did not participate in the Normandy Landing on D Day, June 6, 1944, but landed ashore Utah Beach later in the week. On June 14, they started their combat action with the operational standup of the US Army VIII Corps, led by Maj. Gen. Troy V. Middleton. See the section "The 59th Signal Battalion in WW II." for more detailed information on the role the 59th (and hence Norb) played in the war on the Western Front. Through an internet search, I sadly learned that one of Norb's friends died during the D Day invasion and was buried in the Normandy American Cemetery.

Around October 28, 1944 Norb was taken from somewhere on the Belgium front. In his letters home he stated that he was "having trouble with his ticker" and asked to be evaluated. In 1945, after a medical discharge, he received a 50% Award of Disability Compensation or Pension for "nervous disability in combat." In the American Civil War, this was referred to as "soldiers' heart." Nervous disorders were very real and they created a stigma on the soldier. In all likelihood, he did not want his family to know the real reason he was in the hospital for a few months. To be held that long indicates a more severe problem. Soldiers were usually recuperated at a hotel or safe place near the battlefront, as Norb initially was, and sent back to the field quickly. Norb stated that he hoped he could rejoin his unit but that never happened.

While Norb never talked much about the war, he was adamant in his disgust of Gen. Patton who did not believe in such things as battle fatigue, nervous disorders, shell shock, etc. Patton made it clear he thought these soldiers were malingerers in the hospitals and cowards. Patton had slapped a soldier in a hospital on August 2, 1943 when the soldier told Patton he was nervous rather than physically wounded. Patton slapped him, called him a gutless bastard, and threatened to send him back to the front. It was found later that the soldier had malaria.

Norb served a total of 2 years, 8 months and 20 days in the army, 11 months of which was in the European Theater for which he received a medal.

Time Line of Norb's Assignments and Posts And
HQ Co. 59th Signal Battalion Action in WW II

1942:

August 4	Norb inducted into the US Army
August 18	Norb begins active duty in the Army
August 20	Letter from Norb: from Co. F, Ft. Harrison, Indiana
August 25	Norb is Private First Class, Co. E, 34th Battalion, SCRTC, Camp Crowder, Missouri
October 17	Norb learns he is not a Corporal, as he was told by his CO
September 15	Norb completed basic training
September 20	Billeted in Hotel Howard, Room 217, 1414 Locust in Kansas City, Missouri
September 23	Norb began technical training at Bell South training school. Address: Co. F 804th, Bldg. 3523, SSR, US Army; Mid-Western School Camp Crowder, Missouri
November 2-10	Girlfriend Alma Pierce visits Norb in Kansas City
November 21	Norb graduated from training; received diploma for 240 hours training at Southwestern Bell Telephone Company (Kansas City) in Telephone Substation Installation and Maintenance
November 23	Norb transferred from Clerk duties to Telephones
November 24	Norb assigned back to HQ Co. 59th Signal Battalion, Camp Crowder, Missouri; Clerk at Motor Depot, 126 trucks to track; could cross train to clerk if he wanted

1943

January 3-30	Norb assigned to HQ. Co. 59th Signal Battalion, Camp Crowder, Missouri
February 4	Norb transferred to HQ. Co. 59th Signal Battalion, Fort Jackson, South Carolina
April	Norb promoted to Corporal
c. April 18-29	Norb on furlough in Louisville
July	Norb still in Ft. Jackson but using APO 312 and the service # on correspondence
August	Norb on Furlough in Louisville
September 9	Norb awarded M-1 Rifle Sharpshooter medal

c. Oct 3 – Nov 9	Norb on maneuvers at Camp Forrest near Nashville, Tennessee; APO 402
November 10	Norb at Ft. Jackson, South Carolina; awarded Carbine Marksman medal
November 29	59th Signal Battalion is no longer part of XII Corps at Ft. Jackson
December	Norb on Furlough to Louisville

1944

January	Norb at HQ. Co. 59th Signal Battalion, Fort Jackson, South Carolina
January 29	Norb departed for European Theater from New York, NY on the ship RMS Aquitania headed for an area near Glasgow Scotland; NY APO #9473
February 6	Letter from Norb states he had arrived in England
February 8	Letter from Norb: "Somewhere in England" APO #9473
February 17	Letter from Norb: "Somewhere in England" APO #887
March 8	Letter from Norb: "Somewhere in England" APO #308
May 24	Letter from Norb in England: "Situated by a big lake 4 times larger than Twin Lakes [in Kentucky]."
June 6	✪ Allies land in Normandy on the coast of France for the D Day invasion. The gigantic Operation Overlord begins. Friend Tommy Bratten is KIA.
June 10	Letter from Norb, NY APO#308: mentions 'invasion is on' and that it was the troops' biggest morale booster."
June 14	✪ Gen. Troy Middleton (Commander of VIII Corps) "Report After Action Against Enemy" dated 20 July 1944 states that "a part of the 59th Signal Battalion... accompanied the advanced echelon of Headquarters of the VIII Corps landed over Utah Beach on the 14th and 15th of June 1944." The Army VIII Corps takes over the sector on the west side of the Cotentin Peninsula.
June 15-July 31	✪ US VIII Corps joined the US First Army from June 15-31 July, commanded by Gen. Patton
July 3	Letter from Norb: "Somewhere in France" writing from a 2 ½ foot deep foxhole Norb says he has seen a lot of French cities "blown to hell."
July 5	✪ Heavy fighting continues. VIII Corps captures La Haye-du-Puits railway station.
July 6	✪ US VII and US VIII Corps continue slow advance to the south in the direction of Lessay and Périers against exceptionally fierce German resistance

July 7	Letter from Norb: NY APO #308; mentions he has had nothing stronger than apple cider for a month. The Calvados area of Normandy, France, specializes in apple cider or Calvados. Norb still thinks he will be home for Christmas
July 8	✪ US VIII Corps overruns La Haye-du-Puits.
July 9	✪ US VIII Corps tries to push on beyond La Haye-du-Puits but is pinned down by difficult terrain and stiff enemy resistance
July 25	Operation Cobra commences under Gen. Omar Bradley. Two days later US VII and VIII Corps advanced rapidly isolating the Cotentin peninsula.
Aug 1 - Sep 4	✪ **US VIII Corps joined the US Third Army** under command of George S. Patton
August 1	✪ VIII Corps moves to Brittany
Sep 5 - Oct 21	✪ **US VIII Corps joined the US Ninth Army**
September 8	France
September 19	✪ VIII Corps liberates the city of Brest
October 4	✪ Part of US IX Army/VIII Corps took over the front in Ardennes along the Our River and Schnee Eifel
October 4	Letter from Norb: First letter from Belgium. Writes that Brest was the worst of cities he had "seen." "...seen all the rest nearly. La Hague de Puits, Valogne, St. Lô, Lessay, St. Sauveur, Paris..."
Oct 22 - Dec 19	✪ **US VIII Corps joins US First Army**
October 22	✪ Ops leading up to the Allied Offensive against the Rhine begin with the drawing up along the Allied front of the 3 American Armies which are to take part, from North to South, the 1ˢᵗ, 9ᵗʰ and 3ʳᵈ.
October 23	Last letter from Norb (from a hotel in Belgium) until he is in a Red Cross hospital in England. States he is on a rest and in a real hotel with a bed and mattress for the 1ˢᵗ time since leaving the US.
c. October 28	Norb is taken from Belgium with 'nervous disorder' and heart problems to an American Red Cross Hospital in Paris. Flew from Paris to England.
November 5	Letter from Norb: Sent from an ARC Hospital in England. States he "had a little trouble with my ticker" & has no idea how long he will be there. His later 'Award of Disability Compensation or Pension' show that he received a 50 % disability for "nervous disability (in combat),
December 11	Norb changed hospital to US Army Hospital, Plant #4166, APO #508, NY.

December 15	Norb departed the European Theater of WW II for a hospital in the USA.
December 16	✪ **Germans attacked the US Army VIII Corps with 20 divisions, the Ardennes Offensive.**
December 27	Norb arrived in the USA.

<u>1945</u>

January 9	Norb's Mother died
April 20	Honorable discharge from the US Army as a Tech 5.
	Medically discharged from Wakeman General and Convalescent Hospital, Camp Atterbury, Indiana.
	Awarded battle stars for serving in Belgium and France.

<u>1988</u>	Military burial at Zachary Taylor Cemetery, a federal military cemetery, Louisville, Kentucky

The 59ᵗʰ Signal Battalion in WW II

By Major Earl Zortman, US Army in "Voice of the Arctic," July, 2004

"In a recent letter to the Commander of the 59ᵗʰ Signal Battalion, a Ms. Carol R. Trainer wrote us to enquire about possible battles her dad, Tech Sergeant Norbert A. Rawert, would have participated in as a member of the 59ᵗʰ Signal Battalion in WW II. The first reminder of the history is the five battle streamers the 59ᵗʰ was awarded for service in WW II: Normandy 1944; Ardennes-France 1944-1945; Northern France 1944; Rhineland 1944-1945; Central Europe 1945. But what did our historical band of brothers do during those campaigns? What battles and what ground did the 59ᵗʰ Signal Battalion Guidon once participate in?

The battalion was constituted on 11 May 1942, activated 28 October 1942 at Camp Crowder, Missouri, and then inactivated 24 Nov 1945 at Camp Kilmer, New Jersey. Sometime in late 1943 or early 1944, the 59ᵗʰ Signal Battalion transferred to England to prepare for Operation Overlord. The 59ᵗʰ Signal Battalion did not participate in the 6 June 1944 Normandy Landing, but was brought ashore later in the week. On 15 June 1944, they started their combat action with the operational standup of VIII Corps, led by MG Troy H. Middleton.

As a small support unit, 59ᵗʰ Signal Battalion has not garnered the recognition we might think it deserves. The history books are more concerned with Infantry, Armor, and Field Artillery, but even then, barely going below battalion level, unless it is a small tactical engagement analysis. I could only find three references to 59ᵗʰ Signal Battalion from here in Alaska. The first is from "The Signal Corps: The Outcome," a Center of Military History WW II series book. On page 125, it refers to 59ᵗʰ Signal Battalion, as a part of VIII Corps during the attack in Brittany, France, being responsible for wire communications to three divisions, an extensive fire direction net, the radio co-ordination for naval bombardment of the city (Brest), and the maintenance of radio link contact to two armies, an army group, and a tactical air force. Our Signal battalion was also responsible for rehabilitating over 7,250 miles of existing open wire and underground cable in four weeks. Now that would be a job for today's DCO shop! The second reference I found about 59ᵗʰ Signal Battalion was on the University of Texas webpage, a project to archive information about US Latinos and Latinas & World War II. A Jose "Joe" Eriberto Adame was assigned to the 59ᵗʰ Signal Battalion in the US and then moved over to 86ᵗʰ Chemical Mortar Battalion while in England. The third and final reference to 59ᵗʰ Signal Battalion was on a webpage dedicated to the 33ʳᵈ Signal Construction Battalion Reenactors. One officer and 34 enlisted men (four crews) from Company B were dispatched to VIII Corps on July 14, equipped with two line trucks (K-43), to 2 ½ ton 6x6 trucks, and one ¼-ton truck. Their mission was to maintain communications between the VIII Corps and First Army, and they joined the VIII Corps in a bivouac area near La Haye-du-Puits, being attached to Company C, 59ᵗʰ Signal Battalion.

What is especially interesting about this support is it is likely that these soldiers from 33rd Signal Construction are specifically the reason the 59th Signal Battalion was able to provide the Corps level support described in "The Outcome."

The remaining documented history of 59th Signal Battalion is likely buried within thick tomes of military orders and deep shelves of dedicated military libraries at Fort Leavenworth and Fort Gordon. However, as a support unit for VIII Corps, their battles are our battles, as we provided the communication.

I offered to go TDY to Fort Leavenworth, Kansas for a few days to do additional research, but Maj. McPherson asked about how this supports Active Directory, so I had to let it slide. The next best thing to do is describing some of the engagements VIII Corps participated in, and imagine laying wire and raising antennas during it.

The immediate mission of VIII Corps was the organization of defensive positions from Carentan, France west across the peninsula. As the beachhead continued to expand, VIII Corps was charged with guarding the security of VII Corps southern flank, as VII Corps prepared to move west and clear the French peninsula through the city of Cherbourg of all German resistance. On 29 June 1944, VII Corps conquered the city of Cherbourg, but only after the port, facilities were completely destroyed by the remaining German troops.

July 1944 started with plans for a major offensive, starting with VIII Corps. On 3 July, VIII Corps (Maj. Gen. Troy H. Middleton) opened the First Army offensive. Three divisions jumped off abreast in a downpour of rain that not only nullified air attacks but prevented artillery observation. Enemy resistance was heavy and the 82d Airborne Division scored the only notable advance. During the next three days, slow progress was made in hard fighting under adverse weather. The corps struck the enemy's MLR (main line of resistance) along the line le Plessis-Mont-Castre Forest, La Haye-du-Puits, and enemy counterattacks stiffened by armor helped to slow down the VIII Corps. Though La Haye-du-Puits was nearly surrounded, average gains for the three-day period were under 6,000 yards on the corps front and, contrary to expectations, the enemy had clearly shown his intentions of defending in place whatever the cost.

The slugging match continued through 11 July in both VII and VIII Corps zones. The hard battles of VIII Corps finally produced their fruits in mid-July. As the three attacking divisions broke past the rough La Haye-du-Puits Mont-Castre hills, where they had cracked the enemy's MLR, they found resistance less and less tenacious. On 14 July, VIII Corps came up to the line of the Ay River; it had reached the initial objectives prescribed in its attack order, a gain of 12,000 yards in 12 days of battle. But the corps was still far short of its assigned ultimate objectives when orders from First Army stopped the attack at the positions then reached. Though hard fought, the two Corps, VII and VIII, stopped to solidify their positions and prepare for Operation Cobra. XIX Corps continued to fight through June 19th, as it battled south to St. Lô, France.

Following the action in July, VIII Corps continued to attack along the west coast of the

French peninsula as part of Operation Cobra launched on 25 July 1944 in order to break the stalemate following the Normandy beachhead. As the Third Army continued to move East through France towards Belgium and Germany, VIII Corps continued to attack toward Brest, capturing the vital port city on 18 September 1944. Unfortunately, this left the VIII Corps well behind its higher headquarters, which resulted in VIII Corps being reassigned to the Ninth Army.

Following the taking of the Brest Peninsula VIII Corps was moved into a supporting position, covering the southern flank of the Third Army, as they pushed into Belgium through the fall.

As the winter started, the battle lines were reorganized throughout the Ardennes Forest and VIII Corps moved into the Northern portion. The strongest fighting was occurring in the south, still with Third and First Army, so VIII Corps became the place for divisions to reorganize and new divisions to be placed to get their first experience in combat, as the VIII Corps portion of the western line was relatively sedate compared to the southern portion.

The fighting in the fall was fierce and slow as the Germans fought for every inch as the Allies pushed them closer and closer to their homeland. By 15 December, the Allies had almost completely recovered whole of France and Belgium, through Operation Market Garden. Then on December 16, the Germans launched their last major offensive known as Battle of the Ardennes or Battle of the Bulge, the second greatest American loss in the war.

Without going into depth about the Battle of the Bulge, the VIII Corps took the heaviest brunt of the Germany counterattack, having to dislodge their headquarters from Bastogne, leaving the city to 101st Airborne Division, which led to their historical defense, and famous line by Gen McAuliffe in regards to the German demand of surrender "Nuts!" The Third Army, which absorbed the remnants of VIII Corps, pushed back into Bastogne, and relieved 101st Airborne. By January 18, the German counterattack was defeated, and the battle lines were restored. The Battle of the Bulge was Germany's last serious attack, and 4 months later, once the Allies and Russian armies met in Saxony, Germany surrendered on 8 May 1945.

While a majority of this information is about VIII Corps, a non-divisional support unit like 59th Signal Battalion would have been spread throughout the battlefield. When GEN Middleton moved his headquarters from Bastogne to Neufchateau on 18 December, it is likely that the 59th moved also.

Works Cited:

Cole, Hugh M. The Ardennes: Battle of The Bulge. Washington, DC, Center of Military History 1965 <http://www.Army.mil/cmh-pg/books/WW II/7-8/7-8_cont.htm

Trejo, Frank. US Latino & Latina World War II Oral History Project. 8 July 2004, <http://www.utexas.edu/projects/latinoarchives/index.html>

Phillips, Ed. 33<u>rd</u> <u>Signal Construction Battalion Reenactors</u>. 8 July 2004 <http://members. trpod.com/33rdscb/>

Harris, Dixie H., and Thompson, G.R. <u>The Signal Corps: The Outcome</u>. Washington, DC: Center of Military History, 1966.

German Cousins Serve in Hitler's Third Reich

Josef Effkemann was Norb's second cousin once removed. At the time Norb was in the US Army during WW II his cousin, whom he had never known, was fighting with the Nazis in the SS. In one letter, Norb had mentioned that he might have to go to Germany and kill some of his cousins. Little did he know his cousin might have been closer than he had thought?

After WW I Josef's mother and other family members contacted the family in Schnitzelburg once again. The Rawerts on Texas Street and Cousins Wilhelmina Heitkemper and family came to their aid sending care packages since the war had devastated many families.

In 2000, Josef Effkemann and I made contact with each other, each very grateful for being able to reach out to family after many years. In 2005, Josef presented me with the family history book *Die Effkemanns* that he had just published. In 2002, on one of our visits to Josef's we were sitting around his kitchen table with his family. As he showed us his documents and papers from WW II and started to explain them, he broke down and cried. His children ran to him very concerned. He had never discussed the war and his children had never seen him cry. My father Norb also did not speak of the war and he never cried, at least in front of me. The war took great tolls on both sides.

In *Die Effkemanns* Josef also wrote about his experience in WW II. He was conscripted into the German Federal work service on 12 January 1943 (at age 17). While at a work camp at 7:00 am, he and other selected young men were forced to leave with six SS Officers. They went by a livestock train to an unknown location, which turned out to be Russia. They were housed in Russian barracks in Zhtoymr, northwest of Kiev and Ukraine and underwent a three-month training period. Afterwards, his company unit was assigned to provide protection for the Division and the remainder went to the Front.

In January 1944, his unit was decorated with the SS Panzer "Iron Cross II class, "meaning "Tank Defense." He said there were many decorations, which were used as incentive for the soldiers. He said he, like other soldiers, would have preferred to stay home rather than be praised and rewarded with medals and insignia, fighting to the dictates of the politicians.

After a short leave, he reported to Lemburg on the Front and was deployed to Toulouse, France where he joined a new company. The West Allied forces had landed troops in Normandy so the pace picked up

Around the beginning of July 1944, he was wounded by grenade fragments in his hip. Then as they were being transported to an association place, they were hit by six land mines, which hurled him into a lateral deep ditch. Then the transportation vehicle, the "Opel Lightning," immediately burst into bright flames. Out of the other 16 casualties, Josef was the only one to survive. He was sent to Ronse, a military hospital in Belgium, about 70 km from Brussels. After one week, the military hospital was evacuated because of the approaching Western powers. It is interesting to note here that Norbert A. Rawert, was part of the Normandy Invasion and they (59th Signal Battalion assigned to the VIII Corp,

USA.) were making their way from Normandy into Belgium on the way to Germany. Norbert left the battle in Belgium when he was flown to Paris and then to a Red Cross hospital in England. Josef was sent to Lingen at Elmsland, lowland Germany, where for six months he was billeted in a trade school that was used as a substitute military hospital.

After recuperation, Josef was assigned to a replacement battalion in Prague-Russia and was promoted to senior private. He was assigned as support trainer.

In April of 1945, he was sent to Austria. At Krems, northwest of Vienna, he was wounded in the left foot after about two weeks of action so he was assigned to a new unit in Dresden where he supervised other soldiers.

There was much confusion about the end of the war on May 08. He ended up in Czechoslovakia at a place named Aussig Ustin at the Elbe about 20 km inland and found himself with only civilians. His group then moved further inland and heard reports that the American soldiers had occupied Komotau. He had no confidence in the Eastern powers. As they struggled along on foot marches, they saw much devastation and desperation of women, children and old people. He was affected by it and wondered, "Is this what we fought for?" He mentioned that the Czechs were very brutal and the soldiers' possessions, even their boots, were extorted from them, causing them to have to continue to march on barefooted.

Shortly they were on German soil where they changed from uniforms to civilian clothing that was too small for them. They travelled on until reaching Rotenburg on the Fulda River where he was taken Prisoner of War by the English authorities. He notes the treatment was inhumane and that they were brutally abused. He was imprisoned for a week. After discharge, he was taken away in a truck and made his way home from there by train and truck.

After the war, Josef went to school and learned the building trade. He became a prominent builder in the Ahaus, Germany area. He married Josefa Nienhaus on

Carol Rawert Trainer and Joseph Effkemann, March 7, 2014

May 25, 1953 and they had six children with whom I am in contact today. Regretfully, Josef's wife Josefa died on January 8, 2012 and Josef himself died on October 23, 2016, while I was writing this book. He is greatly missed.

Chapter 1

1942

Norb Begins Life in the Army

Norb voluntarily registered for selective service in the US Army and, according to his Enlisted Record and Report of Separation/Honorable discharge certificate, he was inducted on August 4. He entered active service on August 18. The first letter in the correspondence was from his sister Hermina. Her letters comprise most of this WW II Letter collection. Like many families, they believed it was important to stay in frequent contact with the military member in order to keep up the soldier's morale. It was also important not to mention anything negative in case it would demoralize the soldier. This collection begins with the following letter.

Louisville, Kentucky, **August 19,** 1:30 pm

Dearest Norb,

Although we do not have your address, I thought I would write these few lines anyway. When we came home last night Alma came with us and stayed with us until 9:30 pm Joe and Ann, Shirley and I, and Marge all rode home with her. Today is warm again. I was to see Julia Hellmann; she is on her 2 weeks' vacation and is the only Hellmann girl home. Herman is in St. Petersburg, Fla. and his mother and Rita are visiting him. Red is in Corpus Christi, Texas and Lippy and Aggie is visiting him. Angela is home again. Her husband is in Calif. On maneuvers.

I suppose by this time you are getting shots, more shots, and not your kind either [*reference to his love of alcohol*]. We are all well and everybody is more settled. We had lunch with Cousin Mary. One of her cousins are visiting her so we got a free meal. Tain't bad.

Shirley is gone to Dr. Tully and I suppose you'll be seeing the dentist too. How's the meals? Mrs. Schlegel told me that she was taking Mrs. Mattie Fleig [sp] home with her last night, that is, going to try to get her to come home with her because she doesn't have another relative here. Joe and Ann got a card table from Aline today. Well, I'll bring this to a close, and finish it as soon as we get your address.

Continued, **August 20**

Brother

As we haven't heard from you as yet, I just keep on scribbling. I canned 23 ½ pints of tomatoes today. Until tomorrow.

Continued, **August 21**

Dear Norbie,

That phone call really helped us out. You sounded just like yourself. Those hours of sleep are very much like home. We got those pictures and am enclosing a few, when we get your address we will send all. Your letter was appreciated as much as the phone call.

[Enclosed was a torn, scribbled note in Alma Pierce's handwriting, folded and shaped in the shape of a tiny envelope with a postal stamp and address written on it:]

Hello Norb, Just a few lines to tell you I miss you an awful lot and wish you were here. Honey I won't have time to write very much this time because I'm on my way to work, but will write a long letter the next time. Well, I'll close now hoping to hear from you real soon, Love,
Alma [*Pierce; Norb's Irish girlfriend*]

Continued, **August 21**

Dear Norbert!

We all were glad to hear your voice and that you are well. Joe [*Norb's brother*] would of liked to talk to you but I never thought so far; next time I will. We got your letter at 8:30 am. Alma got a kick out of Papa's story about where he worked a year ago; he was just in the mood of talking. You know how he is sometime, ha, ha. Well, I can't tell you a lot of news. I am washing today. We are well, canned tomatoes yesterday. Alma, Hermina and I are writing the same time. You might read one story 3 times. Louis Bodner is in 1-B2. I spoke to Mrs. Bodner this morning coming from church. She said she would of liked to see you before you left. Shirley is still sleeping. I'm going to wake her up so she can write to you also. Mary said 'Hello honeybunch.' Marge would of written to you also but she's not here, we will call her up at noon and she can write you later.
Love from all and good luck,
Mother, Kate

Continued by Shirley Muth:

Hello Norb, we all are glad to hear from you. Mother is not here so I'll say hello for her. We were all waiting to hear from you. Thursday evening I was over at Norman Maddens. When I got home they said you called and said that you were standing guard duty already. Sincerely yours,
Shirley Ann Muth

PS. Write some more in a hurry. We are all praying for you. We saw Mother in church for prayers on Thursday.

The header to following letter provided the first information that Norb was in Company F at Fort Benjamin Harrison, Indiana.

Co. F, Ft. Harrison Indiana, August 20

Dear Mom, Pop and All,

 Well, it's 3:00 in the morning and I'm on guard duty. I didn't get but three hours of sleep last night and the night before so this is the first time I had a chance to write. I guess you think I'm still keeping my same old hours, but here we have to do it but at home, I caught hell for it. The food is pretty good if they would give you enough time to eat it, but everything goes in a hurry. We got our clothes, shots and everything, and are ready to move out whenever they tell us.

 Enclosed you will find an insurance policy for $5,000 so take care if these papers. You will also find a war saving[s] application. I guess everybody is OK. This is all the time I have now but will write soon.

Thinking of you all,

Norb

Fort Harrison, Indiana [*postcard*], August 23

Dear Mom and Pop,

 I am ready to ship now. I feel much better since I had a good night's sleep. I don't know where I'm going but I'm going. Tell everybody hello and I sure am glad you all came. So until I reach my next camp.

I'm still,

Norb

The Rawert Family Visits Fort Benjamin
Harrison, Indiana, August 23, 1942

Private Norbert Rawert,
US Army, 8-23-1942

Norb with his parents
Herman and Catherine

Norb's girlfriend, Alma Pierce,
with his mom Catherine

Norb with his girlfriend,
Alma Pierce

Private Norbert Rawert, Ft. Benjamin Harrison, Indiana

Norb sitting on Platform at Fort Benjamin Harrison, Indiana, 8-23-42, age 22

The following letter provides the first indication that Pvt. Rawert arrived at Co. E 34 Battalion, SCRTC, Camp Crowder, Missouri.

Camp Crowder, Missouri, **August 24**

Dear Mom and All,

Well, I finally reached here It's a new camp and composed mostly of different kinds of schools. Oh, my god, some of these dumb yaps from West Virginia mining section. We were on the train for about 16 hours. I didn't think we were going near this far. But we got a break at that. The bunch that left before us are going across right away and receive their training over there.

I was sure glad to see all of you Sunday but I was so tired I could hardly move. I don't know how I will like this camp as yet I just have to wait and find out. I feel pretty good but I'm all bound up [*constipated*]. We are way down on the other end of Missouri I believe. We came through St. Louis sometime last night but I don't remember what time it was any more. Tomorrow I get my other shot, then another a week later. I don't think I will stay here over seven weeks because most of them don't; at least that's what I was told. Tell Shirley I didn't have time to write her yet but I will as soon as I get a chance. My address is Pvt. Norbert A. Rawert, US Army; Co. E 34 Bn., SCRTC, Camp Crowder. Well, Mom, that's about all the time I have for now, Missouri
So until I hear from you I'll still be,
Norb

Louisville, Kentucky, **August 24**

Dear Norb,

We are thinking of you and wondering just where you'll be sent. Mom and Pop got home just about 2:00 am and stood the trip fine. Mom's stomach was on good behavior so we are all glad she got to make the trip. The bus came in just at 1:05. Moody [*Norb's Uncle Leo Muth*] and Lip [*Norb's sister, Elizabeth*] was at the Station since 11:30. We figured they would be on the 11:30 bus but wasn't, so they just stayed down there and their bus was ahead of schedule. The 11:30 bus pulled in at 1:00 am. It had a breakdown so I feel they were lucky. That's all about the bus.

This letter will be diary fashion until we get your address. Mom thought you looked swell in your uniform and was glad to know you gained in weight. I thought Mom might have a picture like the 10 cent stores have, 10 cents a picture, but I was disappointed. I also hear you're getting housemaid knees. That isn't so pleasant until you get toughened up. Shirley went to the Amphitheater with Mildred M. The Holy Name [*Catholic Church& School*] gave a concert, all patriotic music. That's all for today. It was swell.
Until tomorrow.
H.R. [*Hermina*]

Continued, Tuesday, **August 25**

I went in town today with Shirley Ann to get 2 more towels yesterday for 25 cents and 35 cents, you know, the ones with "Who's Been Eating My Porridge" and a little brown bear so the lady ordered six more from her and is she thrilled. I am going to start to iron. Until tomorrow,

H.R.

Camp Crowder, Missouri, **August 25**

Dear Shirley,

I sure was glad to hear that you are praying for me. How are all of your boyfriends getting along? Since I'm gone I guess you have found a new one. How are all your brothers and sisters and my sister Elizabeth? I know your old man couldn't get sick.

I guess you are getting ready to start to school pretty soon. I start myself in 2 ½ weeks. I'm going to study to be a Company Clerk. You just study hard like your Uncle and you won't get anywhere.

If you were here you would have a lot of soldiers to flirt with, because this place is full of them. Well, Shirley that's all I know for now so until I hear from you I'm still your boyfriend, Norb

Louisville, Kentucky, **August 26,** 4:30 pm

Dear Norb,

I suppose by this time you have reached your destination or maybe they might send you to Mc Arthur immediately, providing they seen your pictures. Alma was up last night. She showed us the two pictures and pillow top you sent her. I think both pictures are good, but you really look like a tough monkey on the other picture. If Hitler could see it, we'd have peace. I like that picture best tho the other one looks like you on pay nite.

Last afternoon about 4:30, a middle-aged stout man brought 50 cents for you. He said it was coming to you from Park and Tilford and he was told to bring it here, so I bet that will burn you until you get it. Call for 5-'92 [*reference to an ad for the local Oertel's '92 beer*] or can't you get '92 like you used to razz Zip about all the time. We're supposed to go to Johnny's [*Norb's brother*] on Sunday. We'll be called for and delivered, hmmmh! I'm wondering if we'll get pie like you didn't like. Remember?

Until tomorrow,

H.R.

Continued, **August 26,** 9:30 pm

Dear Norb,

Well, I'm a monkey's aunt. You had a plenty of that "Show Me" besides sending you to Missouri but I do hope you like it. We told Joe, and Marge and Shirley are going to Lip's to tell her. I called Mrs. Russell, honey. We just couldn't wait. Pop's gone to Huelsman's [*a Schnitzelburg tavern at the end of the alley*]; has to take a beer on that. I couldn't get Alma at Moore's anymore so that will be taken care of tomorrow. We'll be looking for your letter and don't fail to write as often as you get time. You can write Pee (like Katsy says it). You sounded good on the phone. Your voice is clear.

With love from all. We're OK,

Hermina

Louisville, Kentucky, **August 27,** 10 am

Dear Norb,

Well, we all know you're in Camp Crowder now to get your Company or Division number. I hear Schultz and Geppert is in one of those swanky hotels along the $1,000,000 boardwalk in Atlantic, NJ. We are all OK. Fritz Schmitt was at Camp Crowder. He's in the Signal Corps. Are you in the Signal Corps? I suppose that's right with the Radio Division. Mrs. Schmitt said he liked it fine, and I should ask you if Fred Hacker is with you. That's Fritz's cousin. He left Monday (Ft. Harrison). I called Alma and she was glad to hear.

John bought a G.E. refrigerator. I suppose your basic training is already started. How about your teeth? Nosey, ain't I? The mailman is either smiled upon on looked clear through. Poor feller. What would you like to have? Would you like Fitch's shampoo? Or hair dressing? Vitalis, or anything? Did you go by bus or train to Missouri? Shirley can't wait until she gets her letter and wants to know if she can mail her letter separately.

Mrs. Zipperle just called and wanted your address, so she could tell Edward [*Norb's friend "Zip"*]. She hasn't heard from Zip for a week and a half and said they were moving him to a different camp in NC but now she is wondering if they are going to send Zip. We were hoping you'd be sent to Ft. Bragg but I'm thankful you're not sent to Ft. Knox. I'd rather you weren't with the armored forces but Lip thinks those tanks are safe looking.

Hoping you are well. I'm writing this on the couch on my back. Until we get your address or until tomorrow.

Jerks [*Hermina's self-deprecating reference to her epileptic seizures*]

Louisville, Kentucky, **August 28**

Dear Norbert.

Alma received your letter and called us. We haven't received ours as yet. What's the matter with the Air Mail Special Delivery Stamp [*stamp sent to Norb to use for letter*]? So you're going to set on your rear all day. I thought maybe you'd be doing welding or more of a manual work. Hope you like it and lots of luck ole boy.

Love from us,

H.R.

Continued, **August 28,** 1:30 pm

I was talking to Mrs. Schmitt. She said Fritz, or Smithy as they call him, was in the Signal Corps and he had to take typing too. We received your first Special-Air-Mail today at noon. She said it was 1,500 soldiers there then, this was a new camp and they expected about 35,000 soldiers there then. It was dedicated the middle part of April. We certainly did think you got a break by being <u>a bunch late,</u> to think of those boys being sent off immediately to a foreign port. That's something to be thankful for.

Alma is coming for supper tonight. Henry Rawert has to have his blood test made. I am sending those pictures taken at Ft. Harrison, IN. Keep on writing. Now Momma wants to write. Mrs. Schmitt told me everything about the Camp Crowder. I almost feel like I was there or that I am a WAAC.
Hermina

Dear Norb,

We are so glad to get the letter. Hope next time you can write more about the camp and how you like it. Did anyone you know go with you? I was to see uncle [*Wessling*] yesterday afternoon and showed him the wedding picture. He thought it was good. He said you looked so tall he could not believe it was you. I think he is very absent-minded [*Alzheimer's?*]. Helen said the same. The priest that comes to see him thought that also. He asked me twice where you were stationed. Bud Wessling is stationed at Arkansas. Say, Norbert, the night you called, Papa could not finish talking to you. He was so full of crying. You said tell Pop to drink one for me. He just got through with the first growler; I told him what you said. He said I'm going right now. He asked Joe to help him drink it. He asked me if I could drink a glass, ha, ha.

How is it to get up in the morning? Did you watch the eclipse? Pop watched it till the moon was getting clear. Marge and Joe and Ann all said hello, and Mary also.
As ever,
Mother

PS. Did you go to you-know-what-I-mean? [*Next to her words was a drawing of a grail like in Holy Communion*].

Continued by Hermina:

Tonite for supper we're having fried corn, mashed taters [*potatoes*], maters [*tomatoes*], cucumbers, and to think you get meat. Momma's going to send you some Watkins Laxatives in a little yellow box (glass might break). We're going to send a box. Keep looking for it.

Continued by Shirley Muth:

Dear Norb,

Ever since you called up and told me that a letter is coming, I'm still waiting. When the man that delivered the Special Delivery Letter, he told me to sign it, I told him I was not Mommy and he said he knew it. I didn't know what to do. We have to register to go back to school September 4 and I hate it. Ma [*Margaret*] and I were at Holy Mass last night for you and I went to church for you this morning. And I want to tell you that I kissed Alma like you told me to do. She was so surprised she was wondering what happened. I wonder if she is that surprised when you kiss her. I don't think she is. Alma is coming to stay all night. Mother was so anxious to find out your new address. I hope my letter got to you. Mother and Daddy and all are well. Write to me soon.

Still thinking of you,

Shirley

Camp Crowder, Missouri, **August 29,** I think

Dear Mom, Pop, Sisters and Bros.

I am glad to hear that you made the trip OK. I guess that is about as far as you have been for a long time. How did Pop like it? I guess he missed his beer - that's one thing I got against Indiana [*dry county*]. Well, to begin with I been eating like hell. Anyone in the army can eat. Some of these guys can stick a half of a steak at once (when we get steak) in their mouth at one time. They act like they were holding their appetite back until they were drafted. If you're not hungry, just watching some of these guys eat will give you an appetite. I believe my arm has grown six inches since I been here. I really developed a reach [*to grab food before it was gone*]. Speaking of arms, I got a shot in both of them today and I don't know which hurts the worst when I move them, so I don't have to worry. They won't be really sore until tomorrow though. It's Sunday so I won't have to do much.

I am glad to hear that Shirley is doing so well in her new business. I guess that comes from her old man's side [*Muth's Candy*]. You say, "What's the matter with the air mail stamp?" Well, I can't use the same stamp twice! I used them once so I guess you got the letter.

I start to school the 17ᵗʰ of September after I finish my basic. But after I finish school, so I heard, I think I will take a little trip 'across the pond.' You can't believe everything you hear in the army, though. I could use a bottle of Vitalis because my hair is falling out like hell. I haven't warshed [*sic*] it but once since I been in the army.

We went by train and it took us 16 hours to get here [*Camp Crowder, Missouri*]. Had to go to work as soon as we arrived and it was KP [*kitchen patrol*] at that. I even had to stand guard on the train for a three-hour stretch. They thought one damn fool was going to make a break for it, but he didn't. I tell you they got some goofs in this army. One guy from West Virginia that sleeps with us can't even read or write and when he tries to march it's pitiful. He can't lose his country stride. He gave me my biggest laugh since I been here. But you have to feel sorry for him.

I don't know what to think about Zip unless he just didn't have time to write. That happens, you know. It could be that his mail was delayed for some reason. Please don't forget to send me that half a buck because I sure can use it. You would be surprised at all the nicnacs [*sic*] you need. I sure would like to have a '92. This beer here ain't worth a shit. You know that phone call cost me $1.85. Boy, they sure do slap it to you.

Tell Pop when he gets back with that beer to drink one for me because I'm pretty damn dry. As soon as I get my first pay, I will call again. But I will let you know by mail, then Alma can be there too. I had to wait for better than an hour to get the call through.

Yes, I'm in Signal Corps. That's all what this camp consists of. They can give any kind of signal. But some of these damn clucks have to go to school to learn what the word 'signal' means. But of course they ain't all dumb. We have some pretty intelligent fellows in our outfit also. I believe every state in the Union is represented here. No doubt about it. This place is 48,000 square acres, and that's big enough for a tennis court. The weather has been swell, boy and what a moon. Where the hell is Alma? I surely could do some wow [?] pitching. No, it is really swell here as far as the weather is concerned. I caught a cold in Harrison but I'm getting rid of it now.

I am anxious to see the picture we took Sunday, I bet I look like I'm sleeping on my feet... but that would look natural. I heard that Bud Neuner, that's Crip's brother, was missing in action at sea. I don't know if it's the truth or not, but I hope it ain't. Well, I could write more but it's about time to hit the hay and I can't be late so I guess I will hear from you soon. Hoping you are all well and Horse [*Hermina*] is still fat and arguing with Marge, or does that still go on? I hope so. I would like to hear a good argument again. One thing good about this army, you don't have to think, somebody does your thinking for you.
So until I hear from you I will still be,
Norb

Louisville, Kentucky, **August 29,** 9:45 am
Dear Constipated Brother,

Don't eat so much cheese. I hope by this time you are feeling better. Why don't you open your little mouth and sweetly ask for a pill? We are all OK. You never did say if any Louisville boys are with you that left with you. Did any boys you know get shipped across for their training? (Dr. I.Q. scribbling). Neosho and Joplin are the closest towns to you. According to our Atlas, Joplin has 34,000 inhabitants. Neosho has about 3,000.

The bus wants $19.50 round trip. The train $22.50 R.T. to Joplin. Mary is going to mail your box. Joe took it to Shelby and Oak but they wouldn't accept it after 6 pm yesterday. Mom said you get your dates wrong so she's sending a calendar. You can slip it in your writing kit.

Have you started your basic training as yet? Do the shots make you sick? Is your vaccination sore? I never thought yesterday when I sent your airmail letter I feel like you'll have to pay now because 1 oz. is the maximum weight.
Hermina

Dear Norb,

I don't know any news so I will ask questions. Have you any money yet? Can you get beer? Alma and Shirley are washing the breakfast dishes. It is 10:15 now. Papa said he could not write, we should write for him, but I think he will write a few lines sometime. He got 3 growlers last night, 2 for us and 1 for Joe and Ann. I hope you can get to Mass on Sundays. Mary said hello.

As ever,

Your Mother

Louisville, Kentucky, **August 29**, 4 pm, Saturday

Dear Norb,

My second letter to you today, even if I don't do nothing else you'll have to give me credit for scribbling. I just called Mrs. Zipperle to give her your address. Zip also has a new address and she was waiting for his also, so she received her first letter from Zip since he was transferred. I am enclosing it (see insert). Zip is in the Instrumental Survey School, Officer's Training School, so maybe when you and Zip meet again he won't talk to you and he won't be able to bum with you, counting the chickens will you salute him? She says he's up at 5:45; school begins at 8 until 11:45, lunch period 12:45 to 4, school again 4, drilling 6 to 7, supper 7 and at 9, school again. Do you think the army could keep you and Zip apart? I don't.

Shirley [*Norb's niece*] got her letter today, and I don't think no money could buy it. Lip called her up and told her she had a letter, she took to her heels right now and in 15 minutes she was home and back here. She ran all the way there. This afternoon Alma and her [*sic*] are gone in town. We sure did have a swell laugh at Shirley this morning. She told Alma she liked her name, it sounded so soft, some names was awful hard sounding she thought but Alma reminded her of velvet. Alma laughed tears and Mom's belly did the jitterbug.

She was telling about their birthdays. Mother's was in January and not another birthday until June. June 21st when Margie was born. She was born on the first summer night, and the first night of the picnic. Can I explain better on paper or do I do better telling you face to snout?

Mrs. Gold, you know Emmy, was just here. I had to call Miss Emma so they could go to the graveyard [*St. Michael's*] together. Well, Norb until tomorrow this is all the news. Now, Zip's address: Candidate Edw. A. Zipperle, Battery B., OCDAAS, 2nd Platoon, Camp Davis, North Carolina. It's almost as bad as yours.

Hermina

Louisville, Kentucky, **August 31,** 9:30 pm

Dear Norb,

Tonight a week ago you were traveling - tonight perhaps you're marching. Well, we're glad you're at your destination anyway. I worked today. We listened to the Firestone Hour. Richard Crooks sang the National Anthem. They were presented with a Service Flag for doing a good job in defense work. They played Sousa March, we naturally thought of you then. We have another star boarder, since Sunday, Betsy has been here. They register Friday for school. We had a parade tonight in honor of our heroes of this war. Jimmy was in it. None of us went, doesn't sound very patriotic.

Norb, you will find a dollar enclosed. I imagine you will be receiving your first pay soon. Will it be $50 or $21? I thought $21 until you're in 4 months. Johnson thought you got $50 immediately. Who's right? Norb, with this dollar will you get Mom a souvenir? When you get your first chance, I doubt if this entered your mind but she's been waiting for one since you've been gone and thought she would be getting one today. Just get something useful or ornamental or not, just so she gets something. Later I'm going to send you money to get a formal picture made with a peak cap like Zip's.

Nobody knows I'm writing this letter, so don't answer on it. I hope you don't feel like I'm dictating to you. The Parcel-Post Man stopped and she thought it might be something from you. According to the latest news tonite, all distilleries will quit making whiskey by November. They will make smokeless powder. Would you like the 'Courier Journal' or 'Louisville Times' sent to you?

As ever, your sister,

Hermina

Louisville, Kentucky, **August 31,** 8:00 am

Dear Norb,

Waiting for the water to boil for coffee so I thought I would scribble a few lines. We were at Johnny's last night and we wasn't there ten minutes and Pop was digging in the garden. He wanted to feel how it was to take potatoes from the ground. He bought himself a pipe, cigars were getting too costly he thought. I just got a card from Jr Hubbuch. He's going to be moved. Betsy stayed here overnight, she slept with Maah [*Margaret*]. Mrs. Russell said they promised Jr a furlough the last part of September. She was going there this week but Junior said they promised a furlough, so here's hoping he gets it. He said their liberty cards were taken away from them so if his mother would visit him, she might see once or just a couple times just as things might be. When you receive this letter, you will also have received the one with Zip's photo clipping from the Sunday Courier Journal that is really swell of him. Mrs. Zip [*Zipperle*] called you know, and then she told me about Edward. She sure is proud of him. He has to take 10 different subjects, algebra and courtesy is two of them.

We know from Taps to Reveille is Alma's time but tell us what you must do from Reveille to Taps. What time you arise and retire, the chow and everything? Alma and Shirley went to see Sergeant York Saturday; you know Shirley is willing and anxious to go whenever she gets a chance. She sure was pleased. I'm just about out of news (if it is news). Will write more. I'm going into work. I think they [*Hubbuch Company*] have another large order for Ft. Knox again. Hoping you are well and don't eat too much cheese. Mom's in her glory. You know – washing.

With love from your little sistah,
Hermina

Louisville, Kentucky, **August 31**

Dear Mom, Pop and all,

I haven't ate a piece of cheese since I been in the army. In fact, I haven't even seen any. My bowels have been doing pretty good. I haven't taken but one laxative since I been in the army.

No, there is not a Louisville boy here except one I met the other night at the PX [*Post Exchange*]. He did live in Schnitzelburg at one time but he moved. I am bumming around here with some guy from Columbus, Ohio. And some other guy from Rudolph, Kentucky. They are both pretty nice guys. Why, yes, the guy I bummed around with in Harrison was shipped across. He is supposed to write me a letter when he gets to his station and I haven't received one yet so they must have taken a pretty long ride.

You can tell old lady Smith she is full of shit. There are a hell of a lot more than 1,500 boys here. It's way over that amount. You asked me if I'm broke. No, I'm not broke. I have the amount of 45 cents in my pocket. I don't know when we will get a paycheck.

I started my basic training today and I am pretty tired. I did get me a few bottles of beer tonight [*that's evident from the language used in the letter*]. They sell beer on a Sunday here too, from 1 to 8. I took two more shots but they didn't bother me, only made my arm sore.

That airmail letter had better not amount to much or I won't be able to pay for it. What time do you all get up, doing the breakfast dishes at 10:15? I get up at 5:00 every morning and it's still dark yet. Alma told me that Pop is turning her into a drunkard. What is that house beginning to be? Yes, I went to church last Sunday. I hope it gets a little cooler; it was hotter than hell here today. Did anyone else leave for the army who I know? I guess there is. Well, I have to sign off now so until I hear from you I'll still be at Camp Crowder.

Love to all,
Norb

Camp Crowder, Missouri, **September 1**

My Best Girl Shirley,

I received your letter Tuesday afternoon and I never was so glad to hear from anyone in my life. To me, your letters are an inspiration, but the best thought of all is that I'm you're

A-1 boyfriend. Nothing could please me more. I'm glad to hear that your mother [*Norb's sister, Elizabeth*] is OK. What do you mean by calling her my big sister? That title belongs to someone else [*reference to Hermina, who was very overweight*]. You bet your life I'm going to study hard. That is if I don't fall to sleep. I'm glad to hear that you won't flirt with any more soldiers while I'm away, but what about your other two uncles?

So you and Alma (Irish) went in town to see 'Sergeant York' did you. I thought it was good too. I seen it twice myself. Listen, Shirley, you had better not let Alma watch you write these letters because I don't want her to know that I love you too. She may get mad at me.

Yes, I am worried about your dad. I am worried because he gets '92 [*local beer*] and I don't. I can get Miller's High Life but it's too weak. If I was you Shirley, I would raise heck if anybody opened my mail since you are old enough to flirt with soldiers. You tell Pop that it's all right for him to drink beer, but not to talk about his old girlfriends. Alma might think I'd do the same thing.

In the army every day seems the same, it don't matter what date it is, unless it's getting near payday. You tell Alma for me please that all the pretty girls here are from Missouri – that ain't from Kentucky damn it. Well, it's about 11:00 o'clock here Shirley so I guess I'll have to close for now. So you be good until I hear from you again. I'll still be,
Your best and only boyfriend,
Norb

Louisville, Kentucky, **September 2**, 8:30 pm
Dear Bootsie,

Well, we got your letter and it certainly was appreciated. It seems to me you are kept busy and glad to hear somebody does your thinking for you. It relieves your brain. "What brains?" By this time you know why Zip didn't write, was moved you know. Mom is just feeding the pisses [*faces*]. Certainly am sorry to hear of Bud Neuner. I hope it isn't so. Alma was here last night for supper. I got a card from Alice Butler from Bay View, Michigan. Write Mary [*Cousin Mary Hollkamp who rented the 2nd floor living quarters at 1344 Texas*] a note with our letter if you think of it, honey.

It's the time of the year for hair to fall out, so don't worry about becoming bald and your Vitalis will soon be on the way. Glad to know your cold is better. Mr. Amshoff, the Prudential Insurance man, enlisted too, he told Mom. I do not know what branch of the service. I am also enclosing a clipping from the Society News. By this time you have the pictures too. I think they are all grand especially the one of you setting down, that is being enlarged. Dewey [*Joey Rawert Carter's stepson*] registers for St. X.

Glad to hear of the wonderful reach, boarding house reach, huh? Now about being sent over the pond. Perhaps you'll get a chance like Zip and maybe that was just a rumor. We'll hope it was Freddy Schmidt is in Hawaii. He wrote his mother he'd love to spend the duration there.

How do you sleep? Is your bunk comfortable? I didn't think they took illiterates in the army. Johnny stopped by yesterday. He was vaccinated again. They still are house hunting. Did you see the eclipse of the moon last week? You write the moon gets you down. $1.85 for a phone call 'twasn't [*sic*] bad. I guess it hurt your purse.

Love,

Hermina

Louisville, Kentucky, **September 2**, 10 pm

Dear Norb,

Your letter sure was appreciated. Mom went to Lip's with it and she had one, so it was two very much pleased Mammas. Well, you're drilling! Do you think your high school drills helps you out any? I worked since 12:30 today, just jerked around before that time [*epileptic seizure*]. I hope you can help those W. Virginians out some. Leo, I mean, Moody, sent a box of candy for you. If you don't eat it, give it to one of those poor guys. You can feel fortunate aside of them. They couldn't read a letter if they got one. How many soldiers are at Camp Crowder? That airmail letter didn't come any sooner than a free letter. It got here on the morning delivery where we would probably gotten the free one in the afternoon. How many days does it take you to get a letter 3 cents postage.

Mildred M. gave Ann and Joe a spice set, fits in a rack, 8 assorted spices and a nest of mixing bowls, 5 of them. They are all so cute. The Madden kids are giving a show. Three cents admission. Shirley and Betsy sell the lemonade between acts. Believe me, that's something.

I think we'll have to send the Vitalis and candy under separate cover. Alma is busy writing your letters, must be humdingers. I suppose the Boyer [*movie star Charles Boyer*] type. She keeps them close to her heart, oh so close to her heart, and nobody can read them. Well, Boyer of the US Army, I am sending another clipping, they claim they marched up the aisle in duck or ducky formation [*referring to an announcement regarding the wedding of Francis State and Anna Marie Logsdon*].

I'll finish this letter tomorrow but one thing I must say we find out more from your written than we did snout to snout.

Goodnite dear, goodnite until tomorrow,

[*Hermina*]

Louisville, Kentucky, **September 2**

Dear Son!

I hope by now you will have what you most needed, that is, laxatives. Are you still bound up? If you want anything else, let us know. John said those grape nuts for breakfast helps him so much. He said you should eat that, too, if you could. Mrs. Russell was planning to see Junior but he wrote he might get a furlough in September or October, so she is not going as

yet. Junior is alright. I hope that you will enjoy everything in the box. Papa, Mary, Marge, Shirley and Betsy say hello.
Mother

Continued by Hermina:

Eddie Stevens enters Officers Training school this week in Virginia. Mom said can you can spend the money there. Or not? A foolish question. Mamma is sending Edelweiss.

Continued by Betsy and Shirley Muth:

Hi Norb.
From Betsy

Hello Uncle Norb,
I was wondering how you are.
From Shirley Ann Muth

Louisville, Kentucky, **September 2**

Dear Mom, Pop, Sis's and Bros.,

I received the box you sent me and liked it very much, but I wouldn't send anything like that through the mail again. It's not that I don't appreciate it, but everything was busted up except the cigs and gum. I opened up the box and peanuts went all over the place, but the cigarettes were in good shape, the pills also.

I'm glad to hear that June's [*Junior Russell's*] going to get a furlough and I guess he is too. I guess Zip will really go through the mill, too. They have officer training here, too, but you have to be in the Army 4 or 5 months before you can apply for it.

I arise at five and go to bed at eleven, so I don't get so much sleep. The sun is hotter than blue hell here. I don't know how it is there. I believe it's a 110 in the shade and we never get in the shade.

You have told me about five times that Shirley and Alma went to the show, so I thought I could save you a little trouble by leaving it out of your next letter. I got a letter from Lip today and one from Joey yesterday. I will answer them as soon as possible. The biggest news of all is that Hermina is going to work. Now that is news. Ha, ha. This is all the time I have so until I have again, I'll still be raising hell about these "yaps."
I remain,
Norb

Louisville, Kentucky, **September 3,** 9 am

Dear Brother,

For breakfast, we had kuchen, coffee, doughnuts. I bet you had better than that. You get plenty of chow but just what do you get, honey? Margaret don't like the idea of your reach when you come home. We'll all be left in the shade. You could pick tomatoes without getting up from the table. Mrs. Russell might go to see Junior [Norb's neighbor and boyhood friend]. It all depends on it if he can get a furlough or not. Joe heard Bud Neuner was on a torpedo boat. Poor boy. How did you hear it?

Bye, until tomorrow.

[Hermina]

Louisville, Kentucky, **September 3**

Dear little brother,

Just read your letter and my poor soul almost broke. Well, I think by this time you received my $2.00 I mailed last Sunday morning. Altho [*sic*] I'll think it over by the time I finish this one and another may grow back. I found the bottle the other night that I had of yours the day of Joe's wedding and it's about 1/4 of a quart. I'm saving it - we will have a highball. Alma just called up and is wanting to know if we are going to Holy Hour and she is coming and going with us. It's now 10 minutes of 6 and 7 o'clock is holy hour. We are having sauerkraut for supper. I think it will hold out so I can get to church and back. It really works. How is the boy that can't write? Does he ever get anything from anybody? I sure do feel for him, or does he like it? The children started school, I mean registered, today. Shirley and Hermina are working on a box for you. Papa is going to write some time. He always asks about the letters and really enjoys to know about you. I am wondering who is going to make it with Alma, the Pa or the kid brother. We all like her real, real much. We haven't gotten the picture as yet. Jimmie Huntley is in the Navy. Mr. Russell came over and told us. I haven't been over there since you left. Elizabeth had a letter from you and Wahoo's wife [*Joey, Norb's sister*] also. They both enjoyed them immensely. Did you ever write to Cletus Muerr? He is at Waverly and do write to him. (Cletus Muerr, Waverly Hills Sanatorium, Waverly, Kentucky). Now this is about all I know as Joe told me to tell you this address. Now the angelus bells are ringing and prayer is in the kitchen. I'm praying and writing also.

Katsy is going to start school and is all thrilled over it. Norb, is there anything you want me to do? So you want something? As I told you I'll think of you, so here is about all or else they will eat all the supper for me. We are still busy at work as Mr. Hubbuch has been sick. I haven't seen him since you left. He is back at work I was told, only I haven't been near him. Old man Axe is calling "Vegetable man!" I'm surprised you can't hear him. He's really early tonight. Hoping you receive the 2 bucks I am enclosing.

Love and best of luck. Study real hard and we will pray for you. Queen of Peace pray for us! Your sis,

Margaret

September [or Aug?] 3

Dear Mom, Pop and All,

How are you all? My feet feel like two raw beefsteaks. We have rubber soles on these shoes and I don't like them. I believe they way [*sic*] about 10 pounds apiece. As soon as I get some money Mom I will send you something but I am broker now than hell and I won't get paid for maybe another month and a half because I never did sign the pay roll yet.

It rained all day here but that don't matter, you go on just the same. This whole army is all wet. You can take that two ways if you like. I got a letter from Lip, Betsy and Jimmy, too. That Betsy is just about as witty in a letter as she is to her face.

They keep you too damn busy here to even think. But you don't have to worry about that because they do all the thinking for you. There are a bunch of fellows shipping out of here every day. In about another 3 weeks we will start wearing our winter clothes. They are pretty damn heavy but they are top rate material.

I dropped my watch this morning when I was washing but I don't think it hurt any. I haven't set it for two weeks and I'm only running a minute fast. That sure was a good picture of Zip but I knew that it was going to happen all the time because he told me so. I am pretty sure he will make it. Well, I think I'll get to bed because I'm all staved [*sic*] up (hop-jump-stop-jump).

Well, that's all I know for now so until I hear from all of you again,
I remain,
Yardbird Norb

Louisville, Kentucky, **September 4**, 3:30 pm

Dear Norb,

We received your letter today. So did Shirley. Your letters are coming more frequent, to our utter joy. (How's that?) Did you get the two bucks Marge sent you? So your box was like hash. Well, I did not pack it too good, I suppose because I thought you could get it Saturday. How did you enjoy the newspaper I sent with 'em?

Alma was too young for Mengels [*a company that manufactured wood products for war use*] and Mrs. Russell too old, from 21 - 40. I sure was sorry for Alma as they are working them so long again. She's going to the telephone company.

We, that is, Marge, Mom and me woke up this morning, it was a special delivery at 1:15 am from Eileen Saunders - it frightened us so, we just couldn't sleep after that for a while, it wasn't a damn thing in it. I thought if I could get my hands on her then I could of beat her up. Mom sent you $2.00 too. We got your letter in 36 hours. Your free ones come quicker than Air Mail. Isn't that strange?

The Madden kids' show netted them $1.36. Shirley made 36 cents, she sold kool-ade (1 quart) and fudge, 20 pieces. It was all sold out in two minutes. Sure was funny to watch.

Shirley was the "pronouncer" [*announcer*]. They sang the latest hits and ended it with our national anthem. Some kids wanted their money back.

Mr. Madden said the Lieutenant at Jefferson told the men over there that in 8 months' time all healthy married and single men would be in the army regardless of dependents. Norb, you read that wrong. I said when Fritz Smith entered Camp Crowder it was 1,500 boys there, that was the middle of March. So you know all the dope on going to officers' training. Well, I hope you get the chance. Did you enjoy all the Zip's clippings? That was funny.

Continued, **September 5**

I hope you got acquainted with that James Wachtel by this time. Mrs. Madden's sister is in Cincinnati, Ohio. She's trying to join the WAAC's [Women's Army/Air Corps]. Now they are taking them with high school diplomas, college isn't required.

I just got through waxing the kitchen, hall and bath. My poor little knees. We are sending you a box today, packed lots better. I hear all packages are censored. Is that true? The West End had a pouring down rain after supper yesterday. We had a sprinkle but it's a lot cooler today.

Continued, Sunday **September 6,** 10:30 pm

Nobbe,

I heard yesterday Jonesy is expected back over Labor Day. Cletus Murr received your letter. One doctor told him he didn't know why he had to be there [*Waverly*]. He could receive the same treatment at home, the way I understand he isn't bedfast. They play cards, roll the bones, and play the ponies. They can sit on the sun porch. That's pretty fat I think.

This is going to be a long story. We waited 9 days for those pictures to be reprinted. We had a family picture (with the boys in front) and you sitting at Ft. Harrison enlarged, they sent the films back, it was an oversight. I put these films in an envelope, told Betsy to take them to Hertel's. Betsy drops them in the mail box [*instead*], so I had to call the P.O. and identify what was in it, as the mail collector wouldn't give them to Shirley. So Moody got them last night at 10 pm. They even wanted to know if they were prints or negatives, very particular. Margie is starting young to be a wash lady. She said I'll help you wash Mother, Lip answered yes. Unbeknowanced [*sic*] to Lip she puts in Jim's red socks, so all the good white shirts came out in the 'pink' of condition.

Mom went 7 days too soon to the 3rd Order Conference. Services are next Sunday. Not until she got [there] did she realize she was a week early. There has been no second breakfast so far.

Mary [*Hollkamp*] said tell honey-bunch hello for her. Mrs. Smith [*Ann's mother*] came to see Ann [*Norb's brother Joes' wife*] yesterday afternoon. I suppose your 'timmers' aren't as tired as your 'tup's, unless you keep 'thumming the Serg.'

Norb, I am sending you the $2.00 I promised. Please have your picture tooked [*jokingly*]

38

like Zip's with dress coat, peak hat. We will be waiting. Would you like to have a sewing kit? And a shoe shine kit? I know now every box gets censored so they evidently ripped open the cellophane socks and put it all together. This is all I know for this time, huntsfutza [*Huntfurz, German for dog fart, a favorite expression in the Rawert household*]. I see Mr. and Mrs. Sherran on Lee's porch with their baby, he looks the same. School starts at 9 pm, Market Street cars are going to run again during school hours.

Well, as I am as ever, your sister, or Your daily Diagnostician,
Love and 1,000 ughs or hummhs (how do you spell your answer, the grunt?),
Hermina

[*Typed letter*] **September 6**

Dear Mom, Pop, Sis's and Bro's,

How is everything back in the hills? You know I'm getting to be a city slicker. So Jimmie Hundley is in the Navy. Well, I met him a couple of nights before I left. In the army I think you'll see more. I get tired of looking at water unless I have a fishing pole in my hand. They say there is a pretty food fishing hole down here, so I think I will try it out some Sunday if I get a chance.

I got a letter from Cletus Murr yesterday and he said he likes it fine. I sure am glad he does. It would be hell if he didn't. I wrote to him the first day or second day I was here. I sure do feel sorry for him. That is what you really call a tough break, especially for a guy so young.

I guess when Katsy starts to school she will have to take Betsy along so the teacher can understand her. Don't you think? No, I can't hear Axe quite this far, but I think it's because they are shooting on the rifle range. It's not because he don't holler loud enough.

It's been raining for the last 3 days but it's pretty nice today. I was glad it rained because it was getting hot as hell here. Was it very hot there? That sauerkraut sounds OK but I think I will have something better than that. At least I hope so. We have to mop our floors every morning and scrub them on our hands and knees every Friday. They sure do keep this place clean. I believe it's the first time some of these guys ever seen soap and water.

Is there anything happening around the burg, except new babies? Tell Mrs. Russell I said thanks for the card, I would write her but I have so many damn letters to write, that is about all I have time for. I have about six letters to answer today, but I won't be able to answer them all. You see we are having a beer party this afternoon and I don't want to miss that. It's going to be 5% beer too, so they say.

The Horse [*Hermina*] said she is still jerking around, well you know. it's necessary to take some form of exercise. We have to take exercise every morning and night. Hermina said I should feel fortunate aside from some of them guys. Well, there is room for argument there. They are so dumb that they can't do nothing so they get off easy, except when we drill, and we do plenty of that. I believe it's about eight miles every day.

I would have gave My Ass and Elbows to see that State wedding, oh, if I just had a moving picture of that I could really make some money. That would bring a laugh in a funeral parlor. I wonder if Old Man State had chicken shit on his shoes just for old time's sake. I guess Mrs. State was attired in her usual night gown. I have to address the envelopes in pen and ink I don't think they allow you to have them typewritten. That is to check up on if anybody is cheating the government out on mail.

This is the first time I sat at a typewriter for a long time, but I still remember the key board about as good as ever. This is a hell of a lot faster that using a pencil. So I can let you in on more dope, in a shorter period of time. I am not Boyer of the US Army. I am just another 'Yardbird.' I guess I will be for at least three months. Then I guess me and Mc Arthur will get together. Me as his personal adviser on how to sleep well at nights.

I got two more shots, in my arm of course, and they are sore as hell. I think it might be from the weather because there was a fog in the holler. Ask Pop if there was a fog there. You can tell Pop I'll excuse him from writing if he just drinks a beer for me instead. Yes sir, I am really developing a reach. I can just make the length of a ten foot table now, no telling what it will be by the time I get out of this army. I get most of my local dope. He is about as good with a letter as he is with his mouth. I don't know if it is an advantage or disadvantage but in the army I think it is an advantage. If you can't holler for what you want you are shit out of luck. You know I bet this letter would be ten pages long if it were written in pencil. This typing sure does save space.

We head for the rifle range tomorrow. I imagine that will be a little fun. I hope I make expert. You get to shoot eighty shots I believe. Forty preliminary and forty which goes into your service book. This book means everything when you get out of the army. It tells everything you done while you are in the army. So I guess it's best to have a good service record.

There were a bunch of boys came in from Texas last night, or this morning about 4:30. Woke all of us up. We had to put up beds for them guys, but somebody had to do the same for us. I met another Kentuckian from Highland Park, and another from 29th and Portland. They are both about thirty-two years old. There are quite a few guys from Kentucky around here but you can find them from any state in the Union.

Thank you girls for the assistance. It gave me new life and a couple of beers. Well, I think I am about finished now so until I hear again I'll still be a YARDBIRD.

Love to all,

Norb

Louisville, Kentucky, **September 7**, Labor Day, 1:30 pm

Dear Norb,

I suppose Labor Day doesn't spell a thing to you except the same old routine. It's the same here. I think most people worked. Marge didn't. We washed the same as usual. Katie couldn't think otherwise. Mom is sending you a Dr. Scholl foot outfit without the exerciser. I think your poor feet get plenty of that. Mom said what does a regular meal consist of? Lavada, Mrs. Russell's niece, is looking for a furnished apartment. I never seen the like, on Texas Street near Shelby, a living room, a bedroom fairly furnished and a kitchen in very poor condition [is] $62.50 per month. Wessenger-Gaulbert Apts. One room and a bath $65 s month. How's that for rent?

Ray Gehrig gave Katz [*Katsy*] a lunch kit for school. She was up yesterday. You'd thought it was worth a million. It seems like we might have a shower. Say Norb, your bed is darn hard. That's my spot for the duration. Haven't got any special news. Don't know if Jonesy got a 3 day leave or not. Joe didn't work either. Shirley is staying until tomorrow morning school time. Schlegel brother is going to help his father. The Pastor is going to fix up one of these cottages for him to live in. Tain't bad. Mom is going back to church to give in your name and have those Plaques blessed and also turn in your pledge envelopes Well, Rookie, this is all for this time.

Johnny expects to hear today if they will get that place on Payne. We are going to get your picture at the White Cottage sometime.

As ever, with lots of love,
Hermina R.

Louisville, Kentucky, **September 7**, Tuesday, 8:00 am
Dear Norb,

We just got your letter and your foot soap and salve will be on its way. Norb, you never do say if you received the money Mom and Marge sent. Marge sent $2.00 twice and Mom sent you $2.00 last week. I got a Lane Bryant book. Would you like to see all the fat ladies? Your poor little tups. Don't they give you anything for that? Do you all do your own washing? And can you wear white socks? If you can we will send you some. Why, you dated that letter before you were in the army - August 3rd you had. Let us know if you got the money or not. We heard the President's speech last night and thought he was fine.
Until tomorrow,
Hermina

Louisville, Kentucky, **September 8**
Dear Norb,

I am going to town today to pay my last $33 and I am glad of that. The doctor's office will be closed after Sept. 15th. Dr. Stevens is in army. He sent me a letter and told the name and address of another Dr. if I would need him. Norb if you can write Mary a few lines you can put it in our letter or write her a special one. I know it would please her very much. Papa is well. John & Joe gave him the laugh. Father Marchell is in the hospital. I don't know in what hospital. I hope that your feet and eyes will get better soon. Hope you got to church Sunday

and that you have been to the Sacraments. If you would know how much it worries me, you would go. I went to St. Boniface on Sunday thinking it was the 2ⁿᵈ Sunday and when I got there it was empty. Then it dawned on me it was the 1ˢᵗ Sunday. They gave me the laugh at home. Well, they all say hello to you and I will close with the hope that you are well also. It is now 10:20 am. Norb I send you $1.00. Hope I can give you more next time
Your loving Mother

Continued, **September 8**, 9:30 pm

Dear Norb,

Well, how are those sweaty, swollen, tender feet? Can't you go barefooted? Bernard Hollkamp and his mother was here today. Bernard was examined, you know, so he leaves tomorrow for Camp if he passes the Armory exams. I imagine he will get a furlough. Lou got a V-Letter from William today. You know - the kind they take a picture of. Photo static, I believe the correct name is. Gertie called her baby Nancy Lou. It will be a year tomorrow that William is in the army.

I am enclosing a card you might be a little interested in, I don't know if you will profit from it or not, or if you must be a member. I am also enclosing a clipping.

Jerry Madden told me her mother told her not to pick up a cat or dog, it might have 'macease' [*disease*] Katsy is Twaysie [*crazy*] about school even if it didn't start, they got off at 10:00 am. Muth's [*Candy*] made the second most money of any booth at our picnic.

Lill's nephew and cousin were here over Labor Day but Johnny did not come. Did you get your box sent last Friday with Vitalis? Mom's going to the Sugar Rationing Board. That's all for tonite. Until tomorrow, your daily diagnostician.

Continued, Wednesday morning, **September 9**, 9 am

Dear Brother Norbert,

Just received your nicely typed letter and must say it did a lot of good for Mom to tell you not to use some words, ha, ha. I am enclosing a clipping from the first page of Friday's paper. Would you like the Times? Mr. Clephas died, you know, our neighbor from next door on Clay Street. Here's hoping you do good on the rifle range. You know Chalmers came in first and second on the pistol range, at least that's the dope their church bulletin put out. His mom gave their information with officers and men competing. "Dead shot Chalmers" - that's what he's known as.

I thought of your Godchild when I got this Fish Fry card in [*postcard advertising a fish fry at the All Wool and a Yard Wide Democratic Club at Shelby and Goss, in honor of the Soldier Boys, Ed. Zipperle, Chairman*]. Mass starts at 8:00. They were the first there. Sister told them to come 15 minutes later, 7:45 was plenty soon - doesn't that take you back to your school days, that promptness?

Your fish are begging for food. I think they can see me at the dining table. Mrs. Gyr

[*sp*] is just leaving Mrs. Threedouble's and there are a lot of good byes. You know Raymond Robben is separated from his wife and is trying to get in the Navy.
PIG [*Hermina*]

Louisville, Kentucky, **September 9**, 4:30 pm

Dear Norb,

I hain't [*sic*] got over your typewritten letter as yet. Let that happen more often brother - long and cussy[*sic*]. We are having steak, green beans, maters, taters for supper. On the way home from church Mom met Mrs. Bodner and Tom. She had to stop in and have kuchen and coffee. Louie is in 1-B. He's ruptured. They won $45 at a bingo. *[$1.00 in 1943 had the same buying power in 1943 as $12.49 in 2017, so they won around $642.00]*. I don't know if it was recently or not, Helen is still so backwards yet. I wonder if you know this Tindall. His picture has appeared 3 days out of 4 this week in the paper. He lives in the 900 block of Oak Street and is 22 years old. His father recognized his picture in the Sunday CJ [*Courier Journal newspaper*].

Norb did you ever fix your teeth? I guess you didn't get time to go gallivanting as yet. Are the Missouri women as beautiful as KY? Your typing isn't half-bad. Mom feels like you are going to study harder for Uncle Sam than you did here; she feels you're going someplace. How did your shooting come out? I see McArthur asks every soldier to kill one Jap so when you shoot, think it is a Jap. And you might be known as the Sure-Dead-Shot Rawert. Did you see the Wachtel boy as yet?

We are expecting Alma tonight. How was the beer party? Was you bartender? I am glad Clarence J. writes, especially if he's that windy. We haven't been to the Catalog Store since you been away. So you received the money and new life. How perfectly amazing. How do you sleep at night since you want to advise McArthur? Jimmy gave Mom two Cracker Jack pins for that McArthur pin.

Russell celebrated Labor Day too; instead he began a day ahead and extended it another day. We are all glad you wrote Cletus Murr. It shows your charitable spirit which I think you inherit from both sides, a sympathetic person is always appreciated - like me.

It isn't necessary for you to tell Pop to drink one for you. He hasn't failed as yet. I think he will write you a few lines sometime. Would you like a loaf of homemade bread? That's Mom's idea. We had a shower this afternoon. We can use a few showers.

Mom is enclosing a piece of her new tablecloths she bought in honor of her two Irish daughter-in-laws, and Alma which would have been three, hadn't Uncle [*Sam*] stepped in. Alma enjoys reading our letters but hers she keeps close to her heart. I got a hunch they're the Boyer type, Challie [*reference to Charles Boyer*].

Well, yard bird, how do you like the Missouri mud? Are you still gaining in weight? And knowledge? Fred Kremer says hello. Until tomorrow your daily diagnosis columnist, Sow R. [Hermina]

Dear Norb,

I cannot write much news because Hermina can write faster that I and maybe you cannot read my writing because you have not answered my questions. Alma is reading my letter but she won't let us read hers. I wonder why???? I surely enjoyed the letter. So did Pop - the first letter he read. We always read them for him. We are ready to go to see Mr. Clephas. Joe is going to take Papa and I [*sic*]. Well good-bye so far and so long.

[*German writing*] that means Your Loving Mother

PS. We saw the most beautiful rainbow. It lasted about 45 minutes.

Continued by Shirley Muth:

Dear Uncle Norb,

I have been wondering when you will answer my letter. I guess you are busy though. I sold another towel today. I have found Milton's sister's name. Her name is Sister Leon and Mary Katherine's [*Katsy's*] sister's name is Joan. She was sick in school today. Sister said she was sick and she was crying.

Hope you are well. I guess you don't get enough '92s now. I get mine almost every night and I'm still up at Mommy's yet. I was just covering my schoolbooks. Write soon. I want you to write me when you start to school.

YOUR A-1 GIRLFRIEND,

Shirley Muth

Camp Crowder, Missouri, **September 9**

Dear People,

I picked up a couple of minutes to drop a line or so. Well, I finally got to the rifle range and done damn good for myself. I made "Sharpshooter." I made 168 out of a possible 200. The bull's eye is 10 inches and you shoot at it from a distance of 200 yards. It was really a lot of fun even if my ears are still ringing. Them rifles sure make a hell of a noise when they go off. I guess I will get a badge or whatever you call it in about 2 weeks. I believe some of them actually threw off because they thought if they shot too good they would send them across. But there were very few fellows like that. They were getting up some pretty good jackpots, but my funds were a little too low to indulge. The highest score out of 500 men was 177 so I wasn't so damn far behind.

What was in this letter that was so important that Eileen had to send a special delivery? Well, right now at Camp Crowder there are 50,000 men. So I guess Fritz Smith came over there when this place was a mud hole. Where is Fritz now? I never heard anything of James Wachtel. He must be up the road from me apiece.

No, they do not censor any bundles here. If they do, I never heard of it. Thanks a lot for the package and tell Lip (Elizabeth) thanks also, in case I don't get to write immediately.

Yes, I heard about those pictures three times already. I will be busy all this weekend. I have to stand ground tomorrow night. Damn it! Well, it's time for me to hit the hay; it's 10:50 so I will have to close now.
Love to all,
Norb

PS. Tell Cousin Mary that I send her a special hello with a big kiss.
Just a special note: Please send me what brown or white socks I have. I think I have a few pair. About eight of my handkerchiefs and the rest of my shorts and shirts that still look pretty good. Because I'm short on all of these. I'm getting just like Mom. I have to warsh [jokingly] every day.
Thanks a million, Norb

Louisville, Kentucky, **September 10**
Dear Norb,

Well, Norb, I ain't got no news, so what's the need of writing, huh? I did want to ask you how big your 'low Dutch' feet is getting; perhaps you'll be in Herm. H.'s shoes 'fore long. You must of rented that typewriter. I read Joe's letter - Sugar on Sewer Caps! Well, we all got a good kick out of it. Mom's gone to Mr. Clephas's Funeral Mass; he had Dropsy. How are the army MDs? There must have been plenty fogs in the holler. We had two nice showers yesterday and the most brilliantly colored rainbow I have ever seen. Mary is going to Gertie Bowe's. She has three in the Service. Your foot balm should be there by now. That's all for now.
Your Un-newsy Commentator,
Hermina

Continued, **September 10**, 8:30 am
Dear Norb,

I couldn't refrain from writing you this morning. I am enclosing a picture of myself [*probably a picture of a pig or horse*] as it appeared in the C. J. We are all OK. I read where Frank Stratman is with the Navy Chemical something. It said he attended Speed Scientific School 3 years after graduating at St. X. I guess you hear from Zip. The fish are begging with a terrific wiggle. They sure mean business. I don't know of no new babies either. Alma just called. She's coming tomorrow afternoon. I am also sending a picture of a husky Negro soldier. If you keep on going brother, can we expect you to look like this? He sure looks pleasant.

Haven't heard if Bernard H [*Hollkamp*] has left or not. You have to wait a week to get pictures at Hertel's now. We're waiting patiently. Having our family picture enlarged and you sitting at Ft. Harrison.

Haven't heard from Jr Hubbuch as yet so I presume he's going over the pond. Hoping you are well and that you don't get too fat. That's no good, you know.
Your daily diagnosis columnist,
H.R.

PS. Did you get a picture made as yet? Marge is sending a dollar. Just say hello to Mary in your next letter to us.

Louisville, Kentucky, **September 11**

Dear Norb,

Well, I was in town today, yes sir. I saw more pretty cute little dresses for myself. Seen Dr. Stites and his office. Well, they had chairs in the center of the room. Mildred M. seen Dr. Atherton at Hertel's yesterday. He was naturally in uniform, sunburnt and looking fine. This gossip we heard about his coming back because of the strain on his heart is all idle gossip. The lady that kept his office said he was expecting to go across so perhaps it was a furlough before he went. Dr. Soam is still at Ft. Harrison. Maybe he gave you some of your shots. I passed Kunz's about 1:20 pm today, about 250 Negros were lined up and walking in. I suppose they were from the army. Didn't you go to Kunz, too? Ray Kegabein left yesterday and was not given a two-week furlough. My blood pressure is exactly 100, now I know why I felt so lazy [she had low thyroid]. We didn't go to the fish fry. I am going on a diet again (until tomorrow). Ann had a washday tonight and she said I should tell you she washed everything, flowery or not. Pop said I should tell you he's just drinking Oertel's and he wishes you were here with him to hoist one. He couldn't get a letter together tonight but he's going to soon.

Well, I hear we are going to have gas rationing for the rubber shortage; 5,000 miles per year. Mayor Wyatt is speaking now asking the citizens to keep their cans for the tin collection which is once a month.

I suppose you will hear from Alma saying she has part of Joey's letter. If Joey has part of her letter, I surely would like to have been Joey, "Challie."

Every third Wednesday is tin collection day over all the city of Louisville. Papa's drinking another '92. He certainly obeys your orders [*to drink for Norb*], and hasn't failed yet. Joe's over. Shirley's going home Sunday night. I'm sending you some 'beer cheese. We all sampled it. It's 60 cents a pound. Are you still marching? By this time next week, you'll be going to school again.

That Stuckenborg boy is getting his papers, his sister said. They hated to see him go 'especially' since he's assistant foreman at some distillery. He's about 20 years old. Hoping you're well. Little Danny Burmeister said my pin [brooch?] looks like 'Christmas Eggs.'
Love from all of us to you honey bunch.
H.R.

Write tomorrow. Note: No joking Norb, would you like to have a fountain syringe? Or some laxatives? What brand?

Bye-Bye,

H.R.

Camp Crowder, Missouri, ~~August~~ (pardon me) **September 12**

Dear Mom, Pop, Marge and Meanie,

You will have to pardon the heading of this letter. I can't remember what month it is. You know it seems sometimes as though I haven't been in the army over a week and then again, it seems as though I have been in here five years. I guess it's because they keep you so busy.

We went on a 12-mile hike today and my feet are slightly on the tired side of things. Well, I have to go for an interview with a fellow named Capt. Lauch [*sp*]. I may or may not get a permanent personnel job on the rifle range. I'm sort of in doubt if I want it or not. Sometimes I think it would be a break, and then again, I don't like Missouri so much. I have to learn my 'Military Courtesy' before Monday before I meet with this guy because that's one thing they are pretty tough on.

Say, I met that Wachtel fellow or whatever his name is. I didn't get to talk to him very long though. He seems to be a right guy. I don't get hold of a typewriter all the time. I only wish I could catch up on my correspondence. I am way behind. Mom mentioned Mr. Clephas in her letter. Do I know him?

I tell you I been so busy lately I hardly have time to scribble so I hope you can read this. I seen that about Pappy [Father] Knue, but nobody can change my mind. I still think he is .I haven't begun to study anything yet, and I won't for at least a week. We had Telephones, Chemical Warfare and a lot of other things. We went through the gas chamber, that is - tear gas, first with the mask on, and then you go in with the mask off, and you have to hold your breath to keep your eyes closed - or else. You would be so surprised how that gas burns your skin. It doesn't do any damage but it just burns. It looks funny as hell to see a bunch of guys crying.

I received that foot saver in good order and the eye drops also. I sleep pretty damn good most of the time and so would anybody else, after the shadows begin falling, because you're just a little tired. But I don't get much more sleep because I go to bed at 11 and get up at five.

Tell Shirley and Jimmy I appreciate their letters a lot and will write them as soon as I find time. No, I wouldn't have no use for homemade bread, even though I would like some. You can tell Alma (honey) that there may be just a little more practical news in this letter, but I know she reads them all the time because I could tell by her letters (Sherlock Holmes).

I haven't been over three squares off the barracks except on hikes and going to basic school. I never seen enough of "Missouri Women" to pass an opinion on them, but it's impossible to beat Kentucky women, especially one, and I don't have to say who that is.

I heard I got my letters mixed up. I bet somebody got a kick out of that, even if I didn't.

That just goes to show you how busy I am. I'll have to close now so until I hear from all you again,
Norb

Louisville, Kentucky, **September 12**, Saturday, 8:45 am

Dear Norb,

Well, well, so we got a sharpshooter in our family. Congratulations! Do you think you can thank Wahoo [reference to Joey's husband, Lee Carter, part Indian, who hunted with Norb] a little? That was darn good - 168 out of 200. My, my.

Mom is ending you some underwear. You know some of yours wasn't worth a blow out, so she got you some Hanes shirts, Cooper shorts, and Bachelor Friend socks. I'm sure they'll all fit, she said she better not catch any Gen. [General] in your shorts. If MacArthur wants to, special privileges will be granted. Didn't you get your undies from the Gov? I marked all your things. I hope it will be OK. I also sewed on your cute little unmentionables. I would of been called Hermina for that when you were home. Your weight must be about 177. Well, that isn't bad, boy - you'll get to your father's weight yet (all muscle and brawn). How was the beer party? Did you get your snout wet or did you miss '92? Mom said you should feel free to ask for the things you want. Pop was glad to hear of your shooting average even if he does cry a little.

Charles Meyer is home on a furlough from the Navy. (Mrs. Paul's grandson) We made out that O.P.A. [Office of Property Assessment?] sheet for property owners. Sure were some questions. But you can see why they do it. Pop's getting ready to get a shock of beer. What do you think the initials SCRTC stand for? I heard Shanky Schenkenfelder is across.

Several nights this week a plane flew across with floodlights on. Alma is here tonite. I have no scandal to write of. Fritz Schmidt is in Honolulu, said the army is a lot easier over there and would like to spend the 'duration' over there. I keep watching the paper for boys from Camp Crowder and I never seen but one boy's name - it sounded Jewish and altogether different address. The news sounds very good for us at the present time.
Tu tu tu toot dear, goodnite, sweet goodnite until tomorrow.
[Hermina]

PS. Your bed does fine. I cut down that extra mattress and it lays fine. I'm getting it in shape for you, angel.

Louisville, Kentucky, **September 13**, Sunday, 1:50 pm

Dear Norb,

We included these cards with the letter. They might come in handy, hun. Did you get the box of stationary that we sent you? Alma said you received hers. We are OK. I'm full of watermelon. Did you get the foot preparation and eye drops? Here comes Pop for his dinner. Mom's getting ready to go to church. She went last week, too, you know. It's very warm today.

Shirley wants a bike so bad that she's going to the bingo to win some money so she can buy one. She told Lip she wanted one for her birthday. Your Maw says wanting and getting is two different things. Mrs. Bierbaum's son came home and got tonsillitis. Mary got a very cute card for you. Mom's waiting to mail this.

What's the name of your chaplain and how old is he? Bernard Spoelker signed up to go in as Chaplain under our Bishop, not with the army officers yet.

Anna Hub's former husband is now Captain in the 5ᵗʰ Armored Division in Camp Cook, California. Marge is still got ants [energy] and I have still got lead. Little Nickie next door is an alley rat. He was rooting our garbage cans yesterday with his little pants almost off. He looked so cute, walks all around. Glad you are off on Sunday. No more news, so until tomorrow.

Your Daily diagnosis,
H.R.

Louisville, Kentucky, **September 13**, Sunday, 7 pm
Wonderful Rawert,

You know Norb we didn't see the inside of the flap of the envelope until tonight (got the letter Saturday). You naughty boy - you forgot your pen. Johnny [*Norb's brother*] spied it tonight. Johnny, Inc. is here. They were very much thrilled with your letter. Edgar and family are visiting Joe. I just spoke to them and they asked about you. Edgar said there used to be a little increase in your pay for sharpshooting. Johnny thought that was in the Navy.

Here is a good one on Russell - he sat on his swivel chair and he went thru the front window. He beat it to bed (9 pm on Saturday). She asked him about it this morning - words couldn't express it - he acted like the cat who ate the canary. Mom wants to write some.

Louisville, Kentucky, **September 14**, Monday, 9 am
Monday is washday to you, too.
Dear Abby,

Looked for a letter this morning but were S.O.L. (Shit Out of Luck).
[Hermina]

Continued by Norb's mother:
Dear Norbert,

I just got done with the dishes. It is 12:20 noon. Shirley is still here - can't get rid of her. Ha, ha, ha. She went to town with Anna Saturday. She likes that very much. Alma was here Saturday evening. She stayed overnight, went to 6:30 Mass, then to work. She wrote to you Saturday night, I believe. It takes her about 2 hours. I don't blame her for all the loving words she thinks and writes. I like to tease her - she don't get angry but laughs about it. Papa thinks yesterday was his last Sunday off [*worked as janitor and bell ringer at St. Brigid's.*] He said he might not come home for dinner - he would not get hardly no rest.

I went to the 3rd Order Conference. The church was crowded now. Mrs. Bierbaum and I went. Her son is home on furlough but he got sick, has a very bad throat. He went to the doctor but I don't remember what she said it was. He came last Wednesday and has to go back this Wednesday. He is commander of over 1,100 men.

Well, Hermina just called. She went to work this morning about 10:00 o'clock. She saw Lou Hollenlkamp. She told her that Bernard never past [*sic*] on account of his rupture the doctor said it was not healed enough. He would not be able to be called before January. Gertrude looks bad. Her husband is not called yet. They are staying with her mother. You are surely kept busy writing. Hoping to hear from you soon.

I remain always,

Your loving Mother

PS. I 'm expecting a call from Alma. She is so anxious to get the enlarged pictures.
How do you like your underwear? How are your feet? I hope better. Goodbye. I almost forgot, Father Eagan joined the Passionist Order. We wall were surprised. Did you get to Church Sunday? Father Spoelker signed up to the Archbishop. He was asking for [volunteers]. Cousin Ben don't like it much, he ain't no better than anyone else. It is 110 on the back porch. Alma called about 1:30 asked if we had the picture. She is going to call again this afternoon.

Louisville, Kentucky, **September 14,** Monday, 6:30 am

Dear Norb,

Mom never had no rest until I got this card off. She thought maybe you couldn't get one there so I bought this at Tonini's [*religious articles store across from St. Martin's*]. It cost 25 cents - not a cheap one, honey. She thought it might be a reminder for Alma's birthday, which is the 22nd, and Shirley's is the 24th. So, I bought one for her too. Send them both together. If Shirley's is ahead of time, it's the thought. Can't write much. I'm OK as well as the rest. Nobody but Mom and I know this - we still have our little secrets, I bet you're thinking. Will write tomorrow.

Goodnite brother.

H.R.

Continued, Tuesday, 8:30:

Dear Brother,

By this time, you should have received your undies. How long does it take a box to reach its destination? Oh, why do I ask these questions when my contestant does not answer. Norb, I'm putting this with Mary's card. Saves a stamp honey.

Camp Crowder Missouri, **September 14**

Dear Mom, Pop, Marge and Hermina:

How are all you good people? Just the same as ever, I hope. Yes, my feet are enlarging a hell of a lot, and I ain't fooling either. No, I didn't know that Tindall fellow at all, but it seems to me that he is doing all right for himself. Well, I met that Capt. Lantz today. I might get a permanent job on the rifle range as for as permanent goes in the army. He told me that he was going to put in a request for me, but there were people over him so he didn't know for sure. First time I was ever in a big shot's office since I have been in this army. I guess my salute was alright; at least I tried to make it that way. The only thing is that I don't like Missouri any too well. But I guess it's the same in any other camp. But even the non-coms don't like it here and most of them guys been in the army for a pretty good while.

You know they have Mass here every night at seven o'clock. In order to go to Communion you have to fast from three but you can drink water up til six. The chapel is so crowded on Sunday that you can barely get on the inside.

That Frank Stratman was always a horses ass ['*ass' was blotted out, as if done so by Norb's mother*], so that part of the letter didn't interest me very much, even though I like to hear local news.

I haven't had a picture made yet because I haven't been off the Post., so I couldn't have a picture made. Besides, new cameras run pretty high and I am just a Yard bird. Sometimes this typewriter is setting here and sometimes it ain't, so I don't always get to make youse [use] of it, but it does make it a hell of a lot faster. My basic training will end Wednesday as far as I am aware. But you can never tell what will happen between now and then. They can change their mind so damn fast around here. Actually, sometimes I wonder if they know what they are doing themselves.

A few guys I came in with and been pal'ing [*sic*] around with are pulling out sometime this week, so I really don't know what the hell is coming off next.

So they are going to put a ration on gasoline. That will sure make it hard on my roving 'Brother in law" [*Lee Carter or Wahoo*"]. He will have to cut out some of his Indian tactics.

I don't think I will have any use for any beer cheese because I would look damn funny sitting on the side of my bunk with a big piece of cheese hanging out of my mouth. But one thing, we keep our gas masks right on the side of our beds in case it would produce any unwanted gas, which is very frequent in our barracks. Some of the strangest smells sometimes arise, but we all eat the same thing. It's really hard to understand those gas attacks.

I guess you all get the same news in my letters so there is not much discussion about them, but I usually try to change it around a little. I would like to know how my goldfish are doing and how is my sweetheart Cousin Mary doing? I hope she don't feel hurt that I mentioned the gold fish first. I didn't mean no harm. Who does she kiss besides Pop since I am gone?

Alma told me that her and Mrs. Russell went to see a sick person. Who the hell was it, her old man? Or is his stomach still holding out pretty good? Does he still insist on watering [*urinating on*] the umbrella plants, or has he acquired a few manners?

I got a letter from Clarence Johnson saying that he hasn't seen Joe [Rawert] since he was married. What the hell is the matter? Is he hen pecked already? I thought he was one of those guys who was going to do as he damn pleases. Tell him I said so and tell Ann not to be too hard on the poor fellow for he is not really responsible.

I received Mom's card but I don't like the idea of that mop on that card. It makes me tired to look at it. You can teel (pardon the mistake) [*letter was typed*] I mean, tell Pop that as long as he drinks a beer I'll excuse him from writing. Well, time is growing short so I guess I will have to close for a little while. So until I hear from all of you, I will remain as I always have been, just a Yard bird.
Love to all and especially to everybody,
Norb

PS. Mabe [*sic*] all the hell Mom use [*sic*] to give me for going hunting didn't help. Mabe if I didn't go hunting so much I wouldn't have done so good on the rifle range.

Louisville, Kentucky, **September 15**, Tuesday, 2:30 pm
Dear Norb,

We are sending you the ten bucks, boy. You're not the only soldier that does that, I know. I asked Mrs. Hellman if Red or Herm asked for underwear and she said no, that they didn't but they wanted the stuff that bought the underwear. It seems every soldier is fund-less until they get their pay.

Today is Marge's birthday. Do you want us to intercede with Park and Tilford or ask that Mr. Burke on Mulberry, or will you do your own asking, Sherlock? Red Hellman was operated on for...and is up and doing fine.

Well, more about the rifle range. In a hurry. Mary is going to mail this letter.
Hermina

Louisville, Kentucky, **September 15**, Tuesday, 8:30 pm
Still More wonderful Rawert,

We are all talking about your penmanship. I said it's written like Katsy talks. Your godchild and all are here swapping letters. Katsy got her first "lat" (slap) for "lating" (laughing) and she laughed all over again. She felt like slapping the teacher down. I believe she's going to be a pain to manage, perhaps like her Uncle (*Norb*). She got 2 pr. todees (shoes) and 2 dresses so far and such pride.

That Roman boy on Texas (his mother was a Harpring) - they got word today from the Govt. that he arrived safe. He left the same day you did and must of been in the group that went right across. They believe he is in Egypt. Ft. Harrison is the only place he was at in the US, at least that's how Lip told us she heard.

You must think everybody is full of ****, or is that the only word you can spell correctly? Did your foot balm help you? I never did send that beer cheese. It's a snappy cheese that spreads. I thought I would send it in our next box but Alma's box contained quite a few snacks so I'll just wait.

We got a good belly laugh (Mom's was best) on that 'Shrine to a happy courtship' in Lip's letter. No news about Jr [*Jr Russell, a boyhood friend and neighbor of Norb's*] lately. I don't know if he'll get his furlough or not. Lip said that Wachtel boy is married and has one child, she thinks.

If you can't write to all those guys, why won't you try to drop a card like we sent you? That certainly ought to answer the purpose at times. I got some V-Mail stationary to write to Bill Hollkamp.

Pa's going for beer. Alma read our letter, Sherlock. You should have seen her when you said just one beautiful Kentucky Woman. Her mouth just screwed up and her brown eyes sparkled. It had good effects, Challie. I sure do wish you could get a typewriter. I'm the interpreter of your spelling after a study period, after every sentence, I find every word. I should do good with Ripley. No kidding, we like your puzzles and as many as you can send.

We are all waiting to hear how you come out with Captain Larch and your shooting match. Did you accept, nay or yay? Margie is saying everything, nice or not. She fusses across the street with that 4-year-old boy. She said he called her a "Yitass." We're listening to Red Skelton and Shirley made a B-line for pencil and paper. She wants that song 'Conchita, Rosita-Waunita O'Toole" it goes like that. So far we don't have no left overs. Shirley hasn't went home, staying another week until tomorrow. She can't depart, she said. Good night brother. So you passed through the gas chambers, huh?

Continued the next day, **September 16**

Dear Norb,

Joe heard from the corner Min Elick is coming back on a furlough. He is an instructor or teacher (in October). Well, sonny boy, I'm bringing this to a close because I have to go to work. Hoping you are well as we is, OK. Bernard Hollkamp got a 3-month deferment on account of his operation. Gertie's husband would of left with you hadn't the stork come.

How does it feel to hug a hog? [*one of her nicknames.*]

Love and Hugs,

H.R.

Camp Crowder, Missouri, **September 15**

Dear Mom, Pop, Marge and Hermina,

Just drop you a line and let you know that I am still here. I have about three switches of underwear but they ain't quite enough if you take a shower every night. You at least need five or six. Every time I hang my socks to dry somebody either swipes a pair or else they blow away. If I had a few more pair, I could send them to the laundry every week and wouldn't have to worry about them. That marking Hermina put in there may help but they have to have my serial number in them. My serial number is 34587644. Damn near like a convict, ain't it? SCRTC stands for Signal Corps Replacement Training Center, that's a hell of a lot, ain't it? This whole camp is nothing but Signal Corps. No matter what outfit we get sent to, we will still be in the Signal Corps. No matter if it's tanks, air corps or what have you, we will still be the Signal men of that outfit.

So Fritz Schmidt likes Honolulu, does he? I imagine it would be better than this place myself. I had to quit writing for a few minutes for mail call. I received your box in good order. I have plenty of underwear now. I have about 7 or 8 pairs. Please don't send me any more chewing gum for a while. I have about a month's supply at least. Pretty soon, they will think I am a cow.

I received your letter with the package, Katie [*Mom*]. So it takes Alma two hours to write a letter, does it? She must write awful slow [*sic*] because I can read them in five minutes. You had better watch out how you kid her, Mom, she has an Irish temper. I know. I guess, in fact, I know, she reads these letters, because I catch hell if she finds out something in this letter that wouldn't be in hers. She might get a little mad when she reads this, but she's mighty cute when she's mad. How is Marge and Hubbuch's getting along? I guess they are sort of slack right now, ain't they? Am I wrong?

Glad to hear about Mr. Russell. Did he crack his skull open? If not, why not? Damn, he can't even sit still when he's canned up. Yes, the army used to give extra pay for sharpshooting but they cut that out now. I guess they have enough expense the way it is. In the letter here, Mom said she just got through warshing dishes. Something new has been added.

Well, I'm finished with basic training today. I don't know what I will do tomorrow. Thanks a lot for the sunflower catchers. I hope you can read this letter. I'm in a hurry. That's about all I know so until the next time,
Norb

Louisville, Kentucky, **September 16**

My Dear A-1 Uncle,

Mommy and I are down in the basement. Mommy is ironing and I am sitting at the sewing machine writing. Mommy is telling me what to write. First, I want to tell you that we have got a free day today because it is Sister Cornila's, the principal of the school, name day. And the Sisters [*told*] the children to go to Holy Communion for her Spiritual Bouquet. And the girls in my class had a privilege to sing with a class of 8th grade girls, we have got 3 seventh-grade classes, but just our class of girls got to sing (ain't that something?) A lady was telling Mommy outside of church that when the song which was specially sang for

Sister Cornila (it was beautiful) was sung, a chill went through her. Mommy said the same thing too. The name of the song was "Heart of Jesus Meek and Mild." And your name is on the roster. Your name is the last one so far. Mommy counted on the big board 200 names and on the little board is 18 names; your name is on the small board. And I don't want to forget that Milton's birthday is today September 16, 1942 and he is 13 years old and is in the 8th grade. My birthday is September 24 and I will be 12. Mommy said she thinks Alma's birthday is September 22. Joe said that Min is coming home on a furlow[*sic*]. Min's brother told Joe. Alma came over Tuesday night from work. We are invited over at Joe and Ann's Sunday for supper. And Alma is invited too. And Mommy is glad that you got to speak to that Mr. Wachtel.

It is exactly 3:00 and the Wachtels are blowing now. I made a few mistakes so I guess you can read it (Honey). Well, I guess that's all I know what to write now. So until I hear from my dear Uncle I will still be,
Your A-1 Girl Friend,
Shirley

Louisville, Kentucky, **September 16**, Wednesday, 10:30 pm
Dear Norb,

I was at Lill Klein Kleiner's tonite. Laurence is still with the Medical Corps at Ft. Benning, GA. No more has been called so far, you know they are all married. Eleanor's husband is in the City Garage. They closed up where he was at. He had a swell job in a big garage here. We got Jr Hubbuch's address today. He is in Yakima, Washington with the Army-Air Base. He had nearly a cross-country ride from Keesler Field, Mississippi. I just wrote him a line.

Today is Milton's birthday. Alma is here tonite. She said you went to church Sunday, Sherlock, and it was crowded. Will you explain a little about the services and all? We are anxious how you came out with Capt. Lance. Donaldson [Donaldson's *Bakery with home delivery*] was telling Mom he's a sharpshooter. He goes every week to some rifle range here. He said you had a very good average. He also does something as you pull the gun. He shoots. He got a high average on that, do you understand? Mom don't let him leave so many [*delivered bakery goods*] on the porch since you're gone. Until tomorrow, goodnite my sweet.

Continued, **September 17,** Thursday, 9:00 am:

Morning has dawned. We just got your typed letter and digested it. So doggone glad you get a hold of a typewriter. For then there's no pauses for letter identifications. I believe you boys think if you get moved you will like it better. Well, I heard of three that didn't like Keesler Field, Mississippi.

That sick person that Mrs. Russell and Alma went to see about, well the sick person is in the infirmary. It's Mrs. Benson Butler. She wasn't doing so well. The boy was home by himself and they walked out there and got him. She's at the Jewish Infirmary. Was operated on Sat. for tumors and is doing fine now but is pretty sick. Mrs. Russell stayed with her. I wonder how many she sat with already. That permanent job, well, wise minds run together. We all thought you had Lee to thank some, and we all said to Mom if you hadn't went hunting, well, you wouldn't of had that offer. Donaldson said steadiness means so much. I sure do hope you get your picture tooked [*sic*] like Zip's tho with a peaked cap. Well, almost as big as I am. I wish you could of heard the garbage men. It was a rat in the garbage can and they were going to kill it. The guy missed it and it got away. Did they ride him? We laughed tears. It is raining today. We needed it badly. Mom wants to write so until tomorrow, good day my sweet.

H.R.

Continued by Mommy:

Dear Norb!

Well, I cannot write much news because I don't hear any. Say Norb, why don't you send a card to your former boss [*Park & Tilford distillery*]. It might be a silent reminder [*for care package items*]. Joe and Ann are going to have company tonight. He asked Papa to get him a case of beer, he asked me to cook a pot of vegetable soup. They are going to eat here. It feels like it is as of old. Mary heard your letter this morning. She laught [*sic*] when you said about kissing Papa. Some lines I did not read to her. I never will like it; too many nice words to use that sound better [*than Norb's cursing and slang*]. I am glad that you went to church Sunday. I hope you go to Mass if you can; in fact, I know that you would not miss it you could help it. Did you go to confession since you're there? If not, then please do. So much consolation in it that no one else can give you. Do you have Mass every day or just on Sunday? I mean in the evening. I wish I could see a crowd of soldiers going to Holy Communion. Say, Hermina is telling me they took $20 away from him (Oberhausen) while he was taking a shower. That's something you do not have to worry about.

Norb, would you like a pair of clogs? They are like wooden bedroom slipper to wear to and from the shower. They claim they get down the spread of Athletic Feet Ringworm). They collected eight carloads of tin cans yesterday. They are going to collect every 3rd Wednesday. Tin cans only. It is 70°F on the back porch.

Mary was pleased that you remembered her. She said she did not know what to write. I hope you can read my letter. My eye is blurring so much this morning. Everybody says hellow [*sic*]. Well, good-bye and God bless you. Alma sent your letter before she went to work.

[*Mother*]

PS. Please don't use these (rough) words. I don't see any fun in it

Louisville, Kentucky, Wednesday [*postcard*], **September 17,** 7:10 pm

Dear Norb,

Well, how are you coming along? We are OK. Jr Hubbuch is in Yakima, Washington. He sure had a long ride from Mississippi. Hope you received our letter from yesterday. That Raibel boy is in the Marines. Your name is in Church.

Write more later,

H.R.

Around the time of September 17, 1942, Norb finished Basic Training and was transferred to a 240-hour Southwestern Bell Telephone Company training course on Telephone Substation Installation and Maintenance civilian training for the US Signal Corps. He graduated around November 21, 1942. The course was in Kansas City, Missouri and he lived at the Camp Crowder barracks. His new address was SCRTC. [Signal Corps Replacement Training Center], Co. F 804th Signal Service Regiment, Mid-Western School, Barracks 3523, Camp Crowder, Missouri.

Camp Crowder, Missouri, **September 17**

Dear Irish and FlabBurgasted [*brother Joe & his wife Ann*],

I just received your letter and thought while I had time I would sling a little "more" shit with you. As far as reading my letters are concerned, you're not Mr. Palmer [*English teacher?*] yourself. Besides, it will do you good to use that damn big Dutch head of yours once in a while.

Well, your hopes are right. My feet are getting bigger and flatter. One reason is that I have plenty of excess room in these damn houseboats. Every morning I put them on they feel different. I think they must be made of a Missouri cow. Cletus told me that it was right up his line, setting on his ass and playing racehorses. Which do you think he misses most, Oertel's (*local beer*) or Mary? I think he drank one and ... [*words unreadable*].

So you finally got your rooms fixed up. Damn, you sure must be slow. My God, it takes you about a month and a half. Say, by the way, I have a personal question to ask you. Are you really as henpecked as I think you are? As far as taking a healthy shit is concerned, I would be careful if I were you. Ann would be wondering where her husband went to. The "beautiful Ohio [*River*]" could answer that question. As far as pressing past go, I think you had more practice at that than Ann, so it would do you good to stay in shape. I have to do it.

Damn if that Paglina can't get into trouble. I don't think he's a damn bit better than an ex-con himself. You go ahead and get a quart of '92 and see if I give a damn. I think I'll get my first pass and get me a half pint or pint tomorrow and drink it down in one gulp [*which is how Norb drank all of his drinks for all of his life*]. You had better watch Ann if she's getting hotter than hell and her pants are on the ironing board. Do you have the shades down, or do you get Mr. Paul all worked up? Poor fellow.

Yeah, I seen all those pictures they had at the Cottage - quite a few of them when I left, and that's been exactly a month today. I wouldn't care if they hung my picture in a public shit-house if it helped sanitation any. Well, I better quit and flush the toilet.

So until the next time,

Norb

Louisville, Kentucky, **September 18**, Friday, 10 pm

Dear Norb:

Well, Pop is just gone for the 2nd growler. Johnny's here. We just got home from work. A rush order came in and so many things piled up. Mrs. Russell worked, too. Mom said she didn't write. I wanted to during lunchtime but couldn't so maybe you'll miss a letter. We are OK. Johnny never got that house on Payne Street. Shirley's working very hard with arithmetic problems. Mrs. Butler is just doing fine. It certainly is hot tonite, very sultry. Russell's on the straight and narrow. I am enclosing a few clippings. Does the one take you back a few years hence?

Going to work I seen Mr. Reddle and three of his playmates. They couldn't get too close together for they all had '92 tumors [*beer bellies*]; something was funny. They had a good laugh. I had news, at least some news, and can't think of anymore so will close now until tomorrow.

H.R.

Louisville, Kentucky, **September 19**, Saturday, 11 am

Dear Norb,

Yes, your Maw was disappointed because she didn't get a letter this mornin' but she understands she got two fat ones this week. That ought to satisfy any Mom. It's been so darn hot I believe it would melt the hinges of hell, not the heat alone, but smothery dampness and dryness. We had a shower and then the sun comes out. It rained quite a bit this week but it's still warm. It won't be long before those chilly nites will be coming. I sure will welcome them. Fr. Rausch's daddy died Wednesday. He was buried from St. Vincent DePaul. Father was on retreat when he died suddenly.

Mom is washing the breadbox and just spilled some water and you know her word then. "Oh ****!" Shirley, I believe, is going to be a permanent guest. I asked her about going home and she don't talk too long on that. She wants to get your mind on other things. By tomorrow, I can let you know what kind of meal Ann can put up. We are invited there for dinner.

Do you know we haven't got those pictures from Hertel's yet? It's been two weeks. Their alibi is that so many men were taken in the army, and then on another occasion, the machinery broke down. In town, you still get 24-hour service but can't blame Hertel but we don't believe the alibi anymore. Alma bought a frame for your picture two weeks ago and it still has John Payne's [*actor & singer*] picture in it. BEWARE!

Mr. Schutz is fixing that post on the old house. I think Mr. Rell's car was broke down. I seen him hoofing it to Shelby and Goss but I heard it again today. I worked some this week. Wasn't bad but such long hours for the minimum. If you don't work for Uncle Sammy, you're sunk. What is a Commanding Officer? I know what that means but what is his rank or Title? Captain or what? That's what Norman Bierbaum is. He has 1,100 men under him. I figured it was a Captain but not knowing, it could be higher. He is in Belleville, Ill. I'm going to finish this after a while. Maybe I can dig up a little dirt in that time. You know better than that.

This is Mom's bright one. She gave Johnny some of the stale bread for his neighbors "the Hogs". Shirley sold another towel. I worked on that thing about 7 hours. It was cute. Such work for 35¢!

The football games are starting but Saturday was the first one at Manual Stadium this season. You never did say if you had your teeth fixed. Did you get your undies? Mom wants to know. Until tomorrow.

Continued, **Saturday, 8:30 pm**

Well, it wasn't until tomorrow we got the pictures and they are excellent. I can't see how they can be better. They bawl things up tho. We waited two weeks and then, instead of 4 enlargements, it was 2 they made. We had your picture enlarged sitting at Ft. Harrison and our family picture with you 3 boys kneeling in front and it is grand. A posed portrait couldn't have been better. Would you like an enlargement honey?

Mary was telling Mom how pretty Pop was on that picture and how young looking he was and did he have a kick out of it! He was in the kitchen hearing it. Mary thought he was at work. Donaldson looked at your picture. Marge said, "Do you know Norb?" He said "Do I? Vell, I should say! So, that's a wonderful picture. I'm going to bring my picture." He is in the State Militia. You can't realize how much better the enlargement looks but that don't get you out of posing for a picture in your coat and cap like Zip's. We'll be waiting, honey.

We never did find out where your loose piece of letter went to - did you? Pop just got a shock of beer and Moody is helping him now. Today is Ann's birthday. September is a lot of birthdays in our family. Moody said Naughty's [*Norby's*]is in the army and she salutes. Well, until tomorrow.

Continued:

No extra news. Your name is on the [*St. Elizabeth's Sunday*] bulletin. Also on the bulletin board at church. Your name is with a lot of your old cronies. Kegabein boy is in Ogden, Utah. Bye, bye me Brudder until tomorrow or maybe tonite if I don't eat too much. Sistah Hermina

Camp Crowder, Missouri, **September 20**

My dear Ma, Pas, Maaaa and Porky,

Well, I picked up a few minutes to drop you a line. Ex-Lax excluded. I move somewhere tomorrow but I think it will be to the other side of this camp. I sure will be glad. I worked about 16 hours yesterday and about 17 today so I'm pretty tired.

I left your letter over in the barracks so I cannot answer that flock of questions. I do remember about Joe Oberhausen "looseing" $20.

Now, Ma, you know good and well my lingo is not rough. It's just one phrase of a soldier's expression. And boy, what expressions they do have. Especially some of these non-coms. Well, my good people I have to get up early tomorrow and pack my clothes but I get up early every morning so that won't make much difference. There is only one last wish that I want to make and that is to have the letters "KP" removed from the alphabet.'

Hoping all are well and happy and that Mom still warshes [*sic*] every day - after all, you have to have some pleasure. At least that was my opinion until I reached Missouri. But it could be worse. I'm not complaining. It's just the arguing Rawert instinct that I can't seem to get rid of.

There is one thing I do like to listen to and that is every night at 11:00 pm. Everything is real quiet, and they blow the Taps. You can hear that bugle blow from a pretty far distance. It sends chills up and down your spine. I don't know who blows that bugle but whoever he is, he is really good. This is for Mary X X X X.

Well, goodnight and good luck,
Norb

Louisville, Kentucky, **September 20,** Sunday, 3:05 pm

Dear Brother,

Got a few minutes time until I must get dressed for a dinner engagement at Joe's. Norb, that picture of you is swell. Everybody thinks so. You have that "taking it in" look like you give Wahoo before you say "some [*shit*] or begin pitching it.

We are expecting Alma now anytime. I think I'm going to wear my black dress, might as well be prepared. I think I'll take a box of bicarbonate of soda along. Must close. Cousin Mary Rawert and Frances [*Heitkemper*] just stepped in.

Continued, **9:45 pm**

Well, we are back from Joe's and had a swell time and the cookin' was swell. We had taters, maters, cucumbers, corn and beans, roast beef, gravy, apple pie a' la mode. It was all very, very good. And Ann kept my baking soda - Damn Irish. I want you to tease Ann and Joe about feeding us pretzel sticks with chipped glass. Her dish was chipped and we didn't know it until we ate a lot of them with beer, we didn't get the name of the glass but I told her she must of wanted to get rid of us.

Shirley wanted to learn how to play Military with cards. She meant Solitary. She gets more names mixed up and really is plenty funny. We didn't get to Joe's until nearly 6 o'clock. We got talking, Moody & Lip [*Leo & Elizabeth Muth*] and us Rawerts. Mr. Schultz told Pop he was young looking and he was pleased as punch. Shirley went to the Bingo but so far no luck for her bicycle.

Manual Stadium is going to have a warfare show, I suppose you'd call it. Joe was telling me they were going to take out a whole side wall in order to have this show. I suppose we'll hear plenty of the cannons roaring (Oct 8-13). Alma is filling her pen with ink; she caught my eye and gave me one of those screwed up mouths. Pop believes she likes to come here.

Did you start your company clerical school or don't you go because of your shooting average? Will you let us know if you hear? We were looking at pictures at Joe's and some of Min Elick holding Shirley and Milt. Shirley said she was so glad Min held her as a baby. She was proud of that. Well, sugar, I don't have no more news. I don't think Joe is as henpecked as Clarence J. says he is, but if he is, it's doing him good.

Sending a Sunday [*church*] bulletin to you. Joe was saying when the papering season starts to drop (which it is doing, altho Joe hasn't lost one minute) when there is no more to be papered, he [*Sabel*] offered him a good price. Joe naturally took him up on that. I sure think he's fair and square with Joe. This bulletin gives a lot of names of the boys you left with, don't it? Gemanently [*sp*] you should see this - Alma, Shirley and I all writing to you, and everything is so quiet with so many girls around. It's really cold tonight. We had a hard shower yesterday and today was bright and clear. Tonight it is clear and cold and we'll need a double blanket to keep us warm. Didn't that Rodmann boy leave with you? If he did, they think he's in Egypt. Did that Lawrence J. Raible go to St. Elizabeth's school with you?

What do those other initials stand for, such as AS and SCS, etc.? I must get me a book on army insignias. We are all fine. Mom made Pop some knable [*hard toast*], you know, so I think we'll all have some for breakfast, not just Pop alone. Will close for it's getting late. It sure seems funny when Mary comes in and locks up and we never hear you catch hell at second breakfast time [*Norb didn't wake up in time for the first breakfast because he got in late the night before*]. It hasn't been no second breakfast so far [*since you left home*]. Goodnite dear, goodnite.
Until tomorrow my sweet,
Hermina

Louisville, Kentucky, **September 20,** 10:20 pm
My Dear Uncle Norb

I hope you received the letter me and Mommy wrote. My birthday is September 24. I did not realize it was here so quick. I went to the bingo today back at Saint Elizabeth's church. Jimmy, Mary Ann and I went. We never won anything though. If I would won enough I would got me a bicycle. I been wanting one but it looks like I'll never get one unless I buy it

myself. Well, it's getting late. It is 10:30 pm now so I guess I ~~haff~~ have to close now, so until I hear from you I will still be your A-1 Girl.
Shirley

Louisville, Kentucky, **September 21**, Monday, 8:55 am
Dear brother,

I bet you think you wasn't called dear brother at home. You were, honey, when you was a good little bully. Mom got two letters this morning. This one was postmarked Joplin so I suppose you did a little sightseeing. Well, I want a new fall outfit so I have to work for it. I wish Tommy Tucker would be alive or live close, he might could sing for me. He'd have to sing day and night for a while for my size (you're thinking that). This one letter you couldn't understand - Julia Hellmann had an envelope big enough, so she took it along and mailed it for us. Mom thought maybe you couldn't get out to get a card for Alma. After I bought it I couldn't find an envelope big enough. Went to Hertel and no good, so I met Julia and she mailed it. I thought I wrote that to you. Maybe I didn't. Can't say.

You're moving to a new area and Camp, you think? Well, I wish it would be closer to home. We might could gander up to see you in uniform and I know you won't get a furlough.

How did you like my marks? It taken me about three hours to do that. I couldn't make a straight mark with any pen like this NR but had to dot everything like this...the material wouldn't stand for dashes. Your sunflower catchers, do they fit you? It's for a 32-inch waist and government regulations doesn't permit the whole elastic band if you've noticed it. Those cute little, dainty, sweet, stipends cost 60 cents each now, so don't let those yaps steal them. Would you like a few clothespins? If you have a few more undies, would that help you out so you could send it all to the laundry? You pay for it, don't you Norb? If a few more of anything might help, you let us know. Well, Abby I must move on cause I 'haf a ' (like Milt says) get busy.
So until tomorrow, good day my sweet.
H.R.

A note from his mom:
Dear Norb,

Just so you don't forget my handwriting I write a few lines. Hermina can write faster than I can. If it was not for her, you wouldn't get such long letters. I am glad that she likes to write. Mary said hello and wants to know when you will answer the questions on the card. That's all for now. With love and prayer,
Mother

Louisville, Kentucky, **September 22,** 10 pm
Dear Norb,

Well, you will know now that we sent you a letter Sept. 2 and it taken 20 days to be returned to us because I forgot to put the 34th down. Couldn't be helped but I know you sure could of used those $2.00 at that time.

I felt so newsy tonite, but was out humming and it sort of made me a little worn out, but I have to work tomorrow so don't put off until tomorrow what you can do today (ambitious speaking). I see any school you attend will be signal corps school. I imagine that will be pretty good for you but what worries me is this: can you pull that little diamond mark on your stomach as a sick sign? As you did 8 or 10 years back? Your signal of illness sign.

Mrs. Russell gave Joey a pretty double finger-wave [*V for victory*]. I told her I imagine she'd be good in the Signal corp. She said she was too old for the WAAC (*Women's Army Air Corps*). I suppose you have started school again. Give us the dope on it. You want KP taken out of the dictionary. Well, you add some initials such as Mom's warsh; just omit that R. That's ink wasted. I'll send you a dictionary sometimes. Today is Alma's birthday. We sent her a card. Mom was napping when she called and Lip answered so I don't know what she had to say. I told you 2,700 soldiers were going to be put up in Allgeirs' Field for an Army Air Show at Manual Stadium. Mrs. Hertel told me today that Mildred M. said there was a big tractor cutting the weeds in the field, but 2,700 soldiers is a lot of soldiers.

We want to send Jim Doerr a picture and Hertel's asked for one. They sure did fine work on your picture. We thought after the war you might make good in Hollywood because you're photogenic. What's Victor Mature [*an actor from Louisville*] got that you haven't got (a lot more nerve).

Huelsman's was caught selling whiskey and the nights are cool, and Pop said it was a dead place, too cool for beer and not selling whiskey. But let a warm nite come. It never gets too cool for Pop.

Norb, if I fix up some cards and have names and addresses typed on them, do you think you could put a line on each card and sign your name? If you can't, just say so. My feelings won't be hurt and Mom can't take my part on paper. I hope you will get my letters to your old address. I don't know what to tell you about. Joe's henpeckedness, when Mom went there tonite he was ironing his shirts. Do you think you got in the toughest army?

I sure do want a new pen. Going to try one of those inkographs. They're $1.00. Your letters written with pen are clearer and we don't need a magnifying glass for them. Did I feel funny tonight? I did. I taken some red-stomach drops over to Mrs. Russell. As I walked into the kitchen, Russell was working on his books when the phone rang. I asked for Mrs. Russell and he told me she went out for a few minutes and to answer the phone. This all happened in a split second. I answered and Mrs. Russell was on the other end of the line. I told her I felt funny but I just got there. She's been asking about those Red Drops. She was at Lavada's. They came and got her. Well, Norb, this is all for tonite, so dear goodnite, sweet goodnite.

Your little sister,

Hermina

Continued by Shirley Muth:

All want to know is if you got your pay or not.

Hello from Shirley.

Continued, **September 23**, Wednesday, 8:40 am:

Good morning Norb,

My, the nights are really chilly and the daytime is so pretty and clear. Mom and Ann gone for a sugar ration card this morning. I'm getting ready for work, so must say bye bye. That new housing on Clay Street [*Norb was born on Clay Street*] is going to be called Shepard Place. Joey said she wonders if they could find the black sheep. Good nite Norb.

Louisville, Kentucky, **September 23,** Wednesday, 1:30 pm

Dear Norb,

Well, we did not cut Shirley's cake. No one cared to eat, so we are going to St. Elizabeth's tonite, that is, Marge, Hermina and Shirley and myself. I don't know if Ann and Joe are going. I was surprised to get the mail back and glad that the $2.00 was there yet. I often wondered why you did not write that you received that money. I guess you can use it now, if you like it better. Where are you now? I hope you do not have to work so hard.

Dr. Atherton was in Louisville for 76 hours. That lady that kept his office clean and lives in that cottage said he looked fine and is very tan and liked it [*military service*] very much. Huelsman's was raided Saturday. I feel sorry for J.C. but I think he has another place. Joe came over home about 12 o'clock. He is going to fix the [TV] aerial. The wire would give me a shock if I would stretch the line. I wish you would write Shirley's name on the top line also. I guess you will use your 'longies' soon without the strings. Have you enough winter underwear? There are no new names on the soldiers' list [*at St. Elizabeth's*] yet. You are still the last one. I went to Mass this morning; don't know if I will get there tonite. Papa was teasing Alma last nite when she was writing to you. He said, "Why do you always hold up that page [*a cover sheet*]?" Alma just smiled. Moody said that Carl Farry is in Crowder Camp also. I showed Mrs. Lee your and our family picture. She said they were good. She always asked about you. So does old lady Lerger [*sp*]. Erney Schieman [*Texas Street grocer/ butcher*] was in 4 or 5 different camps. I was mending Papa's gray suit and sent it to the cleaner. Who does your mending? I tried to get you a thimble but could not get them large enough. The moon was shining so brite last night I said to Alma we could read outside. I must close now. Everybody said hello to Norby

As ever,

Your loving Mother

Louisville, Kentucky, **September 23,** Wednesday, 8:40 pm

Dear Norb,

I suppose you got your mail OK. However, they sure are particular. Marge, Mrs. Russell and I went to Mr. Butler's house and cleaned and dusted it. He got us from work. The place wasn't dirty at all. We just gave it a Friday cleaning. The dishes, well I believe he had them stacked since she went to the Infirmary. The house looked just like a man's housekeeping. I bet you could keep house good now, a lot better than you did. Butler really was grateful. He cooked us coffee and got a devil's food cake; was good. He said he really likes sponge cake. Mrs. Butler is supposed to come home tomorrow or Friday. She got along fine since the 4th day. She was sick then but is OK now

Am sending another Oertel's '92 label in case you wore out that other one for an inspiration. Alma bought Shirley a birthday cake all decorated, was very pretty. Shirley's going to get Joe and Ann to come over and get a piece. She said she might get something yet. We all liked Alma's card and thought it was very pretty. Shirley's expecting a letter because it's her birthday tomorrow.

I was talking with Herb Ever. Well, the army didn't take him. He thought he could do something but they thought differently; feel sorry for him. Shirley said it's amazing how fast I can make up a letter. Mom's wondering if she understood you right - did you say you could get a furlough at Christmas? Now, how's the schoolboy? Do you enjoy the smell of the classroom? It's a good thing you're the studious type, honey. Pop's got a can of beer. Russell was out of whiskey tonite, too. Bill said haven't got anything but Russell acted like himself.

I think I told you Katsy's Sister [Ursuline *Nun/teacher*] asked if anyone could sing. She volunteered. She sang "Oh, Johnny" and "Do the Rumba." I would of loved to see her.

They surely must be shipping them out fast. Where are you? Mom got her sugar [*ration*] cards today. I thought I could give you more dope. Do you ever go to the USO dances or did your low-Dutch feet get too darn big? I heard you're a crooner at night. Why don't you try to conserve your strength and sing with a tin can if the army don't pay off? Antoinette Spoelker [*cousin*] lives some place in Missouri. I think it's Kansas City. That's all the dope for tonite, so goodnite sweet, goodnite.

Your little sister,

H.R.

Missouri, **September 23**

Dear Mom, Pop, & Sisters,

Well, how am doing? Good. I will be here two weeks and then I will move again. Ain't that nice? I transferred from clerk to telephone so now I will get out of Missouri and get to go to a civilian school, at least that's what I'm betting on. I will go to school here though before moving out. My school hours are 4:00 pm till 12 midnight. I won't even be able to drink their lousy beer. There are so many new men coming in here and everything is so mixed up I sometimes wonder if they know that the hell they are doing.

I've got about 20 letters to answer but I just won't be able to answer them because I just won't be able to find the time. So you can explain that for me. I start to school today if something else don't start. I will be glad to get started. This detail work drives you nuts because you have nothing to keep your mind on.

I've had a headache for about four straight days now. It must be from the cold I got. With the weather they have here anyone would have a cold. It's so damp that the envelopes stick together.

Well, that's all I have time for now so until I get another chance to write,

Just Norb

Missouri, **September 24**

Dear Map, Pam, [*sic*] Bros and Sisters,

Well, to start off with, I spent my first night in school last night. The study is Principles of electricity, Ohm's Law and all that sort of stuff. Circuits, currents, math, atoms, conductivity, $E=H/R-L=x/m=125$. That's a sample, but it's pretty interesting and time passes pretty fast but I wish we would go to school during the day instead of night. We get up at 8:30 and eat at 9:00. Clean our barracks from 4:15 till 9:45 we are free till 12:30 then we drill till 1:50 and eat again at 2:00. We are there till 3:30 and then to school from 4 to 6:30 then we eat chow at 7:00 and go back to school from 8 to 12. That's the day I have. When I say free, I don't always mean free because there are a million and two things to do. They haven't got the mail proposition straight yet so I won't get mail for a few days, I don't think.

It really is cold here so I guess it's cold there too. This place here is strictly a mud hole. You have a hell of a time trying to keep shoes shined the way they should be. Since I moved, I will miss my pay again. I always run into that kind of luck. I leave here on Oct. 10, as far as I heard, but they change orders here so fast you really never know what to believe.

Well, I have to warsh and shave before I start shooting paper wads so will write when I find time.

As ever,

Norb

Louisville, Kentucky, **September 24**

Dear Norb,

I wrote to Wil Hollkamp in a V-Mail. You did seem in the fighting mood or like raising hell. Poor Termiter. We didn't pay him last year to kill rats that wasn't there. The little pooch next door got some poison and died. We told them to watch the dog. I asked Mr. Lee if Jack got some. He said, in a very sad way, Jack was eating grass and not feeling up to par. But he was frisky as could be today. We told him, too.

Well, they want people not to eat more than 2 ½ pounds of meat a week. [*Words scratched out here.*] Got that a little twisted. Well, that's easily done but when it comes to coffee that will get me madder. Tried to get coffee at six different places and no one had coffee around here. Does Larny Johnson ever write to you? I haven't seen him since before you left. I'll have to go down there and see if I can get any dope for you.

I think you're in a very interesting part of the service but maybe I would think differently if I was there. We thought Min might be back by this time but I guess he still can come yet.

Jimmy wrote that letter all by himself. I read it all over and really think it's cute. Milt got his letter, too, from you. Can't think of no news ao will continue later. Well, Norb it is 7:30 pm. We rode out with Moody to see the soldiers. There isn't much you can see. A lot of tents and some soldiers playing ball, a few trucks and jeeps. We also seen the new Curtis-Wright Plant, and the Gun Factory. Shirley's gone home; you know she made up her mind.

Moody is at the Soupy stage [*lost his teeth*]. He has to eat soup but he got along fine, and no complaints went with it. I sure hope he soon gets his chewers. Mom and Mrs. Russell are gone to see Mrs. Butler. They passed here today and she is doing fine. They came by from church, the Holy Name Society, to get your correct address for the Xmas gifts for the boys in the Service. They told me they were giving a money belt to the boys. It was funny; I was going to ask you if you would like one. So you will get one for Christmas. Ann's nephew in the army got married. He married a girl from one of those islands off Venezuela. I don't know if I spelt that correctly. He wrote Joe and Ann wishing them luck and said he knew how it was himself. Before he could marry, his mother had to sign a paper stating that she would care for the girl, and she is going to try to come to the US. This is a Dutch island; naturally, she is Dutch.

Alma called. She is coming over tomorrow. Ben Hollenkamp from Poplar Level Rd. is called to the army. He leaves the 14th. He's 42 years old. None of those Hollkamp boys are called. Norb, I believe that. How is that boy that was taken to the hospital? For the sixth time Norb, did they fix your teeth? Mom seen Antoinette Spoelker. She's going to come over this week sometime so we can see her baby.

With love from and until tomorrow, good nite my sweet,
Hermina

Missouri, **September 26**

Dear Mom and all,

I'm sitting in school writing this letter and I have to keep a good eye on the teacher because if he catches me he might tan my ass. I wouldn't mind so much though because I don't get to sit on it but very little. No, I have about a half hour until the next period so I thought I might as well make use of my (scarce) idle time.

I received your belated letter today. That's the one I never could get straight. I'm also reading the one today from Marge and Horse. I put that 2 bucks to good use. I bought me some towels, soap and warsh cloths (you notice I say warsh cloths now). You can tell I'm getting up in the world. The only trouble is I don't know how soon I will go down. Ha, Ha, or either Ho, Ho, take your pick.

The weather here is fine tonight but I haven't had a beer for four days. I got heel prints all over my tongue where it's been dragging behind me and there's tramping on it. So you can see for yourself how thirsty I am. But don't tell this to Joe, damn it. He might send me another '92 label and then I know for sure I would go AWOL just for a couple quarts of "Oertel's." After my religion, comes Oertel's. And after that comes more, so long as my bones shall rattle.

The food here is a lot better than what it was at the other place. For dinner today, we had roast beef, potatoes, peas, salad, stewed tomatoes and cauliflower (is that spelled correct?). We also had cake, bread, butter and tea. I been eating so much that our mess hall gets extra rations. The only trouble I have is that all that goes in don't always come out. But that's where Watkins Laxative does the work, but I haven't taken but three of them since you sent them to me, so I ain't doing so bad.

You will have to pardon this paper because it's the only paper I have with me [*the paper had lots of electrical drawings and math equations on it*]. The rest has work done on them that I need. I tell you I get my E's, P's and Q's mixed up, but they put you here to learn so I guess it's natural to make some mistakes.

So Joe feeds you glass, does he? Well, there's a shortage on razor blades so I guess that could be the reason. Just for punishment I wouldn't let him come over and take a crap in the morning; make him suffer. As for Ann, well she's Irish, so I guess there's an excuse there, if I know my Irish as well as I think I do. And I think I do, I do. In fact, I know I do, yes indeed, I do, I do. Sounds like I'm getting married. Well, enough for the Irish. I would rather talk on a sensible subject.

I seen my name on the Parish bulletin with a lot of other goofs. How is old flat foot Dudine [*Parish priest at St. Elizabeth's*] doing now, still popping off, I presume. That's one thing about being in the army, we don't have to listen to 'Bingo' or money sermons.

My feet are in pretty good shape. I haven't been on them as much as I was during my basic training, but I still don't like to go to school from 4 - 12. You don't have time to do nothing, but it will only be for two weeks til I go to civilian school, I hope.

No, I never mailed no letter from Neosho [*some envelopes had postal stamps from Neosho, Missouri*]. It's just that the post offices here are too busy to handle all the mail that is coming in and going out. I think when I get my first pay, if I ever do, I will buy me a small radio so I know what humans are doing on the outside.

Well, folks, that's about all the news I have for the present; at least, that's all I can think of right now. Oh, that telephone call didn't cost but $1.05. That ain't so bad. I was wondering if Shirley got my address straight. Well, I will close for now because I run out of paper but will write more as soon as possible. I could get more paper in the privy but it's already used and besides, that would be carrying things too far.

Going crazy (or gone), Still,

Norb

Louisville, Kentucky, **September 27**, Sunday, 4:22 pm

Dear Norb,

We are listening to a dedication in honor of the Parents and Teachers Association and those southern brogues of Georgia. I haven't got any new dope on anything. I think I'm going down to Lip's a little while. Haven't seen the new soldier's encampment yet. The public is invited. The state is really pushing a metal drive; people are giving iron fences and they are sifting the metal at Ft. Knox for all the bullets used in WW I. Russell was in very good spirits yesterday. Haven't any new dope, will finish when I return from Lip's.

Until tomorrow, good day my sweet,

Hermina

Louisville, Kentucky, **September 28,** Monday, 9:30 am

Dear Norb,

I never went to Lip's. Instead I got some rat poison and Norb I wish you could of seen them. We have never been so ratty; it was nothing to see from 1 to 4 rats in broad daylight. We spent $1.00 on rat poison, Marge laid about 24 pieces where the garbage can sits, and you could see them hauling it in. In less than 5 minutes, all was gone. In the garage, the same way. No kidding, Norb, but the grass at Madden's is about 3 or 4 inches and Madden showed me their path to the garage; a rat path 4 inches wide. I have never seen the likes. Oh, Rats!

We have just received your letter saying you started to school. You seem to like it a right smart. Mom said maybe you could fix her wash-machine if it ever breaks, when you get back. That wash-machine is really a humming. She only washed once last week. She has a heap but she's really in her glory. It is very cold here, too. The thermometer said 30° F this morning but the days are beautiful, clear, and cold and the sky is that beautiful blue. It rained all day Saturday, very hard at times, but we are having a beautiful autumn.

I got a cold, too. My head feels like my body, steam exploded eight times the normal size. Did you get the coconut brittle? I have been writing all along. I hope you get your mail.

I seen Jim Hunley. He must of been leaving with his white canvas bag, he still looks like himself, and has the same walk. He had his blue suit and pea jacket on. Jimmie Bliler left too; I believe they are in the same company. Ann Bliler gave Jimmie a little party so the day before she went in town to get a few things, as she was crossing 4th and Jefferson, a poultry truck knocked her down and broke her leg in 2 places. She's getting along fine. Was at the

City Hospital 4 days and is home now. They left her come home Saturday so that she could be with Jimmie, until last nite, that's really a tough break, but she's doing fine.

You say you have to make paper wads. Well, Marge, Mom and I will make spit balls for you and wrap them in cellophane instead of bathroom conferences [?] if that will help the war effort. I don't think Pa would do good at that. You will collect your back pay, won't you?

They even asked us at Church to go see this War Show. Hoping your cold is better and "keep on writing." Mrs. Russell hasn't heard from Jr in 2 weeks. She started to get a little leery feeling but she heard [*from him*] this morning, but the letter is sealed so I can't give you no dope on that. Hoping you're teacher's pet and your cold is OK. With loads of love and until tomorrow, goodbye my sweet.

Norb, I was going to send you a money order as you never got paid, but they thought it was best to wait for you to know if you are getting your mail OK now.

So until we hear from you,

H.R.

September 28, Time 1:10, weather 55° F

Dear Norb,

I just got through with dinner. Now for the dishes. I know you feel sorry for me now doing KP. Alma called about one hour ago. Hermina called her Friday evening. She had already left. She is coming this evening. She has been sick but she is better now. I don't know if she is going to stay. She would not have any clean apron. Hermina said we could wash it and iron it here. I am glad that you like your work and hope that you will study hard, and not make paper wads. I am sorry that I cannot talk to your teachers and ask how Norbert is doing. I will tell the others to write and not to wait for anyone because you were too busy to write. They will understand. Papa did not have to work yesterday afternoon. He was lonesome. He would like to play cards.

Norb, did it give you a lot of trouble to have that money order cashed? If so, maybe we could send it some other way. There are some men leaving for the army today but I forgot the names. Hermina just called and said her and Marge are going to work tonight. That's all. Third time I started to write. X XXX X - Mary's kisses, she said honey bunch.

Goodbye,

Mother, KATE

Louisville, Kentucky, **September 29**, Tuesday 8:30 pm

Dear Norb,

We have received two letters from you since you called long distance eight days ago. Naturally, there were letters on the way to you. I hope you get them. We kept on writing just the same. On these two letters you forgot to put your return address on them, so I wondered if Shirley got it right over the phone. Alma came over last nite. The address is correct but

Shirley said you didn't give her that building number so we are wondering if you are hearing from us at all. I don't know if you got a letter we mailed back that was returned to us. I wrote it Sept. 2nd. It was returned because I left the 34th off your envelope. Mom put $2 in it. Everything was OK but it was returned to us. Did you get it? It was returned Sept. 22. If you got our letter yesterday, you'll know why we didn't send you a money order. We just never seen your address written, so we are sending you a money order today.

Moody had his upper teeth pulled yesterday Rudy [*Muth, Leo's brother*] went with him. Now we expect him to have some pulled, too, for we feel he has a toothache, too. If he don't he's letting us down.

I got a letter from Jr Hubbuch. He's in Yakima, Washington and likes it a hell of a lot better than Keesler Field, Mississippi. He said he lost 34 pounds at Keesler Field. He didn't even look like a Hubbuch. Marge got a letter from Maurice Slattery. Until tomorrow, goodbye my sweet,
Your little sister,
H.R.

Continued by Mommy:

Marge didn't have this time to write so she asked me to. She is sending you a $10 money order. Marge took one family picture and your picture to work. The ones we have now are a little darker. I am so glad we had those pictures taken. Everybody seems to think they are good. Moody called this morning and told me he was at work. I was surprised. I thought he could not work today yet. I baked him a raisin kuchen. Thought he could bite that - his gums must be very sore. Alma just left for work. Norb, if you haven't got the time to write much, just a few lines will be enough, but of course, the longer the better. Otto Weland is overseas. His mother got a letter yesterday from the government telling her that he arrived safe and well. Let us know as soon as you can when you get the money order. I am going to town today to get my arch support adjusted. My left [*knee*] hurts very bad. How do you like the new paper? Hermina wrote on it.

Norb, did you say over the phone that you was coming home Christmas or did I dream that? Do you want me to go to Mr. Burck and ask why you did not get the money? Mary said she loves you as ever, sends you ten kisses, honey bunch.
Well, goodbye and good luck,
Mother

Missouri, **September 29**

Dear Mom, Pop & Sissies,

Well, I'll start out with saying that it's still mighty cold here for this time of year. The fellow who sleeps next to me caught the flu so he left for the hospital about 45 minutes ago. You could tell he was very sick. He got a package of cakes from home so he told me to eat them for him. I didn't refuse. I told him what he needed was a half-pint of whiskey but he is a Baptist. But I don't think he's what you call a "strict Baptist." Yes, I'll agree, the army is as changeable as women, if not more so, and that's a strong statement.

No, I lost tract of that Wachtel fellow, but I know he's somewhere close around. I believe he's in the company next to mine. But he goes to day school and I go to night school. You can tell Moody that he is more than welcome to use my shotguns if he wants to. But the way he shoots, he could do just as good throwing cream puffs. Tell him he can have the damn thing till I get back because the Signal Corps gets finished with a sub-machine gun. It's just a small gun for close-range shooting. We were told by our Major that the Signal Corps was on an equal rank with the Air Corps. He said, in fact, it's more important. But I think he's nuts but I hope he don't know I think so.

I received that box of candy and it sure was good. Thanks a million. Sometimes an APO address means that you are due for shipment and sometimes it don't. I heard of fellows having an APO address for three months before they shipped. I got a letter from Earl Johnson and he has an APO. So has Louis Johnson. Maybe Louie might be across already, I don't know.

Yes, I believe I do get more sleep, but what the hell is the use of sleeping your life away? But I don't get in bed until about 1:30 so I don't get to bed as early as you think. I would much rather go to bed at 2:30 and get up at 7:30. I guess I'm the type that doesn't require much sleep. Yes, I heard going to civilian school was the 'life of Riley.' I hope I can believe that and I hope the orders don't change again. Maybe by the time the war is over I'll be in the Infantry. But they told us that once you're in the Signal Corps you're there to stay. There is only one way to get out and that is by joining the Air Corps. Sometimes I wonder if I would like the Air Corps. But I guess I'll have a few months to decide that.

I guess Herman Hellman is acting Corporal. I wouldn't be one of those damn things if they would give me $50 more on a month. He's just about shitty enough to be one I guess. Being a regular Corporal is OK but not an acting Corporal. We have a few of them around here who are going to get the hell kicked out of them. Just wait till we start to civilian school and see if that ain't the truth.

Tell Shirley and Milton I appreciated their letters a lot and will write them as soon as I can. I only have time for about two letters a day except on Sundays and Monday morning. And I don't feel much like writing so many letters on a Sunday because that's my only day off. I'm sorry if you can't read this letter, but my hands are really cold and it makes it hard to write. If the weather is there, the way it is here, I guess Pop will see quite a few "fogs in the holler." It's really damp here. We are at the foot of the Ozarks, or whatever they call them. I don't know if that is spelt [*sic*] right or not. We are not far from Oklahoma. X O X O Especially for Mary. Well, that's about all I can tell you for now so until the next time, Just as ever,

Norb

Missouri, **September 30**

Dear Folks,

I received your letter post-marked the 28th on the 30th. Can you get that straight? The days here are swell, too, but the nights sure are cold. Well, I learned today that I won't get paid now until the 31st of October. That's what gets a guy disgusted. Damn, here I was supposed to get paid about three weeks ago and they tell us today we won't be paid until the 31st. Yes, I'll get all my back pay but at the rate, they are going now I won't be paid until after the war and then I'll have to wait about 15 years. I sure would like to have a radio now. The World Series is on the radio. I heard part of it as I was passing one of the barracks.

Since I'm gone, the rats must be getting worse. That just goes to show I was good for something, even if I was good for nothing. Why in the hell don't you tell that damn Termiter about it? I believe he's a breeder instead of a rat killer. Boy, do I like raising hell.

The school is alright but I can't say that I'm really fond of it. I would rather be in something else, I believe. Well, I may get a chance to transfer if I ever make up my mind. I only wish I knew what was going to happen from day to day. They change things around here so fast your head swims. Sometimes I believe a fellow is better off in the Infantry because all they have to do is walk. Well, that's all I have time for now. I guess you can tell I'm in a hurry.
Love to all,
Norb

Louisville, Kentucky, **September 30**, Wednesday, 7 pm

Me [*sic*] Dear Brudder,

Today we have good ole summertime again with the windows and doors open. It's beginning to get a wee bit coolish now. Joe and Ann got their selves a heating stove from Geher's. It's a nice sturdy looking stove that will heat both rooms. It's an Anchor stove, holds fire 36 hours. So that's why it got warm today. Ann had to stay home so that they would place it right, so we scrubbed down the bathrooms and it surely needed it, that's no Ripley.

Helping Shirley with her spelling and I wish I could help you, too. Yesterday you wanted to 'high hat' us with 'warsh cloths' instead of [*wash*] rags. If that don't sound funny! You getting a trousseau ready or you stocked up in your linens or have you all the necessities? Honey, you bought <u>Wash</u> not <u>Warsh</u> cloths. Don't roll your wash so [*joke on rolling 'r's*].

Shirley can really eat, really Norb, I think she can keep up with you. She mopped up on everything tonite, licked the platters clean. She run to Hertel's to weigh herself, 102 lbs. She wants to write to you. Are you receiving your mail regular now? I think your Watkins must think it's funny, 3 pills isn't bad in 6 weeks' time. I think more furniture has been added to your Shrine to a Happy Courtship at last. That's what we heard. Maybe she'll be a war bride yet.

How's school by this time? Did they let you transfer to Telephone School from Clerical

or did it happen that way? What about sharpshooter? Did you hear anything of that? What did you think of the Radio proposition? Mom and Pop are gone over to see Joe's store. Norb, I don't know any new dope and I want to write to Cousin Anna Heitkemper. It's over 2 months since we received her letter, so until tomorrow, goodnite my sweet
Your little Sistah,
Hermie

Shirley Muth added a note, 7:30:

Dear Norbe,

I just came back from Hertel's Drugstore and weighed myself and I weigh 102 lbs. At supper time I ate so much I had to take my belt off - my belly was getting too big. I'm getting almost as fat as you are. I think I eat as much as you do or more. Do you know anything about Volley Ball, that is, for the girls? We have a big net stretched across the court. It's just the 7 and 8 grades that get to play, but just the girls. The boys play basketball. The 8th graders get to go to other schools and play but the 7th grade gets to go along, but they don't get to play unless someone gets hurts (you know what I mean). Most of the 7th grade girls are taller than some of the 8th graders.

Daddy feels much better since he had his teeth pulled. Uncle Rudy went to the Dentist with him. And there was a pint of Old Grand Dad in it. That just reminded me. Did you go to the Dentist yet? We missed Fibber McGee and Molly [*popular TV show*] so I can't tell you about it.

Norb, you are not embarrassed if I ask you, "How much do you weigh, Fatty?" I told you mine. I sure will let you know the next time I get weighed. I got mostly hundreds on my spelling paper. Katsy had to stand in the corner of the room the other day for screaming out loud in school. She can read pretty good. I wish you could see her. It is funny, very, very funny. Hope you are well. It is 8:15 pm. Poppa just went after some beer. Well, that's about all I know so until I write again, I'm still,
You're A-1 Girl Friend,
Shirley

Louisville, Kentucky, **October 1**, Thursday, 9 am

Dear Norb,

Say, your menu sounded good: five vegetables, one meat, cakes and tea. Do you like tea? I know Joe does and so does our own dear mother. Breitenstein asked about you at Best's yesterday. Mom was going to get birdseed instead of fish food. You'd feel funny when you came back on your furlough and hear your fish singing our National Anthem. We got our enlargements from Hertel's. Alma got your mug [*photo*]; her mouth was working overtime in twisting about. They are fine pictures. Pop had guts enough to say the boys looked better than the girls. That's what you call royal guts. Pop thinks you all look so fine. How did you like Pop's letter?

Sylvester Fahringer flew home, he very likely will be sent across, as he will have a New York address. Have you left the reservation as yet? I suppose you got your Olive Drabs, too. We had an upset midnight visitor, you know. He was fighting full. Joe's bed is made good use of. Mom counted her money for the third time. She sat almost too far off Joe's bed. Now she knows she has $9.00. Will write more tonight.

Continued, Thursday, 9:30 pm:

Well, Joe got another wedding gift, a large round mirror over the mantle from Aline. John and sons were here tonight. He spent $25 at Smith's for shoes, etc. They were so cute. He got Hilary black shoes, Vernie brown, so they could tell them apart. He said sometimes whoever gets up first might have on two left's and in a little while they'll yell cause their feet hurt.

Mom just got back from retreat at St. Boniface. Mrs. Heichelbeck was here today. She said Mauurice was in Alaska and was moved this week 800 miles closer to the US. He was first stationed after Ft. Harrison at a camp near St. Louis, Missouri; then to Washington, DC; then the state of Washington. She said she got a letter from him asking if Joe got married. A boy got a box from KY with a CJ in it so he saw Joe's marriage license.

Mom did her share of <u>boy talk</u> today swapping a yarn with Mrs. Heichelbeck, then she met Mrs. Thompson this afternoon and more boy talk. Is Carl Fairy [*sp*]with you at Camp Crowder? I suppose we'll be getting a letter from you tomorrow. Some old man where Joe was at today gave him a 32-caliber gun, so I told him he could look in the mirror so he can be sure, when he shot himself.

At last, we got our pictures from Hertel's. I mean all of them. I'm still promising myself a new pen. This one is terrible heavy. Well, until tomorrow, goodnite my Nobbe.
Your little Sistah,
Hermina

Missouri, **October 2**

Dear Mom and all,

Well, to start off with there must be a hold back in the mail somewhere. Are you sure you only received two letters? You should have received at least six, if not more. But they do have so much mail to handle here, and this being a new camp I guess there is some confusion. I got your money order this morning and I sure can use it. I had exactly 11 cents in my pocket and I was afraid to spend that. You see, I had some cleaning done. Had to have my pants altered. I bought me a belt, some 'Cannon' towels and warsh cloths, a carton of cigs and of course, I had very few beers. In fact, I had about seven beers in two weeks.

I did give Shirley that building number. She must have got mixed up or got it confused with something else.

I said it might be possible for me to get a furlough about Christmas because I will be in the army over six months then. Now I wrote one letter about a week ago telling you that I received that belated letter with the $2.00 bucks in it. Is my handwriting that bad? If it is, I'll get me a secretary.

Since Moody got his uppers pulled, I guess Rudy will have all of his pulled because I think they get jealous when one of them gets sicker than the other one. You say Marge didn't have time to write. Well, that's OK because I know how that is because I'm in the same shoes myself sometimes. Just so you leave me know how many 'warshings' you get done in a week. After all, you are entitled to some pleasure. You say if I can't write,I should get a card. Well, what good would it do to write a card and then not be able to mail it? So you see how it is. I'll write as often as possible and that's all I can do.

No, no, no, don't go too Mr. Burke because I think it's on the way now. But I guess when I do get it, it will take me a month to get it cashed. I still have that Dr. Scholl's foot kit that Marge and Hermina sent to me but I never used it yet. I don't have time to fool around with all that stuff, not that I don't appreciate the feelings behind it. My feet are pretty good since I got my shoes broke in. Now I have another pair to break in. The thing that makes them hard is that rubber sole. I never could stand a rubber sole. Tell Marge thanks a million for the money order and I will send it back first chance I get. XXXXX for Pussyfoot [*reference to 'Cousin Mary' Hollenkamp, who lived upstairs at 1345 Texas*].
So goodbye for a while.
Norb

Louisville, Kentucky. **October 3**, Saturday

Dear Norb,

We received your letter giving the time you received Mom's letter, in other words, Norb, we take it that you received the Railway Express Money Order for $10. Is that right? We were wondering if you received it. So you don't get your first paycheck until October 31st. Well, Norb, that's heck but look how good you'll feel when you do get it. But there'll be plenty what will be deducted. Will you get paid for your two weeks furlough? We are sending you a box. It's a cake I baked. I hope it won't make you too sick. So I guess it will be the last one until your new address. Mom said when you are moved you should call long distance and reverse the charges because you won't have any money to spare for that.

You all must all get the idea that the infantry is the only alternative. Jonesy wrote home and said he was working 18 hours a day. He'd rather walk his *** off than work it off in the Air Corps. A letter from Jr Hubbuch said he lost 34 pounds. He don't even look like a Hubbuch anymore. He gained quite a bit at first and then lost. He likes Yakima, Washington so much better than Keesler Field. He is in the Air Corps. I sure hate to see that on those

Johnsons going across, but they sure was here a long time. Do you hear from Zip? I never heard about the [*All Wool and a Yard Wide Democratic Club*] Fish Fry or anything, how they came out. Gertie Bowe Meyer's 4th son has his papers. The 5th is married you know, he was examined but they reclassified him in 3-A. What do you really think you would like to do? We all thought you asked to be transferred from clerical to telephone, so you wouldn't have to plunk a typewriter all day. We got, I mean bought, a pretty rooster from Rudy. Everybody's getting 29 cents a pound but he's asking 25 cents. It's really pretty.

How is the boy with the flu? I hope you don't get it. I seen in the paper, it said October was a month for flu colds. Oscar got a 36-hour leave. He wrote and said he was going to fly home but he changed his mind. He's going to hitchhike. Quite a bit of difference, isn't it? Mr. Redd from Hubbuch's left for the army. He goes in as a Lieutenant. He was in uniform yesterday and was going to Florida. He is going to have a charge of some books. I think Amshoff is going in with a commission also because he knew he was leaving in November. So I guess he must have specialized in something.

Well, Norb, the supper bell is ringing and she don't sound too friendly 'cause she sounded her alarm several times. So until tomorrow, good evening. Be patient about your radio. We'll hear soon and then let you know immediately.

Your little Sistah,

Hermina

Missouri, **October 3**

Dear Mom and all,

It's a very warm and wet day today and the mud here is ups to my knees. I tell you this **** Missouri mud really sticks. It's even worse than Kentucky clay. It makes it pretty darn hard to keep your shoes shined, especially the way they want them shined.

I also received Pop's letter yesterday and that 'cheer up with Oertel's '92.' That would be a good slogan, if I just had the Oertel's. A pint of good old Kentucky bourbon would bring a little cheer also, because the beer here is hardly fit to drink. Especially on Sundays. They have to sell extra low [*alcohol*] volume beer. This money order is an express money order and I can't get it cashed at the Post Office. I took it to the Post Office this morning because I thought that it was a postal instead an express. The only thing I read on it was the ten; the rest wasn't of very much interest. I think I will go in town tomorrow and get it cashed. Tomorrow is Sunday, but I think most of the stores stay open, because that is their big day because all the soldiers are off on Sunday.

So that Jr Hubbuch lost 34 pounds. Is he worrying that much or is it that they're working him too hard? Or it might be a combination of both. It won't be so much longer here until my two weeks schooling will be over, and then to a civilian school I hope. It will be that way too if the orders aren't changed again. So you can't say for sure what's going to happen.

Listen, Horse, if you are going to correct the mistakes in my letters, I will send you a corrected copy of your own, and you can see what I have to put up with. Ah, and is it really true what they tell me about our own little Marge? I hear that there is a romance in bloom and he don't have to say a word because he has talking eyes. And to think this whole thing started of rats. That just goes to show that rats are good for something anyway.

Well, I guess that's about all for now, so until later then.

Still a Yard bird,

Norb

Louisville, Kentucky, **October 3,** 8:00 pm

Dear Uncle Norbe,

I just want to drop you a few lines tonight. Well, I just got done packing my clothes. I'm going home tonight if Daddy comes. If he don't, I won't. Then I will go home tomorrow Sunday. We are going to have a procession back at church Sunday. I don't know who is going to crown the Blessed Mother. It will be a second-grader. Mary Katherine [Katsy] will march and so will Betsy. The boys don't march. The ones that do march is in the first, second and third grades. Well, well, well, the Muths came in so I will go home tonight. Well, I guess I will close. So good-night. Hope you are well.

Your A-1 Girl Friend,

Shirley

Louisville, Kentucky, **October 3**

Dear Norb,

I am still praying for you and I hope you are doing pretty good in school. We get our report two weeks from now. Do you go to church and pray for me too, Norby? Milton got your letter this morning. I played football this morning and bruised my knee but what is a bruised knee when you win a game? We beat them 21 to 12. I made every point but they gave me interference. We got two dogs now, Norb. We got a little rat and tan and Snooky. Snooky is a big hound now. The rat and tan is about a foot tall. Betsy and Ma is stringing little bitty green and red peppers. We are having a scrap iron drive at our school. We brought about 150 pounds back this morning. Me and Milton went and some other kids went out to that camp [*Camp Taylor*]. on Poplar Level Road We saw a German plane, cannon, two big bombs and that is all now.

From Jimmy [*Muth; Norb's nephew*]

Louisville, Kentucky, **October 5**

Cousin Mary Hollenkamp sent Norb a card:

"To My Soldier Boy - since you are in the army, my only thought is this: Our Uncle Sam's got MAN-POWER that I am going to miss!" The card is old and one side was worn off, making it impossible to decipher the whole letter. Inside: "Dear Honeybunch, I always hear from

you. It's very nice of you to think of me. I think of you every day [even if] I don't write. I heard in your letter you had a X. I don't know what that stands for.
From Pussyfoot to Honeybunch

Louisville, Kentucky, **October 5,** Monday

Dear Norb,

How come Mary or Pussyfoot rates all the kisses and we don't get any? Papa got out of serving the jury. Glad to know you had 11 cents left. That don't make you feel so good does it. Well, now you got 1,000 more cents or do you have several beers and less cents?

Do we feel patriotic, Norb! We feel like Aunt Sam. We scoured the house for metal from attic to basement and we do have quite a bit. The garage too got it. We seen just about ½ dozen soldiers' trucks go thru now all along Texas Street. They are stretching a big heavy cable, looks like Manila rope, but I suppose it's for extra power.

Across from Johnny's [*in Plainview*] the field is full of hemp (that's where we get our rope from as if you didn't know). This is government seed grown up on Hearsch's place. This is raised for seed alone this year and last week as John was passing, a kid was stamping out a fire he said three men in a car like his had started three fires and he was stamping out the last one as Johnny came along.

I got several good ones to tell you. First one: Joe came over and mooched Mom for some coal [*since*] it got a good deal cooler. That is one thing you can get him on. We all give him the Ha, Ha, Ha. Second one: Lee is working with Ray Bliler painting. Mrs. Russell and Mr. Russell went to see Ann and Ray was telling them that Lee's brother was killed in 'action' last week. He got word and he zipped in his car, went to see his mother, and zipped back. Of all the cheerful ones I believe he would take first prize. Don't you think his plate [*implanted in his skull*] would do more good in the metal drive? Betsy came for the scrap and they really have a heap back here at church. Ann Bliler has her wheel chair now and is doing fine. That Dr. Scholl's outfit Norb, Mom sent that. Marge or I never paid for that.

It's about 7:30 and we are waiting for Alma. That foot balm, Norb, is good for chapped skin, etc. Did you ever mail Shirley's birthday card? She has never received it. Herbert Adams has been moved to Colorado. Clifton hasn't been heard from since he left the US. JO has a deferment until Nov. 16th. He is joining the Air Corps then. Mom wants to write. So until tomorrow, study hard my sweet.

Norb we're going to get you a mourning card to send to Lee in honor of his brother who was killed in 'action.' Pop just shook laughing at that and wants you to send that card, that's up to you, but it really was funny.
Love from all,
Hermina

Continued by Mommy:

Dear Norb,

Alma is watching me writing. She said she loves you more and more every day. Absence makes the heart grow fonder. That is what she said. Now I don't want to write about love to you. Alma can do that better than I. Now I am going to talk love to you. I was to church tonight and prayed very hard for you, They gave out prayer leaflets and the priest and people pray them together. I am sending you a leaflet so you can pray that also. I am trying to go to Mass during October. Father Dudine sure does ask the people to come to church. I wish you would write Uncle Wessling a card. His address is Mr. Ben Wessling, 1029 Caldwell Street, Louisville, Kentucky. Guten Nacht means good night, and sweet dreams as ever.
Mother
(Everybody says hello, hello from Papa also)

Continued by Hermina:

Dear Norb,

Here I am back again to tell you the Signal Corps is going to put on an extra show. I looked in the Encyclopedia for the Signal Corps and it said it's the most indispensable part of the Service, sounding important. Are you going to join the Air Corps? That is, are you thinking of or considering it? Well, that's all for now, and Pop gave me 5 cents for a card (mourning) (believe it or not).
Goodnite,
H.R.

Camp Crowder, Missouri, **October 7**

Dear Mom, Pop, and "youngins,"

Well, I don't have much to write in this letter but I just thought I would write and say hello.

I received that cake this morning but I didn't taste it yet, so I won't say thanks until I sample it.

I got a letter from Johnny yesterday and it seems as though he has mice in his pantery [*sic*]. The rates must be getting bad in the Rawert family. All I can tell you is that it's a beautiful day and everything is OK.

I thought of Mom this morning. I had some 'warshing' I had to do. The only trouble is I don't get a kick out of it (like she does). I think I'll mail all my dirty handkerchiefs home and then you can warsh them and mail them back, ha, ha, ha. I'm getting lazy like the rest of the guys here in the army. I think tonight is the last night of school in this camp, at least that's the way I understand it. Well, I haven't much to write in this letter because I wrote it all in the last one so I guess that will be all for today. I "reckon" I will hang around here for a few days yet so I'll close now for a little while. Tell Mary hello.
Still,
Norb

Camp Crowder, Missouri, **October 7**

[*Mom, Pop and all*]

Well, as far as I know we pull out of here the 9th. At least that's the latest. I will call as soon as I reach my destination and I won't reverse the charges because Park and Tilford finally came through. As soon as I can get to the Post Office, I will send a money order for the amount that was loaned to me.

I still don't know where I'm going, but I know we're pulling out because our mess hall just has rations until Friday. I kinda hate to leave this mess hall because the chow has been pretty good. If and when I go to civilian school, I think we eat in restaurants but of course, the government pays for our meals. I just wonder if they know the volume of my appetite.

Yes, I was surprised to get a letter from "Herm" [*dad*] but I wasn't surprised that he told me about "Oertel's '92." I reckon he's a better judge of it than I am now. My main drinks are milk shakes and coffee, believe it or not, but that is an actual fact. I hear they have a big radio and telephone school in Lexington, but I don't expect to get there. But one can never tell, can one? I guess I'll end up in California somewhere. Well, anyway, it will be pretty warm.

It was funny about Morris finding out about Joe being married, wasn't it? I don't think I would like Alaska very much. I think I would rather be in Ireland or Australia. It seems as though people around here doesn't have much use for soldiers, but I don't give a damn what they think of me. It they don't like it, they know what they can do about it. Some of these civilians try to shit on the soldiers and the soldiers won't take it, and so there's hell. These stores around here will always 'up' the prices on soldiers. I heard about it time and time again. I will admit there are some 'no counts' in the army, but there is also a bunch of hell-of-a-nice fellows, and they outnumber the no-counts 400 to 1. I been in the army for nearly two months now and I like it a lot better than I did at first. And I'll bet you a lot of fellows will sign up for a second hitch after the war is over. Of course, as I said before, it's not like being at home, but you can't expect it to be. But you do what is right and you'll be treated fair and square. At least, that's the way I found it so far. [*Later in life, after his experiences in the military and government after his separation, he changed his mind and thought the military/government lied, was unfair and couldn't be trusted*]. If they wouldn't be pretty fair the morale of the army wouldn't be as high as it is. But, of course, there are some types of fellows who would crab about everything, even if it's for their own benefit. I was going to buy me a garrison cap on Sunday, but I thought I would wait until I got to where I was going, and then I wouldn't have to pack it along with me. I did buy one of those heavy leather belts that you wear on the outside of your coat. I have a few more things I have to buy yet, and then my outfit would be almost complete. You would be surprised at the knick-knacks you have to buy.

If you are figuring on sending a radio don't get one that's too large, because I won't have room for it. Get a pretty small one but get a good one and then tell me how much it is and

I'll send the money. Don't get one over 10 or 11 inches square, if you can help it. And don't send it until I get to where I am going because that will be more stuff for me to pack and it might get broken.

I tell you that this Principles of Electricity is really tough and I ain't fooling. It's a mixture of Algebra, Geometry, fractions, and plain arithmetic. If I knew electricity was that tough, I would rather burn oil lamps. I finished DC (Direct current) and am now on ACa2 (Alternating current). Alternating current is a lot tougher than direct current because the current changes sixty times a second.

I have nearly all my shots except one (tetanus). But I have a yellow fever shot coming if I ever cross the pond. I got about seven shots in all so far.

I just got a letter from Johnny this morning. It took a pretty long time to get here because it had to go through my old address first. Well, I guess that's all for now so until I pick up a little more time, I hope you are all well. Pop still drinking his Oertel's? Are Mom's feet in better condition? And Hermina still holding bathroom conferences? Tell Mary I give her a special hello and a hundred XXXXXX.

Love to All,

Norb

Louisville, Kentucky, **October 8**

Dear Norbie,

I'm up at Mommy's writing you a few lines. We are waiting to see lights at Manual Stadium. Milton is selling soft drinks tonight. I might go Saturday. I received your letter today. Heard that you are going to be moved. There is an airplane flying above the house now. I think it will start at 8:00 o'clock. If I'm not mistaken. There is a little baby living next to Manual Stadium and they told the mother she would have to take the baby someplace else because it would break its eardrums, the noise would. I guess that's about all I know. Hope you are well. I think Jimmy's going to write a line or two. So until I write again,

I'm still you're A-1 girl Friend,

Shirley

A letter from Jimmy Muth was included:

Dear Norb,

Mary Catherine [*Katsy*] likes school. But sometime she does not want to study her lessons. Today I had to draw a map. I had to write all the rivers and states. It's getting harder every year. Milton is in the same room that he was in in the first grade. Shirley's Sister, when there is a fight in the schoolyard, doesn't stop them. My sister - she's mean. But sometimes she's nice. Betsy's Sister is pretty good, but she does not like her.

Tonight back at Manual Stadium they are having the Army War Show. Milton has a job at the statim [*stadium*]. He sells candy and peanuts or soft drinks. That show is going

to last six more nights. Milton will make about $5.00 a night. I could do a whole lot with that if Mother would let me. If is a hard world, you know. Mother told me you was getting transferred to a different camp. I hope you like the camp that you are going to. Do you know 'an ounce of pluck is worth a ton of luck?' Bye now, Norb, I haft to go now. But good luck.
From,
Jimmy

Continued by Marge at the bottom of Jim's letter:
An ounce of pluck is worth a ton of luck. Well, I can't beat it. Little Jimmy wrote this letter while we were watching the show. Cute kid, ain't he? He's just like his uncle Norbie is, huh?
Margaret

Louisville, Kentucky, **October 8**, Thursday, 10:30 pm
Dear Norb,
   Norbert Wafzig and Oshie Murr are added to the list of the ones who are called to the army. We seen the "highlights" of "Here Comes the Army," those powerful plane spotters and the shooting "ack ack ack" and the powerful bombs, you could feel the vibration on the porch. Three planes with powerful floodlights would sweep low over the stadium. It ended with the audience singing "Our National Anthem." It also had fireworks. We could see all this from home, but the flamethrowers and all the low things we couldn't see that, and the tank action, and finally the whole army fighting. The band couldn't be heard as good as last night. What we seen and heard was very impressive. We are OK. We don't see hardly any soldiers, a jeep now and then. Tonite the police escorted some private cars, probably army officials, through Texas Street. That's all about the Army Show.
   We are not going to mail this letter until you reach your new destination... Jimmy is so sincere in writing you. I hope you can make it all out. Ben at Schieman's is moved to Tennessee. Ernie [*Schieman; the butcher and owner of the corner store and meat market*] was staying at one of those swanky hotels and he was transferred, too. I don't know where, but he is now sleeping in a cow barn.
   Sure am glad to know you got your money from Park and Tilford. That's fine. Now when the army comes across, I feel a celebration coming on. Well, until tomorrow, study hard my sweet. Until tomorrow, sleep tight my sweet.
Love from all. Your little sister,
Hermina

Continued, **October 9**, Friday, 5:45 pm
Dear Norb,
   News as I get it - Lonny Johnson leaves the 14th, so does that Stuckenburg boy on Milton. Do you get paid in full from Park and Tilford or in monthly payments? Ann was saying that

the way Clarence spoke, you get some every month until you are paid up. I suppose you are travelling. We all spoke of you so much today. If the weather there is as it is here, you have beautiful weather to spend your vacation in. It won't be long and we'll be hearing music and hearing the show. Well, until tomorrow, take in all the sights my sweet.
Hermina Rawert

Continued, **October 10**, Saturday

Barney Dillmann has been called to the army too. I just heard over the radio that they are calling men to the signal corps. Scholtz is still at the swanky hotel in New Jersey. He got his training at $1,000,000 boardwalk. He's in the Air Corps. Well, we lived thru another nite of the Army Show and Manual Stadium. When it's lit up, it looks like dawn, or second breakfast time for you, my dear.

I'm not putting dear on this. I got that card this morning and it calls for a good one in return, so if you get one, it will be in answer to this. Now to get you bored, I still see you roll your <u>warsh</u>. By the time we get your address, you sure will have an overweight letter. That's the only thing you like overweight, huh? I must say I got a laugh out of the card. Everybody did. Should I say I appreciated the thought but not the sentiment? I guess the army will have plenty kuchen [*coffee cake*] from now on - Charles Heitzman [*of Heitzman Bakery on Lydia*] goes next week, too. That Gamelhoft on Lydia is called, too. It seems like the army took another strong dose and is ridding the Burg [*Schnitzelburg*] of all the boys. When you left, you know how many of the boys left then? It's the same way now.

Lip's taking my cards home to show her neighbors. We can't hear a thing tonite, the air must be going a different direction. Marge is going Monday nite to the show. St. Xavier High School wants the name of all the boys in the service so we're sending yours in. Betsy and Shirley are going back home tonite. I gave Betsy the money and she was so thrilled. Milton worked there Wednesday, Thursday and Friday nites. Wednesday he didn't make anything. He sacked peanuts. Thursday he made 58 cents, Friday $1.00. So Jimmy got Lip to make him a money belt so he's trying his luck.

Continued, **October 11**, Sunday morning, 11:30 am

Just got a little more dope. We had more pictures of our family and you at Ft. Benjamin (*Harrison; IN*) made. Mrs. Hertel wanted one. She just had one made; it's hanging over the Soda fountain. He told me there is 39 in the service from that corner. George Herbig is in; he got a card from him saying he was passing thru the state of Texas. Do you write to them? They are collecting scrap today, all kinds of trucks, Railway Express, Gulf Refining, etc.
Loads of love,
Hermina

October 11

Dear Corp.,

Bill Hollenkamp is in New Guinea.

Well, honey we just received that message and "CONGRATULATIONS." Say, do you do things in a hurry. You must have got faster, do you eat dynamite now? Well, I'll be mailing this. I called Alma. She's coming this evening at 5 pm. They are raising the 'service flag' at church with 250 names on it. That's something.

To end with a bang, I'll tell you Deenie Johnson got in a scrap with a bigger guy than he is. He was knocked down. The feller hit him on the head and Johnson was knocked out, but he has the laugh on this guy - he broke his hand in three places. And makes $100 a week.

Pop isn't home yet from work. Norb, when did they make you PFC? We never knew it. So now you're a real Corp., not an acting one. Here's hoping you like Kansas City and keep on liking the Signal Corps. You climbed up quicker than anyone I know. How complimentary and to think you sent me such an unflattering card. You're forgiven so until tomorrow, study hard my sweet. Until tomorrow, don't get the high hat my sweet. How is hotel life?
Love,
Hermina

Continued by Margaret:

Mr. Hubbuch [*Hubbuch Company*] is trying his very best to get a radio. He is as sweet as ever. He called me this morning and said Mr. Lester and another guy are trying to get me one. Say, I got a big complement for you. Have you one to exchange?
Just Mary Margaret Catherine Rawert.

Norb's New Address was Howard Hotel, Room 217, 1414 Locust, Kansas City, Missouri.

Louisville, Kentucky, **October 11**, 5 pm

Dear Norb,

We sure was surprised at the telephone call at that time of the day but we know a long distance ring so we made a beeline upstairs as we were in the basement. Mom had just gone down to Lips about 10 minutes before you called, for a chicken dinner. She said she would of rather missed a days' food as to missed hearing from you. It really does them a lot of good for you to call even if Pop does get a little tearful. I called Mrs. Orrill. She told Mom and of your promotion, so Mom had a crying spell, and when Pop came home I told him, so he was a good bit tearful, but awful proud, Norb. He didn't hardly have the last bit down; he wanted to know if Marge would like a glass of beer. He couldn't wait until he broke the news to Huelsman's. He really thinks you will get some place in the army, if I heard it once I heard it 25 times since he came home. We all hope he is right. When you come home, you will see your picture everyplace: Hertel's, White Cottage. And Marge is so pleased with hers, but Mom is still talking about your picture with a "peak cap" as she calls it, so we'll keep on waiting until someday we'll be getting it. They are all gone to the Service Flag Dedication at church. It has 250 names on it. [*Father*] Bernard Spoelker is leaving for the army in November. They are remodeling his school. Dottie said they had three shacks and are combining them into one and putting the toilet indoors. They never had any modern facilities there, so as soon as it is completed Bernard will be leaving.

Milt made $1.65 last night and Jim, 65 cents. This man asked Milt who he was, and was he related to Rudy. He told him [*yes*] so he said, "I thought so, because you really can sell things."

I was talking with Dottie Spoelker; Antoinette was here and is gone back. She was supposed to come over and she was expecting to stay a week. He came down for 1 day and went back so she didn't get to come over. She gave me Antoinette's address. You should go see her as she lives across the river from Missouri. They live in one of those government houses put up for the Defense workers. He works in a Bomber factory. I'll write Antoinette's address on a card. I know you will be welcome, Norb. Do you think that sometime you could get a 36-hour leave? If you make good time, I imagine you could come home for an hour or two. Or don't you? Oscar was home again today.

Mom wants to write, too, so I am saving a few lines for her. I called the bus station. It takes about 18 hours to make that trip so that couldn't be done in 36 hours. It seems funny to address your envelope as Corporal. We're expecting Johnny here tonite. The Angelus is just ringing. I imagine hotel life is a lot better than barracks. Do you still like your school Corp [Corporal)] since Alma came home? I know you're not the fault, not 100 %, of sending me that card. She selected it. She's like Joey - gives herself up. I'm going to do a little shopping myself and I won't need you to send it either. Mary Elizzie came over with Eleanor. Well, until tomorrow, don't bust too many buttons, Corp. Sleep tight, but don't get tight.
Love XX,
Hermina

Louisville, Kentucky, **October 11**, 9:00 [*dated 'September 11' in error*]
Dear Norb!
Congratulations, my boy, from Papa, Mom, sisters and brothers! I like to write on lines. I took a different paper [*than Hermina's, which was unlined*]. Hermina told you most of the news. It don't take her long to compose a letter. I was really surprised when Mrs. Orrell call me at Elizabeth's little window. I just finished my chicken dinner. It was very good. Of course, I wished that I would have been home.

Oh, the services in church was grand. The United States flag is above the Saint Ann statue and the flag with 250 stars so far, is above the St. Theresa's statue. Then the chaplain had a sermon telling all about the boys and praised them highly, so much consolation for the parents and wives and sweethearts. I hope that you do as the chaplain said, that the men sure show that they were good Catholics. I think they took 4 and 5 pictures or whatever you call it. I will send you the picture if they will be in the paper. I believe I sent you a leaflet. Father Dudine recited the prayers and rosary. Then the people sang the songs that is on the leaflets. Then they gave the solemn blessing and then they sang the "Star Spangled Banner." It is the first time I heard that sung in church. You should have heard me sing. I thought of you all the time in church. Pop sang also. I have not heard Pop sing in years. I was so glad that he did not have to work this afternoon. We want to go to see the war show tomorrow night. John and his family are here this evening and Elizabeth's family; Milton and Jimmy are selling peanuts again tonight.

Alma and I are writing on the kitchen table. We stopped a few minutes to see the powerful light in the air and the planes pass through them. It is so wonderful. Alma and I had to stop again and see the light and planes again and the fireworks. Well, it is all over now. Last night there were 45 streetcars passed our house in a short time. The crowd seemed larger tonight. Papa cried again but you know beer is a help, for if he is tired or in the dumps, I am glad that '92 cheers him up. Are you not glad also? I tell you Muthy had 'em bad tonight [*Moody loved to make people laugh, and often did so with letting gas, or holding his stomach in and dropping his pants*]. He really looks funny when he wants, with his teeth out. We laughed tears at the supper table. Well, Norb it is about all I know so I will close and wish you good luck for the future and God bless you from Papa, Mama, sisters and brothers. Mary sends you a sweet kiss and was glad that you was promoted. Marge is frying fish. Papa getting beer [*for*] Alma, Hermina, Marge, Papa and I. It is 10:40 o'clock. Mother

Rm 217 Howard Hotel, 1414 Locust St., Kansas City, Missouri, **October 12**
Dear Mom and all,

Well, I'm still in Missouri, as you all know. I like it a lot better here than I did in the camp. It don't even feel like you're a soldier. We eat at a restaurant that's under the government and the food is pretty darn good. We have a civilian instructor. There about 40 of us in the whole group but the group is divided into 4 classes. So there is an instructor for every ten men.

My buddy and I walked about 15 miles Sunday so we covered a lot of Kansas City. What we were really looking for was the city limits. You can get beer out in the country on Sunday but you can't get it in the city. Well, we got to the country alright. I will be here for six weeks and then I go to a lateral unit. So there is really a lot to learn in six weeks, and not much time for monkey business except on Saturday. We are off from Saturday afternoon until 10:00 pm on Sunday night, so we at least have a weekend. Our hotel is just about 100 feet from our school so that makes it quite handy. Kansas City is alright but I don't think it's quite as clean as Louisville. It looks like the people are afraid of lawnmowers.

There are only three of us in our room. One of them is a non-drinking Baptist. He will drink one beer but that's as far as he will go. But I guess that's to his advantage if he likes it that way. Enclosed you will find a few goofy pictures. I wasn't drunk either. Neither was my pal. Well, that's about all I have to say for now so until later then,

I'm still,

Norb

Kansas City, Missouri, **October 12**

Dear Mom and all,

Well, to start out with this stuff about Walter Winchell. He might know a few things that are going to happen, but he sure don't know that. Are you sure you got that straight? Are you sure he didn't say 40 years? Ha, Ha.

I just got a note from Antoinette Spoelker today. She must have called while I was at school so they left a note in my box. She told me I should come over as soon as I could, so I guess I will have to go now. I suppose I will try to get there Saturday if nothing else comes up between now and then. It was pretty nice of them asking me.

I got a letter from Lip today also. It was very good to hear about all the kids but not about that ½ pound of coffee she got in 4 weeks. I don't see how the restaurants get hold of it. Well, everything is going along swell and that's all I can write for now, so until later then,

Norb

Louisville, Kentucky, **October 12,** 10:55 am

Dear Corp,

To begin with, Pop's gone to Huelsman's. He, Mom and Marge, Alma went to the War Show and they all enjoyed it velly, velly [affecting a foreign accent] much. George Heitkemper is in the Navy. Shankie is in England. I was talking to Clarence Johnson this morning. He just received this letter from Shankie.

It was 17,783 at the War Show tonight. Giving you the dope, my boy. I was talking with Mrs. Zipperle, too. She was talking with a few of the "actors." They are so sick of performing, she said. They are busy in the morning practicing and taking care of what they must do and then at nite they have to perform. That is tough.

Hertel's has your picture up. Joe Paul, Harold Chalmers, Claude Nunn and George Herbig's pictures are up. We are all OK. I was at Dr. Stites today. Dr. John is a Major in the army, Dr. James a Lieutenant Commander. I asked him if it would be General Frank. He said no. I lost 4 lbs. in 5 weeks. Tain't very good but he said it was swell because this diet doesn't slim you until about 3 weeks.

We are sending you a box tomorrow. I'm sending you some nuts in return for that card and also something else I promised. They sure enjoyed the show tonite. The Signal Corps was fine.

I got a letter from Jr Hubbuch today. Mom wants to finish this letter so it's getting very late. So until tomorrow, sleep tight my sweet.

Heard the president tonite and he sure praised the women. He said the men were the first to look up from their work when he came through on his unannounced trip. So we have F.D.R. on our side. Wonder if Franklin thinks the same about Eleanor?

Continued, Tues, 9:30 am

I'm waiting on the car, so I thought I would tell you Mr. Horne, the lawyer, suffered a heart attack and died this morning.

Continued, 4:00 pm

It is now almost 4 o'clock, the time for you to come home. I did not miss many 4 o'clocks that I did not think of you. I don't know what time you think of me the most. Maybe it's 3 o'clock in the morning. Marge is going to Elizabeth's after work. Elizabeth and Muddy [*Moody*] are going to the War Show. Rudy gave them the treat. I am glad that Elizabeth gets to go. I liked it very much. Your daddy also and Alma and Marge. The 55¢ ticket seats were as good as the $1.10 seats. We had the $1.10. I am sorry we did. Marge paid for us. I was almost broke. You know how that is when 10¢ looks too good to spend. But Papa got the check last night already; that don't happen very often. I had better than 11¢ anyhow. If we have any more rats in Schnitzelburg, it is not our fault, for your picture is well represented. As soon as you can, let us have one with a cap and a peak. Let us know how you like your new home. So many ask me, "How is Norb?" Of course, I can tell them now that you are a Corporal. Makes us feel proud. I want to go to church tonight. I had to miss last night. Pray for us also.
Love from all,
Mother

The first letter addressed to Room 217 at Howard Hotel, 1414 Locust, Kansas City, Missouri was October 13.

October 13, Tuesday, 7:30 pm

Dear Norb,

Well, the show will soon be starting tonight. It is the last performance and they expect to have seated 100,000 people in these 6 nites, or rather, the attendance is expected to be 100,000. Tain't bad for a one-horse town.

Carny Hubbuch tried to get a radio like you, but no gettee. They tried every wholesale house in Louisville. We called Boman-Summers. They are expecting some in, a Philco radio to sell at $13 and $19. We will know if they got that shipment by Saturday. Joe is going to ask Sabel [*Joe's boss*], too. The reason I'm telling you this is because if you can get one you like there, it would be grand because we cannot locate one, only depend on Boman-Summers. Will you let us know about this as soon as you can, Norb? We thought perhaps one in the Service might be able to pick it up quicker.

Marge is down at Lips. Lip and Moody are at the War Show. How was the cake? Tell the truth, Corp. Was it good, or not? I put a soft icing on it. I hope it kept that way. Have you been receiving your mail OK?

Haven't much new, only Alma's mother called here last night while she was at the War Show to know if she stayed Sunday night. She was so worried for Alma. Alma didn't leave her know that she was coming here.

I took my shoes to Abie's at 5:30 and waited for them at Lavern's. We talked about everything until 7 o'clock and Mom got so worried. She wanted to see the show, Pop came home earlier, and did I get it! Well, they got to the show. Alma looked and switched her mouth around cause Kate did spare no words and neither did "Herm." Well, they got to the show and liked it very much. About 9:00, Alma's mother called about her - she was excited too. So Alma and I got holy hell yesterday.

How long do you expect to be in this hotel, Norb, or don't you know? Tell us all about it. I have a good compliment but it might cause you to sew in a few more buttons [*because his chest may swell in pride*]. I took a few of our pictures with me to Dr. Stites'. He said you boys had a nice figure but my poor 200 [*weight*]. Nobody gives me any credit for carrying around such excess. Carny Hubbuch sold Dr. Sites a big order. I told him it paid him to get sick. He took Bernard in today and Fr. Niedert last week. He weighed 260. Ben weighs 204. It will be a dieting bunch down there if we all keep up the good or bad work,
Good nite my sweet,
Hermina

Louisville, Kentucky, **October 14,** 7:30 pm

Dear Norb!

Hello Norb. Got your letter this afternoon. We were waiting with patience for a letter to hear how you like your new place. John stopped in for a few minutes. [*He*] had to go to the office, and wanted to know if we heard from you. I did not have the letter yet. I told him I expected one. Ann and Joe read the letter. Of course, Mary and Hermina also. Papa is not home yet. They [*St. Brigid's*] have services almost every night. You know it's rosary month. Marge is ironing. I did not get done with it today. Hermina is going with Mr. and Mrs. Russell to see Mr. Horne. He is going to be buried tomorrow afternoon. She [*Mrs. Horne*] is taking his death very hard. He died of a heart attack. You said you were going to send me some school...[*words unreadable*], but we cannot make out the word you wrote like this... [*words unreadable*]. Thanks for the compliment that Louisville is a cleaner place. I glory in your Baptist friend that he is man enough to say no. He is a good example for some of them. You write with only 4 beers, then 6 beers. How many more after the 6th one? I hope you can say no before you get too much. Where will you go after the 6 weeks? The pictures are fairly good for being drunk. Ha, ha, ha. Believe it or not, I am going to get Papa supper now. Have to peel potatoes. He is going to have sour kraut. Saturday we are going to have Pannas [*Scrapple in German*]. Do you want some? Of course, you could eat it Friday. Were those 40 men all made corporals that go to your school now? What is the meaning of that medal your pal is wearing? Now another question. Is the church far from your hotel? John and Eleanor got up Sunday morning at 4 o'clock and got the children ready for 5 o'clock Mass at St. Matthews. He asked to get off on Sunday instead of Tuesday but so far, they have not let him off.

Continued, **October 15**

I just came home. Went to mass this morning and prayed for all the soldiers and extra prayer for you. It was very foggy this morning. I guess in the hollow, too. Papa looked at those pictures a half dozen times. Elizabeth and Margie are here to spend the day, I hope. Why don't Mary get any XXX no more?
Well, goodbye and God bless you.
Your Mamma

Louisville, Kentucky, **October 14,** 9:20 pm
Dear Norb,
I just brought an airmail letter to the mailbox. I suppose by this time you've read where we got you a Radio from Sutcliffe's.
I went to see Mr. Horne tonight. He looks grand. I never seen a corpse that looked better. He came home from work at 8:30; he had been suffering with his heart although nobody knew it. He never felt too good so he sat in his easy chair until 2:00 am. Mrs. Horne heard him come to bed then but heard a noise and thought Carl was snoring so she got up and Mr. Horne was gasping for breath. She sat him up and called Carl. He died at 2:15 pm. They take it hard but mighty nice. He sure has lovely flowers.
Norbert Wafzig passed, was just given 2 weeks furlough. Beans rejected - acute alcoholism. Frank Frisch was rejected – tuberculosis. He is going to be sent to Dawson Springs. He served in First World War. I heard Cletus Murr came home over the weekend. Norb, what's your buddy's name? Nosey, huh? The War Show is over. It seems strange. Goss Avenue was a mighty busy thoroughfare today, army trucks, jeeps, etc. passing all day.
Norb did you lose weight? You look thinner to me but very neat. Get a real good picture of yourself. George Herbig has his at Hertel's. Looks fine. You beat everything.
I heard of walking a mile for a Lucky [*Lucky Strike cigarettes commercial line*] but I never heard of walking 15 miles for a beer. Write that one in to Ripley's [*Believe It or Not*], honey. Sure am glad to learn you like Kansas City. Norb, I suppose your shoes will shine now. Mrs. Russell has been staying with Mrs. Horne. He gets buried tomorrow. Now about

the radio. Norb we shopped the town over in at least a dozen places only Sutcliffe and a radio store had five between the two. They quit making radios in April.

Fr. Rauch left today for Christ the King Church. Do you still go to night school, Norb? One instructor for 10 men? I don't think you could shoot many paper wads and get by with it now.

Let the Baptist go, Norb. I suppose he's doing his as conscience tells him, and we all think you did good in Crowder even if your refreshment was milkshakes, but you're just like Pop - a beer cures everything. He's just back from the corner [*Hueltsman's*] now. I believe he'd walk 15 miles, too, Norb. Glad to know you like Hotel life and the chow is good. Until tomorrow and until I get more dope [*information*], study hard and keep walking.
Hermina

Kansas City, Missouri, **October 15**

Dearest Mom, Pop and Sis's,

Well, here I am in a hotel; it's like the 'life of Riley' compared to an army camp. The food is swell, the beds are fine and I am in a room with two swell fellows. So everything is swell as far as the army is concerned.

I had a swell time tonight. I was with three fellows who were shipwrecked. They were hit three times by a torpedo. They wouldn't tell me the name of the ship they were on but did tell me there were about 2000 men on board and I noticed they wore the air corps insignia, so I wouldn't be surprised that in a few days you wouldn't hear about an aircraft carrier being sunk. They showed me pictures and their watches, and what damage the salt and brine in the ocean done to them. It was really interesting. They are on a 30-day survival leave and they really were swell fellows even if they are failures. One was a Swede, the other a German, the other was a mixture of something. They were in England and Ireland both, and from what they said, I think England couldn't be much blacker at night. They also said you have a very, very hard time getting some good cigarettes to smoke, in fact they said you can't buy them. They said it's the first time they have been in the States for 4 ½ months. I just walked in the place and drank a beer and they told me to come over and sit down, and so I did. I don't know if I will ever see any action or not but if I do I hope I will come out of it like they did. Once again I'll say they were swell fellows, even if they did drink, and I wasn't much behind them, and if I was, it wasn't far, because I can keep up with any sailor as far as beer goes.

Well, Mom, I really enjoyed your letter. It was good to hear from you and about Pop. It was good hearing from him also. And as far as his singing goes, I used to hear him sing when I would come home at 3 bells but it was usually accompanied by some gastric tones also, ha, ha.

I'll tell you, it was really nice here, and the food is tops and I do mean tops. I have been eating like a hungry dog. Well, Mom, I do like it here so you don't have to worry - everything is OK. I'm with a bunch of swell fellows, every one of them, at least they are up to now. I didn't come in here expecting a life of leisure. I know I wasn't expecting it, but I did get more of it than I was expecting. After all, I think I really got a break even if it is a short one. I like school very well as far as I have gone, and everything is OK as far as that is concerned.

I was sorry you wasn't at home, Mom, when I called. I waited especially till church was out thinking everyone would be home but that's alright, just as long as Lip's chicken was fried well done. You must be running around on the Old Man lately. You're a little too old for that, don't you think?

I really do hope that Norb Wafzig doesn't have to go to the army. I guess that will leave Mrs. Wafzig by herself, but if necessary, I guess it has to be. Well, I heard so much about the Army Show I almost think I've seen it, but it must have been a great show to draw such a crowd. I would have liked to see it myself.

When Alma comes up there again, tell her not to send me any more dirty beer labels. I got about four letters from her today and that was held up in Camp Crowder. She always tells me she can't write an interesting letter but she has never been to Missouri. Tell Lip and Moody I received their letter and was very, very glad to hear from them, and you can tell Moody I can get good beer now and all the "Bourbon and Scotch" I want, so he hasn't got anything on me. The only thing he has on me are the odds of Kentucky over Missouri.

Now, talking about a leave, I could get a 34-hour leave every weekend but the only way I could make it home would be by plane. Well, folks, it's about 11:00 bells so if I want to be a clear-headed student, I guess I had better turn in, don't you think? So, I will say goodnight, wishing all of you the very best of luck and good health with more '92. Well, so long.

Love to all. And a special love to Alma. Tell Alma when she goes out to Ft. Knox to see if she can find a fellow by the name of Roy Darrlin. I doubt if she could, because sometimes you don't even know the guy in the next barracks. Well, good night and sleep tight. I know I will. Pardon me for being so long winded.
Norb

Louisville, Kentucky, **October 15**, Thursday, 9 pm
Dear Norb,

Well, Larny [*Johnson*] is in the army. He seen Lee and told him [*that he*] got a 2 week furlough. Mom went back to church tonite with Mrs. Hellman. This Inkograph does better on heavy paper it seems. Cliff Ernst isn't at Hubbuch's and the girl Martha in the office is leaving, too. With the ones in the office and the men leaving, the force is quite a bit reduced. They both got Defense jobs. Don't have any special news, my brother. We just got one letter this week. Just what kind of school are you attending now?

Lip and Margie was up today. It seems funny Little Katsy wasn't with them. She likes Tool [*school*]. Our brother-in-law [*Lee Carter*] is living the life of Riley. He's hunting and fishing for two weeks. To hell with his job until that's off his brain. They are giving another

Fish Fry - the All Wool and Dye Club - for Christmas gifts for the boys in the service. I suppose you don't rate there. Mr. Zip [*Zipperle*] is chairman. Did you receive that letter saying the Holy Name is giving all the boys in the service a money belt and religious placket for Christmas? Joe Paul's picture was in last night's paper. Sure is good of him. Hertel's has one like it. So far, I haven't went to the White Cottage to see yours. You sure will help the shoe repairers out if you always walk 15 miles for a beer.

Moody said did Wachtel come with you? I feel this 18 to 19 draft will go through soon. One of those army trucks killed a girl at Logan and Oak streets yesterday coming from the bivouac. They sure do ride some. Mom will finish this tomorrow so until tomorrow study hard my sweet and don't thumb your nose at your teacher, or do you know another signal by now?

Love, your little sister,

Hermina

Do you have a post card of what your hotel looks like? How many rooms is it? Does it compare to the Brown Hotel? Itching for news.

Chubby

Louisville, Kentucky, **October 16**

Dear Norb!

I am always in a hurry just like you are. Mary will soon be going and I want her to mail this letter. The weather is fine here but we could stand some rain. I was looking for a letter from you. Listen, Norb, don't spend your money foolish. I guess you will soon get money from the government. I would try to save something. What you save is yours, what you spend foolish will belong to someone else. Don't think I am preaching. I mean it for your own good.

Mrs. Hellman said she was in the dumps this summer. Herman got married secretly and no Catholic. You know that one of the girls went to see Herman. She said she was awful sick on the way but she was so homesick to see him. Herman and Red are getting along fine. Hope you study hard and get 100 average. I will close with hopes that I will get a letter Saturday. Everybody says hello.

Mother

Kansas City, Missouri, **October 16**

Dearest Mom and all,

Well, I haven't much to say but I thought I would drop you a line. I received the box today, and don't you know I was just getting ready to walk down to the drugstore to get me some shaving cream and toothpaste? And I very well understood the meaning of the dictionary and I don't blame you. I have to write letters so fast I don't have time to look for mistakes. Now if I could take all the time in the world I wanted I could write you a perfect letter (I think). But just so you can make it out. I guess you got two bits of fun out of sending me that dictionary, ha, ha - well, I put it on our table for the other guys to use and I think they can use it as well as I can because they have the same trouble as I have.

I also received "Horse's" airmail and Marge's letter also, and there's nothing I like more than a letter because I get a little curious about the nosey Schnitzelburg Dutch. You know I had a letter all written to Jim and now I can't find it so you can tell him I am thinking about him.

This beer here has a swell taste but it's not stout enough. I found one place here so far that sells Park and Tilford whiskey but they can keep that stuff. Once again, I'll say the food is swell and I do mean swell.

I had my picture taken the other night but it will take me about eight days to get my negatives so when they come through I've got one for "you all" and Alma (peak cap). Good Night. That's all I know until tomorrow, so good-nite and happy landings.
As always,
Knob-Head

Louisville, Kentucky, **October 16**, Friday, 8:15 pm
Dear Norb,

Well, Norb, by this time you might have your radio. It is being sent Railway Express and the batteries will come separate. I called Sutcliffe's and they told me the batteries were in so I stopped there from work. The store hours now are from 10 to 6 because of the trolley service.

Lights Out program is at 7 pm. Frank Nunn, Golden Voice of Radio, is on Friday at 8 pm. The coffee question is a mighty serious one. Joey said her grocer told her in 10 days there would be a sufficiency. The Great Western has kept us supplied but people run from one store to another. Mrs. Madden was at 9 stores the other night and no coffee. Mary Rawert said she was out too, so she went on Jefferson St. As she entered the man said, "No coffee, lady." She calls every now and then to ask about you, Norb.

We are still in the Scrap Drive. Tomorrow the trucks come out again. I was talking with Clarence Johnson. He said Joe Schenkenfelder, the famous Duke Heitzman and Barney Dillmann passed [*and they were*] given a 2 weeks furlough. Robert Lee Steinmetz passed also. Until tomorrow, study hard my sweet.

Continued, Saturday, 9 pm:
Dear Norb,

Charles Heitzman passed the army. He tried the Marines, the Navy - they both turned him down for a spot on his lung. They feel good to think the army accepted him. This came from a reliable person.

I failed to tell you the radio cost $29.95.

By November 1st, the married men without children are supposed to be called. Mamma said from the kitchen that I should ask you if you broke your arm - she only got one letter this week. I said maybe you always got your two fingers up so you couldn't write.
With love from all. Little sister,
Hermina Rawert

Norb increasingly had a distaste and disdain for the US government based on his experience in the army. The following letter shows one example of his reasons for doing so.

Kansas City, Missouri, **October 17**

Dear Mom and all,
It actually hurts to write this letter. I would rather take the worst beating I could get. I am now with 40 of the most disgusted fellows in the Army I suppose and I feel just that way myself. As I think I have told you, the night we arrived here and all met in a government building they told us that beginning now we were all T [*Technical*] Corps, that is the whole class of forty. Well, today a first Louie [*First Lieutenant.*] came through each class and told us we were not Corps' [*Corporals*] but PFC [*Private First Class*]. That took the starch out of the whole bunch of fellows and most of them swore up and down that they were going to quit studying and I don't blame them. That is a hell of a letdown. Not because they care about the stripes, for one thing, but it makes you lose all the trust in your superior officers. Now it sure would be a holy hell if they make mistakes like that in actual combat. If ever I am in actual combat I want to be able to put my faith in my commanding officer, and so would every other soldier. For the first time since I have been in the Army, I am disgusted and so are a lot of other guys. Another thing is none of us have been paid since we been in the Army and a lot of these guys are flat broke. I have about $20 bucks standing out that I have loaned to them, most of it is OK and I don't give a damn about the rest. That's one reason I haven't sent a money order home.
I want to say thanks for all the trouble you had getting the radio. I'm not going to answer any of the questions you had in your previous letters because I'm not in the mood. I am OK and hope you are all the same. I hope you can read this letter, but I am so damn mad now I don't give a damn.
Norb

Louisville, Kentucky, **October 18**

Dear Norb,
I am still praying for you and I hope you are doing good in school. I heard that you are a Corprel [*Corporal*]. I guess that is what they call you in the Army. I hope you get up higher. Maybe someday you will be a Gennarl [*general*]. Do you know ma[*y*]be is a hard word sometimes? If you take it in such and such a way. Well, goodbye,
From Jimmy

Louisville, Kentucky, **October 18,** Sunday 9:35 pm

Dear Norb,

It's almost bedtime. Norb, Alma came from work today. We expected her yesterday but Alma didn't show up. She said she was so late in getting home from town. You know how that is honey. At least we understand. Fr. Dreckman's mother died Friday. Mom went to see her today. Her son died August 2nd.

How many miles did you walk for a beer today? Pop and all are drinking beer. Mom expected you to call today. What do you expect we all asked her; you can't count on your looks can you? (Corp Norb speaking --Damn quicker than you).

We went to see Lavada Thompson Blight today. We went with the Col. on Texas. She is living in Valley Station now. He was sober as a judge, but after he got home you could see him making a beeline for the Corner. Coming home the Col. got wobbly-knee'd.

Momma dreamed about you last night. She said you were walking and walking her, and all what you could see was Negroes. You said that's all what's here is niggers.

Lip asked Betsy what she wanted to write and she said she isn't going to write you and waste paper on the Corp. because you never answer and of her letters. How's that for a lip? Well, Norb, this is about all for tonight so write tomorrow, study hard my sweet love,
Chubby [Hermina]

Continued by Mommy:

It is 10:20 pm. Alma is getting ready to go home. We want her to stay but she said her mother would be worried about her. Papa said he drank a beer for you. I hope it didn't make you drunk. Alma wants to go to see you had asked me to go along but I don't know yet. She will write you about it. I thought if you would stay there I would rather wait a little longer, but she said she could get off 29-31 this month. I thought that maybe that you would get closer to us. We will write more about it.
God bless you,
Mother

PS. How many hours do you study when you start and when are you dismissed? You have only written us 1 letter last week. Did you break your arm or keep your fingers crossed all the time. If you can write, write to Jimmy, Betsy and Mary Catherine, if only a few words. It means so much to them.

Schlegel the Janitor was here on a furlow [*sic*]. Mary went to the bingo this afternoon and he said a fine word to the bingo players. Do you think you will get a furlow? About how many miles is Kansas City, Missouri from Kansas City, Kansas? Antoinette Spoelker lives in Kansas City.

Continued by Hermina:

The railway fare is $22.00. Do you think you could get a weekend off? If this wouldn't happen Mom would forget about making the trip. She told me to write this.

Bette [*Betsy*] wants you to have this. They went to see the foreign planes, etc. at Parkway Field and this is the work of the signal corps. Don't you think Jim's letters are cute? The spelling keeps you guessing.

Louisville, Kentucky, **October 19**, 1 pm, Weather cloudy, back porch, 66°F

[*Norb*]

I did not send the mail away this morning so I am going to write a few words more. Hermina called the air port, or whatever you call it, they said it was $66 round-trip without the taxes. The taxes are now 5% but they are going to raise them. This is my way of thinking about the trip. Alma wants to go very bad, no more than I do, I don't believe, but if you could fly here everybody could get to see you. And me and Alma could be with you just as long as if we would take the trip. What do you think about it? They tell us the soldiers need the coaches and that the passengers have to put up in the hotel til you can go, and that might cost as much as $3 a day without eats.

I don't know what Papa and Marge and Hermina thinks. I just wrote the way I thought. I don't like to see Alma go alone. I think it is such a long trip and lonesome if you don't have anyone with you. Hermina said it would take 6 hours to get here, they told her. I guess she will ask you or tell you more about it. I am not going to tell her that I told you how I thought because they might have a better way. And Alma also. She is going to call us sometime today. I don't know if she is going to stay over nite or not.

Is the church far from your hotel? We got your two letters this morning so I want to take it back that you might have broken your arm or crossed your fingers. I went on the porch, it was 8:30, to see if we got any mail and the postman met me with two letters. Was I glad? You know I cannot work till I know if we got a letter or not. It makes us all happy to hear from you.

Goodbye, God bless you,

Mother

Louisville, Kentucky, **October 19**, Monday 10:30

Dear Brudder,

So you got the box, aye, the dictionary too. I hope you'se [*sic*] all get use out of it but your spelling is improving. Those letters really was good. The ten-sided one where you met the sailors - that letter was a honey. Your Maw was beginning to feel hurt, just got one letter last week. Just got two in this morning's mail. Now you're wonderful.

Jr Russell has charge of 27 beds now. That toothpaste and shaving cream arrived just in time, didn't it? Do you still have to do your own washing or do you get it done hotel service?

I was humming tonite. I seen Lill Klein Kleiner. Lawrence now has charge of a ward. Pop had one can [of beer] and he has just arrived with the second can. You hain't got nothing on him. By the tone of your letter, your beer tastes mighty good. <I think it tasted too good. Mother>

I called the airlines. It takes 6 hours to make it to Kansas City round trip, ticket $66.00 plus 5 cents tax and in the future 10¢ tax. We are all OK and glad you got your picture tooked [*Hermina's attempt at humor was using grammatically incorrect wording*] with (peak cap). That's a garrison cap isn't it? Joe and Ann are here. Joe wants to know what Mamma wants to argue about, religion or politics? It's 20 minutes to 12 so I better bring this letter to a close. My Mom always wants to add a little, you know. Marge just got in 30 minutes late. She had to wait for a [*trolley*] car over 30 minutes. That's a good excuse isn't it?

Those sailors really must of seen something. What did the pictures and watches look like? With lots of love from your little sister. How was that cake, Norb, you never did say. Your loving sister,
Hermina

October 20, 1:20 pm

Dear Norb,

The weather is beautiful - 76° on the porch. The paper said rain but we never had any. Well, Hermina said Joe wanted to argue. I said alright I'll argue. Telephone bill - let's all pitch in. I'm tired of always paying the bill. He wanted to argue but Ann said that was fair, so that's that. He payed [*sic*] for the second bucket [*of beer*]. He sure is tight. Tonight we want to go to St. Matthew Church. They have 40-hour devotion. Jackie is going to march. I hope that I can go next time. I will write more. Send Mary a hello. I'll pray for you tonite.
Mamma

Kansas City, Missouri, **October 20**

Dear Mom and all,

I received the radio last night and I appreciate all the trouble there was in getting it. It sounds pretty good but I haven't had time to connect the grounding wire yet. The batteries came with it. I've been trying to get WHAS [*popular Louisville channel*] but I haven't been able to as yet.

I been so damn mad after all that mix up I couldn't decide if I wanted to write or not but I guess I will meet up with that kind of thing more than once while I'm in the Army. But it just makes you feel like a damn jackass. From now on, I'm going to keep my mouth shut. I thought that was something I could do, but I see where I'm wrong.

Well, for our meals we have coffee, buttermilk and sweet milk. We can have all we want of all three.

I had some pictures taken the other night and as soon as I see the negatives I'll send you one, but it may take about a week and a half to get them, maybe longer.

So the famous Duke [Heitzman] is being drafted. I'll bet he'll make a good soldier. These fellows still haven't heard about being paid. I don't know what the hell is wrong..Once again, I'll say thanks for all the trouble and I may write tomorrow. I may feel more in the mood. It's no use trying to write a letter if you don't feel like it, so I'll be seeing you.
As always,
Norb

Louisville, Kentucky, **October 20,** Tuesday, 7:20 pm

Dear Norb,

Well, I just got thru with my KP. Now, I know you are very sympathetic. You know how it is. Believe it or not, I scoured the sink. We sure had a lovely autumn so far. It is very dry now and could use some rain. Marge and I swept up the leaves after work. It was quite a bit til Mulberry Street.

I was talking with Smitty's sister. He was made a PFC. I told her you was a Corporal. You might be a general if you listen to Jimmy. We all think his letters are really the stuff. I suppose you have received his letters by now. Did you receive your radio, Norb? What do you think of it?

This is one on Jimmy. Lip and Mrs. Orrill was talking over Defence [*the fence*]. Jimmy was whittling on a stick. Orrill said, "What you doing Jim?" "Making a letter opener," [*Jim said*]. Lip said, "What you want with a letter opener? You got one letter in your life and that was from Besendorf's two years ago when you made your First Communion." Jim said, "Just one letter in my whole damn life!" Mrs. Orrill said it was too funny to see him. His [*Jim's*] idea is getting a letter from you. Orrill said when they get a letter they say "just one damn letter."

I can't give you no news on Schnitzelburg what you crave. I suppose I'll have to go to Taps [*local tavern*] and dig up some news, <u>not dirt</u>, tee, hee. I laugh different from you. Lip wanted some coffee. She's out. John got Mom for a pound last nite. We're lucky. Axe [vegetable cart man]is just yelling. Your nephew Milton was in a free for all. It was really something. He was the winner. Lip, etc. are here. Katsy had such a twamp (cramp) in her leg, this morning she had the belly ache so in church at Muniun (communion). She left three [*gas*] and her bellyache was over.
[*Hermina*]

Continued by Marge:

Hermina is gone to Russells' to hear some news from Buehla, Mr. Russell's sister. I am sending you a picture we cut out of the paper - V for Victory and native US Signal Corps photo. Are you going to learn how to take pictures? The picture is nothing like seeing it.

It's almost 10 o'clock and beer is poured out for me. Mom has her Fehr's [*local brewery*] cup and liking her beer. Mom would like to come up with Alma. They might change their minds - just talking about it. Well, we would all like to see you. Do you know when the next place will be? I hope closer, but as long as you like it, it's OK I guess.

Well, Hermina is back from Russells' and, oh my, the gift of gab. And I just had two beers. Norb, I enjoyed your last letter and Mom sure did too. She just looks and looks for your letters and she is so unnerved when she don't get them. But really, I think you do fine in writing. Only last week Mom only had one letter and then she wondered if you could be sick, I guess. Well, that's just like all sweet moms are, and that cross you sent her, oh how she likes it. She's really proud of it and of you. Norbie, now could I say just a trinket for Pop? Maybe just a little bit, only a beer mug would do. How are you on dough? I am always Marge, you know. We are still busy at work [*Hubbuch's*] and Hermina works about five hours a day lately. Well, every bit helps.

Well, my boy, you should see the hat the horse [*Hermina*] bought. Hot stuff [*with*] a big band across the front. And you should of seen Shirley Ann on Sunday. Alma brought her new dress (a formal) and Shirley tried it on. And did she think she was the tops. She really looked pretty. They say she looks like me, ha, ha. Alma had such a kick out of it and it's still at our house in your closet. She only brought it because Shirley wanted to see it so bad. Please, Norb, send Jimmy a letter. He would be so proud of it.

It's now ten thirty. Mom is ironing. Hermina is popping off, no shoes on, and Pop's just saying if he'd stay on beer it would be alright (Mr. Russell, he means) and so far into the night. It's warm here tonight like a spring day. Don't you see? Hermina works so she has something to write, ha, ha? Tell her about it. And she's on a diet. I guess because Connie's husband is losing weight. Hope you are well and happy.

Your little sis [*older but smaller than Hermina*],
Marge

Louisville, Kentucky, **October 21**, 9:30 am

Dearest Norb,

We received your letter this morning seeing PFC. Maybe it is just a trial to see if you can earn [*illegible words*] take it and not let down in your studies. I know that you all are disgusted. Anybody would be, but it is not your fault and you cannot do anything about it no matter how much you worry or how mad you get. I would try mighty hard not to let down with the study and show them that you can earn and will act like a man. Of course, we feel very sorry for you and hope and pray that you will feel better when you write again. Don't give up writing to us for we would be worried if you cannot. Or if you don't feel like answering a question, that will be alright, just so we hear from you. I will start a Novena and you can join us also. It is the best thing. It will give you peace of mind and think Thy will

be done and offer it up. Hermina wants to write a few lines. Don't worry about the money till the Government pays off. I will close and say good-bye and God bless you.
Mother

Continued by Hermina:

For once I can hardly know what to write. Mom wrote how I feel, too. Sometimes I think it is a trial to see if you can take it. It sure is a big mistake on somebody's part. All else seems to be so nice, so what else is there to do but make the best of it? The Army does funny things. Everybody says it and now we know it is 'true. Norb, I feel this way - if it's their mistake they should have left it go at that. Three boys that I know left with you are just buck privates so you see you're above them at that.
Feeling sorry for and with all my love,
Hermina

Louisville, Kentucky, **October 21,** 8 pm

Dear Norb,

By this time, I know you have received your Air-Mail letter I mailed this morning as I went to work. We hope by this time you are feeling different about your disappointment. That was awful. Mom feels like it was a trial to see if you could take it and go on just the same. I believe Mom's got something there. But you never were a PFC. You know, Jr had the same thing to go thru in the Navy. When he left Portsmouth he was sent to Key West. On his arrival they made him Hospital Apprentice First Class and he received his pay that month with the increase. So an officer informed him he was an Apprentice Second Class and deducted the amount paid over the next pay. He was as disgusted as you are. He was made first class since you left.

Jerry Israel, Lydia Street - I suppose you've gotten the clipping, Norb. I thought he went to school with you. They were floating in the ocean seven hours and was too weak to stand up. He is in a Naval Hospital, was operated on three times and is doing fine. His mother got a letter yesterday.

Norb, you sure must of been mad. We said a blind man could read your letter - you pressed so hard you could see all the imprints on the other side of the page. Mom's just getting in from church. She goes practically every nite and I think you got the benefit of a few more Our Father's today.

That Teske boy on Lydia, he's been in the Navy two years. His father was in the First World War. He joined up (his father) with the Navy. Sea Bees is what they call them, for construction work across the ocean.

Now the coffee question, Norb. You know we bought 3 lbs. a week so we got 6 lbs. every two weeks. I'm suffering already. It's getting colder tonite. We had rain yesterday and today. We are still busy at work. I think the brother-in-law has a new job in sight but the paint didn't come in yet. It's a bad time of the year for him. Joe had a little scare - when he got home from work his front door was open. It wasn't nothing missing so they probably forgot to lock it. Mom wants to write, so until tomorrow I hope you are happy and in better humor. From Hermina

Kansas City, Missouri, **October 21**

Dearest Mom and all,

I don't know what to tell you about the trip. All I know is that I can't make it home by plane. We have a bed check now on Saturday nights at 2 pm. So, you see, I couldn't make it. Now as for hotels, well, space is pretty limited. I can tell you that, but I think you may be able to find a room, or I think I could arrange for one ma[y]be. I don't want to tell no one what to do. Do you think you could stand the trip? Now if it would give you a setback, it wouldn't be worth it, because ma[y]be I might be stationed closer after I get out of school, I don't know, but I don't think I'll be lucky enough to get a furlough, at least till about a month after I'm out of school. I know you couldn't get a room in our hotel because there are nothing but soldiers in it, and it is government reservation. All I can say is use your own judgment about it, because you know how things are as well as I do.

What do you think? I can call every day? Ha, ha. It cost me about 11 bucks calling home so far. That one night it cost me $2.25 because I was overtime, so you see where my money goes. I'll tell you Katie [*Mom*] the church is about 6 blocks from our hotel. Not the best, but not the worst, but you can quit your worrying. It's not good for your feet [*reference to her diabetes and foot problem*] I go to school from 8 to 4 and get an hour for dinner and of course, I do a little studying but not over the weekends. I am listening to the radio now and I really do enjoy it. It's good pastime. I heard "Lights Out" last night. Once again, I'll say you will have to use your own judgment. You know I would like to see you but you know how your health is better than I do. As for Alma, you won't have to worry about her because I'll see she gets a place to stay. And I still have horse sense. So, I will be waiting to hear from you.
As Always,
Norb

Kansas City, Missouri, **October 22**, 44°

Dear Norb,

I want to write a few lines and tell you not to worry so much about your disappointment. I told Papa after supper. I thought he would take it hard but he didn't even shed a tear and said, "Well, that's not so bad, he'll get up again if he don't give up his study." And, he knows you won't do that. I don't think that you will, the only ones that get disgusted sometimes. I hope the next letter will sound like yourself again. You said you did not feel like writing. For goodness sake, don't stop writing. Don't take it out on us. I just came home from Elizabeth's.

She was patching. I had dinner with her. She wanted to fry me some rabbit but I did not want any. Joey and Lee were there last night. They brought her two rabbits. They sure look nice. They were cleaned also. How would you like some? I don't think he is allowed to hunt yet.

I used our small coffee cups to make us believe we got some more coffee, one large and two small cups. It is raining, 44 on the back porch. The rain is so cold. I am glad I am home again. Norb, if you think about it, tell Mary Hellow [*hello*]. That makes her so happy. Well, I don't know any news so I will close and hope that you will enjoy the radio very much. I think Tuesday nights is Fort Knox night. So long and be of good spirits and things will go better. We prayed the rosary and extra prayers for you. A Hellow from all.
God bless you,
Mother

Louisville, Kentucky, **October 22,** 8 pm

Dear Norb,

We received your letter today and naturally was glad to hear. You seem to still be in the doghouse. You wasn't the only one and we still think you did good to have the rights of PFC. That's what we expected to see but not so soon.

Jerome Schlegel was on a 36-hour leave so was at the Bingo Sunday afternoon. He said her [sic]was still 'Buck Private J. Schlegel.' George Herbig gained 9 lbs. in a week and hasn't had an attack of asthma since he's been in the Amy in Texas. Today, Norb, for the first time I never had coffee at lunchtime. Did enjoy a cup of coffee at supper tho, could of drank more tho.

I listened to baby Snooks. She was something, but Maxwell House coffee cannot be bought so why break their neck advertising it? I want to listen to Bing Crosby.

Is there more pay in PFC? We are glad you received your radio and hope you get a lot of good from it. Your buddies also. Glad you had your picture made and Mom is waiting for it. Hope they are good. We are all waiting. I heard your favorite dream song - "By the Light of the Silvery Moon" that you entertained the boys at Crowder, MO one night with. I don't imagine you entertained them in the week past with singing. There is no more to say but are all said we feel you will have good judgment and keep on studying as hard as you have.

Jr is in doubt about his furlough. One boy there was given 10 days because of the death of his grandfather, but it taken 6 days to get here and 6 days back so he couldn't make use of his leave. I imagine you'll get paid the 31st as you said the other week. Boy, Bing is really swinging it, and Victor Borge was fine.

It rained this morning and part of the afternoon but is clear and colder tonite. Your radio was in good condition. It was sent from Sutcliffe's Saturday and you got it Monday. I think that's good timing. Bing's Barbershop Quartet sang, "You tell me your dreams and I'll tell you mine." I thought of Katie's dream with Snookie [*family dog*] and jingling her bells. How was that cake you received at Crowder? Here's a cute piece of poetry in the CJ

[*Courier Journal*]. It's true too. "One for the money, two for the show, three to make ready, with no gas to go."

Well, until tomorrow, study hard my sweet. Mom will finish. Toodle loo.

H.R.

Kansas City, Missouri, **October 22**

Dear Mom and all,

I received your airmail letter this morning, but I'm not looking for any sympathy. We will probably get our stripes back when we finish school. I know the other fellows who were here at school before us didn't receive theirs until the last week they were here. So be it, as it may.

It's starting to get colder here. In fact, they had the steam on today. I believe the air don't vary much between here and Louisville. Yes, I received the dictionary but if I looked up all the words that I misspell your letter would be only about a half page long. So you will have to take them as they are and be satisfied - like me, ha, ha. Or would you rather I use the dictionary?

I went to see about my pictures tonight and I won't even get to see the proofs till tomorrow night so it will be at least another week until I get my pictures. I tell you they're really busy. I had to wait about two hours to have my picture taken. If there are too many mistakes in this letter, you can blame it on the radio. I' writing this letter and listening to the radio at the same time. I sure do enjoy it. I believe I would be lost without it, just the little time I've had it. I still haven't succeeded in reaching WHAS.

On Wednesday night we have a two hour course on military courtesy, "Something new has been added." It just started this week. We had a meatless meal yesterday but that's the first one we've ever had. Otherwise, we have meat at every meal, and all the coffees we can drink, too. "An' it ain't weak." So, I got it on you anyway.

When I get out of this school, I'll not only be a telephone man, but a troubleshooter, at least that's the way I understand it. About a week and a half of this course consists of troubleshooting. But don't take me by what I write, that's just what they told us. Well, I'll tell you right now it's nice to get a letter every day, I'll admit. But I don't find time to write every day. Besides, I have quite a few letters to write. And, I didn't break my fingers. I think there [*sic*] still in good working order. Just sit down and try to write about three letters every night. Why, that would be all I had time to do. Well. I guess that's all for now so "Keep 'em flying" until I hear from you again.

As Always,

Norb ...-V

Louisville, Kentucky, **October 23**

Dear Norb,

I hope the storm is over by now - after rain comes sunshine. It is 12:45. Alma just called and wanted to know if we got a letter from you. She asked what did you write? I told her that you was disgusted. She said she got one, too, but oh my, oh my, was he disgusted. Hermina went for a map of Missouri and asked how far the nearest hotel was from the Hotel Howard. I believe the nearest one is the Presented [*President*]. She is coming tomorrow afternoon. Well, Norb, Alma is going to come and see you, the way she spoke over the phone. We did not talk long. I will hear more tomorrow, that is, Saturday. I would like to see you, too, but I am afraid to undertake the trip. I have not been feeling well the last two weeks. I went to Gettlefinger [*family doctor*]. He said I was lacking vitamin B and gave me a prescription. I am taking my second bottle. He said it was the best he could give me. Don't mention it in your letter that I told you that I was not feeling well. They don't want me to worry you. It's nothing to worry about. Dr. said once an ulcerated stomach, always ulcerated. At times you feel better, but it comes back again. Well, maybe that's my Purgatory. It's not so bad. Have to do something to get to heaven. That's enough of that, you think. I wish you would be in the mood to answer the questions I asked you. I will repeat less you forgot - did you go to the Sacraments?

I went to communion this morning and prayed very hard for you. I hope my prayers are, or will be, heard. You wrote you did not like to write if you were not in the mood to write. Anyway, you'll have many more setbacks before you will be 68, so we are expecting letters from you, like we have [*been*] getting all along. It makes us happy to hear from you. Love,

from your Mother

Kansas City, Missouri, **October 23**

Dearest Mom, Pop and all,

Just a few lines to say hello and everything is "Oke, Doke," and I'm feeling swell. It's just about time to go to supper and I bet I have a better supper than you do. Today we had steak, potatoes, green beans, hot biscuits, slaw, chocolate pie, buttermilk and coffee. Not bad, eh? But I sure would like to have some rabbit or at least a couple shots at one. They have those large jackrabbits here in Missouri, but you can't eat them. Their ears are as large as mule's ears and boy are they fast! I would like to have Lee up here and go hunting. Maybe he could hit one of these large ones.

I wrote Jimmy a letter last night so I guess he can use his letter opener now, ha, ha. Boy did I get a kick out of that letter. It was interesting and I ain't fooling. It's a little cool here also, but it just got a little warmer today, but the trees still have most of their leaves. I guess it's just the Missouri in them. My cleaning bill is more than it was at home. You see, we just have two winter uniforms and one of them is usually in the cleaners. I signed the payroll last night but I don't know when I will receive my "first" Army pay. I signed it once before but we moved so I never did get paid. [*He was not paid for two months.*]

Tell Margie I received her letter yesterday and I was very glad to hear from her and exceptionally glad to hear Hermina is on a diet. Maybe by the time the war is over she might lose a pound or so. I also received a letter from Eileen Saunders. What the hell are you doing, shipping my picture all over the United States? I ought to be well known by the time the war is over.

Out of eight tests we had so far in school, I got 5 'Excellents and 3 'Goods," so that ain't too bad. Of course, they should have been all "Excellent." Well, I must quit now and go get my supper. Wishing all are well, and the best of luck to each and every one. XXXX Tell my little honey bunch [*Cousin*] Mary hello for me.

As always,
Norb

Louisville, Kentucky, **October 24**, 5:30 pm

Dear Uncle Norbe,

Guess you are surprised because I don't write as often as I used to. Well, because I stay after school and play volleyball and practice for a team. When I get home, I have to go to the store and help mother and then there is suppertime and after supper I study my lessons, then after lessons is done I have to wash and then go to bed. So I don't have much time, do I? I have a lot of work to do, don't I? I'm up at Mommy's now writing this letter to you and it is almost suppertime. I have to go to the shoemaker's and it is 6 o'clock now. Hope you are well. So, until I write again,

I'm still you're A-1 Girl Friend,
Shirley

Kansas City, Missouri, **October 24**

Dear Mom, Pop and Sis's,

Today is Sunday and I just got back from church. "Render unto Caesar the things that are Caesar's, and to God the things that are God's." Well, here you have to render 10¢ before you can get a seat. One thing about it, they don't charge sales tax. If the State family would ever come down here, I'm afraid they would start charging amusement tax. Ha, ha.

It's getting mighty close to dinner time. We usually eat about 1:15. It turned pretty cool here last night, but the sky is blue and the sun is out, and I expect it will warm up a bit. I guess Pop is still helping out Mr. Oertel [*founder of Oertel's Brewery*] by buying his products, no doubt. I'm about fifteen letters behind in my correspondence. I don't know when I will ever catch up. Once you get behind, it's hard to catch up. Well, I guess that's all for now except tell Joe and Ann and my little Mary hello for me.

As Always,
Norb

Louisville, Kentucky, **October 26**, the Firestone Hour, 7:30 pm

Dear Norb,

Norb, the paper carried the saddest news. I think I'll join the WAACS. Do you think I'd reduce? I suppose you feel good knowing Alma is coming. I bet your mouth isn't hanging - the corners are turned up,"ey?" Military Courtesy? Well, well. Will Emily Post take care of the regular courtesy? That's mighty fine when you come home to be all mannered-up and stuff. You might get so disgusted with us maybe you better buy Emily's book and send it ahead of time so we will all know how to act when you get home. The Marines are going to parade thru town tomorrow -"Navy Day."

Miss Emma [*Grimm; elder friend of Norb's Mom*] wanted one of our family pictures so we sent her one of you too and I'm enclosing her card. She answered in return. She fell, but is doing OK.

Carl Horne got 60-day deferment on account of his father's death. He died Monday nite so he informed his draft board Tuesday and his final papers were ready to be mailed out. He would have been examined that Saturday.

Joey was in at work [*Hubbuch's*] today. I never get to talk things over with her but I know they [*Joey end Lee*] are together. She said Ray called him "Yaller" if he wouldn't drink. You know, you can drive a horse to water but you can't make him drink. He has to fix the blame on somebody. He also had to promise to find work.

Churchill Downs is going to have Charity Races. Larney was high as a kite last night at Huelsman's. Now for Shirley's dream - Shirley dreamed that you were coming thru Shelby Park with your trousers on, no shoes or shirt, from the side of your neck clear across your chest you had a red stripe to your waist that was code. On your arm, you had all the dates with Shirley written or rather tattooed on your arm. It was funny hearing her tell it. Moody hasn't his teeth as yet, but he enjoys it, I think.

Be it as it may, as you say. Well, we hope you have the stripes after this course is over, and you'll be a troubleshooter. I hope not like your dear brother-in-law [Lee]. Mom said she wrote to you today on 'More-Ail' paper, she meant 'Air-Mail.' I bet Alma's mouth will work, I mean twist, overtime when she sees the well-mannered "acting Corporal." This week we can laugh but last week it wasn't so funny, was it honey? This Marge - she does things behind my back. She told you I was on a diet. Well, I hope to be coat-suit size by spring end, not 'lose a pound or two by the time the war is over' as you say. Mom wants to add her line. Well, until tomorrow, goodnite my sweet. Kiss Alma for me. Or don't I have to tell you?
Your dieting sister,
Hermina

Kansas City, Missouri, **October 26**

Dear Mom and all,

Well, I just came back from eating chow and had a real good supper. I don't guess you're interested in what I had, but I'll tell you I had all the coffee I wanted (that's just something to get you mad). Tell the Horse I wish to hell she would quite passing out my pictures, after all, it's my mug and I'll send it to those who I want. Every place I go I'll see my picture.

It was freezing last night but it got a little warmer today. I heard Kuchen Bodner got married. When did he do that? I thought that maybe he would be in the Army by now. It looks like the Army is doing Herbig some good.

Oh, about that cake, it was really good, and I got one piece out of the whole darn thing. "Chow hounds." But really, I couldn't use another now, not until I move into another camp anyway. And besides, don't you need the sugar? Or did they take the ration off sugar? I'm listening to the radio while I am writing this letter. Again, you will have to pardon all mistakes.

So Bill Hollenkamp is in New Guinea. He went for a pretty good ride, didn't he? As soon as I ever get a chance, and got the money, I'll hop a plane home, but I don't know when that will be. One thing depends on where they move me. Flash! It just came over the radio that the Courier Wasp was sunk, as I told you in one of my letters about those sailors who were sunk. I knew they wore wings and they said it was a big ship, so I was right and it was the Wasp. What's Walter Winchell [*newscaster*] got on me, ha, ha? Well, that's about all I know for now. I'll have to quit pushing this pen. So until later then. Tell Mary I said hi-do - XXXX
As Always,
Norb

Kansas City, Missouri, **October 27**

Dear Mom and all,

Well, I thought I would jot a few lines before supper. So, my brother-in (out)-law [*Lee*] is on another rampage. He must have really carried on this time. What he needs is someone to kick him in the ass till his mouth bleeds. So, he was going to shoot me, too? Ha, ha. Maybe a Jap will beat him to it. Well, he had plenty of chances, so why in the hell didn't he do it? I wouldn't try to tell Joey what to do - that is her business and hers alone. If you would take my advice, you would just keep your mouth shut. You don't have to worry. He don't have the guts to shoot anyone and I'll bet my life on it. Maybe that plate in his head is beginning to corrode, or maybe this is the Indian time for call to war. If he's so damn anxious to shoot someone, there are plenty of Germans on the Valga front. I guess his knees would shake if he ever seen one of them - someone who can give him a damn good dose of his own medicine.

Well, it's still pretty cool here. I believe fall has a fairly good start now. Come this Saturday, my course will be half completed. We are now tearing down all kinds of telephones and putting them together, and believe it or not, I had one actually work today. We have to start at the terminal on the pole, connect it to the house and then make all the inside connections. There are about eight different kinds of terminal boxes. There is really a hell of a lot more to a telephone than one would think. From now on, I won't think $1.05 is much for calling home, ha, ha. As usual, I have my radio on. I went to sleep last night and when I woke up this morning, it was still playing, so it saved me the trouble of turning it on. It sounds like I'm getting lazy, don't it? Well, it's getting mighty close to chow time. I can tell by my stomach, and I will drink a cup or three of coffee for all of you. Tell Mary I said hello and a hundred XXXX.

So until later then,

Norb

Louisville, Kentucky, **October 27**, 1:30, 32° F on the back porch

Dear Norb,

I want to write you a few lines. Hermina's letter is plenty heavy so I will make this one short. Hermina went to see Joey at noon hour today. Joey said she thought she would take a few days off. She looked a whole lot better [her husband Lee Carter had beat her up in a drunken rage]. I wish I could go to see her but I think it is better to stay away for a while. I thought maybe I could meet her from work but that's out since she is not working. Joey said he is acting much better. I don't believe it till he proves it. I hope and pray that it all will come out alright. Alma did not come last night, so she is coming tonight. She called while I was at church. Does it appeal to you to pray for us as we all pray for you? Is it too much for you to pay for a seat in church? And you pay a bigger price when you go to a show and don't mind it at all? I must close now. The next time I will write more. It is snowing today and a gloomy day. Everyone said hell low and heaven high. We all feel a whole lot better now since the storm is over [Lee's rampage]. Hermina sure helped her out, for she could never seen to all that herself.

[*Mother*]

Louisville, Kentucky, **October 27**, Tuesday, 8:30 pm

Dear Norb,

Well, today we had our first snow of the season. It didn't stick but it snowed a few hours and was very foggy. We'll excuse you for not writing during Alma's visit. We are expecting to see her in a few minutes. Marge told Joey to take the week off yesterday [*Marge, Joey's sister was the sewing department supervisor at Hubbuch's*]. She wasn't looking the best yesterday. I did a little shopping today so dropped in to see her. She looked 100% better today and had put out a big wash. Lee is on the straight and narrow and says he's sorry, and you know that's all it takes. If he had a million dollars, he would give it to Joey for his acting the way he did. I guess everything is on the mend or mended.

No cab service to Churchill Downs for the Fall Races. You know they are having the Charity Races there. Listening to 'Fibber McGee and Molly.' Are you - 8:30 pm? So you pay 10 cents to a pew? They say that most Eastern churches charge like that. It seems you would like to pay - amusement tax. Jimmy hasn't received your letter as yet. The Marines were going to march through town but we didn't go. Jr Russell sent Mrs. Russell a lamp for her radio. It was a ship. It is really very nice looking. It was her birthday Friday. Mom bought some malt coffee from Lubbers'. Poo! I'd rather have water. It's like medicine.

Mom and I wanted to send William Hollenkamp something for Christmas and it's the deadline Saturday. I thought candy but the post office said no chocolates so we're sending hard candies. I hope he gets it.

Your sailor friends that you met about 2 weeks ago, well, the aircraft carrier Wasp was sunk. I wonder if that is the one?

Joe wondered if you got their letter. We thought you did, by mentioning them in your last letter. Johnny Martin, who used to work at Hubbuch's, is in the Solomon Islands. Pa is still keeping Oertel's a going; he's just got a shock. Larny leaves tomorrow you know. You did fine this week. Three letters. That's swell. You get an Excellent in that too. Dear goodnite, sweet goodnite. Study hard and hope you and Alma have a good time.
Love,
Hermina

Dear Norb,

It is 2:20. I have just taken the bread from the stove. I was short on money, only 11 cents to spend and was afraid to spend it. So Papa brought me the check now. He only left a few minutes ago. Mrs. Krumpelmann was here to get her wash. You know I still take in washing, don't you? But Norb, she is so thankful for it. Monday she came and washed my breakfast dishes for me. When Papa was gone she said, "Who was that man? I did not know him." I said, "Why, didn't you know Herman?" She said she had never met him. Well, if you get this letter you will have met Alma I suppose. I wish you and Alma a good time. I'm sorry that I could not come along but if I would get sick, I would spoil yours and Alma's pleasure. I think it is better this way now. Take good care of Alma and be courteous as a gentleman should be to a lady.
Mother

Louisville, Kentucky, **October 28**, Wednesday, 10:25 pm

Dear Norb,

I almost accidently on purpose didn't put dear on this letter. We got your four letters this week and that's swell, but I'll be damn if I think it's so sweet to get the hell part of them. Here is a list of names I sent a picture to - Agnes, Zip, Miss Emma, and Mary Hollenkamp. I addressed the envelopes and wrote a short note with them and they are all very appreciative. I bet you thought to yourself 'that old Sow is busy sending my picture to everybody.' It was Mom's idea, not mine, I thank you. Bow, curtains, music! Mom said everybody was so bothered with rats so she gave them your picture and you don't hear that much about rats lately. How's that for a wise one? The White Cottage has one, so does Hertel's have one lined up [*a line of many local GI's pictures on their wall.*].

By the time you receive this letter, I suppose Alma will be in Kansas City. I was up all night fixing William Hollenkamp a box. He said that in New Guinea it's hotter there than our summers are here. We sent him a tin of candy and stationary. It has to be hard candy, no chocolates, so I dug up a tin for a fruitcake from NBC. Came in about 6 or 8 years ago. So Muth's [*candy store*] fixed it up very pretty. It's a pity is has to be censored and opened with the pretty fixings it has on it.

Joe said did you receive his dollar? Joey mentioned she sent you a dollar about 2 ½ weeks ago. I believe it was in Crowder. Mr. Lee knew about that. She said she hasn't heard from you in about 3 weeks. We believe they are on their second honeymoon. He's working.

That Monday morning letter sets Mom a going. She sure did watch the mailman Monday and presto 2 letters and washing was twice as pleasant [Monday was her wash day]. Do you like this hanging out with your tattle tale grays? Oh, yes, your letter today was in the mailbox. Katie didn't see so good so about 7 pm I went to Russells' to get a heavy cardboard box so I spied it in the mailbox. That's the first time that happened. Jonesy comes home Saturday. They are thrilled. Larny left today. Donaldson left one [loaf of bread]. He left it on the porch.

Give us a buzz or a wire when you come flying home. Saturday is payday and that ain't hay. Is it? I mean you. Here's hoping you're not moved. Haven't got any real news, Norb. Oh yea - Jimmy got his letter and nobody could appreciate it any more than he does. He opened it, read it and put it back in his drawer with orders nobody should touch it. He takes very good care of it. I imagine it all goes with his McArthur stuff. Just a suggestion. Why don't you address them to the kids? Lip is just as pleased. Let my godchild be next, little Betsy. Lip was up here Sunday and the kids looked so cute. Katsy is still such a whitehead and they [*hair*] were curled. She was so cute. Hoping to hear from you but not in the [*argumentative*] Rawert spirit.
With love from all, your ever sweet and loving sister,
Study hard dear, goodnite sweet, goodnite. Not Confushia, says Mom.
Hermina.

Mommy added a note:

Dear Norb
    I wish you would send a letter or card to John and thank them for putting your name in the weekly High Mass at St. Theresa for the men in the services. I mailed them your address. Mary wanted me to. She gave me a stamped envelope - Mr. and Mrs. John Hollenkamp, 1049 E. St. Catherine St., Louisville, Kentucky. Next time I will write more.
[*Mother*]

Louisville, Kentucky, **October 28,** 9:30 pm

Dear Norb,

Well, Alma just left. Marge, Lip and Milton are taking her to the station. I know you will see Alma before you receive this letter. You try to rub the Coffee Situation in, don't you? So far, we haven't been without very much but I know we will be. Lip hasn't had coffee in 3 weeks but she enjoys tea and does very well on tea. I mailed William Hollenkamp a box today. Moody (of Muth's Candy) fixed up a tin of candy. It must be in tin now. I thought my box was too big but they accepted it. I think you were supposed to have them marked for Christmas. I didn't, so I wonder if it will go away before. Well, it's all in Xmas wrappings and he can enjoy it before Christmas as well. So, you can take a telephone apart. Well, that ain't so bad - and you got it together again. That's something! I imagine it's right smart interesting.

Haven't much news, only it rained today and it was a chilly damp day but it cleared up towards evening. Don't worry, none of us is telling Joey anything. I went to see her Tuesday on my lunch break for a few minutes. She'll have to fight it out herself. He's working and everything is in working order, too, I believe.

Marg

Louisville, Kentucky, **October 29**

Dear Norb,

Well, the first of all I thought of was Alma. I hope she had a restful night but she was nervous when she left. I felt sorry for her but I just could not go. I had a dizzy spell going to church last night. I was going to church Holy Hour near where E. Spoelker lives. I was so dizzy I could not stand. I had to reach for the nearest tree. It did not last long. When Alma came I felt a whole lot better. Today I feel OK. I hope I am alright Sunday that I can go to the cemetery. I asked Elizabeth to send the boys tomorrow so they can help me to cut the grass on the graves. I know they look bad. If I could stup [*stoop*], I could do it myself, but that's out.

Don't write in your letters that I told you that I felt bad. I ate sweet potatoes for supper. I think that caused it.

Jimmy got his letter. He sure is proud of it. He puts it in his drawer. Tis a treasure to him. Elizabeth said that she had not received a letter in 3 weeks. I told her you had so many to write and she could read ours and if you would address the letter to one of the children, it would be the same as if she got it. Only it would give them a thrill. She said that was alright.

I believe we are going to have bad and cold weather. The wind is howling fierce and leaves are all over everything. Well, if you receive this letter and Alma is still there tell her hello from all of us. Now, the other day I got some malt and coffee mixed from Lubbers'. I can drink it. So can Mary but Marge and Hermina can't. I gave Elizabeth a sample to try. The malt is 18¢ and the mixed is 25¢. We will get 1 lb. to last for 5 weeks for each person over 15 years. That's all for today and good luck, God bless you. How often have you used your prayer beads [*rosary*]?

As ever,

Your Mother

PS. Still no answer on the most important question, have you been to the Sacraments? This is the 4th or 5th time I have asked you. If I do not get an answer soon I will take it for granted that you have not been as yet and I know that you have no excuse what so ever. It is indifferent, not caring. I am waiting with patience and praying also.

Mother

Kansas City, Missouri, **October 29**

Dear Mom & all,

I don't have much time but I thought I would just 'scribble' a few words. I guess Alma and I will be going out tomorrow night at this time. At least I hope so. It's raining here tonight, but I sure hope it don't rain tomorrow but I believe it will. By the way, I went down to get a beer last night and I walked in the place and nearly passed out. Believe it or not, I met a fellow I went to school with during second year. I knew him the minute I seen him. He's still a civilian and he's on his way to Portland, Oregon to get a defense job. Well, that called for a few (quite a few) beers and I nearly missed bed check but I made it by four or five minutes.

Well, I made an 87 in written test covering two weeks of school and a '92 in the actual work, so I don't think that's a bit bad. It was a fairly tough test. We start our second period tomorrow. The second period will consist mostly of circuits so that will be a little harder. Well, I hope everything is OK and I'll have to close now so I will see you later.

As always,

Norb V...-

Louisville, Kentucky, **October 30**, 10 pm

Dear Norb,

I suppose you and Alma have had a really good chat by this time. Mom had a feeling you might call tonight. I told her I hope her 'feelin' isn't 'foolin', but I feel like your 'feelin might be foolin.' Well, we feel like you might call sometime soon. Is all our 'feelin foolin' funny?

Angela is with Bill. He is on a 2-week furlough so they are with his people in Sterling, New Jersey. From there he is to be sent to Camp Campbell, Kentucky for two months. Lippy Hellmann was saying that one of her boyfriends flies here from some place east and that if an Army plane is going to Louisville they will take you along for $1.00. She says this boy has flown here several times that way. She said that maybe her schoolmate might be lucky enough. Red [*Hellmann*] is going to be moved to Wisconsin. Hermie is still in Florida and is expecting an heir anytime.

We are having the fall rainy spell. Could be worse tho. Yes, Winchell, we kept watching the paper for that sinking of the Wasp. Six or seven Louisville boys were in it and one of Ann's neighbors by the name of Flynn on Kentucky Street. St. Xavier and Manual battle it out tomorrow. Well, I'm out of [*info*] so I will close, hoping you are OK.

Love from your little sister,

Hermine [*sic*]

Louisville, Kentucky, **October 30**

Dear brother Norb,

It's raining tonight and I suppose you and Alma are together this evening. Elizabeth and I and Milt took her to the train and believe me, Norb, I felt like the coach had magnet in it. I wanted to go along so bad. Well, it's over now and I still hope you come closer so it won't be so far. Elizabeth called me this morning and said she couldn't sleep last night thinking of Alma. Well, Norb, just like a good mother - always worrying about some kid. Jimmy sure enjoyed his letter and Milton was the sweetest little fellow, going along to the station to see Alma off. We were caught in the rain [*on the way*] home. I told Lip I was so worried about her coat. It's new (only 10 years old) and did she laugh.

We just drank Oertel's in our Fehr's cups. It's 10 o'clock and Hermina just came home and Papa said, "What's the news?" Angela Hellman is with her hubby [Bill] and said she wished every girl would get a Bill. She is now in Stanley, New Jersey. He had his APO, and instead is coming to Kentucky, about 186 miles from Louisville. Herman Hellman is in St. Petersburg, Florida. His wife is going to make her First Communion Sunday.

Well, this war is terrible, and still it's good to make us think more of good things. And after all, if we do what we should, it's just one heaven for us all. What a pleasure it must be to all be together. I always think of Joey when I think of heaven. I always wonder, hope and pray. Offer up your trials for her, Norb. No more can we do. Well, maybe we don't pray enough. Mother started to Church last night and got a dizzy spell and came back home. She goes to Church every day, sometimes twice a day. Poor Mom wanted to go with Alma so bad and I believe it got on her nerves. Tonight she was better again. After supper, she lied on the couch and all of a sudden I heard the washing machine a going and I was glad. I thought then will she feel a lot better and now she's parked in Pop's chair and reading the evening paper. Papa just asked did Alma take a camera along. I said no. Pop said I thought we would get some more pictures. Norb, I don't write so often, but this evening I beat Hermina and believe me, she's started a letter now and then I think it's foolish for me to write, too.

Pop's sitting across the kitchen table from me in his same old place and said, "I'm tired. That head Sister [*at St. Brigid where he was the janitor*] ain't got no more sense about moving things than a hog has. And I will keep for the summer. Pop's smoking a cigar. Norb, did you all have a storm today? I heard over the radio today it was a storm at Oklahoma and Elizabeth said maybe you had some of it. Hope not.

We are still busy at Hubbuch's. Hope we will stay busy, but I wonder. Of course sometimes I think we should all do war jobs, but again I think to keep the home fires burning sometimes is a job in itself.

Norb, Elizabeth told me about what might be your next address. Mom or the others don't know, but look at Angela Hellman's husband's, now it's changed to Kentucky. Well, as you said, the Army will make up your mind for you. Bernard Hubbuch got his papers I heard from what Chester said. Well, he had a child; I don't think he will go so soon.

I told Hermina to stop at Joey's and tell her to take another week off so I hope she will rest up and Wahoo will work. I'm telling you Norb, Army life I imagine is hard sometimes but we really had a week and now on the second honeymoon. Norb, I never did like to see you and Lee together you know. Well, I had more experience than you did I guess, and maybe worried about people. Well, if you don't worry about people, you can't care about them. Johnny, Joe, Elizabeth, Joey, Ann's bunch and I are OK. Here's hoping you are, Norb. And say a prayer for me. And me for you, a prayer always. Queen of Peace, pray for us. Your sis,
Margaret

Louisville, Kentucky, **October 31** (It is Halloween)

Dear Norb,

I am sure glad you are praying for me and I hope you liked the letters that I wrote you. I got your letter Thursday morning. It was the best letter I ever got. I was sure pleased with it. Norb, do you know what I am going to do? Well, I am going to try to buy you a Christmas present if I get enough money. Momie [Mommy], Shirley and I went to the cemetery this morning. We fixed Dadie's [*Daddy's*] mother's grave, Henry's, Catherine's, Momie's mother and father's and Popies [*Poppy's*].

Back at Manual Statim [*Stadium*] Saint X and Manual is playing. I hope Saint X wins. I can tell you the score before it starts - nothing to nothing. Do you catch? Well, Norb that's all I can write to you today. Well, good by now. And I hope you enjoy your Halloween. Please write to me soon Norb. Just as always,
From Jimmy

Louisville, Kentucky, **October 31**

Dear Uncle Norbe,

I just want to write you a few lines. I will first start out about my report card. Well, I got 81 in General Average and I'm the 6th smartest in the classroom. And Milton got... Well, I'll tell you if you don't tell Daddy. He got _._. Can you make it out (2.67%)? And he's the 16th smartest of the boys. I wonder what you got on your report card (2.2.2.2.2.2.2)? Hope you are well and I'm still praying for you.

[*Shirley?*]

Louisville, Kentucky, **November 1**, Sunday, 3:40 pm (Feast of All Saints)

Dear Brother,

Well, we haven't sent anymore of your pictures. Today is Cemetery Day. All of us but me went to the cemetery. Services are going on now. Moody, Milt and Margie are here. Margie is a woman that craves service and gets it. Boy what a gal. We think Johnny, Inc. is coming too. Lip got your letter and said you are expecting an APO. We never said anything to Mom or Pop. We'll wait until it materializes but we hope that don't happen. Bill, Angela Hellman's husband, has his APO since the first of August as I said in my last letter. They are going to form another Army so that will keep him in Camp Campbell, Kentucky for another two months. Did you hear anything of the Johnsons? They haven't heard from Larny as yet.

Father Dudine had the services at the cemetery. Just the rosary was prayed and the crowd was slim. The cemetery wasn't decorated as much as other years. The flowers was terribly high but the day is beautiful. Mom met everybody she knew there this morning - Bell and Rudy [*Muth*], the Heitkempers and a gob of people. Really haven't any good dope for you, no scandal or anything. That song "Praise the Lord and Pass the Ammunition," the priest chaplain disclaims it, but I feel like he was the originator of it, don't you? I feel like he uttered those words in his excitement, but I doubt if he passed ammunition. We are all OK. Hope you are well, Charlie. So you like your Baptist friend. I bet he's always clear headed. With love from all of us,

Hermina R.

Louisville, Kentucky, **November 2**

Dear Norb,

Received your scribbling as you called it. It was very interesting though. I haven't much time. Marge will soon be going to work. I came home from church, Poor Souls Day today. Prayed for the poor souls and for you and everybody. I don't know good news, but a sad one. Henry Wessling [*a relative*], I think they called him Junior, was in an accident at 9th and Broadway. Died from a fractured skull just like Henry [*Norb's oldest brother who was killed in a motorcycle accident*] did and I will enclose the paper. I sure feel sorry. I know what it is. It upset me very much this morning. I called them - the Wesslings - this morning and asked if I could do anything for them. Uncle is alright. Next time I will write more.

Love,

Mother

Louisville, Kentucky, **November 2**, Monday, 7:20 pm

Dear Brother Norbert Anthony P.F.C.,

How do you like that salutation? Hain't got much dope but I do know Jonesy got in yesterday morning at 7:30 pm. He don't like it at all.

Well, we were all curious, did you get paid and how does it feel? The lady that was a patient at the Norton Infirmary with me twelve years ago wrote me a letter saying she was at St. Joseph Infirmary with a friend and wants me to come and see her but she is going home tonite and will return Thursday, so I suppose I'll visit her or vice versa. I don't know her from Adam but you know we always exchanged Christmas cards.

We are looking at films. Having more pictures made for ourselves. Richard Crooks sang "Ave Maria," Marian Anderson sang "Angus Dei" and "Deep River." They were grand. That surely was too bad about Junior Wessling, wasn't it?

I don't think Alma had very nice weather in her Kansas City stay, did she? Mr. Russell is in Horse Cave. They are arranging for a tombstone for her mother.

Eleanor and Johnny are gone shopping tonite, you know it's mighty convenient. We are all OK. I don't think you did a bit bad with your examinations - lots better than you did the first year at St. X, tee, hee. Dr. I.Q. is on at 8:30 pm on Monday. Well, I don't know anymore but might collect a little more at Hertel's. At least I'll try. Nose trouble, eh?

Well, I'm back from Hertel's and I did pick up some news. Larny Johnson and Duke Heitzman are at Camp Atterbury, Indiana. Mr. Hertel said it is closer to Louisville than Ft. Harrison. I seen a card Duke Heitzman sent Hertel today so I copied the address for you. It is: Pvt Donald M. Heitzman, Co. B 330th Inf. APO 83, Camp Atterbury, Indiana. He wrote, "I arrived in Camp and like it." They have quite a few pictures up there now. Louie Johnson must still be here Norb. You know you said about two weeks ago that he might be across by now. Hertel was telling Lizzie that Louie's wife was in there and she has never said anything about home going across. I think Larny was lucky being stationed so close to home but the infantry part of it. Do you still think that sometime you would like the infantry? This is a new camp. Hoping you are OK. Mom will finish tomorrow. Until tomorrow, get in in time for bed check.

Your loving sis,

Hermina

Louisville, Kentucky, **November 3**

Dear Norb,

I guess you gave me the laugh the way I addressed your letter [*on November 2, she had addressed his letter as 'PFC US Army' instead of putting his name on it*]. I guess you will get it just the same. It is 11:30. I already had my dinner and am going to see Unckel [*Uncle*] Wessling. I suppose you know Junior. Pray for him, that's all we can do. The weather is cold, 24° on the porch, but the sun is shining bright in the old Kentucky home. We have elections today. I don't know if Papa is going to vote or Marge either. I am. So is Hermina.

Father Dudine asked the mothers on Sunday at their Mass at 7:30, for all to vote and [*it is*] in the bulletin also. We all are anxious to see Alma and to hear all the news. I guess you were surprised to meet your former schoolmate and then almost got locked out? Well, early hours is nothing new for you, to my sorrow. I think of it yet sometimes. I hope you will do good in your next lessons unless you have Alma too much on your mind. We heard that the soldiers will only get off once a day after December 31. Papa said beer went up $1.50 on the barrel. Not so good, huh? You still haven't answered my questions.
Mother

Louisville, Kentucky, **November 3**, Tuesday, 8:30 pm

Dear Norb,

Well, today is Election Day and a very quiet one. Mom and I cast our vote for <u>Scrap</u> Happy Chandler. We went to see Junior Wessling. He really looks fine, looks just like our own Henry did, that is, his head is swollen just like Henry's was. Mom and Pop are gone in to see him now. Bud Wessling is in Seattle, Washington. He had his APO but the Red Cross located him. He has been traveling since Sunday evening and will arrive tomorrow nite. Helen said she thought of Mom the first thing.

Joe got off early today and tried to get in the White Cottage [*local restaurant on Eastern Parkway*] and couldn't so he thought Bud's father was dead, as he has been sick. Marge said today is Election Day. He didn't think of it. Oshie Murr got his final papers [*and is*] to be examined in about two weeks. We heard Cletus Murr is home from Waverly Hills [*tuberculosis sanitarium*] to stay. We supposed he was dismissed.

Milton is on a [*football*]. team They play at Maxwell Field. They played the Negroes - "The Mud Daubers" - they call themselves. The Mud Daubers won. Milton said they were really tough.

I don't enjoy reading too much sob stuff and don't like to write too much but Mr. Burke, your boss, was sick and just doing fine, was up and around. He contracted pneumonia and died today. Will send the clipping. Seen Mr. and Mrs. Zip [*Zipperle*] at the polls. We never had a voting machine here but they had eight machines I think in Louisville. Never listened to any returns but don't think it's necessary. The races are still going on. They had a horse by the name of Hermina running. Wasn't any good (you could of told me that).

I heard Norbert Wafzig is at Camp Atterbury, Indiana, too. Lip and Mrs. Orrill were up this evening. She wants a new stove and Orrill wanted to see Joe's. Jimmie Doerr is having a party for Jonesy Saturday night at his home.

Tomorrow is your godchild's birthday. Katsy didn't think of it and she was so thrilled when Lip told her today. She be 'tix' [*six*]. She spells pea for three. One and two she does OK, but three is pea. I been all evening writing this letter. It's 10:30 now. We are OK. I know

Mom will have an addition to put to this but while I had some so-called news, I thought I would write it down. Love, and study hard on your circuits, and sleep tight with your radio going.

H.R.

Continued, Wednesday morning, 10 am

Joe got his "come hither" card from Uncle Sammy for his blood test. He has to go in on November 9.

H.R.

Norb, I can't write today. Going to Uncle Wessling. Helen asked me.

Mother

A postcard from Alma Pierce, Norb's girlfriend and future wife, from President Hotel, Room 833, Kansas City, Missouri. She was 17 years old at the time and the families were upset that she'd go there to visit by herself:

November 5, Kansas City, Missouri

Hello Mom and all [*Norb's family*],

Just a few lines to let you know I'm having a swell time and I'm thinking of you all. I guess it'll be a little while before I'll get back home because Norb wants me to stay a little longer, so I think I will. I might not get to see him for a long time, so while I have the chance to stay I'm going to. I won't get to see Norb until about 4:30 pm tomorrow because he has to go to some kind of school.

With all my love,

Alma - Irish!

Louisville, Kentucky, **November 5**, Thursday, 8 pm

Dear Norb,

We surely was glad to get your call last night as we received the last letter Monday. Mom had been sleeping and we had to arouse her and without her teeth, she sounded funny. Mom is feeling extra good this week. I think she has stayed with Uncle Ben several days and has just left for Bosse's [*funeral home*]. She's just going to the Wessling, Jr funeral. She was going to stay with Uncle but Lou. Hollenkamp offered so Mom is going to the funeral. That's mighty sweet of Lou. She came Monday and cleaned up Helen's place for her. Uncle's mind is really slipping. You know how keen he used to be. Well, at 12:30 Tuesday he thought it was his bedtime. We are having rainy weather now. Mr. Burke gets buried this morning. He's a native of Ireland, is 66 years old.

Now the Alma question. Mrs. Pierce has only received a card the same as we and was wondering why Alma hasn't shown up. She called Mom and we began to worry about her.

Well, you know Mom, so nothing would do but we had to meet the 5:10 pm train last night. We went from work, Marge and I- and no Alma. Mrs. Pierce called about 6:15 pm so I really think your call last night was a balm to some Irish and Dutch nerves. I called her Aunt this morning at 7:00 and let her know Alma was going to stay until Monday. Oh, boy, what a gal.

I don't have much more time to write but you know the mailman can't do like Donaldson. [*baker*] Hoping you are OK and let's have a lengthy letter me little baby brudder.
As ever, your little sistah,
H.R.

PS. Tell Alma it would be advisable to wear a suit of armor home [*reference to anger towards Alma for not informing them*]. We are all OK and hope you and Alma are having a perfectly wonderful time. Love and hugs.

Louisville, Kentucky, **November 5**, 11 pm
Dear Norb,

Don't have much news, as I wrote it this morning. Had to refill my inkograph [*fountain pen*]. The news looks 'velly, velly' fine tonite. Rommel's Army sure took a spanking. Robert Lee Steinmetz is at Camp Campbell, Kentucky. Norbert Wafzig is at Camp Atterbury, Indiana. Orville Spayed left for the Army today. Lip thought he left some days ago. We are all OK I hope you study hard so you get your circuits OK Mom will finish this tomorrow so until tomorrow, study hard my sweet.
Love,
Hermina

Continued by Mommy:
It is 2:15 and I just received a card from Alma. Tell [*her*] I said thanks.

Louisville, Kentucky, **November 6**
Dear Norb,

I haven't much news but much disappointment that you never wrote all this week to let us know how you all were getting along. I think that if Alma did not feel like writing. You should have asked her to. Mrs. Pierce was very much worried. Mrs. Pierce called me up, think it was Tuesday morning. She thought that perhaps she was at our place. She said she never slept all night. Just on account of a few words to a Mother. Alma or you would have that much time to write and nobody can tell me any different. I am not writing this to tell you all what to do. It wouldn't do me any good. I think if you or Alma would send a card or a letter every day to Mrs. Pierce it wouldn't hurt you all a bit. As far as I am concerned, I was not worried so much til I found out that Mrs. Pierce only got one card, the same as we did. I don't know if Hermina wrote you that the morning after you called. She called, I think it was Mrs. Pierce's sister, and told her to let Mrs. Pierce know that Alma wouldn't be home till Monday. It was about 1 o'clock. Marge was not gone to work yet. That's all of this.

Joe got a notice this morning to be examined by Dr. Nesbitt at 2 o'clock next Tuesday. I hope he will be exempted. All your cousins are exempted.

Goodbye and God bless you all,

Mother

2:15. I got Alma's post card. Tell her thanks.

Louisville, Kentucky, November 6

Dear Uncle Norb,

I hope you and Almy had a good time when she was there. Momie (*Mommy*) got Almys (*Alma's*) post cards. They have the same picture on them. I think she bought them by the dozen. Your A-1 girlfriend hasn't been writing to you since she came home from Momie's - that's Shirley. I am up at Momie's right now. I am waiting for Dadie to come and get me. Norb, I am a [*altar*] server now. Today I just got done with my Confeator [*Confiteor*]. I will start serving in about two weeks. Well, Norb this is all that I can write to you today. Please write back.

Just as always,

Jimmy

Louisville, Kentucky, November 6, 10:00 pm

[*Dear Norb,*]

Jim wrote you a few lines and I know you appreciate that. He's really sincere and is staying tonite. We worked until 9 pm tonite. Mom received Alma's card today and glad to know you all are having such a good time. The news is really very, very good today. Hope that it is all true. If it is, we'll be out of this war in a short order.

Joe got his card for his preliminary examination today, his blood test Monday, and his preliminary exam Tuesday at Dr. Neblett's. Are you getting more courteous? I suppose Alma will answer that after we put her through the first, second, third degree and you can bet your working shoes on that, honey. It is still raining today but not so cold. Hope you are having a good time and study hard and be the first kid in your class. Mom will finish. Marge and Pop are drinking beer and exchanging work ideas, but not me.

Loads of love, your little sister,

Hermina

Continued, Saturday, 9 pm

Well, since I wrote the rest I know a lot more. The first is Zip [*Norb's friend*] is a Lieutenant (2nd) and is home on a furlough. We haven't see him but he was in at the corner. Jonesy party is tonite. They say Zip looks good with his bars on. Well, Chandler [*elected*

Governor] is in but you can see that the Republicans is getting a headway. It was a Negro running on the School Ballot, leading at first, but dropped behind.

Joe bought more junk. He bought a vacuum cleaner - a Montgomery Ward. It really was a bargain, with a light. And it isn't used much, about five years old, but we had a good time razzing him for $7.00. Marge said I should tell you she's just as good as ever and she loves you very much, and soon snow and ice will be coming. She hopes the war will be over so you can help her across the street [*joking about getting older*].

I went to see Mrs. Melcom at St. Joe's Infirmary today. I never knew her but I do now. I was glad to see what she looks like. She reminds me of Nan Gehrig a lot, only she's taller. Mrs. Johnson has 3 stars out now [*a star for each serviceman in the family*]. Norbert Wafzig is cutting meat for the Army. I suppose Irish [*Alma*] will be gone home when you receive this letter. You better write a real nice long letter or letters this week because we haven't received a letter you wrote last week, but we appreciated hearing your sweet voice - that's spreading it.

The Red Front Store on Goss Avenue is got Duration Coffee. You can get that. It comes in 1 ½-pound packages for 44 cents. It is slop. Nobody else has coffee but they sell it to anybody, until people get wise.

I hope you get to OTS [*Officer Training School*] before you get out of the Army. Lieutenant Norbert A. Rawert don't sound bad. Cousin Mary Rawert calls every now and then about you.

Bart [*Beha Cleaners*] is going to get your suits and overcoat next week. He is going to clean them but not press them, and then store them in a cedar-lined bag. The cost will just be half. You can tear this page up. He said he turned our neighbor in as a pro-Nazi. You know - right across the street. He was rejected as an alcoholic heart. He filled in his papers as supporting his mother and dad. He had the dope on him, alright, he heard him talking at Taps [*a Schnitzelburg tavern*] and different places.

How are you coming out with your circuits? Is it much harder as you expected? Did I tell you I lost 6 pounds? Tain't bad Norbie. When I get to Hertel's I'll try and get some dope for you. How did the Baptist and the other boy enjoy Muth's candy? And you too. I hope I get to see Zip.

The Army is taking them with one eye now. Mrs. Melcom said they taken her neighbor's son. He was rejected twice but he left this month. Here's hoping the news stays good. Armistice Day is coming this Wednesday. Father Spoelker [*a cousin*] leaves November 28th for some school or college before entering the Army. I suppose it's Chaplain School.

With love from all, so dear, good nite, turn your radio on, turn your radio on. What time must you be in on Sunday?

Love,

Hermina R.

Louisville, Kentucky, **November 7,** Tuesday, 9:30 pm

Dear Norb,

Well, we worked tonite too and expect to work tomorrow. St. Martin's is having a turkey raffle and dinner so we're going to try to get a dinner for 50 cents. Alma was over last night. I think she saw Pop at 1 am in his cute pajamas, ha, ha. Well, that's a darn swell picture of you. Norb, your physique looks like Victor Mature. Did they let you stand on end so you could throw back your shoulders? I sure like the looks of your roommates. They look like they're good boys. Next time I go in town, I'm getting a frame for it. Now we're waiting for a picture of you all by yourself. Your roommates and you look like you're amongst the youngest in your class.

Here's hoping your wishes will be granted...Some class, I would say. Which one is the Baptist? I would judge Perry [is]; he's got thin lips like Gadley said about the Baptist. If you were second highest in your average, which one of these boys had the highest average? Some look like they can't make the grade. Your teachers are a mighty nice looking group of men.

I see you're waiting to hoist a few with Chaplain Spoelker. Did you enjoy the fudge? I thought it cooked up just a little too much or did you say thanks for courtesy's sake, because I know how courteous you were when Alma was there. I think this month is Bernie Spoelker's birth month. I don't know the day. So, you can say happy birthday to your dear third cousin. He's 34 (Walter Winchell).

Don't start putting bad ideas in Pop's head - putting such an idea as making home brew. We'd have to do without sugar, all of us for a month, to make a batch of beer. Did you hear Wimple with Fibber McGee? That was a scream tonite. Red Skelton was very good, too.

I don't think you did the painting in back of the picture. If you see Pop come marching as the spirit of 1942, don't be surprised, St. Martin's janitor is leaving next week for the Army. Many thanks for your picture. Did you have your other pictures taken there? Well, goodnite, study hard and send your photo.

H.R.

Kansas City, Missouri, **November 10**

Dear Mom and all,

Well, I guess all of you are sore at me a little for not writing but I can't help it, even though you think I could. Every time I wanted to write, I had something to do. So there you are. All the last letters I received from home were about death and sickness. I tell you they were some real "pick'er uppers." Not that I don't like to know, but so many people dying. Sure was sorry to hear about Mr. Burke. He was a pretty nice fellow. Well, Alma left last night. Sure hated to see her leave. She left on the 11:30 pm train and I couldn't go to the station because we had 11:00 bed check, and I couldn't get out of it. Sure had a swell time but I guess I don't have to tell you that, do I? I never did see time fly by so fast. It seemed more like a few hours than 9 days. But I guess that's always the way when you're having a good time.

So Zip's a 2nd Louie. Good for him, but he deserves it. I owed him a letter now for about 4 weeks, never did get a chance to answer it, but I guess I will ...[*Pages are missing from the letter*].

[Norb]

Louisville, Kentucky, **November 11,** Wednesday, 10:10 pm

Dear Norb,

Armistice Day - it surely means a lot this year. Well, I'll start off saying that Lieutenant Edw. J. Zipperle was over until 9:30 pm and he does look swell and he sure did want to know all about you. Alma was over so I called him and asked if he had a few minutes to spare and he came right on over. It did seem funny that we didn't have to holler at you to hurry up [because] Zip was waiting. He goes back to Camp Davis Friday. I don't know if Zip was talking up the Signal Corps but he bragged it to us that he thought you got a break because you really learn something. Say why didn't you let us know you came out second in your class? That's swell. Now before you write home and tell me, we won't bow that around but I feel proud of you. No summer school for Rawert, no siree. I think Mom and Pop felt good about Zip's visit. Zip isn't any stouter but he's got a healthy look.

I made some fudge and sent it to you. Sad news column - they measure beer by the glass at the corner [*Hueltsman's*] now. Jonesy is leaving tonite. He was afraid to risk another nite because that would of been the last train out.

Alma said you look so good. You wouldn't look any other way, I don't think, to an Irishman. We are all OK. I sure hope the mailman leaves one in the box tomorrow. Jimmy wanted to write to you. He's been up here several days. He's a cute young'un. He watched Mom look for mail so he asked you in his letter to write her. Nobody says anything. I'm going to send it to you. He's expecting a letter. Marge is really taking in orders. I suppose it's the Thanksgiving rush.

Pop walked as far as Hertel's with Alma tonite. Razz him about it if you think of it. Zip's one ambition is to be <u>your</u> superior officer. Zip's Nellie got married. Well, dear, goodnite and keep up the good work.

As ever,

Your little sister [*joking about her weight*]

Continued by Mommy:

I have no time to write today, Norbe. Mother

Louisville, Kentucky, **November 11**, Armistice Day

Dear Uncle Norb,

I stayed up at Momie's [*Mommy's*] overnight and today. I hope you are doing good in your schoolwork. I just got threw [*sic*] cleaning the fishes' water. There are only two fish left and they are harder to catch. They go through your fingers and everything. There [*sic*] like lightning.

There was a game out at Manual [*Stadium*] between St. X and Male. Male won six to nothing. There wasn't as many cars parked in the street as when Manual and St. X played. Well, Norb that's all that I can write to you today. Norb will you do me a big favor? Please write to me soon. Norb, do you want to do Mommy a favor too? Write to her real often. Please Norb? Well, I hope you had a real good Armistices Day.

Just as always,

from Jimmy

Louisville, Kentucky, **November 12,** Thursday, Maxwell House Coffee Time

Dear Norb,

Well, we did get your letter. Who said anything about being sore? We thought perhaps you and Alma might write a letter together, that's all. And when you have a good time, you can't realize how the time slips up.

Alma said Clarence Johnson has his papers. We heard it from several different sources so it's bound to be true. Alma really looks fine but she can't ramble off like I can. We don't know a lot more than before she came. We all think she reminds us a little of Anne Beckmann. It takes her a while to get started - like Redle's car. Don't have any news, as you know Zip was over. I tried to get him [*by phone*] to tell him what you said but they must be out. Alma's brother [*Bobby Pierce*] leaves today for the Army.

Hermina

Continued by Mommy:

If you have any time, read "Right and Wrong" in the Sunday Visitor (enclosed).

Louisville, Kentucky, **November 13**

Dear Norb,

Well, I am glad that we got a letter again. Exactly two weeks past [*sic*] without. Received your second letter this morning, Friday the 13th. It is postmarked 11 am. That got here in a hurry. Of course, it was an Air Mail. The weather is beautiful but windy. Joe got his card this morning. He is in 1-A. I don't think he will be drafted if they ever examine him, do you? I hope not. Jimmie Wessling is drafted. He leaves sometime this month. Budd [*Wessling*] likes it very much now. He received several medals. His mother [*Helen*] told me, but I don't remember what for. I do feel very sorry for her. She takes it so hard. Uncle Ben is about the same. He can't keep up a conversation; he forgets what he is talking about.

Hermina called up Zip this morning and told him what you told us to tell. Hermina said he had a good laugh and said he would get even with you, and is going to write you a letter soon. We are glad that you got a 92 in examinations. I thought maybe you had to take more time on account of taking Alma out but that didn't seem to be so. Have you any idea where you will go next? I hope you will stay in the States. Pop's alright but he had to fight the bushels and bushels of leaves he burns up. You both like the number '92, whether it's beer or examination. Pop could not understand, only you thought of Oertel's when you got 92 in the examination. That is fine. I hope you can keep that up, in fact, I know you can if you want to.

Norb, I still haven't got the answer to my most often asked question. I wish you would tell me and ease my mind. Nothing in the world could please me more if you could say 'Yes, I have been to the Sacrament.' You know I would like your picture but I would rather that you would truthfully say yes. November 11 it was 6 months. I look at your picture at home and wonder if you received the Sacraments.

[*Mother*]

Louisville, Kentucky, **November 13**

My Dear, Dear Little Brother,

Now Norb, this is dear Friday 13th. That's why I'm writing. Well, Hermina writes all the news so why should you read them twice? I really do like your typewritten letters. They are so much longer. Don't get me wrong, because your penmanship is improving and, oh boy, that 92 average was fine! School - I always liked it. Kate Smith's on the air while I'm writing. Alma said your radio works fine. Don't worry about it financially - I paid for it. Some time you can give it to me, so don't worry about it. I'm still at Hubbuch's. I don't want you to think you can't ask for something and not get it.

I've got a gal in Kalamazoo [*by Glenn Miller*] - do you hear Kate [*Smith, singing it*]? Maybe you do. You really could step this one. Jimmy's here tonight and is going to stay until Sunday. He's a swell kid. Ann has a cold and hoarse but is working and Mrs. Russell worked this week. Joey came in one day this week and never did say if she intended to come back or not. She told Alma that Lee is a different man. Well, I'm so glad for her, if that's what he is. She don't come home lately. I guess funny like always, I can't like Lee and I was always afraid for you to go with him.

Now do you hear Major John Smith on the air, [he] who knocked down the Jap's ships? Well, Mom's got the doorknob off the front door so I'll stop and fix it.

It's all fixed now and I'm out of news too, so I'll send you a clipping of the Courier. Jimmy is gone to Joe's and he is going to take him out. Will wonders ever end? And Joe also paid 50 cents on the phone [bill]. Do you think I could get a buck from Ripley [Ripley's Believe It or Not] for that one? Norb, did you get your pictures? I thought perhaps the Pho-to-grapher would mail them so you wouldn't have the trouble. Say, boy, Mom's a different kid since you been writing again. "That's what I said to my girls"- famous words of Cousin Mary Rawert.

It's kinda cold here. I called Van Haven [*sp*] the dentist and imagine made an appointment for Lill for quarter after seven for next Tuesday. He said they got him so busy. And I'm going at 12:30 Tuesday. He sounded the same as ever.

John's bunch has the chickenpox. Jackie had them. Johnny is thinner than Joe. Imagine. I wonder if Oertel's is weaker or not so much [drinking] maybe! I guess you got your candy by now. Do you like to get boxes from us? We like to send them, too. You hain't got nothing on us. Say the size of the snozzel of the enclosed picture, you'd think he was our brother. Say, about courting, Alma said you really get it, even the men get helped out of the streetcars. How do you do it? I suppose you get 100 in that subject. The goldfish said 'gulp, gulp.' "Can I Forget you" is now on the radio. That's all dear brother.

From your dearest sister,

Mary Margaret Catherine Rawert

November 13, Friday 13, 10 pm

Dear First Class Jack Ass Brother,

What does that leave me? Sow? Harry Lukins giving the news.Well, Norb leave me tell you I know now why you always took a taxi at home. It seems a streetcar was your blundering point. Remember when you left Mom get off the car first, anything for a laugh regardless of whose expense!

As you know, Zip looks fine. I called him today to tell him what you said. He leaves today, you know. And did he have a laugh. Zip really laughed when I told him you would meet him in Africa. I should ask how you are going to get there. Will it be taxi or streetcar? Did you know that Henry Crip Neuner runs the 6 barber chairs at Ft. Bragg where Zip was? So, you got your dear letter. That was sweet in Emma [*Grimm, Mommy's friend*]. What did I tell you? Even the old maids ask about you. Talk about Joe being like Mom, how about misplacing your negatives? That really sounds like Mom and she has been waiting with patience for your picture. I imagine several poor souls benefitted from that. Your letters are very much appreciated, take it from me. Did Alma help your average up? You would think it would be vice versa.

That's all. Good nite. Study hard Corporal.

[*Hermina*]

Louisville, Kentucky, **November 14**, Saturday, 9:00 pm

Dear Norb,

FLASH: When you get this, call us if you can and reverse the charges.

I suppose it won't be long now that we will be addressing your mail to the Hotel Howard. Perhaps you will be lucky to get in a hotel again. Keep your left finger crossed. We enjoy your letters, you know. Everybody that talks about Winchell has a different story. I hope he repeats it - as if that would do any good. We heard the Hit Parade's "Praise the Lord and Keep on Writin' Letters." Did I tell you James Herbert Adams is on a furlough? I hope I get to see him, the last I heard they didn't hear from Clifton for a long time.

Joe got his A-1 Classification. I heard Deanie Johnson got nine questionnaires of some sort since Larny went to the Army. Joe's letter states you would like to hoist quite a few [*beers*] with Larny. With that in mind maybe your average would be '32', not '92.' We all got a laugh when you stated you got such a high average when Alma was there. Your letters even help an ulcerated stomach. Mom's been doing fine. Pop's gone for some of your average with suds ['*92*].

Tommy Bratten called for your address last week from Park and Tilford. It's for a Christmas present for the boys in the Services. We thought you might be moved. So you can take care of that because we don't know where to report that. Then I told Tommy you expected to be moved.

Someone was telling me that a man out at Standard with a glass eye was taken in the Army. We are all OK. So, Antoinette [*Ante*] asked you to come. That is nice in her. Let us know how her baby is too. I bet that will seem funny to see Ante with a baby. You know Bernard Spoelker goes to Harvard University on November 26 for a course in, well, I suppose you would call it Chaplain Training.

You know bacon is very hard to be gotten. That makes me feel squeamish. Say, that General Clark had some spunk. That's the stuff the Army is made of, eh? And Captain Eddie Rickenbacker was found. That sure was fine, but one man died of exposure. That's sad. I heard that the meat rationing is going to go into effect. Better to be rationed than just a few getting their share.

We have been getting quite a few orders at work. Sounds good and is good. No shop talk. I hope you find your negatives before you leave. Lavern has her little brother George's picture. It's really swell. Joe was just over in time for some suds.

Until tomorrow, goodnite,

[*Hermina*]

Kansas City, Missouri, **November 15**

Dear Mom and all,

Well, this is Sunday and it's about 2:45. Both of my roommates are out with their wives, so I have the room all to myself. I sure did have a swell time at Mr. And Mrs. Hensle's. He sure is a nice fellow, and you feel right at home with them. She asked me if I knew they had a baby. Well, I really didn't, but I told her yes. He's a cute little fellow, looks like Ante [Antoinette Spoelker Hensle]. They have a cute little house and I also seen those lamps that you all gave her for her wedding gift. They really look good. "Chaplain Spoelker" is supposed to arrive here about Wednesday or Thursday, so I have to call Bob [*Hensle*] and find out when he gets in. So I guess we will down a few beers together.

Thanks for the fudge. That always was my favorite candy. [*It was always Norb's favorite and he made the best fudge often as I was growing up*]. Tell Pop that he has my sympathy since they started to measure beer. Why don't you start making home brew again? I guess you couldn't get the sugar anyway. Well, I have till next Saturday here, so I guess I will have to eat my "Thanksgiving Turkey" somewhere else. Enclosed you will find a joke that I thought was pretty damn funny. Well, anyway we have a lot to be thankful for. I'll close now and sign off till tomorrow.

With love to all,

Norb

Louisville, Kentucky, **November 15**, 9:30 pm

Dear Norb,

The reason for this Airmail letter is Mom thought about your photo, so you said you lost it, the photographer keeps negatives and surely has your name registered so maybe you could go to see him and tell him and you could have pictures made from the negatives.

Alma said you showed her the proofs. Could it be possible you left it at the President Hotel? Four dollars is a lot to give to somebody. Hope you found them by this time. Mom thinks a lot of your mug. So you had your sour-kraut. Well, Antoinette never forgot Schnitzelburg as yet. We are all OK. Ann and Joe was here for dinner. Lip etc., Johnny etc. for supper. I don't think the Army is much noisier. Alma is coming over tomorrow. Her brother leaves next Thursday for a week furlough. Oshie Murr was rejected but has to have another blood test. Maybe you will be sent closer to Kentucky. When you see Antoinette, tell her hello. I heard Earl Schaldant is in the Army. Glad you called last night. Your voice was so clear.

Love,

Hermina

Louisville, Kentucky, **November 17**

Dear Norb,

I received the group picture at 3 o'clock and letter, also. Many thanks. I'll take good care of it. John stopped in as I was reading the letter and your roommates are fine and handsome looking young men. I guess their wives are proud of their husbands as we all are of you. You all are in the second row are you not?

Thanks again and lots of love,

Mother

The following letter was an unusually long letter to Norb from his Mom. In this letter, she explains why it is so important for him to go to Mass and receive the sacraments. And she reminds him in most of her correspondence to him.

Louisville, Kentucky, **November 18**

Dear, Dear Norb,

I am starting a little earlier to nite. I don't like to rush. It is 11:45. I am through with my dinner, and while I was eating, Mrs. Rhodes called me over the phone. She was operated on last month. I never asked her what the trouble was. She asked me who was in the Army. She saw the Star out [*a scroll of a star that families put in their window, one star for each family member in the military.*]

She said she thought so often about us, so this morning she called me. We just had so much to ask and much to answer. Her boy is in England. He is in the Army since May. I will tell Hermina to write you about it. She can write faster and better. Mrs. Rhodes asked for your address. I gave it to her. She said she would send you a card. She said she would send the address to her boy. I told her that you would not be there any longer than Saturday. She said she would wait till I would let her know the new one.

Hermina just called. It is now 12 noon. I told her Mrs. Rhodes had called. She said [it was] Lee's mother. I forgot his name. Mrs. Rhodes begged me to come to see her. I told that to Hermina. She said she would go with me some night. I always did like her. She misses Lee so much. She said his friends come to see them quite often.

Joey called this morning. She received your letter Monday and was very glad. She said that he [*Lee*] never drank a drop since he was wild or whatever it was. I said to her just so he don't start when the 30 days are over. I think it is the 28th. I hope and pray he will get some sense sometimes before he dies. Joey did not start to work yet. I don't know if she is coming back. I would not ask her. It is none of my business. I wish you would write Mary [Hollenkamp] a few lines or just mention her in our letter. Norb, try to get your picture before you leave. Maybe if you would tell them you lost them they might take them over, you have your receipt or your bill, have you not? Four bucks lost and no picture. Norb, let us know as soon as you can when you are at your new place. I hope you will like it. I wonder if you all will be Corporal before you all leave. I am very much pleased of course. You are the best looking man of the group??? That joke you sent was a good one. Papa could not make it out so I read it to him and when I said 'homesick,' he was crying. I explained it to him so he claimed he [*understood*] and he laughed about it. Huelsman's sells whiskey now. He got the license. I am going to send you Lee's address so you can write to him. Mrs. Rhodes said if only a card, he is so glad to hear from friends. She writes to him every day.

I did not think I was going to write so much. Well, I guess you don't mind it. Joe got different tires. He said he would sell the car if he had to leave. I think Ann is worrying about it. Joe don't blame her. The girls think that's nice of Joe that he don't show how he feels about it. I mean about going to the Army. Norb whatever you do, go to the Sacraments before you leave. You never know where you are going and maybe would not have the chance to go soon. I don't know why you don't tell me if you went or not. The more you go, the better you would feel that you did all you could do to save your soul. This life is a gateway to heaven. I am not worried about anything as much as I am of that. If you get older, you see things in a different light than when you are young. And thinking my time will be up, have I done all I could towards my children? God bless you and till I get the long [*waited*] for answer!

Mother

Kansas City, Missouri, **November 19,** [Typewritten letter]

Dear Mom, Pop and children,

Well, I don't know what to write because everything is just about the same here, so it makes writing sort of difficult. I could tell you that today was just like a summer day and it was windy as hell the last few days. In fact, I had to give my hat a merry chase about five times, and once it was nearly run over by an automobile that had four tires on it and two gallons of gas in the tank - must have been a capitalist.

I got a very nice letter from Lip today and also one from Betsy. Still the same old Betsy. I guess I will write her a letter in the near future because I hear that she is getting mad at me for not writing to her. I wonder what Park and Tilford are going to give us for a Christmas present. Did Tommy say? I'm just a little bit on the nosey side of things. If nothing happens between now and tomorrow night I guess I will go over to Ante's and see Bern [*Antoinette Spoelker's brother, Bernard*], but I don't know if he is here yet or not. I have to call tomorrow I guess.

So Dean Johnson has got his questionnaire, how many did you say he has gotten already since Red's been gone? Maybe they have caught up with all the Johnsons. Well, I really don't know what else to write about and so I guess I will have to close. Glad to hear that all are well and busy. I guess you think that this is a very short letter but that's all I know of and besides I HAVE to walk down to the corner with one of these guys and drink a beer or two. So keep 'em flying.

As Always,

Norb

Louisville, Kentucky, **November 16**, Monday, 11:15 pm

Dear Norb,

Just a few lines to say hello. Mom will finish this letter tomorrow. Joe came over. He couldn't think of the man who played the leading role in 'Goodbye, Mr. Chips' so I called the Courier Journal. It was Robert Donat. We are OK. Love and dear goodnite and keep your brains a working.

H.R.

Louisville, Kentucky, **November 17**, Tuesday, 2:15 pm

Dear Norb,

I guess I will not write to you many more times to this address. I think [*you*] will be homesick for this place you liked it so well. Maybe you will get closer to home. I hope you do. Have you no inkling where about you are going? Alma spent the night here Monday night. I mean she said she would come Friday night. I don't know if she is going to stay overnight. It takes her a long time to make up her mind. I had fresh bread and raisin kuchen for supper. She liked that. She wants me to tell her how to bake it so she could tell her mother. It is rainy today. All day it is gloomy. Donaldson's don't deliver but every other day. The insurance agent come only every other day, the coffee man also. I only got 3 pounds for 2 weeks. I drink malt coffee and coffee mixed. I get it at Lubbers'. I can drink it alright, then I drink tea and Postum. Plenty variety, eh? It saves a little for the others. Every other week I get a pound from Schieman's [*grocer/butcher on Texas Street at the end of the block*]. They said Ben [*Schieman*] was on a furlough and he looks fine. He is getting fat. A lady told me she did not know him his face was so full. How much do you weigh? Papa weighs 165 pounds, John 151, Joe 157. I weigh 145 pounds. That's not bad is it for an old lady? Marge and Hermina worked night work. They are going to work tonight. Also, I don't have to cook much now. Norb, drop a card to John Hollkamp and thank him. Mary said that they sent you a card. She is waiting for the letter to take along.

So good-bye Dear, Dear, Dear Son. As Ever, waiting for a certain answer.
Mother

Kansas City, Missouri, **November 20**

Dear Mom, Pop and All,

Well, I'll start off by saying that it didn't surprise me that Lee Rhodes is in England. I knew he left with Shank, and I knew that Shank was "Over There." I'll have to drop him a letter when I get time. I tell you, if you knew the number of letters I have to write, you would send me a private secretary. I just can't catch up unless I quit writing to some of the ones I write to now and I don't want to do that.

I found out today that we will be here til Tuesday so I guess I will have a few days to myself. I would make a little trip home if I could, but I know they won't let us. You see, we graduate Monday. This is the first school in my life that I didn't want to graduate from. Wouldn't even mind a little summer school, ha, ha.

I went over to see Mr. Hensle's last night and Ante sure did have a swell supper, and I ate like a hog I guess. Gee, this GI food didn't taste so good today after eating a meal like that. It really was delicious. "Chaplain Bern" was here too and he sure does look good, and I believe he's bigger than ever and makes a swell looking officer. He and his uniform with him also. He wouldn't let me go without paying my cab fare home. I didn't want to accept it, but he insisted that I take it, and Bob paid for my cab fare over there. They sure treated me swell.

We took some pictures about 5:30 and by 10 o'clock, they were developed and printed, so I will send you a few. So I learned how to develop pictures last night. "Chaplain Bern" is supposed to stop by home when he comes back, so be sure to get his address. I think it's Chaplain B. Spoelker, Harvard University, but I don't know for sure, so you get it straight for me.

I think Alma got a big kick out of Pop and his pajamas. She wrote and told me that Hermina left out one of her horse laughs [*how Hermina got her nickname of 'Horse.' Until this letter, I had always thought it was because of her weight*].

Listen, I don't care what you say about my physique because I know I ate a lot of crap anyway, but don't compare me with Vic Mature [actor]. I don't like that guy, see. Some of these fellows on the picture might look sort of stupid but that's because they represent the whole of the United States, darn near. The whole bunch are nice fellows though, and there wasn't a fight since we've been here. It's really been windy here today and all last week. It hasn't been raining though and the skies have been blue, but I look for a big change in the weather now because it's beginning to get a little cool now. I still haven't had a chance to find out about my picture, I haven't had the time. So you will just have to wait, and besides, I believe you have about a thousand of them by now.

I have a little poem about Old man Hitler; I thought it was pretty good, so you can read it and see what you think of it. I really think it's more truth than poetry.

I don't know where I will move after Tuesday, but I will hope it's a little farther than Missouri. It might be, you can't never tell.

Katie [*Mom*], I can't make out what you mean in Lee's address because I don't know what it means, so I will underline the words I don't know and you can find out. I wouldn't want to mail a letter all the way to Europe and have it returned to me. Your letter was really swell though, and your handwriting is much better than mine.

We have a big test coming up tomorrow and it's going to be a tough one, so I will have to do some cramming tonight and I also need a beer to wash it down. The Gay Nineties is just coming on. I like that program pretty well.

It looks like the Army is making a showing for itself, and the Navy also, so we can keep it up for about six or eight months until next winter sets in. And I think V [*victory*] will be ours. I think they will, too, beings that we're on the move for the first time since the war started. Well, I will have to close now and get down to my lessons, so all of you be good, which I know you will be. Find out what Zip's new address is for me. And Red Johnson's also. So,

As Always,

Norb

The newest address for Norb was HQ 59th Signal Battalion, Camp Crowder, MO.

Camp Crowder, Missouri, **November 24**, Tuesday night

Dear Mom and All,

I'm back here in Camp Crowder so you know what I'm thinking. I just love this damn place. I'm awful sleepy; I haven't slept since Sunday night so this is going to be a brief letter. I don't know what the chow is like here because I haven't ate yet at the mess hall. I will write more tomorrow, I'm so tired now I can't hold my eyes open, so goodnight and be good.
As Always,
Norb

Camp Crowder, Missouri, **November 26**

Dear Mom, Pop and Sis's,

Well, today is Thanksgiving and we had turkey, and I hope all of you had the same. It was pretty good too, but it did not interfere with our daily routine. We went on just the same; in fact we don't stop for nothing. Some stuff I'll say. We do a lot of drilling and take a lot of exercises now, and every muscle in my body is sore but I don't mind that because I can use the exercise. But it was pretty tough after being in Kansas City for six weeks and not moving around very much.

I tried to call home when I got there but the lines were too busy so I couldn't get a call through. The long distance lines are pretty busy now. I haven't got a letter since last Saturday so I don't know much what to write about. The officers and non-coms here are all pretty nice fellows so that's one thing anyway. I don't know what will happen now.

I have my telephone diploma and will send it home when I get a chance. I might go to teletype or radio school. I can't say for sure so don't be too sure of anything I write. Oh-by the way, tell dear little Mary I received her cute little card and you can tell her I ate all the turkey I could hold. Well, that's all for now. I'll have to close - busy.
As Always,
Norb

Camp Crowder, Missouri, **November 29**

Dear Mom and All,

Well, I received your letter yesterday morning. I guess you did think that letter was short, but that's all the time I had. Busy fellow. It sure is cold here. It turned cold all of a sudden. I guess that's why it seems so cold. Well, I won't be able to write as often as I have been because I'll be too darn busy so you will have to take it as it is. Friday we went on a road march and it was 10 3/10 miles long and I finally put that Dr. Scholl's (or something) foot kit into good use. Sure was tired Friday night after being in Kansas City, and not doing any marching or exercising. Well, it's just kinda hard on you at first but I'm getting used to it now.

No, I wasn't able to get out Thanksgiving. I think we will be able to get a three-day pass

before long but it would still cost so darn much to come home by plane, and a train would be too slow so I guess I will just forget about it and wait till I get a furlough and then I will have more time. The food here is pretty good and a pretty nice bunch of fellows. Well, that's all for now but tell Pop to keep the Oertel's flowing and tell Honeybunch I said hello. So, so long.
As Always,
Norb

Louisville, Kentucky, **November 29**

Dear Norb,

A gloomy Sunday it is. We are listening to Churchill at present. Elizabeth and her shadow is here. Margie want a bicycle - she means a fudgesicle. By this time, I suppose you have received the addresses you desired. I'm enclosing a clipping from the Record about "Chaplain Bern."

The fire at Coconut Grove in Boston was terrible, according to the latest radio report the deaths have been put at 431 with only ½ of the bodies identified. I don't think war could look worse than that.

Jr Russell sent a coconut home before it was taken from the shell. It was treated naturally, looked glazed and about the size of a very small watermelon. Harold Chalmers is going to be married and I understand it is going to be a big affair. I heard his mother is buying a flag that will cost $35.00 and afterward, that is after the ceremony, she is donating it to the Church. That's pretty nice. Mrs. Zipperle sent one of Zip's pictures over. It was taken at Beckman's. Postcard size. It's very good of him. I also heard Johnny Becker was married which I did not know and his wife has a baby. The last they heard of him, he was in Africa. I think Alma told you her sister Mary Catherine [*Pierce*] had a baby girl yesterday.

The gas rationing goes up on the first of December and they can fill up their gas tanks. At Fort Hill, they sold 8 cents of gasoline. He's keeping his tank filled.

Now about Christmas. I am listing some things. Check what you would like and send this paper back. Sweater, Shoes, Gloves and Muffler, Socks, House slippers, Dopps Bag [*?*], $1,000,000, and 2¢, Hoping to get an answer on this promptly.
Love from all. We're OK.
Hermina

Louisville, Kentucky, **November 30**, raining today, 8:45

Dear Son!

Received your letter at 8:30. Going to write so you get it as soon as you can. I am glad that you had the Dr. Scholl's kit. It sure is good stuff. Alma called after work yesterday, said she never received a letter yesterday, wanted to know if we had got one and how you was. I hope you will like your box. It looks like you could have lots in it but we never had a smaller box.

You said you could not write so often as you have. If you could only write a few lines, it would be alright but if you can't, you have to do the best you can. Well, I will have to close. It's 10 minutes to nine now. We will try and write you as often as we can. So goodbye and God bless you. Still praying for you and all the boys in the services. They sure pray a lot for you all. Little Mary said hello.

As Ever,

Mother

Louisville, Kentucky, **December 1,** Tuesday, 10 pm

Dear Norb,

Gee, I couldn't think it was or is December 1. Well, soon '43 will be here and we will be victorious. It is very cold tonight, the coldest for the season so far and the wind is so biting. We waited for a car [*streetcar*] for 15 minutes. The gas rationing is on. Joe got a C Ration card. Did you hear Fibber McGee [*radio comedy*]? Gertie Bowe's fourth son has entered the Army.

Oh yeah, Mary wants to know why you quit sending her kisses. She misses them. Alma said she was going to look into that, and since then, you left out all the X's. You really got Mary wondering. We have a lot of work for Fort Knox and now Mr. Seb. has some for Camp Campbell, KY. It seems you like Camp Crowder better since you returned. Did Rogers and Perry, in fact the whole company, go to Camp Crowder? How did you do about your average?

No local news at all except Joe made muffins tonight. Mom's been making some muffins. They are swell. She could win a prize on them. Joe is so very fond of them, so he taken a shot. They looked good, but no tastee, no givee. Well, Norb I must close now. Mom will close this letter tomorrow.

Goodnite my sweet,

H.R.

Louisville, Kentucky, **December 2**, Cold, 6 above zero, Wed. 12:30

Dear Norb,

It is very cold and it snowed last night. I think about 2 inches deep. Whether you write or not, I have always looked at that mailbox from 5:15 to 9 o'clock. I just cannot help it - a habit, you know. Gertie Bowe (*Mrs. Meyer*) who has four boys in the Army, has two in the fighting line. She told me over the phone it is hard enough to worry about one, much less four. One day she got 3 letters from her sons. She said it keeps her busy writing. She was crying; I could hear that over the phone. She asked me to pray for her boys and she prays for you. She is the <u>honor</u> mother of St. Agnes Parish, the pastor told her.

Hermina asked what you would like for Christmas so let us know as soon as you can. It is no use to get you something you wouldn't need or care for. Don't you think so? Did you get anything from Park and Tilford yet? St. Elizabeth's is going to give every soldier in the parish a nice present. I don't know if they have sent them already. I know one gift is a money belt and some religious things. Don't forget to write to them and thank them. Elizabeth is coming tomorrow. She wants me to help her with some comforts [*comforters*] I believe. Well, I hope it is not so cold and windy where you are as it is here. The sun is shining brief and you can hardly believe it is so cold. I don't know if Marge is going to finish her letter or not. They might have to work night work till Christmas. They have not got much time then. Papa still waits til 9 pm when he gets a growler so that Marge can get a glass or two. I don't drink beer much. It is too cold for my stomack [*sic*]. Papa said it was good for him. You know since there was a shortage of coffee Papa drinks coffee every night. That's funny. We get a pound of coffee to every person over 15 years, every five weeks. That is not much. I cook the coffee over sometimes so you got that over on us. Hoping that you are well and that your feet are getting better. If you want more of Dr. Scholl's foot comfort just let us know. That salve is good for pain also.

Well, I must close. I have to put the bread in pans so Papa will have homemade bread. The girls take it for lunch now. Alma likes it too, and the raisin kuchen, she told me she wished her mother could bake bread. That's all for today. Mary said hello and XXX Goodbye and be good - I mean, extra good, and pray for my <u>intercession.</u>
<u>Go</u>d bless you,
Mother

Camp Crowder, Missouri, **December 1**

Dear Mom and All,

I don't have but a few minutes so I will have to write fast. This is a fast moving Army. I haven't been able to get a phone call home yet because the lines are always busy. I received a box from Park and Tilford this morning and it really was nice. It had soap, toothpaste, button polisher, mirror, comb, writing paper, cakes, candy, jelly, and two cans of different kinds of meat, 3 boxes of different kinds of cookies and a few other things.

I liked that diary type of letter. It contained a lot of news, and was very welcome. I am surprised to hear that young fickle couple (Rudy [*Muth*] and Bell) was married. Well, it took a world war to do it. No, I won't get a furlough for Xmas. I know that but I might get one later on. You never can tell. I have a nice big blister on the bottom of my foot, but I guess it will dry up in a few days. Don't worry about getting me anything for Christmas, and I mean that. My shoes are still in good shape so I won't need new shoes. So far as Xmas goes, just forget about it. It won't seem like Xmas anyway because it will just be another day for us. Well, I guess you think my letters area short but I do everything in a hurry now. The lights are getting ready to go out so goodnight and sleep tight.

As Always,
Norb V...-

Louisville, Kentucky, **December 3**

Dear Norb,

Well, I decided I would write you a few lines but now I changed my mind. I might as well make use of my womanly right. Tomorrow I'm getting a permanent, at Lavern's of course, so I thought I would have oodles of time then. So goodnite dear, good sleep tight and march right.
H.R.

Dear, Dear Norb,

I don't like to disappoint you so I will finish this letter, if not much news, it is the thought. Saw that you got the Christmas gift from Park and Tilford. Did you write them a card of Thanks? That won't take you long. It means so much. I will have to close. Jimmy and Shirley are here and must go home and they won't mail the letter for me. Elizabeth was here today and I helped her clean. I'm not out of the habit of washing [*laundry*] twice a week. I have to have some fun! Mary said she did not feel hurt for not writing to her if you did not have the time. If you just say a few words, it pleases us.
[*Mother*]

Partial letter, page 2:

...that the country the farmers have twice as much beef and porkies, then why in the holy **** can't we have more meat under those conditions?

We are all OK and we will be waiting for the call to come thru regardless of what hour you have to place it. Norb, Jim and Shirley thought you were made a Corporal. We wasn't going to mail those letters but Mom put them in.Well, Norb I will close. Hoping to hear you or from you.
Loads of ***,
H.R.

Camp Crowder, Missouri, **December 3**

Dear Mom, Pop and Sis,

I just came home from work. Had a pretty long day. I've been punching a typewriter for the last two days. I might stick to it, I don't know just yet. I can if I want to. I'm a clerk at the motor depot. It's going to be a lot of work because when the outfit is complete we will have 126 trucks, so that will mean a lot of work. It's not bad though. I won't have to do any marching and I get home too late to stand retreat. Retreat is at 6:00 pm. I was too late for chow tonight so I will have to run up to the PX and get me a sandwich. OK, by the way, that cake was d-e-l-i-c-i-o-u-s. Thanks a lot. Only thing was, it was mostly paper, ha, ha.

The weather is damn cold here. I tell you this radio sure comes in handy, it's good pastime when the day is done. Once more, I'm pressed for time so be good, see you later.
As Always,
Norb V...-

Louisville, Kentucky, **December 5**

Dear Norb,

To begin with, we are having snow. It is falling fast and I imagine it is about 2 inches deep, and is now sleeting on top of that, so we are really having some weather. Marge is at Lavern's getting a permanent. You sure will have two "purty" sisters.

I wrote to "Chaplin Bern" last night. I asked him how he enjoyed his Harvard "bawths" by now. We sent a box to Will. Hollkamp and I sent a V-letter to him the next day. His mother got an answer on my letter but he never mentioned the box at all. Perhaps by now he received it. By this time, you have received the box. We sent cakes and candy. It seems like Christmas, and it don't. The windows have some Christmas decorations but the streets are not decorated at all. We are all OK.

Mom is fixing Guta [*Goetta*]. You know - with oatmeal. Mom, Marge and I chipped up together and got Alma a chenille robe. It is a pretty blue if you remember what Marge's looked like last year. Well, it is the one just exactly like that. Alma took it along when she went to Kansas City and liked it so much so we thought we would go together and get her something nice. Bette wants 38 things and Katsy burns up when Betsy pops off. She thinks Betsy just keeps adding to her list and watches Katsy gets mad all over. Don't know no more news or gossip, so will close hoping you are well and let us know just how cold it gets there. Loads of love from all,
Hermina

Camp Crowder, Missouri, **December 5**

Dear Mom and all,

Well, it seems as though the water is getting pretty high. I read about it in one of the papers here. I sure hope it doesn't get any higher. It will make fishing bad for my brother-in-law. The weather has been pretty good down here for the last couple days, the sun's been out but the air is pretty cold.

I received that box from the Muth's and in case I don't get to write, tell "her and them" I said thanks a million. Yes, I would like to have some of those cards. I haven't had time to write but ma[y]be I could scribble out a few cards in a hurry. It seems as though Hermina will be a smoked "Porkie" if Pop makes good with all those cigars. We keep our gas masks in our barracks all the time I but I was thinking about sending it home. Perhaps you could make better use of it.

Well, my dear, dear people I hope you are all well, fat and contented, so until I get a chance to scribble a few more lines, I remain,
As Always,
Norb V...-

Kansas City, Missouri, **December 5,** Saturday night

Dear Mom, Pop & All,

Well, this is me. Still very busy. I even have to work tomorrow. I like what I'm doing pretty well. It keeps you thinking all day and it keeps you busy. So, it makes a day pass pretty fast. I don't like to sit around with nothing to do because it makes you feel "time's just a wasten." I not only have to do all the typing for the Motor Depot 59th Bn, but I had some new work added on me today. I have to keep books on the gasoline used by 1,213 trucks. I think I'm going to get an adding machine. The "2nd Louie" I worked for tried to get hold of one today but wasn't able to get his hands on one. I work with a 2nd Louie and a Master Sgt. Both of them are pretty nice fellows. Only the Sgt's a pretty sober fellow, but I'll say one thing for him, he works hard as hell.

It's very cold here and I look for it to continue all night. It's really nasty outside. You can tell Mary that the reason I don't add the kisses at the bottom of my letter is because I hear there will be a ration on ink. Besides, what's an X? Tell her I said just to wait til I get a furlough and I will pay up for lost time. XXXXXXX

Glad to hear that all of you are busy. Hope it keeps up. Did you hear any more from Joe's draft board? Tell Joe & Ann I said hello and that I'm glad and he got a class C ration card instead of class AAAAA, as in Fibber McGee's program.

The chow here is pretty good but there is not enough of it, but you feel better when you don't eat so much. (That's a tip for Hermina.) Can you get chewing gum in Louisville? Let me know if you can't. I can get it here in the PX. We still get coffee three times a day but sometimes it's pretty weak but it still tastes a little like coffee I think. I hate to think about working tomorrow because Sunday is one day I like to have off but I guess it's the Army's way of doing things. I have to do some warshing [*sic*] tonight. Tell Lip, Joey, Johnny, and all I said hello, but just that I can't pick up enough time to write. I only hope that you can read this. Well, I hope all of you are well and still able to kick, but I will have to close for now and turn the radio down because of these fellows are tired and want to sleep. So, be good and I'll write when I find time. Tell Little Mary XXX XXXXX XXXXX XXXXXXXXXX. To hell with the ration.

Just as ever,
Norb V...-

Louisville, Kentucky, **December 7,** 7:30 pm, V...-

Dear Norb,

Listening to Richard Crooks. A year ago tonite, he sang nothing but patriotic pieces. Lip came up today to do her washing. Margie broke out with chickenpox while she was here. I believe Lip had 70 pounds of wash. Moody was going to call and ask if this was Ma Beha [*laundry & dry cleaning company*] but he thought they might be in the basement.

Did you enjoy the papers better than the cake? I was wondering if I should of iced it better that the recipe called for. Well, if the cake wasn't no good I think the pineapples were. You didn't mention the fudge. It was funny. I made that. Pop started on it as soon as he could and so finally Johnny etc. came and we put it in the pantry. You almost didn't get that.

I see you are plunking a typewriter again. Don't feel like you will keep it because I don't think you like sitting that long at one time. Then too, I think you learn more in the telephone work. You can plunk a typewriter. Eddie Spoelker was sweeping the snow yesterday when Joe was. He said "Chaplain Bern" was drilling and getting exercises like a regular soldier. He said he was bumming with his two protestant ministers and they have studies besides. We are OK. Do you think you would get to come home Christmas if you flew home? WE just want to know. I called Eastern Air-Lines, they said $32.40 a one-way ticket, plus 1% taxes and the closest port would be Kansas City. We won't bother you again about that but some say the boys will be given a vacation at Xmas, but I seen in the paper only 10% from any Camp. You don't know what to believe. I heard they are building a place for Jap prisoners of war at Fort Knox. Hope you are well.

With love from all,

H.R.

Louisville, Kentucky, **December 8**, Tuesday, 8 pm

Dear Norb,

Well, we still have snow laying in big spots yet but I think it is warming up some. Kucken's Bodner is in the Army about two weeks I heard today. Say, Walter, [*jokingly referring to Norb as the news reporter, Walter Cronkite*] you're slipping; you never left us in on the latest. You told Alma they were rationing toilet tissue. Now that's something! Alma also told us you were playing football. How does that seem to you and do you always win as you used to?

Fibber McGee is now coming on. They were swell last week. Pop's waiting for this program and then he's going to the corner [*Huelsman's*]. Boy they were swell and Bob Hope's in Des Moines, Iowa, the home of the WAAC. Are you still pounding the typewriter? Nosey, ain't I? Huh, Norb?

Love from all,

H.R.

Wednesday, 1 pm

Brother Norbert, USA. Well, I dug up a little more news. You know, the mailman was swell this am. He brought a "fat" letter from you. You know your last few letters looked like they were on a diet or rations but we appreciated them just the same.

Ante and Bob [*Hensle*]wrote a mighty nice letter. Mighty nice. They said Bobby has 6 teeth, weighs over 18 pounds and was 6 months, 6 days and 7 ½ hours old when the letter was written. That's something. They said "Chaplain Bern" rooms with an Episcopalian and

Methodist ministers. Bob's draft board is thinking about him. He received his occupational questionnaire. He said he should of received it 7 months ago. They have 8 inches of snow there. Often we read your letter today. I think you might hold on to your job. Seems on the interesting side. I hope you have your adding machine by now. About a month ago, I heard the government came to these different concerns and just taken the typewriter away from them, left them have so many. But last Saturday and Sunday there was an advertisement in the paper listing typewriters. That seems ducely [*deucedly, a popular term at the time*] odd to me.

I'm glad the ration has been lifted on Mary's Xs. Boy, she got a kick out of that. Mom told her she felt sorry for her when you do get your furlough. Boy, what kisser. Is it colder there than in Kentucky?
Bye,
H.R.

Camp Crowder, Missouri, **December 8**
Dear Mom, Pop and Sis's,

Well, there is not much to write about tonight because about the same thing happens every day. I like what I'm doing pretty well though. That's one thing that makes Camp Crowder better than the last time I was here. I got a package from St. Elizabeth Church and it contained a small compact case with a cross and a small prayer book, and two small medals and a money belt. I don't know what I will use the money belt for but it's pretty nice anyway. [*It would*] be nice to put cigarettes in.

It's really cold and damp here. I don't mind the cold so much, but I don't like the dampness. Some of these guys from California are wearing two suits of woolen underwear! Believe it or no. I just warshed [*sic*] my head and took a shower. Feel powerful clean. We do have a nice shower room. My feet are in a better condition now. My blisters are just about gone. You know I would like to have a big shot of whiskey now and then hit the hay. Well, I didn't get a letter for these three days now from anyone, so there's not much to write about. I can put all my news in a little spore. So I guess that's all I know for now. So be good.
As Always,
Norb

Camp Crowder, Missouri, **December 9**
Dear Mom, Pop and All,

I guess you get tired of hearing that I'm busy all the time so I won't say it anymore. I must quit repeating myself. It "ain't" good English. I'm going to enclose a list that shows what it takes to equip a soldier. I thought it might be of some interest to you ma[y]be.

I just got a letter from Joe and one from Joey and one from Elwood Wise, the fellow I used to work with. Yes, I know Tony Sgroi very well. It seems as though there is one Dago

[*Tony*] who is letting the Germans know that he is there anyway. That dog sure was a pitiful looking sight, poor fellow.

Alma told me that she was going to get you all a Christmas present and she wanted to know what Mom would like but I told her I didn't know. I don't know much news either. I just thought I'd let you know I'm still alive. Feel sorry for poor Bill, having so much trouble in her, first major slip in life. Poor kid. Well, these young newly-weds will have to learn that married life is no bed of roses.

So, Larni Johnson ["Red"] is home on a furlough. Good for him. Well, will write more tomorrow if I have the time so good night all and to all a goodnight.
As Ever,
Norb V...-

Louisville, Kentucky, **December 9**, Wednesday, 1:45, 34°

Dear Norb,

I am just through with washing and dishwashing. Don't you feel sorry for me? I know if you were here, you would help me! You asked about chewing gum. It is very rare, Papa got me 2 packages Sunday night at Huelsman's. Can't get any at Hertel's, Best and Schieman's. Papa is going to try and get me some up there if he can. At Schieman's [*they*] never had a piece of beef Saturday. I go to Best sometime and get beef if he has it. It sure is a problem to get meat the kind you want. No use for the clerks to ask what do you want. It is for the housewives to ask what kind of meat have you? It looks pitiful, such little meat on the counters. It reminds me of the [1937] flood time. Margie is getting along fine. Elizabeth got fever blisters on both her lips. I never saw anyone with such a swollen mouth. When she was a child here, she got a headache in the afternoon and the next morning, that was Tuesday, she was broken out with fever blisters. Elizabeth and I washed her wash Monday. I believe it was 60 pounds or more but the <u>fun</u> I had. I can tell you it is nice to have some fun and don't have to go out to get it. Well, Norb, I am, in fact, we all are, glad that you like it and hope that you will get more to eat so you won't lose your handsome figure.

Norb we are mailing your box today. They ask everyone to mail packages by the 10th of December. Norb if you could go hunting with your Wahoo brother-in-law you sure could make money. Schieman's sold them 50¢ a piece yesterday. [*Lee usually hunted for birds or rabbits*].

Enjoyed your letter very much. Alma was here Sunday night. She sure has long hours. Alma's niece earned 41 dollars a week at the gun plant. Ain't that something? I am getting bored because Mary is getting all the kisses and I don't get any. She gets more kick out of the few lines. She sure enjoys it. Little Mary says hello. She is going to send you a big kiss she said. Well, I must close now. Mary is going to take the box to the post office - she leaves earlier then, so good-bye.
Hello from all and God bless,
Mother

Louisville, Kentucky, **December 9,** Wednesday, 8:30pm

Dear Norb,

Hain't had any news since I last wrote you this morning. Mom usually finishes it the next day. Joe is a busy man, too. He is preparing a rabbit for a 9 o'clock supper so Mom had to give him the lowdown on that. Joe hasn't received any more word from the draft board as yet. Antoinette said Kansas City had 8 inches of snow with all buses, airplanes, trains and cars halted. The cars were stalled in the street.

H.R.

Continued, **December 10**, 5 o'clock, cold rain

I have to hurry. I want to mail this letter before I go to church at 1 o'clock holy hour. Joe got his greetings today - must report at the Norton Building at 7:00 am, December 19th. I hope he will not have to go. He don't seem to worry about it. I think he does, but won't let on. Ann don't know it yet. I feel sorry for both of them. It is easier to part as sweethearts than as husband and wife. Sure glad that you and Alma did not get married. If you love one another, you all will wait for each other. Marg, Hermina and Ann are working to-nite. I think Marge and one of the girls are going to Camp Knox and work on drapery Monday. They might close the drapery room till they get back. Just a day or two. That is the way Marge said cause it can be chancy yet. I don't know any news and I hope that you will get the box in good shape. Let us know if you get it. Joe ate supper with me tonight, Thursday. Goodbye and good luck.

God bless you,

Mother

Louisville, Kentucky, **December 10**

Dear Uncle Norbe,

You did not receive a letter from me for a long time I guess. I'm sitting in bed writing this letter. Mother and Daddy are out in the kitchen, Margie Lou is crying. I'm sorry but lights out. Daddy came in and said I would have to finish it tomorrow so I'm finishing it now. Jimmy is going to serve [*Mass as an altar boy*] soon. We got another dog. Milton picked it up in an alley. It is brown and white. Margie Lou picks it up and kisses it. Milton made some fudge the other day and it was good, too. I can't think of much to say. I don't know anything new. I wish you a <u>Merry Christmas</u> and a Happy New Year!

So Long,

Shirley

Louisville, Kentucky, **December 11**

Dear Norb,

We just received your letter stating you haven't received any mail for 3 days. We have written you every day. I suppose it might be the Christmas rush. That was a nice gift from St. Elizabeth's even if you don't have any money. We are all OK. You know Joe has to be examined December 19th. Now we are wondering if he will pass or not.

I haven't any news because I didn't just wash my head and take a shower, ha, ha. I wish I could send you a slug of Old Grand Dad. Now, I prefer a cup of Maxwell House. Well, bye Norb. Glad you like your work so well.
Love from All,
Hermina

Louisville, Kentucky, **December 11**, 10 pm, V...-
Dear Norb,

We just got home from work a few minutes ago. Joe comes after us at night all the time. So, you like your money belt from St. Elizabeth's? Don't know what to do with it? Haven't you learned to save yet with your salary? I was talking with Clarence Johnson. Larny was here when Louie was on his furlough. Larny stayed just over the weekend. He looks fine, gained 20 pounds. Clarence said he was boxing at Camp and [*got*] knocked out twice. I guess he's dizzy as ever. I bet those boys from California really feel the cold especially since it's so damp. Do you cough much, Norb?

Joey showed us her souvenir pictures you sent. They look right smart nice. Those towns look better than they really are, huh? Alma came here just now. She showed us her souvenir, too. I like the one of you, the fish, and the guys in the middle with the signal corp. Now that fish – you, has already been caught, don't you think? And no other cute fish better look at you cross-eyed, don't you think, Fishee?

I heard on the radio that over a million men has been sent across. That's a lot of men. George Herbig is in Seattle, Wash. He wrote and told his mother their belongings and clothing were being checked and rechecked. He thinks they might be heading for Alaska. I think you were lucky with your Christmas gifts. Seems as if they were both mighty nice. Did you receive the money I sent you for a long distance call? You said you haven't received our letters in three days. Can't understand it. Wrote every day.Well, tain't no use writing when you are out of news. Mom will finish tomorrow.
Love,
H.R.

Louisville, Kentucky, **December 12**
Dear Norb,

This is Saturday, December 12. Well, this was supposed to be mailed but wasn't honey. You should be receiving your letters every day. If you don't, inquire about it, because there's something wrong in Denmark.

We are having a snow again today and it is getting colder. The weatherman now promises

5 above zero. Lip and Moody are gone in town doing some Christmas shopping. We have the 6 sweets here: Shirley and Milt danced, Betsy put on a Carmen Miranda act. Margie has the chickenpox yet. Katsy called Jim a dat-rat-it (jack rabbit).

Well, we all thought about you plenty today. You know we always told you we thought Bernard Hubbuch reminded us of you. Well, today he came to work with a painted heavier-built brown shoe and a black square shoe. Well, we did laugh some and to beat it all he was out selling in some home and never knew it. Unconscious. Pop is coming with beer. Thinks it will hit zero.

I'll assure you those picture cards were greatly appreciated. Mary Rawert's boyfriend is in the Army now, about 10 days. He's as old as Henry [*Norb's brother who died*] would be, which is 44 years old. I feel sorry for a fellow that age. Frank Rawert went down to see if his blood pressure reduced sufficiently to get in the Army but it hasn't. Eddie Stevens gets to come home for Christmas, he comes the 16th. He's a Cpl.

Milton was telling Alma about that kid in the neighborhood who got a Betsy Wetsy doll. Every time it wet, so did she. That was a swell conversation. You got a letter from Elwood Wise. Is that the one they thought had heart trouble? Well, hoping you are well. We are all OK and warm.

With love from all.

Hermina

Louisville, Kentucky, **December 12**, Sunday, 8:30 pm

Dear Norb,

Weather Report 12° F above. This could easily be a WAAC house tonite. Pop is staying at work. It's really very, very slick out. Well, Emma Grimm was here today. She came right from church. We were so surprised to see her, but a friend drove her over. She said she wanted to see her dear, dear friend she hadn't seen since this summer. She was so pleased with that souvenir pictures you sent her. She was really tickled with it.

Tain't got any news. We are all OK. Shirley came up today after the show. She stays all nite now on Sunday. Emma Grimm had a terrible fall about 7 weeks ago. She couldn't work for 5 weeks but she's on the mend. She fell and hurt her head. It required 3 stitches to close it. The 'Take It or Leave It' program is now coming on the air. We will finish this letter tomorrow. Yes, I want to tell you your next-to-nothing brother-in-law Leo Jacob [*Muth*] now weighs 108 ½ pounds.

Well, this is Monday, 11:30 am. Mom washed and is napping so I thought I would close the letter. Shirley brought one [*letter*] up. It's a little ancient [*dated December 10*] but funny. The weather is cold but the day is beautiful with the sun as bright as a summer day. Hoping you are well and getting more to eat.

Love, hugs, kisses from all,

Hermina

Camp Crowder, Missouri, **December 13**

Dear Mom, Pop and Sis's,

Well, there is no snow on the ground here but it sure is colder than hell, but these GI overcoats are pretty warm. I went in town last night and bought two Christmas presents, one for you all and of course one for Alma. I didn't know what you would want so I just bought a present you could all make use of. I know I won't get a chance to get home for Christmas so I didn't have to worry about train fare. But if I ever get a furlough, I still have plenty to get there and back. I might get a furlough in February sometime, I hope.

Say, in that box from you all, well, it just covered about everything I needed. And those house slippers - they really came in handy, and so do the gloves. I can make good use of the toilet paper also. Thanks a lot. That fruitcake was really good.

So Joe got his greeting card to report on the 19th. That's a nice Xmas present, ain't it? I see here by the clipping that they are starting to eat horsemeat. Meat must be pretty scarce at that. You must keep a good eye on Hermina [*Horse*]. There might be some cattle rustlers around.

I got a Xmas card from Mrs. Russell with a buck in it. Tell her I said thanks. I have some cleaning up I have to do today. I don't get a chance to do it through the week because I'm kept too darn busy. Every day it's more and more work to be done. We get time and a half for all our time too, that's what I like about it.

I sure would like to go hunting, especially this year, because game should be pretty plentiful. One thing, there will sure be a lot of them next year if nobody gets to shoot them this year [*seems Norb thinks the war will be over within the year*]. The gasoline ration will hold most of them back. Glad to hear that Lip's kids are getting along OK. Funny about her fever blisters wasn't it. Never had anything quite like that.

If you were here you could have plenty of fun with my warshing, besides, I have plenty of it. I think I will put in it in a box and mail it home. Then you can warsh it and send it back. I ought to get about a six-day service. You don't have to worry about me getting enough to eat if I have to buy it myself. I broke my pen yesterday. I dropped it and the point hit on the concrete floor and bent the hell out of it. I think I will send it to the factory and get it fixed. It shouldn't cost over a half a buck. If I had a camera here, I would take some pictures because the sun is out pretty bright. It would be a swell day for it. First sunny day we had for a long time so I might borrow Bert's camera and take a few pictures after I have a few beers. So that is all the dope for now and thanks again for the package and the one I sent should arrive there about Wednesday or Thursday. I hope it's satisfactory. It's the only decent thing I could find.

So goodbye and so long till later,

Norb

Louisville, Kentucky, **December 14**, 7 pm

Dear Norb,

Bromo-Seltzer time. Well, I do have a little news for you. Min is here - he's in Louisville. He promised to come to "dinner" tomorrow night. He called from the corner. I answered. He said where's Joe? I recognized him immediately. I think he was feeling his oats a little - he said, "How's Kate? Put Kate on." So I hope we get to see him. He was a Chief Petty Officer and over stayed his leave 3 days. He was knocked down to Second Class Petty Officer and before he got his leave, he took the examinations for Chief Petty Officer again so I suppose he'll be a Chief Petty Officer again.

"Shick" Reem - you know him? Ernie Schieman's friend. He takes his final exam with Joe on Saturday and is worried. Mom asked Min if he would like sauerkraut and pig tails. He said he'd rather have ribs. We didn't get a letter today but got one on Saturday. We are all OK. You never did get your call thru did you? Everybody says it's so hard to get a L.D. [*long distance*] call thru. I seen a piece in the paper where the Army is going to pay off before Xmas. Well, that's nice for the boys.

Russell couldn't get his car started so was walking it today. It started to melt this pm. The street was just snow and ice and scarcely any cars out. It is lots warmer out tonite and the weatherman promises warmer weather. We were dreaming of a white Christmas but I bet it will just be a dream on the 25th. Mom will finish this letter.
H.R.

Mommy continued the note:

Dear Norb!

While I am listening to Richard Brooks, I am writing to you. I have not got much space, though, but a few words will be welcome, I hope. Miss Emma Grimm was to see us yesterday. Sunday she had dinner with Hermina and me. Marge was working and Papa did not come home for dinner. She was so pleased to get a souvenir from you. She told us about 6 times how much it pleased her. Say Norb, can you send one to Little Mary? Joey and Elizabeth got theirs. Alma showed us hers also. Is it a beautiful book!

The fish that you said was you - it looks very good. I asked Alma whether she was going to get that fish. I asked if she was trying. She just give me one of those looks. She stayed Saturday night. Alma, Marge and I went to 6:30 Mass. Then Mr. Hubbuch got Marge and took Alma to work also. I was glad. It was then 8 degrees above zero. Sometimes you have to wait 30 minutes for a [*street*] car.

You don't seem to be worried. I told Joe I cannot think that they will take him. If they do, I will be very disappointed. I never thought that way about you because you were well and with no flaws. Joe never told the doctor about his garter [*goiter*]. I hope they will find it, for I don't think he could take it, do you?

I guess of all my mistakes, I had Richard Brooks on my mind. I will close now. Hermina and I want to pray the rosary for the men in the service. Father Dudine sure asked the people to pray for the boys. Have you ever left Camp Crowder? Do you get the mail regular now? I hope you do.

Little Mary said hello and misses you. When it was sleety, she took the car coming home from church. It was very bad walking. Joseph would have taken me with them to church but I wanted to go to early Mass. I could not buy beef today at Schieman's. It looks so pitiful, two pieces of pork on the meat block. Sausage is the most you can get. Hope if you come on a furlow [*sic*] we can get more different kinds of meat.

Papa just stepped in the house. I asked him what to write and he said he did not know, so he told me to tell you hello. It is 9:15 and 30 degrees above.
Good-bye,
Mother and All

Camp Crowder, Missouri, **December 15**

Dear Mom, Pop, Sis, and Honeybunch: XX

Well, it's pretty damn cold here tonight; the wind is pretty strong also. I have a slight cold with my good old cough. It seems like old times. I'm going to get me some cough medicine tomorrow if I get a chance.

So Red gained 20 pounds. Seems like the Army is doing him good. I sure would have liked it to have seen him. If Red got knocked out, it sure was from 100 proof bourbon and not from gloves of any kind.

A fish is not caught until he is landed and in the bucket. I got a laugh out of that one about that Betsy Wetsy doll. It takes a Milt to tell them.

Well, there is no news here except I'm still typing and keeping books. I can notice my arithmetic improving a lot. One thing, I'm in a warm spot all day. No, Elwood Wise is not the one with heart trouble. Does Pop still give weather forecasts by the "fog in the holler?" Well, there are no "hollers" around here so I don't think his prediction would work. Slightly off. Well, that's all the news, hope you receive your present in good shape, so goodnight and warmer weather to you all.
As Always,
Norb

Louisville, Kentucky, **December 16**, 8:30 am, Joe's birthday

[*Dear Norb,*]

Well, we had company alright last night. Plenty company. Min came and Joe about 6:45. We had given them up. Joe only worked a half day so he drummed up Min and they went to Joe Halring's. They were riding horses and Min falls off. He didn't hurt himself. Min said he is taking care of the kids, 17-year-old recruits. He said that sometimes he has to get tough. He said some of those recruits come to him and say, "I'm homesick." "What the hell am I supposed to do about it?" he answered. He said that he said he was homesick the first night but he never told anybody. I don't think he would burden anybody with his troubles.

Eleanor and Johnny etc. came. Eleanor has four teeth chiseled out of her head yesterday. It required 7 stitches to close the incision. They had to pull a perfectly good tooth in order to get to one, which was the worst one. It was about an inch long and shaped like this [*she drew a tooth*]. That was laying in back of her eyetooth so it was necessary to pull that tooth. Eleanor said he hit it with a chisel and a mallet and that she could feel it at the top of her head. It never hurt her but the noise. The other ones wasn't that way, they came out a lot easier. She was at the dentist office from 9 to 12:30. He X-rayed them last week and yesterday when she came in, he said what kind of a person are you - you know teeth anywhere. Yesterday he discovered a tooth coming in back of her wisdom tooth. These are not baby teeth but excess teeth. He said it's a wonder she had any health at all. He just shot Novocain from the front of her mouth to her tonsils and she watched the whole procedure. She sure did grand. Mom fixed her some soup and she drank it all. She'd bend way over. It wasn't bothering her very much. Dr. Williams said there was no danger of hemorrhage. She's so tickled that they are out. That's all.

Did you ever get a letter from your adopted boy or girl [*adopt a soldier program*]? Shirley's adopted a soldier is Harry Galings and she had to write him a letter explaining, so she got an answer yesterday and she was so thrilled. He told her he knew you and Joe, and you were both fine men. Huh. He went to school with Joe. Shirley wants to go in town and have her picture made for him. Milt said, well maybe you better have an oil painting made for him. Wise guy

You know the Nottermann's? They have 6 in the Service, the 7th registering. I thought it was very nice in Mrs. Russell [*neighbor across the street*] remembering you. We sent Junior [*their son, and Norb's boyhood friend*] some candy. Glad you like your box. We couldn't think of anything else. Mom's washing windows and likes it. Lip and Marge is here. Min thinks he will be sent to Sea again. He said he feels like he's booked to be sent. He's in Anstoccia [*Anastacia*], DC about 20 minutes from Washington. We are all OK. Today is beautiful and the snow is all gone.

Marge, Lill, and Ann is in Ft. Knox fixing drapes. Min reenlisted again, you know, so that's the reason for his furlough. He'll be in the Navy 12 years on 27th of February 1943. That's all I know today. I can't think of anything else. Until we receive you Christmas gift. Your fat letter came today. It was almost a Christmas gift. Very nice letter. Sorry to hear you broke your pen.

Until we hear from you again. Yes, I want to tell you when Miss Emma left Sunday, she thanked Mom for her dinner and her nice prayers. I told Mom I believe that's the first person who thanked her for her long prayers [*long prayers and much daily praying angered some of the family who had to pray with her*]. Cheerio and be a good boy Norbert, keep good company and you'll get along alright, quoting Emma.

Love,

Hermina R.

Louisville, Kentucky, **December 16**, 1 pm

Dear Norb,

Well, hi 'ya Toots? I'm getting this letter ready for Mom to add her bit tomorrow. We just listened to Mayor of the Town. Eleanor is getting along fine, Johnny stopped in today.

I failed to give Mary the letter this afternoon so you probably will receive two together. We are all OK. Eddie Stevens is here on a furlough. His grandmother said he failed in his examination for a Lieutenant by one question, so he's now a Cpl. Do to tell, huh?

That was a Donaldson fruitcake. They say you can't buy better fruitcake. Glad you enjoyed it. You never waited for Santa Claus, did you?

I heard Busath's Candy and Rudolph's Candy Company are both closed due to lack of material. Rudy [*Muth's Candy*] is still going. Johnny said he thought it would try for defense work after Christmas. They seem to be putting more and more work on them at the dairy [*Plainview Farms Dairy*]. Will close so goodnite dear, goodnite.

Your little "Horsy" Sis

Camp Crowder, Missouri, **December 16**

Dear Mom and All,

Just a few words to say hello. I don't know nothing new, except I think they're getting our mail all mixed up the last few days. I guess it's because of the large amount they have to handle during this time of year. It was just a little warmer here today and the sun was out for a change. We had sauer kraut for supper tonight. We also had ribs and they were actually good. That is a large change.

We are going to have to scrub the floor in a little while. I don't know why, just some damn fool's idea. We usually do that on a Friday. Well, we will do it tonight and Friday also. I guess by the time you receive this letter Joe will know if he'll be a doughboy or not. Well, I hope he don't for his and Ann's sake both, but you never can tell. If he does, tell him to get out of all the detail he can at the induction center because they always have you behind a GI scrub brush and then you get to wondering how in the hell is this going to win the war. If they don't have no scrubbing for you to do, they have you pick up rocks and stack them in a neat pile, and then after you have them stacked nice and neat, you'll find out that you have stacked them in the wrong place. Then after you have moved them about six times (and cussing about a hundred times, under your breath of course), you will find out that they were in the right place to begin with. Between shots and rocks, well, that's about your first two weeks in Uncle Sam's Army (or rock masons).

Then, of course, you always have about three or four fellows who are always complaining. That's naturally understood. If it's for a reason or not, they have the ability to think of one, even if it happened ten years ago. If then they can't think of nothing to gripe about there is always ex-President Hoover. He's always a good topic of discussion and cussing.

Bob Burns is on the radio now; I was just wondering if you were listening to him, he's pretty good. If it wouldn't be for this radio, I don't know how I would keep up with the news.

I imagine in about another month or so we will go on maneuver. I don't know just how long they will last. I hear that they might be somewhere in Ten-a-see. We had a blackout here that other night at 10:00 and everybody had to get out of bed and dress and be ready to go. There are about five fellows who have "gone over the hill" [*deserted*]. Haven't found any of them yet. This letter turned out to be much longer than I thought it would. You know sometimes I can sit down to write a letter and can't think of a thing to write, so I just give it up.

Xmas is just around the corner and I still can't get hold of any Xmas cards here. They just "ain't" to be had so I guess I will have to do without. Those slippers sure do come in handy because it feels mighty good to get out of those GI shoes. I had my oxfords at the shoemaker now for two and a half weeks and they aren't ready. This is a very slow place. I bought me a new pen last night. I dropped the other one point down on the concrete. I bought a pretty good one while I was at it because I have to use it all day long and then I have to write letters at night, so I thought it would pay to get a good one. Nothing cheap for me, with all the dough I'm making. I might as well spend some of it for something useful.

Tomorrow we start with some new exercises. Everybody has to take them now before the start of their regular work for the day but I think it's a good idea. When we get finished here were supposed to run a half an hour without stopping. Some stuff, I'll say. All men over forty do not have to participate. I don't know what they want men over forty in the Army for anyway. Well, I hope all of you are in good health and still able to argue as much as usual. That's one thing that always seemed necessary for some reason or other.

Does Mary still pick up dog turds for candles and then put them on the dresser for safekeeping? [*This was a long-standing joke. Mary was old and her eyes were bad, and during a blackout one night, she thought a dog turd was a candle*]. XXXX for Mary. V...-
As Always,
Norb

Louisville, Kentucky, **December 17**

Dear son,

It is snowing & hailing & sunshining today & windy also. My news today [*is*] only that I bought a small Christmas tree this morning at Best and paid 65¢. It is very pretty shape tree. People already dechearating [*decorating*] the window with wright's [*wreaths*]. Marge, Ann and Lill [*Steinmetz*] went to Fort Nocks [*Knox*] yesterday to work on drapes. Came home about 12:20 last night. They were too tired this morning. Joe has but a few more days to go when he will find out his lot. I don't give a snap for Christmas this year. It is the first year that you were absent from home. I know we will be with you during holy Mass and Holy Communion. I hope that you will go on Christmas. Nothing would please me more than if you remember us in Holy Communion. I don't want anything more than that and it would take the glume [*gloom*] out of my heart.
Goodbye and god bless you,
Mother and All

PS. If you got time, send [*a card to*] Mrs. Russell and thank her. I don't think that Mr. Russell knows it. I'm not sure. We sent Jr [*Russell*] candy. He never did send a card as yet. I am glad that you liked your box. It was Hermina's Idia [*idea*] to send you slippers. I thought you could not have them. That was a nice fat letter you sent. Mary ain't got the time tonite. So long. It is 2:00 Thursday.

Louisville, Kentucky, **December 17**, Thursday, 10:15 pm

Dear Norb,

Well, it's getting right smart late and I want to retire early because we want to get to work early. We are all OK. We haven't received your gift as yet but that isn't unusual at this time. Well, we didn't have much Xmas spirit this year, doubtful about having a tree, so this morning Mom went to Best's and she really brought home a beautiful Xmas tree. It's one of the prettiest, bushiest trees I have ever seen. So we're going to have a tree.

We had a 5 x 7 picture made of you and Chaplain Bern and you. It is a swell picture. Both of them. The one of you by yourself is really grand, Norb, really good. I think I might have it tinted. I know Alma will want one when she sees it. Norb Hollkamp said you'd make a better looking Marine. I thought that was funny. The picture is really tough looking. You seem to have the fighting spirit and it reflects in your picture so he thought you'd make a tough looking Maine.

We will let you know as soon as we can about Joe, about how he comes thru Saturday. Marge got in from Ft. Knox at 12:15 am. She was really tired. She asked Chester to get her some whiskey, so Carny sent over a quart tonite. We all had highballs but I can't say I like it. It went to my head and I got a headache afterwards, but never got drunk. Marge didn't even feel it. She can take it. Jim Wessling is in California. He left about 3 weeks ago for the Army.

You said you get time and a half for overtime. Do you really mean that? Or is it true? Hoping you are OK.

With love from

Horse

Mommy continued Hermina's letter on **December 18**, 2.o'clock

Dear Norb

I can't write much because Mary will go to work soon. She said she sent you a real sweet kiss. Also, she sent you a buck and told you to drink a beer for that but not to get drunk. Joe helped me work about the house - put a cover on the divan and put up curtains and so on. Hermina got the jerks [*epileptic seizure*] this morning going to work and fell down the front steps and hurt her knees and put holes in her stockings. She wanted to make a full day but she had to go to bed. She had a nervous chill and I gave her hot milk, hot water bottle to her back and a hot iron to her feet. She felt better later on and Mrs. Mitchell came home after

her. They are so very busy. Don't let them know that I told you. I sure feel sorry for her. Alma called today and is coming tonite. We got your letter from the 15ᵗʰ December this morning.
As ever,
Mother

Camp Crowder, Missouri, **December 17**

Dear Mom and All,

Just a line to say hello. The weather here was just like a summer day. It was really nice. I hope it keeps it up for a while. Well, I got my scrubbing done last night and two nice red knees. If you smell anything, it's because I'm sitting in the privy writing this letter. It's the only place the lights are on yet. The lights go out at nine o'clock everywhere else. Been working late at nights and it cuts down on your free time. Well, I will have to close for now. Hoping you are all well. XXXXX for my Little Mary.
As ever,
Norb

Camp Crowder, Missouri, **December 18**

Dear Mom and All,

Well, I wrote a long letter the last time, but I haven't but a few minutes to write a few lines tonight. It's after 11 pm now and I must get to bed because tomorrow is a long day and I'm pretty tired. I have to write all my letters in the "privy" because the lights go out in the barracks at 9:00 pm. Well, it was just like a spring day today. It really was swell. Hope it's the same in KY. Well, I will have to say goodnight and sleep tight. All is well that ends well. Tell my dear little Mary hello and I am reserving all of these for her XX XX XX XX XX Woe be to her when and if I get a furlough.
As Always,
Norb

Louisville, Kentucky, **December 18**, Friday, 9:40 pm

Dear Norb,

Well. Norb, hain't got much news but I'll scribble a few lines. So far, we haven't received your gift as yet. We thought it would be your picture but since you "went shopping" we've given up that idea. Nosey, ain't I? Norb, if you would write to that photographer and explain I believe you could get your picture from Kansas City. Rally [sic] I do!

Well, Joe goes in for his final exam tomorrow. I'll let you know when we hear. Ann was fidgety today, alright. I'll be glad when we hear - we all will - regardless which way it is. It's better when it's all over with. I just got Ann's name in the Christmas Pie at work. I'm getting her a Stationery box and Inkograph pen. We have to spend $2. They are drinking beer and Mom did something funny. I can hear them laughing. We got Mary an electric toaster. It's right pretty.

So the fish is caught only when you have it in the bucket. Everybody got a kick out of the Fish. Eleanor is having the stitches removed tomorrow. She is doing fine so far. Goodnite Norb. Mom will finish this letter tomorrow

Love,

H.R.

Louisville, Kentucky, **December 19**, Saturday, 11 am

Dear Norb,

It's a hard day, Norbeeee. Joe is taking his exams now. Mom is busy so I thought I would finish this letter and get it off. We received your pamphlet letter. It wasn't going to be newsy at all and, my, what a letter it turned out to be. Perhaps if you get to Tennessee you can maneuver home for a spell.

We are very busy at work I fell down the front steps yesterday and I'm all stoved up today with two busted knees. Just a jerk, squirt. I'll answer more on your letter tonight. We have been writing you every day since you left, so it must be the Xmas rush. We had two deliveries before 10:30 yesterday. This letter don't look good but excuse the scribbling. Will write more later. Oh yeah, Norb, if you want to send that pen home I'll see that it gets all fixed up and send it back to you. Be glad to do it, huh? Mary is not at home during a blackout. We don't know what she saves at work. I bet she'll get a kick out of it. We are expecting Alma tonite.

Love,

H.R.

Louisville, Kentucky, **December 19,** Saturday, 3 pm

Dear Norb,

Well, this is to tell you that Joe was rejected. They were going to send him to Ft. Benjamin Harrison to let them decide there. They rejected him on account of his [*glass*] eye. He said two Docs argued whether or not for 20 minutes. The one wanted to send him this afternoon to Ft. Benjamin. The other one said it was useless, so this is to tell you Joe is not in the Army. I have a feeling they might call him up later if they decide differently. What do you think?

Sheik Reem passed. They taken 100 out of 128. They even taken a guy with an open-leg. Some leave tonite or rather this afternoon at 3:30 pm. The rest leave Monday, so they must of cut out that wee grace period they were giving them lately.

Love from all. I know you were as anxious as we were,

H.R.

Camp Crowder, Missouri, **December 20**

Dear Mom, Pop and Sis's,

Today is Sunday and I had to work again. There is not so much to do on Sundays except see that the trucks that pick up mail and the ambulance gets out. I'm here all by my lonesome so I thought I would type out a letter or so because I am way behind in my correspondence, and I never look to catch up.

It is very cold here this morning and there is a gray overcast sky that looks very much like we're going to have a good snow. It wouldn't surprise me a bit. We haven't had a good snow yet this year, but as far as I'm concerned, we can do without it because it would just mean more work. I'm not dreaming of a white Xmas. I had much rather see a blue sky for a change. I think the weather must have been worse in Kentucky than it has been here in Missouri.

Yes, I am the adopted soldier of one of the Schott's back on Burnett Street. I got a Xmas card from him the other day, so I will drop him a card or a little something the first chance I get.

You had better tell Marge and Lill to be careful with all them soldier boys there in Fort Knox. Ha. Ha. How do they like it working out there? I imagine it would be pretty nice, with all those handsome boys in Khaki hanging around.

We only have thirty-five trucks to take care of at the present but when we get our full allotment, we will have a hundred and twenty-six of them. You have to keep books on every ounce of gasoline and oil they burn. Also, when they had their last grease job, when the tires were rotated, and when they will be rotated again. They get all this work done every thousand miles and it doesn't take long to run a thousand miles. If you think so, ask my brother-in-law.

I received a Xmas card from my instructor in Kansas City. I never had a chance to write to him as yet. How is Pop and his Sisters [*nuns at St. Brigid's where he works*] coming along? I'll bet he is still giving them hell. We could use a guy like him in the Army if they would just furnish him with cigars. Smokescreens are an important thing in the Army.

I hope by now that you have received my Xmas present. I guess it takes a little while to get through the mail as rushed as things are now. I thought it would be nice for the kids to play in the bathtub with. I was just in the same shoes you were. I didn't know what to get either. One thing we hardly ever had around home was correct time. So I just made a point to see that there will be correct time when I get back - if the clock runs, and I think it will.

Well, I guess I will have to close this letter, I suppose this is enough for one time. Tell everyone I said hello and tell little Mary I'm thinking of her. With love and kisses XXXXXXXXXXXXXXXXXXXXXXXXXXXXXXXX

As Always,

Norb (FEEL ME ONCE)

Louisville, Kentucky, **December 20**, Sunday, 3:30 pm

Dear Norb, or rather wonderful Norb,

From the contents of this letter, you can, or will, see your letters were digested. Now you want to know about the necessary arrangements we have? Well, we don't have them so often. We found they weren't necessary since you left. How's that? I thought I was going to hear from Cpt. Eddie Rickenbacker at 3:30. Well, it must of been an announcement from the East because I got the tail end of it and I never heard the Captain. I'm mad. I read the contents of his experiences in the morning paper. My, what an experience. I'm sending you the clipping.

When is a few words a book almost? When <u>you</u> write them, honeybunch? No, Mary don't do funny things anymore. We thought about getting a dog several times, but that's out.

Exercises? And you must run a half hour on the straight? That's something, but look what a powerful gentleman you will be then. You're in the age limit where they have to do everything. You should be glad you can take it. So glad you like your bedroom slippers. They thought it was goofy around here but I knew you didn't want to run barefoot and it does feel good to slip into something light and comfortable. How's the little tups [*sic*] getting along after the blisters? I suppose now you'll get more blisters. When you run just think of your school days and think of when you asked, "Is Ollie working?" I believe you'll win any race with that thought in mind, my boy.

All the advice you gave Joe - and to think he was rejected! Well, I think Joe was sort of jittery when he came home. It seems he was at the crying point. Shirley noticed it and so did I. He said hell, I had my mind made up - I wanted to go. They discovered his goiter and he had to lay down for a half hour. Then the MD came over and listened to his heart and throat with the stethoscope. Joe went thru just like the rest, passed the psychiatrist office or rather test. Joe thought he was in the Army. Then a soldier came to him and told him to see the two Drs. who argued over his eye. If the one wouldn't of held out so strong Joe would be in Ft. Harrison. He would of left with 11 boys who went there for observation.

We are going to have rabbit for supper tonite. Mom got them at Schieman's 50¢ at apiece. We haven't received your gift as yet so we are beginning to wonder if we will get it or not. Did you have it insured Norb? What kind of pen did you get this time? You know they have a pen shop here. I told you I would see to it that yours was repaired if you send it home, or else send it to the factory.

Would you want me to send some New Year's cards to you Norb? That must really be a one-horse town. Even Ex. Pres. Hoover gets hell. You couldn't expect a Democrat to praise him! Sure glad to think you get such good enjoyment out of your radio, brother. I suppose it does mean a lot to you. The radio programs must be different there. They are the same programs I imagine, transcribed, because they seem to come on different nights.

Yeh, I guess rabbits will be plentiful this year. We are all OK. This is the third Saturday it snowed. The most I remember for this early in the season, for three straight Saturdays. It snowed during the busiest time of the year. It snowed and sleeted and snowed again, and hailed. The snow really looks like it is glazed. It has an ice crust on it. Amen.

I'm going to get the Xmas tree and ornaments down; crib, etc. Getting ready for old Santa. Everybody must of had sauerkraut last week. Pop said the eggnog was flowing at the corner. Pop is still puffing away on his 3¢ cigars. Hoping you are well and may God bless you and may the Prince of Peace be with you. I wish Emma would be here now.

So long, as ever,

Hermina

Louisville, Kentucky, **December 21** [*Note inside card*]

Dear Norb,

Our dear mother said to send you this prayer and for you to pray it every day, as I guess you do. We also got your letter today. I haven't read it. We are so busy at work. We worked every night except Saturday and worked two Sundays until 5 o'clock. I guess you think I'm in the dough, but believe me things are high. I got a Lumber jacket for Vernon at $5.95 [*$5.95 had the same buying power as $92.68 in 2017*] and Milton a pair of tweed pants for $4.95, and my goodness, you have a hard time to get a sales person to wait on you. I got a card from Maurice Slattery today and he will be home for Christmas. He said just to say hello to the gang. My mother don't like the idea for me to write on this card, so do take special care of the prayer. We all received one from the church. On the Saturday after Christmas, our boss is taking us to a chicken dinner. I guess where we were last year. It's now 11:30 o'clock and little Mary is not home yet and the snow is quite thick. I know she thinks of you, dear. Alma is coming tomorrow. She is cute. Ask her who took her to work on Sunday (Mr. Hubbuch did).

Margaret

Continued by Mommy:

Alma called from work and said she would not come tonite. She said she received a box from you. I guess they called her up. She had to shop yet tonite. She wanted to know if we got ours too. So far, we have not got it yet. I hope you will have a nice Christmas. Of all the eats you all will get - you will not of gotten that menu at home. We all think that was nice that they send that to the relations, don't you? Good night and good luck.

Good-bye,

Mother

Louisville, Kentucky, **December 21**, Monday, 9:10 pm

Dear Norb,

Well, we received your letter and also the Officers' Letter and menu. What a feed, what a feed! I know that's more than we will have, sir. I don't think you could scrub very much on a feed like that. You have housemaid's knees, sir. Don't feel good, does it sir?

I'm listening to the Contented Hour now. We are all OK. Eleanor is doing fine but the Dr.

wouldn't remove the stitches from her mouth because it was too sore but she's doing fine. I went shopping tonite. Marge and I got Pop a real raincoat. I tried to get him a Mackinaw but two stores were out and there is no more reordering. We also got Mom a pair of Dr. Scholl's shoes. Nothing foolish, you know, this year.

I went to confession at St. Boniface and I didn't forget you. I never go to Communion on Christmas Day because that day almost the whole congregation goes, so that will be my Christmas day. So, you stay well and come out of the maneuvers OK. I know they can be real dangerous. It will seem funny not having you here Christmas but you are still in the States and that's a lot to be thankful for. I really feel sorry for Bill Hollkamp in New Guinea. The Bowman Field boys are now singing Silent Night and O come All Ye Faithful. It's really very, very beautiful Semanently [*sentimental*]. All the kisses you send Mary - and to think where you wrote it [*in the latrine*]! We appreciated that letter just the same.

Alma called. She received her present but she didn't know what was in it as yet, as her mother called her at work. So far, we haven't received ours but we probably will. Hope you enjoy your Christmas as much as you can. I know we will. I feel like Lip will be over, and perhaps Johnny, but that depends on his tank.

I don't know these boys [*Courier Journal newspaper clipping enclosed of St. X graduates: Rudy Klarer, Jimmie Miller & Pat Lenahan*] but thought you might. Louis Johnson went back Friday. Earl is coming.
Love and Merry Christmas,
Hermina R.

Louisville, Kentucky, **December 22**, Tuesday, 10:30 pm

Dear Brother,

Tain't got much news but we have really been having some bad weather. It snowed Saturday, as I wrote you before. I went in town from church last night. It was like walking thru 4 inches of damp corn meal. The sidewalks were very icy here and it rained today terrible. When I went back to church, it rained like heck. I got wet clean thru and the church was cold. It was seven people in church including two nuns. The oil is hard to be gotten, you know.

We are OK and wondering if your Christmas program is being enjoyed. It started Tuesday night, didn't it? Shirley came up tonite determined to trim the tree. She's really anxious. We worked tonite (no news). It won't be long and this Christmas rush will be over with. I doubt very much if you receive this scribbling before Christmas.

Jr Russell sent a Xmas card thanking us for the candy. He said the whole dispensary enjoyed it. By this time, I know or think you received our Airmail letter saying Joe was rejected Saturday. The reason for my repeating is that you might have missed that letter.
Goodnite Dear,
Hermina

Camp Crowder, Missouri, **December 22**

Dear Mom and All,

I only have about five minutes to write this letter in and just thought I would say hello and wish all of you a very Merry Xmas and a better New Year. I was glad to hear that Joe wasn't drafted. Of course, in a way I guess he don't like it, but if he was ever in here he would be glad he was rejected, I think. Because it's different with him, he's married and everything.

Well, folks tell everyone hello and tell Mary and extra thanks for the present, and for that card. It was a darn nice card and it had a lot of meaning to it. I never got to write a card because I didn't get any. Well, good night and sleep tight.

As Always,
Norb

December 23

Dear Norb,

The weather is gloomy and not cold. It is 1 o'clock now. Father Dudine sent all the families that have someone in service a beautiful picture - call it the Roll of Honor. This is the way it is worded: "Pray for all of us in the Christmas Mass and we all will remember you. May Our Mother Protect Our Boys. Roll of Honor: in service for his country, Norbert A. Rawert, on our honor roll, Shares in the Service Men's Special Holy Mass each Sunday and in All the Holy Masses and prayers of Clergy Crusaders and Parishioners of St. Elizabeth Church, Louisville, Kentucky. Fr. John W Dudine. That liberty shall not perish from the earth." there's 14 different flags on the [*card*] picture surrounding the Immaculate Conception and the eagle in front of her. Airplane, ship, and land also. It is thought-full of Father. I'm going to have it framed. Again a Merry Christmas and a happy new year. I think it is about 7 x 11 inches.
All the Rawerts [*from Mother*]

Louisville, Kentucky, **December 23**, 11 pm

Dear Norb,

Well, tomorrow is the day before Christmas. What gifts we didn't get, money will answer. We sure did some work, that is, at night. If it wouldn't be for night work, I wouldn't collect much but the nights help me out. Something to be thankful for. Pop's raincoat fits very good. We are OK and haven't received your gift as yet. I called the Post Office tonite and they told me it was doubtful if we get it before Christmas and that they would send a tracer after it after Christmas. Alma received her gift Monday so I suppose we'll just have to wait. And you explained it in your letter what it was. Your Signal Corps typewritten letter was very newsy, very neat. It seems those capital letters are harder to read.

Well, Norb I hope to be able to do better in a future letter, so I will close with much love from all. If your gift isn't loaded for delivery tomorrow, we will not receive it before Christmas so we'll keep hoping and let you know.

Goodnite,

H.R.

December 24, 30 degrees, cloudy

Dear Norb

Just a few hours, then we will be at Elizabeth's. The children are very anxious to know what they are going to get. John was here last night only a few minutes. He asked me what I wanted. I told him he could not give me that. I meant that I would want to see you on Christmas. I was to confession and Communion this morning at 6:15 Mass. I offered it up for you for certain intention [*that Norb goes to the Sacraments*]. Alma is coming this evening. I guess she will go to St. Elizabeth' with us, I think. A Merry time very few can have [*she could not say Merry Christmas, because it was a very sad time for her*].

Mother

Louisville, Kentucky, **December 24**, Christmas Eve, 7 pm

Dear Norb,

We sent you a night letter [*telegram*] to reach you Christmas morn. Hope you received it. She was going to make it sound very Christmasy but no Christmas greetings went over the wire this year, at least not in a night letter. So we are thinking of you tonite.

We are going to Lip's as usual. Will write everything later on about gifts, etc. We are all OK. Your typewritten letter was swell. Do it more often, honey. Our tree really does look nice. We invested in several dollars' worth of ornaments so it shows up fine.

Junior Russell was made a Petty Officer 3rd Class. I thought that was fine. He's still in the infirmary. I guess that's a rating as a Corporal or Sergeant, don't you think. Yeh, Pop still battles it out with the Sisters but not so much lately. Will write more later on. XXX. That's for Christmas and a finger wave for New Year.

Love and real hugs from,

H.R.

Camp Crowder, Missouri, **December 24**

Sober State. Xmas Eve. Would Like a Drink

Dear Mom and All,

This is Xmas Eve. They have a little party for us over at our mess hall. Just beer and sandwiches. I think I will drop over for a few minutes. I want to get back early so I can get to early Mass in the morning.

The Christmas music really sounds beautiful, doesn't it? Well, I hope all of you have a

nice Xmas and I hope by next Xmas I can get a furlough ma[y]be. Put an extra light on the tree for me and I'll be seeing you, I hope. I hope you have received your present by this time Wishing you a Happy New Year!
Norb

Camp Crowder, Missouri, **December 25,** 11:20 am
Dear Mom, Pop and All,

Ah! It's Xmas morning and the sun is shining bright. It is not a white Christmas and now I'm going to do my duty as a soldier and see how the chow is coming along. As I understand it, we are going to have a very delicious dinner. I believe you received the menu in a letter from the company commander. I haven't had any breakfast yet so I believe I can keep up with the best chowhounds that's in this Army. And there are quite a few.

We did have a couple barrels of beer last night but it didn't last very long. We have quite a few beer drinkers in the Army also.

There doesn't seem to be quite as much Xmas on the radio as there usually is or was. They have land speakers about a half mile, and you can hear the Xmas carol's drift across. It sounds pretty nice. Well, my shoes need a shining and I must wash out some socks so I guess... [*Following pages are missing from envelope*].
Norb

Louisville, Kentucky, **December 25,** Christmas 1942
Dear Norb,

It is 8:30 o'clock. Pop just got home with a growler of beer. He had to take Russell home. Pop followed him home and he fell, so one of the Huelsman's helped Pop. He had bottled beer to pack [*carry*] but none broke. That's awful on Christmas Day. Alma [*17 years* old] is sitting at the table and drinking beer with us.

Suke Heitzman [*and*] Lawrence Johnson are home on a furlough. Herald Shanks is home on furlough and is going to get married.

I got a coat from Mary, money from Marge, a dresser scarf from Joe and Ann, shoes from Hermina, a slip from Elizabeth and a what farty [*sp*] shot at from Pop - ha, ha. Never received the clock yet. Just so it ain't broke when it comes here. I hope you had it insured. Somebody stole [*burgularized*] Butler's Bar and he never had no insurance on it for all the money he earns. You wrote some time ago about you washing your clothes. Did you mean that if you want me to wash and iron them? It never come to my mind again to ask you about it. We thought of you and talked of you a lot on Christmas wondering how you enjoyed your dinner Christmas. It was drizzling rain all day.

You are getting a lot of letters today. I hope you can read them. Did you get the night letter and Alma's telegram? We could not write Merry Christmas. That is a greeting and not allowed, so we had to do the best we could without the greeting. That's all I know so goodbye and be good. God bless you. Little Mary said hello.

I hope my prayers are granted.

Mother

And more Christmas letters and notes from Norb's sister Hermina and Norb's Muth nieces and nephews follow.

Dear Norb,

Well, I have a lot of news but I had to say "how do you do" on Christmas. These few lines will have to answer for today, but I promise you a long one for tomorrow. Let us know what Christmas was like in the Camp from the time you opened your eyes until the time you closed them. Russel is really full of the yuletide spirit and I just came from there. He's on a fighting drunk!

Love from your sister,

Hermina

Dear Norb,

I got an electric iron for Christmas and a doll that looks like a real baby, and an ironing board. Did you have a happy Christmas? I hope you did. We had turkey and all the trimmins.

Happy New Year Norb,

Betsy Jean

Dear Norb,

Santa was good to me. Thanks for your dollar. I am going to get some clothes for that. Thanks Norb.

Your Godchild,

Katsy

Dear Norb,

I am sorry that I didn't write to you sooner. I just forgot to write. I told you about my soldier. I heard that one of the Schott boys got your name. There are 14 Schott kids and I don't know which one got your name. Well, I have to close for now. I hope you had a Merry Christmas and I hope you will have a Happy New Year.

Just as always,

Jimmy

Dear Norb:

I am dumb as ever. I got to [two] flunking notes, 67 & 64, and I think I am going to flunk. Alma and us are playing cards right now. And I wish you would give me a few lessons in how to study and Hog [*Hermina*] is playing cards with us too. And Katsy sure was glad to have a dollar. Jimmy said that she was so happy that she pretty near shit in her pants. And

that is all I can think of right now. And Good-bye first class private. If I was in the Army, I would be a General. Ha-Ha.
Milton the fart

Dear Uncle Norbe,

I hope you had a Merry Christmas and I also wish you a happy New Year. I would have wrote sooner but always forget. We are playing cards now so I will close now so until I write again, I will remain you're A-1 Girl Friend.
Shirley

Louisville, Kentucky, **December 26**, 6:45 pm
Dear Norb,

Well, Norb I will give you an account of Christmas Day but first I will tell you we were at Blue River Inn in White Clouds, Indiana. The Hubbuch bunch was there today. I went to the 10 o'clock Mass Christmas. Mom, Marge went to 4:20 stayed for Solemn High [Mass] that followed. The church looked beautiful. The altar was really something. Shirley sang at 10 o'clock. Jimmy was torchbearer.

I stopped at Russell's from church, came home a little too late for dinner, but I got in time to get me grub. Lip etc. was here in the afternoon for supper. Katsy took her dittus [*dishes*] from Ann to see and she was so pleased with that dollar you sent. "Oh, Mother" she said, "I can't have all that money. I nedur [*never*] had that much money." She said, "Oh, Mother it even mells [*smells*] like Norbie." That's something. We had chicken etc. for Christmas. We are all OK.

We, or rather, Pop received the cigars you sent today but we haven't received the ship lamp/clock as yet. [*It always sat on the buffet in the dining room at 1344 Texas Street and spiked my curiosity as I dusted it*] If you had that insured you should see about it.

Now about the trip to White Clouds. First came all the drink you wanted, then country ham, baked chicken and everything that went with it. It was delicious, and the guy that owns that place is really a nut. After dinner we went in the bar-room, dished out more drinks, so he said excuse me folks but I have to take my music lessons, so Mitch said what kind of instrument do you play and let us hear you. He said I play a zither, so he came out with his zither. Norb, it was a fountain syringe with an extra hose that he had rigged up and put around his neck. He got a couple extra tunes out of it. I'm telling you, we all looked at each other and busted out loud. He's really a clown. Mom is calling us to supper now. I will write about gifts tomorrow.
Love from Hermina

Continued, **December 26**, 10:30 pm
I never finished on the other page and I have a little time. Pop had to help Russell home last night. He fell, so Bill and Pop took him home. Tonite at 11:35, we are going to the 7th

Street Station to see Maurice Slattery, to tell him hello and goodbye. He came last nite and leaves today. Moody got drunk yesterday. Joe said he's still drinking today. Pop went for a shock of beer now and had the pleasure of getting Russell from the middle of Ash Street. He was taking in the sidewalks and the street. Joe is feeling them tonite, is on a 'funny' drunk. He's doing the rhumba, dancing with Mom and laughing all the time. He's really all mouth and the funniest I ever seen him. He held me in his lap, wants everybody to make over him. He's really a scream, the biggest laugh in a year. Bye, Norb, I wish you were here to enjoy him, boy what a man.

Louisville, Kentucky, **December 27**, Sunday, 7:30 pm

Dear Norb,

Can't feel like today is Sunday at all. We are going over to Joe's after-while but we have to bring an additional chair along. Alma has been here since Christmas Eve. Sure seems like one of the family - almost like a little sister. We went to White Clouds yesterday. As I told you when we came home, she [*Mom*] had every room in the house cleaned up and it really looked swell. Housework is her hobby, she said. What a hobby. It is a hobby a husband should appreciate.

Lavern's husband, George Heitkemper, is in Kodiak, Alaska. He called her the day he got word they were moving. The call just cost $23.50 . Her telephone bill was $65.34 [*$1,017 buying power in 2017*] this month - with $5.00 for business phone & the rest from her husband. What a husband.

Two strings of lights went out already. Milton is more interested in the gifts he gave than the ones he received. He had $5.00 to spend so Lip got a Last Supper plaque, Moody an 11-cent tie clasp & two hankies, Shirley a Lady Ester make-up kit, Jimmy a toy. Betsy and Katsy a baking set together, Margie a doll. Really, it was cute in him.

For Christmas, I got a purse from Alma. She left $1.98 price tag in it [*Alma was always been known to get things on a good sale and then leave the tag in to make the receiver think she had paid full price*]. I got a kick out of that. A make-up set for Marge and I from Lip and the kids. A beautiful pair of kid gloves from Lill; she was my Christmas Pie at work. A globe from Ann and Joe. Nothing from Maw and Paw as yet. I always have my doubts when they pass up Christmas Day. Tee Hee. Mom's got her Sunday night patching job to do so we are waiting to go to Joe's.

Well, Norb I'm going to close now. Alma and I are going to Joe's and let the pokies come later. We haven't see Johnny etc. as yet but I guess New Year's Eve is their time. Lou and Norbert. [*Holkamp*] were over last night with a "Happy New Year" as they entered. Larny Johnson was here yesterday. I never seen him. Boo hoo. Goodnite. I'm as bad with this letter as I am when I get started talking. You know how dat iss [*Plattdeutsch for das ist, or that is*].

Love,

Horse

Camp Crowder, Missouri, **December 27**

Dear Mom and all,

Well, I received a letter from you all today, and I received your telegram Xmas day at about 12:00 noon. I wrote to Gold Tone Studios where I had my pictures taken in Kansas City. They will be all paid for except the postage. That is if I get them. I told them to mail the pictures to you, so if they do arrive, there might be postage due. One is for home and the other I promised to Alma. They will both be the same I guess.

I hope you all had a nice Xmas with a lot of spirits. I had six bottles of beer myself so my spirits were lifted. I received another box from Park and Tilford. It was like the first one only it had two cartons of Cigs in it.

Well, this letter is short and sweet but that's all I know for now so I'll be seeing you. Enclosed you will find my diploma from the Bell Telephone School. I never had anything to send it home in before so I thought it would be a good time to send it.

With love,

Norb

Southwestern Bell Telephone Certificate of Completion of the Telephone
Substation Installation and Maintenance Course, dated November 21, 1942

Louisville, Kentucky, **December 28**, Monday morning, 8:30 pm

Dear Norb,

This is to let you know that we haven't received your gift as yet. I called the General Delivery this morning. They asked me to call back tomorrow, for two [*train*] car loads of packages were sidetracked in Cincinnati, Ohio in order to give room to the troops coming thru. So it's a possibility we might receive yours today. Here's hoping. We was at Joe's last night. They treated us really, really nice. Hope you are well. I guess you're hard at work again.

Marge likes your typewritten letters. You beat [*type*] out more kisses. We have just received your letter from Christmas Day, short but very sweet. We didn't have a white Christmas either. I bet that was beautiful to hear the carols floating thru the air.

Russell is on a special diet - three cokes and a can of tomatoes. He never was any drunker, but he feels bad after this one. Is working tho. Mom wants to write so I'll say au Revoir.

Love from you dear sister,

H.R.

Louisville, Kentucky, **December 28**, 2:15 pm, 30 degrees, raining

Dear Norb,

We received your letters. The best and most looked for I ever received, if it means that you received the Sacraments at Christmas. I took it for granted that the way you said you did your <u>Christian duty</u>. I hope that I understood it [*right*]. If I did, then say in your letter 'yes Katie yes.' I [*will*] know then for sure. I could of cried for joy. Then I thought you meant going to Mass, so let me know please. I sure went for you -that is, offered up the Holy Communion and Mass.

Norb, could you give me the name and address of the photographer? Maybe Hermina could write to them. Nothing like trying where you had your pictures made. Johnson was here about 1 hour. Said he wanted to tell Joe goodbye but he never came back Sunday. I surely liked those letters. Norb, did you get your nite letter from us and Alma's telegram Christmas morning? Kiss from Mary. Will let you know as soon as we can when we get the box?

Mother

Louisville, Kentucky, **December 28**, Monday, 10:30 pm

Dear Norb,

I'm getting this letter ready for tomorrow, but I found out a little news, so I thought I'd put it down while it's fresh in my mind. Bobby Lee was rejected on account of his age; he's past 38 years or is 38. She [*his mom*] certainly was happy.

George Schultz is going across. He wrote stating that he thought that he was getting a furlough but he didn't. They are pulling out. He said they were issued very lightweight underwear and short trousers. He feels he's Africa bound.

Last night at Joe's, Ann and Alma sat beside Pop and made over him, and did he get red. That was a $1,000,000 blush. It was deep rose. So I guess you get your pretty blush from your father's side. I read Pop those letters you wrote. He was very tearful over them. And can he lay smokescreens now. Joe gave him a box [*of cigars*] as did Marge and you. Boy oh boy.

I see where the Navy will not release the men over 38 - that's what the newscaster said tonite - because they are all volunteer men. Marge and I went down to Lip's tonite. It still sounds like a Jew school - everybody talks at once. Mom got a chenille robe from Mary - rose colored. It's really very pretty. Marge got a loose powder compact and lipstick set from Lill. It's pretty. Mom got a Pyrex set from Lill, a slip from Lip, pair of hose from Alma, a dresser scarf from Joe and Ann. So far, Johnny hasn't been in. Let us hear how you enjoyed your Christmas dinner and stay at Camp that day.

Goodnite dear, goodnite,

H.R.

Louisville, Kentucky, **December 29**, Tuesday Morning, 9:30

[*Dear Norb*]

Well, it's raining again today. It rained some Saturday and rained steadily for about 5 hours Sunday, off and on yesterday and it's really raining today. It reminds you of the 1937 flood. What I am going to write isn't none of my business, I realize that, but Alma told us you were giving up cigarettes after you received her cigarette case and lighter. [*Unfortunately, Norb did not give up cigarettes until too late in life*]. You wrote her that. Well, Norb I know she gave a good price for that because she had the box insured for $20.00. I told her to write you and tell you to send it back. She could get you something else in return, but she will not ask you. She said maybe you won't get any use out of it, but that you should ask her to exchange it for you. Well, I don't feel that way about it, I think it's in her place to make the offer. What do you think? I imagine she could get a fitted case or something more useful than a cigarette lighter. It keeps raining all the time.

Did you send your pen away yet? The Kentucky Pen Shop had an advertisement in the paper that for any make of pen, a new point is replaced for 50¢ guaranteed. I don't know if you received that letter where I told you I would take care of it for you. Amen. Alleluia.

Lovingly, your sister,

Hermina

Louisville, Kentucky, **December 30**, Wednesday, 2 o'clock

[*Dear Norb*]

I received that beautiful pillar [*pillow*] and many thanks, it surprised me and your diploma and all letters came in good order this morning, Wensday [*sic*] and many thanks again. Alma called us up and wanted to know if we got your presents. She said she received 3 letters. She is alright. Oh, I guess you know that better than I do. I asked Cousin Mary Rawert, Francis and Wilhelmina [*Heitkemper*] to come for supper Sunday. They are coming. Mary often asks about you. Mrs. Lee asked about you also. Mr. Lee was exempted on account of his age. She sure was happy, and so was he. He did not like to go. She said you never feel the sting till you have a dear one to leave. She asked for your address. Bobby [*Lee*] wanted to write to you. I hope you can find time to thank those that send you a gift, if it is only a plain card. Did Dora Hollenkamp write to you? Or Anna Heitkemper [*Norb's godmother*]? You never said anything to us. We all wish you a happy and better New Year. God bless you,

Hermina, Marge, Mother and Pop

(He is in his glory and in the ashes. Three boxes of cigars!)

Little Mary says hello. Happy New Year.

Louisville, Kentucky, **December 30,** Wednesday, 9:00 pm

Dear Norb,

Well, your pillow top sure does look nice. We have a pillow that just fits it. Jr [*Russell*] sent a lamp, a very novel one made from large and small seashells. It is really pretty. It was very late in coming too. If we don't hear any better results tomorrow from the post office, we'll let you know. Amshoff, the man that owns that grocery at Hickory and Burnett? Well, he's called to the Army. [The Amshoff family is related to the Rawert family.].

I'm going to cut a piece out of the paper for you. It wasn't necessary for you to say you stayed sober. Even the Associated Press advertised how sober Camp Crowder men were. It has ceased raining and it is a relief. I guess you noticed that I finished the letter today. Little Mary says hello and happy New Year. Well, Mom answered the door and she wanted Mary to take the letter with her. We are all OK.

Louisville, Kentucky, **December 31ˢᵗ**, Thursday, Weather fine, 40°

Dear Norb,

Well, [*this is*] the last time that I'm going to write to you this year. Hope and pray that next year will be a better and happier than the year 1942. So God wills it.

The more I look at the pillow the better I like it. John and family are coming over tonight and going to sleep here, going to early Mass. Junior Russell sent his mother a lamp made out of shells. It has lights on it. It's very pretty. She brought it over to us last night. The banks are not closing tomorrow. Mary is mad about it but the stores are closing. Hoping that you will stay sober New Years as you did Christmas! I will close now with the best wishes and <u>God's blessings always</u>. Remember us all in your prayers as we do for you.

As ever, Love,

Mother

Louisville, Kentucky, **December 31**, 4:55 pm

Dear Norb,

This is to inform you that we have just received your radio clock. Mom was in town when it came at 4:10 pm so we just opened it up. Mom and I think it is just beautiful, it has a face exactly like our kitchen electric, which is a Sessions clock, too. Your clock is an eight-day clock. Mom said she prefers that to an electric because it really looks good on the radio and just fits it, too. Now we'll have correct time any place we go. It's already ticking off. Thanks a million Norb. It really is something. Ornamental, as well as very, very useful. I got a V-Mail letter from Bill Hollkamp. He still doesn't mention the Christmas gift we sent him October 28th so I suppose he hasn't received it as yet.

Did you hear the doorbell ring? Well, Alma just came and is now admiring your clock and pillow top. I'm telling you, Mom was so thrilled with that pillow top and now the clock. You got your Maw in circles. Many, many thanks Norb. Alma is going to write a few lines. Hoping the New Year will be a happier one to live in, and peace alone can bring it. Wishing the best there is this side of heaven.

As always, your sister,

Horse

Continued by Alma Pierce:

Well, honey, I thought I would write you a few lines. The clock you sent Mom is really a beauty. The pillow top is real pretty too, Norb. I'm going to a formal with Mom and Dad tonight. I would like to be going with you instead, but it's impossible. We'll be spending next New Year's together I'm sure. Honey, I can't send you much love in this letter because your mother will be looking at it. Well, I guess I'll close for now and I'll write to you afterwhile [*sic*]

[*Alma*]

Chapter 2

1943

Louisville, Kentucky, **January 1**, 6:45 pm, Happy New Year!

Dear Norb,

Well, this is New Year's Day. I'm taking this afternoon off by writing letters. Your clock really looks fine. We've got it on the buffet for fear of it being knocked off the radio. I wrote Anna Heitkemper. She asked for your address. Johnny etc. is still here. They came yesterday and stayed all night. Eleanor said she is going to write you in a few days. I wrote Bill Hollkamp too. Mom wants to write to you too, but it is nearly 7 o'clock and they pick up the mail then. Father Spoelker is here [*at home in Louisville*] for a 3-day visit before he is sent to Arkansas we heard. Mary [Holkamp] had to work today and she is mad at Governor Johnson. It's so much noise right now I can't hardly think straight.

Jr Russell sent his picture and it isn't anything like him. We are all OK. Had Guinee [*sic*] for dinner. It tastes a lot like chicken. Mom is waiting to take this to the mailbox. So Toodle Loo until tomorrow.

Hermina Rawert

Camp Crowder, Missouri, **January 1**

Dear Mom and all,

Well, today is New Year's Day but we had to work just the same but we did have a darn good dinner. We had chicken and everything. The chow has been much better the last couple of weeks. Haven't had cold fried eggs for breakfast for a long time.

I had that package insured so I guess if anything happens to it, I will send another just like it. I think I told you about it the other night. At least they told me it was insured so I guess it is.

It was a swell day here today, in fact, it was just like spring. It was warm enough to run around in your shirtsleeves. It's so darn damp here though. Well, it's been raining quite a bit but we haven't had any snow to amount to anything as yet. No I haven't received no box from Lip yet but I haven't been to mail call for two days so that may be the reason. Well, that's about all I know until tomorrow. Busy as hell! So goodnight and I'll be seeing you.

As Always,

Norb

Louisville, Kentucky, **January 2**, 7:23 pm by your clock

Dear Norb,

We received your letter this morning. As you know by this time, we received your clock and it keeps good time. Mom got Donaldson [*baker*] to come in and admire it, also the pillow top. He said "Vell, Mrs. Rawert. I tink [*sic*] Norb did very good for a boy in the army." Everybody gets to see it, let me tell you, Mom wants to write, but at present she is in dreamland. It doesn't take her long to kick off. The river is still rising & the crest will be reached Tuesday. Yesterday a machine could hardly get through at 4th and River Street. Lip was there. Johnny said they are fixing to open up the floodgates on Upper River Road and use that flood road. Well, we haven't had any rain for several days and that's good. The creek is still flowing. The paper states there will not be very great inconveniences.

We are expecting Alma tonite. She called me up and said she was having trouble with her eye again. She said about 3 weeks ago she couldn't make out the picture at the show so had to leave. She told me today she couldn't make out the funnies. She don't take care of her eyes the way she should. The reason for writing you this is because I thought your words could make her do it especially if they are put up in the Charles Boyer style. Perhaps I'd better send you a ½ pint then you really could put up the most beautiful words this side of heaven.

Well, the tree is still up. That's long for us to have a tree up but Frances & Mary Rawert is coming over tomorrow. Johnny, Eleanor, and kiddoes left this morning at 5 o'clock. Boy, oh boy were they so cute. Mom was fixing breakfast yesterday & she said I don't know if you all will like what I have here. You might get something different to eat for breakfast. Hilary said in an assuring way, "Well, Mommy, you put on the table what you got and we will pick out what we like." That wasn't bad.

We are OK. Johnny bought Pop a box of cigars for Christmas. I think he has half of them smoked already. Mom missed one thing this Christmas. You know that beggar that was lame on one side and couldn't talk? Well, he hasn't showed up for about a month but you know we had quite a bit of snow but the weather has been OK since then, so she is wondering if he is dead. Robert Lee Robben is in the Infirmary ever since he's been in the Army almost. He's been having abscesses in his ear and so he isn't doing anything but staying in bed. Raymond Robben leaves Tuesday for the Army.

Lee, Lip, and girls are here tonite. Moody [*Leo*] dressed Margie and my, what she looks like. Mom just got up now. She asked to write you about thank you cards. Quite a few people who remembered the boys are receiving thank you cards from them. And how many did you want? They are not expensive and we will send them to you. Mom said she thinks you should, since you couldn't send Christmas cards. End of quotation. Well, I'm bringing this letter to a close. Hoping you are well and we must say you certainly have been like the NRA. You did your part around Christmas. Mrs. Russell called long distance to Jr Last night. It was his birthday, you know. That was swell in Park and Tilford sending another box wasn't it? The Muths are going to their Uncle [*Rudy*] and Aunt on Manslick Road. The newlyweds are doing just fine and a turkey dinner is in store for them. Tain't bad.

Well, goodnite my dear brother, goodnite. And keep on plunking a typewriter.
H.R.

Camp Crowder, Missouri, **January 2**
Dear Mom and all,

Well, I received your letter saying you received my present. Well, it don't sound quite right to me. In the first place, it was supposed to be an electric clock. The name on it was Yankee clipper and it had chrome sails. I think ma[*y*]be something is wrong if it is not right. I'm sure in the hell going to find out about it. They might have sent something cheaper than what I paid for. I don't like to tell people what I pay for stuff but I paid $18.50 for it and I just want to know if you want the one that they were supposed to ship or not. I trust some of these storekeepers as far as I can throw a house and that ain't very far.

I was just wondering if the water is getting any higher by now. A flood wouldn't go so well now. I just received a letter from Lip today and said that Wafzig and a couple of Geperts were home for Xmas. I was just wondering where they are stationed. They must be pretty close to home no doubt.

Yes, Camp Crowder is a pretty sober camp. You don't see so many drunks. They don't lock you up when you're drunk unless you cause trouble or get smart with an MP. Of course, I don't know that from actual experience. Tonight is Saturday and I haven't been off from work very long and I have to get cleaned up and take a shower and stuff. Well, there is not very much to write about tonight so I hope this letter finds you all well, fat and happy.
As Always,
Norb V...-

Louisville, Kentucky, **January 3**
Dear, Dear Norb,

Pop said he was drunk. He said he did not care what I would write. Well, we had two growlers of beer, 40¢ each. Mary Rawert & Frances were here. We had a very nice time. Alma came also after work. We were just eating supper. First time we had them here for a meal since we lived here. Ain't that a shame? I happened to yawn about 10 o'clock and then Mary jumped up to go home. But she stayed a while longer. Joe [*and*] Ann took them home. It is windy and getting colder. That's all I know and good night.
God bless you,
Mother

Continued by Margaret:

It's 15 minutes of 12 o'clock. Some Katie! [*Mom*]. She sure ate a good supper and at 11 o'clock another cup of milk and now she's going to bed. Doing pretty good for herself. Her stomach is acting real good today. I'm feeling fine.

Continued by Pop:

Had two big cans of beer. Your clock says bedtime. Your cigars are so good that [the] box is empty by now.

Continued by Hermina, 10:45 pm:

Dear Norb,

How do you like Pop's letter? Spelling isn't so good. I said you sure would answer on that. Pop's feeling his beer. He got two cans [pails] and dished it out so he didn't lose out. We all had a very nice time tonite. Mom never had much beer but she put her head back and yawned so loud we all roared laughing. Mom blushed. We had baked hen and the trimmin's. Mom told Marge to write something dumb - write all about Pop. Marge said she would write about her then. Marge is talkative too - Oertel's '92. Wonder what I would do with Oertel's in me? Maybe my speaker would crack up.

Well, until I can write a real letter,

Little Horse

Continued by Marge:

Hi Norb,

Nothing little about Horse. She ate ½ chicken, 2 potatoes, ½ bowl of salad and 2 hot buns, cranberries, etc. [*and is*] still hungry. Cousin Mary Rawert and Frances were asking all about you and they really enjoyed themselves today. Pop was so glad they came over and Joseph took them home. [*Mary Rawert was Pop's first cousin*]. Real sweet of Joe. Joey was not at work yesterday. I guess Wahoo must of went along. Well, you sure sent a beautiful clock. Thanks loads. I like it very much and I just think you're grand.

The wind is rough tonight and it's 11:30. It's getting colder temp, was 56° today and now 34°. Quite a difference. Mrs. Kipperick [*sp*] was to see Mary and she was at three Masses today. Well, Norb, I'm still tired of the Christmas rush and all we did during the holidays was entertain at home. Only place I was at was the Blue River Inn when Mr. Hubbuch took us. I sure do like that dinner. Well, this is all for now.

God bless you and pray for me,

Margaret

Louisville, Kentucky, **January 4**, Monday, 9:10 pm

Dear Norb,

Well, the weather is a heap lot colder, a heap lot. The Christmas tree is no more. I took it down tonite. It was real purty. Earl Johnson isn't home as yet, you know he expected a furlough the 21ˢᵗ of December. Well, maybe you'll be fortunate enough to come when he gets here. Alma went to the eye doctor. She called up, said she <u>must</u> wear glasses. We all thought so. She was too proud to wear them before. So you had your helmet issued to you. Well, Alma was telling me. So far we hadn't heard of Beal California, where Alma says you are going on maneuvers. I looked it up in the Atlas. I cannot find Beal but found Bell, Calif. I suppose it won't be long now and you'll be on maneuvers. Let us know something about it or perhaps a letter is on the way. The Bowman Field Show has just come on. They are now playing "I'm wacky for a WAAC, dippy for a WAVE. Nutty for a nurse, so tell me what can I do?" It's pretty cute. Jr Russell thinks he'll get a leave in Feb., also.

Waited 40 minutes for a streetcar and brother was it cold. And now the meat proposition. Well, it won't be long now and Schieman's will have some. Last week all the meat he had was rabbit and a little sausage. Best had some hamburger. So now, I like hamburger. Jimmy Doerr, in the latter part of the week had tuna fish sandwiches - no sausage, no meatloaf. Hamburger isn't hamburger anymore. It's ground beef. Hamburger really feels big now. Joe said a guy from Fischer's [*local meat packing company*] says they are killing the January quota so I get my appetite up for a good young steak. Ice cream will be cut 50%. I seen the heading in tonight's paper saying at the time of Pearl Harbor they were trying to kidnap our President.

The river situation here is very favorable, but you ought to hear the rumors out. We are thankful for the cold weather, but Florence Paul told Marge she heard they told the officials at the State Fair Grounds to clear out all the tires, as the river was getting worse than in the 1937 flood. All tires are being stored in State Fair Grounds. Sounds like Lee. Well, this is about all I know for sure. Goodnight, pleasant dreams,
Hermina

Louisville, Kentucky, **January 5**, Tuesday, 8 o'clock, 20° above

Dear Norb,

I don't know much news but I'll write the little I know. Gertie Bowe, that is Mrs. Meyer, got four boys in the Army. One is in Africa. She heard from him after three months silence. After Christmas, she got a letter from him [*saying*] that he was well. She was so glad to hear from him. Mary called her up today. When she got through talking Gertie talked to me. I do feel sorry for her. She takes it very hard to give up four boys.

Norb, do you know when you go on maneuvers? Norb, everybody likes the clock you sent. Of course, I show it to everybody. I am so glad that it is not electric. I can move it where I want to. Hermina had it on the radio. I put it on the bufay [*buffet*]. It looks better on there. Throws more light on it. The piller [*pillow*] is beautiful too. Papa got 4 boxes of cigars. Hermina brought Mrs. Lee your address. Mrs. Lee said that Bobby would send you sport news. Did you get a box from Anna Heitkemper as yet? Elizabeth and family want to see the young married couple Sunday. Rudy and Bell treated them swell. Elizabeth Said the house is furnished lovely. Jimmy got his tooth filled today. The doctor (Tully) made a nice job. The back of the tooth is gold, about 1/10 of an inch shows the gold.

I saw Ernie Schieman's picture. He looks stouter on the picture but Mrs. Schieman said he did not weigh any more. He is in Utah. He sure did some traveling. Never had a furlough yet. Your pictures have not come yet. Norb, Joe said he send you a letter with $2 in it but he did not receive no answer weather [*whether*] you got the letter or not. Elizabeth and Moody sent you a box also and haven't heard weather you got the box. If you can, just let them know or write to us and we will gladly let them know.

Papa and Moody are sitting at the kitchen table drinking beer. Well, Schieman had beef today. Never had beef I think in about a week. Could get pork. Some butchers did not even have that.

Today is January 5. We never received a letter Monday or Tuesday. I hope we will get one Wednesday. How are your feet? Have you got some Dr. Scholl's salve and powders yet? If you want some, let us know. May be a good idea before you go on maneuvers. Your feet might need it badly. Are you glad to go?

St. Elizabeth's are going to have a mission in February. Are you going?

Well, I guess I will close for it is getting late. I hope that you are well and happy. We are well, fat and sassy, ha ha. Little Mary said hello. Good night and good luck. It is 9:40 now. God bless you,
Mother

Louisville, Kentucky, **January 5**, 9:50 pm

Dear Norb or Wonderful Rawert,

Mom told me to read over her letter first. I did that and got a kick out of it, too. I know you do too. It taken me a couple hours to deliver your address to Mrs. Lee. We talked of, not about, everything. She told me Mr. Sheeran is not with Peter-Burghout. He is with the Jeffersonville Boat Works. He is in Safety, an instructor. I imagine he must have a nice job. His brother is in the Army, too. You know Mr. Sheeran taught first aid. I think that's how he got his job. Delores is taller than her mother. Herb Ever told her they were looking in the West End for a house to buy. Katie Reddicks got a wristwatch from the Mister next door. She gave him a beautiful ring. Sounds bad.

We are OK but we have been having cold weather, which we are thankful for. I hope you can call long distance before you go on maneuvers but if it can't be done, it can't be done.

I really am glad Mr. Lee was rejected. He said his boss told the men that in a short time men over 38 will be put on defense work. Mr. Lee said he has been making St. Anthony

Novenas for thirteen years. He failed when he was hit in the head last year by a ball. You remember. He said he didn't want to go to the Army but if he had to go, it was different. She said he wouldn't miss a novena for anything.

Mom told you Joe asked if you got his $2 he sent you Christmas. Lip asked tonite. Eleanor did New Year's Day. Well, "feel me once," I'll say goodnite, dear, goodnite.
Love,
H.R.

Camp Crowder, Missouri, **January 5**
Dear Mom and All,

Well, it seems as though the water is getting pretty high. Read about it in the papers here. I sure hope it doesn't get any higher. It will make fishing bad for my brother-in-law. The weather has been pretty good down here for the last couple of days. The sun's been out but the air is pretty cold. I received that box from the Muth's and in case I don't get to write, tell "her and them" I said thanks a million.
Yes, I would like to have some of those cards. I haven't had time to write but maybe I could scribble a few cards in a hurry. It seems as though Hermina will be a smoked "Porkie" if Pop makes good with all those cigars. We keep our gas masks in our barracks all the time but I was thinking about sending it home. Perhaps you could make better use of it. Well, my dear, dear people, I hope you are all well, fat and contented. So until I get a chance to scribble a few more lines, I remain
As Always,
Norb V...-

Louisville, Kentucky, **January 7**, Thursday, 8:05 pm, Your time is our time.
Dear Norb,

Well, I don't know much to write about but I do know that the Sessions 8-day kitchen clock is two dollars higher than a Sessions Electric kitchen clock. Joe and Ann were here for supper. We had 'moss' and it was very, very good. The weather still is cold here. Sheik Reem is still in Ft. Harrison depending on GI shoes to get away from there. He has Hellmann's trouble - big feet.

Lip was back at school today. The first graders had a physical examination and your godchild [Katsy] is in a very good condition. She has two baby teeth that needs filling. That's all that's wrong. Margie has a cold but is feeling better. Mom and I stayed there until Lip got back. Marge is busy patching her corsets and brassieres. Mom just came home from church Holy Hour and I'm writing to you. Which is the most necessary?

Mom's looking for a letter from you about this maneuver business. Maybe you didn't do so bad about the clock anyway. Perhaps tomorrow I can drum up more news for you. So for the time being I say goodnite dear, goodnite. Schieman's never had any meat today.

One lady got a little bacon to buy for supper. There's some changes been made since you left. An 18-year-old boy in Lip's neighborhood had received his 1-A classification already. Nite,

[*Hermina*]

Louisville, Kentucky, **January 8**, 9:15 pm

Plain wonderful,

Well, there still is changes being made. Beginning tomorrow, we will have a Saturday afternoon mail delivery. It is the first time since April 1931 due to lack of help and overabundance of mail. The mailmen will deliver Saturday afternoon and be paid time and a half for overtime. Kapfhammers have closed for the duration also due to the lack of help.

Through Lane Bryant, I got an offer to get a pair of nylon hose, and brother, that ain't hay. Well, we located "hard mett" sausage at Kunz's. It is 90¢ per pound. In your next box, you will receive some. If you slice it thin you'll be able to use them as poker chips. We are all well. Mom is patching Pop's coat. He's sleeping. Marge is reading the sales in the paper. Will say goodnite and sleep tight and maybe I can dig up a little more tomorrow. Last year at this time, it was 4 below zero. Do you remember, Challie?

Bye,

Hermina

Louisville, Kentucky, **January 8**, 10:30

Dear Norb,

Papa is 30 minutes late tonight. He had about 2 hours sleep - ain't bad. I was patching his pockets and lining in his coat. Don't you have some patching for me to do? Send them home and I will be at your service. I wound up your clock yesterday for the second time. It ticks very low. I like it very much. Little Margie was sick again. It was a very heavy cold and a bad cough. Her eyes look so weak. They were here tonight. Moody and Elizabeth had a carpet that they thought I would exchange for mine, a bed carpet, but it was too small and I like mine better and it is larger. I just had some beer. It is almost too cold. Today I bought a chuck roast for $1.10. It looks good to us now and will taste better than chicken. I tell you, beef goes like hotcakes.

We are expecting Miss Emma Grimm tomorrow, that is, Saturday to see Mr. Tanner that died; you know he was a dear old neighbor of hers. I think you know him also. His wife could not speak well, lived next to Niemann's. Frank Jr had to register. He told his mother that if he would have to go he would never come back. Sounds babyfied to me. He works at the L & N about 8 months. I guess he makes nice money. I think Alma is coming tomorrow. Her mother is going to the doctor with her. I guess you know she thinks she will have to wear glasses. I told her she would [*look*] more intelligent. Do you think so also? Do you know

when you will have to go on maneuvers? I want to finish my beer now and then go to sleep. Mary is just coming home and sends a sweet deer [*sic*] kiss. XXXXXXX
God bless you and good night,
Mother

Louisville, Kentucky, **January 9**, Friday Morning

Dear Norb,

Well, I dreamed of you last night. You were very plain in it too. I dreamed Joberson tore out the front and back of his store and the side was doing all the supporting. He had his junk laying out in Goss "St" so that the streetcars had to stop at Bert's. It was so much junk. He had 25 hams laying on the street and he discovered they were getting dirty so he had a toilet in his back room and he dips all those hams in there and takes them upstairs. Ann said to me poooeee I wouldn't want to eat them now. Ain't that something? So when I finish my noseying you were in the back there sweeping like everything. I said, "Norb I didn't know you were home." You said, "Well, I didn't get a Christmas furlough and I promised Larny I would help. I'm used to working so I got my furlough later." And you started sweeping like everything. You wasn't even glad to see me or to talk. Amen.

Mr. Tanner on Mulberry died yesterday, is laid out at Russmann's [*Funeral Home on Goss Avenue*]. We just heard it this morning. I seen him Christmas Day. We are OK. It is rather crisp this morning. Oh yeah, Pop and the Sisters had it. That is, she asked Pop to clean up the classroom as the Superior of the Order was coming thru. Pop said he didn't answer her but he dood [*sic*] it. I don't know exactly what you would call that. The cook left there. Fr. Henry's cook is there. She took Pop.
Goodbye, good luck and God bless you. Good day Norbert, good day.
H.R.

Camp Crowder, Missouri, **January 9**

Dear Mom and all,

From the looks of some of the papers around here, it looks as though the weather was pretty high in some spots, especially through Ohio, but without any more rain. I guess by the time this letter reaches you it will be about down to normal.

I think I will quit worrying about that clock and let clock be clock. You can always expect a gyp when you go to any of these fly shit towns around here. I was glancing through the want ads in the St. Louis Globe just to see how scarce labor was and I came across this clipping that you will find in this letter. It's about the best and dumbest I believe I have ever seen in any paper.

I can see where Pop is beginning to censor Alma's letters. I seen that big 'OK' on there so I guess he thinks they're alright but he hasn't seen the best ones. I suppose since Pop has four boxes of cigars it will be unnecessary for the "termiter" to make his annual inspection.

Maybe that's what killed some of my goldfish, ha ha. By the way, how many of my goldfish are left yet? Still the same three?

Yes, I believe I have all my packages by now. I also got the one from Joe, Johnny and the box from the Muth family. I haven't had time to write them all, so I just didn't write to any of them as yet, but you can tell them for me that all is well and thanks a lot.

Starting Monday things are going to start busting loose around here I think. I don't really know, but that is what I think.

I think I told you I got a letter from Red Johnson. I worked at the Motor Pool til 1:00 am the other day, or night, if you wish. This outfit is beginning to get on the beam. The weather was fine today, only it was cold outside but the sun was out.

Did you ever hear from that studio where I had my picture taken in Kansas City? I really don't expect to hear from them myself. Well, I guess that's all for now but I'll see you later.
As Always,
Norb

Camp Crowder, Missouri, **January 10**

Mom and all,

Well, I was rather surprised the other day when I got that letter. It was kind a funny and then again it wasn't so funny. I'm talking about that war bond. It seems as though I'm getting credit when credit is not due. But if you regard it as a Xmas present, that's just fine. You see, I'll tell you how it is. They take $6.25 out of my pay every month for war bonds. These are sent to the 'beneficiary' or in case I kick the bucket, you will be able to cash them. If you will notice on that paper I gave you, that you put in an envelope when I was home, you will find the paper on which I made out my bond allotment. I hated to break up such beautiful thoughts but face the facts. And I thought I would explain the meaning of the whole thing. Pardon please!

It's warm here tonight and we can get passes so I think I'll take off to Columbia and get me a chicken snack, late snack, because we never had much for chow tonight. Still in the dark about when we're pulling out so I couldn't really say. Well, I'm glad everything is running along smoothly. Things are running pretty smooth here also. Well, I have to get dressed to go in town. Might take in a show. I don't know. Well, so long. I'll be seeing you.
As Always,
Norb

Louisville, Kentucky, **January 10**, Sunday, 10 pm

Dear "Feel Me Once,"

Well, we seen your pictures you sent Alma. They look like you are very cold or else like trouble you had when you were younger and had to shuffle your feet or else. It is colder here, too, but we are as warm as Mom's burnt toast. We, that is, Pop and I took Alma for a dime. We played 500 Rum. Pop won one game and so did I.

Mom seen Duke Heitzman going to church this morning. She said gee, but you look fine and he thanked her so politely. Military courtesy, I presume. I think these pictures look like you but think they are better of the other fellow or is he just better looking?

Shirley bought her first lipstick. Betsy was with her and she told Betsy not to tell Mother. The girl, a schoolmate of hers, was going to the show and she wears lipstick, so Shirley had to follow the leader. Say, how about a little news in a letter or are you lost for words? Is Perry and Rogers still with you?

Cousin Mary and Frances liked Alma very much. At least Mary says so. Alma's got a wacky idea, that is, she wants to join the WAAC. We are listening to the Church of God. It is just the same as usual. They are singing a new song and are clapping. We all thought of you when this came on.

Your last letter was dated "Dec. 5, 1942." Did you know you were in the year 1943 and the month of January? Busy man, eh?

Will finish tomorrow nite.

Smoked Pig

Norb in overcoat at Camp Crowder, Missouri, January 1943

Louisville, Kentucky, **January 10,** Route 6, Louisville, Sunday pm

Dear Norbie,

It's now almost 9:00 but if I don't write to you at night, there's no chance during the day with the eight little hands grabbing my pen, paper, etc. So I now have their faces clean and their pajamas donned so I'm hoping the four little frisky birds will close their heavy eyes for tonight pretty soon. Sometimes they won't give up and go to bed until we just make them regardless of how sleepy they get. They sure keep me busy - gosh sometimes I could pull my hair out with them, then another time I could love them to death. All goes in life anyway, doesn't it? Guess I'm just as well off (better than I think) here doing housework and tending babies, as I would be doing anything so I'm very well satisfied with life. In fact, rather happy to be married to your good looking, as well as good-natured, brother and with these four little brats - should I call them?

Oh, well! I know my letter won't seem a bit interesting to you talking about myself so suppose I speak of something more interesting to you! How is the "brown eyed beauty" and boy won't those pies she is learning to bake now taste good to us when we come to visit you two in your apartment, cottage, bungalow, mansion or shanty-whatever it may be. Anyway, it'll be "Your Blue Heaven" or did you say, "Don't count chickens before they hatch?"

How do you like Army life by now? I don't believe I'd like it all if it were me but I'm happy you're no farther than Camp Crowder and hope you soon get a furlough.

Johnny still works every day [*milkman*] and don't get a day off very often. We spent New Year's Eve and day with Mom, Pop, Marge and Hermina. They got lots of nice things for Xmas as well as myself. I got a pretty chenille robe and bedspread I valued the most.

How is the weather there? It's pretty cold here today - snowed this morning. We are very well satisfied at this place now, considering we have the five rooms, big yard, etc. and rather reasonable rent, so have decided to stay another year anyway. Would love to save up a good size down payment and buy a home but guess that "dream" would be too swell to be true. We really are making New Year resolutions to that effort.

Johnny's got a pint of pretty good stuff for Xmas from a customer and I had been kinda saving it along but he got in to it and guzzled down a little a while ago. Vernie [*Vernon*] wants to thank Uncle Norbie for his Xmas present. He still wears his cowboy suit sometime from last year. The children had a rather nice Xmas this year, more than usual in both clothes and toys. All the Godparents remembered our children this year excepting Red Hellman, and of course, he has a family, and far away, etc.

Well, Norbie, I'm rather tired tonight and don't know anything so special so believe I'd better run on to bed. May write more tomorrow but the mail man comes along around 11:00 o'clock so I may not get time. I have a big wash, beds, dishes, etc.

So goodnight and love from

Eleanor

Louisville, Kentucky, **January 11,** Monday morning, 9:50 am

Dear Brother,

Well, Katie's in her glory very much today. She has a big wash and believe it or not, she never had but one washday last week. Mom is over her Monday morning Runs. She got a letter Saturday but none today. It's really a frosty morning. Did you get your boxes and Joe's money? Kindly let us know.

Hermina

Continued by Mother:

Dear Norb.

I can't write much. Am too busy - washday. I saw your picture that you sent Alma. I don't think they are very good. Looks like you were half frozen. It is 10 o'clock at you clock. Will write you more next time. All are well. So long, good luck and God bless you.

Mother

Camp Crowder, Missouri, **January 11**

Dear Mom and all,

I don't know a damn thing to write about except the weather and the weather today is excellent. Glad to hear that my Godchild is in the peak of condition. Very good. Very good.

Well, I don't think we will go on maneuvers before April the way things look now. Mind you, I said I "think" we won't. Never quote me for the sure thing.

That was a very goofy dream the Horse had but she should have saved those hams even if they was dumped in the privy. I don't know a thing to write about at all except I hope the river [*has*] gone down. Should be by now. Well, I'll be seein' ya.

As Always,

Norb

Louisville, Kentucky, **January 12**

God bless you dear brother,

Just finished dishes and now at the radio. And just now Fibber and Molly are coming on in just a minute. Do you hear them yet, Fibber and Molly? Hermina is visiting Mr. And Mrs. Joseph B. Rawert. Pop is shaving and Mother is patching Pop's coat. So now, Elizabeth was up last night; Moody cut his hand and he just came in about an hour ago. It's swollen. I believe it hurts him more than he says it does but he can move his fingers pretty good. It's his right hand. Say, Mart just bought 250 pounds of horsemeat. Fibber said what's he going to do with all of it-eat it? Answer - no, he's going to ride it to work.

All of the little Muths have a cough or a cold and, say, Shirley Ann is getting big. She bought a tube of lipstick and said to Betsy don't tell Mother (cute, ain't it?).

Norb I heard you are asking for a furlough. I have my fingers crossed. What kind of work are you doing now and what about the maneuvers? Do you go soon or not? Did you get Alma's picture? She gave us one also. It's trimmed in blue. We are still working every day but not rushed. Lil Ann [*Steinmetz*] and I worked today and they are remodeling our place on Gray Street, three floors instead of two. And then everything will be on Gray Street - office, store and all. I sure think it will be nice when [*it's*] all finished. Mr. Hubbuch came home from Chicago Sunday and brought us a box of candy. Mr. Hubbuch sure looks good; he certainly has lost some weight.

Well, by this time did Wahoo ever travel his million miles to see you? He hurt his hand and now has an infection he said. I seen him coming out of his car yesterday evening and he told me. First time I saw him since he chased the (squaw), his dear wife. Well, he drew over fifty bucks last week, Joey over thirteen, and Dewey [Lee's son by a previous marriage] sets up pins [working at bowling alley?]. And Joey is still complaining.

Norb, can you believe this one? Mom seen you later than she saw Joey. She hasn't set foot in our home since you left. How do you think Mom feels about it? It hurts me to think she has no feelings at all for the ones who care for her. Well, God bless her but some days she don't work. She could walk and I know she has money [for transportation]. She gave Mother the goods for a dress and Pop a pair of socks (I guess that hurt too). I was a bundle girl and Mother sent her gloves. I was bundle girl again.

Fibber McGee signed off now. Did you hear it? And how's the radio by now? Did you ever need the batteries? I believe Alma seen a picture show and seen some wacko [WAAC] and she thought about going wackie, so I know she's too young. Just a notion, I guess. I told her someday why not get a defense job? That's helping too. I seen those three positives [*proofs*] you sent to Alma. Little Margie looked at them and said 'Nordie, Nordie.' Any soldier's picture is Nordie [*Norbie*]. She talks real cute and so does Peggy. Now Pop's going away with the basket. Mother wants chewing gum, and it's as scarce as his teeth. How do you like your eats and did you get the second box from the big nose [*reference to Moody*] and family? He said he drew a big nose and wrote 'and family.' That's Moody. Moody and Lip and all the sprouts always ask about you. Joe sent you two dollars at Christmas. Did you get it? Johnny and Eleanor sent a book and comb I believe. Did you get that? I have been hearing of so much stealing lately. I sometimes wonder if you ever got the money I sent you before your first pay, because some you never answered on. It would be a good idea if you would only drop a card and say if you received your crusty box or dumb old money. So if you like it, say 'Got it. Send more.' Talk about sending more - Mary always waits for kisses from every letter. She is getting so bad that she asks for kisses from your letters. Lil Steinmetz said her brother Joe's boy, Albert, is in Cleveland and Lawrence's boys, Robert Lee, is in Camp Campbell, KY and Charles is in Florida and Bill is to be examined the 19th of January.

Pop just came in and said no chewing gum - but that basket he's careful with it - so it's Oertel's. Do you ever see the boys you had to room with? Just thinking I told you Wahoo hurt his hand. It's not bad. He was working, so don't worry about it. I seen him close his car door with the hurt hand (it's clear now).

Your goldfish, that's two, are still living and the cat's tail is growing. Our vacuum sweeper still runs and the washing machine is tops so that's all the family. The Paul girls are as solemn as ever and Mildred Miller has a soldier boyfriend and Katie Reddick has two boyfriends. How's that for the neighbors? So now, I'm going in the kitchen and drink beer and think of you. Christmas morning I thought very much of you and received Holy Communion for you and Mother went with me. So that was two, I'm almost sure. We knelt in front of the crib and, well, we prayed and I do believe you did the same. Anyhow, when you think of it, write Mother and tell her. You sure had a sacrifice to do without your beer and got up so early on Christmas. We went to church at 4:20. Mom's doing fine, better than I thought. I guess your prayers are heard so bye bye. Hope to be seeing you soon.
Just Margaret
God bless you.

Louisville, Kentucky, **January 13**, Wensday [*sic*] 3 pm
Dear Son,

It is cold but the sun is shining bright. I guess because Joey came to see us this morning. Quite a surprise. I told her she did not come since you left. She said she was here one time but I don't remember how long ago. She looks very good. She said she did not have the time. I told her that if I loved someone I would make it my business to visit them. She asked me to come to see her. I told her I would come sometime. Well, that's that. Mr. Girsman's [*sp*], (coal man) boy is in Kansas City, Missouri. Going to school learning radio. Must stay for 20 weeks. His parents went to see him Christmas week. Said he wished he would of stayed longer. They had no trouble to get there. To get home they went by train. His son likes it very much. Norb, did you ever try to call long distance lately? The last letter we got was dated Jan. 5th. How is that? We send you a letter every day. Alma is going to get her glasses today. She said she would call me today. She called yesterday. Norb, did you get those thank you cards? We are all well and hope you are well too. Did Mr. Lee [*neighbor*] write to you? I wonder if you can answer all of the questions. I will close now and get the supper ready - steak, potatoes, gravy, cabbage slaw, and applesauce. Maybe pie, maybe not. Don't sound bad.
God bless you,
Mother and all

Hermina added a note:

Dear Norb,
Just saying HOWDY. I'm lost for words and believe you are too.
Smoked Havana Porky

Louisville, Kentucky, **January 14**, Thursday, Noon
Hunt-fut-sa [*Hundefurz is German for dog fart*]

I thought I would say hallo and it's a cold day in Louisville. It was hailing this morning but yesterday was heavenly. The plumbers were at Hubbuch's yesterday so Marge did not have to report yesterday until 1:00 pm. Seemed ducely [*deucedly*] odd to have Marge around the house that long. As you know, Joey came over yesterday. She still has little secrets that she tells everybody but I guess she always will. She looks very good. Moody's hand is still swollen but the Dr. said it looks fine.

Mom and Pop had it at 5 o'clock this morning. Pop did some soldering in his good pants and spilled that fluid on his pants and the outcome is a ruined pair of pants. Mom can't see why he does it, but he 'dood [*sic*] it. Poor Pa. His alibis don't work. The earlier part of the week was Mom's legs' exercise time. She just felt like a letter had to come and we was all getting a little uneasy, as your last letter was dated Jan. 5. Mom thought that perhaps you were gone on maneuvers.

Bud Wessling has been put in charge of 11 barracks to see that these men who leave for Africa has their equipment. He has a permanent job in the US. Jim Wessling is in the Coast Artillery. We received your letter this morning saying you worked until 1am. That's some hours to put in and what do you mean you all will be on the beam? That certainly was a funny advertisement in the paper but I also noticed the midwife advertisement. I haven't seen any of those appear in the papers here. You know they deliver babies.

I'm going to send you our want ad column. That is really something. Mr. Hubbuch is back from the Chicago market [*cloth and textiles*]. Always before, they lasted two weeks. He said they closed when he left and that was one week. Organdy has gone to war, they use it to camouflage ships and the market as a whole was poor. They made no promises. And furniture was promised by May. The hotels aren't kept as clean and restaurants the same way. He said at one place, the dishes didn't even look clean, all due to the lack of employees.

You have two fish left so one must have died since you left. They are both fine, ha ha. It was the longest that we have been without a letter since you left for the Army August 18th. Johnny just stopped in. It hailed, snowed and is now raining. John said the river is now down to normal. Mom is making some petticoats for herself. I got the goofiest telephone call yesterday. I said hello and she said, "I'm the radio reporter. Are you listening to your radio now?" "No, I'm not." "Thank you." Now ain't that something? Well, too da loo till tomorrow. Hope you won't have to work so hard and write soon.
Hermina

Continued:

Please don't worry about that clock, Norb. We are all tickled with it and Mom [*would*] rather have it than an electric one, so she's got what she likes. Moody asked if you got a kick out of his nose and family. I just called him up and asked about the kids and him, and his hand. The swelling is going down today. The kids are all on the mend. Hope you receive the box we sent you Monday. And we are glad to know that you got all your Christmas boxes.

Good afternoon 2:30 pm.

We just received your other letter. That makes two in one day and Mom is pleased as punch. I wish I could of saved those hams. Mom will be easy to get along with for the rest of the week. I have no more news so goodbye for the third time.
Hermina, Smoked Havana and Philipina Porky

PS. Dear Norb, You are a good boy sending us two letters in the same day. If you don't know much, write anyhow. I gave Alma a badge like yours.
Mother

Louisville, Kentucky, **January 14**, Thursday, 9:00 pm

Dear Norb,

Well, we still are glad to get your un-newsy letter. It's a letter. Tuesday morning's paper carried a writing about Pvt. Oscar Geppert. He said his Captain asked him what paper was here in Louisville so he is supposed to have put it in the paper about him. I'm trying to get a hold of one of those. I'm anxious to see it and I'll send it to you.

Do you think all those long hours you're putting in will get you home sooner or perhaps a longer stay? Lavern and Marlynn were here tonite. Believe it or not but Marge and Ann are making Joe and Ann a wedding present, a satin bedspread. Joe was here, Ann at work, so they came over here. Joe is taking them in to work.

I see where they sank the Aircraft Carrier Hornet. Howard Nunn, friend of Jr Russell, was out on it. He was among the survivors. Jr Seen this craft before he went to Key West. I am listening to Costello [on the radio]:

This little pig went to market,
This little pig stayed at home,
This little pig had roast beef (he knew the butcher)

Since you're in the office, perhaps you might be able to write your own furloughs like Zip's. Mrs. Hertel said Zip told her the last time he was here he thought he wouldn't ask for another furlough because all his friends are now in the Service and he don't have anybody to bum around with. I bet if they told him they were giving him a furlough he would take it.

Dr. Atherton is a Major now. When you have to work so late, must you stand revile the next morning? What about those exercises you all had to take? Do you take them?
[*Following pages were missing.*]
Hermina

189

Camp Crowder, Missouri, **December**

Dear Mom, Pop, Marge (Bank), Meanie (Horse), and Mary (Pussy<u>fut</u>),

Well, so sorry I don't get a chance to write very often but you know how it is. You know we are going to have a big inspection here Monday by some General so things were really buzzing here this week. And when I say buzzing, I mean buzzing. A couple of nights this week we went to bed about 1:30 and got up at four so that will give you a general idea as to how things must shine for this inspection. A few more inspections like this one and I'm ready to go AWOL. [*The letter was torn off at this point. He may have said some words that his mother didn't appreciate hearing or it was censored by the Army.*]
[*Norb*]

Norb sent a "Notice of Change of Address" postcard from the War Department from Colombia, South Carolina on January 14, 1944. This was his notice that he was going overseas and to the European theater. His new address was HQ CO 59th Signal BN, APO No. 9473, c/o Postmaster New York, New York.

Louisville, Kentucky, **January 17**, Sunday, 5:30 pm

Dear Norb,

Listening to the Great Gildersleeve. What a Gildersleeve! Lip, Betsy and Margie are here. What do you think Margie is? A peach today - really cute. Alma called here about an hour ago. If you want to bore her - rooster is on his back again. She told me their furniture is all packed up again. I asked about the rooster. She said "Smarty." I just have to tease her that way. You ask her.

That Robmann boy that left the same time you did is in New Guinea. Katsy enjoys a cough because she likes "caught dots" [*cough drops*]. She asked Lip for a nit-el [*nickel*] for Mitt's [*Milt's*] caught dots. She don't like Vitt's (Vicks). I see where you can't send anything across to the boys anymore. You have to use V-Mail stationary only. The news has been on the good side lately or don't you think?

We are all OK. We heard Doc. Atherton has just arrived in Africa. That's all for tonite, so until tomorrow,
Porky

Contined by Mommy, 9 pm:

Dear Norb,

Beer time now. Papa is going right now. Wish you could drink with us but I think you are busy, don't you? Papa buys cigars at the drug store near St. Brigid's so he can get one pack of chewing gum. Don't you think that is thought full [*sic*]? Gum is getting less. Everything [goes] for the service men. That is the way it should be. I do miss it very much. It helps my stomach very much. One-half price now, it is cut in half, soon won't be any. Norb did you receive a box from us? If you did, let us know when you write.

Have you got your rosary yet, that you taken along? If you haven't any, let me know and I'll send you one. They ask for rosaries and medals, even broken ones. They can't get any more, or so we were told.

Norb, what are your old roommates doing? Are they doing office work also? What time do you get up and what time do you start work? You never have told us. If you haven't the time, it will be alright too. We received your last letters Thursday, Jan. 14th. I know you are busy but a few lines. That will be alright, Goodnight and PS. It is now 10:30. Just got through praying the rosary for all men in the service, especially for you.
God bless you,
Mother

Louisville, Kentucky, **January 18**, Monday, 34°
Dear Norb,

Hermina's birthday is today but it don't mean anything but another day. Like all our birthdays. Elisabeth's is 28 January. The weather is so gloomy today at 8:30. It was no good day light yet, [*when*] this insurance man came this morning. I said to him "My, you are early." He said, "It is 8:30 already." I asked him where Mr. Amshoff was. He said in Georgia but he forgot to bring me his address. I saw the Stuckenborg boy yesterday after 5 o'clock services with his mother. He sure looks fine. Think he put on weight. Tomorrow the 19th, a lot of boys are leaving. Dr. Atherton is in Africa. He is a Major.

Today it is 5 months already that you left. I always think what 18th means to me, [*one*] more month-longer gone. Hope that you will get a furlough soon, but if you can help it, don't surprise me. I don't think I could take it. I told Elizabeth that I would want to know. She said that I would be worried if you would not come the time that you thought you would. I thought we would get a letter today but I guess we will get one tomorrow.

Alma called yesterday and said she was coming today. I mean, tonight. It is 8:30 o'clock. She is not here yet. Maybe she is working late. Haven't seen her for almost 2 weeks. I think we all miss her if we don't see her once in a while.

Today is Jan. 19th, 2:00 o'clock. Sun is shining but very cold. I wish you could of seen little Mary when she saw it was mail from you. When she opened the envelope she looked disappointed, [*no kisses*], just your name. Then she opened the card and saw the letter. She was so happy she couldn't read it fast enough. I was in her kitchen [*upstairs*] when Hermina brought the mail. I am glad that you are sending them.
Mother

Over -Alma didn't come last night. Don't know why. I will answer you on KP duty some other time. Hello from all and Mary.

Louisville, Kentucky, **January 18,** Monday, My Birthday. 2 pm

Dear Norb,

Well, I went to Hertel's and got your much thought of fish some food. We are all well but news-less. We can't get sliced bread anymore. You have to slice it yourself and Mary is mad. Angela Hellmann's husband is at Fort Knox for a month. Gen. Devers of Knox is in Africa they think. Everyone is going to Africa.C

Continued, Tuesday at noon

Brothah,

I am listening to Balkage. I think he really gives the news and what news! The Russians are all gleeful, he said, because of the recapture of Leningrad [*German Cousin Josef Effkemann's brother died in the Battle of Leningrad. There is a memorial to the dead in the Ahaus town square*].

We did not know that Mrs. Lee was sick. That's news to us. I am very glad he wrote you. I can't write good because I have Balkage on my mind. Balkage is signed off. We received your letter this morning and what a letter. I think Pop knows better until the next time to solder in his good clothes. He wants a pair of coveralls now. I'll bet he'll never change clothes then, he'll just add to them.

Moody was over here. You know Lip hangs her clothes up here [*laundry to dry in their spacious basement*]. He got a hell of a kick out of all your tickled sympathy. I think he might backfire on that but he thinks you write swell letters. Pat your back. Mom said she wants to answer you on the KP questions. I did not know you were doing special duty work. Sounds big.

Of course, we tell you as we are told. That's what Helen Wessling told Mom and guess she is as green as we are. I wouldn't know any better. I guess I have to join the WAAC to find out but they wouldn't want me - too fat. That's what Barb Lauyans was rejected for. I hope your toothache feels OK by now. Did you have some toothache medicine [*liquor*] like Russell takes? On second thought since you are on the beam I suppose you can't take that kind of medicine.

Eleanor got along fine after all that cutting and chiseling. Her mouth is healed swell. Your Katsy is doing fine in school the Sister said but she talks continuously even in church. Sister had to poke her. Mary is tickled with her thank you card and all the love that goes with it. I got a buzz from Mrs. Russell too. She received your card and she was tickled with it.

Now the weather officially, I think, is 8° above 0° F. It is 6° on our register. Saturday was 62°, Sunday 32°, today 6° or 8°. So you can see what a 'de-jump' it made here. At 4:00 o'clock this morning I heard the wind howling and at 8 am it had all the windows frosted and 8° above.

That's swell in Park and Tilford sending all those smokes. Yes, Pop is still puffing away. Usually falls asleep with a cigar. He's more trouble than when he chewed. That was nice in Bill's wife sending you smokes. Did you say or send her a dank-a-shane card? Moody is doing good but I never in my life seen such a big mitt on such a little fellow. We were a little worried about it. He still has it bandaged but the swelling is gone. Glad to know of all your medals, General Rawert.

There's a piece in today's paper about Chaplain Bernie Spoelker. He is in Camp Chaffee, Arkansas. Sure glad you got to see the dentist. Mom wouldn't want you to walk in on her if you got a furlough. She don't think she could take it but I think she could. If you do get furlough, perhaps you could wire her you were leaving. Otherwise, if you think you're going to get [*one*] and something unforeseen happens, she would be greatly disappointed.

Hoping you are OK and knowing you are on the beam I will close with love from all the hell raisers.

Hermina

Schnitzelburg, Kentucky, **January 19**

Dear Size 7 ¾,

"Lights Out" is on the radio now. It's about 7:30 and that made me think about writing you a letter because the play was about a woman turning into a cat. It was the same one we heard about three years ago over home. Damn, it sure was creepy as hell.

I read your letter that you sent Mom and you said it was cold down there. You should be here. I'm damn near sitting on top of the stove now and by morning, they say it will be 10° below and that's getting plenty cool. It wouldn't be so damn bad but I have to get all the coal in.

I seen Red Johnson the other weekend. He looks pretty good. I didn't get a chance to talk to him though. He was on his way to church I guess and I was riding up "Goss Street."

We are getting pretty busy up at the store. Now it's just about time to bust loose but we didn't lose but about two weeks altogether so that ain't so damn bad. All the news in the paper here looks pretty good. If all that stuff can be believed the war can't last much longer and I hope the hell it don't.

I saw Clarence Johnson the other night down at the corner. It was the first time I seen him down there for about two months. He said he was kept pretty busy acting like a big brother to Kate. He said the Dutchman, you know Shanky, said for him to take care of her so she won't get lonesome while he's gone. Well, he sure as hell is doing his part in the war effort in that respect.

Well, I guess Annie and I will open a quart of Fehr's [local beer] and then jump in our little, brrrr, cold bed and shiver our asses off. That's about all I know now, will write sooner next time.

So long,

Joe

Continued by Joe's wife, Ann:

Dear Number 10's,

How is my dear, dear sweet brother-in-law, and I don't mean Carter or Muth. We are fine and working hard every day. Sorry we haven't written sooner, but honestly, the time goes by so fast we hardly know what day it is.

We got a letter from Laurence Janes last Saturday and said he is now on maneuvers down at Biloxi, Mississippi. Likes them OK except the rainy days, then the fire goes out and they have to eat out of tin cans. (Maybe Joe would like that now.)

I haven't seen Alma since the Sunday after Christmas and that night she and the family came over to see us. We are finally getting our big kitchen filled up a little now. I just bought a porcelain top table, looks really nice in our kitchen. Also got a pretty new bedspread from Marge and Hermina. It was our wedding gift just about 6 months late-that's not so bad but Ann Beckman did beat them. We got her gift a couple months ago.

It is so cold here Joe had to work for about an hour getting his machine to run and then came in the house and the water was froze up so you can imagine his English for about the next half an hour but everything is under control now.

Jim Doerr got on a good tear and went in town and met in with a soldier and got him all conored [sp] up. Then the soldier left so Jimmy goes and buys the kids a big loose sack of blocks and starts home, seeing the soldier sitting on the curb at 4th and Jefferson. Trying to help him up he dropped all the blocks and there they were both staggering around picking them up. Said they were a big crowd of people watching them but no one would help them and then by the time he got home, he had about 7 or 8 left. But look at the fun the people had watching them.

Well, Norb as I haven't anymore to write I guess I had better close. With lots of luck. Your dear, dear Irish sister-in-law,

Ann

Continued by Joe:

This is another late-night-edition news report. I just about burned up the damn place. I went to light a cigarette and I caught the fringe on the tablecloth. Damn, we a fanning like hell for a minute. It ruined the table cloth and blistered the table a little. The spots on this letter is from beer that got spilled in putting the fire out.

Louisville, Kentucky, **January 20**, Wednesday, 11 am

Dear Norb,

Well, I looked like a stick up woman. I had four butcher knives that I had to take over to Krebs last night. Donaldson Bread looks so different in a loaf. Mrs. Lee had kidney trouble.

She is up and about again. I think they got in touch with four MDs before one called at her home.

Moody was here this am. He said St. Elizabeth's had their first 'Gold Star,' a Friebert boy, 30 years old from Ash Street. He was killed in action in North Africa. His people should of received a message from the Chaplain who buried him the 8th of December. It seems everybody is going to Africa. Well, the news is good and that's something.

We are all OK. I read your pamphlet letter to Pop last night. He just shook laughing when I read about the argument. He was eating but he missed his mouth and it fell on his plate. He got a kick out of that. I really think he should of been an actor. When I finished the letter, he was crying. What do you think? Mom will finish this as Marge called me in for this afternoon. This will be the first time since Christmas I worked. One thing for sure, I won't have to pay income tax. Well, 'tooda loo' til tomorrow.
Love,
Hermina

1:30 pm. Wednesday, **Jan 20th 1943**, (not like you had – 1942)
Dear Norb,
Hello from Papa, Marge, Hermina, Little Mary. I hope you received the box by now. I'm afraid that the muffins are stale by now. That is the expensive sausage, only 95 cents a pound. That is 45 cents worth. I believe you will like it. If you get anything that you don't want us to send, let us know, or if you want something.

You seem to understand Kitchen Duty. I hope you will think by now it is not as easy as you thought when you were home. What about a few pieces of socks and clothes? Going in my footsteps? I'm glad you find out how nice it is, as you always thought and said 'that's nothing.' Ha ha. I had a few weeks [with] only one washday. I can't get used to it. St. X laundry does not take any new customers. Joe and Ann get their washing done by them.

I am baking today. I baked a small loaf of bread for Mary and a small raisin bread. I like to give them to her because she takes your boxes to the Post Office, a small Post Office on Jefferson Street. She likes homemade bread very much. It is almost 2:00 now and I must close so Mary can mail it for me.
As always, Your Dear, Dear Mother to her Dear, Dear boy.
God bless you always. That is our prayer for you
Mother

Louisville, Kentucky, **January 20**
Dear Mom and All,
Well, I don't know how it is in Louisville but it's about 10° below here. It is really cold. These barracks are so cold that after we mopped the floor this morning there was a sheet

of ice all over our floor. We could skate right to bed and that's where we went too because it was too cold to stay up. Well, so much for the weather but I do hope it gets a little warmer.

If I can, I will see if I can get you some gum here on the post. I doubt if I can but it don't hurt to try.

I asked Alma about that rooster but it wouldn't surprise me if it wouldn't be an actual fact, because it gets plenty of training. Still busy as hell and I expect to be that way for quite some time. Of course I can't tell you everything because we have military secrets you know. (Time out, the cook just came in with a bunch of cakes and apples.)

Now that I have finished gorging down a couple of cakes, I will continue. My radio is still going strong but I don't get to much time to listen to it. Send me Anna Heitkemper's address. I lost it, also Bernard Spoelker's. I lost that one too. Just like me. Well, kids I have to '<u>warsh</u>' and take a shower so I guess it would be a good idea to close this letter so I will see you later, hoping all are well.
Norb

Louisville, Kentucky, **January 21**, Thursday, 2 o'clock
Dear, Dear Norb,

Today I am the first to write. Hermina went to work at about 11 o'clock. It was cold in the building till the plumbers got done. Marge went later also. They are not busy now. Mr. Russell and Joey are not working. Ann did not go to work today. Mary left [*sic*] Alma read that thanks card you sent her. She said she wanted to get Alma jealous. Norb you surely wrote some letters. We all enjoyed them. Papa came home with about 3 or 4 gallons of spagttie [spaghetti] last nite. They had cooked too many at St. Brigteds [*Brigid's*] for a spaghetti supper dinner. We called up Orels [Orrills] next door to Elizabeth and told them Elizabeth or Moody should come over but did not tell them what for. It did not take long [*until*] Elizabeth, Mr. and Mrs. Milton were here. They never even blew the horn, so quiet they came in. Marge said we wanted you all to have those spaghettis. Elizabeth looked surprised. They thought something happened and the children thought you came home. Moody was all slicked up. Elizabeth was dressed better. Marge said it looked so funny the way they acted. We all had a good laugh. We thought Papa did not want anybody to know that he brought them home so we gave [*some to*] Mrs. Russell, little Mary and Joe and we have plenty yet. I wonder if Papa is going to eat some tonite. Going to have Sauer meat. They will go good with that. Well, that's all for today.

Hope that you make good use of all your medals and rosary and prayer books. Do you listen in Sundays at 1:00 o'clock am? I think it is in the Catholic Men's Hour. Rev. Mgr. Schanar [*sp*] speaks. If you listen in it is sure worthwhile. It is 3:00 o'clock now and I received your fountain pen but no letter. What do you want me to do with it? I wanted to let Marge take this letter and mail it but Mary Krumplemann came just then and I did not have it ready. A walk to the mailbox will not hurt me.

Marge and Hermina, Joe and Ann, Elizabeth and Moody are all invited to Bell and

Rudy's shower Saturday nite and to meet at Preston and Eastern Parkway. I guess I will have to be Nursie. I do not want to take care of Margie. She would cry all nite for her mother. Gertrude Stengel invited them. She said [*it is*] a supposed surprise party. Did you send Anna Heitkemper a card of thanks, even if the candy did not taste like Muth's? It is hard to beat their candy. I repeat that I will close and get supper. Want to have early supper. Holy Hour tonight. Very few I missed and I pray for the men in service, especially my son. All are well. God bless you,
Mother

Louisville, Kentucky, **January 21**
Dear Uncle Norb,

I guess you thought I have forgotten you so I am up at Mommy's writing this letter. Mother, Daddy, the Stangels, Hermina, Marge, Hammer the Will and some girls - some Brod as [broad ass?] Gheens are invited to Uncle Rudy's and Aunt Bell's tonight.

We are having examinations at school now. We had arithmetic, spelling, English and vocabulary. Monday we will have Religion, History or Geography. So will you pray that I pass because it is real hard and I'm not kidding? You ought to know. Well, I can't think of anymore dope. Katsy has got something in this letter.
You're A-1 Girl Friend
Shirley

Louisville, Kentucky, **January 21**, Thursday, 5:30 pm
Dear FlabBurgasted,

I seen your letters, Joe's and Lip's, and my, what letters! I know right now it will not be Park and Tilford for you after the war is over. It will be the Courier Journal or Louisville Times. Norb Rawert feature columnist but all these things could not be carried in the daily paper. We all got a heck of a kick out of them. Moody took your letter down to the shop [*Muth's Candy*]. He tore off the part about Bill and Rudy so Rudy read it and got a kick out of it too. He said "Say, Leo it looks like this letter was censored. Was it?" Moody acted innocent as hell, "I don't know if it was or not." Moody said that was double funny.

I rode in the car with Mary Jane Nunn. She said Claude is still in Australia. He has been there 8 months. They sent him homemade fudge and a ring. It reached him after Christmas but the fudge was molded. Say, you and Claude must really like homemade fudge. Elbert has received his first examination and Nelson has received the questionnaire. She said my, it will be so lonesome when they all go.

Do you want me to take your pen to the pen shop and send it to you? I presume a letter will give the necessary instructions. Hope you are OK and take it from me, Russell hasn't seen roosters with red spots since Xmas because it almost put him with the daisies.
Love,
H.R.

Louisville, Kentucky, **January 23**, Saturday 5 pm

Dear Norb,

We received your letter this morning and I see right now where I'll have to oil up those old ice skates for you so you can skate to bed. Personally, I think it's goofy to mop unless it's that it's just that filthy. The Army does everything the hard way they say. Oh well, the weather is very beautiful here. It's like a beautiful spring day but the weatherman said it was 4 above Tuesday morning.

We are OK. Mom had the headache this morning. I think she went beyond the straight and narrow diet list but is feeling better this pm. Mom has been doing splendid tho. Those vitamins she's taking helped her more than anything. She said she's going to try and get Pop to take some vitamins but Oertel's is a cure-all for him. Mom is going to be Nursey [*babysitter*] tonite. Lip's brood is coming over while we go to Bell and Rudy's tonite. We got a chenille bedspread, white and blue - Joe, Ann, Lip, Moody, Marge and I went together to buy it. It is pretty. Here are the addresses you requested. Anna D. HEITKEMPER, 604 Holcomb, Mobile, Alabama. Ch, 1st Lt. Bernard A. Spoelker, Station Hospital, Camp Chaffee, Arkansas.

I was talking to Mary Louise Spoelker. She's as crazy as ever. She said Bean is 10 miles from Bob Burress's homestead and that their house looks better than Bob Burns' so she's getting a pazooka and is going to make money. Ch. Bean took to long underwear too. Ante said it was 16° below zero there Wednesday. Ante is going to come here if she can the last part of February. Maybe you can visit her if you go to Kansas City. Well, this is all for tonite, sleep tight and I hope you won't have to skate to bed, but if you do, skate fancy. Mom said could you smell the pork chops she's frying.

Love from all.

Hermina

Louisville, Kentucky, **January 24**, Sunday, 4 pm, 80° on back porch

Dear Norb,

Well, we are sitting here with windows and doors open. The men are sitting outside at the White Cottage. It's the warmest I have ever seen it at this time of year. It's unbelievable to think Tuesday was so cold.

We were at Bell's and Rudy last night. Had a very enjoyable time. It was a gang there, lot of Schnitzelburgers. Moody took all the Willenburgs, Soup and his two sisters in the [*Muth's*] truck, and little Moody. He said he had 1,000 pounds of beef in his truck but no baby beef. They really had a nice feed, plenty of it, and it was all so good. Plenty of beer too, high balls, coke and a Dutch lunch with nuts, candy, big cakes and cookies. It was fine. They almost crammed it down you. And hot coffee, which I relish. Everybody did. It was a treat. I had three bingo games, so did Lip and Marge but I drew high so I got first gift, but they gave 13 prizes. Well, it was all swell. They surely have a cute furnished home. It's beautiful, not alone, cute. We got home at 2:30 pm thru the most dense fog I have ever seen. Joe had to drive with his head out the door and follow the white line on Preston Street. Several had run off the road. I was really afraid. Pop took a taxi to work and you couldn't begin to make out the curbing. The driver said he never seen anything like it. He just kept turning his lights off and on. You couldn't make out the garage from the kitchen.

Shirley wrote you a letter last night. She said she wrote you two letters but Mother never enclosed them with her letters and you might feel hurt because she writes to her adopted soldier boy. I thought that was very sensible.

Did you hear of Mr. 5 X 5 marrying Miss 4 X 4? They walked up the aisle two by two and had children one by one. Mary Spoelker told me that one. Walter Orrill got his papers last week and she is taking it terrible hard. He was 18 in October or November. We are all OK.

I don't think Dude [*Russell*] was seeing Roosters with red spots. I think they were white spots. He was no pale-face. He was on 2 gin drunks last week. Well, Norb I guess I'll sign off. I don't know any news. Do you have your teeth fixed up? Today you could use roller skates, not ice skates. Milt had his kite up with 4 balls of twine out. It was really up there. Well, until tomorrow, "good day" my sweet.
Porky (failed to mail yesterday's letter)

Fort Jackson, South Carolina, **January 25**

Dear Mom and all,

Well, I finally found a few minutes to jot down a line or two. I can truthfully say that it's very cold here, in fact, damn cold. I believe the tempeture [*sic*] here in our barracks is about 45° and that ain't very warm. It makes it rather difficult to write. If this letter looks a little shaky, it's because of the cold.

My radio has a short in it somewhere but I haven't had time to give it a going over. I'm just a little afraid to - you know I can take a thing apart but I can't get them back together. I was just thinking about mailing it home and see perhaps if there's a radio shop where I can get it fixed and perhaps you could mail it back when I could use it. I don't hardly get a chance to use it now and I don't like for it to sit around the barracks just for nothing.

So Rudy thought my letter was censored. Well, it seems to me as though it was. Well, I don't see a chance for a furlough for quite some time yet. All of my hopes have vanished. It's too much work to be done and it seems as though the work comes before the furlough. That's the GI rules and regulations.

Well, we had liver and onions for supper tonight and they really were good. First time I had liver and onions for a long time. We also had coffee and that was pretty good also, of course, I don't mean to rub it in. Well, my dear, dear people it's just a little too chilly to write much longer and I believe the ink in this pen is turning to ice so I'll write tomorrow if it's a little warmer. Good night. Tell little Mary I said hello. XXX.
As Always,
Norb

Louisville, Kentucky, **January 25** (not '42 as you write)

Dear Norb,

It is 2 o'clock pm. Cold - 22° above yesterday and 80° on Monday. We received your letter from Jan. 21, 1942. You write that you need a few '92's. Come home, then. You can get all you want, that is, not too much or then you get drunk. So you don't think you will have a furlough so soon. <u>Grin and bear it.</u> We had the doors open yesterday. It was so warm then, and today so cold. That is too much change. I see you are going to write Milton a letter. I am glad if you would. I told you some time ago to write to him. Maybe it would do some good because he thinks so much of you. In fact, they all do. I asked Margie 'How does Norby salute?' She puts her little hand to her head. She had your negative in her hand and she gave it to me and said 'Norby, Mami. [*Mommy*].' So I put it away. I was surprised she knew you from the negative.

Tea is getting scarcer too the way I heard. I am going to Plest [illegible] and try to get some. We can't get no Postum [*coffee substitute*]. I think we will have to drink hot or cold water or '92s. What would you like best? Norb, did you get that box? I would like to know. I'm afraid that the muffins got stale. Maybe it would be better not to send homemade cakes. How did you like the sausage? Schieman's has some sausage. It's called beer sausage. It is good. Forty cents a pound. We all like it, but can't always get it.

I filled my pen twice writing this letter. Don't know how to go about it. I am not asked to write this but I thought Alma would not care - in fact, I should think she would like it. Alma run a splinter in her finger and she had to go to the doctor. He told her she should dip her finger in alcohol up and down. She called us up this Monday morning and told Hermina about it. Infection set in, the Doctor said. She is not working so she cannot write to you, she said. Hermina offered to write to you but she did not OK that! Ha ha. I am sure she [*will*] write as soon as possible. The doctor said the splinter is out. She hurt herself at work. I don't know when it happened. I guess I am going to call her this evening and find out how she is. Will let you know in tomorrow's letter. Hermina went to work about 11 o'clock today.

We did not get in town yet to have your pen fixed. I want to go sometime this week. I have to have my feet tended to. Now listen, 2 corns, one on each little toe, ingrown toenail and 2 corns on my left foot. They hurt so bad I put my real old shoes on today.

That's all. So Well, well, well. Goodbye, be good. Daddy and Honey bunch send you XXXXX (and Marge and Hermina). Well, well, well, I think that's all for today. I guess you think if it is not much news it is a letter and hearing from us.

God bless you,

Mother

Camp Crowder, Missouri, **January 26** [typewritten, all capital letters]

Dear Mom and all,

My time is very limited so I won't be able to write very much. It is nearly seven o'clock and I haven't had supper yet because I have to wait for two trucks to come in [*Norb was the depot clerk*]. They seem a little late tonight. They probably have a lot to do like everyone else around here.

It seems to me as if Missouri should be known for bad weather rather than for mules. I was just wondering if it was quite as cold back there in ole Kentucky. I don't see how it could be.

I have to go to the dentist again tomorrow, which is not a very pleasant thought, but at least a very necessary one. I guess I will have a couple filled. At least I hope so. The other day I was down there for four hours and never got a lick of work done. That is how busy they are, but I hope it's not the same tomorrow

As Always,

Norb

PS. I didn't get a chance to mail this letter so just a little more crap. As far as I know, we are pulling out of Camp Crowder to a new station but it's still in the USA. I have to pack yet tonight. I don't have much time so I will let you know when I reach my new homeWell, my dear people you will have to pardon this short letter but it's the best I can do for the present. So long.

Louisville, Kentucky, **January 27**, Wednesday, 8:05 pm

Dear Norb,

Well, I just heard that Zink, the meat man next to Slim, is closing his door. Saturday is the last day of business for him. I told you there is a changes being made.

I'm waiting for the bathroom. Maah [*Marge*] is scrubbing her scales and I'm next. There has been some changes made here too. The heater at work went out bad again today so no work. Marge and I got busy at home. She cleaned the wallpaper in the two front rooms and I did the scrubbing and waxing. I also scrubbed the bathroom. It's Lilly white again but you have to wash that down every month for it to keep clean. I don't like a white bathroom in winter. It ruins my beautiful hands. Now if you come home everything will be shining but we didn't do it for that reason, but I hope you can come home.

Well, the paper tonite states that the German press called the President and Churchill's meeting a "Hollywood Pow-Wow." I thought that was sort of funny but I bet they would of gave a lot to attend such a "Pow-Wow."

Did you get that last box we sent you? I bet those muffins were like baseballs. How did you like the sausage? We are all OK. Alma has an infection in her finger. She told me Monday. I tried to call there a few moments ago but nobody answered. She told Mom it felt a lot better after she opened it.

Our snow is melting today. It was 22° above at 5 o'clock this morning but it isn't so cold tonite and the snow melted in the sunshine today.

Did you get to Kansas City as yet? Well, I got Alma on the telephone and she worked again today. She said her finger feels OK. I am glad to hear that. Alma was telling me you are expecting to be sent across. Did you hear that for sure? Or is it just floating around? I hope you won't be sent to Africa or New Guinea. You might get a cold "butt," but I hope you are Alaska bound. I'm glad you didn't tell Mom or it would have worried her. It's bad enough she has to know it when the time comes.

Scally or Skallie I think he went to St. X with you. Ann read a letter he wrote his mother. You know he lived on Kentucky Street. He is in North Africa and was with that Company that the Friebert boy and Speckner boy that were killed were in.

Another of Ann's neighbors on Kentucky Street joined the Marines. He also wrote to his mother. He said they went on 15-mile hikes for two days so on the third day two other boys and him got the idea that they could reduce the mileage so they took a short cut. A dear Captain met them and he said "Mom I never in my life seen so many dirty dishes - we three had to wash them all." Gee, Mom better not join the WAAC.

Did you hear Fibber McGee? They were a scream. Pop is going after beer now. It is now 9:10 pm. Mom's looking at The Globe, Marge is rolling her hair. I'm writing you, dear brother. Jr Hubbard don't like New Mexico at all. He said he will go back to Idaho in February. Well, Norb I'm out of news if you call it that. I think my Inkograph is going bad but it did its duty, so dear, good nite, sleep tite [*sic*] and I hope you won't have to skate to bed. Hoping to hear from you soon. We received your letter Monday.
As ever,
Porky

Louisville, Kentucky, **January 28**, Thursday, 8:30 pm
Dear Norb,

It's Lip's birthday. Listening to Bing Crosby. We are thinking that if your radio is now on the way we'll be looking for it and do as you requested.

George Herbig is on the way to Alaska. Boobie [?] Heintz is supposed to leave too according to Kate's last letter. The gals [*at Hubbuch's*] still couldn't work today so they taken some work home. Mom looked at the thermometer on the porch. It was 31°. Mom said if it freezes [*32°*], she isn't going to church. We all gave her a very loud laugh. She would get out of going for one degree. She did.

Now, that radio is it being sent for two purposes - to be repaired and to keep - because you think you'll be sent across?

Dr. Stites's father died Tuesday and Soup Willenburg passed away today. I hate for a letter to sound like an obituary but Marge said it will be the first time she'll see Soup in a casket. Did we laugh? We are OK and listening to the radio. So you are still cold. Well, it has warmed up quite a bit; I hope it has there too. I really haven't got any more dope for you my fren [*sic*]. I'll say goodnight.
H.R.

Continued, Friday, noon:

Dear Norb,

There was a Fuller Brush man here - a German-Jew - and he couldn't get the right meaning, I don't think. He'd go, ya, ya. Well, you had to hear him. I suppose that was the only way he could make a living. I wanted a duster mop for Joe.

How was the sausage? And did you get all your Thank You cards sent out? Haven't got any news, only we are all well and it's a gloomy day in Louisville. Mom had you enrolled in the Sacred Heart league for that Morning Prayer.

Bye now,

H.R.

Louisville, Kentucky, **January 29**, Friday, 9:30 pm

Dear Norb,

Well, this is the last of the papers. I had to drum this up. We are keeping Lip's kids while they are going to see Soup. He had a cerebral hemorrhage. We had a blackout for ourselves for a minute. I heard a train whistle and I thought it was Durkee coming up so I said "blackout" and I turned out the lights. The whistle stopped. The kids got scared and then we all had a big laugh.

Well, I heard on the radio today that the Government is taking 150,000 men from camps and putting them in college for special courses. They will make their selection from the camps. I hope you are amongst the favored "few." Our president really does get around. I think very few could have taken his place.

Marge found a new way to get a man. She had a fight with the revolving doors at work. They wasn't hooked up or wasn't in the groove so they fell down. She said she never heard such noise. All the men came running. It broke the plate glass. A piece flew up and cut Marge's hand. They took her to the Dr. so now she has bandages. The Dr. said she can work so she came home early tonight. She said the cut wasn't very deep but she shouldn't get it wet. Picture this - Mom said that she would wash her dishes for her. Can you think of another way to get a man? Raymond Robben is in Florida. We are all OK.

I'm telling you Mom and Pop are so sociable. They are both sleeping. Pop came in the front to find out what was wrong with Marge's hand. Marge is priding herself on how she can get the men. I doubt if Marge could pick candles tonite but the cut don't hurt and it isn't swollen at all.

Hoping you are well and that we hear from you soon.

As ever,

Your little sistah "Porky"

Louisville, Kentucky, **January 30**

Dear Norb,

Do you remember way back when these were printed? [*Referring to the heading on the stationery she was writing on: "Joseph B. Rawert Wall Papering, All Work Guaranteed, 1344 Texas St., Magnolia 6072-J"*]. We have been expecting a letter as you said you were writing the next day. I went in town today with Betsy and what do you think - we couldn't get ice cream at the 10¢ store. I took Betsy to Dr. Stites. She had a lump in her chest and a fluid came out. He told me to take her to a child specialist, Dr. Bruce, which I did. He said it wasn't anything so we feel OK. Betsy is OK. Dr Bruce said only a little pekid [*sic*] looking so he gave her vitamin pills and took a blood count, a tubercular test. So Monday we have to go back and take a specimen of urine. Betsy thought that was too funny. Johnny just came in to stay tonight. Eleanor and the kids are staying at the Smiths.

It took nine men to lift Soup. Bosse [*Funeral Home director*] said he weighed 300 pounds. We are all OK. I am writing this at Joe's house. I think Mom will lose her tenants soon. Joe and Ann bought two overstuffed chairs. I told them that they'll soon need more room. They are beautiful. I haven't got any more news.

[*Hermina*]

Louisville, Kentucky, **January 30**, Sunday

Dear Norb,

Katsy makes a wonderful saleslady. She was selling a magazine for school called the "Twistin Family" (Christian Family). Did we laugh! We are expecting Johnny, etc. for supper. Our mission opens tonight. Shirley got a handkerchief from her adopted soldier. She sure is thrilled. It was silk with 'remember me' on it. Lip's kids has got Valentine fever. Well, that's all for yesterday and today.

Love,

Porky

Louisville, Kentucky, **February 1**, Mon., 4:45 pm

Dear Norb,

Well, to begin with we received your letter this morning. I don't know if we should say we're happy or not that you are leaving Camp Crowder, but you say you will still be in the States. That's something to be thankful for. This letter will be diary fashion again, you know. I have quite a bit of news today. I seen Mr. Johnson and he said Larny is at Camp Atterbury yet. He was taking up surveying but gave that up and is taking up telephone work, which he likes very much. Larny's fine. Earl is at Camp Livingston, Louisiana. Loui's at Camp Claybourne, Louisiana. They are just 18 miles apart. All are OK. Frank Niemann Jr is got his paper and will get his final examination on Feb. 20th. Mrs. Russell received a letter from Jr saying he'll be home Wednesday at noon. He said he thought he'd have two days at home, perhaps three. I know she'll be disappointed if they happen to change their mind again. We are all OK.

I also received a letter from William Hollkamp, he said it was one year that he's been in New Guinea, and that he received the box we sent him for Christmas on Jan 10th. We mailed it Oct. 28th.

I taken Betsy back to Dr. Bruce today. He said her heart, lungs and all were fine but that she was a bit anemic. He gave her some vitamin pills which cost 5¢ apiece, and capsules - 84 for $2.75, which is for anemia. He said that medicine worked marvels with kids. Betsy said the one pill looks like a little football, the other a Mexican jumping bean. So it ought to do something.

As you know, our Mission started yesterday. I believe you might get some missionary quotations, even if it is for the women.

Well, I'll say goodbye now and add my bit every day until we get your address. We are grateful you are in the USA.

[Hermina]

Continued, Louisville, Kentucky, **February 2**

Dear Norb,

Ground Hog Day, Tuesday, Noon. Well, it's a beautiful [*day*] in Louisville. The sky is like a picture of early spring although it was frosty. Mom, and of course the ground hog, seen his shadow. We are all OK at 1344 Texas. We thought perhaps we would get a card from you, but know it's impossible when we don't, but no harm to hope though.

Joe was housekeeper at our house last night Mom asked him to come over "in case" you might call us. He was a dear one too and washed everything, I mean dishes (seems like Ann is doing good). Mom told him she was sending him a bill for tissues. He said she should, but what did he get for keeping house?

Margie and Lip was up here this morning. She looks more like you than any kid I have ever seen. She's so chubby and really cute, got two plaits now, with red hair ribbon on each. She's a doll.

Junior [*Russell*] comes home tomorrow at 4:10 pm. She's [*Jr's mother, Mary*] still afraid yet to think for sure. I'm inclosing [*sic*] our former neighbor's picture. That's grand, isn't it? I'm glad when a fellow like him gets what he is deserving of.

I just heard Balkage News. He's good. I think all men between 18 and 38 will soon be called in the Army or else do defense work, according to the latest reports.

Mom's gone home with Lip to cut out a pair of pants for Jimmy. That's all for today I think.

Bye and happy landing

[*Hermina*]

Norb transferred to Fort Jackson, South Carolina and his new address was 59th signal Battalion, Fort Jackson, South Carolina

Fort Jackson, South Carolina, **February 3** [*Norb wrote January 3, 1943*]

Dear Mom and all,

Well, I finally arrived in South Carolina, Ft. Jackson. We traveled over 1,400 miles to get here and we went through 7 states. I tried to get a phone call through but was unable to do so because the line was too busy as usual. I don't know how long we will stay here but it may be a couple of months. There will be no furloughs, as I understand it. The fellows are pretty burnt up about it also.

Had a pretty nice trip. We were on the train for two and a half days and we had to sleep siting up because we had day coaches. We went through Oklahoma, Arkansas, Mississippi, Tennessee, Georgia, touched N. Carolina and ended up in S. Carolina.

Well, there is so damn much work to do yet so I have to quit writing. My address is 59 Sig. Bat., Fort Jackson, S. Carolina.

As Always,

Norb

Louisville, Kentucky, **February 3**, Wednesday 8:45 pm

Dear Norb

Well, we haven't heard from you as yet, but we keep on hoping and praying. You are our topic and will be until we get your address. Well, it seems everybody in the age limit is taking the news serious. Sabel [*Joe's employer*] guesses he will close the place and get a job. He's 38 but all his men are younger and then Hubbuch is in the age limit and all the men excepting his uncle and Tony, so we'll just have to wait. That's all you can do.

Jr Russell came in around 7 o'clock tonite. He was over 2 hours late. So far, I haven't seen him. His Detroit girlfriend and her mother came at noon today. He is still thin as ever. He said he had some extra poundage but lost it worrying about whether or not he will get a leave. I think Johnny's work will be termed essential work, but I think if the Army doesn't take Joe he will be working for defense too, don't you?

Well, I seen where the Germans gave up or died in Stalingrad. That's good news.

We are all OK. Pop didn't get home until 8:30 pm, so Mom called. She forgot it was St. Blase, the blessing of throats.

Did you hear Bob Hope Tuesday? He said he didn't realize that Washington's hotels was so crowded that the President had to go to Africa for a conference. They never had any trouble finding the way - the pilot just followed the Wilkie buttons. And said that some people will really go out of the way for a second cup of coffee. He really pulled them cute. [*Hermina*]

Louisville, Kentucky, **February 4**, Thursday, 4:45 pm

Dear Norb,

Before I forget - Mrs. Redle told Marge of a woman that lived over there. She is a bookkeeper and typewriter. I thought I might forget that.

Yes, we seen Jr Russell and his bride-to-be, I suppose. He came over with her this morning. I went over there this afternoon and met her mother. She is from Belgium, speaks with a definite accent. I doubt if she is as old as Mrs. Russell is and she's fat. I think this girl is pretty sensible. So does Mom. Jr Looks the same. Skinny as he always was and I don't think he's quite as handsome. Jr and Madlyn went in town to see about a marriage license, so now we all wonder.

We never heard from you. Mom is getting jittery, but it consoles her to know you are someplace in the USA. That's something to be thankful for, also that you're sensible.

Betsy is already showing a peppy sign. She's jumping and playing, I really believe those pills work miracles. I guess it was something her system lacked. It's very warm today.

We are expecting Alma over tonite. She said if she got here in time she wanted to go to the Mission with us. Keeping our timmers [*fingers*] crossed.
H.R.

Fort Jackson, South Carolina, **February 4**

Dear Mom and All,

Well, here I am again and it won't be long til bedtime and I'm glad of that because I am all "broke up" but there's no "fog in the holler." I like the climate down here much better than I did in Missouri. It's a little warmer than it was there. The ground or earth or whatever you want to call it is very sandy. I guess that's because we're not but 140-150 miles from the ocean.

You know when we were on the train I never ate but two meals in the same state. I had breakfast in one, dinner in another and supper in still another. Some of the country looked mighty poor. Perhaps farmers have defense jobs.

I thought perhaps I could get Falls City beer down here but I don't think there is any. But if there is, I'll find... [*Pages missing.*]
[*Norb*]

Louisville, Kentucky, **February 5**, Friday, 4:30 pm

Dear Norb,

Well, we haven't heard from you as yet, but we keep on hoping. This is to let you know that the last chapter in Mrs. Russell's book will be written at 7:00 pm tonite. Jr is going to be married. She was just here and asked us to come over. Write more tomorrow.
H.R.

Louisville, Kentucky, **February 6**, Saturday, 2:30 pm

Dear Norb,

We haven't heard from you today either. Mom is wondering if you are going to be sent across, but she is OK. So is Pop.

Well, Jr was just married last night. Reverend Peek from Milton Avenue performed the ceremony. Lavada and Jack, Mr. and Mrs. Butler were witnesses. The minister was very nice and Mary was there. Mom, Marge, Joe, Ann and I were there and Mrs. Clay, Madlyn's mother and that's all. This all went in a very big hurry you know. The most amusing of all was to see Russell Sr. eating a pink and white ice cream and wedding cake with the minister. Did we razz him after the Rev left. Elmer said Russell would never live that down. Then he asked how did he do, we told him he ate that as if he was accustomed to it. Russell was swell, he really was. It did look funny to us to see all the men eating ice cream and cake [*as opposed to the usual beers and alcohol*]. After the Rev left, Russell got out the beer, but only one bottle. He's been sober as a judge all week. That was something to be thankful for. Jr leaves this afternoon at 4:10 pm and has to take duration luck. He might get a seat on the train, and he might not. He has to report Monday at 8 am. My, my, what a bustle all these three days. I think Jr aged quite a bit. He was as sensible as you think you are yesterday and his bride is a sensible, nice little girl. She is going back with her mother for 2 months and then to Key West. Jr said he's on the personnel there and is sure he'll be there another year according to the commanding officer. Jr wished for you to be there. He showed the minister your picture and added how he used to come over and eat. He was nice as could be. They both asked Jr to wait until the war was over, so did her mother, but no good. Now this afternoon he has to leave again. It is foolish in a way. Clarence Koebel's marriage license was in the paper onThursday. All of us together gave Jr and bride $5.00 [*$71.43 value in 2017*]. Hoping we hear soon. Mom, Marge, Ann, Russell and the Rev sat at the table together. Mom wore lipstick for the first time. I told Elmer to rib her about it and you know he don't leave anything undone in that way. Mom felt like everybody was looking at her. I fixed her hair. Mr. Butler told Mom how good she looked. She got more compliments than the bride did. Joe said he was going to let Mom know about attending a night wedding and not going to church, to make the Mission alone. I'm waiting for it. Mom did look nice if I have to say so myself, and compliment myself halfway.

I must also say my, my, what a letter. If there is any questions you want to ask, just make out a questionnaire. Joe and Ann don't think the marriage will last. You can't tell. It might, but we would all hate to see you go into it like that.

Until tomorrow, good day my sweet,

Hermina

Louisville, Kentucky, **February** 7

Dear Norb,

Well, no news is still good news. Our Mission closes today at 2:00 pm. It is a beautiful day too. We're OK. I don't have a speck of news. Jr had to stand on his trip back to Key West. I certainly hope we hear from you soon, especially tomorrow. You know that Monday morning jitters Mom has. Pop's puffing away. I'll sign off for this day.

Love and kisses from all of us.

Porky

Continued, Monday Morning:

Dear Norb,

Well, there wasn't any jitters. Mom got two letters and boy we certainly did appreciate them. Let me know how you like this [*referring to her 7-day letter that she kept adding to*].

Cletus Murr's father died Saturday. That Mr. Gorman, head of your draft board - he died last week. End of obituary.

Dorothy Davis's wedding announcement was in yesterday's paper. She is marrying Charles Klapeke, Jr of the US Naval Reserve. Didn't you go to school with him? We are all swell and I bet on your weekend off you take in some ocean sights.

Love and hugs, kisses, squeezes, pinches and pats, that's all,

Porky

Louisville, Kentucky, **February 8**, Monday, 8:30 pm

Dear Norb,

Well, we sure were glad to hear from you. Mom got the letters on her first trip to the mailbox. We all thought New York was your destination. Oh no, I take that back. Mom and Pop thought California. According to the Railway, you are not any further away from us than Missouri. We are all OK.

After your letters today, I got busy on the phone. I called Mr. Orrill for Lip, Johnson for Johnny, Mrs. Russell, St. Brigid, and Marge. Joey called, so everybody knew today you were in South Carolina. Now, bring on the Maneuvers.

Mom picked up a little dope [*gossip*] while at Schieman's. That is, - Ernie's in Omaha, Ben's in California. So is Jack in California. J.L. Tucker is in Pensacola. I haven't no other news out-side of that. I imagine Jr Hubbuch might be heading for the Big Pond. His father received a wallet, his sister a piece of jewelry, his mother something too. And he told them not to write until they hear from him. I got a feeling he's going across but I hope my feelings are fooling.

We are expecting Alma tonite. She went home from work to read your letters. Then she is coming here so it will be late. Hoping to hear from you soon.

I got a little more to add. Lill [Steinmetz] said Bill was at Jackson in the First World

War so that is an old camp. You bet we waited for a long distance call. I wish you could get a call thru sometime. We all do.

With love from all,

"Porky"

Louisville, Kentucky, February 9, Tuesday, 10:10 pm

Dear Norb,

Well, Mom intended to write you but she had to go in town and get herself a pair of shoes, her Christmas present. She didn't need a ration coupon for that. Mom's going to have her corns out tomorrow.

How did you come out with the dentist? Is your mouth well taken care of?

Alma told me last night that Bud Kaiser was going to be married. Well, I seen him at Shelby and Broadway, but he denied it. He admitted he was going with a girl, but he wasn't getting married. He said I was the 5th person to ask him that. Still gossipy, huh?

Yankee Doodle Dandy is in its 6th week run. How do you like Fort Jackson by now and how warm or cold is it there? That's a permanent camp isn't it?

Red Hellmann's home. I heard he's wearing a braided rope on his shoulder. What does that indicate? We got a nice Valentine card from Alma. So did Joe and Lip. That is a card-sending gal. We are all fine. Hoping to hear from you soon. With love from all,

Hermina

Louisville, Kentucky, February 9

Norb,

Just received your nice letter and the pictures. I like the one of you sitting at a table the best. It is 2:30 now and I had a hunch that you would send a letter. I addressed the envelope and stamped it but left the letter open. Then I looked in the mailbox and lo and behold a letter from you. It makes me and all of us feel so good. If we can't see and talk to one another, we can exchange thoughts, and that is a whole lot. But if you can't write much, just a few lines will be enough.

You look very stern just like your Papa. Ha, ha

[Mother]

Louisville, Kentucky, February 11, Cold, 22°, 1:15 pm

God bless you. Dear Norb.

I just got through cleaning the fish bowl. On Jan. 18 I bought them a box of fish food. They don't seem to like it very much, sheet wafers. There are no more worms.

We are all well and hope you are also. Sorry you won't get no furlough. I don't know if Hermina wrote this to you. You know Mrs. Russell received a letter from Jr telling that they were never told that 90 percent of the boys were going across the big pond in about two weeks now. Jr wants them to come to see him. She is all nervous and broke up. I feel sorry for her. She is waiting for a letter from Jr that is more definite before she will go. I hope that he not have to go. Norb, they got your name twice on the church roster. I'm going to have that corrected.

I was in town twice this week. Tuesday I got my shoes that Hermina ordered for me and paid 1 dollar down. If I would wait, the Salesman said over the phone, I would have to use my ration card. You know shoes are rationed now. Three pairs of shoes in a year. That is all we are allowed. It's all right for most of the people but not for the children. I bought Papa two pairs at Besendorf's about 2 weeks ago and had a pair half-soled at the Jew on Goss Avenue. Cost $1.50. Good job. Just bought those before Christmas.

The men have a Mission this week and it is crowded every night. Joe goes every night but not in the morning. Papa goes also. Father lets him off at 5:30 pm so he can attend the Mission. Some men went up in the choir. Good attendance.

I am not sure but I think it is Cletus's Mass, the one that was in the T.B. Hospital. He is going to the mission and going back to church and get married over again. He said it was not his wife's fault that they were not married right.

Norb are you working in the office again? Did you find a '92 or not? Are your classmates with you again? Why did you not send your radio? Can you go to Mass? Let us know if you received the box of Valentine candy please. How are you getting along with your teeth? Have you got them all filled? Wednesday I had my feet tended to - corns, ingrown toenail, and callus. My feet feel like I could dance a quadrille.
Goodbye,
Mother and all

Louisville, Kentucky, **February 12**, Friday, 7:40 pm
Dear Norb,

It was beautiful in Louisville. We hardly had a fire all day but yesterday it was blistering cold. We are all OK. Pop is getting over his cold and he really has the sniffles.

Well, your letter today was dated a year and a month later than the one yesterday. Your years sure pass by quick so I suppose your next letter will be on date.

Mom said if your hine [*hiney*] is so sore from horseback riding, she could send you that rubber pillow. No kidding, can you ride good? If you can, get us a picture of yourself on a nag. Are any of those hosses [*sic*] KY saddle hosses?

From the contents of your letter, it seems you like it at Ft. Jackson better than you ever liked Crowder.

Jr Hubbuch is coming home Sunday for a few days furlough.

Ann wanted to add a bit of sarcasm. She said I should tell you for once she read your letter with a correct date. I told her I had you told already. Then she discovered you were a month behind time yet.

This beats all news - Joey said today Lee is in 4-H. He was reclassified and that 4-H comes before 4-F. How do you figure it? [*4-F was the Army draft classification for a physical disability*].

We heard the president [*Franklin D. Roosevelt*] tonight and he was grand. I hope you heard him too. Say, is your radio working or not? We have never received it you know.

Your godchild Katsy is a tricky one. Her teacher told Shirley she and another girl got into her crayons and printed each other's face all colors and had the biggest kick out of it.

That's all for tonite, goodnite, sleep tite, and hope your hine's alright.
H.R.

Continued, Saturday morning:
Well, it's snowing again today. It's really cold. Jimmy's in a Boy Scout show at the Armory today. I dreamed you came home last night and you were as skinny as could be. Well, this is all for this time,
Bye,
Porky

Louisville, Kentucky, **February 14,** Sunday, 5:10 pm

Valentine Day

Dear Norb,
Well, I'm inclosing a picture of your clock. Looks good, doesn't it? I just wrote to Bill Hollkamp. It's hard to write those censored letters you know. The pictures we took of Jr's wedding did not get good.

Did you go horseback riding today? Well, Is it as cold there as here? I doubt very much if you did. It was 20 below this morning, the coldest yet this season. Margie got the biggest kick out of playing with the "pinnies."

I sent Moody a Valentine on the Chronic Complainer. He guessed it too. Alma called yesterday saying she was coming over today. I wouldn't blame her if she didn't, because it's too cold. We are all OK. Moody is going to get the blessing tonite. It's the closing of the men's Mission. Margie calls him "hee-ho" for Leo. The kids are going to mail this and I will bring this newsless script to a close.

I suppose we will hear from you too. We are OK. I hope you are too.
Valentine Greetings good and true I send in friendship Name to you.
Antique looking and sounding, isn't it?
"Porky"

Louisville, Kentucky, **February 15**, Monday, 1:05 pm, 10°

Dear Norb:

Yeh, man it's still cold. I don't know how cold it was early this morning. You don't expect that of me, do you? Nope, we never got a letter this morning but we did get one Friday afternoon. We don't have Saturday afternoon mail delivery anymore either. They delivered about 3 Saturday so they cut that out again last week.

I didn't know there was a 4-H classification. Moody is in that too. I thought that was a tall one of Lee's, but I seen Moody's card last night. "Judge not lest you be judged." I would certainly like to see how the good Lord will judge him.

I guess you can enjoy the good - more southern - sunshine, while we shiver. I heard Louis Heintz is going to get married. Don't know if it's the truth or not. I will say bye-bye for now. Mom will finish
"Porky"

Continued, 2 pm:

Dear Norb,

The weather was 2° below yesterday but not so cold today. We have had our kitchen door locked yesterday and today. I weather-stripped it with silk stocking. Going to give Uncle Sam lots of old silk stockings. He is asking for them. Norb, did you get the box of candy?

Papa had a very bad cold and the head sister at St. Brigdet's [*Brigid's*] asked him if he would take some whiskey. He said he did not care for any but his wife liked it, so Saturday she brought a pint of good bottle in bond for 5 years old whiskey to him and told him to drink it. That would do him some good I think. That was very nice of her, don't you think?

I was at Mary's for supper last night. Mrs. Griffin and Mrs. Moorcamp and Miss Toby were there also. Mrs. Griffin's son left for the Army last Tuesday a week and she has not heard from him as yet. She is worried about him. He went to Camp Fort Harrison. I can't make it out why he did not write. Well, Mary Wilson came down to go to work so I must close. Mary said Hello. Papa is better and all are well, so good-bye and be good. Don't forget to pray.
Mother

Louisville, Kentucky, **February 16**, 1:45, 12° above 0° cold

Dear Norb,

Yesterday it snowed and the snow was so fine, like I never saw before. Hermina is ironing. I was patching Papa's pants with your old pants that you wore to work in. It sure pays to save junk. Your green pants are minus patches also. Thursday every schoolchild is supposed to collect 5 pounds of clothing for the Russians so I am going to get busy and rob my wardrobe in the basement.

Elizabeth was here quite early this morning. Muthy brought her and the baby and 3 tubs of clothes to dry them. She has Berney's laundry to do also. He gave her his wash machine and ironer and told her he would give her $2 a week in or after March. I don't remember. He has some man staying with him. He works and he cooks and Berney cooks sometimes. They get along fine. Rudy told Berney that he could work for a defense job so that he would not be drafted. He said he would not do that - people would think that he did not want to serve. I would not doubt that. Elizabeth would not take him.

Joe and Ann also. Hermina wants to write too so good-bye, God bless you and pray hard for us as we pray for you every day.
Mother and all

Mom said send the photographs please. [*H.R.*]

February 16, Tuesday
Dear Norb,

I see from Mom's letter it's 12° above zero. Cold, but the sun is shining bright. The sky is a deep blue and this pretty. White snow makes a lovely picture.

This drafting from 18-38 is causing a many serious looking expression. Well, the sooner the better and get this darn war over with. I think all of these businesses of luxury will certainly be out. Jr Hubbuch did not get to come home. His furlough has been postponed until next week. You surely can't tell for sure anymore.

Joe and Pop got their Valentines from Alma. Of course, Joe blamed me for it. It was a henpecked husband. She was pinning dress material on him. It was funny and fitting. Pop's was a cigar smoking politician. He had cigars in every pocket, but it didn't the Papa. We are all OK.

You never did say a word about your pen you sent home. Also, did you receive your Valentine box? How did you like that sausage we sent you at Crowder? Do you still work in the office?
Hoping you are well as ever,
"Porky"

Louisville, Kentucky, **February 17,** 9 am
[*Dear Norb*]

We have been waiting for a letter from you but no letter yet this week. Sometimes I think your [*sic*] probably in maneuvers. Is my thinker on the right track? We are all OK.

A person don't know what to think, they are taking men from the Curtiss-Wright Co. and inducting them in the Army so I wonder if any job will keep a man out, because that's really defense work.

Antoinette Spoelker's husband is afraid that he will be drafted. The work he had been doing is non-deferrable now and they are taking these men so he is going to try and see if he can find something that will keep him out. It's government work he's doing, too.

Well, that's about all I know. Jimmie Beiler [*or Bliler*] is out on a leave and is going to be sent out when he returns. I thought they kept these 17-year- olds awhile, at least before they send them out. He's in the Navy.

Katsy came home. She needed some (fises) prizes for school. Well, that's all for this time. Hoping to hear from you soon.

Hermina

Continued by Mommy:

Dearest Son,

Having not heard from you this week. Was thinking you may be ill or on a lull of waiting, or too busy. You never stated if you do office work again? Did you have your exercise Sunday going horseback riding? How many miles are you from Louisville? You are not so far from Kentucky, west as you are from us. I hope that we will hear from you soon. Well then, goodbye and God bless you. Don't forget your prayers. If ever, we need them now.

Mother and all

In the following letter Norb wrote 'Jan 16, 1942' and then crossed out 'Jan' and added 'Feb'. He forgot to correct the year to 1943. His sister would kid him about that in a later letter.

Fort Jackson, South Carolina, **February 16?**

Dear Mom and all,

Just a line to let you know I received your valentine and thanks a million. It was 15°above yesterday and I believe it broke a record here in SC.

Alma was saying she might have to have her eye operated on. I sure hope not. It would be pretty tough.

I'm going to apply for a furlough again but that is about all the good it will do me I guess. It will be about 15 days before I hear anything about it. So I guess I might as well hope for the best.

Well, I hope all is well at home. It is here so far. Well, I must get going so I'll see you again when I get a chance. Tell MaryI said Hello.

As Always,

Norb

Louisville, Kentucky, **February 18**, Thursday

Dear Norb,

It is 10:30 am. We received your letter stating that you were waiting for the General. Well, did the old buzzard come?

Well, it warmed up quite a bit yesterday and today is warmer also but pretty crimp. But it is a beautiful day. Well, I do think with all this scribbling I could rate better than a "horse." You could have called me a "news-casting thoroughbred." I would have been proud of that, but I overlook that you really know how to make sistah feel good, not that I don't think she rates "Bank" to you, but she was pleased with that title.

Pop is over his cold but still [*sniffles*] a little to let you know he had one.

The news really isn't so good right now for the US boys. It sounded mighty grim last night. I imagine a lot of Ft. Knox boys are there with the Armored Division. Well, there's a lot of boys in N. Africa from the Burg [*Schnitzelburg*] that we know so there's no telling how many is there.

Why in the **** don't you answer some questions? I and Mom both asked about where you posed for your picture. We, that is Alma and us, want a picture, and you said it is paid for. I thought Alma said it was Gold Tone Studio. Will you kindly tell us dear angelic brother (phooey)? Are you going to some school again in Ft. Jackson do you think? Or don't you? Jonesy said he was going to see if he could take up the course that leads to a 2nd Lieutenant.

Your sisters are getting pretty active as I wrote saying they were remodeling our place [*Hubbuch's*]. Well, yesterday they yanked the steps down, so we all came down on the stepladder with round rungs like painters use. We came 3rd to 2nd floor. They rigged it up securely, but you could see to the dirt below, looked scary but Porky made it. Marge did swell. I didn't work today for that reason. I'm not paid to climb ladders so I'd rather wait until steps are there.

I hope the inspection was fine. I hope you are all thru with it by now because I wouldn't want to see Norbie come drooping home before the war was over.

Well, we start on food rationing now. Everybody is allowed 5 cans per week of food. You can get by on that. So far, I don't see where anybody has a squawk a coming.

I'm sending a card under separate cover. Mom's birthday is Feb 27. She'll be 69 years old. It would be nice if you could get a long distance call through around that time.
Hope you are well, honey.
As ever,
"Porky"

Louisville, Kentucky, **February 21**, 3:50 pm

Dear Norb,

Just another month until spring. Seems everybody is looking forward to spring. Today seems like a pretty Easter Sunday. We are looking for Alma to come soon now. Jr Hubbuch got a 3-day furlough so he's coming over tomorrow night. I think that's mighty nice of him.

Mrs. Russell just called and said that all of Ruby's boys are in. You remember that little puny twin, Paul Allen? Well, he joined the Navy and is in Great Lakes. JO Is at Fort Harrison, Herbert is in Utah, Carl is across. That's giving all of them. Everybody, even Ruby. I'm going to finish this letter tonite.

Well, it's nearly 9:00 pm. Alma didn't show up. She worked later so apparently her eye isn't bothering her too much. She called and said she was coming tomorrow. Mom had an awful cold too this week but she feels OK today and got to church. Nearly everybody has a cold since that cold snap. I never seen so many colds in all my life. Jackie's got the measles so I guess all the kids out there will get them too, but he isn't sick.

We are thinking of your furlough and still hoping. Haven't any news as you can see so I will close. Pa and his beer drinker Marge just finished a can of Oertel's. We are OK and hope you are too.

With love from all,

"Porky"

Louisville, Kentucky, **February 21**, Monday, 7 pm

Dear Norb,

Well, we got three letters from you today. From the contents of one, Mom said she'd have a popping good time. For once since August 19, '42, you had your date right and that's fine. Perhaps you need a little praise and you'll do better, but what's the diff?

We're expecting Jr Hubbard tonite so we got a few quarts of Oertel's and Pop said I could have some of his Valentine for highballs. Tain't bad. But I just don't like the idea of serving whiskey to anybody so that's out, I know.

Well, this ration business is a serious thing. Tonight's paper carried what you can get. Everybody is allowed 48 points a month but I guess we can get along because we only ate partially on a can. We are wondering if the fast and abstinence of Lent will be lifted this year.

I guess Alma is working late because she hasn't gotten here as yet. She called from work today and said she had taken the second treatment.

That proof was grand of you Norb - the best of them all. I called Acorn service. They said they would charge 35¢ to take a picture of that and an 8 x 10 photo would cost 45¢, the same as any enlargement that size. Mom and I haven't said anything to anybody about it so it's down at Hertel's already. If or when you get your furlough, Mom said to Reiger's [*photographer's studio*] you must go. To Reiger's you must go and smile pretty. She didn't say anything about smiling but she was going to see to it that she had a good picture of you. That's her aim in life when you get your furlough. We are going to listen to Richard Crooks now.

"Porky"

Continued, Tuesday 11:00 pm:

Well, by this time you received and airmail letter I hope. We are all OK. Mom received a letter addressed to her from you this morning and it was Dear Lip, Beak and kids. It was Lip's letter. We got a kick out of that. You said the mess sergeant had syphilis. My stars, that's terrible. We were glad to know you had a blood test already and your weight isn't bad either.

Love,

"Porky"

Louisville, Kentucky, **February 23**, 8:10 am

Dear Norb,

    This is the first time for a long time I wrote a letter so early. Joe was feeling 'em last night as you could hear. He tried four different times to write you when Alma was writing and all the letters ran together, so he gave it up as a bad job. It was a bad job. Alma is going to try and call you long distance tonight. This Tuesday night. In case she is not successful, you try and call Wednesday or Thursday. You know last night everybody was so anxious to talk to you. Your voice didn't sound so clear, I didn't think. Well, Norb we are all OK and we'll let you know when you talk to us if we find out.

Love,

Hermina

Louisville, Kentucky, **February 23**, Noon

Dear Norb,

    This is the third time I'm writing to you today. We all know you're worried about Alma. She called a few minutes ago. She's taken another treatment and also got the diagnosis. She has a tumor on her right eye. They are giving these treatments in order to save the eye. Mom thought I could write that better than her but I think Katie does OK. We are making a novena for her to the Blessed Mother. Mom is having a Mass said. It seems strange there is always so much eye trouble in the family. And you say a few Our Fathers with us every day. Then Alma will benefit from spiritual and medical attention. How was your telephone call last night? We intend to pay some on that call. Let us know now.

Hermina

Continued by Mommy, Fine weather, 12:30

Dear Norb,

    All I want to tell you is that I want you to join us in the novena for Alma. Say a few Our Fathers and the Memorare. That's the prayers we are going to pray. I told Alma that she should join with us also. I told her I would go to confession and communion for her. She said that she wanted to go to the Sacraments, too. I hope that you will do the same. Receive the sacraments of love of your God for her, for the one you love and [*who*] needs your prayer. That's the least we can do. To show and feel how near and dear she is to us and you. If it does cost a little effort on your part, it will make you feel you did all in your power and she will be grateful for it. So I will close with the hope that you will not disappoint Alma. I told her I was going to ask you.

    I thank you very much for the chewing gum and I will think of you when I take a chew. I never told anyone but Margaret and Hermina. I want to tell what Margie said. She was mad at Elizabeth and said 'go to hell.' Elizabeth said who did you say that to? The dog was just there so she said 'You go to hell Daisy' to make her mother believe that she was talking

to their dog. Don't you think that's smart? Elizabeth was here when her letter came. How much was that call last night? We will help pay for it.
Mother

Louisville, Kentucky, **February 24**, Friday, 1:30
Dear Norb,

I said yesterday that it was spring weather. Well, the thermometer today says about 25° above. It's real "blizzardy" out. It snowed and now the wind is blowing it all around. Nuf said.

From the contents of your letter there must be plenty horses asses around Ft. Jackson. Oh well, I guess he just wants to show his (atoritah) authority. With timmers and tups crossed and wishing for you furlough, I will bring my next to nothing letter to a close. We are OK. It's Mom's birthday tomorrow. Hoping to see you soon but I wouldn't be too disappointed if you don't get your furlough.
"Horse"

Louisville, Kentucky, **February 25**, Thursday, 8:50 pm
Dear Norb,

Well, it's a beautiful night in Louisville. It looks like spring is here. Yeah, man. Mom got the ration books today. Looks like a lot of bingo numbers. I seen in the papers where mothers are going to be arrested if they leave children home by themselves while they attend bingo parties.

Mom said if you get your furlough don't forget to bring your radio if it needs repairing. She just thought of that. We haven't had a letter since Monday. Marge is working tonite. There is so much to be cut and you know Marge does all of that. Mom and I was bored at her. I made biscuits and Mom tried to dig up a meal she would especially like - and she don't show up.

I see they are thinking of taking single and childless men up to 45 years. That would get Bobby Lee then. Do you ever get to see any radio actors and Hollywood shows at Ft. Jackson? Jr Hubbuch said he saw one the week he came home and it was pretty good - Noble Sissle Orchestra. I haven't got any special news at all.
So goodnight,
"Porky"

February 26
Dear Mom and all,

Well, there is a very strong wind blowing outside tonight and for once, it's not in the barracks. But the wind is very strong. I wouldn't doubt it a bit if it's not the tail end of a storm. I sure wouldn't want to be walking guard tonight because when that wind and sand gets to beating in your face it's not the most pleasant thing I could think of.

Well, I got a letter from Alma today and she said I didn't sound any pleasant over the phone. Well, for one thing, it scared the hell out of me and for another thing, the office was full of officers, captains, majors, just any kind you wanted.

We have another inspection tomorrow. Inspections, inspections, inspections! I heard one officer make the remark that this outfit was worse than Officers Training School. And he ought to know; he had to go through it. It's very silly and most of these officers will say the same thing. There is such a thing as being too damn clean, too. You can't even have a shoe a quarter of an inch out of the way unless you get gigged for it. And beds – well, if they aren't made just to a tee, that's the next thing to a court martial. Just because they found two coats on a hanger that had a button open we had to scrub barracks night before last. Now that's something. It'll be good to [*go on*] maneuvers and get away from all this chicken shit. Because when you're on maneuvers, anything goes. You don't have to shave for a week if you don't want to. Not that I wouldn't but there's no inspection then.

I still haven't heard anything further about my furlough but I hope to hear something this week. If I do, I'll let you know. I put it in for the eighth of next month, but weather [*sic*] it will go through for that date or not I do not know. Nor I don't think anyone else does.

There are some very happy, happy men in our outfit today. I am talking about the ones over thirty eight. Five of them went home today and another bunch goes home tomorrow. I think it's a very good thing because they can't keep up with a young fellow in running and exercises of which we have plenty of. And after all, that is what you'll need, but I hope the running ain't always backwards.

Well, as you know we have a new mess sarge and the food for the last few days has been excellent and that is saying a mouthful for Army chow. We also have coffee twice a day. That don't get you in the humor of joining the Army, does it? Tonight for supper we had roast pork, potatoes (mashed), carrots and peas, Well I can see that I'm working up another appetite just thinking about it so I'll close for now and I'll see you-all later.
Still holding the same lust for food,
Norb V...-

Louisville, Kentucky, **February 26**, 1:30 pm

[*Dear Norb*]

I'll start about the weather. We have snow, sunshine, wind and plenty regular snow flurries. Well, we are looking forward for your furlough but I am not going to bank on it. I wouldn't want to be disappointed if you could not come. So, as God wills it. Don't know any news but that things are looking better for us, as the paper and the radio says. I seen in the paper that the President is ill. I hope and pray that it is not serious. Norb I wish you would tell Alma that she should follow the directions of her doctor. She sure don't follow them as she should. She was here the Wednesday night. She came after work. She should have had her prescription filled but she would not. She said that it would be all right the next day. I don't want her to know that I wrote about her to you. Of course, it's none of my business. I understand that but I thought that she would pay more attention to you. I also called her sister and asked her to see to it that she would take her medicine. She told me that she has to stand right aside of her and make her take it. So again, I asked you not to tell her that I called her sister. She seems to be very nice.

Papa and I got an invitation to Bro. Joseph Sandford's First Solemn Holy Mass Sunday Feb. 25 and to the reception [*at*] his home Sunday from 2-5. I guess maybe you don't know anyone there, but for love's sweet sake, I'll have to go. I'm sending you a leaflet. Pray the morning offering. That's all you have to do. I had you enrolled in it. We get a leaflet every month. He is a Franciscan. So I guess we will go. Papa wants me to go. I don't care to. I learned it by heart.

I'm afraid Joe will have to serve now, don't you? I have no questions to ask. You don't answer them no how. But wait til you come home. Then you have to go through the mill with answers for the questions you did not answer. Well, that's all for today. Mary wants to know if you're rationing the kisses for only one today for her. Goodbye and good luck. God bless you and don't forget to pray for Alma. We are making a novena for her - two Our Fathers and one Memories [*Memorare*], so join in with us. Mary wants to know where she could get the kissing ration book.
Mother

Fort Jackson, South Carolina. **February 28**
Hello folks,

How do you do? I hain't got much news but the weather is a little cooler than it has been for a while. I got a letter from Lee Rhodes. He's in N. Africa now. He wants to know when I'm coming over to pay him a visit. Should I tell him? Now about that furlough business, I just put in for March the 8th but expecting and getting are two different things. It looks as though they had a pretty bad blizzard in Alaska. So, Wahoo has another car? Perhaps he needed one. Who knows except him? Well, this is a short letter but that's all I know for now. But I'll see you later.
As Always,
Norb

Louisville, Kentucky, **February 28**, Sunday, 3:45 pm
Dear Norb,

It's a heavenly day in Louisville. Mom and Pop are gone to Fr. Mark Joseph Sanford's reception. You know Pop wouldn't miss that for anything. They have fine kegs of beer there. So that's the reason, you know. Betsy is writing also. I don't know what she's cooking up.

We are expecting Alma. Mom called her yesterday to thank her for the card and dollar she sent Mom. She really appreciated that but thought the card would do as Alma is under a heavy expense now. Talking about cards, Mom never received the card I sent you. I thought perhaps you didn't receive it or it was just late coming.

Bottom of letter on page one. The top was neatly torn off:

Mom and Pop are problems to get out when there is such a special place to go. I fix up. Mom and Pop needed finishing touches, too, but they're off! I bet we will see a lot of front yard gardens this year. That's what all people are talking about since the point rationing system is going into effect.

Antoinette Heurle's husband got a deferment again so she is visiting here now. I hope when you get your furlough she will be here yet but I doubt that very much. We are all OK. We are going to have a blackout Tuesday night. The whistles blow different now, so they have been blowing every day at 12:30 am. Even today, Sunday, to get the people acquainted with it. I didn't write yesterday as I always do because so often I fail to mail it, then there's two on Sunday.

With fingers crossed. Love,

Hermina

Louisville, Kentucky, **February 28**

Dear Norb,

I hope you get your furlough. It was so long since I saw you that I barely no [*sic*] what you look like. We get our reports in a couple weeks. I might make a few mistakes in your letter. I haven't wrote you a letter that I can't remember it. Well, I haven't got very much to write.

I am up at Momies. Margie tries to write but she just scribbles on a valentine that Mrs. Orile, Mary Ann's mother, gave her. I will have to close now.

As Always,

Betsy

Louisville, Kentucky, **March 1**

Dear Norb,

Received two letters today. Pop just came home. It's 9 o'clock and it's 24° and rather windy. Pop said it's going to be 10° above and the bucket [*porcelain pail used to collect beer*] and Pop are going out the front door. He just came in and is going out again. Well, Norb the little ones are asking about you and Johnny called today to find out. Well, we all will be glad to see you if it is for you to have a furlough. I hope anyway. Maurice Slattery is home from the Navy until the 12th and his brother John was so happy this morning. Alma was over yesterday. She looks good and we are praying for her, and she prays along with us. When she's here, she gets on her prayer bones [*knees*]. I'm glad she's Catholic. I believe she likes Mom. And Dad also. She always calls him Pop. And Mom too. Well, Norb if you come in and you feel like stopping at Hubbuch's. OK. Do you need anything or have you got enough? How about your income tax? I haven't paid mine as yet. Only until the 15th to pay. I have four war bonds - $25 each ($100). This pen isn't so hot anymore. It don't write as good. Are you making use of your money belt? Hermina just came in from Edgar's (Ann's brother). He wanted to know about a truck and Johnny knew about one and called to tell him about it. He was glad to know about it.

Pop just came in and Hermina is reading your letters to him and I'm glad your dad had the hell scared out of you. We will have an angel brother coming home. Say, you have good eats, don't you? Swell. Glad to know it. Hermina worked since 11 o'clock. Well, I work about the same yesterday. I worked and got my bath about 8 o'clock Sunday. Just as every busy Sunday. Joey is working. And Wahoo, too, has a new machine. He never comes home anymore and Dewey is growing. Lee has a large car again. He wants a B ration card and is going to get riders. Maybe they like to fish. Ha Ha. Say Norb, when you get home you will have to go to the Ration Board and get your coffee. And also you are allowed so many cans of cans of canned goods. It seems odd - shoes, canned good and coffee so far. Our trolley car stops at New Lydia and Goss Avenue. (Exercise? Ain't so).

Well, Norb that is about all for tonight. Hope to see you soon. Keep praying and be good. Your loving sister,
Mary Margaret Catherine

Louisville, Kentucky, **March 1**, Monday, 10 pm
Dear Norb,

We are now getting in the "stretch" of thinking of your furlough. We are all hoping for the best. Marge has written her pamphlet [*letter above*], I see. We are all OK. I told Mom she'd have to do some cooking with you coming home. She would have to sling the hash. She said that didn't worry her because you was easy. You do eat nearly anything. We are listening to the "News." Mom will finish this tomorrow so I'll say goodnite. I hope you are over your telephone scare by now. Under the conditions you stated, I would have sounded sour too.

Goodnite, sleep tight,
"Porky"

Louisville, Kentucky, **March 2**, 21°, cold, snowing
Dear Norb,

I haven't got much time. The bread is ready to put in the pans and that must be on time like the Army - to the dot. Tonight we have a blackout. Everything is going to be over with at 9:30. I guess we will sit in the dark living room or in the lighted hall. The last blackout was no success. John did not know anything about it. Some people did not even hear the alarm. It gets E's [*Elizabeth's*] little ones afraid of the blackout. Jimmy got an altar boy medal. He is

so proud of it. I thought you was going to write Milton a letter. At least you said you would. I think he is doing somewhat better. We are all alright. That's all for today. Two letters in one day. That's fine. Enjoyed them both. Close with a wish for a safe homecoming.
Mother

Louisville, Kentucky, **March 3**, Wednesday, 10 pm
Dear Norb,

Listening to Dick Fisher News. We are all OK. I suppose you have answered Lee Rhodes' letter but I'll enclose a V...- Mail letter in case you haven't. I think it is about 5 above tonite. It's plenty cold.

Well, it seems as if we've touched the Germans' nerve center. The news is good. If you can call war good. To tell the truth, the blackout last night was rather pretty. It was really a study in black and white. We worked tonite until 9:00 pm. We are hoping for your furlough but Ernie Schieman hasn't had a furlough as yet. Jr Hubbuch just had 4 days and was gone over 9 months so don't let your spirits get too low if you're not successful in getting yours just now.

Antoinette Huesel said she was coming over Saturday night. Well, Mom can finish this tomorrow and we're hoping.

According to the paper tonite we will get 1 ¾ pounds of meat a week per person. That isn't much. Cheese will be rationed also. So will butter, oleo, fats and oil later. Porky will be a sparse name in the future. Goodnite. Sleep tight and don't roll out of your bunk.
Love,
"Porky"

Fort Jackson, South Carolina, **March 4**
Dear Mom and all,

Well, what are you doing? Hey, hey. I'm doing pretty well. I was to the dentist today but this is a slow and painful process in the Army. They don't do enough work on you at one time. The weather has been pretty chilly down here for the last couple days. I believe it broke a couple records.

Well, I still don't know when I will get my furlough. It might not be for some time yet because all these men over 38 are going home and they don't allow but one third of the manpower to be on furlough at one time. So I guess that will slow things down a little but I don't guess it will be for very long. There were sure a few smiling and happy faces here today because three men left to go home today and five will go tomorrow, so it won't take them long to clean these guys out. They didn't belong here in the first place. So I guess my furlough will be delayed a couple of weeks.

I forgot that little Shot [*Schott*] boy's name and address or I would have written him a card or something. Suppose you ask Milton what it is. He ought to know the Shots. I believe everyone does because there are quite a few of them.

The chow is still pretty good and I am doing my bit of damage to it after it is on the table but I sure could use a beer right now. I laid down tonight after supper and didn't wake up til kind of late, so I thought I had better write a few letters instead of drinking beer, but I still could use one.

Things are rolling pretty fast down here now that we are here for a while. Now I want to see it get a little warm like the south should be. There is not much more that I know for now so I guess I will close for now. Hoping all is and all are well.

Y-ust [*sic*] about the same,

Norb (feel me once) blotch blotch

Louisville, Kentucky, **March 4**, Thursday, 10:30 pm

Dear Norb,

How do you do, not as you please. I know, otherwise you would of had your furlough papers signed. Well, we're thinking of it.

I met Mrs. Nunn on the [*trolley*] car today. Claude is still in Australia. Nelson and Elbert both have [*had*] their blood test and [*are*] waiting. Mr. Nunn is at the Marine Hospital since Tuesday, she said, his lips were swelling so. I don't know just what's wrong with him. She said you should come to see her when you're home on furlough. Don't have any more news to tell you so will sign off and let Mom finish tomorrow. Too da loo, goodnite, sweet dreams. "Butterball" (expensive name) [*Hermina*]

Fort Jackson, South Carolina, **March 5**

Dear Mom and all,

Well, how is everything? Everything is fine here including the weather for a change. I went in to see the Company commander today about the furlough. After we talked about fifteen minutes, he said he would try to get it for me on the 9th but not for sure. So, I can't bank on it, but here's hoping. I gave him a couple of good excuses so maybe or maybe not. Can't say for sure. Now if it does go through, don't expect me to start running around [visiting] all the relatives because that's out. I didn't do it when I was home and I'm not going to start it now. That, my dear people, is a law of my own and a good one also.

As Always,

Norb V...-

Louisville, Kentucky, **March 5**, 9 am

My Dear Beloved Uncle,

I am sitting by the fishes writing this letter. Mommy is laying down. Hermina is waxing the floor and Joe is reading the paper. It is snowing but it's not sticking. You have not got anything over on us. The only days we have to fast are on Ash Wednesday and Good Friday and of course on Fridays. I just got through washing the windows. I sure hope you get your furlough because I want to see that big, glorious hunk of a man you are. Joe just left to get Poppie. I guess I will sign off.

Shirley

(Over)

The faultfinder is cleaning wallpaper. I am referring to Joe. Poppie is sitting in his easy chair resting like a millionaire. Hermina is ironing curtains, Mommy and I washed the dishes, Ma and Ann is working tonight. I don't know who else is. Hope there are some good radio programs. I know Kate Smith is on. I don't know what to write. Hope you are feeling fine and not drinking too much beer and sure hope you get your furlough. Poppy is just getting a bucket of Oertel's '92.

Your A-1 Girl Friend, V...- V...- V...-

Shirley

Louisville, Kentucky, **March 6**, Saturday, 7:30 pm

Dear Norb,

Well, here I am again. Have just had my Saturday bath, so sweet and clean. We certainly are thinking about you. As we never received a letter today. We don't know which way to wonder. We are all OK. It snowed yesterday but never stuck. If it had we would have been under a foot of snow. It turned to rain last night but it is very much colder out and snowing fine so with the cold wind that's blowing I believe by morning it will be close to 10°.

Of all the different things we seen this past week were Donaldson has a woman on the wagon [*female employee*] on Gray Street [*and*] a woman driving a florist truck. Alma was to see Dr. Von Haven today. I called early this morning; he said he would put a temporary filling in for her, which he did. I think she has to go back next Saturday.

Antoinette Heusle is going home tonite so is not coming here. She was at Ed's Wednesday and one of his little ones took the measles the next day so she took her baby to the Dr. He gave him a shot and told her to go home because he stands a chance of taking them. Then she would have to stay here at least a week longer. So, she called and told us. I called to tell Mrs. Rhodes you heard from Lee so Mr. Rhodes answered. He thanked me for calling. He said they got a letter and he appreciated getting it. He said you write a letter exactly like you talk. So that's news that travels to N. Africa and back and then to you.

All of Johnny's [*family*] got the measles now. They are up again, wasn't real sick. That's all you hear is 'measles.' I guess they are at camp too. Hoping to hear from you. Will close.

Love from all,

"Porky"

Louisville, Kentucky, **March 7**, Sunday, 8:45 pm

Dear Norb,

We have just finished "dinner." We were rather late you know. We seem to be having wintertime with no let up. Lip and family are getting ready to leave. As for news, well, I do have some. Lip said she seen Henry Paul's marriage license in Tuesday's paper. I also seen an account of Louis Heintz's marriage to Dorothy Kamber on Ellison Avenue in the Society News. Bandy legs, remember? Milton said he has a chance of passing the grade so he was very busy tonite with his lessons, seemed deucely odd. We are all OK and still thinking of your furlough. Milt taken my pencil home and the pen seems to be doing fine tonite.
[*Hermina*]

Dear Feel Me Once a Million Times,

Well, I see vere [*where*] you yust [*just*] get your furloaf (like Jr Russell's mother-in-law calls it). Well, in couple of weeks we might see you. We were all sort of looking for you to walk right in on us. Do you wish to be 38 [*to be sent home from military service*]? Mom says you wouldn't but I hope you will get it in a couple of weeks. I will close now. We are all OK. Mom's in her glory and I will mail it as I go to work. These dam [*sic*] cars stop at New Lydia and Goss so we have to hoof it and that's quite a distance in this cold weather. March hasn't been this cold for I don't know how many years. Sort of set a record. And we had a few days when the trees that are early bloomers. Almost blossomed. We are wondering if they will be hurt. Time will tell.
So long,
200 or over [*Margaret*]

Louisville, Kentucky, **March 8**

Dear Mom,

Well, today I was all packed up and ready to go and a half hour before I was going to leave, they called off the furloughs. Oh my God, was I mad! Something like that is damn hard to take. So, I guess I won't get a furlough for a while. I had my papers all made out, and ready to go and then they pull something like that. Well, no furlough, so there's not much you can do about that. So goodnight and I'll be writing.
As Always,
Norb

Norb was granted a three-day leave but he was not close enough to home to make it home for just three days.

Louisville, Kentucky, **March 16**

Dear Bootsie [*Norb*],

How are you? I just turned on the radio and guess what the song was? When You Look in the Heart of a Shamrock. Irish, I bet. Tomorrow is St. Patrick's Day. All the Irish will celebrate. Alma sent us all a card and now the radio is singing 'Mother Dear O Pray for Me.' It's so sweet and oh so much meaning and bright in bliss above, and well, I'm not going to pray all. But really, Norb, we do pray more [*for you*], I guess. And do pray for us also. I just hope you are hearing the radio. Pop is singing and eating his supper. It's about 6:30 o'clock. Mom's waiting on Pop as usual. I have been working at nights and I am so terrible tired tonight. Mom said it's too much work, but well, we need the money. My income tax was plenty. I only paid 1/4 of it, $20.04 for 1/4 of it, and tonight I'm paying the taxes for the house, $125.04. [$1,759 in 2017 value]. Say, don't you think I need a little dough? Now Hermina is tuning to a different station. She didn't like Lights Out.

Did you ever find the address of the boy who writes to you? I do hope you send him something. You can imagine how tickled they are, Norb. Little Margie is getting so sweet and says everything, and Milton got 83 in his average - and Norb, he was so proud of it. All of the kids are looking forward to you coming home and are planning to sleep in Joe's bed to be with you. Milt and Jimmy both want to stay. Were you surprised to know Harry Paul was married? You can't tell a thing about this neighborhood. Katie's house next to Mrs. Russell's is empty so I haven't heard about the marriage. Now I am hearing a boy talk to his mother over the radio and he said he's growing up to be a hog.

Norb, what do you think of Norbert Hollkamp? It might help him. I sure hope it does anyhow and to think Joe Hollkamp was here Saturday and Sunday night. Alma met Joe. Are you jealous? Well, anyway, I feel sorry for Joe. Nobody cares for him, it looks like. I haven't seen Eleanor for a long time. Joe Rawert is going to do some papering for him Sunday a week and I was thinking about going along and cleaning for her so her place will be all cleaned and pretty. I think we should help her because it won't be long before the Stork will be there - the last of April, I think. Oh boy, they sure have a sweet family, don't they? Well, I want to sew a little tonight. I guess I'm nuts, but I'm so tired. I still feel like doing something. No rest I guess.

You had a three-day leave. What did you do, Norb? I wish you could of been closer. Well, Mom wanted to go to church Wednesday, Ash Wednesday it was, and she was thinking her baby [Norb] might be home. Well, I guess God didn't want it that way but I hope the Blessed Mother will send you home soon. Norb, I must be wound up tonight and I can't stop, I guess. Did you know Mom and Alma went to the Passionist Fathers and she was blessed? So was Mom. Joe took them out there. I believe Joe thinks more of Mom and Pop since he is married. Well it really makes me feel good. Ann is as sweet as always. Well, if you think of all in our family, I think they are all sweet, don't you? A family to be proud of - dear, dear ones. Say, spring is around the corner and to think I haven't bought a thing. Alma has a cute suit and blouse. She wore it Saturday to go with Mom to the Passionists. We made a Novena for her. Norb, she lives with her sister now. Sometimes I wish she was with us here. Her sister don't go to church, she told Mom. I do hope it won't make Alma careless so you

ask her to pray for you Norb because Alma is a sweet kid we all like her very much. She did not used to like her brother-in-law and now, thank heavens, she told me he was a changed man. Alma looks good but still doctors with her eye. I hope it will soon be OK. We call her almost every day. Mrs. Ridgeway was here. Does that interest you? Ha, ha. She asked me about you dear. Are your eyes tired? Well, goodbye now. It's 25 minutes of 8 o'clock. Mom's washing dishes, Papa's sleeping in the chair, and Hermina is barefoot. So bye, bye. Pray for me and God bless you.
Margaret

Louisville, Kentucky, **March 17**, 8:35 pm

Dear Norb,

St. Patrick's Day, Wednesday. Just a line to say how do you do and how are you? And, how did you enjoy your three-day 'vacation?' It's a shame you couldn't of been at Camp Atterbury or someplace closer. We haven't heard from you since Monday. Are they putting ink on the ration list too? We thought we'd get a letter today. Are you still expecting your furlough? We are OK. Mom went to see Uncle Ben. He's fine. That old man in those back rooms moved in with his son now. I don't know any news so I will close now until tomorrow. One moment please - Bernard Spoelker never did get to come. He said he was going to California as I told you and that if he is sent across and you are sent across he hopes to meet you there. That's all for this time.
Goodnight and '92,
[*Hermina*]

Louisville, Kentucky, **March 18**, 10:00, beautiful weather

Dear Norb,

I do not know any news today. I want to go see Uncle Ben. Haven't been there in about 10 weeks or more. Helen told me over the phone that his mind was a whole lot better. Well, here's hoping and praying that you won't be disappointed again about your furlough, but please let me know if you can. If only you call when you get to Louisville. The rest all think I could take it but I know it would make me sick, or what I mean, upset. Papa said it would not. I told him why do you cry for every little bit, but he said I can't help it. I said do you think I liked to get upset that day when we thought you were coming? I got real nervous, but that's natural. Never received a letter since Monday. I am trying to make a novena of nine Masses, if I can, for Alma. I hope that she will get alright. She sure has to have plenty of patience. I hope that you pray for her. We don't have to fast. Pray for us and we pray for both of you.
Mother

Louisville, Kentucky, **March 18**, 2:20 pm, cloudy weather

Dear Norb,

You don't write. How is that? Thought we would get a letter today for sure. Don't Alma get any either? I hope she does. Haven't seen her since Saturday night. I took her to the car. While we were waiting for the car she said, "I passed your place many times but I never thought I would ever enter or leave it." She meant that she would not get acquainted with you and the family, I guess. She sure looked cute, had on her new spring suit. I still asked you to pray so she gets well soon. I go [*to*] the Way of the Cross for the poor souls so they pray for her and so God [*will*] help us. Well, I must close for now. Mary will be going soon. Want her to wait for me. Did you ever get the picture with the clock? So, goodbye and God bless you and good luck. Mary says hello

Mother

Louisville, Kentucky, **March 18**, Thursday

Dear Norb,

We received your letter. You never said a word about your three-day pass and how you enjoyed yourself. Will write more tomorrow. Hope you enjoyed your ice cream. The ice cream we get here ain't what it used to be. It mustn't have the cream in it and it isn't as sweet. Margie wanted a pudge cicle [*fudgesicle*] Sunday. We all got one and the chocolate coating stuck to your mouth like paraffin. You couldn't get rid of it.

Goodnight and '92.

[*Hermina*]

Louisville, Kentucky, **March 19**, 9:00 pm

Dear Norb,

Yesterday we had 2 thunderstorms. Neither one was severe but it rained incessantly since noon. It is storming now and the sky is heavy. We are OK. Talk about the coffee going far. -We are on a ½ pound for more than a week, brother, but Pop really rates since the ration [*started*]. He gets it at night too but Mom really puts the coffee stretcher in it. Don't know of any news. Did you get your boxes we sent you? Last week? You should have them by now. I imagine you had a laugh at the one box. We just had a 5 or 10 minute downpour and at 5:30 this morning, the sky emptied itself all at once. The crocuses are in bloom, the jonquils are thick with buds, the weeping willows are a faint green and the grass is beginning to "green up" in spots. The birds have sang sweetly but the rain today must have changed their mind.

Good day and God bless you,

Hermina

Louisville, Kentucky, **March 19**, Friday

Dear Norb,

We just received your letter this afternoon thanking us for the box of candy. You're welcome, but did you get the shaving kit? I had that insurance. Let us know about that. That's nice in Park and Tilford remembering you that often. Mighty nice. It has been storming yesterday and today. The water is just standing on top of the ground. I guess spring is coming soon although we still need fire [*heat*].

Say, how do you get that US Air Corps on your stationary? You didn't switch over did you? I think that's the best too. If you get a furlough, you get it, Pop said. Well, in fact, Mom and Pop argued over your furlough. Mom said if he just calls me up from the station when he arrives in Louisville, I'll feel alright. Pop said, I think I'd like to see him just walk in. That's foolish, Mom, to get that idea in your head that you have to have the word he's coming. Mom said she don't think her stomach would stand it. Pop laughed. Mom said all what you would do is tear a little. Pop said he thinks he would too but still thinks it's foolish for Mom to get the bellyache over it. So if you get it, come right ahead brother. We'll be glad to see you if it is 4:00 in the "morning." Or 5:00, perhaps. Good afternoon and '92.

We are all OK. I thought I would write tomorrow but Lizzie came up with the kids' photos. She said maybe that would bring an answer to some of her letters. She wants you to have a picture of them all. Aren't they fine? You better brag a little about all of them. Y,ou know how Mommas are.

You never said a word about your trip to Columbia. I just called Alma. She said you enjoyed being away from army life for 72 hours or 3 days. Mom would, as well as all of us, appreciate a word about your trip. I said to Mom, I bet he even forgot about that trip. Now, the water they say, is really coming up. Beargrass Creek has flown over its banks at Ellison Avenue, Joe said. They are placing sandbags at 4th and 5th Streets but the weatherman said it was not dangerous. It's getting colder tonite so I guess that will take care of the rain. That's all I know for tonite. So goodnight and '92. Mrs. Orrill cut this clipping for us to send you. That's all. Write soon.

"Porky"

Fort Jackson, South Carolina, **March 19**

[*Mom, Dad and all,*]

Well, I really cleaned up on the mail today. I got about seven letters in all. That's the way it usually works though. It all comes in bunches. You know it don't pay to mess up in this outfit now, or [you'll] be brought in by the MPs. Now if anything like that happens, you start off on Saturday afternoon at one o'clock, take 30 minutes of exercise, followed by a 20 minute run, and then 30 minutes of exercises. Then just to make you feel better you go on a ten-mile hike with full pack, eat supper and fall out again for 70 minutes of dismounted drill. That's just Saturday. Sunday morning you are up bright and early for 30 minutes of exercises, a 20 minute run (I don't know if you ever tried running for 30 minutes without stopping, it ain't so easy) and 30 minutes of exercises followed by 70 minutes of dismounted drill, then you get enough time to go to Church and eat dinner. Then after dinner, you fall out with full field pack for a 14-mile road march. Then after supper, you get exercises and then drill again. You see, you get all of this during what time you are supposed to have free. Nice, ain't it? Well, I don't have to do it as yet.

The chow hasn't been worth a damn. The last few days we only had meat once except for bacon for breakfast. You know I could really go for some "Gutta" [*Goetta*], or whatever it is. Why wasn't I informed sooner that I was going to be uncle the 1st of April? The suspense will just kill me. We are going to have a beer party tonight in the Recreation Hall but never enough beer but it may be tonight. I could drink a keg by myself right now and I ain't fooling. I got a letter from Joe and Ann today also. That's what made me think of writing about the beer party.

Well, be good and I'll write as soon as possible and tell Marge not to work too hard and write a little more. Mighty fine letter, mighty fine. Well, I'll be seeing you.
As Always,
Norb

Fort Jackson, South Carolina, **March 21**, 1:35 pm
Dear Mom, Pop, Sis's, and Mary,

Well, it's Sunday afternoon and a very wet one at that. I believe it's about the most water I've seen since the 1937 flood. It's really coming down in sheets. It cost me about 40 cents to go to church this morning because I'll have to have some of my clothes cleaned and pressed. The wind is pretty strong also but I guess it's just the March weather.

The beer party came off pretty well - only about four fights but nobody hurt seriously. But, it was hard to get a seat in the crapper this morning because all the beer must have had a laxative effect on the boys.

Right now, the wind sounds as though it is going to blow the place down and it wouldn't take much to do it either. We have a new member in our outfit. It's a little puppy about a month and a half old. It's a cute little squirt. I believe they are saving him in case of a blackout so we will have plenty of candles, but Mary's not here to pick them up for us. [*Once during a blackout in Louisville, Mary Hollkamp picked up a dog turd and put it on her table thinking it was a candle.*] I don't know who will install the wicks.

Well, one thing nice, we don't have to shine our shoes any more. They gave us a Lublin [*sic*] to put on them. It looks something like lard, it makes the leather soft, and it makes them dull as hell also. I guess next week we will get orders to shine them up again. That's the way the army works, you know. Its mind is never made up. I guess that's what makes an army. Well, my dear, dear people, that's about all for today, but I'll be seeing you and tell Mary I said how-de-do.
As Always,
Norb

Louisville, Kentucky, **March 21**, 3:15 pm

Dear Norb,

Alma's eye is doing fine, Dr. Maupin said yesterday. She also told us the Dr. said her eye seemed to bulge or extend. Now it seems to have gone back to its proper place. We are all very happy over that. Next, I'll talk about the flood conditions. It seems the river is still rising. They were pumping at Ballard's yesterday. The creek has overflown the concrete wall. They opened the floodgates so that made the water go down 12 inches but it will also be hard on the ones at Shippingport. Mary Rawert said water was in the basement at the cold storage on Logan Street. It has to get to 44 feet before it comes to Hubbuch's on Broadway. I'll send the first page with this letter. We are all OK.

We are listening to Winston Churchill. Cousin John Spoelker died at St. Joseph's Infirmary yesterday at 5:05 pm. Vincent is in Camp Walters, Texas. Joe [*Rawert*] is going in to get new glasses and new eye tomorrow. This is quite a story. His eye has been a little inflamed looking. I think it is as every year this time. He is working every day and it is strained. He used Argaral [*sic*] and it cleared up but his glasses broke so he wants to take the proper care of it. Dr. Baker doesn't make appointments. He and Junior papered the "White Cottage" early this morning. Poor Joe. He was pushing a case of soft drinks and a bottle burst and Joe's wrist was cut. He said blood squirted. Bud bandaged his wrist up and Joe went back to working. He saw his blood on the floor and he just keeled over. He tried to make it to the door, couldn't, and scraped his back terrible. I put Tri Merthiolate on his back and the poor boy cried tears - as big as light bulbs came pouring down. But he feels OK now. Joe just can't stand to see blood. I told him I was going to tell you what a pantywaist he was. Lip and Margie are here. The rest are at the show. I don't have any more news so I'll sign off.

Good afternoon and '92,

"Porky"

Louisville, Kentucky, **March 22**, Monday, 9:50 pm

Dear Norb,

Well, this is a crimp day even tho it is spring. We all thought it was that Laurence Dishlnow [*sp*] as you said. We received your letter this morning. Alma called. She said her sister has the measles. Everybody that didn't have them certainly had them this year. Jr Niemann has them at Camp. We are all OK. Alma also said she hear from you fifteen times today, 3 letters and 12 cards. What a sweetheart! What a lover man! What a soldier! What a man! You know that didn't surprise me a lot when she told me that. I seen the cards.

Dr. Baker told Joe he had a marvelous eye, excellent vision, perfect balance but that his work [*painter and paperhanger*] was rather close and it was eyestrain. Joe had to get an eye made. Never had an eye to fit him. They are sending his old eye with a few corrections and Joe is going to have to pay 20 bucks for it. He also is getting new glasses with invisible rims.

Well, all fats are now rationed or rather frozen until rationed. Do I feel squeamish? I do. I made chocolate pie tonite, the first since you left I believe. It was delicious if I have to say so myself. Mom said this censor business really gets you thinking. She meant ration. Well, Norb that's all I know for this time so goodnite and '92.
Hermina

Louisville, Kentucky, **March 23**, Tuesday, 2:00, 20° at 5 am
Dear Norb,

Enjoyed your letter stating that you are well and I hope that you won't get the measles. You had them twice if I remember right, also an attack of appendicitis. You know that white diamond, ha ha. Will that help you out in the army? I am looking for John this afternoon. He wants to see Cousin John [*Spoelker*]. Hillary and Vernon have a breaking out again. Eleanor is not feeling so well, John said over the phone last night.

Elizabeth is coming at 8:00 tonight and I guess Marge will go to see John Spoelker. Also, Papa and I went to see him Sunday night. Vincent came home at 5 o'clock Monday afternoon. He is going to be buried Wednesday at 9 o'clock. He had a requiem Mass this morning at 8 o'clock. Father asked the children to pray for him. Everybody speaks so well of him. He played cards til 12 o'clock Thursday night. Saturday morning at 10 he had another stroke. He was sent to St. Joseph's in the afternoon. He was there one hour and died at five after five. He looks so nice, and is laid out very nice. I ask you to pray for him also.

Norb, did you ever get that Watkins shaving set? If you didn't get, it please let us know. We had insurance so we can see in to it. Did you ever send that boy a card or something? It makes them feel bad and I don't blame them. It's only a few words to let him know you are thinking of him. You ought to see the nice letters Shirley Ann gets from her soldier boy. She surely is proud of him and rightly so. She brings them here so we can read them.

Father Spoelker telegrammed home that he arrived OK at San Francisco yesterday.

The river crest will be reached today. They think it will reach 38 ½ feet today. It won't be near as high as they thought. The government froze the taters [*potatoes*] this morning. Mr. Schieman [*corner butcher and grocer*] said the seed potatoes got mixed with the other taters. Don't know how long it will last. Well, that's war time. I am glad we have potatoes, about 1 bushel and 2 pecks but I cannot hug you around the neck and squeeze you right tight [*reference to a little ditty of "I love you a bushel and a peck, I love you with a hug around the neck"*]. I am sure chewing chewing gum. I enjoy it immensely and while I am writing this letter, I am chewing.

You ought to see Papa - what he is abstaining from this Lent. He said he was going to abstain from chewing tobacco, when he has all his pockets empty, but he is always buying more so they will never get empty. He is laying smoke screens since his birthday 72 years young.

My letters are four times as long as yours. How do you like to camp out, or does that remind you of you and Wahoo?

We were so glad of the good news from the Dr. about Alma's eye. We are still praying for her every day. I hope you went to Communion for her also. Good luck. God bless. Mary sends XXXXXXXX

Mother

Louisville, Kentucky, **March 24**, Wednesday, 1:30 pm

[*Dear Norb*]

Quoting PFC Norbert Anthony Henry Rawert's letter to March 19, 1943: "Tell Marge not to work too hard and write a little more. Mighty fine letter, mighty fine letter." End quotation. That's a fine way to treat, or rather, ignore a sister that's been writing a letter every day since August 18, 1942. Not even an honorable mention does she get but let one explode several times annually and she's put on the "E" rating. But that's life, even in a big city. Now I'm wondering if I should continue writing but I won't waste this 3¢ stamp.

Mom said [*asked* if] would you like some sausage meat but she can't wait for an answer on that because the ration will go into effect Monday. It came over the radio that we will get 16 points per person per week and with that, meat and fats must be bought. That would amount to 2 pounds of steak a week and no lard or butter could be bought. Lard I think is 5 points per pound, butter 8 points per pound, steak 8 points per pound but cheaper cuts will be less points. Pigs' ears are 1 point per pound. So you see, tain't much Norbie.

Johnny came in last nite to see Cousin John Spoelker. Vernon wanted to know why he was cleaning up so for. John said, "Why, I'm to see a dead man." Vernon said, "Then, why are you cleaning up so for, Daddy? He can't see you." Yes, the stork will visit them the latter part of April. We was not going to mention it (did you say I couldn't keep a secret?) In fact, I thought Marge knew it but she said she didn't, or else she forgot about it. We are all hoping it is a girl so Peggy will have a partner and not get too much attention from Johnny. Eleanor doesn't show a preference. She is cute. We were going to telegram you then but Marge just didn't know that.

This is a swell one on Pop - Joe and John was here last nite and played pinochle. Johnny [*goes to*] get a bucket of beer and then Joe [*goes to*] get one. Joe came in with the bucket empty. "Beer is frozen," he announced. We all thought it was true. Pop said got some at 8:00 yet. Joe said it was frozen at 8:00, so we all had the laugh on Pop. Finally, he jumped up, scratched a little and said, I'm going down at Bill's [*Hueltsman's*]. So, Joe came in with his bucket full but Pop was really worried. He was itchy and everything. Mom thought Joe should of left [*sic*] him go down there. She really got a kick out of that. We all did.

What's the most embarrassing thing you can do at the table? <u>Eat</u> the last bean and pea in the bowl. The senior moron took a yardstick to bed with him to see how long he slept and the junior moron ran around the bed to catch up on his sleep. A moron threw his watch in the crapper so he could s[*hit*] on his own time. How do you lika dat [*like that*] or doess [*those*].

Cousin John had a solemn high Mass. Fr. Knue preached the sermon. He looked so nice. I didn't get to see him. I had diarrhea Monday nite and Tuesday so I really felt washed out. I took a big dose of Castor Oil and it did the work. I sure was sorry I could not see him. Vincent [*Spoelker*] has a 15-day furlough. Bud Schneider was here on a furlough and he got a very brief stay. Very brief.

Anna Heitkemper wrote Mary a letter saying, or rather asking, how everybody was and about you too. She told her she sent you a box of candy but she never heard if you received it or not. You know you asked her for her address right after Xmas and some thank you cards to send. I know Mrs. Russell got hers from you. If you want one, let us know. Her address is Anna D. HEITKEMPER, 607 Halcombe, Mobile, Ala. Joe's new glasses look swell on him. Joe said you really know all about the exercises, drills, and marches. I told him I was letting you know that. Here's hoping you'll never have to experience any of those "mess marches." Will getting drunk put you in that? I think you'll agree - I got my 3¢ worth.

Good afternoon and '92,

"Porky"

Louisville, Kentucky, **March 25**, Thursday morning

Dear Norb,

Just 3 months since Christmas. It's a beautiful day in Louisville and I feel the urge to get out and rake, rake, rake. I [*sic*] better put that urge into motion since that terrible rain last week the hills look like kids have been digging in them. I'll finish tonite so too-da-loo until tonite. [*Hermina*]

Continued, **March 26**, Friday, 12:30 pm:

Well, I didn't get down to writing last night. I got the whole yard in, as you would say, damn good condition (I never say that.) (I wear wings [*angel*]). It's a same old story; we can't find our rake, the one we bought last year. After we ask the neighbors and relatives, we might find it.

Marge stopped by Lou Hollkamp's. She just received Norb's [*Hollkamp*] clothes so I suppose they will keep him. He's still at Ft. Harrison. Miss Niemann was saying Louis Heintz was classed 4-F. He has a slight rupture. Catherine wrote to her. Louis wept from sorrow and his wife from joy. It's a mad scramble at the butcher's today, believe you me - 16 points for butter, lard. And meat - a pound-per-week per person isn't very much. We're all OK.

Forty Hours starts today at St. Elizabeth's. Joe wanted to know why Mom wasn't going to the opening this morning. Mom said because she didn't want to. She went to an earlier Mass but wouldn't tell him.

Henry Paul bought his own home on Clarks Lane. Tain't bad for Heinie. Mrs. Paul's brother, the one that boards over there - "Unk." Do you remember? He finished work at one defense plant so they sent him to Curtiss-Wright and they are sending him to school two nights a week. He's about 67 years old. He said he thought they would graduate. Mrs. Paul told him she hopes he don't fail. I thought that was funny.

It's been raining all morning, not very hard tho. Well, I'll be saying Goodbye and hoping to hear from you. That sure was a fat letter Joe got and to think you was so dry, too.
Love, more loved than ever before,
"Porky"

Fort Jackson, South Carolina, **March 25**

Dear Mom, Pop and all,

Well, there is not much new, only another big inspection coming up. This one is going to last for four days. Lame stuff I'll say. I know I'll be happy as hell when it's over. I've been working nearly every night this week and all work and no play makes Jack a dull boy. I didn't get a chance to have to write Lip yet but those pictures were swell, but there were none of Margie. I thought ma[y]be you forgot to put it in the envelope. In about 10 minutes, the lights are going out. In fact, they are blowing the Taps now.

The weather has been fine for the last two days but it's been a little chilly with a fog in the "holler" but I believe it'll clear up OK. Well, I must say good night now. Will write when I get a chance.
As Always,
Norb

Louisville, Kentucky, **March 27**

Dear Mom and all,

Well, tonight is Saturday - bath night. In just a darn few minutes, I'll be under the shower. Well, I received that box of Watkins toilet articles. I didn't know who it came from. The box of powder came apart so I had a large box of powder.

The weather has been swell lately, just like summer. I think I'll buy me a reel and pole and do a little fishing if I can get hold of any.

You say I don't write much anymore. Well, there isn't much to write about. Just the same things over and over and over. And I don't want to keep writing the same thing over and over. We had a gas alert. You should have seen the tears that were shed from the tear gas until we got our gas masks [on]. Well, folks, there ain't much more but tomorrow is Sunday. I'll write more then. Well, I'm still,
As Always,
Norb

Louisville, Kentucky, **March 28**, Sunday, 10:30 am

Dear Norb,

I'll start where I left off Friday. Seen Mr. Johnson. He said Louis had his APO San Francisco, so they are expecting him to go across. Earl is at Camp Livingston, Louisiana. He said they got a letter from him. He wants to go across and get it over with. Larny is at Atterbury. Those Henry Ford Union delegates are at their camp. Larny said they are putting them through army life. Couldn't write last night. Lou, Gertrude and Nancy (Gertie's baby) was here. She's got one of the cutest babies I've ever seen, chubby, fat, and smart as heck. Looks like William. We're OK. Norb's [*Hollkamp*] at Harrison yet waiting for shoes. He wore 12's. Never had any trouble getting them here. Lou brought his clothes along. He likes it. He was standing guard and for a half day; chopped wood. Writes a sweet and very nice letter. Will still sounds homesick. In the letter he wrote Xmas day, he said the day couldn't be worse, he doesn't think. His girlfriend got a letter from him yesterday telling her to listen to the radio. He couldn't tell her what it was. We heard last night that the Allies scored a direct hit on the Japs' convoy in New Guinea. I feel like that was it. Bud Kleiner on New Lydia is in the Air Corp (Klein's nephew).

Pop cut down the Holly-Hock [*sic*] and hedge on the Texas Street side yesterday. Mom got him some chewing tobacco. He chews intermittently you know. I think cigars runs him too high. It didn't take him very long to saw them down. Mom said she had him spitting like a grasshopper. The more he chewed, the faster he worked. We haven't heard from you since Wednesday but did hear Mon., Tues., and Wed.

Now about this ration business. At noon yesterday, Schieman was sold out of meat. People milled in and out from one store to another.

Joe was papering at Johnny's yesterday and is going again today. Getting the house fixed up for the blessed event. We all think she should of went to the hospital. But her. And it's her business. Ann's other sister had a baby about a month ago. She went to the hospital one day. The next day they brought her back in an ambulance. The hospital is so crowded and the Dr. so overworked he couldn't deliver the baby at home. That's in Lebanon, Kentucky. Both are doing fine. It was a boy. Most papas are getting their wish today.

Green peppers 10¢ each, cucumbers 25¢. I don't think I will be able to get my snitch of raw beef before supper anymore. The meat question I think hit the hardest. People made a lot over the coffee question but that's only secondary now. We got a good coffee-stretcher. It's malted barley, 24¢ a pound, but it's fine.

That State boy is home on leave. He looks very nice in his Sailor's uniform. Joe was saying Hilary likes Hill-Billy music. He knows the time and stations when they come on. He gets up early and turns it on. If Vernon wakes up, off it goes. He dislikes it but Hilary was telling Joe about it.

All the Rawerts [*John and family*] on Hurtsbourne Lane are OK. I think tomorrow will be the biggest headache for the butcher. We in the East End cannot get any because delivery

is made on Tuesday and Friday. I think Mom will have a lot of names coined by the time you come home. She calls points "penny." Like pig ears a penny a pound. It is confusing. Well, I think I'll close. Hoping to hear from you and cheerio, goodbye and '92.
"Hermie"

Fort Jackson, South Carolina, **March 28**

Dear Mom and all,

I was very sorry to hear about Cousin John's death. Well, all you can say is that he was a hell of a nice guy. So Knue preached the sermon. Well, he wouldn't have to preach a sermon for me but I hope the rest of them liked it.

I'll tell you, Hermina ("Horse"), you know you have plenty of time to write. That is to be considered also. I notice that this letter I received today was written at 1:30 pm on 3/24/43.

I imagine it [*rationing*] helps out with the dishes but I don't guess you dirty many dishes anymore, but then again, when Mom cooks, there are always quite a few dishes even if only one eats.

One break we got here is that everything is so close. The mess hall is just about 14 yards from the barracks, the PX is just about a block and the Chapel is just about a block and a half. We did have some red headed Irishman for a Chaplain but he wasn't there this morning. Mass here only lasts about 30 minutes with a sermon. Pretty nice, eh?

Mom, don't send no sausage. You can use it better than I can. We was just without meat for a couple days because the rations got messed up. We had a pretty good dinner today. We had baked ham, green beans, sweet potatoes, salad, pineapple and ice cream so there's no reason for complaint there.

It sure is a beautiful day today. It makes you want to get out in the open but I guess we'll have plenty of that before long. I wrote a letter last night but I forgot to mail it so you should get two at one time. I will try to type the next one so you will be able to read it.
As Always,
Norb V...-

Louisville, Kentucky, **March 29**, Monday, 5:30 pm

Dear Norb,

Well, this is the first day of meat rationing. It doesn't mean a thing to the East Enders anyway because there is no meat up here.

The reason you didn't get a picture of Margie is she didn't attend school as yet but Lip is taking her in town and having one made. You'll get one if she has small ones made, I'm sure.

Well, I sure thought of you today. I saw more fishing worms. I could hear Wahoo say, "There's one Nobbie. There's one Nobbie." I dug up Mom's garden spot and put in 70 sets of onions. The ground is mighty damp and cold feeling. Then I dug up 2 ft. wide along the drive and got 2 packs of Old Fashioned Garden Seeds like you got one year, and planted them. I hope they are as pretty as yours were. I'm going to call Lip and tell her you're a very busy man. I know Lip will understand.

Cletus Heim is in the Army since Thursday. He has left Ft. Harrison already. We are having splendid weather. Today was ideal for outdoor work. Shirley's adopted soldier hasn't been sent across as yet. He said 50 of them failed physically. His eyes kept him back but he cannot leave the Camp grounds now because he might be called up anyway.

Mom said, "how is the chow by now?" I heard this one Senator say a defense worker needs more meat than the government is allowing them, so they might eventually let us have a little more. I hope this inspection won't have anything to do with you being sent across. We're all OK. Jackie will receive his First Communion May 9th. Eleanor is helping Jackie with his spelling. He stumbled on a few words. Hilary said, "I can spell, too." Joe said, "Heck, you can't spell anything. You don't know how." Hil said, "I can spell Louisville." Joe said, "If you can spell Louisville, let's hear you." Hilary spelled 'WHAS' and said "Louisville" [*WHAS always announced 'WHAS - Louisville*]. I think that's a daisy. We also might get to keep Vernon and Hilary when Eleanor's taken down. They are like one another's shadow. Funny little squirts.

What's the name of your outfit's Pooch? Mary got a kick out of that candle business. Same ole Mary. Donaldson just left one [*loaf of bread*] on the porch.

Katsy was a flower girl last night. Betsy marched too, at he closing of 40-hours prayer. Katsy was as proud as a peacock. She would take no amount of money for her flowers. She was very cute. Lip was dressing her, so she ran in the front room to put on her shoes and socks, and she looked at me and said "Meenie, don't it feel tunt-able?" I asked her again and she said, "Oh Meenie it feels so tunt-able [*comfortable*] to walk barefoot on the rugs."

Well, I think I'll bring this to a close now. It's chow time here too. We'll do OK with meat this week. You know Wahoo is laid up with his back. He collected $15.00 compensation last week. Do you think he hears the River calling him? Or Goose Creek? I wouldn't mind having some good fresh fish tho. You can get coffee-stretcher, fix butter with gelatin to stretch it, but you cannot stretch you money today. So long and write when you can.
Loads of love,
Hermina

Mommy added a note:
Did you get that shaving kit? The time will expire on the insurance. Kindly let us know.

The following letter was accepted by Walter Cronkite and team to be included in his book "World War II Letters" to be published by Alfred A. Knoph. However, on November 8, 2001 in a letter from Tracy Quinn McLennan, a freelance writer of the book, to Carol Rawert Trainer, she announced "through a bizarre set of unfortunate circumstances" that the book was resold to St. Martin's Press. She had no information on what the outcome would be. Later it was learned that the letter was unfortunately cut from the book by the new publishers.

Fort Jackson, South Carolina, **March 29**

Dear Kate, Herm, Ma, Meanie;

It's about 9:30 pm now and I just came over from the mess hall where I had two cups of delicious coffee and a tenderloin steak sandwich. Just a late snack. You see, one of the cooks here went to school with me in Kansas City, so I knew him pretty well but what's got me worried is that he's over 38 and he'll be going home before many more weeks pass. It may stop my evening snacks. Well, my gut is big enough now so it won't hurt to quit eating for a while. Besides, it's Lent and I should do a little fasting, ha ha ha! It seems like I never will have to fast because there is always something that comes up to stop it. Pretty nice, ain't it?

I'm sitting here with a bunch of bums writing this letter and shooting the shit at the same time, so if this letter smells that will be the reason for it.

Well, the way things are now we will spend three days in the field next week digging foxholes and such. We got some very pretty, new rifles last week. They're beautiful jobs. They keep telling you in the army that your gun is your best friend and that you should treat it as such.

Ah, the weather was beautiful today. A wonderful day it was.

So, Mrs. Paul's brother is going to school. Pretty good, pretty good. I hope he don't get Brother Carl for a principal - it would be rough on him.

I'll be glad when this inspection is over. We got orders to get strictly GI haircuts, and I do mean GI. So, I guess I'll show the barber a good time, that is, if you want to call them barbers. I think they would make better plumbers, myself.

Well, folks, I think I'll call it a night and turn in. See you tomorrow if I get a chance to write.

As always,

Norb

Louisville, Kentucky, **March 30**

Dear Norb,

Papa is going to get a bucket of '92. Marge, Ann, and Mrs. Russell was working tonight. I hope you can read this. My eyes are blurring but I wanted to write a few lines. You know Alma worked till 9 o'clock last night. I do think that is too long for her. Hermina talked to her over the phone. Hermina told her that she needed more rest. It takes her 1 hour to get home. Then I know she won't get to bed till 12 o'clock. I think she ought to be more careful about her eye. We are always telling her about her working too much. Don't you? She does not seem to realize it what rest means to her eye. I know what the Dr. told me when I had my eye trouble. I understand she is doing well so far. She is going to have another x-ray made. I don't know when though. Don't mention this to Alma what I wrote you. Maybe she won't like it. I am sending you a Benedict medal. Wear it if you can, otherwise put it in your pocket and try to say a little prayer. I'm sending you a leaflet. I had you and Alma enrolled in it and Papa and I also are enrolled. It is for homeless girls and boys.

Did you write Cousin Ann and the Schott boy? Well, I must close. It is 10:30 o'clock on your clock. So good nite and God bless you and we are praying for you every day. Goodbye,
Mother

Louisville, Kentucky, **March 30**, Tuesday, 1:55 pm
Dear Norb,

You know we want to be different. I planted some Sweet Pea seeds - if all comes up, we'll look like a flower garden - and some balsam seed. They will vine over the fence, you know. The Apricot tree is blossoming forth today. It is a beautiful day in Louisville. Is South Carolina more beautiful than Kentucky in springtime?

That Lester Wright - I imagine you remember him. He's in the Navy. Mom was talking to his mother. He's on convoy duty and has seen action. We're all OK. Mom is going to finish I'll say adieu.
H.R.

7:40 pm
Mom didn't finish, so I'm back at it. We are having "Dinnah" tonight with the door open. I finished my garden work by moving the blue hydrangea in front of the side fence. Now I'm waiting for the seeds to come up. If they do, boy, I'll be peddling flowers. Tomorrow is the last day to register for unessential workers within draft age. All from Hubbuch's had to go except Tony, Mr. Seb. and Charlie Redle. I believe six others had to register including Corny.

Mr. Hoering gave up delivery of milk about 2 weeks ago. He went to work his farm, but the Cream Top [Dairy] kept delivering so we called Hoering's and they said he gave it up. So we called Johnny to start delivering. Joe got 2 rooms prepared for John. Now Johnny is finishing the other 2 rooms. Eleanor was talking to me on the phone. She said Johnny is papering, got the ceiling up and ½ of the room. She heard a few bad words every now and then but she'll have to stuff her ears because Johhny's determined to get it finished tonite. Well, I thought that was funny. I would like to see the performance. It is too late to mail this so I'll say goodnite and might add a little more tomorrow.
Nighty Night,
"Porky"

Louisville, Kentucky, **March 31**

Dearest Norbert,

How's everything? We are all OK and Alma is getting so much better, I heard. I haven't seen her for over two weeks now but we always call her or she calls us. We are so busy at work and Horse don't feel so good and hasn't worked for some time. I worked every night this week until 9 o'clock and I just finished a letter to Thelma Saunders. Maybe you'd like to read it.

OK. The news sounds good over the radio. Hope it [*war*] will soon be over. Mrs. Russell is still working with me and she wants to go to see Jr for Mother's Day. She said he is begging her to come. So, I would go if I was her and I think she will.

We had Forty Hours Devotion last week and Betsy and Katsy marched. Katsy said just look how many people will see me. She thought she was so pretty. She looked like an angel, and so did Betsy, with her golden locks. Katsy was flower girl and she sure loved her flowers. Soon the flowers will be up. Our apricot tree is starting to bloom and the goldfish (2) are OK. Betsy brought us some pretty rocks, all colors, for the bowel. You can't see the nasty stuff at the bottom - now it's between the rocks.

You should see Leo Muth with his false teeth. He likes to take them out and show then so much when he comes over. That little Margie is sure crazy about her dad. Say what do you think about the meat ration? What I'm worried about is "Horse." Joe got a new eye today and Mamma said it looked good. Norb did you ever get a letter from Bob Lee? He always asks about you. He's a darn sweet somebody. Every time I go to devotions, he's there. And I seen the State boy in his sailor uniform, He looks good. It's the one that went to St. Xavier. He was in church Saturday night (Forty Hours). That sister of his looks pitiful. I imagine she will land at Lakeland [*psychiatric center*] the way she walks it almost shows it.

The clock you sent has 11:27 on it. Pop is asleep. I haven't had a song as of yet. Mom is in bed and so is little sister. And all is quiet. Mary is still walking upstairs. I heard her turn out the lights. The trains sound so loud. I guess a rain is in store - it's so warm tonight. Well, here's hoping you will be coming soon. Walk in at work and surprise me. I'll like it. Lawrence Shaughnessy next door to Lil is in a camp in Missouri. Good night. God bless you.
As Ever,
Margaret

Louisville, Kentucky, **April 1**, Your Day, 8:30 pm

Dear Norb,

You know I read your letter over again and damn if I didn't see you quoting me. Your letter is written 3/24/43 at 1:30 pm – "That's a good time to get out of dishwashing" (end of quote). You know I wouldn't have answered so sweetly if I seen, or rather, understood that then, but my letter is off and I don't want to keep on feuding. But if you want a good argument, I'll keep it going. Pick the topic.

Grants 5 & 10¢ [*drugstore*] have remodeled and are opening today. They have pasted wallpaper on sale. Joe [*a paperhanger and painter*] got a kick out of that. Joe got his new eye. Looks grand. You know they have to order most of their eyes, 20 bucks, so it looks good. Joe ordered another one. He said they scarcely received any eyes since Pearl Harbor.

Here is Bernard Spoelker's address. Ch. 1ˢᵗ Lt. Bernard A. Spoelker 0503484, APO 4090 c/o Postmaster, San Francisco, California. Mary told me his clothes are on ship already but he don't know when he will leave. She also specified to put those numbers aside his name as I have them.

Ann got Joe bright and early. They had company. It was past mid-nite when they got to bed. Ann said did I hear somebody knocking. Joe said. "You go and see." She said, "No, you go. It might be somebody from over home." Joe gets up and answers and then Ann hollered, "April Fools." Joe got her right back tho. He said Russell couldn't take them to work this morning. I don't know what excuse he gave her but Ann came over in a rush, her good clothes on from last night. I guess they were the handiest. She was here at 7:30. Russell usually gets here at 7:50 darn near to the second.

I don't like for you to have to be digging foxholes. Don't sound too good, does it? We had a storm at 5 o'clock this morning. It wasn't a bad one but it rained quite hard. It has stopped and the sun is shining beautifully again.

Damn that tenderloin steak sandwich. Do you realize that would have to do us a ½ week? Snot! And coffee too. Blah. What kind of whole do you think I would have to dig? Well, I don't know any more. I'll sign off hoping you get more steak sandwiches. Somebody in our family should get a break sometime. Joe never registered. He said he thought he would have to go to the Army anyhow if they decided to take him. Well, fill the gut and come home rolling.   Joey sent a can of pineapple, sugar and butter for me to bake you a cake. I don't think I'll get to it today but you can look for it next week sometime.
"Porky"

Louisville, Kentucky, **April 2**

Dear Norb,

Well, it's a beautiful day but a little crimp. I haven't got any news. Lip and girls were here last night. She's having trouble with Easter being so close and to have to still outfit four gals. That's something. Shirley wants a coat-suit. Every girl in her room is getting one. Leave it to her to spend all of Moody's money on an Easter attire. I know how that is tho; Moody got us eight plants of Spirea from Sears Roebuck to put in front of the porch. I hope they do good. [*In fact, the hedge in front of the porch was beautiful and provided for many crowns for the May parades and church celebrations.*] It cost $2.00. Will close. Too-da-loo til tomorrow.
H.R.

Continued, Saturday, 10 am:

Dear Norb,

Well, it's a beautiful day and cold. The temperature says 22°. Aggie Hellmann went to Texas to marry her soldier-boyfriend. So that leaves Mrs. Hellman with the two nurses and beautician at home. Seems like the professional stick with Mamma. I told Betsy I would give her a nickel to dry dishes. She did. I paid off. Before she went home, Momma paid off so she collected twice and looked at me and laughed as hard as she could. I really got tickled. Will close. No more news. Say, when are you going to Officers' Training?
H.R.

Fort Jackson, South Carolina, **April 2**

Dear Mom and all,

The wind is really blowing tonight. It picks up that sand and throws it all in your face. It feels like someone sticking you with a million pins. I got a GI haircut yesterday, and - what I mean - it's really GI. It's just about a quarter of an inch long. There is no use for a comb anymore. All I have to do now when I get up in the morn is wash my hands and face and scrub my teeth. My hair takes care of itself. Very nice.

Hell, no! South Carolina is not half as pretty as Kentucky in the spring. Most of the soil down here is sand, so there is not much grass. And I don't like the trees as well. I guess that's why all the birds come up Kentucky way when the winter is over.

Seems as though the English are doing pretty well for themselves but all you see is what's in print and you don't know how much of that you can believe. Well, our big inspection is over. That's one thing to be thankful for. It lasted for two days and that's a hell of a long time for an inspection to last. I don't know just what we will do now for the next few weeks.

Well, that's about all I know for now but will see you later. I been busier than hell for the last week. Good night and good luck.
As Always,
Norb

Fort Jackson, South Carolina, **April 3**

Dear Mom, Pop and all,

Well, it's Saturday night. Thought I would stay in and write a few letters. Not much to do anyway. It's a little cool tonight, cooler than it has been. It seems to me it should be warming up by now. But I guess that will come pretty soon. They told me it gets pretty warm here in the summer and I believe them. I got that "April Fool's" letter today. But it's a crime to be wasting 6¢ on such foolishness. I don't see what you were thinking of living these "trying" times. Ha, ha. You know I was going to do the same thing but it slipped my mind, so you beat me to the draw.

Well, I guess I got a Corporal rating. At least I'm up for it. I would give my left arm to see

Norbert Hollenkamp. I can see where some bunch of soldiers have a hell of a bunch of fun. It will really do him good, watch and see. He will be a hell of a lot different when he gets out. One thing nice about it, he won't have to ride his bicycle when he feels like traveling. I can just see him trying to keep in step with those strides he takes. I see where some Corporal or Sergeant will go absolutely nuts and he'll catch hell about 50 times a day, but he'll snap out of it. Poor guy, poor guy. I can just see a lot of KP staring him in the face. Well, I'll see you tomorrow if I get time to write.

As Always,

Norb

Louisville, Kentucky, **April 4**, Sunday, 3:50 pm

Dear Norb,

It's turned out to be a beautiful day in Louisville, but it rained this "morning." Russell got his whole backyard spayed up and he got some seeds. They'll really have a beautiful Victory Garden. Mrs. Russell is going to see Jr for Mother's Day. She's got her mind made up. We dug worms for the birds and put them in the birdbath. They crawled out and no birds came. Boohoo. Joe and Ann's gone to Flecks. I asked him if he wanted to take that sheep manure along in case he ran short, 'cause he really can shoot it [*reference to Joe's bull-shitting*].

Anthony Oberhausen is now a Lt. In the Army. I believe they'll all be officers before long. By the time Joe comes back, I might have more news because I'm plum blanktey-blank until I gather a little gossip, honey.

H.R.

Continued:

A big mistake about Oberhausen. He's a Sergeant not a Louie, Lip told me. Kenny Flechler is in Detroit working in an airplane factory. He has punctured eardrums and a slight rupture. Bernie is in Texas. Paul is running the farm. We received your letter this morning. Inspection is over, I see, and you got a GI haircut. Well, could we have a dime-store picture of your beautiful haircut? I bet the barber said "What a dome! What a dome!" Did you pay time and a half?

We went to Lip's last night. She's got your picture hung on the front room wall and the kids put a little flag above it. A patriotic display. Margie mooches just like her old man. He takes her to Haberstein's; Eddie Kirch gave her a piece of candy and chewing gum last Sunday. So this Sunday he gave her a piece of candy and she asked for the chewing gum. He never had any, so after supper, he went again and she spied some. She said "Heddy zoo dot some chewing gum now." She's really crazy about Moody. She gave everybody a piece of gum and ran out when it came to Marge, so she said, I haven't got any chewing gum. She took Lip's piece away and cut it in half and gave the other half to Marge. We all thought that was thinking far for a 2 ½ year old. I bet you were busier than a cat on a hot tin roof last week. I'm going to Schieman's and get the seeds this morning for the garden and finish it up.

Mom's in her glory. Mary had a hen party yesterday with some women she worked with. They made more noise. It seemed so funny, but it did seem alive upstairs. It's a beautiful day in Louisville. How about a picture before your cowlick comes back.
Love,
Hermina

Louisville, Kentucky, **April 5**, Monday, 8:25 pm
Dear Norb,

In retaliation for your two cups of coffee and tenderloins steak sandwich. I must say Mom made a bowl of Panas and Gutta [*Goetta*] and does it look good. And we got 6 quarts of Oertel's '92 also. Your cake is on its way. Let me know how good it was or if it wasn't any good. I never made a cake that had such a delicious smell. To date I have planted onions, lettuce, beets, bush beans, carrots, radishes, a few pole beans and that's all in the vitamin line. I got a pack of pansies and trying them out in a bowl in the house. Hope I'm successful with them because I think they're very pretty.

I'm inclosing a piece of paper. I wrote you about it. Joe told this guy at the White Cottage and he turned it in to the Editor. I do think it's cute and original. Tomorrow is Army Day. Let us know how you celebrated it or how the Scrubbing 59th celebrated. Digging foxholes, huh? How about that picture brother? You know we sent you a dime about 5 or 6 months ago to have a dime-store picture taken, so favor us now if it is convenient for you (an elephant never forgets). We are all OK.

Dewey [*Carter*] started to work at the L&N today. I think he weighs in the 140s. He's a muscular boy. I hope he sticks it out. He made Joey beneficiary of his insurance. He might be the breadwinner from now on. It wouldn't surprise me. Joey also has a Lee haircut. She had her haircut as short as possible and a permanent. She looks like a frizzle top.
That's all for tonite, so goodnite, sleep tight and as always,
H.R.

Continued, Tuesday 2:30 pm:
Mary is about ready so I "taut" I would finish this. We are sort of expecting John, etc. this pm. He spoke like they might come in today. Mary Rawert was here this morning for a little while. She got a few Balsam seeds. You said in your letter yesterday that the inspection was over and you didn't know what you would be doing for the next few weeks. Do you think your [*battalion*] might be sent across? We all wondered over that statement. It's a beautiful day in Louisville but cool. Well, I can't think of anything else at present so will say good afternoon General.
H.R.

Fort Jackson, South Carolina, **April 6**

Dear Mom, Pop, Marge, Piggier,

Ah, ah, it's a beautiful sunset. I have just eaten chow and taken a shower - so full and clean. Well, I got a promotion to a Corporal yesterday, or did I tell you. Lt. Baustert the new Motor Officer gave it to me. He's not from the last war. He also has the Purple Heart. We don't hear much about furloughs as yet, that's something I don't understand about this outfit. The rest of the outfits get them. I am going to start raising a little hell. Nothing like a little hell to start the ball rolling.

I got a letter from Johnny and "Elenare" the other day so tell them I said hello and I hope it's a boy. I like to be different. I don't know much that's new and besides I have some washing to do so I had better be at it.

As always,

Norb V...-

Louisville, Kentucky, **April 6**, Wednesday, 5:45 pm

Dear Norb,

Mrs. Niemann got a card from Norbert Hollkamp. He's in the Field Artillery, Camp Leonard Woods, Missouri. I knew it was something I wanted to tell you. Eleanor thinks you might look funny with your quarter-inch haircut. She can't see why that's necessary and what did I think. We got tickled. She asked if you received her letter.

[*Hermina*]

Continued later that night, 11:40 pm

Dear Norb,

Well, we're still poking the fire [*furnace*] in Louisville, but it's a beautiful day. The Rawerts of St. Matthews [*John and family*] were here last night. Boys got new shoes and haircuts. For those little squirts, haircuts are 35¢. They all look swell, are getting that first red sunburn. Hilary looks swell with it and Vernon's cheeks were like apples. They all were so cute. Peggy is still as sour as ever. She sure talks plainly.

I sent you that piece "Off the Record." Hilary isn't pleased at all. He said to Joe, "Why did you tell that? Everybody in Louisville will know how dumb I am," and he meant it, for he found out the proper way to spell Louisville.

Why did the moron salute the refrigerator? Because it was General Electric.

War news is still very "good" sounding. Pop had his game of Pinochle last night. He still walks like he's looking for a garbage can. It's a shame they are overflowing today and it would be good rooting now. What are the latest developments at the Camp?

Continued the next day by Mommy, **April** 7, 1:15 pm

Just got through with the kitchen duty. Going to the dressmaker soon to have two housedresses made. She lives in the home where Spoelkers lived. It seems nice, what I saw of it. [*She made*] Madden's two girls a coat and only charged $1.25 apiece. That's too cheap. I don't see how she can make them. I know I wouldn't. Jackie is going to make his first Holy Communion on the 9th of May. Jackie said that [*on*] Mother's Day Johnny will give a party if the stork party is not in the way. He said he was trying to save all the points so he could buy a ham. He gets 96 stamps a week. We get 6. It is not enough. Lard is 5 points, butter 8 points, and oleomargarine 7 points. All must have points. That's all I know now. God bless you.
Love,
Mother

Continued, **April** 7, Thursday 8:20 pm

So you got the April Fools letter. Did you get a card from Alma on Thursday? She sends cards for everything, you know. So I see Marge got her letters mixed up. You're not the only one. I'm reclining so you'll have to overlook the scribbling. Mom's gone to Besendorf's and Lip's, too. You know that's a must. Glad to hear you might be promoted. We congratulated you on that before but nevertheless we'll keep on hoping your next letter will have Cpl. More money tain't bad. We'll keep timmers crossed. I'll even cross my tups. We're OK. Mom weighs more than she ever did, looks swell. She had a hard time getting a belt from last a year's dress buttoned. She looks like she gets all the Oertel's. Pop is dusting the statues. Mom gave him heck, but Herman's got two ears which function properly [*and she didn't need to raise her voice*].

The paperboys are soliciting for the Red Cross. Did you get the cake? It's chilly here. It snowed and hailed at 2:00 am yesterday but the paper never mentioned it.
Love,
Jerks

Fort Jackson, South Carolina, **April 8**,

Dear Mom and all,

There is just a few minutes till "Lights Out" so in just about a half hour I'll be in bed. It turned a little cold here the other day and I caught one hell of a cold in my head. It feels like a bass drum and it looks just about the same with this GI haircut, because my hair stands straight up. Very funny, very funny. We are going out in the field for a week pretty soon but I don't mind living in the field, but of course, the snakes and I don't always agree with each other, but we get along with each other.

That was pretty cute with Hilary, wasn't it? Some student, I'll say. Well, there isn't much new around here. Everything is just about the same. Except the temperature is fairly warm tonight and I think it's going to rain. Well, let it rain. I like rain.
As Always,
Norb V...-

Louisville, Kentucky, **April 9**, 12:30 pm

Dear Norb,

Are you, or are you not, a Corporal? We are mighty anxious to know. Well, the war-news is very, very, very good. Russell really has a Victory Garden. Even if he likes to hide the bottle in the brush. He was really feeling them. He wanted to know why I never did get married and has an extra line with eenie, meenie.

Here is Norb Hollkamp's address: Pvt. Norb Hollkamp, Btry C 889 F.A. Btn., APO 451, Ft. Leonard Woods, Missouri. If you find time, drop him a few lines.

Mom said if you are made a Cpl., kindly let her know immediately. Bart was just here. We had a good argument on beer. He said it was back 12 years ago. Mom said 10 years. He got thinner. We asked him if he didn't get as much beer. That started the ball, now he's going to find out for sure and let us know who's right. I know we are because at Fr. Spoelker's reception was the first time I seen it in Kegs at a house and he will be priest 10 years in June. That's what you call a little knatty [*sp*]. I think he overlooked the fact that Roosevelt is in Office only 10 years and it was dry under Hoover.

Continued, 1:25 pm in his mother's handwriting:
Just got through washing. Can't overcome that twice a week duty. It is awful if you cannot stop working. Now I am going to do kitchen duty. Don't care for that much, as you told me in a letter some time ago. No offense. You say it is no compliment. I am sure. Ha, ha. I hope you got to be Corporal. You deserve it, I'm sure. Alma is coming Sunday.
God bless you,
Mother

Louisville, Kentucky, **April 10**, Saturday, 10:30 am

Dear Norb,

Well, we had a good thunderstorm last night. It tore that Aerial Stict [*sp*] down. It made plenty noise. You must be very busy. We received a letter from you Thursday that was written today a week ago so we figured you're about digging foxholes or such. Believe it or not, Milt and Jim went to Rudy's last night and stayed "all nite." Can you imagine Milt doing that? He also has chickens and bandies and pheasants just hatched out, so it's really interesting time of the year. I think that lured Milt out there.

Lip was up last night and she had to call out there. You would of thought they were gone a month. Milt is getting so big and mannish looking. I think you'll notice the biggest change in him. Still nuts but mighty sweet, without a doubt Lip's pet. We are all OK. We thought we'd get a letter from you today, announcing your promotion but we are fooled.

Mom ordered the coal. You can't get any more than you got last year. St. Brigid's got notice to install coal furnace because of the oil situation. Hoping you are well.
Love from all,
H.R.

Louisville, Kentucky, **April 10**, Sunday, 7:25 pm

[Dear Norb,]

Well, I was talking with Alma last night and she said she got two letters saying you were Corporal. Well, congratulations for the second time. I hope it is for keeps this time. I know it will. It was just a mistake the last time, that's all. We received the letter you wrote Saturday a week ago on Thursday but the mail is as funny as everything else is. We might get two letters tomorrow, which has often happened. I hope so.

Milt and Jim stayed last nite at Rudy's too. He left them from 6 to 9 pm last night. Milt got homesick in that time and called. He was crying, had the bellyache and everything while he was talking to Lip. Then Rudy came in. He said they got homesick and with dark coming on, the frogs croaking and the hoot owls hooting, and that they got that "all alone feeling," so Rudy had a good laugh. He said all the lights were burning but Milt forgot all about the bellyache when Rudy came home and they stayed all night. Haven't come home yet.

Ann's nephew from Venezuela and Trinidad is home on a 10-day furlough. He came in this morning and was traveling since Friday a week ago. A lot of the way by plane. He's been in the Army 3 years and 3 months. Now he reports to Florida. He's seen action. He also traveled by ship and train. He said for 15 minutes after his arrival they did nothing but laugh and cry.

Boy, I can really make good ice cream. Marge wanted more. I gave it to her, then she wanted more. I never had any more so she licked the teaspoons first, then licked the saucers. I'll say goodnite and finish tomorrow. With pen or pencil in hand, can't you pen out a few words to Lizziebet?

H.R.

Louisville, Kentucky, **April 12**, Monday, 9:30 pm

Dear Cpl. Norb,

Well, we got two letters this morning. Sure are glad you're a Corporal, Norb. Mom had the runs. The mailman was late. It was terribly windy. About 8:30 am, it felt like the house was rocking and now it's getting colder. And guess what? Matthew Kendrick was walking across the street. I even called Mom out of her glory to see it. Someone said they saw him waiting at the 4th and Market Streets for a streetcar. He looks about the same. Did your whole outfit get the Cpl. rating or just you? Because your work is under a different commanding officer. The weather is damp. It rained like everything last nite and this morning but I guess you can expect it this time of year.

Don't you want Peggy to have a little partner [*baby girl for a sister*]? But you can't tell any difference [*between Peggy and a boy*]. She bams right and left and fights with all of them. She's really tough and stern. I hope you get your furlough with your short haircut. Boy I would love to see that head, but it looks good in a cap. Looks better than 6 5/8 . Hell, why am I so complimentary to you when you always try to de-compliment me? Damn if I know.

We are all OK. You know your letters are just a week old when we get them. It seems from your date and postmark that you're late in posing them, and they are 4 days in coming for the last 2 weeks.

Piggier, Sou, Horse, Porky

Louisville, Kentucky, **April 12**, Monday, 1:00 pm

Dear Norb,

The weather is windy and gloomy. I am writing you a wide letter. Out of writing paper. Isn't that too bad? So this must do for now. We are all glad that you are promoted and all wish you luck. We are happy with you even if we are far away. As the saying goes - so near and yet so far. But you can reverse it and say so far and yet so near. I enjoyed your letters very much but had to wait long for them. When we were disappointed, I offered it up. Maybe the poor souls got the benefit. Norb, you know the 9ᵗʰ of May is Mother's Day and you could not please me any better than by going to the Sacraments. And you would make your Easter duty also? Maybe you will get a furlough. I want you to remember all of us in your prayers. We pray for you every day. Sometimes when we pray the rosary [*which was almost every night*], Papa falls asleep. Then he will answer again when he gets awake and wants to pray the rosary when we are already finished. So, that's good-bye and good luck and God bless you. Mary said hello honey bunch.

Mother

Fort Jackson, South Carolina, **April 12**, Monday, 9:30 pm

Dear Mom ad all,

Well, I haven' been able to write much for the last three days because we have been in the field and when you're in the field you can't do much writing. It's a mighty funny feeling when a tank runs over your head and you're in a foxhole about 5 ½ feet deep. But it's really a lot of fun. I would just as soon live in the field if I could take a bath a little more often, but water is just a little scarce.

It don't look as though I get a furlough for a little while because of a new training period. But I'll be glad to see maneuvers because I think they will be a lot of fun except for the tank and snakes. Well, I haven't slept very little for the last few days so I am really a little tired so excuse this writing and I'll write more later. XX for Mary.

As Always,

Norb

Louisville, Kentucky, **April 14**, Wednesday, 12 noon

Dear Norb,

Well, I'm not dreaming of a White Easter but it's possible. It has been snowing for two hours or more. It isn't sticking though. Our birdbath is a solid sheet of ice. It is 24° above zero now. This letter will sound like another weather report but yesterday it rained hard. Then the sun shown at 10:55 am.

I was standing by the front room side window. So was Mom, Lip and Margie. When for a half moment the windows shook. We all looked at one another. We thought it was a mild quake or an explosion of some kind. The evening paper came out with there was no report of a tremor. The FBI was investigating. This tremor was felt more on the South-west outline of Louisville from Shawnee Park to Eastern Parkway. After the tremor yesterday, it snowed and the ground was covered in spots this morning early. It also sleeted for about 15 minutes. How is the weather there? I have never seen such diversified weather.

John H. Rawert, Jr [*Jackie*] makes his first Communion [*on*] Mother's Day, May 9th. Here's hoping you will get to come home then. Gee. you will keep us always keeping our fingers crossed. I hope you get your furlough boy. I was talking to Mrs. Zip [*Zipperle*]. She wanted to know if you got your furlough. She never seen you. She said Zip is at Ft. Fisher, North Carolina. Do you ever hear from him? She said she didn't know if Zip and you wrote to each other. He never mentions you. I told her you never mention Zip either, so we were both dumb.

Lill Steinmetz's nephew Eddie, Joe's boy, is going across. He's about there by now. Baukhage [*news reporter and radio commentator*] reported that the Japs are reported to be starting a big offensive. I guess those slant-eyes got something up their sleeves.

I seen your letter, or should I say scribbles, today. You don't play pinochle anymore? If you get your furlough, Pop will scratch until you play with him. You know, sometimes I think it makes a letter more interesting if you have to ponder over the words. Just keep on scribbling. Let [leave] the pondering for us. Some people seem to think it was the rock quarry that caused that tremor; others think it was an explosion from a defense plant; still others think it was intentional. You know there is a War Bond Drive going on. A 1,000 [*sic*] people and a 1,000 ideas. Well, will close.

With love,
"Cold Porky"

Continued by Mommy:

Norb, did you get that cake? Does your radio work again? Would be nice if you could come for the day when <u>Jackie</u> makes his <u>First Communion</u> on <u>Mother's Day 9 May</u>. Answer these questions for once.

Good-bye and God bless you always,
Mother

Louisville, Kentucky, **April 16,** Friday, 2:11 pm

Dear Norb,

A gloomy day in Louisville and we are still feeling like wintertime. Katsy was in a "pay" [*play*] last nite. The PTA had a meeting so Mom went with Lip. Katsy was with the widdum [*rhythm*] band. She had to shake a "tangerine" (tambourine). She was so tickled. Announcing that the last fish died yesterday. You know we had two fish left. The other died Wednesday so we don't have any more. It seemed they both died with the same thing that was in, under, and on back of their gills. It showed blood spots. Perhaps they had a hemorrhage.

I don't have any more news. We haven't received a letter since Tuesday or Wednesday. We are beginning house cleaning but this weather puts a damper on everything. I don't think I'll mail this. Tain't enough news in it. I'll wait till tomorrow day, as Milt used to say. I think he will graduate the first Sunday in June. He got a very good report. Mom said I should mail these few lines because a little news is better than none. I believe that's a hint. She still watches the mailman.

Love, hugs, kisses and hints,

"Porky"

Louisville, Kentucky, April 17, Saturday, noon

Dear Norb,

Well, I see where you are in the field. Just a preliminary to maneuvers I suppose. Betsy thought it was "Removers," so you'd better take care. I suppose she has the right slant on it anyway. What do you think of your picture? [*Norb was pictured in a clipping in the Courier Journal showing local troops who had received promotions*]. Everybody thought it was fine. Mom showed it to Donaldson. He just said, "dots him, looks 'chust' like Norb." He's a first class private in the Kentucky State Militia. Mom thinks you're the most handsome and Pop doesn't give you enough credit. Why don't you go for Mr. America 1943?

We are all OK. I am going to close. Mom wants to write also so will say too, da, loo and a block buster or love.

"Porky"

A letter from Norb's mom was added to the envelope for this day but it was ripped in half so only half of the letter on each page can be presented here:

...if you did not, so we can trace it. We had it insured. We are sending you an Easter box so keep an eye and your mind on it and let us know because it wearies us till we find out. The weather is beautiful today but we had so much rain, even it was snowing. I mean snowing and the sun was shining. Alma said she was coming tomorrow believe it or not she's not been to see us for 5 weeks. I would like to...

...is using good judgement. I thought he [*Pop*] would cry a little bit, but he forgot he was very tired. He has so much work- and hard work - this week. I feel sorry for him. but he gets a bucket of beer and waits for the 10 o'clock news. He won't go to bed before the war news is

broadcast. That's all for today so goodbye and be good. Norb, write to us if you can, if only an "I am well. Hello and goodbye. As Always,
Norb."
Mama, Papa, Ma, Meanie, Mary xx and Betsy

Continued by Betsy Muth:
Hello handsome uncle Norbe. Do you still believe in the Easter rabbit? I am helping him with your basket. I think it will be very nice. Mommy said that you youst [*used*] to believe in it. I think that you look that dumb. I wish you a happy Easter,
Betsy

Based on letters, Norb received a furlough starting April 18 until around April 29, 1943.

Louisville, Kentucky, **May 1**
Dear Mom and all,
    I have been very busy the last few days. Didn't have any time to write but I have a little time off now and I'm going to the Bob Hope Show. It starts at 10:00 pm - Jerry Calonia. You know him? He's always on Bob Hope's show. Well, he came through our barracks today. He don't look as crazy as he sounds. Only he wears a GI haircut. We are going to have an IG inspection (IG means Inspecting General) this Thursday. Things are getting rather hot down here. It was about 110° yesterday. I hope we pull out of here before July or August. If we don't, I see myself weighing about 100 pounds. Well, I'll be seeing you later and Katie [*Mom*] take good care of yourself and goodnight.
As Always,
Norb

Louisville, Kentucky, **May 2**, Sunday, 3 pm
(Saw this U Boat scene. It sort of got me)
Dear Norb,
    Well, we had more rain today and to think how beautiful it was yesterday but it is clearing up. I suppose you'll want to know about Joe and Moody at the track [*Kentucky Derby at Churchill Downs*]. Well, neither of them cashed a ticket so that was another bad investment for me. I never win on ponies. Sounds big doesn't it? They got in at 7:30 and left right after the Derby. Joe bet on Gold Showers. They estimated the crowd at 60,000 to 65,000 people. The paper claimed Rochester [*comedian Jack Benny's sidekick*] taken the publicity away from [*Kentucky Governor*] Chandler. Bunky and Joe hoisted Moody on their shoulder and he called the numbers as the hosses [*horses*] passed. They claim to have had attentive listeners. Pop was awful shaky. He told Russell to drive to a saloon so they could get a beer. He had to go to the toilet.

I seen these pictures in last night's paper and thought they were very cute and thought of you instantly. Do you moan high or low? Or always? Boy, oh boy, does that birdbath draw the birds. Six of them but the robin fought it out. The robin wanted privacy until the sparrow got tired of it and they fought it out. Was quite a scene. Don't know any more. I suppose you're nearing your destination by this time.

Love from all,

H.R.

Louisville, Kentucky, **May 3**, 10:30 pm

Dear Mom and all,

Well, it's very, very hot down here but it gets pretty cool at night, which is a great help. I went to the Bob Hope show and if you were listening to what he said it was just about the truth. I had a seat about 15 feet from the stage. A very good seat. A better seat than most of the Majors had, but I was lucky. After the show, I and "Barnaski," some guy I know here, stumbled into the dressing room and I got the autograph of Bob Hope, Jerry Colonna, Francis Langford Vera Vogue, Bob Allen and Wendell Niles. It was really funny and we were in there with majors, Lt. Colonels, Admirals and all the big shots. Some time I will send this little book home and let you see it if you would like.

Things are getting tougher right along. We had a General Inspection today and it was tough just like all big inspections are but everything was all right. You'll have to pardon me for not writing but been just too damn busy. I haven't written Alma a letter since last Friday, May 27, I think. I'll enclose a picture I had taken a little while after I came back from furlough. Thought maybe you would, or would not, like to see it. Well, I'll have to close for now. Hope you're feeling just a lot, lot better Kate and Pop still drinking his rationed Oertel's.

As Always,

Norb

Louisville, Kentucky, **May 4**, 9:15

Dear Norb,

Just a few lines to let you know that I hope that you will keep your promise that you would go to the Sacraments on Mother's Day as you promised me when you kissed me goodbye. I hope and trust that you will not disappoint your mother.

We are all well and hope that you are well also. Papa is drinking '92. Marge is reading. Hermina is going to Maddens to tell them what came over the radio just before Fibber and Molly came over the radio. It was announced that people should not take Fletcher Castoria and druggists [*should*] take it off the shelf and tell the neighbors. What happened, we do not know.

Goodbye,

[*Mother*]

Louisville, Kentucky, **May 5**, Wednesday, 8 pm

Dear Norb,

We haven't heard from you as yet. We thought by this pm we would, but tomorrow we might be successful. We are having summertime and could sit outside for the first time this spring. Got the screens up today and we have seen a few flies. My garden? Well, it's better left unsaid, but you can't tell. Norb, about your radio tubes. Send us the name of your tube or numbers. Mrs. Butler got one for Jr at Sears and his neighbor is in radio business is going to get the other tube. I think it's the same thing you need.

We are all OK. We haven't heard from Eleanor as yet. Jackie makes his First Communion Sunday. Mrs. Russell leaves tomorrow at 11:20 am on the Pan American [*train*] for Florida. She used fingernail polish for the first time and don't know how to hold her long fingers. Funny.

I scrubbed the front of the house and my hands are so stiff. I guess you can tell from my scribbles. Will say goodnite and might add a few more lines tomorrow. Goodnite, Sleep tite, oh yeh, does the bed bugs bite?
[*Hermina*]

Louisville, Kentucky, **May 6**

Dear Norb,

Just received your letter and see that you had to stand so long. I am going to the foot doctor today. They hurt me very bad. I hope you will like it better again. Tucker is going back again on the train with Mrs. Russell. She doesn't know how long it will be that they will travel together. Your letter was very welcome as it is always. Hermina is sewing at home on the draperies. Chester brings them and takes them back [*to Hubbuch's*]. Don't forget the Mother's Day promise.
Mother

Fort Jackson, South Carolina, **May 6**

Dear Mom and all,

This is Thursday evening 6:40 pm to be exact and it's pretty damn hot here now and this is just spring. No telling how hot it will be here this summer. You might raise hell about the ration points but I would rather have those than the army chow. But it should improve this week after we get these new 77 rookies straightened out.

I have been pretty busy since I came back. I had a lot of work I had to catch up on and things are really buzzing now. Well, I did have my share of Oertel's when I was there but I sure could use one now. I guess I'll start losing weight again since summer is coming on, but I can afford to lose a few pounds. Well, that's all what's new for now, so until later then, I'm As Always,
Norb

Louisville, Kentucky, **May 7**, Friday, 8:30 pm

Dear Norb,

We received your letter saying you arrived OK, but tired. I bet that was a tiresome trip. We are having more rain. Every other day it rains. Today we had two heavy showers. Mrs. Russell should be in Florida by this time. Mom was talking to Cousin Mary. She told her Mrs. Russell went by the "American Flyer" that was the fastest train. She meant Pan-American.

Lip was cleaning house and run a splinter in her hand. She went to [*Dr.*] Gettlefinger. He couldn't locate it. He lanced it and dug deep around. She suffered a bit until suppertime, then the pain eased up quite a lot. She went home feeling a lot better than when she came. Dr. said it would come out OK. Eleanor is still on the go, poor child. This is some news on the Muth's - Katsy is going to confession soon. She told Lip she had pour (four) sins. She was d-bee-e-cent (disobedient) to her mother four times and she tussed [*cussed*] seven times. Shirley played volleyball today against St. Martin's and I believe she feels important. She spelled the smartest girl down in her class so she's class champion. I imagine she can teach you a few words.

You have Mom's key. I think that will come through the mail OK. I feel like you are thinking of that Mother's Day card. Joe and Ann sent one of the cutest ones I have ever seen. If you did forget it, send it later. Ray Kegebein, friend of Mrs. Orrill, was made Sgt. last week. I'm sure glad for him. Hoping you are OK and back into the routine of army life. Did you arrive in time or not? You never stated that in your letter.

Say, what did you tell Alma? She said you said she was getting as fat as Horse. She told me she would die if she'd get fat and went 'phooey, no I don't want to get fat.' I quit talking for a minute and she asked if I hung up [*the phone*]. I said no, I just died 'cause I'm fat, and considered the source.

Betsy thinks it's funny whenever she was at Fontaine Ferry Park. She never seen racehorses at the Racing Derby. Some thought, eh?Hoping to hear from you.
With love from all the Rawerts,
"Porky"

Fort Jackson, South Carolina, **May 8**, Saturday

Dear Mom and all,

It's Saturday night and it's hotter than hell outside but it's beginning to thunder and lightning and right now it has just started raining. It can rain down here for a whole day and the sun can come out for 15 minutes and everything is dry again. Well, we have to work tomorrow all day long, which is a very unpleasant thought. I do like one day a week off but that's the way it is, so I guess we work. We had about 150 new men come in our outfit. They were only in the Army for about five days and it's really funny to think how dumb you are when you were first inducted. It nearly seems impossible but we do get a lot of laughs out of them. There is one fellow among who eats razor blades and toothpaste tubes. He is strictly nuts. I think they are going to give him a mental examination. I think he needs one.

It's beginning to cool off a little since it started raining. That's one thing to be thankful for because it was really hot today out in the sun. We go out on the rifle range next Friday so we had to get a little practice. I get a big kick out of shooting a rifle though, so I'll be glad to get out on the range and see how good my nerves are. See if that '92 hurt them any, which I know it didn't. How that lightning does carry on. I wish it would rain a little harder.

Just from the looks of things, I imagine that I am an uncle by this time. Am I right or wrong? Right! Well, my dear, dear people the sound of the rain on the roof is getting me very sleepy so I think I'll retire for the night. Tell everyone hello for me because I just got too damn busy to write all of them a letter. Well, goodnight.
As Always,
Norb

Louisville, Kentucky, **May 9**, Mother's Day
Dear Norb,

Oh, what a day this one started out to be! Mom, Marge, Joe and Ann, Lip and Mrs. Smith are gone out to Trinity Church to see Jackie. At 5:15 am, our phone rang. It was Johnny. He called to tell them to get there early so Joe could take Jackie, as Eleanor was feeling bad, as he had to call the MD for her. It didn't take them long to get away either. To top it all off, the girl that was staying with Eleanor went home yesterday to be with her kids. She's coming back tonite. I bet Johnny was going in semi-circles. I guess Johnny won't make it to church either. That's a pity it all had to happen today but we felt like everything would happen at once. We might have a nephew, niece, or both by this time. I sure am living in hopes everything will be OK.

Mom has been having so many dizzy spells. Four yesterday, three on Friday and she had a couple the earlier part of the week. So we're going to see what they are all about. They are of short duration, usually after she eats. Mom's new hat really looks swell on her. I think Eleanor's baby picked a mighty opportune time to be born.

I guess I should say Milton represented you this morning at Mass. I think this was a very nice idea. They asked the 7th and 8th grade boys to volunteer if they wanted to represent the Servicemen at Mother's Day mass so Milt did. They wore small flags in their lapel. Mary is just back from church. She said two servicemen walked beside the priest going in church carrying the two flags. Lip's finger is still very, very tender. So far, no sign of the splinter but I think it's just rotting away. Will sign off until I hear more. You have all the dope to the minute, Sir.

Continued later:

Hold your breath! Announcing Boy Rawert! Born at 6:00 am, weight 11 pounds, dark blue eyes, on the fair side, built like a boxer. Just why couldn't my godchild been a girl, but I kind of like it this way. I was Betsy's godmother. Vernon said they got four boys and a kid now, but I say making a first appearance at 11 pounds is something. Hilary don't go near his mother. He 'don't want that disease.' Will bring this to a close now. It's all the news I know for this time. Congratulations Uncle Corporal!
Love,
Aunt Meenie

Fort Jackson, South Carolina, **May 9**

Dear Mom and all,

This is Sunday afternoon and not much to do but I am going down and drink a few beers at the PX [*Post Exchange*]. I have a key in my pocket that I drug along with me when I left and I don't have no use for it so I'll send it back. Well, I'll see you later.
As Always
[*Norb*]

On a US Army postcard marked May 10:
"Chapel Sixteen, Fort Jackson, South Carolina. Mother's Day 1943.
Mother Dear: Today I remembered you in a very special way. I went to our Chapel for services and asked God to reward you for your unselfish devotion to me, your soldier son. I hope and pray that God will spare you for many, many years. Your devoted boy." [*Norb left it unsigned. It makes the author wonder if Norb really went to "the Sacraments" like his mother was always reminding and begging him to do since he couldn't sign his name to it.*]

Louisville, Kentucky, **May 12**, Wednesday, 2:20 pm

Dear Norb,

First of all, I want to thank you for the card. It is very nice. The weather is so changeable. I made a fire [*in the furnace*] this morning. Now it is too hot and we have the window open. Norb, what I would like to know is if you went to the Sacraments on Mother's Day as you promised me so faithful and I sure took your word of honor. I pictured you with the other army men going to Holy Communion, thinking of us at home, and praying for us. I hope you will not let this question unanswered as it means a lot to me, and Papa also. I wish you good luck and god bless you from your mother's heart. Goodbye.
Mother

Continued by Hermina:

80° Dear Norb,

Wait a minute. We got two letters from you at the same time - 2:30 pm. The one is a nice big fat one. No, you were not uncle at that time when you wrote that, but by 6:00 the next morning, you were. I think you got the Airmail letter by this time. Johnny is really so tickled with "Gene." He's a big beautiful boy, not a wrinkle on his body. If he keeps his weight, he'll be a whopper. I don't think he looks like any of the rest of them at all, but he has long fingers and toes like Eleanor, with long nails. I think Moody will be godpoppy but I don't know for sure. Johnny likes the name Eugene and calls him Gene. I don't think Eleanor bothers. She said she picked out plenty names already.

Your other letter contained Mom's key. It came very nicely thru the mail. I tell de world Norb, I'm sick of our weather. We're still poking a fire. This pm is turning out beautiful. Monday and Tuesday we had showers all day and thru the night.

I hear Winston Churchill is here again. I bet a lot is being cooked up in Washington, DC during this visit. We are going to be put in a zone or whatever it might be. A numeral will be added between Louisville and KY such as Lou. 5 KY (enclosing clipping). Also inclosing a clipping of serious air-crash at Curtiss-Wright. That happened near Manslick Road. They claim the wings fell off and it sort of blew to bits. That's close to Rudy's.

The CSSMC meets at Shelby Park, then they go to the St. X Alumni Field this pm.

Lip still hollers ouch when you look at her digit cross-eyed. The splinter hasn't come out as yet. I think it might pop out from the looks of it someday. This is Muth's talk: Katsy said this one girl in the neighborhood is "engraved" to a soldier. She also cried Monday morning. She didn't want to go to school and that St. Elizabeth's never has "pee" days. Betsy, she's as bright as ever. Lip can't pound the steak so Moody fried it. Of course, it was supposed to be better than ever. Betsy said, "Well, Daddy, if you think you're such an expert steak fryer we can all sit on our asses at night and wait for you to fix the meal."

Well, honey, I'll bring this to a close. I'm not saying this to boss, but if you sent Mommy something for Mother for that three bucks I gave you on Saturday, she never has received it. With love from you affectionate sister,
Hermina Mary

Fort Jackson, South Carolina, **May 13**

Dear Mom, Pop, Sis's and Mary,

Well, there's not much to write about, just the same old routine. The weather has been excellent. It's been a little warm though, but it really gets cool at nights. It gets cool enough that you have to use a blanket.

Congratulations to Johnny and Eleanor. I told you that it was going to be a boy. I guess Johnny was running around there like a chicken with his head cut off. I don't blame him. Sorry to hear about Lip's hand. I haven't had a chance to write to anybody at all yet because we have rifle practice from 6:30 to 8:30 pm every night and there's not much time left to do everything after you get your own work done. It all takes time you know.

We had a bunch of new fellows to come into our outfit and one of them is absolutely nuts. He eats razor blades and old toothpaste tubes. I really don't think he has them all or else he's putting up a front trying to get out of the army. It's either one of the two.

The beer here is just as rotten as ever. Not half as good as Oertel's, but it's still beer and so long as it's beer, I'll have to drink it.

Been trying like hell to get some chewing gum but they have limited it to two packs per person. I'll do my best

Well, folks there's not much more to say so I'll sign off until later when I have a little more dope or a little more news. So, so long & I'll be seeing you.

As Always,

Norb

Louisville, Kentucky, **May 13**, 7:50pm

Dear Norb,

I thought I would miss Bing Crosby but I looked at the clock wrong. They really got the Germans in N. Africa. I know I acknowledged your two letters yesterday and today Mom got a "Chaplain" Mother's Day card from you. It really pleased her very, very much Norb. She thought that was a swell idea. Mom still has been having "dizzy" spells. I have begged her to go to the Dr. but I still think she will go tomorrow. She's afraid of high blood pressure I think, but she can't be dizzy all the time.

We got a card from Mary [*Russell*] today. She must be having a wonderful time. He [*Mr. Russell*] got a letter Tuesday. She said Jr went fishing and caught 35 pounds of fish the Sunday before she got there. Jr got the weekend off so they were going fishing Sunday again. I could eat a good fish sandwich myself.

Ann, Joe and Marge are gone to Johnny's. My godchild is the drawing card. Really a swell looking kid. We will send you a snapshot as soon as one is taken of it. I think it will be soon. We are still having rain and more rain at 5:00 pm. It got so dark we had to turn the lights on. And we had a really hard shower and it is still raining. The grass had its official first cutting yesterday by Maddens and Joe. We were all busy and it does look good too, I must say. Looks like velvet. The lawnmower said, "Where's Norb?" I been purty busy myself. I put in 33 hours at home working on drapes this past week. I'm going to leave this letter open. Maybe I might have more news by tomorrow. Goodnite brother.

Before I forget to tell you, that Redmann boy on Texas Street that left the same time you did, well he is in N. Africa. His parents received notice yesterday. He was wounded in action. They don't know how serious. No details came with it. That's all you could think of yesterday was that fighting and at 6 pm yesterday news came over that the fighting has ceased. Now that's something.

[*Hermina*]

Continued, **May 14**, Friday, 8:00 am:

Well, I do say some changes has been made. The baby is named Norbert Henry Rawert. I think that's mighty nice. Moody and I are going to take it to church. Godchild is as big as godfather, but oh the godmammy [*Hermina*]! I'm going to make sure Fr. Knue sees Moody; otherwise, he might ask if Moody is the one to be baptized. I think they are going to call him "Bert." The Dr. has the name and he is taking Vernon and Jackie to St. Joseph's Infirmary the last of May for their tonsils to be removed. That is a heap lot of news me fren [*sic*]. Good day

And another note added from his mother before mailing:

Dear Norb.

I received your Mother's Day card yesterday, May 13. And thank you very much. Hope what you prayed for will come true. We are praying for you every day.

Well, I will close. I can't wait to go to get me a tablecloth. I gave Elizabeth mine to use on her kitchen wall. It was green and it matched her paper. We are all well except I don't feel so well so I am going to the doctor. Well, so long.

Goodbye,

Mother

PS. What do you think about the Africa war? Thank God for that and hope that we will have peace soon. I am listening to Breakfast at Sardey's [*Sardi's*]. It is good. He is just interviewing a lady 96 years old today and she is grand for her memory. I know I won't be that if I am 96.

Louisville, Kentucky, **May 16**, Sunday, 9:25 pm

Dear Norb,

Well, I really don't have any news excepting Norbert Henry Rawert was baptized this afternoon at 1:30 pm. Fr. Hautledge of Holy Trinity baptized him. It was just Norbie and another boy baptized. His father was an F.B.I. man, his godfather a Lt. in the Army. Your namesake never whimpered and is just as husky looking as can be. The other baby was delicate, not as big as Norb and a month old. Eleanor looks and is swell is going to get up tomorrow.

Mom is in bad need of a sun-suit. If you think about it, tease her about it. Dr. Gettlefinger gave her pills for dizziness. So far, they have never helped her but he said she needs a good dose of sunshine. I think Mom would look cute in shorts cutting the lawn, don't you? Dr. Gettlefinger got Lip's splinter out. I'm inclosing a $3.00 piece of lumber [*the splinter and the cost to remove it?*] Lip walked the floor and cried Friday but the finger is really healing up good now. He cut to the bone, that's where it was lodged.

Margie told me she planted tomatoes and soup in her garden (just bring your spoon).

We are still having rain and more rain so it's terrible. You could see the fields with water standing in the rows. Everything is pretty and green tho. Well, Rudy got that pony but I don't know whose it is. Milt has been there since Friday. We are all OK.

Milt graduates June 4th. Will say goodnite. Tuesday 2:30 pm. Out of stamps so couldn't mail it. It's 9 months today you're in the Army and a month yesterday you were on furlough. How the time does fly. Don't have any special news. Hope you're OK. We are. Lip is too.
Love,
H.R.

Fort Jackson, South Carolina, **May 19**

Dear Mom and all,

Just a line to say hello and how are you all doing? How is your dizzy spells and how is Pop and his beer? I guess you have went to the doctor by this time, at least you should have. It was hot as hell here today. We were out on the rifle range yesterday. I shot a 136 out of a possible 150 so I didn't do so bad. I see in the paper where there was a flood in Indiana. Well, rain down here has been scarce. Well, folks I have to sign off for now so goodnight and I still sing in my sleep, as I was informed. So, I am,
As Always,
Norb V...-

Louisville, Kentucky, **May 19**, Wednesday, 11:40 pm

Dear Norb,

We are thinking or wondering if it is going to rain. We haven't had as nice a day as Derby day since you were here. We are listening to Winston Churchill. He pledged full assistance to the US for the war with Japan. Thanks Winston! Mrs. Russell will come home today if she does as her card states.

Johnny came in yesterday afternoon. It seemed like old times almost. Joe got off early yesterday. He and John went to Johnson's [hardware store]. Now here comes a story. Joe bought a kerosene lamp-stove for $1.25. Clarence said it was 30 years old. They had six of them. This was the last one. Mom had one to use before we had piped gas on Clay Street for heating our milk for bottles. I don't remember it but I do remember when the gas was piped. Joe had it going when Ann came home. She stopped here first. I told her Joe had something new. Is it a radio, she asked? I can't tell you. When she got home, nothing but soot balls greeted her. He was reading in his bedroom and had it going full blast. It was necessary for Joe to mop up the kitchen and it was just mopped Saturday. Ann don't think it is worth a damn.

Sad news: beer is now rationed. I can't tell how much Jimmy is allowed but I know it's below his quota. Lip's thumb is healing grand. I got a nice letter from Norbert Hollkamp today.

Little Norb is just A-1 and so is Eleanor. She got up a little yesterday. The Dr. told her she was just fine, but being she got along so swell, she should still take care of herself.

Churchill really gave Isenhauer [*Eisenhower*] credit for his work. He also said that the "Huns" are either at your throat or at your feet. I think he is right.

Katsy didn't feel too good Monday. The warm days got her. She said she had a bellyache so she didn't go to school. Some playmate passed and called her about 9 o'clock, told her the first and second grades didn't have school because of First Communion class. Katsy said, "Doody, Doody (goody), I didn't play hootie (hooky) after all. She was well immediately. A little like her uncle but without a diamond [*Norb had a diamond shaped birthmark*].

Russell went 8 places before he got tomato plants. You know he's choicy. Pop spotted a place on his way home so they went there. They really are beautiful plants but Pop's got them planted too close and he was thrilled with them. You'd think he found $1,000. I cleaned the boys' room yesterday. Took out one bed. Now I intend to get to the attic. Mom got Pop coveralls. She thinks he'll put them on top of his best suit now.

Churchill called Hitler a Corporal. Does that make you feel too bad Cpl? Hoping for sunshine so Mom gets it out of her joints. It started to rain again.
Love from all,
Hermina

Louisville, Kentucky, **May 20**
Dear Mom and all,

Well, you will have to pardon this paper. This is GI scratchpads. It looks like I'm going to grammar school yet. It might be a good idea, who knows? It rained a little down here today and then it really did get hot and I ain't fooling. I wouldn't mind a bit if it would rain a little more. Well, Katie [*Mom*], what was the doctor's verdict? What did he say made you dizzy? That's a funny question to ask.

We are going out in the field next Monday for a week. I guess it will rain like hell then. It always does. So I might not be able to write, but we will receive our mail just the same. I have a little work to do tonight so I guess I'll have to quit writing for now so I'll see you later.
As Always,
Norb V...-

Louisville, Kentucky, **May 22**, Saturday, 8:30 pm
Ya darn smart eleck [*sic*] snot!!
(No offence) or Dear Norb,

Whatta ya mean, I should get busy and help Mom? Brother, you should of seen me this week. I did get a start at chasing germ-ans [*Germans*] too. I got your room - or my room, which is it - all cleaned. And that darn bathroom since it's painted white, is nothing less than a pain. I scoured the whole thing. Nothing would clean it right so I had to buckle down to it. Looks good. Mom never got a dizzy spell today at all. The first time in weeks, she went a whole day. We really had a dizzy Mother but the weather we're having is enough to make anybody have aches and pains. Mom said she doubts if she'll go to church tomorrow if her knee don't stop aching. It's swollen. Dr. Gettelfinger told her it was arthritis and sunshine is the only thing that will make it feel better so we're hoping for sunshine. Everything is beautiful, green and tender looking, but does that grass grow! I wish you could have weekend furloughs just to cut the grass (now that wasn't a nice remark was it?) (H.R. SOU!)

Did you get your buttons sewed on since you heard about Norbert Henry [*so proud of his namesake, that he'd pop the buttons off his expanded chest*]? He really is a big boy. I guess Mom was too much in her glory, you know. She pudded [*sic*] so much in water doing Johnny's [*laundry*] and helping Lip with her washing, and these damp days in the basement, is just too much. Marge said nothing doing with washing Monday, so I can't say what Mom will do Monday.

Yeh, man, Pop is still rushing the bucket [*beer pail*] while I am writing you. He's talking about the beer ration, which I believe he's a little worried about. Bill never had any whiskey tonight. He said it's very hard to be gotten. Well, we put up the porch swing. I painted it and the old chair. We're still talking about lawn furniture but it never materializes. You know how dot iss [*'that is'*].

Mrs. Russell came home yesterday from Key West. She said her trip home was very, very tiresome. She left Tuesday morning, got in Friday Morning at 3:00 am. She missed the bus from Key West to Miami and the next time the Pan American came thru was Friday. It was all reserved so it would have been Monday, if she was fortunate enough, before she could have left. She sure enjoyed her trip. I wish I could write it all (but no, maybe you don't). Jr and Madlynn are just fine. She took the slow train home. She said she asked three different people and they all wanted to route her differently. She said she appreciated the looks of a good Kentucky tree. I told her you said the same thing. She liked Florida but give her Kentucky. We had a beautiful day today but Pop expects rain tomorrow. I think it will rain too, just from the feel. It has been two years since they had a good rain in Key West.

Did I tell you Mr. Res been and is very sick? He was sick when you were here. That next Monday he was anointed and they called his five children home. He has Uremic Poisoning, but last week he improved quite a bit. I heard he was worse again yesterday but I never heard it from them. We miss Chuck-de-Chuck [*clunking sound of his car*].

John Hollkamp gave Mom some tomato stocks, 17 of them. Pop bought 22 and we got 12 from Werx thru the mail. Boy will we be full of acid if they all bear. Pop buys lettuce from a man with a little hot house on Shriller [*Schiller*] Ave., and he really eats it too. It's the best lettuce you can buy. Marge just put sheep manure on my precious garden and ruined it, boo hoo, but my sweet peas are beautiful. I can't wait until they bloom. The okra looks good. Mrs. Russell said she never seen a garden as pretty as Russell's. It is picturesque.

Walden Orrill gets his final exam the 27th of May and so does the youngest Kegebein boy.

The oldest one was made a Sarge and she received all his personal belongings, so I guess he's on his way over. Moody was coming for Lip. Betsy said, "Mother here comes 'aches and pains.'" A lady died in their neighborhood and the undertaker came. Besty seen them take the body. It was covered natural - all but the hands. She said, "Mother, it looked like the ghost of Frankenstein." Lip was pleased with your letter. Her thumb is healing swell.

Well, the flood hasn't affected us. The river gauge is 16.8' but John said they were going to open the wickets. I doubt if this will affect us. The creeks are barely flowing.

You didn't do too bad on rifle range. Let us know more about it. We are all interested in your shooting. Don't you think I had better stop? Hope you are well. We are OK.
Love from all,
Hermina

Louisville, Kentucky, **May 23**
Dear Mom and all,
It's Sunday and I took a half hour off to jot down a couple of lines. We've been getting up at four o'clock every morning and working to 10:00 & 11:00 at night. Tomorrow we get up at three. You see we are going to spend a week in the field. I guess we'll have about a 19-mile march tomorrow morning because that's about how far we are going out. I don't know how much writing I'll be able to do next week but I don't look for it to be much.

The weather has been swell down here only it's hotter than seven hells in the sun. We have an occasional shower every now and then. We were on the rifle range all day Friday.

Say, Kate, they tell me you are looking for a "Sun Suit." Well, I'll tell you what I'll do; maybe someday, if I ever get to Hawaii, I'll send you a grass skirt. I think that will answer the same purpose. Well, how has little Norb been doing? OK? Well, you talk about beer being rationed. Well, it's also rationed here at the Post. They only sell beer from 6:30 pm to 9:00 pm and that's not very long, and you get quite thirsty after you get finished working. Well, Mom, I hope you get to feeling better and take good care of yourself & I'll be seeing you.
As Always,
Norb

Louisville, Kentucky, **May 24**, Monday, 9:00 am
Dear Norb,
We received your "yellow letter" this morning. We bought that kind of paper when we went to school, called it "Klondike." It keeps raining all the time it was raining and gloomy yesterday and today. I can't tell you how tired we are of it. The "Doc" never said exactly what made Mom dizzy. She never had it Saturday at all and once since yesterday but that arthritis bothered her yesterday a lot, so I hope that sun really comes out. Then I think she'll be OK then.

Your old girlfriend Emma [*Grimm*] here yesterday. Poor soul. I feel for her. Sure we all do. I think Mom's inviting more junk. Her niece told her that it seems the woman she's staying with needs her more than they do, so she hasn't been home since January 26th. She's staying with a schoolmate of Mom's. She's got one boy. All relatives are dead. The Army took the boy so Emma stayed at nite with her. She's still keeping house for this one lady and stays with "Renee" at night. After the war, she is going in a home. Mom told her she could put her wardrobe in the basement. She was sorry she didn't get to see you. You were such a dear boy. I never will forget when you left, when she looked at you and said, "above all, keep good company." Moody gets so tickled at Mom's women friends. I do think Mom's grand to them. I don't know if it's the lure of having more junk or not? We razzed her.

Milt worried about not having no clothes for graduation. That's surprising but he's going in town today. I can't believe he's ready for high school. He's so babyish. Margie got her first spanking from Moody yesterday, just a few slaps, but Milt couldn't stand to see that.

So they got you in the field now. Well, take care. Did you average one of the highest on the rifle range? We all wonder. Tony Oberhausen is on furlough now. He's a big one too. Lip's thumb is doing fine. I'm writing this in bed with a carpenter pencil. I think Mom and I are going to Dr. Stites tomorrow. Dizzy and Jerks [*Hermina makes fun of her mom's dizzy spells and Hermina's epileptic seizures*]. Mary told Mom she has a heck of a time with her old maid friends. Can't think of any more at present.

Love,

H.R.

Louisville, Kentucky, **May 24**

Dear Norby,

Well, how are you? I am not as well as I was when you left. I have Rheumatism in my right knee. Sometimes it hurts very bad at night. Now I am getting ready to take a nap and put the hot pad on my knee. I could not walk to church yesterday. I hurt so bad. I think I am going to Dr. Stites tomorrow. Mary did not want me to help her. I just helped a little. She said if my knee hurts more she would give me the laugh, so if I see her, I tell her that my knee's worse. Then she laughs and I told her it sounds like a jackass laugh. When she was sick this winter, she wouldn't stay away from the wash either. It surely is pitiful how slow things are growing. We had a fire yesterday and Hermina is going to make a fire today. It is 66° only and the sky is so dreary looking. That's all I know for this time.

I hope and pray that you will not have to go across. St. Elizabeth has another service flag. It is where the United States flag was. They have 3 stars in each corner. So far, it is the same size as the flag that is filled. Fr. Dudine sure prays a lot for our soldiers, as he puts it. I sure enjoyed your letters. It is 1:15 now and nap time also. Maybe I will be dreaming of you. So goodbye and good luck. Joe took Marge to 11:00 Mass at church

You never answered my question.

God bless you.

Mother

Continued by Hermina:

Norby, you asked what caused those dizzy spells. Dr. Gettelfinger told me over the phone that it sounds like hardening of the arteries. I thought I told you but when she went there, he never said the cause of it. If we go to Dr. Stites, I'll let you know exactly what he says. Mom don't know that she has hardening of the arteries, if that is what it is, so never let on in your letter. She wasn't dizzy at all today. Promising to let you know. The sun is starting to shine thru. This yellow paper really travels.

Love,

Hermina

Louisville, Kentucky, **May 25**, Tuesday, 8:10 am

Dear Norby,

Just seven months til Christmas. What a pleasant thought in war time. Well, it's still raining. We had a very heavy shower last night. It really poured and it's gloomy as can be. I wonder if the sun is doing defense work. We never see it. It keeps raining all the time.

Mr. Johnson was up with some swing hooks. He said Zip is on furlough. Came in yesterday morning. Louie is on a southern Pacific island. Lanny is going on maneuvers in Tennessee. He has never gotten his furlough but expects to get more weekends off after maneuvers. Lil [*Steinmetz*] told Marge she heard Earl is going to be married but Mr. Johnson never said anything. Clarence still sits on his buttock.

Milt got his graduation suit yesterday. It's a mingled light and dark blue. He's very easily pleased. Lip said he wears size 17. Got it at Levy's with two pairs of trousers. We got an application for the third War Ration Book. I suppose you're out in the field by this time. We keep thinking of you always. Lip is up here washing. She hasn't a good place to dry clothes. Her thumb is healing fine but the tip is a little numb as yet.

Mom is going to Dr. Stites this morning. I'm glad for that and will let you know when she comes back.

Love from all, your sister,

Hermina

Continued, 2:00 pm

Dear Norby,

Mom just got in from Dr. Stites. He said she has high blood pressure. It is 178. Rheumatism in her knee and ankle and ringworm on her finger. He prescribed for all three things. Gave her some of that new Sulfa Ointment for her finger, told her to rest a lot. She feels like Stites knows everything. He told her he would bring her around OK. Well, that's all I can say for this time. I had to bust open my envelope to put this note with it. We are all OK. With love from all,

Your little sister,

Hermina

Fort Jackson, South Carolina**May 26,** Wednesday morning, 7:50 am,

Dear Mom and all,

Well, here it is Wednesday morning and most of the fellows are out on a problem, so I have a little time to write a few lines. We are on maneuvers just about 35 or 40 miles from Camp and it's really in a beautiful spot, all surrounded by pine trees. It looks something like a park, only a little more natural. I've been looking over the place to see if I could find a fishing hole somewhere but I don't think there is one nearby. I think the closest one is about two miles from where we are now.

It rained like hell last night and I woke up with water trickling in my face. Now if it had been somewhere else, I would have been accustomed to it and I wouldn't have woke up. This damn tent I got leaks so I guess when we go back to Ft. Jackson I'll turn it in and get a different tent. I sure would like to have a camera with me. Some of the shots you could get.

Getting out in this air makes one eat like a horse. I've been eating too damn much. I think I will have to cut down a little. Ma[y]be we should have point values on everything. We had "beans" for supper last night and it sounded like a machine gun barrage. Lucky we have our gas masks with us at all times. Those gas masks are handy contraptions believe you me.

Well, folks, I really don't have much time so I'll close for now. Tell Marge to watch out for Mrs. Brown (Brownie). Everybody knows what a brownie is. Tell Mary hello XX. I'll be seeing you,

As Always,

Norby

Fort Jackson, South Carolina, **May 27**

Thursday afternoon, weather: hot as hell, Location: in the woods

Dear Mom, Pop, Sis's and Mary,

So you're getting ready to take a nap, eh, Katie? A very sensible idea I should think. I might even do the same thing myself if these sand flies give you a chance to sleep. They have more speed and they sound like dive-bombers. When they clamp their jaws down on you, you know something has landed. Well, I hope you are getting the same sunshine there that we are getting here. This sun is really bearing down. Hottest day we had yet and there's no "Fog in the Holler," so I suppose there's no rain in sight.

You and Mary sure must like to wash. I wish I could feel the same about washing because I have a little washing to do myself, you know, and I don't use Lux on my undies either. It's just the same as that OK soap that you can buy for a nickel a bar. It takes skin and all off at the same time.

My tongue is strictly hanging out for a bottle of beer, or should I say, bottles of beer? How is Pop making out now since the stuff is rationed? So my old girlfriend Emma was there. Don't tell Mary that. She might get jealous and there's no sense in Mary and Emma [*two old maids*] fighting [*over me*]. Well, folks that's about all I know for now so I'll be seeing you later.

As Always,

Norby V...-

Louisville, Kentucky, **May 27**, Thursday, 8:15 am

Dear Norby,

Above everything, I must tell you we had two days of sunshine without a drop of rain and the sun is shining again today. I hope it will last all day too. We cut the grass yesterday again. Does it grow! We received your letter yesterday that was written Sunday. Mom got a kick out of the Hawaiian grass skirt idea. While I'm writing this the sun is playing peek-a-boo so I betcha we get rain today. Katie Reddick got married Tuesday night.

Margie always wants cookies when she comes. It was a few left so I refused her, for sometimes you can't get them, and Pop's sweet tooth is still there. I told her they were for Pop's lunch. She waited a few minutes and told me "Tookies" make her good. That was so cute.

I got a letter from Bill Hollkamp yesterday, written <u>March 11, 1943,</u>-telling me even if the Xmas box was late how he enjoyed it. Let us know how you came out on the rifle range, how good you did.

Mom wasn't dizzy yesterday but her knee bothered her some. That medicine has some Luminal [*barbiturate*] in it, and does Katie puff 'em away. She told me all she could dream about was Karl Muehling across the Street. She'd wake up, doze off, and dream of him again. I told her that was bad. We haven't heard from John this week. I imagine little Norby is OK.

We got Miss Emma's wardrobe and enough junk to fill it but she is coming back to look over her things and dispose of it. Pop got Rheumatism in his arm. A man told him to take lemons. That was good. He ate three lemons and thought it was better.

Bob Hope will be at Fort Jackson this coming Tuesday he announced. Zip is here you, know. We haven't saw or heard a thing of him. This is all for this time. I'm started with the basement you know, but I still have a couple days down there, I know. Will say goodbye, take care of yourself, dearie.

As Always your little sistah,

Hermina V...- V...- V...-

Louisville, Kentucky, **May 28**, Friday, 2:30 pm

Dear Norby,

Can't you smell peppermint? I was out pulling out the mint. Mom hasn't been having as many dizzy spells as she has had but it seems strange to see Mom limping around with Rheumatics. That has not cleared any but I think the sunshine is all what a lot of people need.

Omar Hollkamp passed for the Army yesterday. His name was on Buddy Kegebein's list. They leave next Thursday. Walter Orrill was sent to Fort Benjamin Harrison for further examination. That makes three boys for Lou and I bet Bernard is in there before long. Barney was here trying to sell insurance. He's with another company. By the time this letter reaches you, I suppose you'll be out of the field. Do you think this is just to get you all in trim to go across?

I was correct yesterday. It rained quite a bit after 5:30 pm but today is a beautiful and heavenly day if there ever was one. Say, why never no kisses to Mary? She is going to mail this for me. Well, this is all the news for today. With lots of love and good luck to you,
Your Sister,
Hermina

Louisville, Kentucky, **May 30**, Sunday, 4 pm
Dear Norb,

Well, it's raining again today. We were halfway expecting John and Eleanor but I doubt it now. Norbert Henry is doing fine. Johnny called Thursday.

Mom is doing as good as can be expected. Yesterday afternoon she suffered with her leg but she feels better today, that is, she gets the pain in spells and then they pass over. Dr. Stites told her to go to bed and stay there for a few days. It will relieve her pain as well as reduce the blood pressure.

Tomorrow is Memorial Day. They are decorating at different cemeteries today instead Marge don't have to work tomorrow. The stores are closing in town but I think the defense workers will work. By this time, I suppose you will be out of the field. How do you like the wide open spaces? Betsy is writing a letter also. I wonder about its contents.

I don't have much news, only stuff that's like a cow's cud and been chewed before. I must tell you my radishes did fine. They look like the package. Strawberries $9.00 a crate or $6.00 if you pick them yourself, or 40¢ a quart. Joe and Ann were invited to Sabel's [*Joe's employer*]. Louie received his First Communion today. Mrs. Niemann was worried about Jr but she heard from him with a bushel of oranges. He is in Florida. She also got a letter from him.

Well, I had about an hour pause. Lou, Omar, Bernard [*Hollkamp*] were here to tell us goodbye as Omar leaves Thursday at 11:25 pm for the army. They hear from Bill weekly now. The mail seems to come better. He said he don't know if he'll get a furlough or not. He has had 7 days leave and the farthest he gets is Australia.
Love from all,
Hermina

Louisville, Kentucky, **June 1**, Tuesday, 12:30 pm

Dear Norby,

Well, we are still having rain. "It keeps raining all the time" but maybe June will do better. Emma was over yesterday and we helped her sort and assort. She got rid of lots of things, honey, and Mary said she has faith in you. It's perfectly OK that you ask about Emma. Yes, and Emma is going to write you sometime when she gets settled. We all feel sorry for her. You can't help but feel for her.

Mom had her best day yesterday that she has had in a long time. I don't think she had a dizzy spell and her Rheumatics were a lot better. Now this morning she had a dizzy spell. She don't stay in bed either - but it looks like she can't - but she does rest awhile.

Marge, Pop, Joe and Ann were out at Johnny's Sunday. They were all swell including Norbie. I would try and call him Bert. We are expecting Lip's kids up here this pm, that is, some of them. Lip told me to tell you that she would write soon. On account of her thumb, she couldn't do so well. Yesterday her and Moody washed and Lip was feeling pretty good but in the afternoon Lip got to feeling bad and had a miscarriage, Dr. Gettlefinger said. So now she'll be laid up a week and won't get to see Milt graduate. That hurt her so. Don't let on to anybody that I told you what was wrong, but I know you won't get your letter this week from her. Moody is home with her today and school closes this noon.

Well, I suppose that's all the news I know for this time. That's mostly grief but Lip is doing fine and Mom's feeling some better. That's still good news. Alma called Sunday, and was supposed to come out yesterday but didn't show up. But we didn't expect her as she put in 24 hours straight on Sunday. Are you out of the field now? We still cover with blankets. Love, all the Rawerts,
Hermina

Louisville, Kentucky, **June 2**, Wednesday, 2:30 pm

Dear Norby,

From now on, address our mail thus: Mrs. Herman Rawert, 1344 Texas Ave., Louisville 4 Kentucky. Every resident of Louisville got a bulletin in their box notifying them what station they are in. We are in "4" as you can see. If you forget, just think of "Hup, 1, 2, 3, 4." School closed today instead of yesterday. It is sultry hot today. We have been able to sit outside since Saturday nite. It never rained yesterday or today but I believe it will before today is over.

Lip is obeying Dr.'s orders and staying in bed. She is doing fine. Milt graduates tomorrow nite at 7:30 pm. I believe I told you. He thought if he had a party, he could make enough to buy a wheel [bike]. Wise, eh? Mom still has her Rheumatics but she don't have it as often as she did. Jack Nunn graduates too.

Well, Norby, I think I will close. I have a lot of work to do as yet and Mary will soon be leaving. Are you still in the field? Betsy told her one playmate that her mother's sick in bed but no baby.

Love, as ever,

Sister Hermina

Louisville, Kentucky, **June 4**, Saturday afternoon, 2:30 pm

Dear Mom and all,

Yes, it's an actual fact; they gave us the afternoon off so I think I'll get dressed and get off Camp for a while. Boy, oh boy it is hot down here. You don't have to work up a sweat down here, you can stand still in the shade and you sweat just the same. It still gets cool at night after 12:00. Most of the fellows take their bedroll and sleep on the outside. We haven't had but two rainy days since I've got back from furlough. It's a wonder we didn't have more with all the rain you've been having.

We are going out in the field for two weeks again pretty soon. I think about the 15ᵗʰ of this month. I hope so anyway. Well, I really don't know much so I guess I'll close for now and I'll be seeing you.

As Always,

Norby

Louisville, Kentucky, **June 5**

Dear Son!

Now this is not nagging but only to remind you to go to the Sacraments as soon as you can. Only tomorrow two weeks I asked whether you kept your promise on your word of honor to go to the Sacraments on Mother's Day but you forgot to answer.

Joe takes me to church on Sundays but I went yesterday by myself and got along alright. I keep the First Fridays. I did not ask anyone to go along - otherwise I know they would. My knee still hurts but it is the dizzy spells that I am afraid of, to get in the way. I didn't get to Milton's graduation in church Thursday but we went to the house and had beer, ice cream and cake. I do feel sorry for Elizabeth. She is looking better, Mrs. Orrill said. I wish I could do for her but the way it is now, I can't do so much. I hope everything will be better soon again. Papa is alright. As long as he likes his beer, I think he don't feel so bad. His shoulder hurt him. Somebody told him lemons were good for that. He took two and felt better. I think I will try it also. Well, this is all I know for now. I must get at my work, working for Hubbuch's, you know. I am helping Hermina with the drapes. Didn't go in the basement this week to wash. [*the large basement had two sewing tables for drapes, a few sewing machines, a crude bathroom and a washer.*] That was penance for me. Now, that would not have been penance for you? Mary is alright and so said hello. Goodbye and God Bless and xxxxx you. I am thinking of you always. Hellow [*sic*] from all,

Mother

Louisville, Kentucky, **June 5**, Saturday, 8:00 am

Dear Norby,

From the contents of your letter, we judge you feel as though you might be sent across soon. Did you all have the IG Inspection Thursday? If so, what was the outcome? So you met Jerry Colona. He is really silly. Of any night, we missed Bob Hope Tuesday but we heard him last night. He was on some kind of Victory Entertainment I believe. Joe said after the broadcast that he heard Bob Hope puts on a show for the boys. I guess that would be an off the Record show.

Well, it was very hot here too and we never had rain for four days. That is off the record also, dear brother, but I thought surely we were in for a storm yesterday but we just had a "penetrating" rain, a slow drip, I should say. And to tell you the truth we all welcomed it because it was so hot and sultry. Mom had a good day yesterday. She was sewing some by hand and Lip is doing OK too, poor girl! Sure has had some misfortune lately. She had to go to the Dr. Tuesday and she said she made up her mind to go to the hospital if necessary and get herself put in tiptop shape. Shirley does real good around the house I think.

Joe heard Johnny Beeker was wounded seriously in North Africa. Our tomatoes are beginning to blossom. Milt looked very nice on his graduation day. Believe it or not, he was worried if he looked OK or not and asked if he looked OK. He couldn't get brown and white sport oxfords so taken mahogany colored shoes and blue tie and blue suit. He reminded me of the dollar I promised him last fall if he would graduate. So he bought swimming trunks with that. Betsy thinks he should have an extra present because he's the first Muth to graduate. Rudy never remembered him or come to see him graduate. I thought that was a darn dirty trick. Well, I'll have to sign off,

With much love as ever,

Porky

Louisville, Kentucky, **June 6**, Sunday, 2:30 pm

Dear Norby,

Thinking of you dearie, sweet ain't it? Or is it? Huh? Well, it is hot as hell as you would say. I have never in all my born days seen things pop out of the ground as they done during our "dry spell" last week. Every seed is a miracle. That certainly is true. Our garden looks fine. Beans (3 plants) are in blossom. All the tomatoes looks swell and some are in blossom. I planted sweet peas and they are really beautiful. I put them by the back fence and this morning they are all opened in full bloom and they are all opened in full bloom and all colors. No kidding. It is a pretty sight. Our potatoes are so strong and big and healthy looking are ready to bloom. Pop is just looking on the porch. He said it is 100 degrees to the dot!

Mary asked for Pop. They put on another night watchman. I believe Pop's age would be against him. It was too late however, but it would just be 40 hours per week. He didn't get the chance and he didn't want it because he would make only $20.00 per week and there would be no extra work. Such ambition for a 72-year-old youngster. You know he likes those extras. Next Sunday is Father's Day, I believe. You know, Norby, you talked about your "pretty" pictures taken and send that for "pappy's day." If not, why not?

Mom still has her dizzy spells after each meal. Stites told her to take Milk of Magnesia after each meal so we're waiting to see how that works and she has to go there Tuesday. Lip is doing fine but feels very week. She has to go to the Dr. Tuesday also. Mom's Rheumatics is a lot better. Mr. Redle is up on the porch again. Pop's going for beer now. It looks as if a shower is blowing up again. We would welcome it, by gravy. Well, I'll close for this time.
As Ever,
Porky

Louisville, Kentucky, **June 6**

Dear Norbert A. Rawert, Dear, dear Brother,

Oh boy, we are going to have some rain. Plenty dark and Mom is asleep. It's now 10 minutes of 3:00 and Pop is coming down.

Well, I said it looked like a storm and now it's 15 of 4:00 and still raining. Joe took Dad to church. Ann and Hermina went along. It's still lightening and thundering (it's Sunday) and I hope the last Sunday for Dad to go back [*to work*] for a while. There is a large branch of a tree down in the front of Russell's porch. Somebody will need a saw, I know. The temperature dropped about 32°. It was very hot this morning. Well, Mother woke when we [came] too close to the window and said, "Why didn't you all call me?"

I guess you noticed how far I got with this letter and Pop did come in with his beer in time. And Joe and Ann came over too. And so, the storm goes on. Not bad anymore. Anyway, I had a glass of beer. I never seen a storm come so fast before. Hermina had a letter from Jr Hubbuch and he knew all about the fuss we had. Can you imagine it? Miss Brown or Miss Berry is still down at work but speechless. Poor thing, she wears those trolley glasses - and talk about funny! A comic valentine if you ask me.

Milton graduated last Thursday. I thought of you when you did. It was more then - 80 boys and girls, all in church and Milton looked very nice. Elizabeth is getting along fine but was heartbroken not to see Milton graduate. Eleanor didn't see Jackie make his First Holy Communion either. Those are hard things to take, don't you think so? The roosters are crowing for more rain and Mom just said 68° - that's the temperature on the rear porch. Mom is making it pretty good. When she goes up the church steps it's one step at a time. She walks very stiff. First Friday she got back to church by herself. I never even heard her leave and was I surprised. I worried about her though. (Of course, she was in a good place.)

Our garden is doing fine. Lee Carter must be on a fishing spell. Joey only worked one day last week and said to me, " I don't want to lose my job but I'm going to tell Lee that I am not going to work unless he does." He is putting on a spell of Rheumatism. I call is f i s h m a t i s m. Ha, ha. Do you know a better word for it? Dewey is still at the L&N and wants to move from there. They had both rooms papered last week and the paperhanger was run away by Lee a few weeks ago. And now he came back and apologized to Lee. Can you beat it? So now I guess they have a clean house. Joey bought 1 chair and 2 rockers and paid $30 down on them. I guess I'll have a nice job to cover them for her but undecided. She don't want me at her house. She wants it done at work.

Say Norbert, they sure are rolling tin pins above and I wonder how scared dear little Hermina is. And her Mother is not with her. They must be riding around seeing the sights. Hermina is one herself. She scrambled for her shoes under the couch and took a comb along for her hair, put on a coat and gone she was. Oh boy! They are just coming in and Joe said it hit pretty hard in some sections. One whole tree down on Shiller Avenue and one on Hepburn Avenue. Well, I guess Hermina will tell you more about the storm tomorrow. Joe said it was not so bad by the church (St. Brigid's) and we called Johnson's and asked how Johnny was and they said the storm was not so bad out there. It's 25 minutes after 4 and I'm still writing. Are you getting tired of reading? Say - Hermina got bawled out by her dear mother, believe it or not. You should of been here last Monday when Miss Emma was here and I told her you asked about her and she said, I must write that dear boy a letter. So here's hoping, dear Brother.

How did your inspection pass? Well, all the Steinmetz boys are gone, Charles, Robert Lee and Billy left last Thursday for the Navy Air Corps. Their dad is walking around the house. I wonder what the boys will do to support their parents now? It's darn hard. Well, I guess you know Omar <u>Turkey</u> is gone. He told us goodbye last Sunday.

Fr. Nord read his first mass at St. Elizabeth's today. The bells just rang at 4:30 and it reminded me of it. So here is hoping you had time to read this scribbling and hope you are in the best of health. Good luck and God bless you. Pray for us and we will be praying for one another. Hope to see you soon and our boys are doing a fine job.

God Bless you and so long.

Margaret

Louisville, Kentucky, **June 7**, Monday

[*Dear Norb,*]

I thought your picture was good but is that whiskey [*in the bottle he was holding*]? Mom said no, you can't get that at Camp. Jimmie said yes, but you can get it at other places. Thanks for the money, honey.

[*Hermina*]

Monday morning, 11:00 am

Dear Norby,

We received your letter this morning. Was glad to know you enjoyed your Bob Hope show so much. I told you we forgot to listen. I could kick myself until I was Ann's size that I didn't hear it. Well, that letter had a very pleasing effect, very pleasing indeed. I know an elephant never forgets but I wasn't sure about a bull. I told you yesterday a storm was coming up. We seen three trees down, and branches too numerous to count, on our way to St. Brigid's. Russell's big tree in front, a Sugar Maple - a big brand, is off that and also the Buckeye. It's still gloomy today. Mary and I just got thru with washing. Katie is completely left out. Poor child. Elizzie [Elizabeth] is about the same.

Don't you think I would make a good businesswoman, or don't you? Joey hasn't even called or come home to see Mom. I think that's damn dirty. You know she has forgotten when Mom ran after her a few years ago. Well, I don't care to hear a lot of gripes and neither do you. I know I will be looking forward to next month - something to look forward to. Ha, ha. This baby needs new clothes.

Goodbye Angel???

[*Hermina*]

Louisville, Kentucky, **June 7** [*Norb wrote 'May' 7*]

Dear Mom and all,

Well, we're just having a storm right now and the wind is really blowing and I do mean hard. It's just beginning to rain now. I hope it does rain like hell because it was really hot today and I do mean hot. I sent my watch to Alma so she could have it fixed. I broke the crystal out of it and I think it needs a cleaning also.

Well, tell Milton I said congratulations and all that goes with it. I don't have much time anymore. In fact hardly any at all. We are going out in the field again for two weeks pretty soon, starting the 15th of this month, but I like the field. I'd like to get somewhere near a lake so I could do a little fishing. Well, the lights are going out so I'll have to say goodnight.

As Always,

Norby

Fort Jackson, South Carolina, **June 8**

Dear Mom and all.

This ain't going to be much of a letter because I don't know very much. Because things are usually the same old things or sixty-six. I could say the weather is hot but I get tired of writing the weather reports.

I see where Churchill said in tonight's paper that invasion is near. Well, I hope he knows what he's talking about, and I hope he's telling the truth. At the rate things are going, we'll be in war for two years yet and that's just a little longer than I care for it to last. I say let's get it done in a hurry. "Efficiency Man."

Well, Mom, how you been feeling lately? And how is Lip getting along? Glad to hear that Eleanor is up and about and that "Feel Me Once II" is doing OK.

It looks like more rain for tonight. I hope so anyway. It may keep things a little cooler. Well, I'll be seeing you and good night and good luck.

As Always,

Norby

Louisville, Kentucky, **June 10**, Thursday, 8:50 pm

Dear Norby,

Well, we have been receiving your letters right along. So, you go on the E rating. Glad to hear but I see where I have to send you the month of June.

Earl Johnson gets married Saturday at St. Joseph Church. He is home on furlough. I don't know who the lucky girl is (or unlucky). Norbert was here yesterday. It was the rest of the Rawerts. Johnny and I did their washing. Then we went to the Cemetery. We cut grass as high as my waist. We had to cut and sickle before we could run the lawn mower. Then we cut the grass. We had a very full day. Hilary liked the cemetery. He had a lot of monuments to scale. He also carried the grass away. Jack was a big help. Hilary said, Hermina, we really had a trip, didn't we? He enjoyed it immensely. It was the first time they were in a cemetery and they thought the dead was buried under the tombstone. The baby weighs 11 ½ pounds now. He has very dark blue eyes set like Vernon's. Other than that, I think he looks like himself. I enjoyed myself in the cemetery. Next time I go, I'll ask Hil to go along.

Johnny's garden looks swell, they say. I asked Peggy if she helped in it. She said little girls don't help in garden, but when she gets bigger and is a Daddy she can work in it and Daddy can help her. I told her she'll be a momma, not a daddy, and she won't have it. Eleanor said she got that from the boys and she wants to be just like them. They were all as cute as a button yesterday.

We all got 6 chance books from St. Elizabeth I think they're swell - 5¢ a chance, 6 for 25¢ on $1,000 in war bonds. I see you're putting the Station number on the envelope. You get 100 % on that too.

Hilary just wouldn't leave the hose alone. He was dripping wet. He really loves it. Jackie asked me if I found the "Snozzle" [*nozzle*] for the hose. As I was putting it on Jack asked again if that was the Snozzle. A man passing by laughed so hard. I think I am going to call Alma and ask her if she seen Norby yesterday. He was in here a few hours. Lip is doing OK. Mary said hello. My sweet peas are picturesque. Picked the past few days a bouquet from them. Next summer they will be along the whole back fence.

So you are busy. Well, my dear child, we will congratulate Milt for you. Uncle Rudy sent $3.00 in a card. He don't know what he wants to get with his money. Well, beef is getting harder to be gotten right along, and round steak is 12 points per lb. now instead of 8 points so I guess we'll eat on the porkies more. Walter Orrill left Monday for the Army. Mom wants to scribble a few lines too so I'll be seeing you.

V...-

H.R.

Continued by Mommy:

We have June now - not May. 10:00 am, 1943,

Dear Norby,

I am starting to write. The war news started so I will wait till it is over. I cannot write and listen at the same time. Breakfast At Sardy's [*Sardi's*] is on now from California. I like it very much. I don't miss it often. I met Mrs. Johnson the other day at Schieman's. She asked me if Red came to see us. I told her no and she said, "I want him to see you all and I will tell him myself about it." I said, "Norbert would not go either. Maybe he is 'as bully as my son was?" She said, "I'll see to it all-right." So I don't know how long he has the furlough. Mrs. Johnson told me but I forgot. She was telling everyone at Schieman's that Earl was going to get married at St. Joseph's Church at 9:00 o'clock. It seems to me that she wasn't very happy about it. I am feeling somewhat better but get dizzy about once a day. That's not so bad but my knee is not much better. I walk up and down the steps like Mrs. Paul. Getting old, you know.

God bless you,

Mother

Louisville, Kentucky, **June 11**, Friday, 8:30 am

Dear Norby,

Well, we got your letter. Mom had a big kick out of "Feel me Once, the Second" [*baby Norbie*]. I did too. He's swell. They sure got good-looking kids, the Rawerts have. Yes sir. Emma was here last night with a few coats. She had to run for a streetcar. I enjoyed that. She's bluer than indigo. I ironed from 9 to 5:30 yesterday - a two weeks' ironing.

I seen Mrs. Redle sitting on the porch. Carl was full [*drunk*] last nite, his truck came across the street by itself, and his mother screamed. She turned on the porch light and was in her nightgown. She looked like Maggie does in the comics. Sure did scare us - the truck.

Lip is doing fine. Mom is about the same. I got to get busy and get some 'kleening" done.

I seen in the papers where they have Italian Prisoners of War at Camp Atterbury, 89 miles from Louisville. Well, Feel Me Once the first, I'll close hoping you are well and give our best regards to the General. Good day Corporal.

[*Hermina*]

Louisville, Kentucky, **June 13**, Sunday, 2 pm

Dear Norby,

Well, it's a very hot, sticky day. I hope we don't have a storm as last Sunday. It really uprooted some trees. The papers said it mussed up several airplanes at Bowman Field and nearly demolished two.

Well, you know how different saloons aren't selling beer in buckets. Jimmy, for one, isn't. Pop still gets his can [*pail of beer*] yet at night. That's something to be thankful for I imagine.

I planted butter beans 10 days ago. Every one showed up and some are 6" high and real sturdy looking. I put some more in today. Russell's twin sister has come to live with them. We are storing her sewing machine in our basement. Pop went over with me to help Russell carry it over. Naturally, he [*Russell*] was feeling it. He introduced Pop to her as his twin sister and added she's 78 years old. It was too funny for words and he put on airs doing it. He was on his vacation this week, painting the house and feeling it the whole weeklong.

Pop just got home with bad news. He said Bill is all out of bottle beer excepting a little Falls City.

The war news is really on the good side, isn't it? I suppose you will be out in the field again when you receive this letter. Do you think you'll be going over soon, or don't you? We are going to have an Air-Raid practice Thursday. I heard they will drop flour from planes. I heard a sham of some kind Thursday nite. The paper never carried an account of it and I don't know just where it was located. It seems as if it was in Camp Taylor. You could hear the whistle of the "bomb."

Feel Me Once II is fine. We were expecting them again this week but they didn't show up. Mom hasn't had a dizzy spell in two days now. That's the longest she has ever gone. Her Rheumatic's is bothering her today.

Lip got a new carpet. Well, Marge got it for her. It's a beautiful thing. It was on display and half price. Marge is making new drapes so Lizzy will be all fixed up.

I was about to close this letter after I left the main part out. Teets Harman married that Vetter girl from Kentucky Street. Pop knows her mother. They married Thursday at St. Brigid's. He was in the Philippines. I suppose Earl Johnson got married yesterday as his mother told Mom. Well, I will say goodbye and keep on scribbling.
As ever,
H.R.

Fort Jackson, South Carolina, **June 14**

Dear Mom and all,

Well, I just want to say "Howdy" and stuff. The physical fitness test I was telling you about - well, we beat the Infantry and that's something. Our Major asked the (IG) Inspector General's Office if they thought this was an infantry unit and they told him that if the 59th Sig Btn was going up to stay in the XII Corps they would have to be able to do what the Infantry does. I guess we "dood it."

Now once more for the weather report. Still hotter than hell Monday thru Sunday each week. The scenery is real pretty from where I am writing. They really do have some tall pine trees down here and plenty of them. I guess they're about the only thing that will grow in this sand.

So "Feel Me Once" #2 is gaining weight, eh? Well, just wait til he gets in the Army. I see where they're not going to draft as many as they have been. I guess this Army is getting big enough and I don't doubt it. Seems as though the boys are receiving a little hell on the islands off Italy. Sure hope they can keep it up.

Sure could use a beer right now. My tongue is touching my toes, so you see how dry I am. They usually run out of beer here on the Post after about an hour and a half. So that crap about everything for the soldiers is getting to be more crap every day. [*Sad that it is still the case today*]. Well, I'm still thirsty so I'll have to do something about it. So so-long and I'll be seeing you.

As Always,

Norby

Fort Jackson, South Carolina, **June 15**

Dear Mom and all,

Well, it's still hot as hell but I just had something happen to boost my morale about 75%. The company commander, Capt. Mayer, asked me to step in his office so he could have a talk with me and so I did. He asked me how come I had not stayed in telephones since I made excellent marks, and I told him that I was just supposed to stay at the Motor Pool office until a telegraph class was started. He said he don't think he's going to let me waste the training I had in telephones, and I agreed with him. Well, there seems to be a teletype class gotten together and shipped out here to go to school, and he said that if one is gotten together I would be on the list. That my dear people made me very happy. I only hope that this thing holds water. Because I would be more than glad to learn something about teletype. Another thing, I'll get out of SC and probably go to Camp Crowder or Ft. Monmouth, NJ. They say it's really swell up there. I imagine it will take a little while for this to get under way. Ma[y]be three or four weeks and ma[y]be never, but I sure am hoping.

Well, it's just about chow time and I thought I would let you in on the news, so I'll have to close now hoping you are all well. And hoping Mom's knee is being helped by that Kentucky sunshine or does the sun shine in Kentucky? Well, be good folks and I'll let you in on all further developments.

Just as Always,

Norby

Louisville, Kentucky, **June 16**, 8:00 am

Dear Norby,

We received your letter from yesterday. You know more than we did about the Lifeguards at Shelby Park. I suppose that's because they have "wimmen" guards. John was here with his wash again yesterday and we dood it, then we put [*white lime*] stone dressing on the foundation. The shack looks right nice. We had a shower Monday and yesterday but that's all. The grass looks like velvet. Joe got some wooden lawn chairs painted white and really looks good from the dining room windows.

Clarence Johnson got his blood test and is in 1-A. I don't know when he goes in for his examination. Earl married Mary Rose Kinzer. Clarence said he thought you knew her and went fishing with them. Alma came out Monday night or rather afternoon. Her eye looks grand. It's just a shade darker than her other eye, that is, not the eye itself but the lower lid and where you would get circles under your eye. Is that plain enough or more complicated? That extra little piece of skin, well, that has disappeared. Her eye looked better than we've seen since she went to the doctor. Her left eyelashes are growing in. Johnny said he hopes it isn't that way with Feel Me Once II. He'll really have a job ahead of him for how many years, Norby.

What have you been doing that you couldn't shoot better than 42 out of 50? That's the worstest you have ever written you poor dear. We haven't gotten any beef from Schieman's in a week. Saturday he got bacon and a piece of pork chops. Margaret brought a hen along. It weighed 3 ¼ pounds, cost $1.90, and we never had a good meal on it. You might see your sisters come in as a WAAC just for a good meal. People are looking with anticipation for Thursday's Air-Raid Practice.

We got the rest of dear, dear Emma's things, her trunk and wash stand. She wants to write. We know you received our letter telling about Emma because you started out with too many dears, my dear, dear Norbert. I don't know if I told you but she was telling how she cleaned and sunned her drawers [*actual dresser drawers but Joe and Ann thought of drawers as the underwear type*]. Joe and Ann had to hold back an explosion. We were really full of laughter.

Lizzie is doing OK. Mom is feeling pretty chipper this morning. She hasn't had a dizzy spell in three days now. I don't see what makes you wait for the time when you get to Hawaii. Just send shorts. Pop told her to sit out in the back yard and let the sun shine on her knee but Katie doesn't like the idea.

Will bring this explosion to a close. Hope you are well and able to shoot better the next time. I wonder how Poppy would come out on the Rifle Range? Will close with a hi-dee [*howdy*] from all. I think you'll make the physical fitness test alright. So you think you could make it home in three days?

Love from all the dears,

[*Hermina*]

Fort Jackson, South Carolina, **June 18**

Dear Mom and all,

Today is Friday and I'm dreaming of a big steak for dinner. All I do is dream about it too - those dreams never come true. Well, so far as I know I think ma[y]be I might be able to get out of Ft. Jackson and go to school for a while again. Happy days. I'd like to go somewhere where it is just a little cooler. Yesterday it was 101 here and that's not in the sun. So you see it's fairly warm here, sir!

They're not quite as tough on the boys as they were there for a while, ever since we had that General Inspection. I think the inspecting officers found out that morale was pretty low in the 59th. Instead of scrubbing barracks on Friday nights, we scrub them on Friday afternoon from 3 to 5. We haven't had any 25-mile marches since then either. They are changing Company Commanders in HQ. Co. And "C" company. I hate to lose our company commander though, because he and I get along pretty well together. He gave me a few breaks. But if he didn't like you, he could be pretty damn mean. I hope this teletype school doesn't fall through since he's leaving. I don't think it will.

Well, I hope "you all" are alright and it's not quite as warm there as it is here and I'll be seeing you. Tell Mary I said hello. XXXXX.
As Always,
Norby V...-

Louisville, Kentucky, **June 18**, 10 am
Dear Norby,

Well, it's a beautiful day in Louisville, a beautiful day it is. We're waiting for the painter Milton to come. He painted the back picket fence yesterday and did a swell job. So far, he has not showed up.

Well, we had the Air Raid Practice last night. I bet 500 or more people milled back and forth. They put up a tent at the cemetery and burnt it. Anybody could volunteer for a casualty. About five Red Cross ambulances kept going back and forth and an army ambulance driven by a woman. They would give First Aid and take them to the St. Elizabeth's basement. No traffic was allowed. We were on the main thoroughfare; saw a lot of Air-Raid Wardens. That was about all you could see. We were expecting to see a lot more, especially airplanes taking part. Amen.

Russell was stopped last night by the Air Raid Warden on Shelby Street so he had to hoof it home. Seemed ducely [*deucedly*] odd. At 10 o'clock, she went after it [*car*].That's about all for this time.Well, I want to get started on house cleaning again. Seems as though I never will get done. Lip is feeling a lot better. Mom is doing pretty good too.
As ever, with love,
Hermina

Louisville, Kentucky, **June 18**
Dear son,

Thought I would get a letter this morning. I guess you're busy as always. While I am waiting, I am listening to Breakfast at Sardey's [*Sardi's*]. It comes at 6 or 6:30 pm but I have never heard it at that time. Never think of it at that time.

Say Norby, why did you wear those glasses when you had your picture made? Maybe your eyes were a little dazey. So I thought it was a pistol or something to shoot with. The other thought was that it was a bottle of beer or whiskey or wine. Was I right?

I am feeling somewhat better. I am going to call him today. My medicine is all [gone?] so I don't know if I have to take the same again. Norby, if you can, don't forget to write a few lines to Papa for Father's Day, even if it is later that June 20th. He will sure like it very much and shed a few tears also as always, so please don't forget it. The paper said Wednesday morning that we would not have no meat in July. We don't know if that is true but we can't not get no beef this week. I had to order pork for Saturday-Sunday, 15 pork chops, half of ham does not sound so bad but you get tired of it. Did you all have meat last Saturday, day before Pentecost?

Norb playing 'cool' Fort. Jackson, South Carolina. Mentioned in letter from his mother on June 18, 1943.

We [*St. Elizabeth's church*] are going to have a picnic. Each got 6 books [*of chance tickets*]. Don't you want to take some chances? The prizes are:

1. $250 War Bond and $250 cash
2. $100 War Bond and $100 cash
3. $50 War Bond and $50 cash
4. $50 War Bond and $50 cash
5. $25 War Bond and $25 cash
6. $25 War Bond and $25 cash
7. $25 War Bond and $25 cash
8. $25 War Bond and $25 cash

Eight prizes in all. How do you like the outline? Hope you are well and contented. I remain as always your linbn Muther
[*lieben Mutter or loving or dear mother in German*].

Continued by Hermina, **June 18**, 4 pm, Friday:
Extra! Extra! ME DEAR BRUDDER, we just received your two letters. The one sounds velly velly [*sic*] good and here's hoping you get to go to teletype school at Ft. Mammouth [*Monmouth*], NJ too, or if it would be Camp Crowder. Just so you get to teletype school. We are sure glad it boosted your morale 75%. Your oldest letter stated you all would be placed with the Infantry. Well, I suppose if you get to go to school, you will be unattached to any company. Did I say that right? These military terms keeps me in a quandary.

Mom had the feel of the Suds in "Soap suds." Dr. asked her if she was taking it easy. She said yes. You know she had a few unnecessary things to wash. She felt shaky but I believe it helped her morale too. She only had one dizzy spell this week. That's very good I think.

'Porky, Porky, Porky, without a streak of beef' should be the civilian cry. I feel squeamish. Today your oldest brother would be 45 years old [*Henry, born in 1898, died in a motorcycle accident in 1922*]. Mom and Pop will be married 46 years next Wednesday, June 23rd.

Mr. Redle was picking up ash cans with the hook of his cane. He takes it slow but is hopping around. Mom said it don't take 110 in the shade for you to get thirsty. You're like your Paw. He's still getting his [*beer*].
Love,
H.R.

Ft. Jackson, South Carolina, **June 20**, Sunday morning, 8:15 am
Dear Mom and all,
Well, it's Sunday morning - aaah, and it's a beautiful day, it is -with the sun "beaming" down. It's about an hour and fifteen minutes before Mass so I thought I would jot down a few lines. I got a kick out of the way Emma washed and sunned her panties. I could use a few instructions because I have to do the work myself sometimes.

Monday, or tomorrow, we are going out in the field for sure. It's going to be on a combat range, what you call a Nazi Village. There is going to be machine gun fire over our heads, about 18 inches, so it's best to keep your nose to the ground. We have to crawl through bob [*barbed*]-wire and all kinds of crap. Oh well, it should be something different. The Captain told me yesterday morning that he put my name in to go to school so I might be pulling out of here before long. He said it wouldn't be so long before it started.

I have a hell of a lot of work to do this afternoon yet. I have to get all of the files ready to take out in the field and I have to get up a list of drivers for next week. We got 117 trucks so it's going to take quite a little while.

Well, I'll see you after church. Well, tell Emma to keep her pants clean and I'll be seeing you.
As Always,
Norby

Louisville, Kentucky, **June 20**, Father's Day, 8 am

Dear Norby,

It seems if you don't get a letter written early it don't go off on Sunday. Well, it's a beautiful day in Louisville. The sun is shining brightly. It has all indication of being a very hot one too. We had two light showers Monday & Tuesday but no rain since.

Since this is Father's Day it's very significant that I write about Pop - and what a Pop! He heard yesterday that St. Theresa's was advertising for a janitor. He asked me to call. I did. They pay $150 per month, the priest told me by phone. That interested Pop so he took to his heels and Fr. Nieters was very nice to him. Pop said he always is nice whenever he passes there. He never fails to speak or throw up his hand. He wanted to know why Pop wanted to quit St. Brigid. Pop said if you could better yourself wouldn't you? He said yes. They have a flunky there. Also, they pay $30.00 a month to pull the bell in the evening, I think. And he will be thru with work after 9 o'clock Mass on Sunday. He will know if the job is his Monday night at 9:30 pm. I think their idea is of a younger man [*Pop was 72*], but Pop's got a good record of 13 years that stands out. We all thought that was spunky in Pop, married 46 years and changing his job. But here's hoping. He said if he gets it, he will inform Fr. Maloney [*of St. Brigid's*] that if he gets $40.00 per week from him he'll stay there, but not otherwise.

Joe had a few extra beers and left the cat out of the bag. He had $20.00 put away for an anniversary present for Ann that she never knew about. In his hilarious mood, he tells her all about it. Joe and Moody are gone fishing today. Pop was figuring just how much he would make per week on the other side [*of this letter*], so I'll just leave his figure as is. I don't think an explosion [*long letter*] from Marge is coming up too. I'll sign off saying Mom still feels her old Rheumatiz but isn't quite as dizzy.

Will let you know about further developments. Watch the mailman. Mom said were you that thirsty that your tongue could reach your toes, or were you kissing the clodhoppers? With love from all, 20 points more,
Porky

Louisville, Kentucky, **June 22**, Tuesday, 12:45 pm

Dear Norby,

Well, it's a clouding up, it is. We really could use some rain now. I sprinkled good last night and pulled up weeds this morning. Our lawn looks good, believe it or not. Everybody thinks Joe's lawn chairs is such an improvement and it's a cool stretch through there.

Well, Pop hasn't heard from St. Theresa's as yet. He was supposed to have heard last night at 9:30 pm but there's still a possibility, but I think Pop's age is against him. Mom is sounding the dinner bell. Will continue after I put on a few more pounds, ha, ha. That wasn't funny, was it? Huh?

Well, I just feasted on a pancake and a little piece of ham. Listen - don't ever call me Porky again. We have had nothing but pork for our breakfast, pork for our dinner, pork for our supper, lest we got tired of all that old pork. We have had nothing but pork for two weeks and not a sign of beef in sight.

Joe and Ann bought a Philco radio and record player combination. It cost $179 [*$2,557 at 2017 value*]. It plays 8 records. I am anxious to hear it I am. Katie's leg bothered her yesterday quite a bit but is doing swell today.

Norby, could you have a record made of your sweet voice? Then we could play it over and over. It would be nice to play an argument, wouldn't it?

Margie was 3 years old yesterday. Mrs. Paul said Dr. Gettlefinger isn't interested in old women. All the trade he wants is pregnant women. He still guards Texas Street.

Love from all of us,

The former Porky

Fort Jackson, South Carolina, **June 22**

Dear Mom and all,

Howdy folks, howdy! Well, here I am out in the field with all the nice little chiggers. I believe they called a family reunion and decided to hold their dinner party on me. One thing, they sure keep your mind occupied.

We went through that course today, the one where they shoot about 18 inches over your head (I mean ass) because you're crawling just as close to the earth as possible and you're not on your hands and knees either - you're on your belly. It's really some experience to go through. It's just the next thing to actual combat. There are also holes that feel like bomb craters and they set a three-stick charge and set them off as you crawl by and you can feel the earth tremble beneath you. You also have to crawl under bob [*barbed*]-wire at the same time. One poor fellow was creeping along very slowly and very close to the ground and he came face to face with a snake and it scared him so bad that he raised up a little and got shot in the butt. I really know it wasn't as funny in action as it is on paper. Just another day.

Well, I'm going to have to quit for a while but I'll get a chance to write tomorrow. So that's all that's new and I'm... [*unreadable words*].

As Always,

Norby

Fort Jackson, South Carolina, **June 24**

Dear Mom and all,

Not much to write about but it has been raining off and on. Last night I was sleeping on the ground with just my blanket and it started to rain about 2:00 am so I had to move into a cab of a truck after I was all wet. It's a good thing I got used to a wet bed when I was but a child or should I say nearly a man. Take your choice folks, take your choice. Sticks and stones may break my bones, etc.

Well, I might be pulling out of here about the 5th of July. I don't know for sure so don't quote me on that. In fact, don't quote me on nothing because this is the army - and the army has strange ways - very strange indeed. I heard today that we might go to Kansas City, MO. Boy, oh boy, I sure hope so. But I know I couldn't be quite that lucky. Oh well, we'll wait and see.

I'll be damn glad to get out of the field because I'm covered with chiggers. You know how I was once before. Well, they're not quite that bad, but bad enough. I write a word and scratch a chigger. I put some iodine on them and it helped a lot.

Lest I forget, what did Herman do about St. Theresa's and St. Brigid's? I hope he can tell Maloney to kiss his ass and mine for good measure. He always likes a good measure anyway. He should be a chaplain in the Army. He would lose some of his high hat and nervous system. I think I'll see what I can do to promote it. Do you think I could have any influence? I don't, ha ha, but I would if I could.

I have a lot of work to do tomorrow. I have to make a report on every vehicle we have in the outfit. So you see, I'll be pretty damn busy. So ma[y]be I should get some sleep. Well, I'll be seeing you good dear people and Katie I want you to take good care of that leg and not get dizzy anymore. That's an order from the US Army. So be a good soldier or I'll draft the horse [*Hermina*] to do a little KP and I know you wouldn't like that. Well, good night, good luck and God bless you all. PS. You need it.

As Always,

Norby

Fort Jackson, South Carolina, **June 25**

Dear Mom and all,

I just have a few minutes before supper to drop a few lines about my chiggers. Well, now I am full of them, and when I say full, I mean full. I have more than I can count so I am very busy writing with one hand and scratching with the other. I'm just as bad off as a one armed paperhanger.

Well, we'll go back to Ft. Jackson in the morning. I'll be glad to get back to work there so I can get some clean clothes on. We had the same clothes on for a week now and in this hot weather it's none too comfortable, believe you me. A good bath would be just the thing now. I look more like a wild man than a civilized one. I'm painted with iodine all over. I scare myself a little even. That is, when I look in the mirror. But it will all pass away with no harm done except to the chigger. It costs him his life - and me just a few scratches.

I seen a plane crash today but no one was hurt. It landed in a lake about a block from where we were at. Our medical officer was in the plane and he just got a few scratches. They were pretty damn lucky if you ask me. Well, they are blowing the bugle for chow and when that thing blows, I start running. So goodbye and I hope we have beef, but I doubt it.

As Always,

Norby

Louisville, Kentucky, **June 27**, Sunday, 1:30 pm

Dear Norby,

Hot as the hinges of...! We had a good shower yesterday but that sun at 6:00 this am was blazing hot. Alma is here. She came for dinner and is getting ready to go to Churchill Downs for Corpus Christi Procession. I'm wondering what congregation will come in first. I hope it cools off some. The sky is getting promising looking. Remember last year that terribly hard rain and how the women's dresses did the shrinking act?

I'm inclosing a piece that was in Thursday night's paper in the Walter Winchell column. Is the sick one a Pvt. or is he an officer? I said a Pvt. or a soldier under a Sgt rating. Joe said he's an officer because the medic said he had the bellyache. Joe said he complained of his abdomen. Kindly answer on this. My answer is that bellyache is below stomach ache in the matter of speech. That's what made me think he was below a Sgt. in rank. Answer please, pretty please.

Alma looks fine. Her eye looks better than we have seen it. In fact, you can't tell anything was ever wrong with it. We were so glad to see how good she looked. Walter Orrill left Ft. Harrison. It will be 2 weeks Tuesday and she hasn't received a word from him. You know, that's a long time.

Your Poppy got the news to ask for more money yesterday. He said he popped 3 or 4 bottles of beer in him and then told him [*Fr. Maloney*] what he thought. There's a promise of a raise next week. Here's hoping he gets it. Alma said she called you last night and couldn't get you so she called this morning. We were glad to know you were off those maneuvers. Hope you will soon be in school again... [*the letter was ripped off here*].

...If you have time sometime, maybe you could call home some nite. I think it would do Mom a world of good. We had a funny ring yesterday. It was long distance but wrong number. It looked like it thrilled Mom so, until we found out it was a wrong number. Mom always did get a kick out of it when you called. Mom feels pretty good today. If possible, hoping to hear your dear, dear voice soon. I think Mom's rheumatism would disappear, at least...[*the letter was ripped off here*].

[*Hermina*]

Fort Jackson, South Carolina, **June 27**

Dear Mom and all,

Well, I got a few minutes to scribble a line or two. It's just after dinner. We had some damn good fish, about the best I've tasted since I've been in the army. I'm still scratching like hell with these chiggers. I put everything on them from toothpaste to gasoline. I think that Watkins Antiseptic done the most good. I think alcohol taken internally would be the most beneficial.

From what I hear, we are pulling out of here the 5th of July - that is, me and the other fellows who are going to teletype school. But you know things change fast in the Army. Our outfit is supposed to go on a 125-mile march from Columbia, SC to Charleston, SC. That's some walking believe you me. 125 miles is not just around the block. Ma[y]be I'll be out of here by the time they do that. Here's hoping anyway.

Well, my time is up and I must go back to work. I'll drop you a line later. Alma called me Sunday wondering if I could get home for the 4ᵗʰ of July but there's not a chance that I can see. Well, I'll be seeing ya. Tell Mary hello and many XXXXXX

As always,

Norby

Louisville, Kentucky, **June 29**, Tuesday, 7:15 am, Notice the 7:15 am!

(As good as the best, "Wetter" than the rest.)

Dear Norby,

Well, our house has the morning after look. We really did some entertaining yesterday. We have some relief this morning. The breeze is really cool, but it does feel swell. It has been so hot here we would have a storm and it was just as hot afterward, so we're praising the Lawd for the relief.

Antoinette Hensle was here yesterday. She's really got a cute baby. He's 13 months and he dances, not at all shy but is just cute. He seen a fly, well, he calls them "bucks." He's got eyes like Cousin Ben and I think he favors Eddie a little too. Yes, we looked at pictures. She said if you remember the name of the studio that took your picture she would find out about it, as she always goes to Kansas City, Mo. it wouldn't be any trouble at all. She offered her services. She said she'd be glad to do it. It never struck us. Her husband is back in Kansas City and she's leaving next Monday. They had to stay until a storm passed over. Then Lip and her three youngest came up. Margie is so cute and plump and she wants to really baby Nicki next door.

So about 8:30 in comes Johnny. We really laughed. We had a picnic with Hilary. He's so suntanned and he really sings the hillbilly music. I cannot describe it on paper, but this is what he sang. I mean Hilary and all his motions. The song "He's a high geared daddy until he got a sweet mamma that can cool him down. He would go around breaking women's hearts and keeping them in tears, but now he's got a sweet momma that shifts his gears." Hilary was terrific. Pop shook for 15 minutes. Thereafter Johnny said he was working in the back of his garden and his neighbor was working in the front by his fence. Hilary was sitting on the porch singing that song. He noticed the neighbor lay down his hoe and hold his sides. So, Hilary had to sing that one over. He also sang Frankie and Johnny were sweethearts. He's a bang.

I had better tell you now Antoinette said you were welcome to come whenever you feel and she hopes you get in Kansas City. They got Jackie's proofs. They are real good, I think.

Couldn't get no beer late Sunday afternoon. They were all out. Beer is becoming scarcer all the time. No bottled beer either. We got hamburger from Best's. It went as good as chicken, I'm here to tell you.

The Corpus Christi Procession was nice at Churchill Downs. I never seen yesterday's paper for pictures of it. Norbert is really pretty. I do think it's the prettiest one so far. Lip couldn't wait until she got to hold him. Is Peggy a tomboy? She is. Eleanor bought new silk panties for her. They all climb them big trees, so Sunday she got her washed up and put on her new drawers, and it wasn't 15 minutes before she had them all torn by a limb or tree. She's really a beautiful kid. We got your two letters yesterday. Hope your chiggers are gone by this time and glad you're out of the field. Marge said she would of loved to have your picture. A week without a change of clothes. I imagine you were a little scary looking. Mrs. Orrill got 2 letters from Walter from Camp Cook, Calif., so that's the reason for the delay. Wasn't Gold-Tone the name of the studio where you had your picture taken? Bye, Bye. Be a good boy. Mom's feeling pretty good this morning. It's 70 degrees. A relief I say.
H.R.

Louisville, Kentucky, **June 30**, 12:30 pm

Dear Norby,

50° and what a day! Boy, oh boy, did we have a drop in temperature and how we do welcome it. Yes, we even covered with blankets. It's a heavenly change, believe me. Jimmy just came up. He went blackberrying. He got about a quar. By Monday, he said, they will all be ripe because they're red now. Remember the chiggers you got Norby when you went? Now that you have them again I was thinking didn't you use ammonia water on them? Just happened to think of it. Or ammoniated water?

Seems like Mom's Rheumatism is not getting any better. Some days it does a lot better than others. She called Dr. Stites. He said for her to have an X-Ray taken of it so Mom's going to wait until she completes her bottle of medicine and then if it doesn't show any more improvement she will have a picture made.

Joey was here today. The motor of her [*sewing*] machine is broken at work and they don't know if they can get it fixed so she is off for a few days. Lee is started back to work again today. We're having everything fixed it seems. Well, Mom's been making good use of the heating pad, so it broke. I took it and an electric percolator that Marge brought from work (electric plate) and fan down to Johnson's. We got the heating pad back so now we're having the sewing machine motor fixed but we had to call six places before anybody would fix it. It sure will be shocking having everything in running order.

Well, I couldn't find the pen and it was laying right before me [*the letter had been written in pencil until the pen was found*]. This will be garden talk. Johnny brought in a big mess of turnips. They really are the prettiest I've laid eyes on. He has been picking tomatoes since last week, the first one I know to do that around here this year. Now my butter beans really look swell, too. They aren't blooming yet but they look healthy.

Well, I suppose I'll close. Mom wants to pop off to you, too, so I'll say bye, bye.
H.R.

Continued by Mommy:

Dear Norby,

I haven't much time to write. Mary is getting ready to go to work. How are your pets [*chiggers*]? I hope they have left you by now. Would you like to have Father Spoelker's address? I will try and send it to you. I am going to write you a longer letter next time. I have a sweater on and don't feel a bit too hot. Cool headed- you know I am like my baby - if you know him [*Norb was her youngest*].

Papa shed a few tears when Hermina read your letter to him that stated that you drank a beer for him on Father's Day. Papa will find out Saturday when he will get more [*pay*]. He said if he can't make the extra as he does now, he won't consider it. He told Father that he could get plenty of work repairing and he would not have to work there. Papa said he had four beers to get the nerve. I asked him if he had any beers when he proposed [*to me*].

Now goodbye and be good and pray for me so I will get rid of this pain in my knee. God bless you and good luck. Everybody said Hellow [*sic*].
Mother

Louisville, Kentucky, **July 2**, Friday, 8:30 pm

Dear Norby,

We were listening to the news so before I started the day I thought I would write you a few lines. You come first. Now don't you feel important? Well, the news isn't much different. It's been so cool we haven't been able to sit outside since Monday. It's a relief, but yet you do wish to get outside of an evening.

Shirley's adopted soldier left on August 18, 1942, too. Do you remember him - Harry Gerhrig? Ha, ha. Never gotten a furlough but thought he would be getting one soon. He asked Shirley if she would go to the show with him. Then Shirley never answered, so in his next letter he asked if that movie date still held good but Shirley never answered. She started to say, if you take Mary Ann Orrill along but she rubbed that out.

We haven't received any mail from you since Monday. I think the mailman has gone for this morning. Carl Harstern from Shelby Street is in the Infantry in Texas. He definitely did not want the Infantry, or Texas, so he met with the reserves immediately. The mailman was late this morning. I see they might have you on a long march or would you say getting a little exercise? We got your letter [*dated June 27*] this morning. You're out of luck I think if you think internal alcohol would help your chiggers. I'm the real Porky now, no beef yet. We had bacon for supper last night. It was good bacon but we're so tired of Sow. Did I tell you Tuesday night there was no beer available in the Burg? Pop had to drink Lemonade.

Alma just called and said her brother-in-the-Army's wife just had a baby Monday. I suppose you got my letter about ammoniated water for chiggers. I'm quite sure that's what you used it for, don't you think? I also heard to rub a piece of fat bacon rind would do the work also. Hope you get out of the 125-Mile March but you can't tell.

Love,

The Real Porky

Louisville, Kentucky, **July 3**, Saturday, 9:10 pm

Dear Norby,

Well, the past few days has warmed up quite a lot, with a good breeze stirring. It was suffocating close, but tonight is real pleasant. Pop got an increase in salary this week. He got a $5.00 raise per week. That isn't bad, do you think? Joe and Ann got some records this week: I Dream of Jeanie With the Light Brown Hair by Richard Crooks, Ave Maria by Marian Anderson and about six other pieces. They do sound swell.

Ernie Schieman came home today on furlough. Bernard Hollkamp got his card to be examined July 6 & 7th. Omar is in an Army hospital in Danville, Kentucky. He's in a medical unit or whatever you call it. Did you or did you not go on the 125 mile hike? According to our Encyclopedia Ft. Mammoth [*Monmouth*], NJ is listed as a Signal Corp School (Army). Frank Niemann is in Charlestown, SC now. He was sent to the "Citadel." He's studying engineering. Do you think that's an especially good break? His mother did. They call it the West Point of the South. She felt honored, I know.

I'm sending you another picture of the Corpus Christi procession. Marge said she knows that's her and Alma. The morning paper was larger and clearer but we don't have it. I have to make out the [*chance*] books for the picnic. I just got thru with writing out all of those stubs. I know what writer's cramps are. Well, it seems like the Yanks are really going to it. Tomorrow is the 4th. I can't believe it. Mary seen Omar. He looks good but I heard he didn't like it with the sick. I think he's with the veterans of the last world war.

Carl Besendorf's wife gave birth of a boy yesterday. I guess that will keep up the Besendorf's Dry Goods. At present, I cannot think of anything that would interest you so will say goodnite dear, goodnite thee.

Porky

Louisville, Kentucky, **July 4**, Sunday, Hot as !!!!!

Dearest Norb,

Marge is busy writing some letters she owed. I believe it's fixing to rain. I don't have any more news. Rudy Muth has a party today. It's his 49th birthday. I doubt if you get this letter at Ft. Jackson if you leave as you expect.

Now the salutary 'Dearest' is there because it's close to the 6th of the month. You become sweeter then. "No hard feeling, just jesting." Mom still has trouble with her knee. I suppose will go in town and have an X-ray made Tuesday. Hoping your 4th was a pleasant one and next year we'll have peace and then we can celebrate it. Listening to Sousa Stars and Stripes Forever.

In housecleaning I came across some of those notes you wrote Lee Rhodes at St. E. Would you like to have one to send to Lee? You can send them Air Mail you know. If you want one, say so. Until I get more interesting dope, Bye.

Your sweetest sister,

Meenie

Louisville, Kentucky, **July 5**

Dear Norby it is 8:30 pm.

I just came in from the porch. It was getting too cool for me - cool headed, you know? Well, 4th or 5th of July is over almost. We all hope that we all will be together next fourth. Hoping and praying. I pray that we will be together sooner than then. It all sounds good for us but I think we have lots to pray for. I sure miss that I cannot go to Mass on weekdays. I am going to Dr. Stites tomorrow. He is going to recommend an Ex-ray or whatever you call it. My knee is no better than when I went to the Dr. the first time but the high blood pressure is lots better. I will find out tomorrow about that also, so here is hoping that I will get better.

Elizabeth is here and some of the children are here, Moody also. Pop came now, too. Beer is out. They have the saloons closed. No beer, no trade, so Pop cannot rush the bucket tonight. It's awful how the men complain. You'd think they did not have beer for a year. I don't drink beer now so beer does not bother me.

Maybe this letter will find you in another state. I hope that you will like it and study hard. You can if you want to. I know that. Pop and Joe and Ann went to see John and Eleanor. They are all well. Norbert the II is looking fine and sassy like you. It seems he wants to" goo goo" so sweet.

The Irish picnic was today. It rained around 6 o'clock a little but the rest of the evening is gloomy but no rain. St. Theresa had a picnic Saturday a week and it poured down raining for a while but they made $7,000 and sold supper for 35¢. St. Elizabeth's is going to have a picnic next Saturday. Supper is 75¢. I don't think that I can go. I couldn't stand long. It is going to be on the school ground. I hope that the weather will be nice. Father Maloney offered Pop $2 more a week. Pop said $3 a week or I will quit. So he said alright, so Papa is satisfied. Papa told him about St. Theresa's. He said you ought to be glad you didn't get it. Why, we don't know.

John Hollkamp met Papa and Papa told him that he spoke to his Pastor so John asked him [Pastor] why Papa didn't get the job. He said the job was halfway promised but if he [*person who was hired*] didn't do the work right he [*Pop*] was on the list yet. Papa said he wouldn't change.

Love from all,

Mother

Fort Jackson, South Carolina, **July 5**

Dear Mom and all,

Hello and how are you all and how was the 4ᵗʰ? I had a darn good time myself. We were off Saturday and Sunday so three of us guys went to Chester, SC and we really had a good time. We went to some country-dance and there weren't many soldiers in Chester so we were treated royally.

It's pretty warm here tonight - in fact, it's damn hot. I don't know much of anything that's new so I'll send you a 59ᵗʰ Signal Brigade paper. It's just a little paper that the boys here started up. I think you find me in there a few times. I don't know if I told you or not I have a driver's license. I had to make quite a few trips to Battalion Headquarters through the course of the day and it took too long when you have to walk, so I do all my running in a jeep.

Well, I'll send you the paper and I'll be signing off with saying I'm

As Always,

Norby

Louisville, Kentucky, **July 7**, Wednesday, 5:30 pm

Dear Norby,

I'm writing this at Lavern's [*Cousin George Heitkemper's wife who did hairdressing in her home*] under the dryer, but no kidding, I'm really going to be beautiful - I mean, more beautiful. Well, this is the longest I've ever waited in writing to you. The reason is your new address. We haven't heard from you since Thursday unless Mom gets a letter this pm.

I haven't did a thing today but squat. We waited from 10:00 to 2:00 to see Dr. Stites. He looked at Mom's knee good, pressed and pulled around on it, and decided it was arthritis. He wanted to see her before the X-rays so he said today he thinks X-rays wouldn't show a thing but gave her a prescription that he thinks will help her in time. She has to stay off the foot as much as possible. He said it helped a lady 75 years old. It cured her in two years' time. He told her it was a slow process but it certainly is worth trying because the knee has bothered her more this week again. Mom's blood pressure is 140 and that's about normal. She gained 4 pounds, weighs 156. Mom looks fine.

On July 4ᵗʰ and 5ᵗʰ the Saloons were closed, all day on the 4ᵗʰ and sold just what they could get which wasn't much on the 5ᵗʰ. That's the talk of the Burg now. That's one thing I don't suffer from is lack of beer. In fact, I think it's a very good thing that Russell got a case without bottles, which everybody needs now – bottles, in order to get a bottle. He's also got a quart of Four roses ($5.00), or least he told me that on the 4ᵗʰ. I believe him too, because she [*Mary, his wife*] spent the 4ᵗʰ and 5ᵗʰ out of his sight. I was over there the 4ᵗʰ. He got to the point he wanted his gun. Boy, you should of heard him cuss her out loud on the porch. So she got her purse and told him (she stomped her foot and she had her lower teeth out), and she said "'Dude' Russell there's not a grain of man in you. You would support me if there was and not let me work." And that's not music to his ears. As anxious as I was to clear out, I had to laugh. I thought you might, and might not, get a kick out of that.

We got a card from Bernard Spoelker today. He's still in the Philippines and he said he's enjoying his stay in the Islands. He asked about you and where you were located. Where are you located? We also got a letter from Alma. She is with her mother and dad again in Valley Station, KY.

We sure have been with you this week in thought. Wondering if you're traveling on your own power or by train, or should I say Locomotion. Dr. Stites closes his door a few minutes before 12 o'clock or 12 noon. I heard him say he wouldn't get out before 4:00 pm and he's there at 9:00 am. He certainly works hard.

In case you don't know it, Norbert H. is referred to by Margie as "Naudy's (Norbie's) baby." We really had the April showers today but could use it. The things will look so nice by next week. We're expecting to see some ripe tomatoes. Our potatoes are all dug out. They were about the size of a head of a match. Johnny's got some nice big ones. Hilary's got a stone bruise showing how tough his feet were so the MD had to lance it. It's doing OK. It's just about well. They came in last night. Eleanor was careful to bandage up his "sore" foot and he wore a bedroom slipper on it, so when he got at our house he told her she bandaged up the wrong foot and he really got a kick out of it. It was funny.

Is there anything you would like us to send you, for your chiggers or anything else? Well, I'll close this letter, as my hair is just about dry and will finish it at home.

At Home, 8 pm

Lip and kids are here. We're chewing the fat. Emma Hildebrand has a boy since Monday. Well, I will close. Hoping your chiggers are OK and you too. What's your address honey? Love from all,
The Genuine "Porky"

Fort Jackson, South Carolina, **July 7**

Hello Mom and all,

Very busy, very busy, no time at all. I still look forward to that 125-mile road march if they don't call it off. I haven't heard any more about going to school but it will happen one of these days. We'll have to pack up in 20 minutes and get out, I guess.

It's very hot down here and I ain't fooling. I done took two showers today and in just a few minutes, I'm going down and take another one. It's one way to keep cool. I received that clipping of Marge and Alma at the Corpus Christi. It could be them ma[y]be. It's a very funny setting [*Churchill Downs*] for the Corpus Christi. I wonder how the betting sheds done. Well, I know this ain't much but I don't know much.

As Always,
Norby

Louisville, Kentucky, **July 8**, Thursday, 8 pm

Dear Norby, or Chigger-in-Person,

Still getting Pork. We received your letter today also the 59th Hi-Lite. It did us all a lot of good to see your name in print. Mom was really pleased with it and this being Thursday and Pop not home as yet I expect a few tears on that. Don't forget to send us the next copy especially when your name is mentioned. We will look forward to that. So you think the chigger is a lovable little parasite. You sure sound big to do all your own driving in a jeep. Alma called and is coming out tomorrow. or so she said. I suppose she told you she quit her job. I brought the prescription to Hertel's [*drugstore*] yesterday at 6:30 pm. The medicine wasn't in stock so Mom got it today at 2:30 pm - 25 capsules for $2.75. Now we're looking forward for it to cure her. Stites told her to positively not be on it, only when she has to. So she wasn't feeling so hot today and was really off of it. Since supper, Katie is perking up and is feeling a whole lot better.

I got 2 weeks ironing to do tomorrow. I don't care though. I can sit to that. This week is boomp [*sic*] week here, it seems. Shirley fell off Rudy's pony. She's OK but has a long scratch on her arm, which is healed. Joe fell off the stepladder yesterday. It folded up on him. He wasn't hurt a bit and Johnny fell delivering a bottle of milk, cut his little finger on his left hand. It had to be stitched. He said it bled terrible and he had to go to three different Drs. before he found one home who could do the stitching. It bothered him since yesterday but he worked today. He drove the [*Plainview Farms Dairy*] truck and had a jumper [*a person to carry the milk to the doors*]. The Dr. said it was a clean cut and thinks it will be OK.

We'll save that Hi-Lite for you. In later years you may enjoy reading it, even if you hate the lovable Parasite. We haven't heard from you for a week. Thought by this time you would be in a different location. Glad to hear you had such a good time at the Country Dance and they treated you royal. How many Brenda's and Copeva's were thar [*sic*]? How are the SC gals? I think you had a better time than most civilians. You didn't see any fireworks hardly and no beer made it a very bad holiday. Of course, I didn't feel that. I'll close this letter tomorrow. Mrs. Madden said if you rub with coal oil, the chiggers never bother you and if you got chiggers, to rub with the rind of a bacon. It will kill them. That's all the chigger dope I know. I guess by this time your chiggers are gone "any ha" [*sic*].

Until tomorrow, goodnite Chigger

H.R.

Louisville, Kentucky, **July 9**, Friday, 2:00 pm

Dear Chigger,

Well, it's a hot day in Louisville. John came in last night around 9:30 pm. He went to the company doctor. Johnny said the other doctor didn't take care of it right. His wound is closed but that's all. The tendons are cut and the finger falls limp to the palm of his hand. It's his index finger left hand. Dr. Richardson advised him to go to the Deaconess Hospital for 3 or 4 days. I just came back from the hospital and Johnny is doing fine. The Dr. made an L-like incision from the top of his hand like this [drawing of hand & incision]. The operation lasted 30 minutes. Before he sewed it shut, he asked John to move his finger and John was able to move it, so the Dr. said he would get along OK. We all think he will. It's the first time he could move it since the accident. It's nothing serious but I do think, well I know, he would of had a stiff finger. Lip and I went to hospital and Eleanor and Norbert was there. He laughed loud for the first time. He's really a handsome scrapper and smiles when you talk to him.

Mom is feeling oodles better today, at present is in dreamland puffing like the old 97. Don't worry about Johnny. The reason I wrote that is because someone else might not mention it, so now you got the straight of it. The Dr. said this morning he might be out in a day or two and Compensation is paying for it.

Well, that's all for this time. We never heard from you this morning but maybe this pm we'll be more fortunate.

Love from all. Mary said hello and 10 X's.

Porky

Louisville, Kentucky, **July 11**, Sunday, 2:30 pm

HOT AS AN ITALIAN IN SICILY!

Dear Norby,

Boy. it's a blazing hot Sunday. Johnny just called. He said Charley Brown is going to bring him here from the hospital in about an hour. Sure glad to hear that. We expect to see him home today. I just wrote Fr. Spoelker. Well, our Picnic was last night and it was given on the Church grounds. Pop went there last night and walks to the Swiss thinking it was given there. But then he went to the Picnic, however, he got some unwanted exercise. But Pop looks swell. Mr. And Mrs. Nunn stopped by on their way to the Picnic. She showed us a snap of Claude and he's as hefty as he always was. She said he was gone 19 months onFriday, and is 15 months in Australia. He's a cook there, still a PFC but is expecting Sgt. stripes any time. The second boy is in Ft. Leonard Woods, Missouri. I cannot keep Nelson and Elbert apart. Which is the oldest of the two? The third one is in Tacoma, Washington. He was just 18 and very homesick. He left June 3rd. I think he's the one in the Infantry.

We sure was looking for a letter from you yesterday so we think you might be traveling. Alma was to see us. She said she did washing on the board this week. I told her I would of loved to seen her. She don't like country. She's going to be godmother for her brother's baby this pm. I think I'll wait til tomorrow day (as Milt formerly said) and finish this. We had hamburger today for dinner. It was a whole skillet full and before it was done it was just ½ its size when ready to serve. It looks like it has cereal with it. I know the dairies put out something to mix with ground meat. I know I don't want any more of that. It's course looking common liver pudding. It's going on 6 weeks and still no beef. Joe and Ann are gone to the country today. My cow! My cow! My kingdom for a cow!

Continued, Monday, 10:30 am

Received your letter this morning. Well, we had a big wash and an early start so now I'll start ironing and catch up on some from two days ago. Mom feels pretty good some days and some days not so good but it's a good one today. John just couldn't wait until he got home. The MD told him it would be three weeks before he could work. Naturally, it's healing fine or otherwise he would not be home as yet.

Well, the Russells are still a feuding. He actually threw her out last night. It was still light about 8 pm. I seen her on the porch. Then she went towards the screen door and all of a sudden we seen Mary come a sailing and land on her butt. A few moments before that, we heard glass break but Mary threw a bowl at Dude and got him. So that was too much for Dude and he just threw her out. He was a pale face. It was gin. She wasn't hurt but I believe the situation there is beginning to be like the war, "the beginning of the end."

Believe it or not, the Street is being repaired at Mulberry. Mary Rawert came to see it yesterday. Well, that's all for this so until I get more scandal I'll close, hoping you'll be sent to school rather than on a march. I suppose by this time you're exempt from the chigger. Love, your vegetarian sister,

H.R.

Knoxville, Tennessee [a *postcard*], **July 12**

Hello everybody,

Just arrived here in Knoxville. Will leave in 45 minutes. My brother and I made it in good time to Nashville. I'll be in Columbia, SC at 1:15. I'm so nervous I can barely hold this pen. I can say I'm really tired for once and will be glad when I get to SC so until later, I'll be seeing you.

As always,

Alma

Louisville, Kentucky, **July 13**, Tuesday, 8:30 pm

Dear Norby,

Well, it's a beautiful day in Louisville - a beautiful day! And Mom seems to be starting out good this morning. Jimmy is coming to help me cut the grass. It really needs it. I waited until the mail man came before I wrote to see if we had a letter from you and we did not, so Norb, I am going to ask if you sent the five dollars or not. If you have, I haven't received it. You know I am not working. I couldn't work for two reasons. Mom is one and myself is another. Since I quit I don't have no difficulty in sleeping. That sewing really got on my nerves. My funds are running low, as I have managed to pay for my own medicine and that costs plenty, so if you haven't sent it I hope you will do so when you can, as you know there's no payday when you stay home.

I got a letter from Anna Heitkemper yesterday. I can't scrape a bit of news together. Betsy is 9 years old today. Jimmy has to serve Mass for two weeks and today he's a prompt somebody and that's all for this time. I heard we might get beef but I doubt it.
Love,
H.R.

Louisville, Kentucky, **July 15**, Thursday, 8 pm
Dear Norb,

By this time, I know you received the telegrams. We were shocked when little Elizabeth [*Rawert*] called and said they found Uncle Frank [*Rawert*] dead at 5:30 pm. I think little Henry found him. He had the groceries sitting by the door and he was sitting in the kitchen by the table - dead. She was all to pieces naturally. That's a terrible shock. Pop, Joe, Marge and Ann are gone in there now. Joe got Pop from work. I feel he will be buried Monday. The Coroner wasn't there as yet but I imagine it was a heart attack.

We haven't received a letter from you since Monday and that was written Wednesday a week ago, so we will probably get one tomorrow "we hope." By this time I suppose you have had a pleasant surprise, or wasn't it a surprise?

Joey gave Milt Dewey's old bicycle and he is thrilled. Mom's knee was on the very good side today, the best yet, but yesterday Mom ran a temperature all day, but she feels a lot better. I wonder if the new medicines could produce that? Johnny's hand is doing fine. The Dr. permitted him to sit in the truck and direct, so he doesn't do no actual work. He removed the stitches Tuesday.

Pop took it [*his brother Frank's death*] pretty good. He said, well I'm the oldest and lived the longest. Mom is sending you a sympathy card and said please don't forget to send it.
Love,
H.R.

Fort Jackson, South Carolina, **July 16**
Dear Mom and all,

Well, Uncle Frank's death came as a surprise to me. I received the telegram about 11 pm last night. I can't get home because they won't give me a furlough. The excuse was that presence was not necessary. I have told you all about six times that whenever anything like that happens, for God's sake, send it through the Red Cross! I don't know why you didn't. That damn fool we got for a company commander now, I could shoot him in the back of the head and think I done a good deed. I called up the Red Cross, they checked with the Louisville Chapter, and the telegram that came back said that a very close relation had died and that is good grounds for a furlough but that damn fool wouldn't give me any. I'll get even with him for that if it takes me the rest of my life to do so.

Well, Alma's been here since Tuesday and I just seen her for about two hours. I was out in the field when I received the message, so yesterday I met her at the gate. I got a ride in from the field. I don't know why in the hell she don't let someone know what's cooking. I think she got as much of a surprise out of it as I did. That is the most foolish thing you can do. I hope I get a pass tomorrow. This outfit is bearing down. Probably last minute fixings.

About that five bucks, I'll send it the first thing next month. After that guy bating me out of ten, and I had two months of insurance to pay and then the Fourth of July, well, I was broke by the tenth. I have exactly $1.65 to last me to the end of the month. I'm writing for one of those Park and Tilford Packages with the cigarettes in it. I'm due for one pretty soon.

I guess you don't think it gets hot down here. Just ask Alma when she gets back. It's really not as hot as it was. Well, we're working long hours now, and I'll have to quit and go to sleep with those damn chiggers. So good night and I'm... [*Words are missing here*].
As Always,
Norb

Louisville, Kentucky, **July 20**, Tuesday, 9:30 pm

Dear Norby,

I suppose you realize that Sunday you were in the army eleven months. I suppose you're wondering why [*I sent*] the orange wrappers. Well, August 1st Joe and Ann will be married 1 year. I thought you could send that to them as an anniversary gift as 1st anniversary is paper. We are going to cook up something on that order. If you have something else in mind, send it.

We are sending you a bottle of Watkins antiseptic. Let us know if you get it. We are also sending you a box. Mom is going to Dr. Stites tomorrow. So far, she has shown no improvement at all with her arthritis but her blood pressure is down. Mom is thinking about taking those baths like Joey had taken some years ago. Some people are relieved quite a bit by them.

Are you still in the field? And, how did you make out about the pass? Well, I see where Rome has been bombed. That really does make history. They said most of the boys were Roman Catholic. I see where Sec. of the Navy, Knox, said it would take until 1949 before we would get Japan. I imagine they feel the news was too favorable for us and people were too optimistic.

Tony Hoffmann sprained his ankle last week and was hopping around and Monday he broke his left arm so they have him at St. Anthony Hospital with weights on his arm. Now that's double trouble.

We certainly could use some rain and a cooling off period but the stars are many and bright in Kentucky so I guess we won't get any rain and I never hear lately if there was a 'fog in the holler.'

Will say goodnite and sleep tight. Well, will close, can't think of anymore.

[*Hermina*]

Louisville, Kentucky, **July 21**, Wednesday, 1:30pm

[*Dear Norb,*]

Mom came home about an hour ago. Dr. Stites thought she's a little impatient. Mom said well it's two months now and no relief. In fact, her other knee is starting. You know sometimes she don't do as well as Mrs. Paul, other times she does a little better. Today Stites sent her to Dr. Hudson, a home specialist. He told her it was arthritis and 3/4 arch trouble. Dr. Hudson took care of Dewey too, you know. Mom hasn't been wearing her arch supports lately, not at all. Her feet didn't bother her at all. Her knee is swollen some. She has a prescription and has to have her shoes built in so now we're in hopes this will do the work.

Another thing. Mom is in the dumps about the Pumpernickel. The baker from Lubbers' is in the army now so none for the duration.

Pop is real tickled with his find; you know he has such thick toenails. He found a pair of pruning shears and it cuts the nails. That's something. Well, will close for now, hoping you are well and scratch less.

Love from all,

Still on a pork chop

Continued, Thursday, 8 am

Mom got an early start. At 7:45 she was on her way to Stites. She's like her son [*Norb*] - now she taxis everywhere she goes. But Joe was sure nice to us while Uncle Frank was laying a corpse. Love, keep 'em scratching, still eating Pork,

Sistah H

Louisville, Kentucky, **July 22**, Thursday, 9 pm

Dear Brother,

Lay that Tommy Gun down! Lay that Tommy Gun down! And write a little oftener. Vots da motter? Lip was just here. It's getting so cool tonite. People are sitting on the lawns with sweaters on but the porch is real pleasant. But I could not think of a thing more pleasanter than writing to you. (Says the Corporal, you're full of HORSE). Lip said Freddy Keller, USN, Nan's nephew, Clarks Lane, is reported missing. His mother received the government notice yesterday. Lip said you went to school with him.

Milton's ambition in life is lifeguard. Lip said that's the only thing she even heard him say he would like to be. Shirley gives him credit for being a good swimmer and diver. Jim said he asked him to take notice of him as he drove off, if he looked good? Jim said his trunks were as low as could be. He said he's sunburned and it was natural skin showing above his trunks. He lost his belt, but unconscious Milt don't give a hoot. Lip don't know where he is going to school as yet. I don't like the idea of Halleck Hall. Shirley and Milt has been working at the shop [*Muth's Candy*] and another unconscious thing he [*Milt*] did was put on Shirley's new jersey blouse thinking it was a sport shirt. He was going to pick blackberries in it. I believe he'd go in Mahatma attire, but he did like his new suit. This is kid talk, but Watkins [*sales representative*] was there, and Katsy goes to the toilet and lets the door open so she could see what her mother was buying.

Mom seems to have some comfort today. Dr. Hudson taped her leg with adhesive tape From arch to knee. She has to go in Monday.

Johnny had his finger dressed yesterday and will have it dressed tomorrow again. He can wiggle it now. "I" put up 2 ½ gallons of blackberries today, some jam and some jelly. Looks good too. (Patting my own back) and expanding my chest. Johnny brought in the blackberries, a head of cabbage, about a ½ peck of tomatoes and a mess of okra. It all went good, I say. Tomatoes are 25¢ for 2 pounds. Will say goodnite boy, will add tomorrow day. Oh yeah, Moody said there was no beer in the Burg tonite. Sad but true.
[*Hermina*]

Louisville, Kentucky, **July 23**, Friday, 8:30 am

[*Dear Norb,*]

Say, lay that pistol down, we haven't got any mail from you this morning. It got so cool last night I couldn't stand the breeze blowing in on me cute little head. It was beautiful sleeping. In case you don't know, to date, your bed has two mattresses, one feather bed and one feather mattress from Emmy. Lays good, brother.

We are going to have an Air Raid Sunday afternoon at 3:00 pm. They are going to drop pasteboard bombs over the city. Hoping you are well. Mom is still blowing away. I know I'll catch hell for not calling her sooner but she's supposed to be off her low-Dutch feet anyhow.

Bye, bye, and quit scratching chiggers long enough to say howdy. Mr. Paul sat for 2 hours yesterday on the front porch and read out loud. I could make out something from the living room.
[*Hermina*]

Louisville, Kentucky, **July 25**, Sunday, 2:00 pm

Dear Norb,

Just five months till Xmas. Thought perhaps the thought would cool you off. Alma called around noon today saying she got in last night. We were all glad to hear from her and especially that you are OK. She said you wrote a letter. Perhaps we'll get it tomorrow, as we haven't received any since you acknowledged the telegram. It's terribly, terribly hot. Has been the past two weeks but one nite was very cool. I had to close the window. I suppose we have picked about two dozen tomatoes. They are smooth and firm and little better than medium size. Did I tell you my butterbeans are in bloom?

This afternoon at 3 pm, we are going to have an Air Raid so we are sort of anxious to see how the thing will work. I believe 12 planes from Bowman Field will do the "dirty work."

Believe it (it's no nots about it) we had beef today. The supermarket - Red Front on Goss - had it so Jimmy got the Rawerts and Muths some. It went good but from the fat, you could see it wasn't a young boy. You have to stew it a little but it beats pork. First beef we've had in nearly two months.

Yeah man! Pop seen a "fog in the holler" for two mornings. That's words of encouragement we might get some very much needed rain. The lawns are beginning to show the need of it but they have never been more beautiful.

Ann's niece, Eudora Mattingly, joined the SPARS [*US Coast Guard Women's Reserve*].

Ann went with Edgar blackberrying at his place yesterday. They are beginning to dry up now. He said last week he got them an inch long. Ann got about 2 gallons so Mom went over there last night to boss the jelly making. Joe and Ann really worked hard. It taken two to do everything. Joe said, "Gee but it's a lot of work," and they had about two dozen more quarts washed than they could fill. They must of thought it was magic in those berries. Milton is writing, too. I'm anxious to know what he is cooking up.

Mary Rawert said they were coming over this afternoon. Marge made biscuits for dinner. Brother, any Jap would run from them. I asked Pop how he liked them. He said he wasn't so stuck on them. Ask Pop how he made out on the beef. I'm telling you, that one tooth had to do double duty. Maybe triple.

I just read Milt's letter I hope you can do the same. He wants to go to Ahrens Trade [*School*] but he needs a year of high school first. Lip said they all brag about Shirley at the [*Muth's Candy*] shop. She practically takes care of all the store trade. She's interested and a willing worker. A little girl can't make money like a boy so she's real tickled. Milt, it gets too hot for him. Lip said they claim he's a little bully. He wants to help Bernice all the time. It really does get hot in the Popcorn room. Jimmy wants to get down there too, to make some money but I think the kindergarten is filled.

Well, I must close. Little Mary has just come home so I'll say bye, bye, hoping to hear and are you going to school?
Goodbye,
Hermina

Louisville, Kentucky, **July 26**

Dear Norb,

I am working down at the candy shop now but I am going to quit the damn dump because I got the hottest job in the whole place. I pop popcorn. Dewey gave me his wheels. I have got it all fixed up. I don't know if I am going to St. X or not. Sunday we had four chickens for dinner and I am full to the top. Dad is having a hard time with the beer problem. St. Elizabeth cleared on their picnic $6,311.26 and I wonder how you are feeling up there. I wonder if you are sweating your little tail off. I am glad they have got you in the field because you did not do anything around here. And when you are finished in the field I will sure the hell laugh if they would put you on KP. Joe killed a chicken Sunday and it made him sick. I been in swimming almost twice a week since it opened, to cool off. And when you get time, you better write a letter to Betsy or when you get home, she will tear you apart. I am growing very fast. I am as tall as Mark. My note on my report was 84 average. Well, I hope you get home soon. Everybody said I write like you so I guess you can read it. Milton [*almost 14 years old*]

Louisville, Kentucky, **July 26**, Monday, nearly noon

[*Dear Norb,*]

We received your letter this morning. Was surely glad to hear. We almost called you yesterday because in your last letter you mentioned last minute fixings so when Alma called we knew a letter was on its way. Can't you call sometime and reverse the charges? We'd be so glad to hear your dear, dear voice. Your last letter was very embarrassing to Mom about Johnson's haircut. I imagine Larny's letters are A-1 daisies. I bet he is a happy soldier.

Mom is now at the Dr.'s office. Ann went with her this time. Mary and I have just finished Mom's glory [*Monday washing*]. Mom can have it. Here's hoping the Dr. fixes her up soon but it could be worse, but Mom likes the feel of the suds. So does Pa, but a more concentrated kind. There was no beer in the Burg yesterday. Moody, etc. passed by. He told Pop he knows where he could get beer. Pop had just come from Joe's so Pop said I can round you up a few more. So Joe, Madden and Austin, the young "feller" next door went to the Swiss. It was warm so it was a picnic at the All Wool [*All Wool and a Yard Wide Democratic Club*]. They proceeded there. It was warm but it was beer.

So you expect to go on maneuvers soon and Larny is on maneuvers too. Could it be possible you two might meet? Then what would happen!!!! I received a letter from Will Hollkamp. He said he was on a furlough in Australia and had just gotten back and 35 letters were staring him in the face. He said he has answered letters for three nights. Norbert [*Hollkamp*] never writes anymore. I suppose he has plenty to accompany his mind.

Well, we heard yesterday where the Il Duce [*dictator Mussolini*] was kicked out of Italy. I wonder if his successor will be any better. Your godmother is coming to visit in Louisville for a while, so you might write a "right nice" letter that we could read aloud to her, not like the one today.

So the three looked like a million. Well, you forgetful animal, why in the world didn't you say whether you would like some open work bedroom slippers or "no?" With pen in hand, answer that.

No rain yet. We need it badly. No fog in the holler yesterday but the sky looks threatening for 5 minutes then the sun come out. The strangest you have ever seen or felt. I got a right nice suntan. Spoelker's move to their new home on Kaelin this week.

Mom just came in. The Dr. taped up her leg again and said she was doing OK. Well, I am just about out of news casting. That's all there is any more. Walter Winchell [*fast talking newspaper columnist and radio personality*] says when in Rome do as the Romans did.

Norb, I am not sending clippings because we never intended to send this letter Air Mail. After I discovered the APO 312, we thought we should sent it Air Mail. That might give you time to call before you go on maneuvers. Hoping to hear from you in person very soon. Mom said you should call - it's not my makeup.

St. Teresa let roses fall, not Oertel's bumpers. A few clippings and Uncle Frank's death card.

I just happened to look at your envelope and discovered APO #312. What does that mean? You never mentioned it in your letter. Now we're wondering so please call us up when it is convenient to you, day or night and reverse the charges. It's a command. Mom said how did you feel when you seen Alma? Did you get the Watkins Antiseptic and our box?

Well, hoping to hear your dear voice, sweet or not, soon. As Always, your dear, sweet, angelic, plump, baby sister,
H.R.

Fort Jackson, South Carolina, **July 27**

Dear Mom and all,

This is a Tuesday morning and not much to do so I thought I would write you a few lines. I received the box you sent me yesterday. The peanuts were really good. I haven't had a chance to sample the rest so I'll pass my opinion on them as soon as possible.

Well, well, well, I see where Il Duce took to his feet which is very good news. But that's as far as it goes. I tell you when you're in the army you don't even know there is a war going on. There's too much to keep you busy. I imagine in about two weeks Italy will be out of the war altogether and that's when things will really start moving. I hope, I hope.

I also see in the paper where Mrs. F.D.R. sees that the draft of women may be necessary. It seems as though the women don't think so much of a uniform after all, being they now have a chance to wear one.

We had a little rain last night, which was very welcome. It cooled things off a little. It gets pretty warm down here you know. I don't think it will be so long before we go on maneuvers, at least I hope not. I'll be glad to move from Columbia, SC. For my part, they can give it back to the Indians. You can ask Alma what kind of town it is. It's all soldiers. A civilian is a rare thing. And prices, whew! They know they got a good thing and they really take advantage of it. Well, I guess I had better get back to work and get a few things done so I'll be seeing ya.

As Always,
Norb V...

Louisville, Kentucky, **July 27**, Tuesday, 8 pm

Dear Norb,

I'll begin answering your "yaller pamphlet" tonight. How long did it take you to concentrate? Can you still do that, huh? Goodnite, sleep tight.

[*Hermina*]

Louisville, Kentucky, **July 28**, Wednesday, 8 am

[*Dear Norb,*]

You have more numerals in your address than Pres. Roosevelt has initials, in effect. The Pres. is going to speak tonight at 8:30 pm. I got a letter from Norbert Hollkamp. He said he's expecting to get a furlough in September. I can't figure him in the army 6 months yet.

By the time I get your envelope addressed, I want to "holler" Bingo. We still haven't had any rain. We need it badly. So your chiggers have left you. Well, that's a better thought. Say, you must of played "possum" on the Commanding Officer. Love, oh love, oh Army love. Did you feel like Romeo [*sneaking out*]?

Yes, Mary Rawert's boyfriend is about 44. I think he went to school with our Henry. Your godmother [*Anna Deloris Heitkemper, b. June 3, 1879*] was here yesterday. She was very nice. She looks older than Mom and don't look good. She has been very sick. She's had acute neuritis. She said in a half hour she would stiffen up so that she could not use her arms or, in fact, use her arms & limbs but she feels lots better. I believe that damp climate has a lot to do with her condition [*she lived in Mobile, Alabama*]. Maybe the good Kentucky sunshine will help her. I'll suggest that she gets a good sun tan and run around in a playsuit, she and Mom together.

I met Aggie Hellmann's husband, Lt. Klein. He's on a furlough. Aggie looks good. He seems to be an ordinary, nice fellow.

Last night I had a lot to write but it got too dark on me. I must have acute neuritis of the brain this morning. Yes, Johnny's address is R.R. [*Rural Route*] 66, Louisville, Kentucky. Marge got a letter from Agnes [*Hollkamp*], such scratching. I do not know the contents. It seems as if it is Hollkamp week. On Monday I got a letter from Bill and on Tuesday from Norb; today Agnes.

Chester [*Hubbuch's employee*] has brought a lot of drapes this noon so I guess that means get busy. Say, that's terrible about those guys losing their minds. Are they clamping down on you all so hard and they can't take it? That's terrible. I don't appreciate that remark about Pork. At least you ate it. That's more than I could do with some of this tough old Bull they have in Louisville.

We just got our third ration book this morning The Nattermanns have 9 stars in the window. Five boys in the Navy, two in the Army and one daughter in the WAVE and the other a WAC. It was announced over WHAS this morning. An airplane is really cutting up this morn.

Bernie Crimmins looks lots older than you do from that picture. We thought you might call last night. Perhaps you did not get the Airmail letter. If you do not call we will try and see if we can contact you. Mom is cooking up something to write to you, too. I don't think Bourbon would help Mom at all. I don't think Bourbon is a cure all like a lot of lovers of bourbon think.

Sardi's is on so I'll say bye, bye and don't sweat too much.

Love,

H.R.

Louisville, Kentucky, **July 28**

Dear Son,

We have been waiting for a call from you - reverse charges. Received your fat and welcome letter yesterday. Glad that your chigger friends left. Don't entertain any more. We sent you a bottle of Watkins Antiseptic but I do not know if you received it. And a box also [*and you have not*] acknowledged it as yet. Alma called Sunday morning. I answered the phone and was surprised. Was just thinking of her when she called. She said that you was well and looking fine and she saw you almost every night, but it was very hot there. She liked the Old Kentucky Home better. She promised to come sometime this week. She said she was going to her parents and see if she could get work there. I believe her father is trying to get a job for her. As you said, her eye is looking fine.

Well, if you can get a furlough I don't blame you for trying. I am sorry you don't hear anything about your schooling you was promised. So we will hope and pray that you will get your wish. We haven't much time. Want the mail to leave at 9 o'clock. I have my right foot and leg taped to the knee. For the second, it gives me comfort and have to exercise my feet twice a day. Dr. Stites won't give me no medicine till he sees how I am getting along. I have to have my shoes built up a little bit. I did not wear my arch supports for about 2 months and was glad that I did not feel any discomfort but I think that had a lot to do with it. I asked Dr. Hudson. He said that it could but he would not say positive.

Mary Rawert and her friend and Elizabeth and her husband were here Sunday afternoon for a little while. Mary told us they received a card of sympathy from you and it pleased them very much. See what a little effort can do to make someone feel good? Mary takes Uncle's death very hard. She sure babyed [*sic*] Uncle. I don't think that she could have treated Uncle any better. She said to me, I am glad that I have treated Papa as good as I knew how, now I have no regrets. I thought maybe the boys would walk with their girlfriends but they didn't. Mary, Henry and Frank walked together. Bernard and Johnny, then Elizabeth and husband and then Papa and I. Then Mary Rawert & Aunt Elizabeth's [*Lichtefeld*] relatives. Papa insisted to stop at Rawerts. Mary and Elizabeth were crying. Then Papa had his crying spell. Also, I felt sorry for all of them.

Received your letter this morning so this letter will probably not go till this afternoon.

Please do not use any vulgar words. It don't sound good.That's all for now and hope you keep the spirit of writing if only a card if you have no time for a letter.
God bless you,
Mother

Louisville, Kentucky, **July 29**, Thursday, 9:30 pm

Dear Norb,

I doubt seriously if I get to take pen in hand tomorrow so I'm at it twice today. We have been looking for you to call. I should say waiting. We thought last night you would have the letter where we asked you to. I wrote it Monday. Well, today we didn't hear from you but you have been put back on the E rating this week. So far we haven't seen Alma since she returned but I doubt seriously if we will see her until Saturday or Sunday because I feel like her dad was able to get her a job the next day the way things are now.

Mom is now wearing the shoes she had built up. They throw her feet to the outside. She had a very good day today. She mailed that card this afternoon. She wanted to know how it felt to walk to Lydia Street. That's farther than she's walked in 2 months. She made it OK but was a little tired.

We are going to put up two bushels of tomatoes tomorrow. Renn was in today with them. That's all he had so we have a very busy day to look forward to. They are $1.50 a bushel this year. That's pretty steep I think but I doubt if we get them any cheaper and Indiana tomatoes are better anyway. He's farming this year and not working at all. He said that rain we had yesterday was worth thousands. St. Joseph Orphans picnic was yesterday. It rained from about 7 to 8 pm, just when most people would be coming. So they served supper and after 8:30 people came in so they sold chicken for 35¢ and announced the picnic would be given over tonite. And tonite it rained harder than last night. Marge did take the kids but I feel like they rode to Shelby and Walnut and rode back, and she is now back at Lip's. It's too bad it had to rain on these days but this rain is really worth something. The Kosair Picnic is Saturday.

We all got a kick out of Joe's card. I thought it was that when I seen the envelope. Pop shook and Mom thought it was funny, too. I don't think you should ever think of going back in the whiskey business [*but should get a job as a reporter or writer of some kind*]. I bet the Commanding Officer didn't put his OK on that. Marge just came in. They made it out to the Orphanage and it was raining when they got there.
Goodnite, finish tomorrow.
[*Hermina*]

Louisville, Kentucky, **July 30**, Friday, 8:30

[*Dear Norb,*]

We got you letter this morning. I see you didn't get the antiseptic as yet. I can't understand this pen. Yesterday it wrote good. Why are all the Italian people flatfooted? Because they lost their heel. Carny said that yesterday. He also said Hitler won't die with his boot on. Both are good I think. Well, I'll finish with a pencil. Renn is going to bring Mom some Silkweed root. He said take a 6 inch root and put it in a pint of whiskey. It's good for Arthritis. He knows of a woman it helped. I guess Katie will try it.

That was really a storm last night. Wish we had the morning paper. It thundered and lighteningned [*sic*] from 7:30 to 11:30. I'll let you know how my maters [*tomatoes*] got when we get thru. Perhaps I better wait and see how they keep.

Good day, Corporal,

H.R.

Fort Jackson, South Carolina, **July 29**

Dear Mom and all,

Whew! It's hot tonight, very hot indeed. I'm sitting here with sweat just rolling off me. I won't, or I mean I didn't, get a chance to call. Sometimes it takes six hours to get a call through. We have to go to a lecture on "bombs" tonight. I sure can think of more interesting things to do.

Tell Mary I received her card and was very surprised. Give her my love and kisses XXX (Rationed). We won't go on maneuvers for a while yet. I don't know how soon but don't write me any card saying "So you're going on maneuvers." I may even get a furlough before we go. Who knows? There are clouds coming up and I can hear the roll of thunder. It sounds very good to me. I wish it would rain for a week. If it would, it would help anyway.

I see where you can buy all the coffee you want now and sugar will soon be the same. I understand there will also be more gasoline for civilian use. Well, that's something anyway. I didn't get to hear the President last night but I sure would have liked to. I guess he just repeated something we already knew.

I sent Joe his greeting card so I guess they have a wipe by this time anyway. My address is Cpl. N. A. Rawert, HQ. Co. 59 Sig Bn, Fort Jackson, SC. You need not put my ASN 55487644 on the envelope. Well, I don't guess I'll call because of the time it takes to get a call through so I'll say goodnight, good luck and God-bless you all.

As Always,

Norb

Fort Jackson, South Carolina, **August 1,** Sunday afternoon, 2 pm

Dear Mom and all,

Well, I was on guard last night but I was Cpl. of the guards and they don't have to do nothing but post the guards so I got my regular amount of beauty sleep. (I can use all of that I can get.)

Well, this morning I got up, went to church, came back and now I'm in the pink of conciliation. Waiting for 6:30 pm so I can go down to the PX and drink some beer. I can stand a few, believe me. It's very warm here today. There's no breeze blowing at all and that's when it really warms up down here, because there's usually a breeze. But the heat don't bother me much. It only makes me smell like a horse at the end of the day but we got beautiful showers and plenty of water. We get a 30-minute run twice a week now and that is when the sweat really pours off. We get that before breakfast. You couldn't run it on a full stomach.

I put in for a furlough. Whether I get it or not is doubtful, but keeped [*sic*] tuned to this station for further developments. (I doubt it very much myself.)

Well, the Italians don't seem to be able to make their mind up, but I think they will before very long. I never expected them to hold out this long. They're making it hard on themselves. There won't be no more "Govt" after this war is over. Well, I close for now and I'm,
As Always,
Norb

Louisville, Kentucky, **August 6**, Friday, 9:30 pm

Dear Norb,

Well, well, well, so you have the furlough approval. Glad to hear. Mom is tickled pink. She had to call Marge immediately and I know Elizzie is on the calling list. You know Norb, I am getting your birthday box ready. It seems as tho every time you get a furlough you're getting a box at the other end of the line. You know how it was at Easter, my boy. We haven't seen hide nor hair of Alma as yet. If you wrote her the same, perhaps we might get a buzz now.

Jr Hubbuch is home too. He said he's just an old Private, doesn't have any stripes at all. It made his dad and mother feel very bad but he's hopeful of getting them back in a few months. He and two more were acting smart with an airplane so that's the outcome. I wish you could meet him. I believe you would like him. I appreciate him coming to see me because I know he has to put himself out to do it.

Well, we're happy. The letter boosted my morale. So I'll scrub like hell on the bathroom. It should be gleaming white. Well, too-da-loo me brother and until we meet again next week, I hope, I hope.
Love, your dear, dear Sistah,
Hermina Mary Rawert

Norb was on furlough in Louisville for his 23rd birthday on August 17, 1943.

Aug 17, 1943

Norb at home on furlough for his 23rd birthday, August 17, 1943

Louisville, Kentucky, **August 27**, Friday, 11 am

Dear Norb,

Well, we are now having a swell shower. Oh my, it's almost too hot to live. Guess I better start mending my ways. We received your letter this morning. Always glad to hear, short and sweet or long and explanatory. Mom is like Annie Roonie. She's got the wim-woms [*sic*] because she really feels that you are going across in the very near future. I have always felt that way since you first wrote about your second furlough. We will be looking "forward" to getting your personal belongings now. Well, you will be the first to cross the ocean since your grandparents [*from Germany in 1870*]. I heard it was announced over the air this week for civilians not to use the train unless absolutely necessary for two weeks. They are going to move troops in mass numbers.

Mom is in her glee at present. Vernon and Jackie are doing swell. We have them all here. They aren't saying a word. Eleanor is trying to get Peg to quit crying. If she were mine, she'd have her butt blistered like Mom's foot was. She's rotten and nothing is ever enough for her.

If there is anything you would like for us to know, write it to Lip or Joe. Specify to tell us - but not Mom or Pop. We are OK. I hope. Am really very busy. Your namesake is always hungry.

Mom is sending two dollars for the postage as I imagine you are broke. Don't forget to have it insured. We sent radio thru American Railway Express. If there is anything you want, please let us know.

Love,

Porky

Fort Jackson, South Carolina, **August 28**

Dear Mom and All,

Well, I'll start off telling you about this insurance. (We're having a storm right now and the lightning just struck something about two blocks from here.) This insurance covers death. It doesn't have nothing to do with a pension. Now, just say I would get hurt - I would get the same amount of pension even if I had no insurance at all. I have $5,000 worth now and I was intending to get more when I heard the boat whistle blow. Of course, I don't know when it will start blowing. One thing it sure is cheap traveling. We can take out more insurance at any time. I was intending to take more out but I don't expect you to pay for it. I'll take care of that part of it myself.

Well, we're getting things in order to move out and we are definitely going to Tennessee. The Motor Pool (126 trucks) is going by truck and the rest are going by rail. I think we'll be on maneuvers about 6 weeks. It's really a very short maneuver. Ma[y]be I'll bump into Red Johnson if he's still there but that is very doubtful. The way we're going it will take us three days to get there. The Army always takes the long way around. We're short on drivers so I guess I'll drive a 2 ½-ton truck down. I'd rather do that than go by rail.

I never did get a chance to pack my radio and stuff yet so it may be a while before you receive it. I'll mail it the first chance I get.

It's really raining outside and it's cooled off a lot. It was so damn hot down here this afternoon you could hardly breathe. It's been pretty busy the last few days. I'll have to work tomorrow which is Sunday to get all my papers and books in order. I got about two days' work to do in one. I guess I should work tonight but I thought I'd take time out and write a few letters. I am a little behind (now don't get me wrong when I say I'm a "little behind"). You know the "Record" you sent? Well, there was 3¢ postage due on it. I can't understand it. It wasn't very heavy. But I did have 62¢ so I had plenty to defray all expenses.

I have to take a shower and shave yet tonight so I had better be getting at it. Oh, I also got a Tetanus shot, a Typhoid shot and a Vaccination today. My arms are full of holes. Three shots at one time is two too many. My left arm is pretty darn sore. Well, I say goodnight and hope it keeps raining.

As Always,

Norb V...-

Louisville, Kentucky, **August 29**, Sunday

Dear Norb,

Well, it's now 17 minutes of 8 o'clock and Pop and I are home. Mom is at Wessling's and Johnny and family went home. Been here since Wednesday and, oh my, I am still shaky. Poor Johnny. What a life! The baby had grand attention. Hermina sure worked and kept him spotless. Jackie is a sweet little fellow like a man. And such crying and carrying on.

Well, it's all over (dirty Irish) is that what you'd say? Now, I wonder if you are going to enjoy this note. Well, I worked from 7:00 to 6:00 pm yesterday, came home and washed dishes and about 8:00 I was finished, so I was wishing to be in the Army. We are all well, Norb. Elizabeth was up today and all are well. So is Joey and she went to the country.

Just want a laugh and Pop is talking all the while I'm writing. He is cutting the lawn and cleaning the schools. No fog in the hollow as yet. A few gurgles of beer and now he said he guesses we will get a letter from Norb tomorrow. So I don't have no news – only, enclosed find $2.00 for whatever you need it. Well, maybe for your birthday? You never did tell me. Well, Mom had a sailor boy loving her last Monday night - Maurice. Did you hear me talk of him? Well, I finally ended up being main attraction. I wish I could tell you all about it. It's better than the funnies. Maurice is a good guy, only was tipsy. Well, so now I will come to a close and say goodnite. Pray for me and I do likewise. God bless you. Hope the two bucks look good to you.

From your loving sister,

Mary Margaret Rawert

Louisville, Kentucky, **August 30**, Monday noon

Dear Norb,

Well, it's a beautiful day in Louisville. The air is cool and pleasant and the sun is pleasingly warm but to me it's like a lull after a storm, if you know what I mean. We sure had our hands full last week. Vernon and Jackie did fine. They left yesterday about 4 o'clock and I can't say I'm sorry, only I really miss the baby. He was the cutest thing and very good.

Mom collected some relics again yesterday. Helen Wessling asked her to come over to help assort some pictures. We got all of our pictures back including your First Communion picture. We really had a washday. Norbert can look at every bed and say I went there.

I just got a letter from Jr Hubbuch. He thinks he will be released from the Army by September 10, 1943, if he gets released. Shirley got a letter from her adopted soldier and he enclosed some German money. He's guarding German Prisoners of War. Did you get the money for the postage, hon?

Helen [*Wessling*] told Mom that 3 ½ years ago there were 10 in the house. Now, by September it will be three left. Her third one leaves for the Service in September. She will have the baby and he is as old as Milt. Milton registers at St. X today - if he didn't take another notion - but I really think he is going there.

Peg napped in her good dress and when she woke up she said just look how I inkled [*sic*] up my dress. Hilary starts to school September 7. Milt has another pup. It's a bull like Lee's dog, Jack. That dog is exactly like Snookie. He takes 'em all on and last night he must of taken on an elephant. He's really chewed up. I seen Zip's brother and he told me he's in England and OK.

Love from

Porky

Louisville, Kentucky, **August 31**, Tuesday, 3 pm

Dear Norb,

Well, I have just finished ironing. We sure had a heck of a lot this week. It's a very warm day but the basement is right cool, which I sure appreciate. We are OK. I "heerd" you might be sent to Memphis, Tennessee on maneuvers. You'll be on the Arkansas border. I don't think you'll be much closer home, or will you? Huh?

Cousin Ben Spoelker was here today. We had a "right nice" chat. You know, he was here several hours, for Mom and him were reminiscing about their childhood days and he was talking about the "black snake," a strap his daddy used on them and hell it didn't hurt 'em at all. It did the work even if they were uncomfortable for a little while. Afterward, neither he nor Mom liked how the parents bring up kids these days. So you can see they enjoyed one another's conversation. He looks better than he has in years. He felt like hell until they bought this place. Then they had to get busy. Now he's feeling good. They moved in about a month ago and like it fine. He said it wasn't anything to be done to the inside except the usual cleaning. But the outside, they had too much shrubbery, so he took them down. Bernard [*Fr. Spoelker*] is moved. It's still farther away but he has a newly put up church but not many parishioners. He said hardly anyone knows there's a church there. He says three Masses on Sunday and is stationed at a Hospital Base. There's a new law now that you must be in a year before you can get a higher commission. Bernard's Commanding Officer put in for a Captain Commission for him, so he was told the new law went into effect two days before. So, by Thanksgiving, he's expecting a promotion then. Amen!

I'm inclosing a clipping. Pop just chuckled when I read it to him. I thought it was funny. They must come from a fighting Irish family. BEWARE [*reference to Alma*]. Maurice Slattery was here last week one night. He was full of bourbon, I think I told you, and all what he wanted to do was make love to [*make eyes at or flirt with*] Marge. He'd snap me real short. I must of been too big of a bundle of charm. I helped the course along by singing, "Put your Arms Around Me Honey." If you write just a few words to Marge, say this, "Yum, Yum, What a Chum!" He was like Russell with eenie, meenie...Amen. We got a bushel of tomatoes from Renn, Ketchups for $1.25 a bushel. So far, we cannot get a hold of beans. We intend to put up a bushel but if we don't get rain, we don't get beans.

We haven't heard from you this week. According to Mom, vacations are furloughs.

Katsy hates to think of school. She "dust hates it." She don't know what she could do. She takes after Moody, keeps on the move always. It's really hot today. We are having some of the biggest tomatoes on our vines yet we are having rambling tomatoes. This one stock is entwined around the butterbeans and is in blossom over the fence. It also has some tomatoes hanging on the "wrong side of the fence."

Mr. Redle wants to travel about again in his chuck-chuck [*sic*] but I don't think they will let him.

Your godchild is very wise. Mrs. Russell gave Vernon some pennies Sunday and told him to count to ten and then she would quit [*giving them to him*]. He counted to 9. She gave him the 10th one but he quit on 9 thinking he would profit from that. Wasn't dumb.

Hoping to hear. Love from all,

Hot Porky

Louisville, Kentucky, **September 1**

Dear Uncle Norbe,

Just a few lines to let you know that I haven't forgotten you. First, I want to tell you that I finally paid for my bicycle. I paid for it myself. It cost me $18.00. I had saved up $25.00. Mother said it was the only way I could get one, so I paid for it myself. Oh! It is also 2nd handed. If I got a new one, I would have to swear my life away. You also need a permit so I just got a 2nd handed one. Well, I guess that is enough about the bicycle.

Well, how have you been these days? Alright, I guess. Ma [*Marge*] is making a dress and also a petticoat. I am up at Mommy's writing this letter. It started to rain but it didn't rain after all. How is the weather where you are? Well, school is going to start September 7 and I don't like it a bit. We have to register tomorrow. Milton and Mother went down at St. X today. Mother went to register Milton. The brother Mother was talking to asked her what was Milton's average. Mother said 77%. He said don't you think he could have done better than that? Mother said that of course he could. The Brother said, "I wonder why people think we got a 6 foot, 210 pounds behind the desk for." He meant the Head Brother I think. Weren't the Brothers hard on you at St. X? Mother thinks Mary Catherine [*Katsy*] is going to cry when she has to go back to school. Mary C. hates it. Well, I don't like it neither.

My adopted soldier, Corporal H.J. Goeing sent me some German money. You see, he guards German prisoners from Africa. We are listening to the news now. It is thundering again so it might rain after all. I hope it does. Well, I guess I'd better close for now. I will write soon.

I remain,

Shirley

Louisville, Kentucky, **September 1**, Wednesday, 9 pm

Dear Norb,

Well, your nephew is definitely a freshman at St. X. He registered today. Lip went with him. The Brothers said to him, or rather, asked him what his general average was. He said 77. They asked, "Don't you think you could do better than that?" Lip said, "I know he could." He said, "Why do you think we have 6 foot, 230 lbs. behind the desk for?" The Parochial school kids register tomorrow.

So you know positively you are going to Tennessee? That's fine. When you go to Tennessee what part of Tenn. will it be? We were talking about hopping a train if you are going to be that close. I read that Insurance paper over, but for anything that happened last week, excuse us dear. Vernon and Jackie are mending swell, playing around again but last week I just called them [*Silent*] Henry's. They began to talk Sunday.

I made 6 quarts of chili sauce today and the smell is still lingering in the house. Tain't bad. Would you like a pint (of chili sauce, I mean) and I mean it. After this, address Joe as "Blister." He is painting on the outside now. Feature Joe doing that! Marriage license does strange things.

I just heard about Doc and his wife about 2 weeks ago and I believe she is back again as her oldest boy is there. And she answered the phone Friday. If things were as I heard, I think she has guts. Did you get the two bucks Mom sent? I think she sent them the same time The Record was sent. So, it cost you 3¢. Now you have 59¢ left, or do you? You're a poor boy and I mean it.

Pop just got a can [*pail*] of beer and Joe helped down it, so now Joe bought a can. I bet we'll get quite a few pretty tunes and some not so pretty. So, you got your three shots. By this time, I suppose your soreness is past [*sic*] over. You'll be driving a truck. Could you drive by home, do you think? That was a boresome question, wasn't it? On your way to Tennessee, send some cards on your way if you can. You know Mom likes cards, scenic cards. Mom isn't so good on the hoof this week, even if she was on her toes last week. I think it was just too, too much for her. Did I tell you Mom "dreamt" last week she was a dancer and young? Well, she said she did but she never tied any more "jingles" bells on dogs.

Do you remember that policeman by the name of Bryant that lived downstairs from Joey? Well, he was killed. I am enclosing the account of it.

We have been having some hot days. It lightninged [*sic*] and thundered but still we never got any rain, but the days have reminded you of fall. The nights are nicer. Well, I'll wait til "tomorrow day" to finish this. Goodnite and sleep tight.
Tired Porky

Continued the next morning, **September 2**

Good morning dear brother and how are you this gloomy morning? We had a good rain last night. It was lightning at 7:00 and started to pour at 10:15, and rained heavy and light up to 2:00 am. The sky promises of more. The grass is beginning to green up since last week, but where Joey goes to the country and in Horse Cave, everything is dried up. They haven't a thing to can. They are hauling water out for the stock. I hope this was an all-over rain. Hain't got no more news. So, good day, Corporal

[*Hermina*]

Louisville, Kentucky, **September 3**, Friday, 9 pm

Dear Norb,

Did you try to call at 8:30 tonite? Shirley answered the phone and the operator told her to hold the phone, a long distance call was coming thru and nothing happened. We were happy and excited about nothing.

Schieman got a 530 pound [*piece of*] beef today. That's something to write about. Shirley saw a whole "cow body" go in at Hick's at Shelby and Burnett. We sure did laugh. We haven't heard since Wednesday, then we received a "my size" [*large*] letter from you. I don't know if Larny is in Tennessee yet or not. Clarence leaves Monday.

Well, all the Muth's Sweets are registered. Milt was bored when he got home. He decided he didn't want to go to school. He wants a working permit. I believe Lip might have a time with him. Katsy has Sr. Rose. She taught Betsy. If Katsy was as good as Betsy, she would make a wonderful student. She asked how old she was, Katsy said "Tix", and she was born November "port" (fourth). Sr. Rose asked Lip and Moody's names and she said "Lit-a-budt" [*Elizabeth*] and Leo. She got a kick out of hearing her, even if she might be a headache later on. Margie liked the Sisters' dresses [Ursuline order habits] but don't know why they all wear rain capes.

When Lip was in at St. X she seen Brother Noel, in fact that's who she had to see. She asked him if he knew you. Oh yes, he said, I believe he was in the 1938 class or around that. He asked how you were. Lip told him all. He said tell me why in the world didn't Norb come to see me? Lip said she didn't know. He said, well, some boys come and some don't. We always get a kick out of seeing them and really appreciate their coming. Lip put in an excuse you were sick half your furlough - she didn't know you went down there. Lip liked him. Perhaps you could congratulate him on his promotion and tell him maybe someday he might be "Mother-General" of the Order. He told Lip to tell you that on your next furlough to be sure and come and see him. Lip said they have a boy by the name of White, framed in black. He was killed in this war. It's hanging up in the corridor someplace. Do you know him?

Could you find time to write Milt some words of encouragement? Will say goodnite and finish tomorrow.

[*Hermina*]

Louisville, Kentucky, **September 4**

Dear Norb,

Your last farewell words to me was "Do you go to the Sacraments?" Well, that should be

a very sincere question. I hope you go more often than you went at home. There's nothing makes you feel nearer to God than a good Confession and Holy Communion. I hope that you pray for peace. I hope that you experent [*experienced*] that every time you went. I know I do. Try to go often and pray for peace. I thought of the words you said to me so often and made up my mind to write you about it. I am not feeling so well this week but I will get alright soon again. Goodbye and God bless you. Next time I will write more.
Mother

Fort Jackson, South Carolina, **September 3**

Dear Mom and all,

We've been so damn busy lately that I haven't had a chance to do hardly anything. We've been working until 10:30 nearly every night getting things ready to move for a while. I imagine it will be for about two months.

I received those 4 bucks but I still haven't had a chance to get my things together to mail. I hope to get them packed up over Sunday. We ought to be off then. It's really been pretty warm down here but we did have some rain so it cooled off a little.

So, Zip landed in England. Well, good for him. I'd like to land in England myself, just to see what the old place looked like, "by Jove," so I could compare it with Berlin. The headlines said today "ITALY INVADED," which was very, very excellent news. The sparks will really begin to fly now. I hope. The only thing is that I don't trust those damn Russians and I don't think anyone else will about two years from now. If I had my way (ha, ha) there would be a hell of a lot more pressure on the Japs because we'll be alone after this war is over if we depend on England, or so I think. Well, we'll wait to decide that. Well, the lights are going out so good night.
As Always,
Norb

Louisville, Kentucky, **September 4,** Saturday, 8:15

Dear Norb,

I just heard Frank Sinatra on the Hit Parade sing "I Heard You Cried Last Night." He can't hold Bing's [*Crosby*] hat. Give me boop, boop, Bing. Say, what about those pictures you had taken and promised to send home in your helmet, fatigue suit and leggings? Or have you forgotten so soon?

I didn't think I'd have much to write about but I want to ask you to get this war over in a hurry or soon, so you can help keep peace on the home front. Tonite about 6:00, a man ordered the conductor to stop at a corner where the car doesn't stop. The car stopped at Mulberry and Texas. They say he started to fight the conductor so the conductor hit him in the head with a crank. They taken him in Kendrick's. It held up four cars and I bet three hundred people gathered there. Last night a man was nearly disemboweled at Shelby and

Camp in a streetcar too. A man got on the streetcar after he spied a man with his wife on the car, so he let the man have it. Sounds bad, doesn't it?

Now, this is really something to write about, brother. Mom went to Huelsman's two times today to get Pop three quarts of beer so he would have some on Labor Day. Don't you think that is true love at nearly seventy years old? It was her first time in a beer parlor - the first time they never had any. Pop had to work late and they're usually out, so on his way home he got three. We'll have beer anyway. (Mom really got four, but putting one in reserve, Aunt Annie style.) Will say goodnight and remember those pictures, those pictures, those pictures, pictures, pictures.

Porky

With the following letter on September 6, Norb announced that his new address was HQ Co. 59th Signal Battalion in Nashville, Tennessee where he was to go on Maneuvers for about 5 weeks. However, his first letter from Nashville was not until October 5. He arrived back on Fort Jackson on November 10.

Fort Jackson, South Carolina, **September 5**

Dear Mom & All,

Hi 'Ya All.' I'm pretty damn tired myself but other than that & having a hell of a good appetite, I'm OK. We're here in Tenn. waiting for maneuvers to get going. I can see five weeks of work ahead and ma[y]be more. It gets cold as hell here. Last night I found that out but I guess it's time for that. We only have three blankets too, and that ain't much because you use one to lay on. This morning when I got up, I was so cold I felt like a dog shitting peach seeds. Well, that's all for now but I may need a few things later on. You can't get a damn thing down here. My address is HQ. Co. 59 Signal Battalion, APO# 402-ASN-35487644, Nashville, Tennessee.

As Always,

Norb

Louisville, Kentucky, **September 6**, Monday, Labor Day, 8:30 pm

Dear Norb (scribbles),

Well, dot your 'x' and cross your 'i.' That's the latest in your address now. At least, that's the way your letter came through. I almost had to take it to the bank to get a handwriting expert to tell us but never the less it makes a letter more interesting when you must stop and ponder a while. We appreciate scribbles anytime. We are OK. From your letter, you must be working your "little behind" off and soon you will be moving. Well, I'm hoping you get to come home my "deah," if it's possible. Say, you must really think the US will get Greta Garbo's wish, but don't want it: "I vant to be alone." I don't trust the Reds either but I believe England will be OK because she has quite a bit of interest in the Far East territory such as Hong Kong, etc. We'll just have to wait and see what happens and be glad if we live to tell about it.

Bernard Hollkamp leaves today as does Clarence Johnson. I don't know if Larny Johnson is in Tennessee or not. Norbert Wafzig is home on furlough.

I'm putting 6 cents on the envelope now. You should have a balance of more than 59 cents if you have to pay additional. Do you think you will be made Sergeant before you go on maneuvers? Or after? Huh?? Doris Heinz Beyer has a 6 ½-pound girl. Don't work too hard, my deah.

Love,

Hermina

Fort Jackson, South Carolina, **September 7**

Dear Mom and all,

Well, so they took old Clarence Johnson in the Army of the United States. Well, well, well. Behind every dark cloud, there's a silver lining. I can't get hold of those pictures as yet because the guy who took them is not here right now, but as soon as I can, I'll see what I can do.

Oh boy, but it's hot. It really is. Perspiration is just running down my back. Anyone who says it don't get damn hot in SC is a damn liar. It's too hot to work but, speaking of work, we have to work tonight. Well, ma[y]be we won't pull out of here before the 22nd. You hear so many rumors you don't know what to believe. I still haven't had a chance to mail my radio home. I'm going to try and send it this week if I can get something to mail it in. Well, I'm going to close for now. Write more later.

As Always,

Norb

Louisville, Kentucky, **September 7**, Tuesday, 8:30 pm, 56°

Dear Norb,

Brrr, Brrr, we got a gas burner going, but it's really a very pleasant relief. Yesterday it rained practically all day, which was very good. The Times said the last Tater crop is saved, at least in some sections. The farmers were packing water for about a month. Today is a day when you feel like you want to keep looking at the sky and wish you had a dress just like it. It's a heavenly day.

That train wreck yesterday must have been terrible. They have never heard from Freddy Keller as yet. Another boy from out this way was on the same ship with him. A Summershein boy - he said the part Freddy was on was blew to bits. They were all forced into sea but he hasn't heard or seen anything of him since. He said miracles happen. It could be he's still alive.

Today Milt starts at St. X. I'm anxious to hear him tell it, and Milt would like a baby brother just like Norb H. He said since he seen him, Margie looks so big. Whatta Milt! Pop's ambition or desire is to go to Europe after the war. He said he'd given anything to see the lights there. I think he ought to join the Army.

Talk about waiting. Since the first week in June, we are waiting for a gasket for the refrigerator. We sent our fan and sewing machine motor about the same time. Well, that was never fixed. Pop went and got it and for three weeks we're waiting for a repairman for the wash machine. They promised to come today. Too da loo for now.

Continued later in the evening:

Good news. We got our "Katie's Glory" [*washing machine*] fixed. We're OK. Marge and Ann are going in down and are going to mail this.
Goodbye, good luck,
[*Hermina*]

Louisville, Kentucky, **September 8**, Wednesday, 8:20 pm
Dear Norb,

How are you all? Whooping it up tonight? "Italy Surrenders Unconditionally!" What news! Mom and I were listening to 'Living Can Be Fun.' It succeeds 'Breakfast at Sardi's,' when they interrupted the program. My, you couldn't hardly believe it. We had a parade to open up the 3rd Bond Drive at 1:00 pm today. According to a Post Exchange manager at Ft. Knox, he said they would make enough noise in Ft. Knox to celebrate the good news, that it could be heard in Louisville. Tell us how you all "took the news." I am inclosing a clipping which was in tonite's paper - a letter of Dr. Atherton to his brother. We are listening to the war bond drive program from 8 to 9. The President certainly was good. Everybody was. Do you think you'll get to England to compare it with Berlin? As you thought or wished last week.

I got a letter from Norb Hollkamp. Lou & Bernard visited him the week before last. Now, again, did you send those pictures of yourself as a fighting man, my dear?

Lee isn't working as yet. Talk about the life of Riley. I think he can count the minutes he worked this year. I think it would be good for him if he'd feel the sole of a boot.

Milt thinks he has to start using more Brilliantine [*hair pomade that made hair manageable and shiny*] on his hair. Lip's wondering if St. X has that effect on him so soon. They had to go in a body today to the Cathedral. He's wondering what church he'll belong to now. He goes to Bernie's, mops up his kitchen, and starts supper for him. He's really dizzy.

This is a good one - Watkins was there [*at Lip's*] and all the kids came bursting home from school. He told Lip he couldn't understand how she could stand all that noise. Milt said I think she can put up with the noise I make as well as she could put up with a drunken slop like you. Lip was out of the room then but Shirley said she hear every word he said.

Margie had her first experience of eating out. Betsy and Margie went to Taystee's for a frosted malted. Margie didn't like it and got some on her hands. Betsy takes some paper napkins and wipes her hands good, but she was still sticky, so in a loud voice she said to Betsy, "Get me some more toilet paper Betsy, I'm still sticky!" Betsy was so tickled. They all were who heard her.

Pop is sorry all 3¢ cigars are now 5¢. Well, this is all for tonite. Well, with one down and two to go, how long do you think the war will last? Goodnite and don't forget your pictures. Pesty, huh?

Pesty Porky

Continued, Thursday noon, **September 9**

Well, that's all you hear is the Italian Surrender. I wonder how it feels to be in "Reversia." No news today except the thermometer reads 56° at 9:00 am. It's a heavenly day but it is going towards fall you can tell by the crackle in the leaves. It's a day you feel like you can get the smell of the classrooms. Mom feels like we'll get two letters. She feels a little lost without them, but we understand, or at least think you are a very busy man if you work till 10:30.

Did you have the Bellyache anymore and how does that apron fit, or do, or answer the purpose? We want to make a few more if they are convenient and satisfactory.

Those photos!

Loads of ...., Love,

Porky V...-

Fort Jackson, South Carolina, **September 9**

Dear Mom and all,

Hain't got much to say except it's still hotter than hell and we're just waiting to see what's going to happen. Well, what do you think? The old grease boys in Italy finally gave up and threw in their chips. Well, it's pretty good news anyway.

I still haven't mailed that stuff home, so don't look for it for a while. Just for your information. Yes! That was Edwin P. Kaiser of Ash Street that is getting married. He was going to get married but I didn't know just when. More power to him.

Well, Mom, the lights are just about ready to go out, and we have a 30 minute run in the morning at 5:30 so I had better close now. Good night and good luck etc. I am,

As Always,

Norb

Louisville, Kentucky, **September 10**, Friday, 8:30 pm

Dear Norb,

Well, we received your letter today. So you don't think you'll pull out until the 22nd. I am listening to 'People are Funny' [*hosted by Art Baker until October 1, 1943 when Art Linkletter took over*] and it is funny. They sang "By the Light of the Silvery Moon." So you still sing the boys awake? The latest news at the Muth's house is Milt took his first bath voluntarily, believe it or not, and he asked Lip if he looked clean and neat before he went to school today. Goodnite, will finish tomorrow day. Oh, yeah, Kuchens Bodner is on maneuvers in Tennessee.

Continued, **September 11**, Saturday, 4pm: Greetings from the Gateway to the South under blankets and no horse blankets either, just blankets and caterpillars. Boy, they are lousy. My, my. Would you have time to answer this - that is, would you want us to send you a box so you could send us your radio? My dear, couldn't you call long distance and reverse the charges if you think that would go quicker. Anyhow, try to call before you leave for Tennessee, no kidding.

Boy, it sounds like the Italians are really in Soup. Mary said some think they got out of it too quick. That shows how much she knows.

I gave the clock a good cleaning yesterday with silver cream and took all the things off. It really looks right smart pretty. I got all the things but I can't get those strings in position, but never tried too hard. Pop is getting ready to go so will mail this.

Hoping to get a nice long letter from you. You know - the kind you always write where you flatter the whole family (imagine a Rawert dishing out sweet nothings to another Rawert!).

Renn said the hot weather kept the potato vines from growing. Now that we had some rain, and the days are considerably warm and the nites cool, that will cause the potatoes to grow larger. Everything will go to the seed instead of the vines.

Good day Corporal. Good day. Be a good boy.

H.R.

Louisville, Kentucky, **September 12**, Sunday, 5:40 pm

Dear Norb,

Well, this is Sunday and a little warmer which we all appreciated. We sat on the porch the first time in about ten days. Joe and Huber and Moody went fishing, at least they went to Fairfield to go fishing. When they got there, the Lake was dried up. Joe said it is normally about 35 feet deep. Now it is about 2 feet right in the center and dead fish laying all around. He said the farmers saved all they could and stocked their own places in an effort to save all they could. Amen.

I heard that in Camp Breckenridge, KY they have German Prisoners of War. Fourteen and fifteen years old. I wonder if that is true. Do you all have prisoners there?

Anna Heitkemper and Rose Bader was at Mary's for dinner and does Ann look bad. My! So many think she has cancer. She is doctoring for gall bladder trouble but she's too weak to walk to and from from church. She's going to try and make it back to Mobile.

Jerry Israel from Lydia Street was awarded the Purple Heart. They haven't heard from

Freddy Keller as yet. Milt finally decided to come up and have his picture taken. We still were reserving one from the film we had when you were here. If they get food, we'll send them providing you send us your mug in your "work outfit." I hope you have seen that "feller" by this time. Well, Hilary started to school and on the 2nd day he ripped a new pair of pants. Jackie said, "Mother I sure was glad he had underwear on."

I thought I had a lot to write about but I seem blankety blank. So will finish tomorrow. Good day Corporal. When will it be Sergeant?

Continued, 7:00 pm:

Well, I had to tell you this. Mrs. Threedouble was talking to Nickie next door. She asked him how "Duck" was [*in a German accent for Doug*]. They named the new baby John Douglas and call him Doug for short. I think that's one "Duck" that won't quack, but he might squeak a lot.

They came around from St. Elizabeth for the boys' addresses for Xmas gifts. They have 420 names turned in but there are some that are not turned in as yet. Have you heard from Zip lately? Nite!

[*Hermina*]

Fort Jackson, South Carolina, **September 12**

Dear Mom and all,

Howdy folks, howdy. How are you all? It's turned pretty cool here also. In fact, I used a blanket last night and it wasn't any too warm with just one. I think ma[y]be I need just a little more alcohol in my blood. I've only had about five bottles of beer all week and that ain't much, especially the military beer. It's pretty damn weak.

Well, those Italians finally threw in their chips. Well, no one said anything about it here. Someone came in and announced it in the mess hall and there was no more to it than of someone would have said Mrs. O'Leary's dog had pups. It's just one of those things that everyone expected to happen in the near future.

Dr. or Captain Atherton seems to be doing alright for himself. I wouldn't mind having a meal like that myself, but I don't know about eating chicken with one hand. Rather a problem, I would say.

So, Milt is going to St. X. Well, I don't think he will go for it so well after the first 4 months, but I hope he does. That Brother Noel is quite some guy - pretty tough if he wants to be.

Yeah, the apron works OK except the strings are a little too short. They should be long enough so you can tie them in the front.

It is still undecided as to whether we move out of here on the 17th or not. Sometimes I wonder if we will or not. I got a letter from Red Johnson yesterday and he said they're packed and ready to move out of the maneuver to Camp Breckenridge, KY. He is supposed to get a furlough the 15th of this month, so ma[y]be the maneuvers are over in Tennessee unless they just jerked his outfit out of the maneuvers. They do that sometimes and replace it with another, or it could be that they will start a new maneuver. I wished the hell I knew.

Did I understand you when you said that Wafzig is here at Ft. Jackson? I thought he was in the same unit Red Johnson was in, but I don't guess he could be if he's home on furlough. I think I know that Summershein that was at the same ship with Fred Keller, I think his first name is Joe. I went to school with him also.

Ha, ha, ha, you can just tell Pop that they have a recruiting station in the Post Office ma[y]be he could get in the Army if he tried, but he would have to take all those exercises and a 30-minute run which we get over once a week. It's very bad when that 30-minute run falls on Monday. I don't know why but some of the boys just don't seem to be able to run so well on Monday mornings. They say they develop a certain thump in their heads and also a sick stomach.

I went to a football game last night but the 59th was beat. They played some college here in SC. We were outclassed just a little but I enjoyed it quite a bit. That's the first football game I've seen for a hell of a long time.

Well, I got my radio packed and ready for shipment just as soon as I can get to the Post to mail it. I also have a bunch of letters in there. It just served the purpose. You will also find some of those rations I was telling you about. I thought you might like to see what the army calls a breakfast, dinner and supper when you're in the field. They're alright for just a couple of days, but when you have to eat it then for a week straight, they get tiresome. The boys had to eat them for a week while I was on furlough and they all had their tongues hanging out for a good meal and I can understand why. Well, I guess I had better close before I get the writing cramps, so I'll say so long and remain,

As Always,
Norb

Louisville, Kentucky, **September 13**, Monday, 11 am
[*Dear Norb,*]

Just finished washing. We received your letter this morning and must say they are getting more interesting (to dope out). Well, we have Italy but still must fight for it. No wonder they say everything is fair in love and war. I imagine Hitler will protect Rome, just like he protected the Checks [*Czeks*].

We can't imagine it being so hot there, for it's really cool. We can't stand the windows and doors open and be comfortable. The beer has been holding out this week. As you know, it is cool, a sure sign, and the Gov't says no more beer can be made than what has been made lately. Well, that's OK. I think everybody got a little bit.

Mr. Johnson closes from 12 to 2 now. That Schaefer boy is home on furlough. His mother told Mary that they told the Soldier not to use the trains for traveling. I wonder if something isn't twisted there.

Well, I leave you with this thought. How iss [*sic*] Duck? Goodbye me brudder. The best scribble the US Army has ever known. Keep up the good work, kid.

Bye.

Hermina

Louisville, Kentucky, **September 14**, Tuesday, 8 pm

Dear Brother,

Did I acknowledge your letter of yesterday? If not, here is acknowledging it honey. I am sending you some cards when you're on that maneuver business but letters are always appreciated. You think the same, yes? Milton is taking school serious, buckling down to study periods at home.

Mom got her new bonnet and it's a right nice affair. Black felt and nifty looking. $4.00 please. It has warmed up quite a bit today. We had a good thunderstorm last night of which we were grateful. I suppose you've seen where the Horse Show will be given at Churchill Downs for the benefit of the Nichols General Hospital. I heard that George Heitkemper is coming home for a furlough from Kodiak, Alaska. Gabriel Heatter [*radio news announcer*] is just telling of the German occupation at Rome. Isn't that terrible. It came over they are mounting guns at St. Peter's Cathedral in Rome.

Well, Chester Lander at work [*Hubbuch's*] got his blood test. It doesn't seem as if they are waiting for Congress. I know of four married men that has been examined and all has kids but one. That hurts but you can't let that stand in the way of winning this war I think. Some think it's so terrible.

Omar Hollkamp comes home sometime next month with a medical discharge. I wonder if Norbert will get to come too. I just read about a half column of news carried by the Indianapolis paper on the Ruby Adams family. They surely are patriotic. Clifton, 22, has been promoted to 1st Lt. Some time ago he was in the Battle for Sicily and has received a Meritorious Award. (They are all in the Air Corp). Sgt. Herbert, 26, is with the ground crew at Pocatello, Idaho. He has a home for himself. Carl, 25, is in training for a Pilot. I forgot where he is, but is in the US. J.O., age 23, was in North Carolina but left for an embarkation point some time ago. They think he is over there by this time. Seaman First Class, thin-twin Paul, 19 - he's the only one in the Navy, is in Australia. Papa Adams, Gladys (21) and Pauline (19) are doing defense work and Louise (15) is in High School and helping Mamma. Mrs. Russell heard Gladys and Pauline are taking private flying lessons. Amen. Well, Mom wants to write so will say goodnite Cpl. Goodnite.

H.R.

Continued by Mommy:

Dear Norb, (EX-LAX WEATHER) [*shitty*] censored.

Well, Norb the weather is just rite, not too warm, not too cold, 70 degrees. I hope that the weather will be cooler in SC. Papa is going after a growler. Papa said Hueltsman said he had plenty of beer now. Had a barrel left from last week. Sounds good to Papa.

It came over the radio that the Germans were in Rome. I hope that Hitler won't do his dirty work and get by with it. We all have to pray more and hope in the Lord. I will write some other time and close with your farewell words. Did you go to the Sacraments? I went the first Friday and while I was kneeling at the Communion railing, I prayed for you. I hope you will do the same for us. God bless you.
Mother

Fort Jackson, South Carolina, **September 14**

Dear Mom and all,

I guess by this time you have received my package. If not, it should be there by tomorrow. I sent it by Railway Express, so it may take just a little longer. Well, a new order came through that we will remain here till about Oct. 3 so I guess we will be here till then. It's cool here at night, but it's still warm during the day. In fact it's hot during the day but it's good sleeping anyway. Well, I don't know very much tonight. My mind is blank and it's just about time for beer call (that's a new call they have in the Army) so I will close and have a few beers. Good night and good luck.
As Always,
Norb

Louisville, Kentucky, **September 15**, Tuesday, 9:30 pm

Dear Norb,

Well, I just tried to get you on the phone about 1 ½ hours ago. Mom was so anxious to talk to you before you went on maneuvers. Well, we all were anxious. Lip was here but she went home. They called me back about 10 minutes ago and said the circuits were still busy. We received your "Jumbo" letter. It isn't only small things that come in little packages? Do you think you might leave by the 17ᵗʰ? Well, you only think when you're in the army "anyha."

Yep, Kaiser gets married the 22ⁿᵈ. I think I'll send him a garbage can. I believe he's still putting on weight. It's a Maier girl and her daddy runs a saloon, Mrs. Zipperle was telling me. Mrs. Zip says that Zip has been in England two months now. Today he is in the Army 26 months so he left July 15, 1941. Just another time as long as you have been. You can't think it was that long. She said she heard from him twice and it's 4 weeks since she last heard so she's at an anxious standpoint. When he was home on furlough, he got notice the next day he arrived back at Camp that they were leaving. He said he wrote a dozen letters telling her he was going over but couldn't get the gumption to send them, so he said 'well this letter must serve the purpose. I made up my mind to send it and break the news to you.' He said they asked for two Officers to volunteer for overseas duty and none did so all the eligible names were dropped in a hat and two dropped out. His was one of the two. He said eventually they would all be moving so now was as good a time as any. She said she bought him a watch last year and it never did good so she bought him a Service Man shock proof and sent it to him. Told him to return old watch in same box. So she received that three weeks ago, but no acknowledgment as yet. Amen.

There is a Carnival going on for 6 days at Preston and Woodbine Street and you can hear those spielers here, and sometimes make out just what they're singing.

Milton shovels 'manure' for Bernie on the way to school and does his marketing for him. All for the sake of looking at that pony. Milt likes three uncles, he told Lip (beware buttons) and you're on the top of the list. Katsy had school fever and Sister sent her home. Lip put her to bed, so around noon she said, "Mother you know how I get so sick in my stomach when I sink (think) of Margie?" "Why?" asked Lip. "I sink [think] she maybe she wants me to play with her." Lip said it wasn't a darn thing wrong with her.

Writing paper is very high I think, so I bought this stuff [*lined tablet paper*]. You're just like the Army. Why don't you write on both sides? Bossy huh? Well, goodnite brother, will finish tomorrow. Goodnite.
Hermina

Continued, 10:12 pm:

The operator said it would be 15 minutes before they get you at the phone.

Louisville, Kentucky, **September 15**, Thursday, 8:30 pm

Dear Norb,

Well, we did hear your dear, sweet, "snotty" voice last nite. I'll tell you I had so much to say but when you were there, I just forgot some, I guess. I tried since after 8 o'clock to get you so you lose some enthusiasm. Sorry to hear of your cold. It sounds like a honey. "Snuve [*sic*] up." Marge got two silk handkerchiefs from Yum Yum [*Maurice*]. I'm teasing her quite a bit. Those cards I'm sending you...send Mary one of them - the one where it says I'm a little behind. You never send her kisses anymore.

We finally got somebody to fix up the house. He does the work for Mrs. Madden's mother. It's a time and material job and it needs plenty fixing up. He charges $1.25 per hour. After you get on maneuvers, we will send you a box to help out that K-Rations.

The news is a little more encouraging this morning. Donaldson [*baker*] says that he thinks this is Germany's last time to show she can show strength. Hope he's right. I'm sending an aspirin for that cold. Will say goodbye Cpl. and call us up sometimes. It's more thrilling. Reverse the charges. Call us when you get in Tenn. if you can.
[*Hermina*]

Louisville, Kentucky, **September 16**, Thursday

Dear Norb,

By this time, you know we have received the radio, etc., etc., etc., and did I get into some of my old letters. My, how stale some sound. I read about five. But what we can't understand is how that one letter reached you that Mom sent giving the account of Jr Wessling's death. She had it addressed up in the left-hand corner like this: PFC, US Army, Howard Hotel, 1414 Hertel St., Kansas City, Mo. She never had your name on it, but on the back, she had hers. So you must have received it through that. Do you remember? Mom was pleased with the Scenic Souvenir Folder. Tanks! [*sic*]. I counted the letters, 214 in all, including the telegrams. We were so shocked to see all of them, child. We thought you burnt them as soon as they were consumed.

I am listening to Bing the first time in months and months. The K-Rations are being saved for Pop tonite. Those are hard looking cookies. Are they hard tack? I imagine they are. Pop won't want that I'm sure. We got some candy that I'm ready to send Bill Hollkamp for Xmas. I hope you will remember to answer this. Did any outside remember you last Xmas that we could send to this year? Did Spoelker's send you anything? Mrs. Russell sent a buck and so did Mary. Am I right?

This is a good one on Russell. He came in very early yesterday afternoon, very well preserved, so he fell asleep on the cot. She came in with a small bundle under her arm. He was busy shaving. He had on a clean white shirt and getting ready to go to work. He thought she had her lunch. He said Mary go over and tell Marge and Ann I'm late this morning. Was it Rye or Gin?

When did you send this radio? We got it this afternoon, Thursday Sep. 16, 2 pm. Today is Milt's birthday. Now he can work with a permit. Don't that sound awful? Clarksdale said he could fix it by doing something to the circuits. Do you want us to send it back to you?

No more news dear, so Goodnite. I forgot to send the aspirin and how is that cold honey? Is it cool there? It's really cool here. Can't sit outside.

Love,

H.R.

Louisville, Kentucky, **September 17**, Friday, 8:30 pm, 44°

Dear Norb,

Well, I will start off about those K-Rations. Pop liked the supper can of meat. He ate it and liked it. I said <u>dog</u> food the first nibble I took, but I didn't think it was so bad. Them [*sic*] hard tack ain't nothing to brag about, phooey no. I had the honor of drinking nearly all the Breakfast coffee. Boy that's swell. Better than we can get. That candy ain't worth a damn either. Or the fruit roll. I think that fruit roll must have a laxative effect. Marge and I taken a piece about as big as a thimble. It sort of gripped me but no other effects, thank you. The chocolate candy tasted stale. We all enjoyed relly, relly [*sic*] much. It was the first time any of us seen anything like it and many thanks. I emptied the contents in a separate bowl so I put the boxes with them. I sat it on the table. It looked like St. Nicholas, only there wasn't a banana in it. The next thing we're anxious to try is Bouillon and lemonade but not today. Thanks a million. It was very interesting.

Well, my dear we also found your old wallet. Did you want that in there? Inside of the radio was a pocketknife. It's in pretty good shape and a dried or semi-dried SC leaf was in the back of the radio too. I feel like you got a wallet from Alma for your birthday, as we were talking about sending you one. She said they had those patriotic wallets in town so I guess that's what happened. We got those pictures. None are too good and two didn't take. Will send them as soon as Lizzie sees them.

H.R.

Continued, **September 18**, Saturday, 9 am

Am sending one picture. Marge took the rest to work. Your letters are neatly packed as well as your books and Crowder map. Will say goodbye Corporal. I'm a very busy woman this morning.

Continued, pm:

Well, tonite is the last nite for the horse show. At 10:15 they will announce it. Well, it's still very cool. I doubt if we get any more nites to sit out. We are OK. Hope you are too. I'm inclosing the rest of the pictures. What was your discussion of your lone weasel photo? Now what about your pictures in your fighting suit? Did you ever see that feller?

Before you go on maneuvers, couldn't you have a posed portrait made of youse? We really would all enjoy it. I think if you knew how it would please the folks back home; you would do it, wouldn't you, huh?

I am going to tell you of a very happy occasion in St. Louis. You know Lill's two cousins the Shaugnessy twins, Joe and Laurence; the one was in the Army about 8 months before the other. They were both heading home on furloughs. Neither of the two were aware of the other coming home. When they both stopped at St. Louis to change to the same train, Laurence spied Joe getting on the same train. He said he yelled so loud all eyes were fixed on him. So their mother was down at the station to meet the one and it turned out to be a double header. Don't you think that was a happy occasion?

Will say goodnite. I don't know any news dearest. Yes, wasn't that explosion Norfolk? Marge's "boyfriend" is stationed there.

Love,

Hermina

Continued by Margaret:

I brought the radio to Mr. Hibbit [*sp*] to be repaired so I'll let you know when it's ready. Norb, look at the family group. It looks like a miners' convention. I see in the paper where it's been a blast at Norfolk, VA and that's where Maurice Slattery is, so I'm wondering how he is. It's darn cold here tonight. I'm writing this with Ma's old brown coat on and it really feels good. It's 11 o'clock and Good night, God Bless you.

Margaret

It is unknown if the girl from South Carolina who wrote the following letter was seeing Norb while he was there, or if it was a friend of his sister Margaret. Norb was corresponding with his girlfriend Alma Pierce in Louisville but he was encouraged by his sister Joey Carter to date other girls when he could. Alma really never forgave Joey for that.

Richburg, South Carolina, **September 18**

Hello Norb!

Just a few lines to let you hear from me. I guess you think that I have forgotten you entirely. Well, Norb, that's not exactly true because I've been working in Rock Hill for the past three weeks but I'm home now and I'm going back and forth from home. I hate it. Bad by me not writing any sooner. Well, honey, can't you forgive me one time? I sure hope you'll say yes.

Darling, that was a real natural picture of you, you sent me. You'll never know how much I appreciate it. I'll send you one of me soon, as I have promised so many times. Norb, when I think I'll be in Chester again I'll be sure and let you know because I really do want to see you.

Honey-child, it is really cold up here now, I believe it's not too long until winter. Norb, there's plenty of girls from Rock Hill that have friends from Ft. Jackson to visit them on weekends. How would you like to come to Rock Hill instead of Chester? Because some Saturdays I work from 7 o'clock to 11:00. Write me back and I'll let you know what weekend will suit me best. Well, since time is short I guess I have to close for this time, so answer real soon.

PS. Write me real soon if you still love me.

Love,

"Mary" [*Gillespie*]

Fort Jackson, South Carolina, **September 19**

Dear Mom and all,

Well, I ain't doing so well. I got a good dose of what is commonly called the "GI" shits. If you notice any brown spots on the moon, you know my aim has been good. They're a lot better though. I started cramping Friday night so I went on sick call Saturday morning and got a dose of oil and some other stuff which fixed me up pretty well but my gut is still a little sore and we're going to have chicken for dinner.

Well, you kinda surprised me with that call the other night but I managed to get out of my "fart sack" (bed) and struggle down to battalion headquarters. I guess I seemed a little sleepy, didn't I? Yeah, my cold is gone now, but the weather has taken its place. It was 56° here last night, which broke a record since 1887. Some of the fellows have put on their long underwear this morning.

I see you have received my radio by now. What did you think of those K-Rations? Some meal, eh! Well, as I told you on the phone I don't suppose we will pull out of here before the last of this month.

I got a letter from Zip yesterday. He says England is alright but it's raining all the time. He also said he wishes I was there. He wrote that letter on August 26 and it got here on Sept. 18, which wasn't bad at all. Well, I will close now because I haven't much room and Miss Jones is calling pretty hard,

So, I remain Shitty,

Norb

Louisville, Kentucky, **September** 19, Sunday, 2:30 pm

Dear [*clipped photo of a bull's head pasted where name goes*],

Well, it's a gloomy old day, very gloomy. I seen [*sic*] Kaiser's marriage license in the paper today. If I can find it, I will enclose it. Mary Jane Nunn and George Bancroft's marriage announcement was on the bulletin for the first time. I can't imagine that. She can't be more than 17, can she? Would you like a wedding congratulation card for Kise? For 10¢, I'll send you one as your credit rating is in the II B Class. Ha, ha.

We are entertaining your God Mother [*Anna Heitkemper*] tomorrow at lunch. She is going home Thursday. Hello Norb from Irish Annie. Ann snuck in on me, but being it's her birthday, I'll permit it.

Continued, **September 20**, Monday, 7:45 pm:

Well, my dear, it's a damp coolish day and we did our entertaining. Your Cousin Annie was here. So was Dora Hollkamp and little Mary. Anna looked a lot better today to me but still is far from par. Did you want to know what we had for lunch? Well, we got talking about the "boys," Annie and I did. I sure blew you up. "Steam exploded eight times normal value (not size)." I said, well, Norb has his first gloomy letter to write home. They sure are cheerful and swell and if he don't write, it's because he can't. We all sure do appreciate that. (How are you doing, chest?) Now for lunch we had creamed peas and carrots, mashed Taters, cranberries, slaw, tomatoes and fried chicken, coffee, homemade apple pie. It all tasted damn good too, if I must say so myself. So after they left we started to wash so we were in reverse today.

Hold your breath or sit down, my dear, but our sister Margaret bought herself a fur coat today and she's so talkative. I imagine she pinched Lincoln [*penny*] so hard she had to release him.

Richard Crooks [American tenor in Metropolitan Opera] was surely good tonight. We're waiting for Dr. I. 2 [*French-American operatic soprano and actress*]! You get to listen. Mrs. Horn is going to see Carl Friday. He's in the Navy at Great Lakes, Ill. She looks sort of down in the dumps. It's compulsory that they know how to swim. He struck his head in learning so was hospitalized for a few days.

Lip was over yesterday. Of course, we got kid talk. She said Shirley was acting snotty so she said to Betsy she wishes Shirley would go to the convent so she would lose some of that and I hope you go too. Betsy says well if I do, I'll sure be a fussin' and a cussin' Sister. They say Milt rides that pony beautiful. It's a 5-gaited one and he rides it at every gait.

I'm out of news so will close as Lilly Pons is closing the program and Dr. I. 2 is on his way. We did not hear from you today. If you can, send Betsy one of those cards, will you honey?

Love from all your sister,

[*Hermina*]

LAST MINUTE NEWS!

Mom was trying to get Pop to take a laxative. He's complaining about stomachache "in the bowels." Mom said keep some of that cold beer out of your system and I bet you wouldn't have it. Pop said no, beer's a bracer. It braces me many a time. My bowels are moving plenty. They are really moving often. Your need oril [*oil*]. I'll fix you up a dose. No, I need aspirin. Well, she said, if it's still the Shits, oil makes it quit. And boy did we laugh. Papa sure shook on that one. 'Twas funny but Pop took aspirins. I really think Mom backed the Attack (*gas*) often. Tear this up please!

Louisville, Kentucky, **September 23**, Thursday, 9:45 pm

Dear Norb,

We received your letter this morning. My stars, and what a letter! I guess you did do some laughing. Which of the two felt the worst? It's cool, damp and drizzly here. Dewey was over last night to spend the evening. He sure is a sweet kid. He helped with the dishes. You can't help but like him. Joey is spending her vacation in the country. Lee is still vacationing at home. Can you beat that? Dewey spilled himself. He said he thinks Lee is taking advantage of him. If I were Dewey, I'd turn him in to the draft board.

Well, Pop took a dose of Castor Oil last nite - in cake. I don't know the results. Tell you tomorrow. Mom is making some grape preserves this morning, about a quart. Seems ducely [*sic*] odd to cook in such small quantities.

My, at present we're hearing of so many boys being sent over, or on their way across. Presumably for the second front, I imagine, because the second front will be started. For according to Churchill, it was promised to "Joe" [*Stalin*]. Lip said he [*boy who was being sent* across] used to live on Mulberry St. Do you remember him? I think he went to St. E School. He's about 21. Sister Anthony told Jimmy he was the "dependable type." She could tell. I guess he sets in pretty good. I think Betsy is going to write a few "liones."

First Lt. Messmer across the street was raised to Captaincy yesterday. From the contents of your letter, we can see you 'tell' Mamma everything. Kindly burn my letter I sent yesterday. What will be the next thing brother?

Apples 12¢ a lb., eggs 5¢ each, Grapes are $1.75 a basket, which formerly were 60¢ or 75¢. Sounds like a silent axe.

If your bowels are still loose, take another dose of oil. Sometimes it takes several doses my dear. I don't think it's bad to take it in coke. How about that Milk of Bismuth? You know that helps put a lining in your intestine. It also helps to check loose bowels.

Well, Mr. Hibbit couldn't fix your radio. It's something there needs fixing besides tubes, which cannot be gotten at present. I think they are going to try Clarksdale's [*TV and radio repair shop on Shelby Street*]. You never answered - do you or do you not want us to send it to you? Well, Ducky, and I do mean Goosy, I will close now. Hope you are up to par by this time. How about a posed "pitcher" of your Low Dutch mug? Come on now and dood it!
Love, hugs, kisses and arguments,
Porky

Fort Jackson, South Carolina, **September 23**

Dear Mom and all,

Well, I haven't got much to say. Everything is just about the same except for the weather. It's quite a bit warmer than it has been the last several days. I received those pictures. I thought they were pretty good considering the time of the day when they were taken.

That sounded like a pretty good meal you had when "godmother Anna" was there. I wouldn't mind sitting in on one like that myself but the chow here has been excellent for the last month. It really has. Just as good as you could get anywhere. We had apple pie for supper tonight and I can say it was the best apple pie I have ever ate and that's no fooling. Of course I'm not running your cooking in the ground but it was good pie. We also had Chopped-Suey, which was very good. Well, we're slated to pull out of here about the second or the third if that isn't changed again. I don't think it will be this time, at least I hope not.

Did they have the tubes to fit that radio? You couldn't get them down here nowhere.

Well, I don't know much more so I'll close for now and say so long.
As Always,
Norb

Louisville, Kentucky, **September 24**, Friday, 3 pm

[Dear Norb,]

What do you think of Zip's papa? It must be something new. It's not connected with the 'All Wool and Yard Wide,' do you think? It doesn't mention it.

Lill was saying that Charles got an honorable discharge. She said his mother got a letter with his thumb print and praising him telling him of his good character, but Charles hasn't showed up as yet and that was some weeks ago. I think they got something wrong. What do you think that could be? We can't figure it out.

Jr Russell is in the hospital with a nervous upset before your last letter. He "was given" a new commanding officer and he's so terribly strict. He said he had been getting every other night off so he made it one nite a week. Jr slipped out and was caught, so he was busted. He was told that he was going to be sent over in a short time, so now Madlyn has gone home to Momma because it's nothing but Cubans there [*in Florida*].

Milton is up here popping off now. Beginning October 1, the Shelby Show will have just two shows. I mean just two different shows a week and close Wednesday night all night. The shows change - Sundays and Thursdays. Yep, Milton's getting on the neater side of things. That one change we can see. That's outstanding. We are all OK. Will finish tomorrow. [*Hermina*]

Louisville, Kentucky, **September 25**, Saturday, 9 am

Dear Norb,

Just three months till Christmas my dear. It almost seemed like Xmas yesterday, devoid of gifts tho. Everybody came or was heard from but you. Lip and Margie came yesterday morning and stayed until school was out. Joey called up about 3 pm. Johnny, Jackie, Hill and Vernon came at "Supper Time." They had their hair cut. On Fridays, it's 50¢ for kids too. That's too dern [*sic*] much. Slim said if you brought them in yesterday you'd of saved some money. Johnny was the only one in there, but rules is rules. I forgot to say about Joe and Ann. Well, Joe still comes you know. I just got a nice fire built. It's a heavenly chipper morning.

I heard Kaiser had some celebration. Joe told Mom they had open house. You know her dad has a saloon also. They had 300 fried chickens. Now I just wonder about that. Fryers are 40¢ per pound but could be true.

Well, this is Saturday and I have to get started but nothing makes the day more pleasant than when I write to you first. If you'd be here, I'd argue foist [*first*].

Boy, I really had a dream. I dreamed we at home were getting ready to see a corpse. Mom primped for hours. Pop was even powdering his face. We never seen the corpse but the ocean was there. I said to Joe how beautiful, I'd love to get in it, so Joe took me swimming. He held me tight around the waist and I paddled with his other hand. It was very an enjoyable dream. Imagine poor Joe. I never was in such deep water for such a long time. Amen.

Well, dearest, we're OK. I bet this is the coolest September on record. How's your bellyache? Gone, huh?

H.R.

Louisville, Kentucky, **September 27**, Monday, 11 am

Dear Norb,

A beautiful day!.

According to the news, the Nazis are getting it from all sides. I believe we had the coldest September on record. As you can see [*letters from Katsy and Betsy in the envelope*], I had them writing. Katsy does real good I think. Betsy thought she wrote too much not to get a reply. I got a letter from Bill and Norbert Hollkamp this morning. Mom also received your letter this morning. So you think you all will pull out Oct. 2?

Norbert [*Hollkamp*] tells me he weighs 188 lbs. He said he gained 11 lbs. this past month. He don't know if he'll be released or not. He is guarding prisoners now, not German P of W. Bill's is just about the same. It was postmarked Sept 21 and I got it this morning Sept 27, which is the quickest I have ever received one from him. He's in New Guinea you know.

Mary Jane Nunn is 16. I believe she is marrying Fr. Bancroft's brother because he's going to marry them. We're going to try at Clarksdale's to see if we can get a tube for your radio. A power tube, I believe it is.

Schegel's son, the one that left with you, is across. I think this father draft will really take some effort because they want to get all the single men out of defense work, and fathers since Pearl Harbor, which is the best.

I heard one of Gertie Bowe's boys were wounded slightly over-there. I know he's in N. Africa. It seems it was something interesting. I wanted to write about it but now I'm too thick to think deep. Lip and girls were up yesterday. Joe and Ann went to the country yesterday and bought a pumpkin, so tonight we're having fresh pumpkin pie, I think.

Love from all, your sweet and adorable sister,

Porky

Louisville, Kentucky, **September 27**

Dear Unk,

I made up my mind I was not going to write to you again. I wrote eight times and your never did answer but since you're going to help fight those yellow bellied Japs for me and us. How are you? I heard you had the bellyache again. Those Japs don't amount to anything. Take that from me Unk. Shirley had a birthday Friday but she never got a damn thing. Don't let Katsy know that. I have to do tall studying because I am in the fourth grade now. I am going to try to get first honor. I got a good start. Mary C. [*Katsy*] is in second. She's got Sister Rose; I got Sr. Robert; Shirley got Sr. Anthony. That's supposed to be Aunt Bill's friend, Sister Anthony. We got the best Sisters back there. Daddy is working at St. Peter Claver chicken supper for our dark-skinned brothers and sisters. Yassum.

Well, good-bye,

Betsy

Fort Jackson, South Carolina, **September 27**

Dear Mom & all,

This is Monday night and it's fairly cool but she warms up during the day. Well, were supposed to pull out of here next Sunday morning at 4:00 am. We are going to Lebanon, Tennessee so I won't be but about 160 miles from Louisville. We're supposed to be down there for about 5 weeks but we won't be able to get a pass. Sometimes we'll be maneuvering in Kentucky. You know that was a good picture of Milton. I've been wanting to write him a letter but I never got around to it. Well, there's not a damn thing to write about that's interesting so I guess this will have to do for now, so I'm

As Always,

Norb

Louisville, Kentucky, **September 28**, Tuesday, 8 pm

Dear Norb,

Well, to begin with I had an appointment with Von Haven at 10:30 am. Waiting for the streetcar, I saw Mrs. Zipperle. She said she hasn't heard from Zip since last week. She looked some thinner to me. She asked about you, of course. When I got on the car, who beckons me to sit by them? Was Lill Klein. She tells me her son Bob is across. He's a parachute rigger. He sews and patches parachutes. He landed in Scotland, now is in London, England.

Well, when the trolley proceeded to Tap's Corner who gets on but Ray Harmann and Red [*Larny*]Johnson. They both look good. Larny stopped and talked. He said they went to this side of Nashville, Tenn. on maneuvers. I said you've lost weight, Larny. No, I've gained 2 lbs. He surely doesn't look it. He looks like he did when he was 17 years old, that slimness, so I guess Oertel's is a lot of puff because he really did look lots heavier in civilian life. He said you'll have it easier on maneuvers and laughed, but you can't tell about Larny's laughs. He's all grin. Clarence Johnson is in Oklahoma (Camp Pruitt I believe).

I got to tell Dr. Von Haven - he asked about you - how old you are, where you're at. All the while, I was getting my teeth cleaned. I managed to answer Dr. I. 2 afterwards. Larny said he was coming to see us but you should understand how that is. So in less than a half-hour four different persons asked about you. From Von Haven's I went to Lip's and stayed until just now. I ironed. My, all them pieces. Shirley is waiting for a birthday present from her soldier boy. He promised that and Friday was her birthday. Lill also told me her brother

Laurence Klein was married a few weeks ago when he was home on furlough. He's the youngest of the boys, about 26 I think.

We're OK. Pop got a dirty bump on his head Sunday when he stooped to pick up a nickel and bumped his head on the votive stand, but it's healing up now. You know how he heals up right now. It's a little warmer today. It was beautiful. Pop is going after a shock of beer. Well, my dear I'll say goodnite. At 8:30 Fibber and Molly come back tonite from their vacation. Good nite.

Sweet Porky

Louisville, Kentucky, **September 29**, 86 degrees

Dear Norb,

The weather is lovely today, like summer time. I just got finished putting the bread in the pans. Thought I would write a few lines lest you might forget - <u>have you been to the Sacraments</u>?

It is the first Friday of October. The Third Order is asking everyone to go to Mass next Sunday at the Cathedral at 10:30 am and go to Holy Communion also, if they can, and to ask our friend and loved ones also. So if you will, please join your intention with the Third Order. This is asked of all the members of the Order of US and Canada. Intention is for <u>Peace</u>.

Good-bye and god bless you Norbert,

Mother

The following letter was yellowed, crumbled and hard to read.

Fort Jackson, South Carolina, **September 30**

Dear Mom and all,

Well, the weather is fine and so is my appetite. We're packing and getting ready to pull out of here Sunday morning. I don't guess we'll even go to bed Saturday night. I am sending some more stuff home in my suitcase. I hope it arrives OK. Put those books somewhere where they won't get damaged. I didn't think you would be able to get tubes for that radio. Those are pretty hard to get. You can't get them nowhere. Well, time is short and this is all I know. Anyway, goodnight and I'll be seeing you. Tell Betsy and Katsy I got their letters.

As Always,

Norby

Louisville, Kentucky, **September 30**, Thursday, 1 pm

Dear Norb,

It's a heavenly day it is. It's really a hot day but the nights have been very cool. Until 11:00 am, you debate whether to make a fire or not. If you wait that long you don't want a fire. We received your letter this morning saying you all were pulling out. So you don't think you can get a pass while in Lebanon, Tennessee? You don't know if you can have visitors or not, do you? Mom has been talking about going to see you if you went to Nashville. Train fare is about $8.50 round trip. I suppose this will be the last letter you receive before going to Tennessee.

Mom is going to the bank to help back the attack. She has almost enough for a $25 bond. Pop would of bought bonds too but the old house [*1137 Mulberry Street, their old house next to 1344 Texas Street that they still own and rent out*] needs repairs and that's costly. The news has been very encouraging today, very good.

I heard Sen. Taft of Ohio wants to take the pre-Pearl Harbor fathers under thirty. I think that's pretty sensible. I think he's got really good sense. Pop caught it this morning. He was cutting down a Chinese Elm tree on his own accord. I believe he's on retreat. Mom don't have to pack a pistol, heck no.

Mom was talking with Helen Wessling yesterday. She said her third boy left for the Marines Tuesday night. She was very blue. She got word from Jim. He's in Australia and "Butt" is in the US as yet. Lee is 18, graduated from St. X in June. He's going to San Diego, California for basic training. He had two teeth that needed filling. He wanted Army but they told him they needed Marines, so he took that.

Shirley and Katsy march on Sunday but Betsy don't. She feels slighted. Shirley has to carry a banner and Katsy is a flower girl. Mom just got home from the bank. Stopped at Lip's and Milt has your letter. You're a good man, Norbieeeeee. I suppose you won't pass thru Louisville to Tenn. Will you? If you do, bring the "Drunken 59th" in.

Mr. Redle has got his 'Chucka Chuck' out in front. He was banging around on it. I suppose we'll soon see him pulling out. When you're in Tenn. call us up. Do you think you'll get a furlough after the maneuvers? Well, I'll bring this letter to a close. I'm working in the yard. We got about a bushel of green tomatoes on the vines. I believe by the time they all come down, it will be more than a bushel.

Mom's instructions are don't forget the Money-Man. He's up to $96 now to give away. Boy, if we would win that! Well, I hope you have a safe journey to Lebanon. I wish it were Kentucky instead of Tennessee, then we would get to see you my dear.
Love from Porky

Continued by Mommy:

Dear Norb,

Well, it's 2:45. I am getting ready to go to church. First Friday, you know. Will pray hard for you. I hope that the war will be over soon. I thought so often of you the other day. At night, I dreamed that you was fighting a Negro girl with an eggbeater and I made you stop. That's all now.
Mother

On October 3, 1943, Norb was on Maneuvers for five weeks in Lebanon, Tennessee. His mail was addressed to Nashville.

Louisville, Kentucky, **October 4**, Wednesday, 4:30 pm

Dearest Norb,

Well, I was just about ready to sit down with "pen in hand" and tell you it was two and a half weeks since we heard from you, when the mailman handed me a letter from you. The last letter was written the 8th, this one the 12th. This one was very short but unbelievably sweet. We were beginning to feel uneasy. Mom shed a few tears of gladness between the time you wrote the letter and the time we received it. The war has taken on a different outlook, although it looks better again. Everything was looking so favorably for us when that setback of the English troops at Arnhem was flashed. It seems everybody's feathers dropped but people were really feeling optimistic. It put a damper on all optimism, believe me, but I still don't think this war will go into 1945. Gen. "Ike" said it could end in this year. I believe he knows. Clarence Johnson rolled in this morning. Bernie Werner was killed in Action. They got word Monday night.

It's another beautiful day. The plasterer has the undercoat on and the chimney torn down and back up, so will finish with the skein [*sic*] coat tomorrow. I know they will be glad. Well, I see Al Smith passed away this morning at 6:20am. He certainly has a big write up in tonite's paper. He deserves it.

Pop is still using Kremel [*hair tonic*]. I told Pop he and JoAnn had a lot in common, a toothless smile and an "oiled" scalp. To be continued.

8:00 pm

Well, Gabriel Heatter is on. His news is very encouraging. He is elaboration upon Alfred E. Smith. It sure is swell to hear so much good about anybody. His family can certainly be proud. Well, Lip is here. Betsy is going to mail this. I suppose we will hear from you soon, as I think this letter was delayed. You can't write so often you know. We are OK. Hope you are well.

Love,
Hermina

Louisville, Kentucky, **October 5**, Tuesday, 2 pm

Dear Norb,

We received your grip in very good condition about ½ hour ago. We will pack your hat, shoes and "tablespoon" away also. So, I see how useless a money-belt is to a soldier but it's a nice one. We enjoyed the snotty handkerchief the most. We're wondering if you're at your destination or not by this time.

Eleanor, Jimmy, Johnny, etc., was in last night. She was outfitted from head to toe - undies, slips, dresses, shoes, hose, hat, purse, and coat. Marge got her fur coat yesterday. It's a lot like Ann's. We'll pack those books securely. I never knew you got your grip back. We were wondering how that happened. I think I'll wash and wax up your grip. It would improve it a lot. Johnny's kids look swell and that and that baby is the prettiest thing I've ever seen. It's like Lucky Strikes, so round, so firm, so perfectly blended. I really did gain some since they were here, so did Jack and Vernie. Hilary likes the bus. He likes to go because he knows he'll get rode back.

Pop and Ann fought a round. She put water in his pipe but he had another one in reserve. He's feeling a lot better. He dropped to 158 pounds. He looked tuckered out but he's going again. I don't think he deserves too much sympathy. He cut down 2 Chinese Elms. We were so bored. Hoping to hear from you real soon.

Love,

Porky

Lebanon, Tennessee, **October 6**

Dear Mom & all:

Well, this will have to be a fast letter because the lights are going out in a few minutes. I just got a letter from Alma today and it seems as though she had an attack of appendicitis. They had Dr. Liken for her and they said that if she wasn't better by Tuesday, they would have to operate. Well, tomorrow is Tuesday so I guess I'll know by tomorrow. I'll leave you in on some news. I was supposed to leave yesterday for furlough but they were "postponed" so I'm still living in hopes that ma[y]be they will release them in a week or so. We have two weeks of intensive training and I do mean intensive. We have about four combat courses to compete, which will include the night infiltrations course. That's a pretty tough one. Well, time is short and the lights are getting low so good night. Tell Mary I said Hi. XXX

As Always,

Norb

Louisville, Kentucky, **October 8,** 4:30 pm

Dear Norb:

So you think you start every letter with well, well. Well, I believe I do too. It is a very cloudy and gloomy day and getting colder. We are glad for a little cooler weather. Some days last week it was mostly warm. If you're not hanging your clothes on the Siegfried line, well, I think that is something to be thankful for.

It seems the news in the past four days has been very good. We are mailing you another Xmas box. I suppose that will be the last one for the 1944 Christmas Season. If there is anything you want a 'repeat number' on, let us know and we'll do our best to get it for you. I'm sending you some Christmas Cards. Even if it's late by the time you get them, it's better late than never.

Joe said Clarence Johnson was in a scrap. He has busted knuckles. He hasn't changed a bit. He said he was introduced as mayor of Bragg, Oklahoma a few months before he came home. He said it's a community of about 3,000 people and they threw a party. So, as mayor, he signed about 500 programs. He said they really had a big time. I bet he's a lot of fun anyplace.

Father Rueff died this morning at 10:30 am. He had been ill a few days. Marge put in about a dozen rose slips. I believe there will be more roses than tomatoes next year. I believe I acknowledged your letter of Sept. 18th. We were very glad to get it. You seemed to be feeling OK and in good humor. So you are on maneuvers? We didn't know that before this time. I didn't think you all would have to go on maneuvers after you've been in the "real stuff" but I suppose you don't get rusty that way.

Betsy, Katsy and Margie just came. They took Margie with them to the Shelby [*Theater*]. They saw Snow White and the Seven Dwarfs. Margie got a kick out of the show, but war pictures were out so they came here. We are OK. Hope you are too.

Love from all. Your dear, dear sister,

Hermina

Lebanon, Tennessee, **October 12**

Dear Mom and all,

Well, I haven't had much chance to write for the last week because we were kept pretty damn busy. As a matter of fact, I haven't had my clothes off but once in eight days. I think I'm beginning to smell a little. I don't think we will get any passes for a while and be lucky to get one then. We're back in the hills too damn far. I don't know how long we will be in these maneuvers. It might not be so long as I think. It's hard to say.

The weather is a little warmer down here than what it has been and it's very welcome because it gets rather cool at nights, believe you me. I am with the Blue Army [*Blue Laws prohibited alcohol sales*]. I kinda like it myself except you can't get nothing to drink or go anyplace. But I wrote Red Johnson a letter and asked him to give me some dope on the situation and he told me you can get something to drink in a lot of these farmers' houses. They sell it. So I think Rawert will investigate.

We have everything under blackout conditions and it's funny as hell. The other morning a pig woke me up rooting in my tent. I don't know but I believe he still has the imprint of a GI shoe on his ass. Well, time is drawing short so I had better close for now, so I'll be seeing you. Tell Mary I said hello XX

As Always,

Norb

Louisville, Kentucky, **October 14**, Thursday, 12:30 pm
Dear Norb: or, Honorable Sauerkraut Maker,

We miss you very much (got the kraut cabbage ordered). It's 4 or 5¢ per pound. Haven't got anything of much interest to report but I will say this. I think Milt is doing very good in school. He got 2-90's, 2-80's and 2-65's on his report card. Science and Algebra were the lowest but the Bro. said it usually is low for the first two months.

Lip, etc., was up last night. Katsy went in the basement. Mom was down there by herself. She wanted to know if she wasn't afraid. Mom said, "No, Jesus and my Guardian Angel are with me. She asked what angels eat. Mom said, "Nothing." Katsy said, "I don't want to be an angel then 'cause I like to eat."

Pop's got 4 down and 2 to go, Chinese Elm Trees. He told Mom he learned something cutting those down - to get them to fall the way you want 'em to. It's interesting. Oh boy, whatta boy. Mom wanted to know how many trees he thought he would cut down yet. Jonesy broke his wrist on the obstacle course last Saturday.

Did you have to sleep on the damp ground last night? We had rain here yesterday but it's a beautiful day today. The news is really good today with the exception of the sinking if 2 destroyers (in the Atlantic I think). We're all OK and with no news, relly, relly [sic] good news I hope. Today is Eisenhower's 54th birthday. It should be a happy one. That's all for this time. If you don't write - you're busy.
Love,
Porky

Lebanon, Tennessee, **October 21** (I think)
Dear Mom and all,

Hi you folks. How ya all? I'm damn swimming myself. I was just wondering what a good bath would feel like and also some clean clothes and a bed. This ground seems to be slightly harder than marble and darn near as cold. It was really cold here last Friday I think. In fact, it was sleeting about 12:00 am midnight, but it has warmed up quite a bit.

I haven't had much of a chance to do any writing. In fact haven't had a chance to write at all. Everything is blackout at night so you can't write then even if you had a chance. We're back in the woods but I expect we'll move up any time now. Sometimes we move the whole outfit up or back 2 and 3 times a day and that's quite some job. Yesterday I was going after some automobile parts in my jeep and I had just made a slight turn, it was hardly a turn, and doing about 45 and the damn steering rod let loose so I taken a ditch, and also a nice fence along with me. All I got was a little cut on the knee. Just lucky nothing was coming the other way.

Say, that box really hit the spot. Everything was delicious. This air makes you hungry as hell. I sure could use a drink right now. I believe I could drink Louisville dry in a couple of hours and I ain't kidding. But ma[y]be that wouldn't be such a hard job. They tell me you can't buy a drop of whiskey in Nashville. There's just none to be had. You can get gin, brandy and such but no bourbon. (Pardon me. I got to scratch.)

The other morning I woke up with a toad frog staring me in the face. I think the frog thought about as much of me as I did of him. We put a dead snake in some guy's bedroll and he was laying there very comfortably when all of a sudden he stood straight up in the air. How in the hell did he get out of those blankets? I don't see. It's a dirty trick but it sure was funny as hell.

These planes down here really come close. Sometimes they just clear the treetops. The maneuvers are supposed to end the 8th of next month unless another one starts. I don't know much else except my appetite is good and I'm feeling swell. I'll sign off now until the next time.

As Always,

Norb

Louisville, Kentucky, **October 24**, Sunday, 3 pm

Dear Norb,

As you know by this time, we haven't heard from you but hope you are well and OK. We have unexpected company. Papa's pet, Jackie and Hil came for dinner. The etc.'s are at Mrs. Smith's but I do want to see Norbie. Norbie Hennie (as Margie calls him, always by both names). Mom, like the President, had a cold but is past that sick feeling, But still plenty snotty, plenty! Jonesy's boyfriend from Keesler Field, Mississippi is here in Louisville. He has corresponded with Marilyn for a year and is spending the weekend here and everything he (Jonesy) told him was one enlarged lie. They were at Joe's last night. Joe said it's plenty funny to hear him tell of it, believing 159th thought he was an advertising man from Coca-Cola. He also wanted to go to Harrington Lake to see Jonesy's private cabin and private pier for his yacht. A letter from Lavern is on its way to Cpl. Jones and as soon as he gets to camp, he said a good letter from him will be in the mail. He said everybody believes him, as well as likes him. He said all the guys feel sorry for him to leave such a good position of $350 per month. Joe said this guy told him there was one funny thing about all of his lies. He would borrow money from him every month and he thought if he had money in the bank why didn't he use that, but he was quick to build that up, saying it's too hard to get back. Nuf is nuf.

Mary took Eleanor's watch to have it repaired. They told her she could get it in January 1944! Margie was real cute the other day. She asked Lip if she could play with Danit (Janet). Lip not hearing the first part and Margie repeating with Danit Mudder, Danit Mudder. Lip said, what are you saying Margie? She said, Mudder can I play with Danit? Not Danit, Mudder, Danit, across the street. Realizing Lip thought she might be saying damn it, she looked and said "Dot danit," not danit, but Danit. It was too cute for words. I really think she talks worse or more babyish than she did a year ago.

Hilary and another boy was sent to Fr. Knue for fighting in the classroom. He said the other boy hit him and he was not taking it. He said he fussed with him a little and told him to go on.

It's a rainy day today. Did I tell you Chester was deferred awhile? Bernard Hubbuch will be called up in April the draft board told him. He's a Pre-Pearl Harbor father and sought a Defense job so it will be April for him. January for Carney. He's an unessential papa. Figure it out.

Do you need or want anything? Say so. Well, my deah [*sic*] brother, I will close. That's all I know for now. Hoping we hear soon.

With love from all the arguing Rawerts,

Little Pork

Louisville, Kentucky, **October 25**, Monday, 10:45

Dear Bootsie Boy or Scum Belly!

Well, we got your letter dear brother and we were glad to hear from you, believe you me. Maw began to look down in the mouf [*sic*] :-(but now she looks like a pumpkin face :-). I think she'll be easier to get along with too. We really were beginning to worry, no kidding. We could of gotten that letter Saturday I think. You all, or youse guys, must of had colder weather than we had. We never had frost as yet in this neck of the woods but in Horse Cave and at Johnny's and Okolona they had a "killer" frost.

"Intermission."

Noon, I was to Hertel's and Schieman's. Hertel said he didn't think he'd have anything in the way of Xmas goods at all. At Schieman's I was allowed four bars of Lifebuoy and only one box of Rinso [*detergent*], so we'll have one wash day. But we won't have to worry - Katie's got a few bars put away. But she only has one washday a week now. Sometimes there's an extra one.

That was a dirty trick what you all pulled, putting a snake in a bedroll. Shame on youse all. I believe by tonite we might have snow. It's damp, drizzly. How do you all keep dry on these damp nites? And do you feel at ease damp? Huh?

Now about your accident. I think your Guardian Angel was working overtime, and perhaps, our rosaries are helping there. I really think you were lucky. My!

Hilary was a rat in a play for Fr. Knue. They played the "farmer in the dell" and they all had their costumes. He had to keep saying "eek, eek" and eat the cheese. I bet that was a well-nourished looking rat, I would of loved to seen him. I asked Jackie what he would do if Daddy was called in the Army. He said, "Well, Aunt Meenie, I couldn't keep him out." I don't know if they'll accept Johnny or not. Epping loses 3 drivers Saturday. One is a man with 3 kids. Jackie said his partner at school's daddy has to go and he has 2 sisters, so you can see they're taking them. Thanks for the dried leaf. Hilary was the only one in his room that can write to 50 so his work is on the board. I didn't think that was so small. He and another boy are the smallest in the class. Jackie is the opposite.

Since you enjoyed your box, I'll see what I can do for you. I got a veal bone from Schieman's and it's pretty. He gave it to me for 20¢ and no points. Do you think my beauty startled him? I really felt good about that. Hoping your cut is now on the mend and you are OK. So maneuvers will be over the 8th? That's not even 5 weeks, is it? Do you think you'll get to come home then? Huh? Let us hear if you get an inkling that you might get to come home. Every time the phone rings odd, we think it's you calling. Well, will say Toodaloo till the next time, but don't wait so long.

Love from all,

Porky with a veal bone

Louisville, Kentucky, **October 25**, 44° on the back porch

Dear Norb,

I sure am glad to hear from you. I thought sure you were sick or hurt. Well, the way your letter read, you were hurt. I hope that you will get along alright. I am glad that you enjoyed the box.

Hermina told all the news if you can call it that. Papa is feeling a whole lot better after he got through playing cards til 10 at Joe's last night. He said sitting so long makes a fellow so sift [*stiff*] kneed. Complaining about too much rest, but he enjoyed the game. He [*illegible word*] quite often. Then John and Joe would give him the ha ha.

The weather is cold today. Maybe it will freeze tonight. Mary is almost ready to go to work so I must close. When did you arrive in Tennessee? You never wrote that did you pass close to Louisville. Well, that's all for this time. I thank God that you was not hurt any worse and hope that you will get along all right. Did you ride the jeep to Nashville?

Next Monday is Poor Souls Day so don't forget to pray for them. Mary sends you xxx honey bunch.

God bless you and good luck,

Mother

Lebanon, Tennessee, **October 26**

Dear Mom & all,

Well, I sure can't say the weather is fine because I never seen such miserable weather. It's hard as hell to keep anything dry, especially when you can't have fires. But the mud ain't so bad, it's only knee deep with two more feet to go. I sure hope this rain stops. These mountains are so bad that they had to put chains on all the vehicles.

I never got a chance to call the other day. We got a pass for about 6 hours. We went to Bowling Green, Ky and there was the usual delay in getting a call through and I had just a few hours so I never got the chance. I don't know just how long we will be on maneuvers yet but it won't be so very long I don't think.

I got that Halloween box. Thank you all. I don't know much that's new except that I'd give $10.00 for a comfortable bed and a warm room with some dry blankets. I'm not complaining. I'm just thinking. I could also use a quart of bourbon to offset this cold weather. Well, as time goes by I run out of writing materials so I suppose I'll close for now, and have a few raindrops and a cup of coffee. See you later.

As Always,

Norb V...-

Fort Jackson, South Carolina, October 31, 10:00 pm
Weather: excellent. Place: damn if I know

Dear Mom, Pop, Marge, and Hermina and Mary and ???

Well, to begin with, I received the package you sent me and that cake was simply delicious, believe you me. The pink elephant medicine was very well taken care of also, although I had a quart of it in my tent at the time. I bought it when I went to Bowling Green, KY and it didn't go bad with the weather we've been having. I used it for medical purposes only. But I'll have to say this is a pretty rugged outfit. I'll say out of the 975 men that are in the "59th" Signal Bn., only about two of them got sick and I know damn good and well everybody got wet (so much for my bragging).

The PX truck came in tonight (PX consists of candy, cig's, razor blades, <u>beer</u> and such}. Believe it or not, they have Falls City beer - or should I say they had falls city beer - because they are closed again for a week, as they do not stay open while the problem is going on. I bought a carton of double mint chewing gum and I'll send it the first chance I get to wrap it up and get some stamps. So don't be too expectant, you poor civilians. Believe it or not, but that beer went very well even though it was warm, but I'm getting so used to drinking warm beer that I actually believe it tastes better that way (mabe it's the Dutch in me).

The weather has been swell for the last couple of day, which came in very handy. It sure was hell there for a while though. These hills got so damn slippery that the trucks had to put chains on. You could hardly stand up on your feet. Sounds funny but it's true (honey).

I'm sitting in the back end of a truck writing this letter [*all in capital letters*]. I have an extension cord hooked up from the battery, so I have an electric light. All the comforts of home. Even our meals are on time. The chow has been very good and you would be suprized [*sic*] how your appatite [*sic*] builds up when you hit open country. All you feel like doing is eating, because sleeping ain't any too comfortable.

I suppose we'll pull out of here sometime next week because the maneuvers are supposed to end in a couple of days. The latest latrine rumor (latrine is - shit house to you) is that we are going to Camp Forrest, Tennessee so we'll just have to wait and see what happens.

Camp Forrest is not but about seventy miles from where we are now. I was in Nashville, Tenn. yesterday but it was strictly on business. I had to pick up some automotive parts at the railway express station, so I didn't have long to hang around. Ma[y]be if we go to Camp Forrest I'll get a three day pass and I might be seeing you folks but I couldn't say for sure. In fact, I've quit saying anything for sure.

Tell me what is this I hear about Marge corresponding with Maurice? You had better watch these soldiers, Marge. Some of them are pretty nasty boys but of course, they have their good points also.

I think Hermina said in her letter that Rudy and Bell were there, and you had some pretty good laughs. But at whose expense? It seemed to me that "Katie" rubbed it in on Rudy just a little. Well, you can tell Rudy that the old Amy couldn't hold a candle on the side of the new Army, not only because the rations are better, but it's just a better Army. I know because there are some officers who were in the last war who are in our outfit, and I hear quite a bit of what goes on.

Well, I have a chunk of ground with a couple of blankets waiting for me so I guess I'll hit the "hay" pretty soon as it is getting late and tomorrow is a pretty tough day because things become tactical again tomorrow. So I guess I had better wind up the alarm clock and go to bed. So goodnight and good luck, and god bless you. Blame all mistakes on the Falls fitty shitty Citty [*Falls City beer*].

I'll get the old corncob out tomorrow

As Always,

Norb

Lebanon, Tennessee, **November 3**

Dear Mom and all,

LATEST REPORT: The 59th Signal Battalion will proceed to Fort Jackson sometime this or next week. That is the latest dope. I seen a written order that came out saying we were going to Tenn., Camp Forrest, but it was changed by a later order, so I guess we will go back to Ft. Jackson and join the Corps. We will go by truck. Well, that's the way it stands until the orders are changed again and that's quite often. If I get a chance, I'll call before we leave the maneuver area. It'll be cheaper. (Thrifty).

Today was sure a nasty day. It started to rain last night and it just stopped a few minutes ago and it's about 8:30 pm now. My uniforms are in a hell of a shape but I guess everyone's are after being in the field for a month. It will take me a couple of weeks to get them straightened out and cleaned. I have to turn in all my fatigue clothes in for new ones because they are shot to hell.

Everything is under blackout conditions now but I'm in my tent and have a piece of red paper over the glass and have both ends of the tent closed as well as possible, so there's really not much light.

Right now I can hear some guy calling his pigs and I'll bet he's a mile away. You can just make out the "sau, sau." The sky seems to be clearing up quite well so I don't think we will have any rain tomorrow, at least I sure hope we don't. These maneuvers ain't bad if it wouldn't be for the rain, but you just have a hell of a time keeping things dry. We get plenty of chow and plenty of sleep. In fact, I think it is a fattening process. It's been better than two and a half weeks since any water touched my body except rainwater. A bath would really feel swell, but you really don't feel so dirty when you live in open air like this. If you wash your face once a day, you're considered a gentleman. Well, I'm usually a gentleman because I've managed to wash and shave every day except a few when we were moving up and back towards the front lines. But two weeks ago when I took a bath I was amazed at what little water you can take a bath in. I'll tell you what I done with just one helmet full of water. I washed my face and hands, shaved, took a bath, washed out three pairs of socks and then washed all my boots, all with the one helmet full of water. Of course, it wasn't a first class job all the way around but it sure served the purpose and that's all that's necessary.

I was kind of hoping to go to Camp Forrest because I could make it home on a three day pass from there but if we go back to Jackson ma[y]be we will be lucky because I hear that Camp Forrest is mostly tents and I'm getting tired of these pup tents because there's just enough room to crawl in.

I had a bad night last night, and then, it was funny, too. You see, I pitched my tent and stretched it tight as hell and you can't drive your pegs very deep here because you hit rock bottom. So, during the night the rain softened up the ground and due to the strain on the pegs about five of them pulled out with the result that my tent was no longer pitched very well. So I had to get up and tie rocks on the bottom and then stretch it with that means, but it worked very well that way even if I did cuss at every rock I seen last night.

I still haven't had a chance to wrap that chewing gum but will do so the first chance I get. I'm a little slow in getting around to things. I suppose by this time next week I'll be sleeping on a mattress again and it really won't feel bad. But there are really no privations on maneuvers except on passes and drinks and a pretty rugged life. If we go back to Ft. Jackson again and join the XII Corps we will probably go on maneuvers again in January because they're supposed to start a maneuver somewhere by the eighth of June but I don't know if it will be in Tennessee or not. It might be a desert maneuver and it might be held in California. So waiting and seeing is the best policy I found yet in this Army.

I sure could use a couple of beers tonight. Sometimes we get beer on the weekends when the problem is off but that's the only time. But I believe a few shots of whiskey would go better because it has a warming effect.

I thought of my brother-in-law the other day. I walked through just a small field and I kicked up six rabbits in just about 100 yards if it was that much. This area we're in now is just loaded with them. Well, I don't suppose anyone has hunted down here for about three years because of maneuvers. The government won't allow it. But I looked all day when I was home and never seen as many rabbits as I seen in ten minutes here. This would really make Lee go nuts. He wouldn't be able to speak for ten minutes. He would be like a dog with worms. He wouldn't know what to do.

Well, this letter is getting rather long and my batteries are getting dim, but we have more, so I guess I'll close before I get pen-itis, so good night and good luck and God bless you.

As Always,

Norb

Louisville, Kentucky, **November 4,** Thursday night, 10:30 pm

(Katsy's 7th birthday)

Dear Norb,

Well, my dear we will have a Republican Governor of Kentucky and probably a Rep. President in '44.' Far as Kentucky goes, so goes the US. I think the change will be beneficial. We are all OK and the weather is beautiful but we had a very heavy frost this morning.

I guess you know by this time that John Epping, the soft drink man, is dead. I wish I'd be a favorite niece.

Do you think you'll get a weekend soon? Mom and I have a feeling you might. Here's hoping. I just heard over the air that Tommy Harmon, "the all American Half Back." is missing in action since October. I seen in the paper where the Japs used poisonous gas.

Pop brought a load of logs from those Chinese Elm trees home. He had the iceman haul them. He said they are having the yard graded and fixed and he said this one bulldozer got rid of the one he didn't in a mighty big hurry.

Eleanor called this afternoon. She said that we won either a bushel of groceries or a wagonload of groceries. They raffled them off this afternoon and the kids heard Mom's name called so we were really anxious to know if they were right or not. I'll let you know for sure. Marge covered a bedroom chair for Bell. It really is beautiful. Did you hear any more about Camp Forrest, Tennessee?

Well, I'll finish this tomorrow and say goodnite dear, good nite. I guess by this time that mud ought to be shaped to your "curves" isn't it? Nite!

Continued, **November 5,** Friday morning.

Well, we got your "pamphlet" this morning and was glad to hear. I guess Mom's hunch and mine didn't amount to a darn thing. Miss Elizabeth, Fr. Knue's housekeeper, called from Holy Trinity and we won the two baskets of groceries, not the wagonload. Mom says she's bingo bound now, her luck's beginning.

I guess you're what they would call a clean pig, no bath in 2 ½ weeks and still not dirty, sez you. Mommy is going to have another washday. The dear child thinks it's necessary. Miss Elizabeth told Mom those groceries have a dozen eggs with them. From all the newscasters we're really making progress, we really are. If it keeps up this good, I don't think you'll fight the Dutchmen.

So you think Lee would go nuts in your neck of the woods? Do you think he would "just go?" Mom says she wants to write some but she's deep in the suds [*laundry*]. The material cost $50 for the old house thus far.

[*Hermina*]

Louisville, Kentucky, **November 5**

Dear Norb,

I couldn't write any news. Hermina is the news reporter, as you know. I am glad that she likes to write and let you know all about the whole family's business. We have a carpenter here. He only charges $1.25 an hour. Some price, ain't it? The house is in a bad shape and taking longer than a new job. I thought that you might get to come home if only for a short time. I have you on my mind so much hoping that you could come. Well, if you can't come, then as God wills it.

What do you think about me winning 2 baskets of groceries? Elizabeth called. Phoned us that the little ones would come. She wants to get to town to get Milton a coat. Mutty [Moody] is going to get the baskets for me. He will go to the Sacred Heart School anyhow so that will be fine. I will close now. The carpenter is waiting for roof paste so want to get it from Johnson's.

Good by [*sic*],

Mother

PS. Prayed very special for you this morning for you and for peace at the Communion railing first thing, you know

PS. No. 2. <u>Do you go to the Sacraments</u>?

The following message from girlfriend Alma Pierce was on a 1¢ postcard depicting the Memorial Square looking toward the state capitol in Nashville, Tennessee with the Andrew Jackson Hotel on the right. The return address was 3006 Vanderbilt Place, Nashville. Alma had gone to visit for a week. She was 18 years old. This surely wouldn't have set well with the families of Alma or Norb.

Nashville, Tennessee, **November 6**

Hello Mom [*Norb's Mom*],

How is everyone? Fine I hope. I guess you are surprised to hear from me. I didn't know I would coming till Thursday morning when my boss said I had two weeks' vacation coming to me. So, I came here to see Norb. I'll be here for a week, so if you want to write I'll really be glad to hear from you all.

Love,
Alma

Louisville, Kentucky, **November 7**, Saturday, 9:30

Dear Brother (fooled ya),

To begin with, you will find the enclosed itemized list of what Mom won at Fr. Knue's. Boy, Mom was tickled. Lip thinks some of the prices are higher by a few cents so I guess it's something to win in wartime. A taxi rolled up by our door. We could see a soldier in it. We held our breath for not too long. It was the boy across the street. Will a taxi soon roll up by our door, do you think?

A Nurse's Aid of the American Red Cross called by phone yesterday and wanted to know if I knew Alma Pierce. I said yes. She said they were calling for reference about her. I said, well, what I know of her I think she's a very nice girl. Do you think she will make a good nurse? H.R.: I said yes I do, I feel like she'd make a very good nurse. RC: What we want to know is she as good as her word, that is, if she says something does she usually do it and stick with it? I said yes. RC: Then you think she will make a good nurse and will go thru with the training if she begins? H.R.: I said yes I think she will, but as far as knowing, nobody could tell you that. RC: Well, that's all we wanted to know. Amen. You can tell Alma they called to investigate. It might help her to make further plans. Alma always did say she would like to be a nurse and this is really an opportunity for her because she can never be a R.N. without a High School education. If it wouldn't be for what I have to put up with [*occasional epileptic seizures, hormonal problems*] I would be in there, because I believe I could do that.

Lip got Milt a Finger-Tip coat. It's really cute. It might not be long before you'll have to look up to him. My, he is really shooting up. The saleslady told him the blue one looked so nice on him; it matched his pretty, blue eyes. Lip said Milt didn't know how to look. He has got two sweet looking eyes.

Well, are you pulling out of Tennessee soon?

Did you get that box of candy and another box with a marble cake in it? How was the cake? I had a few crumbs. I picked it up. I thought the chocolate part tasted bitter but Lip tasted too and she said it didn't so I sent it. Let me know if it was bitter, please. I want to know and my "feelins" won't be hurt because you was too complimentary in your last letter and thank you. We really got a letter yesterday. Wow, that was some letter! The war news is good, very good. Boy that must of been some celebration in Russia that "Uncle Joe" [*Stalin*] ordered.

Well, we got a radioman to look at your radio. Mom asked him to put a bulb in it and the thing would not play. He worked about 45 minutes on it so he had to take it home. He sure hated it but that's all he could do. So he took it home to fix it and left us a little one to use. Marge is having the circuit changed in it but you can't do anything about getting tubes.

I guess you can always have it put back again. But I think that after the war all the radios will be so much different.

Tomorrow is Cemetery Day. Mrs. Russell brought over a nice bouquet. Well, I want to press out some curtains and get them up, so good night beautiful Soldier.
Goodnight as ever,
Hermina

The list of items and estimated value (cents) mentioned in the above letter were:
Canned goods: 1 Scott County Trout .15, 3 Peas .36, 1 large milk .10, 1 beet .10, 3 corn .36, 3 puree .30, 1 pear halves .18, 1 mixed veg .15, 3 tomatoes .30, 1 grapefruit juice .29, 2 qt. jar of kraut .35, 1 milk .10, 1 turtle soup .25, 2 green beans .26, 2 soup .22, 1 lb. Del Monte coffee .35, 2 matches .10, 1 qt. homemade carrots .25 (end of canned goods). 1 sm. Super Suds .10, 1 Octagon .06, 1 sack tobacco .05, 2 cleansers .16, 1 savory sauce .25, 3/3 pecks potatoes .40, 1 qt malted milk .35, 1 starch .10, 2 Pancake flour .20, 1 Grape Nuts flakes .10, 1 bran cereal .15, 1 Wheaties .10, 1 Kix .10, 1 Puffed Wheat .10, 1 Rice Gems .10, 1 Raisin Bran .15, 2 rolled oats .20, 1 lb. brown sugar .10, 7 macaroni .70, 1 macaroni dinner .10, 1 dried peas .14, 3 Jello .25, 1 box tea balls .10, 1 crackers .10, 1 salt .10, 1 soda .05, 1 bottle vanilla .05, 2 spaghetti .10, 1 dozen eggs .65. All counted, it was $9.30.

Louisville, Kentucky, **November 9** [*postcard*]
Dear Son,

Have not heard from you this week yet I hope you got the box. You never stated if you got the last box we sent you. Are you coming home? I wish you could if it would only be for a short time. Would like to know. Hoping to hear from you soon.
As Always,
Your dear Mother

November 9, Tuesday night
Hello babe,

How is every little thing coming along? I sound like one of the boys, don't I? HA, HA. Well, Root, I guess you are off of those things they call maneuvers now but I guess you will get this letter if I mail it to the address you had on that letter, won't you? HA, HA.

Guess what I did last Saturday? I went to Louisville and didn't get back until 3:30 Monday afternoon. Boy, did I catch hell. I still don't know what is going to come up. I didn't go up home. It was a couple of other fellows with me and we just pitch a bitch. I didn't even go up in the neighborhood. If you ever get to Louisville let me know when you are going and maybe I will be able to meet you there (maybe), but will try like hell.

You are getting to be an old rum hound aren't you? HA, HA. Well, it's not bad at all, is it? I believe the Army drives you to drink because I just love my liquor now, don't you? It's a darn good thing you are not in the Air Corps or you would be jumping out of those damn things when you get loaded. Maybe it would sober you up when you hit the bottom. I told some of these fellows about that time we got drunk up at St. Brigid's and your ball hung out. They liked to laugh their ass off about it, but I told them it was more fun being there, wasn't it? I sure wish we could get the gang back and have one of those tea parties. Couldn't we raise hell with... pinball machines? HA, HA.

You asked me about my uncle in Camp Taylor. Well, the last time I heard about him he was building another house next door for a mess hall so he must be doing all right. Well, Norb I haven't any more to write about so I better stop now because I have some good ass laying on the next bunk to me and I can't refuse it, so be a good soldier like me and I will see you soon.

How are you and Alma getting along lately? Fine I hope. HA, HA. Good luck and good night.

The tea hound,

(Redtop.) [*Larny Johnson*]

Norb arrived back at Fort Jackson, South Carolina after 5 weeks of maneuvers in Tennessee. His new address was HQ. Co. 59th Signal Battalion, APO #312, ASN 35487644, Ft Jackson, SC.

Fort Jackson, South Carolina, **November 10**

Dear Mom and all,

Arrived at Ft. Jackson late tonight. Can't write much now, too busy. My address is HQ. Co. 59th Signal Battalion, APO #312, ASN 75487644, Ft Jackson, SC.

As Always,

Norb

Louisville, Kentucky, **November 10**, Wednesday, 2:30 pm

Dear Norb,

I'm going to relay to you some news as I heard it. Pop has another nephew. Little Mary [*Rawert*] got married this morning. She married that Willie Hunn. We never knew about it until Cousin Mary Rawert called. She heard it in the grocery. Thought maybe you might be interested but she certainly wasn't interested in their only uncle [*Norb's dad*] but I don't blame her. Psst - they say he makes big money and she is going to continue working.

And the phone rang again. It was Renee Alberts who dear Miss Emma stays with. She was at her neighbors so she called Mom and told her Emma fell down some steps and is laid up. She didn't break any bones but tore the ligaments loose. She's getting along alright I guess because she is beginning to hobble with sticks. I'm sending a card for you to send to her if you want to. I think you will be dear, dear seven times more there! Nothing more she enjoys I know.

Well, where are you? And where will you be sent to? It's a crimp day but beautiful. Mary's getting ready to leave (I hear her coming) so we'll give you Emma Grimm's address: 717 Baroness, Louisville, Kentucky. Hope you are OK as we all are. I was too late. Mary left. Love,
Hermina

Louisville, Kentucky, November 11, Armistice Day, 11:15 am

Dear Norb,

So you're back in SC. Well, well, we thought perhaps you might get a weekend leave at home but we were thinking wrong. Mom got a card from Alma Monday saying she was in Nashville. Did you get to see her? Mom answered the card. It's a beautiful day. Your letter arrived at the eleventh hour but it wasn't much whistles blowing at all, and no holiday at all. We are all OK.

I was talking with the Spoelker girls and Bernard was promoted to Captain about 2 weeks ago, Bob Hensle expects to go to work next week but is still weak in the knees and wears rubber kneecaps. He was fortunate tho. The Dr. Said if he would of waited until he collapsed there would of been no hope for him.

It's really cold out, very cold. How did you enjoy the trip "back home?" Norb, do you want any Christmas Cards? Kindly answer on that because the P.O. wants them all mailed early so let us know before they are all sold out, that is if you want us to get them. And don't be shy about what you would like for Christmas. If there is something, say so, say so. Would you like an identification bracelet? Or is that excess jewelry to you? I think they look nice. I guess you are enjoying a mattress again. I hope so. Your letter was [*postmarked*] last night at 10:00 and we had it today at 11:00. That's fast traveling, my boy. Write soon and more. Love,
Hermina

Continued by Mommy, November 11

Dear Norb,

Just a few lines to write. My dear, dear Hermina is writing the news. I am going to see Miss Emma this afternoon. I feel very sorry for her. We were surprised that you are in Ft. Jackson again. I think you will like it better than in Tennessee. We all thought we would get to see you but it was <u>so near and yet so far</u>. Well, I guess if just has to be that way as <u>God wills it</u>. You will not have to wish for a good drink to get you warmed up. Will you please let us know if you got a box with a marble cake and apples in it? Papa is taking vitamins now. Two capsules a day. I think he eats more but he would not admit it. How did you enjoy your trip home? That's all. The next time more,
God bless you,
Mother

Louisville, Kentucky, **November 11**

Dear Norb,

　　Armistice Day 1943. We do not have any school. I am up at Mommy's. Shirley is gone in town to the National show with Mary Ann Orrill to see the two dead-end kids in person. My old man [*Leo Muth*] is working very hard. He said last night that his hands were swelling with hard work. I wonder if it could be from too much exercise from Oertel's '92. He did have a few ounces of fat on his Low-Dutch frame but he lost it all. Today Mommy [grandma] Muth is dead nine years.

　　I found a tube of lipstick on Mommy's front grass, almost a full tube and plenty of red. I guess we will all have pretty rosebud lips. What do you want from old Santa Claus? Will be here in a little while. I am being good anyhow even if I don't believe in him. Anyhow, it might pay me. You can't tell. Mary said she was fat and sassy and she hopes that you are the same way.

　　Well, my traveling Unk [uncle] I hope this letter finds you on the beam. And see the next line for Petey sake answer one of my morale building letters, otherwise I'll lose all faith in the US Army. Gimme a gob sealed with a little [*here Betsy had a big kiss mark from her new lipstick*] and spit mixed.

Love,

Betsy

Fort Jackson, South Carolina, **November 12**, 9:30 pm

Dear Mom and all,

　　Well, it's a little warmer and dryer here than it was in Tenn.

　　Well, Alma came down to Nashville but I didn't get to see her. We pulled out just the next day after for Ft. Jackson and I couldn't get a pass. So I guess it's just a plain case of "T.S." (Tough shit).

　　I got a letter from Betty Bratten today and she said Tommy has been in England for quite some time. She said they have a baby four months old. Damn time sure does fly.

　　I thought ma[y]be we would get a furlough after this maneuver but I guess that's a case of "T.S." also, because they are only giving furloughs to those who haven't had none in the last six months or those who have had none at all. So I guess I'll wait my turn.

　　This is a short letter but I guess it's better than none at all. Blame all mistakes on this typewriter. It's in bad need of repair. Well, I'll write more later when I have more time. As for the present, I'm pretty damn busy, so good night, good luck and god bless you.

As Always,

Norb

Louisville, Kentucky, **November 14**, Sunday

Dear Norb,

　　It seems ducely [*sic*] odd to address Ft. Jackson again, it does. It's rather cold today. It was 28° this morning. We never heard from you as yet. We got your "notice." Robert Lee Robben is on his way across. It seem this Father Draft is really getting them now. Robert Roth, the Air Raid Warden, got his greetings and the young lady's husband that runs "Kendrick's" place is slated for the Navy. You can't realize how it is getting them now. It seems like the Marriage Feast of Cana. It seems like they are keeping the best (trained) until last. Charles Steinmetz is home on furlough and look how long he's been in the army.

I'm hopeful you will have a letter ready for the morning delivery. It's been 10 days since we last heard, not counting the notice. Chester really grieved about going. He looks pale faced. He said the Dr. told him he got two things to really be thankful for-good feet and all sound teeth. And told him he will have to run around barefoot and grin all the time. Carl Horne is in the Naval Sound School at Key West, Fla.

Do you think you'll get a furlough Christmas or Thanksgiving? My wrong "hinch" gave me a lot of unnecessary work but then I got some exercise week before last. Mom and I thought you would show up on a weekend leave so I got busy on the two front rooms. So we were wrong. So what! I've gained all lost.

I'm wondering if we won anything at St. X. Their Fall Festival was Friday and Saturday. Pop is gone after a shock of beer so you know it's between 9 and 10 pm. Goodnite.

Monday

We received your letter this morning. It's sort of gloomy (the weather) out today. Mom is in her glory. I got a card from Bernhard Hollkamp. I think he likes it better. I suppose by this time you've gotten all the mail we wrote to Tennessee and the envelope you sent today was really something. What did you do with those cards I sent you? We never got one, but we enjoy letters better. So you never got to see Alma. I suppose if she went a week sooner she would have gotten to see you, if you were a certain woman's son that would be written in Love Book No. 1.

Now what about Xmas cards? Norb, don't forget that in your next letter, yes or no. It seems you appreciate SC better. We have music with our meals. We have your radio on the kitchen table. Say, that has a good sound for a little radio. And we ain't blaming no typewriter for mistakes. Who could I blame all of these on?

That Tommy Bratten sure got across in a big hurry. Mom put out about $150 and there's more lumber coming today but this rounds it up. Well, too-da-loo til I scribble again.
Love,
Hermina

Louisville, Kentucky, **November 16**

Dear, Dear Son,

Chewing 'chewing gum' from my dear Son. I received the gum this morning and many thanks. I was altogether out of gum. We already sampled the gum. It is very good. I enjoyed the gum very much. I think of you every time I chew. I don't know how it is I have you in my mind so much this morning. It is 12:30 now. I made Papa some under britches. I cut out 4 pairs. I have work for today. We are listening to your radio. It is on the windowsill in the kitchen on the side where Papa sits. It plays fine. The war sounds good for us this morning. The weather is very gloomy today, 32 degrees. May be we will have snow by this evening. So you like SC better than Tennessee? Are you booten [*booting*] any more hogs and eyeing toad frogs and throwing rocks?

Papa is taking vitamins now and he has better appetite. Yesterday he ate some of his supper for dinner. He didn't have to go back Sunday afternoon. The lady that plays the organ was sick and Mr. Winter who drives the taxi had to work so Papa did not have to come back. The [*St. Brigid*] schoolyard is getting fixed with asphalt. Papa likes it very much and it keeps the school's floor cleaner. Well, Hermina is ironing. Marge starts at 7 o'clock instead of 8 now. I don't like it. It is dark when she leaves. They are so busy now. There's a quite a few married men with children called.

Margie calls your namesake "Norty Hermy [*Norbert Henry*]." she is crazy about him. Well, so long and God bless you.
Mother

Contiued by Hermina:

Hello Nobbie (say it quick).

Tain't got any news. Only I want to "boss" you a little. Did you get Margie's card? If so, kindly mention as she heard from the rest. She sent one too and she asked if you ever said anything. Did you get a box of candy at Nashville and a cake a few days after? A marble cake? If so let us know as it was insured my dear.

More kid talk: Milton brought Lip and Margie a bar of candy from work. He said they were the only ones he liked and they stank. Margie was quick to realize that there might be more Friday. As Milt came home, he went to the bathroom and she kept laying outside of it telling him how much she loved him and everything sweet she could think of. I'd say she's showing her womanly intuition young. She's been wearing knit shirts and woolen pants and Lizzie thinks she looks just like you did. She does but is without that intelligent knot, or should I say that added good for nothing? Huh? Well, toodaloo my deah [*sic*]. I'll be a seeing you when? So good luck and God bless you.
Your little sister,
Mary Hermina Bernadette Rawert
What about Christmas cards??

Louisville, Kentucky, **November 19**, Friday, 3:15 pm

[*Dear Norb,*]

As the old saying goes, all things come to those who wait. I suppose that's true. Last night I tried twice to get up a letter but I couldn't so I quit. If it would of been your first days at Camp I might have had nerve enough to send it. So today, I have something to write about. Norbert Hollkamp is home on a 14-day furlough. He looks fine, weighs 193 pounds. His "ways" are different. The most settled I have ever seen him. He gained 30 pounds and walks like a "Sergeant's headache yet" and it's not so dreamy eyed. We asked him over for a meal on Tuesday. He has a date. I think the army helped him a lot. I was really surprised to see him look as well as he did.

I also got a letter from Bernard. He said he thought about us the whole next day after Halloween as that Pumpkin face like I sent you netted him a day of KP. He said Halloween he lit it up, put it on a post outside the barracks and played cards and forgot about the pumpkin until they smelt it. It was in flames. He said it was plenty of holy hell, or not so holy, that he caught but he had a lot of fun over it. The next time I won't send him a paper pumpkin he can call his own. I'll send him a pumpkin that is real. You're not sick are you? We have only received one letter of short form since you are in Ft. Jackson. Do you think you'll get home over the holidays, my dear? The mailman has been here so we won't hear no more today.

At 1:15 am on Wednesday morning, our phone rang. Well, it was the wrong number. They wanted Krebs [a neighbor]. I was back in bed and it rang again. It did that four times. It was a darky trying mighty hard but never used a dial phone. I never grew impatient. "Hum, clear your throat on that." I told him to dial the operator, which he did and we slept ever after but a phone ring sounds so sharp at nite. We are still waiting for you to call honey, we sure are. If you can, call us and reverse it.

We have windows and door open today. It's really heavenly. We still are eating tomatoes out of our garden. We put them in a basket unwrapped and they really go good. They are 20¢ per pound. I heard over the air [radio] that oranges and citrus fruits were going to be sold by the pound. That must be some way to wriggle out of something. Well, Norb we are all OK on Texas Street and hope you are too. Waiting to hear from you or receive a few scribbles. I know this is sort of scribbled too, but the pen is sort of going "Democrat."

The next day after election Sen. Barkley stopped in at Kentucky Hotel as he always does for a haircut and shave and to chat with his old friend the barber who he knew for years. The barber informed him he would have to charge him more. He asked why. He said because your face is long this morning, Senator. A true Kentucky yarn. Write soon.
Love,
[Hermina]

Fort Jackson, South Carolina, **November 22**

Dear Mom and all,

Well, I wrote a letter the other day and just found out I forgot to mail it. Forgetful ain't I? We've been pretty busy because half the outfit is on furlough so that leaves just half of the amount to do the work. But things are pretty quiet. I think this is just a waiting process. Yeah man, looking for bigger things to come. I think I will get a furlough in the near future ma[y]be. Sometime within the next 30 days, I would like to get home over Xmas if I can. And then again, I might take it as soon as I can get it because this will be the last one I can get for quite some time. They're giving everyone a short furlough. I'm afraid if I wait until around Xmas I won't get it at all. So I guess I'll just sit tight and see what happens.

Alma came down and stayed a few days and she's on her way home now. She didn't have a very long stay though due to financial matters. I was just about broke myself but we made out OK. She stayed at the Guest House here on the post.

The weather is really warm here. In fact, I was sweating yesterday. I think we'll get some rain tonight because it is very cloudy outside.

I lost 3 uniforms when I was on maneuvers so I guess they're in Tenn. I hope I don't have to pay for them because if I do I won't have enough cash to make it to Louisville if I do get a furlough. Ma[y]be they'll make out a Report of Survey and I won't have to stand the expense, but if they don't, old Rawert will have to pay. But I hope not. Well, I'm running out of paper so I'd better close for now. (Tell my little darling Mary hello for me XXX). Remaining,

As Always,

Norb

Louisville, Kentucky, **November 23**, 1 pm

Dear Norb,

I suppose you have Mom's letter by this time. Mom has felt a bit leery because she hasn't heard from you. It was a week yesterday, then it was short and sweet but not enough of it. Mom, I suppose, told you that John etc. was here. The baby weighs 19 ½ pounds. Johnny couldn't go home until he weighed him so he "fit" him in a dishpan. He's really a doll. He looks the most like Jackie only it's more of him but he's friendly as Hilary was. They all look swell. Lip and daughter Margaret was here too. Joey and Lee was here Saturday. You know they are in a dither - don't know where to get shells for hunting. Joey called every place she could. I don't think he's working but you wouldn't expect him to at this time of year [*hunting season*].

We are sending a little Thanksgiving treat. Let us know when you get it. Also about the "two" last boxes we sent. The news sounds good. I think people are getting a little too optimistic but when you hear things like this, it makes you feel good (when you put two and two together). I heard that the Standard Co. were going to start part of the Brass Works up again and a man in the neighborhood went to the Government Employment Agency here for a Defense job. They told him if he had a job within reason to stick to it. Now don't you think that sounds good?

Gertie Meyer's boy is home from Nome, Alaska. Took him 13 days to make the trip. He was in the Attic and Kiska battles, has those stripes. He said he traveled by plane, ship and train. He had dinner at Mary's as well as Mom and I and Lou and Norbert. Norbert sure does look good. So does Gert's boy but he said so many has gone balmy up there in Alaska. He said one boy went bugs on the train coming here. He couldn't believe he was coming to the States.

Lip was telling me you have a brand new future brother-in-law. She seen it in the papers. That's more than I seen. Did Alma go in as a Nurses Aid? Your Godchild was "really" proud yesterday. She got a gold star and two smaller ones for working arithmetic problems. She worked down 18 boys and she feels very good about it indeed. Some girl told Betsy, "Your sister thinks she's smart." Betsy said, "She don't only think she's smart, she KNOWS she's smart."

Hilary's Sister asked someone to sing a song for her so Hilary got to do it. He sang, "He's a high geared daddy until his sweet Mamma put him in low." He said Sister laughed tears and asked him where he learned that song, so some other boy ups and says. "Sr., he heard that on the Saturday night Barn Dance because I heard it over there two weeks ago." Hil said that's where he learned it.

How about looking not too stern at the Birdie for Mom for Xmas, huh? Go ahead and make up your low Dutch block [sp]. Don't forget to scribble a few lines.
Love and more love,
H.R.

Louisville, Kentucky, **November 23**
Dear Norb,

What is the matter? You are not forgetting me, or are you sick? I hope not. We are all well. The weather is fine, 27 degrees cold. John and his family was here Sunday. Papa, John and Joe played cards all afternoon. Little, or big and fat I should say, 'Norty Hermy' is fine. Weighs 19 ½ lbs. He surely is a fine looking boy like you were when you were a baby. Well, you are yet! I am worried that we didn't get a letter for 8 days. We received the book telling all about Ft. Jackson. Very interesting and many thanks.

Walter Orrill is not coming home for the Christmas. His mother is very disappointed. He thinks he will come home on January 15. I hope he will. We are going upstairs to Mary's for dinner. The Hollenkamps and Norbert are coming also. We are going to ask them, also Norbert, looks good.

Norbert, I guess you like it better than at Tenn. I am only sorry that we could not get to see you but we was afraid that we would be disappointed. You didn't write that we could or we could not see you. We thought that maybe you would surprise us and come home.

Well, I hope that you will write soon and so we know how you are. Hermina will write more news tomorrow, so good-bye.
God bless you and good luck,

Mother

Louisville, Kentucky, **November 26**, 1 pm

Dear Norb,

We received your letter this morning. So you think you will be going over soon and expecting a furlough. Well, I think I would take it when offered because you might not get it later on. Perhaps you might get it by Christmas time, we hope. We hope you'll be on the late train.

Well, they really made something of the Gen. Patton happening. Some think it should be kept under cover but I don't. It has been rehashed over the air for the last three days, which I think is too much. I believe the reason for making such an issue out of it is because Pres. Roosevelt is in conference, don't you think?

Ann is gone in town with Mom. She [*Mom*] is going to some Dr. but is going to get Mr. Krebs advice first. Pop wants her to go to Dr. Ritter but Dr. Townes recommended Dr. Wynn so it will be someone. For the past 2 months, she's been having difficulty with getting her eye out and the lids look heavy and partially closed, so she thought she better see about it as it waters so much. I don't think it's anything serious.

Jackie is well on the road to recovery. He has type 7 pneumonia, or bronchial pneumonia to us. He had to save his sputum the first night and take it to the hospital to have it analyzed, as there are 22 types of pneumonia and a serum for every type. And if the sulfa drug didn't act properly, they would give him this serum also. The sulfa drug did the work and the serum wasn't used. They went to see him yesterday and he was doing swell. His fever is broken. That sulfa drug is a miracle.

Mr. Johnson [*Johnson's Hardware*] was here with sand and cement for the old place. Larny is expecting a furlough soon and so is Earl. You might have a buddy dance on your furlough. Furlough, furlough, is all I hear at present. Jr Russell is expecting a leave the first of Dec. He said the C.O. told them they would be going over after this one.

Mom and Ann just came home from Dr. Wynn. He said Mom has an inflammation in her eye and lid. He gave her some drops so it's just an irritation and nothing to worry about he said.

I'm sure glad peace and contentment, such as the one pig is enjoying [*on Norb's last letter stationary*], reminds you of me. Just a piggie [*sic*] of peace I call myself now. As fer [*sic*] you I never seen a picture at present that would fit you, but if I do, I'll send it pronto!

We are all OK. Male beat Manual 26 to 7. It was really crowds of people walking yesterday but they claim yesterday's crowds was the largest ever at the games. One young girl passed [*by*] drunker than everything, the only one we seen that looked canned up. Shirley said you can see that the women have more money this year. Well, Cpl. Rawert I'll sign off hoping you are OK.

Love from all,

Pig of Peace [*Hermina*]

Fort Jackson, South Carolina, **November 27**

Dear Mom and all,

Well, there's not much to say. Only that things are buzzing pretty well and we're very busy. In fact, tomorrow is Sunday and we work tomorrow. You can leave the APO number off my address now because we expect to change it to a new one sometime in the near future. I can't truthfully say if I will get a furlough before I smell the old salt water or not but I do believe I'll get about 10 days but don't bank on that because the army comes first. If I do OK and if I don't OK (bull shit). Well, it's a tough night and it's getting late so old Rawert will sign off as of now.

As Always,

Norb

Louisville, Kentucky, **November 29**, 2 pm

Dear Norb:

Well, it's a gloomy day in Louisville, rather snappy it was, but it seems to be clearing up some and a little warmer. It seems everybody and his cousin is coming home on a furlough. Jonesy is here on a 10-day one. His whole outfit was sent across, with the exception of 27 of them, and he was lucky enough to be one of them. Maybe that's why he's here too. Can't tell, can you?

Now. Mr. Redle fell last week and cut his chin. He fell on Goss and Railroad tracks. This goes to show you how tight we are on MDs. The police took him to General Hospital and it was no MD available that could give him first aid. They put him in an ambulance to St. Mary's and Elizabeth's Hospital where they took 9 stitches in his chin and 4 inside his mouth. Maybe that will make you feel good to be in the Army. I seen where Gen. Patton didn't get his promotion [*uproar over his slapping and belittling of a soldier in a hospital for being a coward, but later it was proven to be malaria*]. Well, if a soldier does something wrong they bust him, so why not an officer? Did you get your medal for a year's service with good behavior? Jonesy had one on. Did you have to pay for your uniforms?

We are all OK in this neck of the woods. We bought you a few things for Xmas but will not send them now because you might come home in time for Xmas. Let us know if you can. You got that Airmail envelope.

Love from

Hermina

...Let me add this. I can't think of much news, sort of thick-skulled today. I couldn't blame it on the weather. We all thought you broke the news swell and I don't care how many fat pigs reminds you of me. I think it helped break the news better for you and us. Momma is writing now. She's been wanting to ever since Friday. She just had a good crying spell and that always relieves her, but Mom takes it swell. She always did take every knock as a boost

I think. Let us know of any developments as they come. We know you are now praying to go across, so the news is broken. I think it was a hard letter for you to write but you made a good job of it. Mom is over her bawling spell and I know she feels better. Norb if you could call us and reverse the charges I know Mom would feel good to hear you, as she waited so long for you to call when in Nashville. Call us if it's convenient and reverse the charges. Love and best of luck from all of us,

Pig of Peace

Louisville, Kentucky, **November 29**

Dear Norbert:

Well, Hermina is writing about the weather. No use to listen to the news twice. We are all well and your letters tells us that you are well also. I believe that your furlough will be not so short as you think. Here's hoping it won't. I don't blame you for not taking it when you can. Of course, Christmas would be better if you can get it to our way of thinking but let it be the way is can.

I believe that you think that you will go across the way you worded your letter. It makes us all feel sad, as you know, but we cannot do anything about it. Only the one God can, and to Him we have to pray and have confidence in. Norb, please go to the <u>Sacraments</u>. That's the only way to have peace and consolation. If we go to the Sacraments often, we have nothing to lose and fear for, everything to gain. A clear conscience is everything. The way I hear, the boys don't have a Chaplain for two months sometimes so make good use of the time you have. I always think and pray for you. Whatever God has in store for us we don't know but we can say and pray Thy will be done. Hoping to hear from you soon if only a few lines. It will make us feel better so good-bye and <u>God bless you</u>.

Mother

Mary sends XXX & Hello

Fort Jackson, South Carolina, **November 29**

Dear Mamy, Papy and kinsfolk,

Monday night and all is well, in fact, too well. We worked all day yesterday for an IG (Inspector General) we had today. It was pretty tough. Yep, pretty tough. It rained down here all last night and most of today. I believe that's the first time since we came back from maneuvers. Well, I'm still undecided about this furlough. Wouldn't say yep and wouldn't say no. It's just a waiting process to see what happens. If I thought this furlough would be like the last one, I'd refuse to take one, and if this one is like the last, I'll never take another. I can't ever remember being so damn sick in my life.

Well, there's really no news except you can leave the APO #312 off my mail because we're no longer attached to the XII Corps. We're subject to a change in station at any time. The lights are going out pretty soon so I'll have to sign off for now. Remaining,

As Always,
Knob head [*Norb*]

Louisville, Kentucky, **November 30**, Tuesday, 1:45pm

Dear Norb,

We received your letter this morning and are living in hopes you will get a furlough but if you don't it will have to be OK as you said. You at least had two furloughs and nice ones and that's more than some boys got, but we will keep our "timmers" crossed. Could you make it on a 3-day pass with an added day if you could just get one day at home? But it's the Army and you can't do anything about it yourself.

We got some things for you for Christmas (kindly answer if you can). We will send it immediately or wait until you get your furlough and receive it at home. Which way do you want it?

Mom's eye socket is getting to feel better but when she strains to write, it smarts. She wanted to write but asked me to do it (important, huh?) She said if you thought you couldn't get a furlough and she could make it up to South Carolina, do you think your Co. would pull out? That is, have you a way of knowing? She wouldn't want to make the trip for nothing but would like to see you. Marge would probably go with her if she can get off. Let her know. We are all OK in Louisville and Jackie is doing fine.

Love from all,
Hermina

Louisville, Kentucky, **December 1**, Wednesday, 5:30 pm

Dear Norb,

We never heard from you today but didn't expect that much of you (considerate). It was gloomy all day but you can't do anything about that. It seems so odd at 8:00 am. It wasn't good and light yet this morning. I was up at 6:40. We are all OK.

Lip's kids are all thrilled about Xmas. Shirley and Milt have a few dollars so they are interested in a spread for Mother. Shirley said all the rest would have to put in a nickel if they want their name on it. Milt's giving everybody something and for Moody and Lip, he's going to wave his report card before them and sing Miltie got a "zero." I nearly died laughing at him. We thought about getting Mom a crochet tablecloth if we all pitched in. Mrs. Smith (Ann's mom) would make it but we kicked that in the head.

Bill Miller at work got his greetings [*from Uncle Sam*]. He has five children. Seems like they are really fighting at present. That Mrs. Stoll kidnaping case is up in Louisville. They have five women jurists on the case, the first time in Kentucky in a criminal case. I suppose you remember that Thomas H. Robinson was the kidnapper. Johnny sells milk to them (Stolls). He said they are nice people.

Beef was cut to 2 to 3 points a pound. Something to write about. We're going to have rabbit for supper. The first time in two years. Mom got it at Schieman's. It was a young 'un and tender and very, very good. I was really anxious for a good "hassa." No red points was needed. It cost 60¢. That's some price for a bunny. They say they are plentiful. You can imagine that.

I suppose Jr Russell will be home Friday. His wife is in Detroit for almost two months. I feel like it might be a case of separation or semi-separation, but fickle-minded might make up her mind again.

I thought this was good. It appeared last night in "Off the Record." The incident was overheard. Two Negro's were talking about Thanksgiving. One said to the other, what are you going to have? He answered 4-F. What do you mean 4-F? Chicken.

Papa said this sounded like Sabel's make up. It could be - Joe told me. Here goes: Hitler and Roosevelt died and met at the gates of heaven. The Lord said to them I don't want you all here. We'll go to hell then, they said. So the devil opened the door and told them he didn't want them either, so Roosevelt looked at Hitler and said Adolf! You start another place and I'll finance it.

Pop had some woman tell him he's happy. The war news is good, isn't it? Joe came over with a little undershirt. It was cute, cut differently again. Joe thought it was the cutest thing. We did too. I thought this idea of Katie's is really cute. She said she was going to get a lullaby on record for Joe and Ann and "Jr" Don't you think that's cute?
Love,
Hermina

Fort Jackson, South Carolina, **December 1**

Dear Mom and all,

Well, if everything turns out alright I'll be seeing you in a little while and I think everything will. The only thing I don't like is that long train ride. It gets pretty tiresome. I was thinking of ma[y]be taking a bus. It takes about 25 hours on a bus if they are on schedule and about 23 hours on a train so I guess I'll just flip a coin and see which one I take.

We're extremely busy at present, very busy indeed, with half the men on furlough and now the other half going. I don't know what's the matter but the chow has been louzy [*sic*] the past week or so. I think we overdrew our rations when we were on maneuvers so now we have to cut down until things even up a little again. We only get coffee for breakfast and the other two meals we get water or that damn sickening orange drink made with powder.

I think they played that story about Gen. Patton up a little too much because there are good-[*illegible word*] in the Army and then on the other hand if the guy was really in a bad way Patton was all together wrong. But he's too good a man to be demoted or reclassified [*Norb changed his mind about Patton later*]. I guess his nerves were getting him down.

They are sending two more men home from our outfit because they went batty, or are going batty.

The weather has been very cool down here. Will have to close now, running out of paper so hope to see you soon.

As Always,

Norb

Louisville, Kentucky, **December 2**

Dear Norb,

We received your letter this morning and by this time, you should have a surprise by Air Mail if you didn't let Marge know. Mom wants to write. Good-bye Corporal.

[*Hermina*]

Continued, 1:30

Dear Norb:

Weather is fine. My eye is some better so I will write a few lines. Write as often as you can no matter how short or long as long as you are there. If you can come, it would be so consoling to us and you also. But we have to pray. Thy will be done. We are thinking of you all the time. E. [*Elizabeth*] is here with Katsy and Margie. Katsy had a tooth pulled so E. stopped by. We are all well and hope that you are also. Hermina bought pears yesterday - 1 peck 60¢ - so I am cooking preserves. Papa goes fifty/fifty for pear preserves but if you want some, we will have some for you also. Let us know if you got the money that Marge sent you.

We had the other house repaired. Cost over 100 now and we are not through yet. I guess the carpenter will work a week yet. He gets $1.25 [*$14.29 in 2017 value*] an hour. Well, if you need any more money, I can help you out some. I don't like to borrow any more than I can help to repair. So far, Papa had it, but I know he will not have it all. I don't want you to have to go empty-handed. Margie said you was a dumbbell. Katsy said hello.

God bless you. Good luck. Good-bye.

Mother

Fort Jackson, South Carolina, **December 5**

Dear Mom and All,

Well, to begin with, I received that $15.00 that MAA (Marge) sent and I wish to take this short message to express my deep appreciation and gratitude for doing same. Once more, I say thank you, Marge. Whether or not I will get to use it, I do not know but if I don't, I shall send it in an envelope and mail it back at the earliest possible time. I will get the furlough even though they were postponed for a short period. I have my fingers crossed anyway.

I wouldn't doubt it a bit if we will have to quit writing pretty soon, that is, after everybody gets back from furlough. I thought I would mention this just in case it would happen so you wouldn't be wondering. I don't think you're allowed to write after you reach the POE (Port of Embarkation). That's done for our protection. There are a lot of spies you know. Of course, it may be some time yet. I couldn't say. Ma[y]be this is just a dry run or part of the training, but I don't think so. But my opinion don't amount to much.

It's a beautiful day out today. It's warm enough to go out in your shirtsleeves. There's not a cloud in the sky. I was sorry to hear but glad that your eye is getting along OK. If it strains your eye to write, don't write. It's better that way because I get all the scandal and such from Hermina. But if it doesn't bother your eye, I'm always open for a letter.

So Emma [*Grimm*] gave her blessings on the "one to come." I imagine she had a few deaths mixed up in there also. In case I get this furlough, I dropped Red Johnson a letter. I think he [can] make it on a weekend pass. I'm sure that great occasion would call for a few drinks, or should I say quite a few. I got a letter from Zip about a week ago and he said he's been working pretty damn hard in England. Well, I just heard the cooks yell "CHOW" so I'll have to be closing and get my vitals [*vittles*].

As Always,

Norb

Louisville, Kentucky, **December 6**, Monday, 2:30 pm

Dear Norb:

Well, we have been looking for you since Friday. Mom bought 3 rabbits so you could have your fill but you didn't show up as yet. Oh well, have to give you time. We always did, you know. Hope you are OK.

Jr Russell came in Friday. Looks fine. Is gone up to Detroit for his wife. Ann is following in Mom's footsteps. She went out with Mom to Dr. Stites and Wynn. They stopped by Cousin Mary Rawert's and now Ann is taking her to the Doctor so I guess you'd call Ann an Angel of Charity. Mary is getting ready to go so we have been waiting and wondering. Hope all will be in your favor that you can come home.

Love,

Pig of Peace

Louisville, Kentucky, **December 7**

Dear Norb,

We are waiting since Saturday when we got your letter. You said you would see us in a little while. I hope that we all won't be disappointed. Margie is not so well. Elizabeth took her to the doctor today. They were here Sunday. She coughed almost 4 hours steady. I think she has a bad cold. I am going to call Elizabeth] after a while. John and family, Lip [*and family*] and Joey and Lee were here Sunday. They all thought you was coming home. Lip's little ones asked, where is Norb? Where is Norb?

Norb, Marge sent you money on November 30th. You should of got the money last Thursday but you never let us know. Please let us know if you got the money.

They are really busy at Hubbuch's. Marge is sending work home. Dr. Wynn said it would not hurt me to sew. I am glad for that. Did you have to pay for the uniforms?

Important! Don't forget to let us know if you received that money. It was $15.00. Everybody says Hellow [*sic*]! I hope to see you soon. Mary XXX
Good luck and God bless you.
Mother

Louisville, Kentucky, **December 8**, Tuesday, noon
Dear Norb,

Well, Mom wrote yesterday but forgot to mail it this morning. She is now at Dr. Wynn's again. Dr. Stites said her urine "analysis" was fine. Her blood pressure just a trifle high, 158. That's nothing to worry about.

I tell you all kinds of thoughts race through our minds. The newest is we think you might be on your way over since we didn't hear this week but we're still hoping to hear in person. I hope. I hope. I hope. I was disappointed when you said you wouldn't be sent to Europe but to Asia for jungle fighting but it might be the safest after all, who knows?

It's been gloomy all week. I sure hope we get more rain as the farmers are still carrying water for their stock. Mr. Hertle is going to get me a box of cigars for Pop. They sure are hard to be gotten and Pop is depending on Xmas for some. You can tell it on him; of course, he didn't come out boldly and say so.

Well, Norb I hope we see you soon. "Kippen" (Christmas) or no Kippen. It will be Kippen any time you show up. Mom hopes you'll have a "pitcher" taken this time. Margie is feeling lots better. She had a rising [*lump*] in her ear. Dr. Gettlefinger lanced it and she's got relief. Hope to hear or see you soon.
Love,
Porky

Fort Jackson, South Carolina, **December 8**
Dear Mom and all,

There is nothing new I know of except the weather is absolutely excellent. I've never seen a better day than today. It really is swell. We went on the range today and I shot a 24 out of a possible of 24, which was excellent. My nerves were extremely calm today for some reason or other. I'm sitting here listening to a "bitching" session. These guys are talking about veterans of the last war and how shitty they were treated. Also raising hell about John L Lewis. I don't know of a soldier that has any use for that "son of a bitch. (Period).

I'm still wondering about my furlough. I have heard of no further development. Tomorrow night we go over the night infiltration course where you crawl through bob [*barbed*] wire and shell crater holes that has charges of TNT in there and there is actual machine gun fire about 18 inches above your head. I went through this course in daytime but never at night. But it's really a lot of fun. Nothing to it.

I'm patiently waiting for Turkey to declare war on Germany. That day won't come too soon. That will be one of the biggest breaks the Allies ever had. I myself look for Germany to be on her knees in another 7 ½ or 8 months. That will be around my next birthday. You know I'm getting older than I think. Things have been happening so fast I didn't even think. I imagine I'll put about three years in this Army or ma[y]be a little longer, if I don't get a one-way ticket. If I do that, there won't be nothing to worry about and everything will be "honky dory." I don't know but I think we will have to deal with the Japs instead of the Germans. Well, I feel like I will be doing a better "act of charity" if I kill a Jap.

Well, I'm still wondering how Alma is doing. Didn't get a letter from her for two days, which is exceptionally long. Well, I hope everything is OK. Ha, I live on hopes. Well, it is exactly midnight and I had best be getting to bed because we arise rather early in the morning so I'll say goodnight.

As Always,

Norb

Fort Jackson, South Carolina, **December 11**, Saturday night

Dear Mom and all,

Well, how are you all? I'm OK myself. How is your eye getting along? Have you been to the doctor since the last time you wrote?

Things are truly busy as hell around here. I believe I'm just about as tired today as I have been since Aug. 18, 1942. We've been going from 7:00 am to 10:00 pm every night this week and we do the same tomorrow, which is Sunday. They are really putting us through our paces. I am wondering about my furlough, It still may be or it may not be. I couldn't say. So all I can say is "Be it as it may."

I don't look to remain in Jackson over another month. Could be we may be here longer. Couldn't say for sure. But that's just my viewpoint and I may be able to get home that time if possible.

Tell my "Darling Mary" I received her Xmas card and present, I am very appreciative, and at the earliest possible date, I shall repay all those kisses twofold and then some! If you think you can send me some Xmas cards, do so, because I'll have to mail some in case I don't get in the old burg [*Schnitzelburg*]. Well, most people are dreaming of a white Xmas. I'm not because the weather has really been swell here although it has been a little cool since last night.

Well, as I have a few more letters to catch up on and it's about 11:15 pm. now I'll have to close so I'll be seeing you ma[y]be.

As Always,

Norb

Louisville, Kentucky, **December 10**, Friday, 2 pm

Dear Norb,

Well, it's a gloomy old day and that's something to be thankful for. I believe it's nearly a week since the sun shone. If I would of waited two minutes yesterday the mail man would of been here. As I got back from the mailbox, we had a letter from you. So your furlough was postponed. Well, I'm hoping we'll see you by next week, but then we thought you might have to finish your two weeks of intensive training.

Mom called Alma yesterday and she is doing velly, velly fine. Expects to go to work Monday. Her dad is going to try to get her on where he works. That won't be hard because different distilleries have been advertising for help, which is unusual you know. Mom got a letter from her Monday saying she was in bed with appendicitis so Mom called her Monday too, but I told you that. She said by Tuesday she had to go to Dr. Likins. So they must of been successful in scattering it. We don't know how to get to Southern Ave. If Joe would be home when it's light Mom would have went to see Alma and you may have to transfer three times to get there I was told. And since Mom knows what's wrong with her eye, she is taking 100% care of it. She hasn't worn her glass eye for a few weeks I know. I'm telling you, this has been a hectic week. It was very few days like Monday that I lived through.

I got Mom a Signal Corps pin with one star in it. Looks real nice I think, but I wish she wouldn't have to wear it, or ever get the chance to wear it. I think that would be money well spent and I know you'll agree. Sure wish this was over. Jr Russell is home again since yesterday, he and his wife. He leaves Monday or Tuesday. He thinks he'll head off to Australia. But who knows. He was anxious for you to get your furlough. There isn't a boy here that you and him played with or bummed with. He asked me if I knew of any. Then too, he's really anxious to see you and what kind of warrior you are. He told me that his in-laws are like us. They believe in eating and Momma really cooks homemade bread and all.

Moody got Mom the last four sacks of Aristos Flour [*that*] Ben Klein had. They told him they wasn't making it any more. I don't think Mom got it from Schieman's for three months. Pop sure hated to hear it. Mom said she'll have to find a substitute because she don't like "baker" bread either. She admitted to it, so it wasn't Papa alone.

Well, Norb I have got a lot of work to do, rally [*sic*] I have - "extensive work." Hoping to see you real, real soon or otherwise answer a few questions, which you don't do anymore. Love from all, your sweet, plump sister,
Hermina

Norb had a furlough between December 10 and December 31 and was home for Christmas.

Louisville, Kentucky, **December 28**

Hello Norb,

Well, it certainly is close to Christmas and a person doesn't realize it over here. Hope you are having better luck. I certainly laugh every time you try to squirm your way out of the predicament you are in with Alma. Brother, you are potentially a married man. Mr. and Mrs. Rawert. How does that sound?

Say, damn it, whenever you address me, call me "Sir" and put emphasis on that word. Either you know how to address your superiors or I'll Court Martial you. I guess that will hold you.

All kidding aside, hope you have a Merry Christmas and a Happy New Year. You don't deserve it. I don't know who will buy your drinks for you this year during the holidays but I guess you have found a sucker by now. Keep your chin up and I wish you were here. Nice country. Why don't you visit shortly?

Zip

Fort Jackson, South Carolina, **December 31**, New Year's Eve

Dear Mom & All,

Just arrived about three hours ago. Had a pretty nice trip. Had a seat all the way and done quite a bit of sleeping. Well, this is New Year's Eve but no celebration, but I think we had a Merry Christmas, which paid up for it. Time is short and I have to get my things together so good night, take care of yourself.

As Always,

Norb

Chapter 3

1944

The letter below, dated January 1, 1944, was the last correspondence from Norb's family or friends saved in the WW II Letters collection until September 2, 1944. Regrettably, the letters were either lost, destroyed or left behind during Norb's service on the Western Front. Thankfully, Norb's letters (the one that were fortunate enough to arrive home) were saved by the family.

Louisville, Kentucky, **January 1**

Happy New Year "Lou's style" to the "Awe" of the old maids

Dear Norb,

Well, right now I'm listening to dear Frankie Sinatra. He's grand. Might as well start the New Year off in boring you. Not a one of us heard the whistles last night, not a one, but I hear there wasn't anything blowing. Why didn't you stay a little longer? Well, how did you stand the trip? Was it very tiresome? And, did you get a place to park your "bunsus?" Here's hoping you got the load off your dogs.

Marge wrote to Maurice and so for an inspiration she wound up the music box. Kid her about this. I know Marge told you all about Mom. Well, I think she is doing fine. I'm just anxious to hear what Drs. Nunn and Fugate has to say, the latter is the one that will give the X-ray treatments.

Ann was thrilled with the kiss for Jr I thought dat [*sic*] was nice. So thoughtful. Yesterday was the sleepiest day I have ever seen. Mom slept all afternoon. Did you have a thru train honey? And how do the S. Carolinians celebrate New Year? For dinner today, I was cook. I got a nice fat hen from Schieman's and it was swell. We had all the trimmins' with it too. Why be a cook if you can't blow about it? But it was so good. It just goes to show you what a little fat does. [*another self-deprecating joke and reference to her weight*].

Well, Cpl. I won't keep you any longer. I presume you're a busy "man." Hoping all is well and what about you being late? Happy New Year. Write soon.

Love from all,

16-point Beefy

Louisville, Kentucky, **January 1**

Dearest Brother,

This is my 2nd letter this year, and does my music kit play! Boy, it's hot. And how are you, Norbert? Swell, I hope. Mother is doing nicely. Now she is lying on the couch. Pop is up at St. Brigid's running the heat thru it. It's New Year's today so you see I guess he will ring 6 [*ring the church bells six times for 6 pm, one of Pop's jobs*] and come home. Hermina and Mary are on an errand. So that's that. Johnny called & wanted to know how everybody was.

What time did you arrive? We taken Alma to her Aunt [*Virginia Mitchell*] on Schiller Avenue. She was to have a party & the next night her aunt she stays with was to have a party. Alma never even called & asked how mother was getting along. We never heard a thing of her. That's not the way mamma was to her when she had a bad eye. Well, I guess I feel like she could say thanks, call up, or act like she enjoys us. I can't understand if you try to do all you can for somebody and they don't appreciate it.

Joey and Lip were over. Lee and Moody are hunting. The 10 o'clock Mass was so crowded today. People were standing over ½ the way up the aisle. Norbert, whenever you need anything don't hesitate to ask me for it. I'll do my best. This week the boss is taking us to dinner at the Blue River Inn. Norbert, just a real happy new year from your loving sister. Good Luck and god bless you. Pray for us, as we will for you.
Margaret

PS. Mamma wants to write a word:
Hello Norb, my loving boy. I wish you a Happy New Year. Please pray hard for me so that I may get well soon. God bless you.
Mother.

PS. I am doing good so far.

Ft. Jackson, South Carolina, **January 3**

Dear Mom and all,

Well, how are you all & how is the eye doing? I never wrote much over the weekend, in fact, I didn't write at all. Frankie and I went out so I never got a chance. The weather is a lot warmer here now but they had that sleet down here Xmas morning also. It sure is hard to get back on the ball again after having a furlough, and I ain't kidding. It's just like starting in the Army all over again.

I guess you have received my air mail letter by this time. It wasn't very long but it served the purpose. Tell Mrs. Russell I received her card and I know how things were. There's nothing new to tell, we're mostly doing the same as when I was here before my furlough. Can't say just what you can expect to happen but I imagine we'll be here for a couple of weeks or more. Can't say for sure about anything. Nothing for sure, nothing for sure.

Well, take care of yourselves and if anything should turn up that is not for the best, just get in touch with the Red Cross and I'll high tail it there. Well, be good and don't forget your Carter's little liver pills.

As Always,

Norb

Fort Jackson, South Carolina, **January 4**

Dear Mom & All,

I am enclosing what I think to be the most beautiful headline since the war started. Of course, I've read the same headline some months back but it had a different meaning then. I was glad to receive your letter, Mom. It wasn't so long but it served the purpose alright. I was very glad to hear that you are doing alright. Just keep taking care of yourself. I wrote Lydia a short letter yesterday and I'm waiting for an answer. I bet it will be a good one with plenty of 'that old time religion' mixed in with it.

I think I told you I was a day late in getting back, didn't I? Well, I got back OK. I knew I would be in the first place but it didn't worry me much. I've quit worrying over small matters like being a day late. I was always late anyway and there's no use changing just because I'm in the Army. Right? Yeah, I changed trains at Danville, KY and caught a through train from there right down to Columbia. It took me about 23 hours to get back here.

The Company Commander said to me the following morning, "Rawert, do you know you're a day late?" Rawert said, "No sir." "Well, you are," he said and proceeded to explain the time to me and I said, "I'm very sorry sir. I had things figured a little different." So he said, "That's alright everything is fixed up. You don't have to worry." And I said, "Thank you, sir." Now, you know, it's pretty nice to have a Company Commander who will go to the front for you. I was a day too late to get paid but I'll survive through it alright.

Tell my darling little Mary hello for me and I am sending all my love and many XXXXXXXXXX. Well, I'm getting tired of talking about the weather and there's not much else to talk about, so folks I'll say good night, good luck and God bless you. I remain,

As always,

Norb

Fort Jackson, South Carolina, **January 4**

Dear Mom & All,

Things still remain about the same here. Everything is running very slowly. The weather is fine though. It's just about right outside and the sun is shining brightly and not a cloud in the sky, except for maybe one or two.

Well, how is your eye doing by this time? I wouldn't doubt that you're not down in the basement with the wash machine going. It wouldn't surprise me a bit. I got a card from Pappy Von Bogart the day I arrived back here. I'll mail it with this letter if I think about it. I haven't been doing very much of anything since I got back from furlough because there's not very much to do but I guess business will pick up before long ma[y]be. I hope so anyway, because just sitting around gets on my nerves, believe it or not, I'd much rather have something to do. I wish the hell they would start that invasion of Europe. The sooner the better. I hope it comes before the end of February and I imagine it will. Well, there is nothing new I can think of right now so I'll close til later.

As Always,

Norb

Fort Jackson, South Carolina, **January 5**

Dear Mom and all,

I guess you think I've made a New Year resolution to write more. Well, it's not that at all. It's just that I have time on my hands and nothing to do with it. They should have given me another extension on my furlough. I guess this is what one would call a waiting process. But I imagine business will pick up in a few days.

We're getting all new clothes. It's a wonder they wouldn't wait till Easter to give us new clothes so we could join the "Easter Parade." I don't know, but I've got a hunch that we'll end up in the South Pacific somewhere, but that's just a guess. I had much rather cast my lot with the Germans but you can't be too particular who in the hell you shoot these days.

It's a little cooler here today - more than it was yesterday. Well, I'd rather have the cool weather myself. It makes you feel better. All you feel like doing down here in the summer is sleeping but we got to do very little of that this summer. I got some junk together last night that I'm going to send home as soon as I can. Can't say exactly when that will be.

Oh, yes, I just taken out a $10,000 worth of insurance. I haven't signed no papers yet but I expect to sign them sometime tomorrow. I thought now would be the best time to take more insurance. I know for sure I'm worth more dead than alive. It cuts down on the payroll quite a bit but I'll get by. Let's see, I have about $12.75 for insurance, $6.75 for war bonds, $1.50 for laundry and about a $4.00 cleaning bill, $1.00 to the Company fund, and beer is 20 cents a bottle. Ha, ha. No wonder my waistline is going down, it's not from the exercise either. Well, that's about the cheapest and best insurance a guy can have, and you can continue the policy after you are <u>once</u> again in civilian life, but the policy will cost a little more and there are a few changes made. I don't know just what they are but I'm going to find out. Tell Honey bunch hello for me XXXX. Well, I don't know much more that's new, so I'll close for now. See you later.

As Always,

Norb

Later in life, Norb was an insurance salesman for Lincoln Income Life Insurance Company in Louisville. He was always concerned about having enough insurance. Whenever I flew out of Louisville, he bought a life insurance policy on me at the insurance kiosks they used to have at Standiford Field airport. It always made me feel strange as if he was taking out a bet on me not to die in an airplane crash. He got a laugh out of it even if it made me feel squeamish.

Fort Jackson, South Carolina, **January 6**

Dear Mom & All,

There's nothing much new around these parts, nothing much now. I expect we'll be here for ma[y]be two weeks or so yet, the way I see it. Still haven't much to do. I'll be getting lazier than hell if they keep this up. I'll be getting fat also.

The weather is a little cooler than it was yesterday. In fact, I'll say it's about 10 degrees difference but the sky is blue and the sun is out. I'm supposed to take a physical exam for my insurance sometime today, I believe. Well, there's not much to that. Not much at all.

The chow has been pretty good since I've come back from furlough but I believe I could do as good myself with just a little practice. We got one cook here though who can really cook good pies. I never have tasted such good pies in my life. He's really good when it comes to baking.

Tell Joe and Ann I received the first edition of the 'Readers' Digest' yesterday. I got most of my junk packed now. All I have to do is send it. I don't know just when that will be but I imagine sometime after the 10th of the year. I don't think I can send it before then. We're taking marine exercises now and they're pretty hard on your shoulders and stomach from what the boys tell me. I got out of them so far because I have to write a report every morning and turn it in to Battalion Headquarters just at the time when the exercises are going on. I don't mind them a bit. They haven't made me a bit sore. Well, how is the eye doing Katie? Alright I hope. I guess you're taking care of it the way you should, aren't you? Or else having it taken care of.

I never ate much breakfast this morning and it's about two hours to dinner and my guts are really growling. I guess they wonder what's wrong because I usually eat a big breakfast but I think I've been eating too much for the amount of work I've been doing, so I cut down a little in order to keep my waistline, or should I say wasteline. Well, I want to get this letter off in the next mail so I'd better quit for now. So be good & I'll be seeing you.

As Always,

Norb

Fort Jackson, South Carolina, **January 6**

Dear Mom & All,

I was a little busier today than I have been for the last week. All our supplies are loaded and we turn in our trucks tomorrow so I guess there will be still less to do next week unless they start taking us on long hikes to pass the time away while we're waiting. Of course, I can think of better ways to pass the time away than hiking but it ain't what I think.

I took that physical examination yesterday for my insurance and my blood pressure was a little high. It was 152 when they took it first and then I jumped on one foot 25 times and it went up to 160. But that doesn't matter much. I got my policy just the same. It starts the first of February. Tomorrow is Saturday so I guess I'll go to take a look at Columbia ma[y] be. I imagine it will be the last time we will get a pass for a while. I don't know very much more so I'll say Amen Brother and sister, drop your nets and follow me.

As Always,

Norb

"South of North Carolina," **January 7**

Dear Mom, Pop, Sis's and Mary,

Well. I'm still just a little bit south of North Carolina. It is a very beautiful day outside, or else it's just that I'm more satisfied in the south. There's not a cloud in the sky, and the temperature is just about 62 degrees, just comfortable in a field jacket. The barracks we moved into were very dirty, but when the scrubbing 59th moves in we really get cleaned up. So things are just about under control now. One thing nice about it, I don't have to do any scrubbing or KP so I definitely do not have dishpan hands, but I have had them already. I knew we were coming down here about five days before we ever moved out, because I seen the order come through, but "mum" is the word you know. Its best to keep your trap shut until you find out where you are going and get there. (Enclosed you will find the proofs I had taken in Kansas City. Alma has seen them already. I thought I would scare the family also.)

Well, how are things in Schnitzelburg? About the same I guess, except for the rationing? This camp has everything in it including tanks, horses, anti-aircraft, artillery, and the last and far from least, the infantry. And of course the best of all - the "Signal Corps." The Signal Corps rates next to the Air Corps you know, but where would the Air corps be without signals.

It won't be long till chow time, I can tell you by that empty feeling I have in my stomach. Still no furloughs, we were told there would be none, so don't bother about asking for any. Well, nothing you can do about that except wait, and I'm used to waiting, it just comes natural after you're in the army for a while. XXX (for Mary). Well, folks I must close now but see you later so I remain

As always,

Norb

Fort Jackson, South Carolina, **January 9**

Dear Mom & All,

Well, there's not much that's new that I know of. There was a pretty heavy snow down here last night but it's just about all melted now. We are restricted to the Post now so we can't get any passes. We did go out last night for a while to Columbia and had a 'few' drinks. I had a rather heavy head this morning, yes I did.

I was surprised to hear from you and I think you have improved on your writing. We're just in a waiting process now. I don't know how long this will go on - no talking. I went down to the PX a while ago and had a few beers but this military beer doesn't taste very good. I don't care much for it. I prefer Oertel's. We are going to have a picture taken of our Company and if I we have time, and if I do, I'll let you see it. I doubt it very much being a good picture but I would like to have one for future reference. Well, that's about all I know for now so I guess I'll close for now, be seeing you,

As always,

Norb

Fort Jackson, South Carolina, **January 10**

Dear Mom & All,

I got a letter from "you all' today so I thought I would drop you a line before retiring for the night. I was glad to hear that your eye was doing so well. If those radium treatments help you like they did Alma, why, everything will be OK.

We're still bumming around here waiting for further orders. Don't know when they will come through. Our mail came through. Our mail clerk pulled a fast one. He signed for and opened up two registered letters containing $80.00 and spent it. I guess he'll go up the line for quite a few years for doing that. They have three charges against him. It surprised everybody because he seemed to be a hell of a nice fellow. He sleeps right across from me but he don't anymore. He's been in the guardhouse since this afternoon.

I got another package from Park and Tilford containing the usual amount of stuff, cig's, cakes, etc. Well, I have to take a shower and shave before going to bed so I'd better close for now and get to work. Be seeing you,

As Always,

Norb V

A section of US Army photo of Norb's graduating class, "HDQ & HDQ Company
59th Signal Battalion, Ft. Jackson, South Carolina, November 1, 1944.
Norb is in the top row, 8th from the left, with a cocked hat.

Fort Jackson, South Carolina, **January 14**, Thursday night, 8:00 pm

Dear Mom & All,

I received your 'AIR MAIL' yesterday. It's raining here tonight, in fact, it's been raining all day long and it's really nasty out. It's about the worst weather we've had since we've come back from 'Maneuvers' or the worst I've seen anyway.

We're still here yet and haven't the slightest idea when we will pull out. I imagine they will give us all a two-hour notice to pack up. I hope this invasion busts loose before long because they have been talking enough about it now. I imagine action will take place any time now before long. We had to hand in our overcoats and they gave us mackinaws instead. The Signal Corps is not supposed to have overcoats but I like them a lot better. I'm sending some clothes home. Put them away for me because I might be able to wear them when I get back, provided I don't get any fatter than I am now. You can hardly wear out these GI pants, and that long underwear is the stuff, if you like long underwear. I did wear them in Tennessee but that was the only time.

I went in town last night and had a chicken supper and it was pretty good. It should be for $1.60, not including a drink. But it was really a meal. There's one joint down here yet where you can still get half of a fried chicken for $1.00, but that place is usually so crowded you can't get in. They have the best Southern fried chicken in Columbia.

I have a pretty good idea where we're going, yep, a pretty good idea. I know where the advanced party is and it won't be in the South Pacific if my calculations are correct.

Very sorry to hear about Lydia. I didn't think she was quite that bad off. I guess my letter was in vain. Ma[y]be it was better that way but I did feel sorry for her sister.

I guess we will get a poker game under way pretty soon, because no one went in town because of the bad weather so I guess I'll close for now. Be seeing you,
As Always,
Norb

On January 14, Norb send a "Notice of Change of Address" postcard to his parents. His old address of HQ Co. 59th signal Battalion, Ft. Jackson, South Carolina was changed to HQ Co. 59th Signal Battalion, APO 9473, c/o Postmaster New York, NY. It also shows his rank as T/5 or Tech 5.

Fort Jackson, South Carolina, **January 15**, 12 midnight

Dear Mom & All,

There's nothing much now that I can (I started to say can't) think of, except the weather is a little better. Well, I got a new coat today and a lot of other new clothes that fit me a little better than my last uniform. I had them all pressed tonight which took me about 3 hours. I also had a couple of drinks and you can tell it according to this writing I imagine. Well, we're still waiting for orders to move. That's all I can say for now.

Yeah! If Milton wants that sweatshirt, give it to him. I just sent it along to take up space.

I'm sorry I got my letters mixed up. I went to let Gillespie's out. Didn't mean anything anyway but a lot of writing. Here's goodnight and God bless you all.
As Always,
Norb

Fort Jackson, South Carolina, **January 18**

Dear Mom & All,

Well, I imagine by the time you receive this letter I should be on a train well off to somewhere. I'm all packed and ready to go. I think we'll leave tomorrow morning sometime.

The weather is really swell out today and I hope it's just as nice tomorrow. There... [*letter is ripped at this point and continues on next page*]... don't know where we're going but I have a fair idea it will be New York. We should get those pictures this afternoon sometime so I hope I can get them off in the next mail. I am going to send the front door key along in this letter because I don't think I can use it right now. Well, take care of yourself and I'll do the same.
As Always,
Norb

Somewhere on the East Coast, **January 22**

Dear Mom & All,

How is everything getting along in Schnitzelburg and how are the radium treatments coming along? Fine I hope. All I can tell you is that I'm somewhere on the East Coast. That's all for now.

I signed up for a new bond allotment today. I'll get a bond a month now. It's hard to say if we'll even have a place to spend any money, but I sure hope so. I haven't had a drink for so long I forgot what the stuff tastes like. I could really go for about four double headers of Bourbon. These bonds I'm telling you about won't come out of my pay till March, so a bond should arrive there about the 15th or 16th of April, and a bond a month through each month. When I get to cash them in, I'm going to buy half interest in either a brewery or distillery. I know it for sure. Well, I have to fall out for a formation so I'll say so long.
As Always,
Norb

New York, **January 25**

Dear Mom & All,

Just a few lines to let you know everything is running smoothly and I'm waiting for pay day so I can take off to New York. Well, it's just as I said, everything is OK, so I'll be seeing you.
As Always,
Norb

According to Norb's Army discharge papers, he was transferred to England on January 29, 1944. And according to the 1944 World War II Troop Ship Crossings he was on the ship Aquitania. His new mailing address was Cpl. N.A. Rawert 35487644, HQ. Co. 59 Signal Battalion, APO 9473 c/o Postmaster, New York, New York, US Army. Because ship transport took so long and army life was hectic and chaotic, there are no letters from January 25 to February 6.

Somewhere in England [V-Mail], **February 6**
[stamped date, may not be actual date of writing]

Dear Mom & All,

Well, I'm somewhere in England among the bloody, blimey blokes. I can't tell you what I think of the place yet because I haven't been around it yet. We're living in some pretty nice barracks though. It's much better than I expected. Had a fairly good trip over across but the ocean got pretty rough at times but I was lucky that I never was seasick. I believe that English money will be a problem for a while, but it's not hard to catch on to. Well, things are just fine over here so far and I'll tell you what I think of the Englishmen later. Take care of yourself.

As Always,
Norb

Somewhere in England, **February 8**

Dear Mom & All:

Well, how are "you all?" I'm just fine myself and everything is running pretty smooth but I'm still waiting to taste this English beer. They tell us it's very good. I guess I'll find out tomorrow night if they issue passes. Wiskey [*sic*] is pretty scarce but you can get it by the drink over the bar in the "Pubs." Pub is what we would all call a beer joint.

The food is pretty good and there's plenty of it, although cigarettes will run a little short I think, and so will soap. Before you send any of them, I would understand that you will have to show this letter to the postal authorities. You can get the cigarettes for about 75¢ a carton at a tobacco store if you can prove they are for overseas shipment.

The weather here is very changeable. One minute the sun is out and the next minute there's a fine drizzle. I don't believe it ever rains hard. I think it would be best if you send all your mail air mail because I got a letter from you today dated the 1st of February which is very good time although I couldn't guarantee [*illegible word*] to do the same.

We really have better barracks here than we had at Ft. Jackson but the toilet and shower is about a half block [*away*]. I would suggest sending regular airmail rather than "V" Mail. I think it's faster. Well, that's all I know for now so I'll say so long.

As Always,
Norb

Somewhere in England, **February 13**

Dear Mom & All,

Well, the weather is a little misty but everything else is fine including the chow. We had turkey for dinner today and it was pretty good. We're in a nice set up as far as I can see. We get quite a few passes and I've visited a few of the towns and also drank my share of this English beer, which is pretty darn good. It's something like home brew, only a lot better than some of the home brews I've drunk already and it packs quite a wallop. It's not rationed either.

The people over here are very friendly and we've all been treated swell so far. At these dances in some of these towns, the girls break the boys instead of the boys breaking the girls. It's a little hard to catch on to their way of speaking but it don't take too long.

As soon as I can I'm going to get a three-day pass, if possible, and see what London looks like. Of course, that will be some time after payday, which is the 28th of this month. Might as well take in all you can now that you're here and get something out of it. I'm going to try to get in touch with Zip and Tommy [*Bratten*] if I can but I don't think I'll have much luck but it won't hurt to try.

How are the radium treatments coming along on your eye and how many more do you have to take? Well, I'm running out of paper so I'll sign off for now. So long. Tell Mary Hello X.

As Always,

Norb

Somewhere in England, **February 17**

Dear Mom & All,

Thought I would write a few lines before hitting the hay and when I say hay, I mean hay. You see, our mattresses and pillows are filled with straw, but they do pretty well after you get your shape down in them, but then by that time you have to shake them up again. The weather is pretty chilly here right now and on these cloudy nights, it's blacker than an ace of spades outdoors. If you don't believe me, you can ask that lamppost I came in contact with the other night. I received that letter that Marge wrote today. It was postmarked February 4 so it made pretty good time.

You talk about things being rationed in the United States; well, really you wouldn't know there is a war going on. Over here, an Englishman is allowed one egg a month and sometimes they don't even get that. But the American soldier eats pretty well considering that it's army chow. We've been having pork chops for breakfast the last couple of days. You know there is one thing about this English beer, you can drink a lot of it and it don't bloat you like the German type beer. I like it every bit as well, but I'm looking for some real Scotch. That is rather scarce but it can be gotten from what I hear. They sell it by the drink but I'd rather have a bottle so I can break the seal myself.

I still haven't written to Zip or Tommy as yet but I'm going to try and get in touch with them pretty soon if it's possible. It's a hard thing to do over here. Well, I hope everything is OK back in Louisville because it is here. I'll close now till sometime later. Give Mary my regards from England

As always,

Norb

Somewhere in England, **February 19** [*postmarked March 4*]

Dear Mom & All,

This is Saturday night and I'm staying home due to a bankroll that is badly bent, or it would be more proper to say busted. I received three letters today and I see where Mr. Redle died. I wonder if that will stop her from window-shopping.

Well, Mom, I can't get hold of no birthday cards but I'm wishing you a happy birthday and many more and hope this gets to you before your birthday. The weather is chilly here and there's a "fog in the holler" so ma[y]be it will change before long. Everything is OK here, couldn't be better unless I were back in the States, but that will come later.

As Always,

Norb

England [*V-Mail*], **February 24**

Dear Mom & All,

Just a couple of lines to let you know that everything is OK on this side of the Atlantic except for some burnt stew every now and then. It just about rains over here constantly, although the sun was out for a while today for a change. I received two letters today that were dated 13 February 1944 so you can see that they made pretty good time. Tell Lip I received her letter and will answer it when I get a chance. Well, here's so long.

As Always,

Norb

England [*V-Mail*], **February 25**

A form filled in by Norb:

Dear Mom,

Please address me as shown below until otherwise advised: T/5 Norbert A. Rawert, 35487644, HQ Co, 59th Sig BN, APO No. 887, c/o Postmaster NY, NY. The above complete address should be placed on all mail sent to me. My code cable address is AMBIHO.

Norbert A. Rawert

Somewhere in England, **March 2**

Dear Mom & All,

Well, everything is just fine here. Plenty to eat and drink and some of the drinks are pretty good. A lot better than some I've drank back in the States. This weather is harder than hell to get used to. It changes almost every fifteen minutes, but tonight the sky is clear and there's a bright moon.

I hear that Mom didn't think much of that statue that Alma bought her, ha, ha! [*Alma bought her a statue of a classic Greek sculptured figure. Since Mommy was ultra-religious, she did not allow nude figures in her home and she draped a cloth around it.*]

I received a letter from Joe and Alma today so tell them I'll answer it the first chance I get. This ain't much of a letter but there's really not much to write about but when I have more time I'll write you a letter telling you all about England from what I've seen of it. And I've seen a little.

Well, Mom I hope your eye is closing alright by now. I hear you're doing pretty darn good. I hope so anyway. They even tell me you are washing dishes, which makes me sad because I know how you and dishes get along together. Tell Pop I have something here that's as good as his Oertel's any day and much better than home brew, although it does resemble home brew.

I'll close for now but before I do, I haven't received that package which you said was on the way. Just wondering. Well, goodnight and good luck and I'll be seeing you.
As Always,
Norb

Somewhere in England, **March 8**

Dear Mom & all,

Just a few lines to let you know that everything is OK on this side of the Atlantic, except for the weather, but I expect that to change pretty soon. I'm going to put in for a 48-hour pass to go to London as soon as possible just to see what the place looks like.

I don't know where you get your information that Scotch was $20.00 a quart over here but I got a quart for a little over $6.00 and that was buying it by the drink and leave me tell you it was really smooth. It really was - until revile the next morning. But it's very scarce and they don't like to sell it to the Yank soldiers. They save it for their regular customers.

Tell Hilary, Jackie and Joey I received their letters today and will answer them as soon as possible as we are rationed to four air mail letters a week although we can write all the V-Mail we want. I think I told you I hit the jackpot the other day. I received 16 letters at one time so I had quite a bit of reading to do.

Well, Mom I'm glad to hear you're doing alright. I'm not losing any weight over here myself. So just keep in good shape and you and I will make a dance when I get back. My

new APO number is APO #308. Well, as the time goes by it's getting later and I must hit the hay and also kill this bottle of beer so I'll say goodnight and remain,
As Always,
Norb

Somewhere in England, **March 15**

Dear Mom & All,

I thought I would drop you a few lines to let you know that everything is OK in England and I hope it is there also. The weather is beginning to break over here a little. Today was a swell day, one of the best since we've landed in England and I also hope it remains this way for a while.

I was surprised to hear that you weren't doing so well but glad to hear that you're doing better now. You had better take good care of yourself and also of Herm.
I received a letter from "Miss Grimm" and is it a honey, etc., really warmth-packing. Along with me, she writes just like she talks and I was even to a few undertakers and doctors, etc.

I haven't been to London yet but I guess I'll get there before the war is over. I have been receiving your letters very regularly but I haven't received the package as yet and I haven't received the Readers' Digest that Joe and Ann sent me at Xmas but I informed them of my change in address so ma[y]be they will come through.
[*Third page is missing from this letter*]
[*Norb*]

Somewhere in England, **March 22**

Dear Mom & All:

Well, here's just a few lines to say hello and hoping everything is OK at home. Things are about the same over here, except I see where Hitler decided to move in a couple of more spots so he could be pushed further when the time comes and I hope it is not too far off.

Yesterday was the first day of spring but it's still rather cool here. I guess it will be for a few weeks to come. I still haven't received that package yet. There were some that came in tonight but mine was not among them. I was just wondering if it's in Davey Jones's locker. Things are about the same here and I'm still making a pretty good go of this English beer. I received a letter from Lip and one from Shirley yesterday, so tell them for me. Well, time is slipping by so I'll have to close for now, so for a while then, I remain,
As Always,
Norb

Somewhere in England, **March 29**

Dear Mom & all,

I'm sitting just about as close to this stove as I can get tonight because it is rather chilly on this side of the Atlantic. I hit the jackpot yesterday. I received ten letters and eight postcards at once. Tell them all thanks. I also received the package yesterday and it was in good order. I have a good supply of cigs and soap now, enough to last me a pretty good while. I don't know if I should let the censor know that or not. He may pull an inspection, ha!

Yeah, I read that article in the Readers Digest and it's just about right except for the chow is a lot worse, but so are the Limeys.

You can tell Pop that this birthday greeting's a little late but I wish him many more and hope I do as well. Also to stick to Oertel's. It's really much better. You know beer gets rather warm over here in the summer. I hope before next summer that I'll be drinking beer in Berlin. I think the climate is better, although last Sunday was a beautiful day. There's only one thing that I could really use - and that's a pair of oxfords - so I can get out of these GI shoes once in a while. It's hard as hell to dance in these boots because they have rubber soles. In case you get an extra coupon, or can get them without. You can bust that check that they sent for the bonds.

I've been trying to get hold of a souvenir or something but it's the next best thing to impossible. It would probably be made in the USA anyway. But I'm doing my best. Seems as though the draft board is cleaning the old Burg out, eh? Well, they haven't got many more to go. Well, things are still running pretty smooth. Yeah, I said pretty smooth, and payday is just around the corner and that's a morale booster. It's getting rather late now and I guess I'd better hit the hay because reveille rolls around pretty soon, much too soon, in fact. So I'll be seeing you and take good care of yourself. So long for now.

As Always,

Norb

Somewhere in England, **April 3**

Dear Mom & All,

Well, here's just a couple of lines to say hello from the "King's Soil." Everything's just about the same except of course the weather has changed again. A rain over here is just a damn heavy fog nearly, but it's pretty wet just the same. Easter called around pretty fast this year. I didn't realize it was so near, I guess. By the time you receive this letter, the old rabbit will have been on its way. Well, I'm not going to try to catch him this year but he'll get a hell of a merry chase next year if all goes well. I don't know what the kids over here do for Easter. I guess they do without because an egg is a rather scarce item. We get about one a month.

Well, how's things around Schnitzelburg? Just about the same, I hope. I guess the old walk is still pretty hot between 1344 [*Texas Street*] and Huelsman's. You can see that I'm running out of paper and it's just about time to hit the Beauty Rest, so here's good luck. I remain,

As Always,

Norb

A corner of the letter was cut out either by the military censor or by his mother the censor.

Somewhere in England, **April 5**

Dear Mom & All,

It's about nine o'clock and it's still daylight. In fact, the sun is just starting to go down. But I'd much rather not be on daylight savings time. It makes the day too long. I'm enclosing a poem which I clipped out of "The Yank." I thought it was one of the best I've read for quite some time. It's more truth than poetry.

Bob Hope is on the radio right now. We get the program about a week later on recordings. They have an American Forces Station and we do get some good American music and all the popular programs. There's not much that's new on this side. How's everything over there? They are having a coal strike over here, which you already know about. Getting more like home every day. Well, I hope everything is OK so take good care of yourself and I'll be doing the same. I expect I'll hit the hay early tonight so I'll say so long for now and I remain,
As Always,
Norb

Easter Sunday, Somewhere in England, **April 9**

Dear Mom & All,

Well, this is Easter Sunday and I just got back from church about an hour ago. It's been raining all morning but I think it will clear up this afternoon. Thank Mrs. Russell & Mrs. Orrill for their Easter cards for me. I don't have time to write individual letters. From all indications, this is going to be a very quiet Easter. Much too quiet, in fact. You don't see many new clothes over here as you would back in the States. I guess they postponed the Easter Parade till after the war. I'm sending home a couple of English newspapers. I thought you'd like to read them. There's nothing special about them, they're just papers.

How's things in Louisville and how's the eye doing? OK I hope. Say, is Dick Fisher still announcing for WHAS? I was just wondering because on the American Forces station that we have over here there's an announcer that sounds just like him and I would lay two to one that it's him. We have a loud speaker in our barracks and we get all the programs, of course, they're a little late because they're taken off of recording, but they're sure good to hear. I don't believe there's a good swing band in all of England. I mean a high-class band. But I understand Bob Crosby's going to be here in a couple of weeks. I guess I'll close for now because there's not much doing and there's not much news that I could write about. Hope you had a happy Easter.
As Always,
Norb

Somewhere in England, **April 10**

Dear Mom & All,

I got back a little late from a trip tonight so I decided to stay home. Yeah, I keep my hat hanging here. These English over here celebrate Easter from Friday till Tuesday and I never seen so many bicycles as I did today. I was reading in the paper where they called off the war for fifty-five minutes on the Aegis Front on Easter Sunday morning. Sounds rather foolish to me. It's raining here again tonight, it's not exactly a rain but one of these English drizzles. I haven't seen a hard rain since I left the POE [Port of Embarkation]. I see where the Russians took Odessa, so the news really looks pretty good. More power to them. By the way, you can tell Bell that 'Bootsie' is just fine but damn thirsty for some good American beer.

You said Katie cooked dinner. Well, you know that sure gives me an appetite, I can almost smell the aroma over here. But as far as washing the dishes are concerned, I do not believe that. I would have to see that first. Well, that pile of straw is calling me so I'll sign off for now and be seeing your letter and if I get the chance I'll send a picture with that Scotch effect, so be good, remaining,

As Always,
Norb
Tell Mary hello XX

Somewhere in England, **April 14**

Dear Mom & All,

Here's a few lines to let you know that I'm OK and hope you're the same. This new place we moved to is quite a mud hole compared with the last one but when we get finished with it will look like Yellowstone National. It's raining over here again tonight and not for a change either. It does that just about every other day. There's nothing new at all, nothing that I can write about anyway, so I'll say goodnight and I'll be seeing you.

As Always,
Norb

Somewhere in England, **April 26**

Dear Mom & All,

Here's just a few lines to let you know all is well in the United Kingdom so far. Can't ever tell when things will be popping through. I never wrote for the last five days. There's just not a damn thing to write about. I received a letter today that was written Easter. First letter I received in three days. Well, I'm going in town and get a few beers tonight so I'll close for now. Hoping all is well. I remain,

As Always,
Norb

Somewhere in England, **April 30**

Dear Mom & Al,

Thought I'd drop you a few lines while I have time to let you know that all is well. It's a beautiful day out today, one of the best since I've been in England. I hope it keeps it up for a while. You know it stays light over here till about 10:55 pm. You really don't see much of the night at all.

Well, it seems like the invasion scare is really on. Well, I hope it does start pretty soon because to be frank with you I'm getting pretty damn tired of the place myself. But there's one thing about it, I'm not alone.

There's a good program on the radio right now. It's Sammy Kaye. That guy really has a band. I haven't heard a good English band yet. They just don't know what Swing is.

Well, how is everything in Louisville? Don't forget and send me the Derby edition [*of the CJ. Norb was always an avid reader*]. I'd like to see it.

In the morning, there's a German propaganda program that comes on air. It consists mostly of the conception of the previous days happening and in between broadcasts, they play American songs and I'm not so sure it's Guy Lombardo's music.

Tell Mary I said hello.

Well, there's really not much more news I can send you from the King's Soil, so for the meantime, I close, and the best of luck. I remain,

As Always,

Norb

Somewhere in England, **May 4**

Dear Mom & All,

I thought I'd drop you a few lines to let you know that all is well in England. So Ernie [*Schieman*] ended up in Italy. I thought he was still in the States. It seems as though Betsy is doing pretty well for herself, doesn't it? The studious type, like I was, ha, ha.

It was raining most of the day today and it's really chilly. I don't think it gets warm over here to the last of May... [*10 lines were cut out of the letter - censored*]... Oh yes, I received the candy and chewing gum and thanks a million. My jaws have been moving ever since. I don't have to stick it behind my ear anymore. I received about nine letterson the day before yesterday. It seems like I get them all in bunches. Tell everyone hello because I don't have time to write everyone. I'll sign off for now until the next time.

As Always,

Norb

Somewhere in England, **May 9**

Dear Mom & All,

I just got finished eating supper, so it's about 6:30 pm. It really was a swell day out today for a change. One of the best we've had for quite some time. I missed the Kentucky Derby. It was broadcast Sunday, so I understand, but I didn't hear it. Don't forget to send me that Derby Edition. I'd like to see it. I was trying to get something for Mother's Day but no luck. You just have to accept this letter and the wishes that come with it.

We're pretty busy. I got a 300-mile trip to make tomorrow so I won't get back for a couple of days. It's a good way to pass time though. But these GI vehicles aren't any too comfortable. I'm taking it easy tonight. In fact, I think I'll hit the hay in about an hour or so. So I'll sign off for now, so good luck.

As Always,

Norb

"Mother's Day" Somewhere in England, **May 14**

Dear Mom,

Well, here's a special message on Mother's Day hoping you have many more. I had all but the carnation today. Zeller's Florists don't sell them over here. Since I'm not there, I thought I would write and let you know I was thinking of you, wishing you the best returns of the day. It's very cool over here today. It was warm this morning but it got considerably cooler this afternoon. We had a few beautiful days last week. The weather on the whole has been pretty good.

I got a kick out of your selection of patterns, Katie, but I thought you were a better judge of size. I received my shoes yesterday. Thanks a million. I wore them last night and walked about eight miles and have a couple of blisters but that's due to the fact that my feet are no longer accustomed to oxfords, but the fit is fine. It's just that the heel cap rubbed along the top but they'll soon soften up. It's just good to get out of these GI shoes for a change. It almost makes me feel like a civilian. Well, it's getting around beer time and that's a very important item you know. So by Jove, I'll say cheerio then. Tell Mary I said Hello X.

With Love,

Norb

Somewhere in England, **May 19**

Dear Mom and All,

Hi ya folks. How you all? Here I am just a "shootin" ya a couple lines from "this here" side of the ocean and a leaving you know that all is "Oke Doke." I'm sorry about the picture. I haven't gotten around to it yet but I will as soon as possible. Of course, I don't know how soon that will be.

There must be something wrong with the mail somewhere because I acknowledged the receipt of that picture of you and Pop, the candy, shoes, etc. [*Norb's letter was postmarked May 19 but was received in Louisville on June 12, per a note his mom made on the envelope*]. Maybe the letters were lost somewhere because I know I wrote and thanked you for them. I distinctly remember that, even though I am a little absent minded at times.

It's been mighty cool over here the last week or so. In fact, it's been damn cool. About that cross or whatever it was that was supposed to be in the sky, well, I read about it in the paper and there were a few people who said they seen it but just like some of these Englishmen they're full of shit also.

Everything is very peaceful over here even more so than back in the States because the pubs close at 10:00 pm. They're closed a lot of time through the week due to the shortage of beer. Well, I guess I'll close for now. Oh, yes, I'm going to look Red Johnson up as soon as I hear from him. So long for now and I'll be seeing you. Tell Mary I Said Hellow [*sic*].
As Always,
Norb

Somewhere in England, **May 21**
[*received in US one month later on June 12*]
Dear Mom and All,

I just finished sinking my molars (as Knue called them) in a piece of chicken which must have made a nonstop flight from the USA to here or else it was a commando because he was pretty tough.

I thought it was going to rain but I guess it's not because the sun is out. But it's very cool here. In fact, they had a very severe frost two nights ago. Well, Mom I'll have a good job for you today. I'm going to try and wash my wool uniform I don't know how it will fit or not when I get finished. I think a lukewarm water and a mild soap should do it. Here's hoping anyway.

I received two boxes from Park & Tilford this week but one was a long time in getting here. I wish they would send a big sample of their "Bourbon" along with it. It wouldn't go bad. Not at all.

Well, I'll close for now letting you know that all is well on the King's Soil. Tell pussy foot I said hello and send my love.
As Always,
Norb

Somewhere in England, **May 22** [received in US on June 12]
Dear Mom and All,

Well, I just finished my washing. It's rather late to be washing but better now than never. It's about 10:15 pm. I'll have my wash on the line first I betcha! The weather was pretty nice today. Even the sun was out for a change but it's still not warm. I don't mind telling you that I'll be glad to go where the climate suits my clothes. I was listening to the radio tonight.

The program was "Command Performance." You know that's a pretty good program. I was wondering if you ever listened to it or not. I think it's one of the best on the air.

Tell Marge I received her letter today and also one from Porky and two from Alma, so the mail was pretty good. It's not going to be too long before I hit the hay, because that bugle always blasts loose about five hours too early. So I'll say goodnight, hoping all are well, because I'm feeling pretty damn good myself, and not from anything I had to drink either. Well, Bye You All.

As Always,
Norb

Somewhere in England, **May 24**, Wednesday night

Dear Mom and All,

Here's a few lines coming your way to let you know that all is well here and hope it's the same there. I'm still waiting for the weather to get warmer so I can do some fishing, as we're situated by a big lake that's about four times as large as the Twin Lakes. I'll leave you know what I catch. I wish to hell I had my equipment over here but I haven't so I guess I'll do without.

The weather is still cool over here. I don't think England ever has warm weather. If they do, it mustn't last very long. Well, it's time for beer call so I'll bring this letter to a close and go over to the PX and dampen my throat (a few years ago it wouldn't have been my throat) ha! [*reference to bed wetting*]. Well, here's so long for now. Tell Mary Hello.

As Always,
Norb

The letter below is one of the few surviving letters to or from Alma Pierce, Norb's girlfriend in Louisville, who later became his wife on June 22, 1946. Alma must have been embarrassed and did not want her children to read the letters later in life.

Somewhere in England, **May 25**, Thursday night

Dearest Alma,

It's about eight o'clock over here and all is well. I just came back from the shower room and did I give my scales a hell of a scrubbing. Is there anything I want? Yeah, honey, suppose you jump in the next envelope, and put a few extra airmail stamps on it. And you had better send it special delivery, just to be on the safe side, you know.

Well, honey, I think I located Red [*Johnson*]. He don't know it, so I think I'll jump in and give him a little surprise. I imagine he will be surprised, don't you? I think he's just twenty miles from where I am.

I've been waiting on that picture you were talking about, Alma. So let's get it on its way, what do you say? I want to see if you've changed any in the last five months, ha. I believe I have. I don't know for sure though, but it's all for the good, of course.

I received news today that my brother (Joe) is the father of a six-pound baby girl [*JoAnn*]. That chalks me up for another uncle. I'll bet he busted all the buttons off his vest. Let's see now, about eleven times I've been an uncle. Right now, I'd like to be the father of about nine, ha, ha. That's pretty good batting average but my old man done it, so why can't I? It would look like a line of ducks walking down the street.

Well, darling, I'll close for now, ma[y]be I'll have more news tomorrow. After a check up on Johnson. So in the meantime be good and remember, Alma, that
I'm always Loving You,
Norb

May 25, Thursday night
Dear Mom & All,

Well, I received news today that I was an uncle for the eleventh time (not ten times, as you informed me in your letter). What's the matter - are you losing count? I was expecting the news any time. I'm glad everything came out OK. Sounds a little funny don't it? Tell JoAnn I said hello. I think I know where Red is at. He's just about 20's miles from me, so I think I'll look him up over the weekend if possible. Maybe you'll get that picture with two drunks instead of one. Well, this ain't much of a letter but there ain't much news, so here's hoping all is well. I'm feeling fine myself.
As Always,
Norb

Somewhere in England, **May 30**
Dear Mom & All,

Here's just a few lines to let you know that all is well over here. It's raining tonight, just a thundershower. It also rained last night but it's been very warm through the day. It's really the first warm weather we had. It feels good too, more like SC, only not quite that warm... [*two lines of the letter cut off, either by army censor or Norb's mom*] ...sign off for now so here's so long & I'll be seeing you.
As Always,
Norb

The D-Day Invasion at Normandy, France occurred on June 6. Tommy Bratten, a friend and co-worker of Norb's was killed in the invasion but his death wasn't known until much later. According to 116th Infantry Regiment Roll Of Honor blogspot.com, Tommy was drafted in November 1942 and assigned to B Company 116 Infantry. Sometime in 1942 he married Lizabeth (Betty) Groeble and on July 5 they had a son who himself was later a decorated soldier in the Vieitnam War. On June 5, 1944 Tommy was promoted to SGT and on the next day, June 6, he was killed in action in the D-Day Landing.

Somewhere in England, **June 10**

Dear Mom & All:

Just a few lines to let you know all is well and I do mean well. Well, the invasion is on and I believe it's the biggest morale booster that any of the troops had here for a long time. It shoved morale up quite a bit.

I'm enclosing a $40.00 money order in this letter. I want you to get Katsy something as I never get around to it, and then do as you like with the rest of it. Don't fail to do so. Maybe you would like a permanent or something, so as I said, don't be backward. Ha. Well, this is all the time I have. Here's hoping you are all well and I'll see you around Xmas [*what an optimist or the youthful thinker Norb was to think that due to the invasion the war would be over by then*].

As Always,

Norb

Military documents show that Norb's company C was part of the invasion of Normandy and went over with the HQ Co. [HQC] 59th Signal Battalion most likely on June 14, 1944. It was still a bloody time as they made their way on the trail to liberate France and Belgium. His mailing address was HQ Company 59th Signal Battalion (HQC 59th SB), APO #308 c/ Postmaster, New York, NY.

The HQC 59th SB was attached to the US First Army under the VIII Corps from June 15 to July 31. In a Report After Action Against Enemy (11 August 1944), Commanding General of the First US Army, Troy Middleton reported that "during the period 15-30 June, 1944, the VIII Corps gradually expanded the line across the Cotentin Peninsula from Carentan to Port Bail on the West Coast, with the mission of protecting the southern flank of the VII Corps, while the latter advanced north and captured Cherbourg." On June 26, Cherbourg fell to the Allies. Afterwards Norb's unit participated in the push southwards to St. Lô and later Coutances as part of. the German resistance became tougher and many cities were bombed by the Allies (source: Wikipedia).

Due to being on the move and caught up in battle his letters became infrequent. Not much about the daily trials were mentioned. Norb's family didn't say anything that would upset him and he couldn't talk about what he was doing or what he saw. Many letters were very short and perfunctory. By July 1, the date of the next letter, Norb mentions he has seen devastation and quite a few French towns blown up. And in his upbeat morale, he thought he'd be home by Christmas, but the war dragged on.

Location unknown, **June 26**

Dear Mom & All,

Just a couple of lines to let you know that everything is OK. I haven't written much in the last couple of weeks. Never got around to it [*putting it mildly!*].

Well, Kate, the way things look, you had better have roast turkey for Xmas dinner because I'll be there to do my share of damage to it. It's about 12:00 pm now and I'm drinking a cup of coffee, in fact, I've started my second. Yeah, it's good coffee for a change, but I'll gladly leave it for a double header of bourbon. Well, here's so long for a while. Take care of yourself and the rest of the kids. Ha, ha. (Hermina), and I'll be seeing you.

As Always,
Norb

Somewhere in France, **July 1**

Dear Mom & All,

It's raining out tonight, or I guess I should say this evening, although we've had pretty good weather for the last couple of days. Well, it won't be long till the Fourth, will it? Well, one consolation, we've got plenty of fireworks [war] and we can get the cider.

Since I've been over here I've seen quite a few of these French towns, or what was French towns. They are really blowed [*sic*] all to hell. My heart goes out to them French, though you can't trust them all. But it really is something to see. Your stomach does a couple of flips. You can get souvenirs by the truckloads but they're too much to pack around and you can't mail any so I just forget about them. I had a bunch of German letters I wanted to send home but they got wet and the ink ran so I threw them away. Well, I'm well and happy and hope you are all the same so I'll say Au Revoir for now.

As Always,
Norb

According to Maj. Zortman's report on the 59th HQC SB, July 1944 "started with plans for a major offensive, starting with VIII Corps. On 3 July, VIII Corps (Maj. Gen. Troy H. Middleton) opened the First Army offensive. Three divisions jumped off abreast in a downpour of rain that not only nullified air attacks but prevented artillery observation. Enemy resistance was heavy, and the 82d Airborne Division scored the only notable advance. During the next three days, slow progress was made in hard fighting under adverse weather. The corps struck the enemy's MLR (main line of resistance) along the line of le Plessis-Mont-Castre Forest and La Haye-du-Puits. Enemy counterattacks stiffened by armor helped to slow down the VIII Corps. Though La Haye-du-Puits was nearly surrounded, average gains for the three-day period were under 6,000 yards on the corps front, and, contrary to expectations, the enemy had clearly shown his intentions of defending in place whatever the cost. The slugging match continued through 11 July in both VII and VIII Corps zones."

The hard battles of VIII Corps finally produced their fruits in mid-July. As the three attacking divisions broke past the rough La Haye-du-Puits-Mont-Castre hills, where they had cracked the enemy's MLR [main line of resistance], they found resistance less and less tenacious. On 14 July, VIII Corps came up to the line of the Ay River; it had reached the initial objectives prescribed in its attack order, a gain of 12,000 yards in 12 days of battle. But the corps was still far short of its assigned ultimate objectives when orders from First Army stopped the attack at the positions then reached. Though hard fought, the two Corps, VII and VIII, stopped to solidify their positions and prepare for Operation Cobra. XIX Corps continued to fight through July 19th, as it battled south to St-Lô, France.

Somewhere in France, **July 3**

Dear Mom & all,

Here's just a couple of lines coming your way to let you know that all is well. The only thing that worries me is where in the hell I'm going to get the drinks to celebrate the Fourth of July. I would even settle for some of my Godmother's homebrew and that always was rotten stuff, especially after she put the cap back on it.

I'm writing this letter from the hole I sleep in. It's about six feet long and about 2 ½ feet deep. It's not the most comfortable place in the world but it might be one way to keep from getting a Purple Heart. It's pretty cozy though. I got my bed roll on the bottom and my tent over the top. The only thing is, I don't know who is going to give it up - me or this ground mole. He sticks his ass out and I gave him a boot and he crawls back into his own hole. Ha. Then in about an hour he's digging back out again.

General Patton said he'd be in Germany in 90 days. I sure hope to hell he knows what he's talking about. Forty-five days from here to Paris and barter five days to clean the rest up. Well, tell everyone I said hello. I don't have time to get around to them all. I'll say so long for now and I'll be seeing you ma[y]be before Xmas. Tell Mary I said hello X. I remain, As Always,
Norb

Somewhere in Normandy, France, **July 7**

Dear Mom & All,

Here's just a few lines to let you know that all is well. Looks as though it may rain again. It usually rains a little every day but today was a swell day as far as the weather is concerned. There's really not much news that I can write about. I'll have to read a paper before I could tell you how the war is going. Well, I hope everyone is feeling well. I'm feeling pretty good myself, even if I haven't had nothing stronger than apple cider for a month. Well, I'll say so long for now. I'll be seeing you. Tell Mary hello.
As Always,
Norb

According to Major Zortman of the 59ᵗʰ Signal Battalion, information on the 59ᵗʰ HQ Signal Battalion, Company C is sketchy but since they were attached to the VIII Corps it is safe to say that whatever the VIII Corps was involved in the 59ᵗʰ HQ SB was also. The VIII Corps was attached to the US Third Army from August 1 to September 4, 1944. According to a history of the 33ʳᵈ Signal Construction Battalion's campaign in France (www.33rdsignall. com) the 33ʳᵈ joined Company C of the 59ᵗʰ Signal Battalion in a bivouac area near La Haye-du-Puits on July 14. According to a mention in 'The Signal Corps: The Outcome,' page 125, their mission was to maintain communications between the Corps and First Army. The 59ᵗʰ participated in the attack in Brittany, France, being responsible for wire communications to three divisions, an extensive fire direction net, the radio coordination for naval bombardment of the city, and the maintenance of radio link contact to two armies, an Army group and a tactical air force. It was also responsible for rehabilitating over 7,250 miles of existing open wire and underground cables in four weeks.

France, **July 17**

Dear Mom & All,

Here's just a couple of lines letting you know all is well. Some of the mail came through today. I received about ten letters. The weather was swell today. It usually rains a little everyday but it skipped today. Well, I'll sign off now and I'll be seeing you.

As Always,

Norb

France, **July 21**, 8 pm

Dear Mom & All,

Here's a couple of lines to let you know that I'm OK. The chow is pretty good. The weather is wet. I see where one of Adolph's men tried to get him but he missed. Well, that's too damn bad. It rained just about all day today but it stopped raining now for a few minutes anyway.

I just finished washing and showering. Feels good for a change. And I also trimmed my mustache. You should see that. It's really a honey. One of those football types 11 [or "] on each side. I was considering growing a goatee but I changed my mind.

Well, I still think I will be there for Xmas so you can still plan on that turkey but I just want that turkey floating in beer. It's been over a month now since I've had a drink except cider and you can't call that a drink, so I prefer a pretty wet reception. I believe our battalion alone could drink New York dry.

I guess I'd better go wring out my blankets and make me a place to sleep for a while. Here's hoping everything comes out OK when you go to the hospital in August. I think it will because you are pretty hard-boiled Katie. Well, I'll say goodnight for now and I'll be seeing you.

As Always,

Norb

France, **July 27**

Dear Mom and All,

Well, I got up rather early this morning. The rain was coming down and I was heading for higher ground. It was a swell day yesterday as far as weather is concerned. The mail is coming thru pretty good but it comes in bunches. One day you get five letters and then it stops for a while.

There's really nothing I need. I have about 40 packs of cig's in stock and we get a weekly ration of seven packs. The only thing I could use would be a barrel of beer and a Beauty Rest mattress.

There's not much doing except the Germans lob about twenty five to thirty 88's [*8.8 cm German Flack anti-aircraft and anti-tank weapons, the most common sound of WW II*] in our direction every night. The other night only about seven went off. You could hear them scream but they didn't go off, so the French must be doing some good in Germany anyway. I was reading some kind of chart where a fellow had this war figured to end on or before Sept 7, 1944 and Winchell said it will end sooner. I hope to hell either one of them are right. The Sky Pilot [*Chaplain*] was here last Sunday and I went to Confession and Communion. Getting good, huh?

Well, I'll close for now so be good and take care of yourself and I'll be seeing you. Tell Mary I said Hello.

As Always,

Norb

By August 1, 1944 "the Operation Cobra attack begun on July 25 by First US Army had developed into a major breakthrough. And elements of VIII Corps had smashed out of the Cotentin Peninsula and were racing through Avranches headed for the important Brittany town of Rennes. Meanwhile elements of the VII Corps (First US Army) were also cutting south in a zone east of Avranches. Twelfth Army Group ordered Third US Army, commanded by Lt. Gen. George S. Patton, Jr., to become operational at 1200 on August 1, and to assume command of the VIII Corps which was far to the south of Army Headquarters" (from Patton and his Third Army Living Historians). The 59th HQC SB was now attached to the Third Army until September 5, 1944.

On August 1, Lt. Gen. Omar Bradley directed the VIII Corps westward into Brittany, France with the object of liberating the Breton ports for Allied use. On August 7 the Corps took the port of Saint-Malo. After an involved battle lasting almost six weeks and characterized by urban combat and reduction of fortifications, the VIII Corps liberated Brest on September 19. Ironically, after so much effort, German demolition proved so effective that the liberated Breton ports were unusable for the remainder of the war.

France, **August 8**

Dear Mom and All,

Here's a few lines to let you know I'm well. I had a surprise the other day. Of all people to run in to I ran into Zip. He was traveling the same way. He looks the same to me. We just talked about two minutes and had to get running again.

Well, I'm fine myself and hope you're all the same. I don't write so often so don't let that worry you. If anything should happen the government would let you know so no news is good news. This cognac packs quite a wallop. It's about 120 proof. About a quart of that stuff and you can whip a lion. Tell everyone hello because I'm cutting down on my paperwork. Well, here's so long for now and I'll be seeing you. Tell Mary I said hello.
As Always,
Norb

Norb wrote about French liquors and specifically Calvados, an apple brandy, which is from a specific region in Normandy called Calvados. His birthday was August 17 and he was 24 years old.

France, **August 17**

Dearest Alma,

Well, honey you'll have to excuse me for not writing. I found two letters I had written to you that I forgot to mail. I'm slipping. I was thinking I mailed these so I'll drop them in the box with this letter. Well, today is my birthday. I'm getting to be an old man. I have a two way celebration tonight, two years in the army and twenty four years old. I hope to hell I don't see twenty five in this man's army.

I was reading in the Stars and Stripes (an Army paper) where they are intending to use the troops that are over here in the Pacific. I hope it's all a mistake. Ha, ha. I agree with General Grant when he said war is hell. I've been receiving your mail regularly honey. We've been getting some mail in eleven or twenty days. I got hold of a quart of French champagne the other day and it was really delicious. Their cognac and Calvados is a pretty rough drink.

Well, honey... [*words scratched out*]...until...and I do... I'm going to have a...when I do get back to the States again.. [*Scratched out maybe by the censors, or maybe by Alma so no one could read it*]. So you're going to take a month off, too, when I get back. Well, that's a darn good idea because you won't be able to work and stand the strain also. Viva la France. Well, I'll close for now so be good darling and I'll be the same. I remain always
Loving You,
Norb

Southern France, **August 17**

Dear Mom and All:

Well, I have a two-way celebration today [*Norb's 24th birthday*] but there's not much of a celebration. But there is plenty to drink, but some of it is pretty rough stuff. Although, I have had a couple quarts of Champaign with a pretty good vintage. Everything seems to be going well on the new front they started in southern France. There is nothing that I need. We get plenty of cigs and candy. More than we know what to do with. We give most of it away to the French. You could send me a pineapple upside down cake. I could go for one of them right now. I was reading in the Stars and Stripes (an Army paper) where they are figuring on using the troops that are over here to finish up the South Pacific. I don't think much of the idea but it may all be a rumor. The mail has been coming through very well. I've received letters from August the sixth, that's just 11 days, so that ain't bad at all.

I imagine about two more months will see the end of things over here. At least I'm hoping so. Well, I sure hope everything's going well in Louisville. It's been swell weather here the last two weeks. It couldn't have been better. It's getting pretty dusty now though. Well, it won't be long till I go on guard so I'll sign off for now and write more later although I have been slipping in my correspondence I catch up when I find time. Here's so long for now and I'll be seeing you.

As Always,

Norb

France, **August 20**

Dear Mom and All:

We had a mail call today and I received five letters in all so my morale went up a couple of notches. The weather has been swell although we had a shower yesterday. First rain we had for over two weeks. Everything seems to be going our way. I still say if we don't go to the South Pacific I'll be there for Xmas. If we do go to the South Pacific it will be about five months more. So it goes. I think I'll head for the States myself.

The women over here are beautiful, that is, the majority. I wish to hell I could speak French. They make the English women look sick. [*This comment infuriated Alma who never forgot it*]. Well, I won't mail this letter now so I'll finish tomorrow nite.

Continuation of August 20 letter, **August 22**

Well, I'll try and finish this letter tonight. It rained all day yesterday and last night and we had an occasional shower today. If you don't like the color of this ink you can blame it on Hitler because this is German ink. I received five letters tonight so the mail is coming through pretty well. There is nothing I need. If there ever is, don't worry, I'll let you know. The one thing that I could use if you can get your hands on would be a cigarette lighter. I had a good Ronson but I lost it in England right before we crossed the Channel. I'll close this letter for now, so so-long for now. I'll be see'in you.

As Always,

Norb

The following is a partial letter from a friend to Alma. It was unsigned and with no envelope. In the letter, the writer said that it took so long to write his letter because he had to stop so often. Norb also mentioned it took him eight days to finish his letter. They were seeing a lot of action as they pushed through France on the way to Belgium and Germany but they couldn't talk about what they were involved in and they didn't have time

Somewhere in France - (Lots of luck!). **August 25**

Hello Alma,

I received your card a few days ago and sure was glad to hear from you again. I hope this finds you very well. Well, how is everything back that way? Are they working you hard? They can't do that to you.

I guess you know I was in France. I've been here for a long time already. So you say Norb is over here? Well, did he come over on the big day? If he didn't then I beat him over here. I thought I saw one of the trucks that belong to Norb's outfit the other day. It had his Signal Co. number on it. But no trace of Norb. I haven't even heard from him since I came over. Next time you write to him you tell him to keep that big ass of his low or he will get it shot off. I will try to write him when I get some more time. I am having one hell of a time writing this. I have to stop so often. Now I don't know what to write about. What I'd like to tell you I can't. It sure is a lot of things over here to see and a hell of a lot going on. But you can't say a damn thing about it. I guess Norb already told you that.

[*Unsigned*]

France, **August ~~20~~ 28**

Dear Mom & All,

Well, as you see I am still mailing this same letter. I thought I would add a few lines to it since it's eight days later. Everything is OK. The only thing I could use would be a beefsteak about an inch thick with mushrooms of course and a big slice of apple pie. With coffee if you don't mind. These "K" rations get a little tiresome. I've eaten enough cheese to last me for a long time - the cows even look at me a little slant-eyed.

I'm enclosing $50 money order in this letter. Take care of it for me the best you can see fit. The weather has been excellent. It couldn't be better. Tell the "Rawerts" on Logan I said thanks for the package. Tell Mary hello and thanks for the card. There is nothing I need for now. Here's hoping all is well. So long for now & I'll be seeing you.

As Always,
Norb

France, **August 30** [*mailed on September 3*]

Dear Mom & All,

Here's a few lines to let you know that all is well. It rained most of yesterday and today, so things were rather quiet. The weather has been exceptionally good the last month though. I hope it stays that way for about another month. I don't think this would be so cozy in cold weather but they tell me it never snows in France. I don't know how true it is.

There is nothing I could use except that cigarette lighter I was talking to you about. But don't go to too much trouble finding one because I have plenty of matches. I'd like a blackout lighter if there is such a thing. I've seen a couple of them but have never been able to get my hands on one. Well, I suppose that's all I know now. Thanks for the cards before I forget. Hoping all are well. Tell Mary Hello. I remain,

As Always,

Norb

September 2

Here's an additional note. We got paid yesterday so I thought I'd better send $50 home. Take care of it for me. All is damn good. Be seeing you soon. Take care of yourselves.

As Always,

Norb

The following letter from Norb's family was the first since January 1944 that was saved in the collection. The letters from the family were most probably left behind in Belgium when Norb was transferred to the Red Cross hospital in October, 1944.

Louisville, Kentucky, **September 2,** Saturday

Dear Norb,

Well, here I am at it again. Mom and I think the guy in the middle looks like you. It's the way you stand when you have something to lean on. Let us know if this fellar is you. Lee's getting a "new" car again. I wonder what trouble he will buy this time. I think you should interest him in a jeep. He probably could go hunting in that as it can take the hills and hollows.

Monday is Labor Day. You can't imagine it being time for school to open. The weather man promised beautiful weather this weekend but I think he's full of good promises. It looks like rain. (But it didn't.)

September 3

Well, it's another pretty day. It's warm too. What do you think of Tony Oberhausen? Seems like he's getting plenty of publicity. It's strange he could wink a lot better... [*pages missing*].

[Hermina]

On September 5, the HQC 59th Signal Btn. was attached to the Ninth Army under the VIII Corps. The envelope of the following letter was postmarked Sep 9 and Sep 19. Censor had stamped inside the letter on Sep 19. The mail was slowed down by censors and war.

France, **September 8**

Dear Mom & All,

Here's a few lines to let you know that everything is OK. I'm sorry to say that the picture you sent me (clipping) was not me. He wasn't in a bad position at all. The news is all excellent, couldn't be better. They even had false rumors the other day that the Germans had capitulated. That will be damn good news. One down and one to go. I was listening the other day to how the army is going to discharge the men after the war ended with Germany. It sounds pretty fair to me, but I think according to that I have a little more army life ahead of me than I suspected. Well, come what may, at any rate it won't take too long now.

It rained off and on all this week and its beginning to get a little cool. I guess it's about time for that now. Say, how about sending me about four packages of TUMS. Some of this chow don't agree with you sometimes [*probably caused by nerves*]. That's all I could use for now. I received the candy about three days ago. The mail has been coming through pretty well. Well, the sun's going down so I guess I'll close for now. So be good and I'll be seeing you. Tell Mary hello & X.

As Always,

Norb

Louisville, Kentucky, **September 12**, Tuesday, 1 pm

Dear Norb,

To begin with, we received your 'three in one' letter yesterday and the checks too. And today we received another letter and check with a German Officer Swastika emblem. Wasn't that from a German officer or do they all surrender? Ha, ha.

Well, it's raining. It's really like fall weather. They claim in New York that the fall breezes are blowing.

I was [*went*] to see Mrs. Lee. She's doing swell. They want to buy a home and the Butlers are going to sell theirs so I had told her about it. She's very much interested. Butlers are going back to Georgia. That's where their heart was all the time.

If you see Zip tell him that his distant relative, Carmel Sheer, eloped Saturday. I heard she packed her duds Saturday and went to where her boyfriend was stationed and Sunday morning her mother got a telegram stating she was married. I called Mary [*Rawert*] on Logan. They never call or come out, but I called to thank her for your package. She said she sent one about Easter and another one in May. Which one did you get? The first one had cigarettes and chewing gum, the last one just chewing gum. Could you smoke and chew it?

Now, we'll do our darnndest to get a cigarette lighter but I doubt seriously if we'll be able to get a blackout lighter. I called all the best shops and nobody but Sutcliff's had any. They were one buck and only had a few. We tried to get a Ronson lighter but the Gem [*sic*] told me they weren't manufacturing them. They haven't had any Ronsons for a long time. All these men shops never had any so I hope we'll be able to get one for one buck at Sutcliff's.

Your checks will be taken care of tomorrow as mom and I are going in town to the Dr. I heard Stites enlarged his office to twice its size. Madden was expected home today but she got a letter stating that it would be sometime after September 15th.

You must be living in a "liberated Utopia" if all the French women are so beautiful. I bet you do wish you could speak French. How many hearts have you broken with those great big beautiful eyes? And to think of the men as Charles Boyer's, ooh la, la. You did a pretty good Boyer act here. Don't you think the French girls would fall for an imitation? Or do they want the genuine? I sure do hope that the war business in Europe will be settled before the cold weather because foxholes with ice cycles wouldn't be very pleasant. F.D.R. and Churchill are meeting in Quebec this week.

Hoping you are OK as we all are. Mom has felt a lot better since Saturday and is going to wash dishes, two cups, two saucers. Do you need any undies? Did you get our birthday cards and birthday cablegram?

Love and hope to see you Christmas and great big fat X.

H.R.

France, **September 12,** 8:00 pm

Dear Mom & all,

Here's just a few lines to let you know I'm OK and hope you are all the same. The weather here has been swell although it looks like it's going to rain any moment now. The news couldn't be better than what it is. Hoping to be drinking Oertel's in the not too distant future! Tell Mary hello X. I remain,

As Always,

Norb

Louisville, Kentucky, **September 13,** Wednesday, 2 pm

Dear Norb,

Well, I can't make mistakes because this is the last full page I have. It's a beautiful day. Clear as a crystal. I got a nice job. I'm washing the dining room furniture so it can be waxed. I hope the waxing will be easier but I doubt it. Well, we got your cigarette lighter. I hope you will like it. It's the only thing we could get. We'll fix up a box and it will soon be on its way.

Well, the kiddoes are all in school. I'm anxious to know how Vernon likes it. Grandma Threedouble [*neighbor on Mulberry Street*] died Sunday nite and was buried this morning. I really don't have any news as you can plainly see, can't you? The news seems swell. They claim in about 10 days they'll know a lot more about the invasion of Germany. I sure hope it doesn't take that long for things to shape up. We are all OK. Hope you'll soon be off K-rations. For lunch mom and I had her Sunday Special of a few years ago - tomato and bacon, lettuce sandwich. Remember?

Love,

Hermina

Louisville, Kentucky, **September 14**

Dear Brother:

How's everything? I hope you are in the best of health. I was down at St. Elizabeth's tonight. It is 11:00 now, Thursday night. I got two curtains for Elizabeth and hung them tonight. Betsy is nutty as ever and Katsy is still the dancing girl. She was in front of the mirror dancing and singing and little Margie is as sweet as ever. Milton is back at St. X. Shirley is proud to be at Hi School and Jimmy Muth is OK. Now, the dog didn't behave so good. They put salt on the rug. Oh, the kids sure are cute.

Did you hear about the storm along the coast? I heard it on the radio. In New York the wind was 95 miles an hour. We are as busy as ever at work. Points [*rations*] are going off lots of canned goods. Well, Saturday we can send you a Xmas box. Anyway, September 15 is a day to celebrate and Milton's birthday is the 16th. I wish you could see that string bean - almost as tall as Joe and he is a nice looking boy. Shirley weighs 126 pounds. This was the first time I went to Elizabeth's since Decoration Day...the kids said they had company. Ha, ha. Mom and Pop are fine and so is baby sister. Joe and Johnny and Joey and family are also. Lee has a 2-door V-8 ford. Good luck Norb. God bless you and we will be seeing you real soon.

Marge

Louisville, Kentucky, **September 14**, Thursday, 9:50 pm

Dear Norb,

Alma called yesterday. She said she moved again. I laughed but she laughs with me. I sure hope she likes it. I always felt sorry for her. How do you keep her address straight, or don't you? Well, it seems the Allies are making progress in Germany but our news is not as newsy as we would like but you can see why that is done. It was a beautiful day but the storm or hurricane struck in New Jersey. Since yesterday they have been warning the people along the coast.

Goodnite,

H.R.

Continued, Friday morning

Well, I didn't start the day very well. At 7:00 am the plasterer called, asked if it would be OK to come today. I told him yes, gladly, so then I called Mrs. Madden [*renter at their adjacent property at 1137 Mulberry Street*]. She said she didn't want that mess while Bill was home. She's expecting him any time now. I said well there's no telling how long you'll have to wait then. She said she didn't care - she lived in the damn mess this long and she could live in it a little longer. I said there's no telling. It might be Easter. She said she didn't care, so I had to call Schnurr back. I was bored [*upset*]. She griped all summer but I don't blame her now. But she better not gripe to me later on. Nuf said.

Milt came, said he would add a bit: "Norb I am going to St. X again. I went to summer school and I flunked Science. We have a new Principal, Brother Edwards. I didn't want to go to St. X again this year but mother made me go. Meanie [*Hermina*] said that every time she sees me I get bigger. I am just about as tall as Joe. Well, I haven't much to say and that is about all."

As always, he's in a hurry doing nothing. He wants to go to the YMCA to shoot pool. Your first Xmas parcel is on its way. I hope you enjoy it but I won't say what's in it. You let us know when you get it. Love and hope to see you Xmas.
Hermina

Louisville, Kentucky, **September 17**

Hello Norb, Dear Brother,

How are you? Mary just asked where is Herman & he is on the porch, so Mom said go out if you want to see him. Now pop come in and he has so much trouble with his pipe. I said I wish I could get him one the size of a tub. He is continually filling his pipe. Cigars are rare. Cigarettes are also. Joey can only buy 2 packs at a time.

Norb, the airplanes are flying very low tonight. They look like they come on top of Russell's trees. It's 7:30 Sunday night. Yesterday Milton was 15 years old and Friday I was 16, ha, ha.

Wednesday, September 15, was the day we could send Christmas packages,so you have one on the way. A cigarette lighter, which is rather small, a fruitcake and candy. You will get more though, Norb.

Mrs. Able's grandson was in Rome and he sent a rosary, miraculous medal, a chain with St. Theresa's picture for his mother. Mrs. Able works with me, that's Mrs. Bank's mother. Hermina is also writing letters. It's 15 minutes of 8 and news is on.

Well, while the news was on, Lip, the old man, Jim, Betsy, Katsy and Margie came in and they all know something. Lip has a new purse. Oh, my! Here comes Ann, JoAnn and Mrs. Russell and we have 14 in all. Well, now it's 10:55 and all quiet. Pop and Hermina are in bed and Mom just put out the kitchen lights and I am anxious to get this letter in the mail tomorrow.

I heard they [allies] are in Holland. With God speed and prayers all will come to a good end. Joe has a cold so he didn't come over tonight and Johnny has not enough gas, he can't make so many trips.

We are still as busy as ever at work. Our new lady in the store seems to be very nice. Anyway she doesn't seem to think herself more than anyone else. Robert Lee Steinmetz has a NY address and Charles is in India. Charlie Boy across the street had a falling out with his lady friend. Well, I might think of something in the morning and then I'll write again. God bless Norbert. That's the way the children pray.

[*Marge*]

Continued the next morning by Hermina:

Oh, what a beautiful morning! We are OK. We seen our first flock of birds going south yesterday. Mrs. Paul's little tree (Dogwood) is beginning to turn but the other trees and grass looks very, very green. We received your letter this morning and sorry, very sorry, to learn that you think you will not be discharged from the Army as soon as you thought. Perhaps it might be Easter then. If you hear more let us know. Yes, you'll get your Tums dear. Are you still on K-rations? Your next box will be on its way with Tums.

Love and keep your chin up. X

H.R.

Maj. Zortman of the 59th *Signal Battalion reported: "Following the action in July, VIII Corps continued to attack along the west coast of the French peninsula as part of Operation Cobra, launched on 25 July 1944 in order to break the stalemate following the Normandy beachhead. As the Third Army continued to move East through France towards Belgium and Germany, VIII Corps continued to attack toward Brest capturing the vital port city on 18 September 1944. Unfortunately, this left the VIII Corps well behind its higher headquarters, which resulted in VIII Corps being reassigned to the Ninth Army.*

Following the taking of the Brest Peninsula, the VIII Corps was moved into a supporting position, covering the southern flank of the Third Army, as they pushed into Belgium through the fall. As the winter started, the battle lines were reorganized throughout the Ardennes Forest, and VIII Corps moved into the Northern portion. The strongest fighting was occurring in the south, still with Third and First Army, so VIII Corps became the place for divisions to reorganize, and new divisions to be placed to get their first experience in combat, as the VIII Corps portion of the western line was relatively sedate compared to the southern portion.

The fighting in the fall was fierce and slow, as the Germans fought for every inch as the Allies pushed them closer and closer to their homeland. By 15 December, the Allies had almost completely recovered the whole of France and Belgium, through Operation Market Garden."

Louisville, Kentucky, **September 18**

Hellow [*sic*] Norb,

I am at Mom's, alias Mrs. Rawert's. I went down and got examined for the Army Saturday August 19, 1944. They put me in 2-B until February 24, 1945. The doctor said I had ankelosis [*sic*]. I really wish I could get in the fight. How are you getting along? I heard you liked the French women. When you learn the French language you will be alright. Let me know how you are getting along. I will have to close now but not for long.

Dewey Carter [*Joey Rawert Carter's stepson*]

In the following letter Norb asks about the address of his cousins in Germany. These were the Effkemanns in Ahaus (called Heitkemper in Louisville) that the Rawert family had occasionally corresponded with after WW I. In the year 2000, Carol and Harold Trainer traveled to Ahaus to meet Josef Effkemann and his family and later met other family members. Norb did not know the family. His cousin Josef and some of Josef's brothers were in the Nazi army serving under Hitler.

France, **September 18**

Dear Mom & All,

Well, I don't know why I always start my letters with "Well" but will anyway. Here's a couple lines to let you know I'm still on maneuvers. There's Yank washing hanging on the Siegfried Line but it ain't mine. I send mine to the laundry. The weather has been swell but I believe it's going to rain tonight. The mail has been coming through fairly well. Can't complain, anyway.

The paratroopers that landed in Holland seem to be doing alright according to reports. It won't be long now "I'm a thinking." What did you say my cousin's address was in Germany? Might drop in and see the boys. With my carbine loaded, of course. I think we could get to Berlin a lot faster if they would give these Yanks a sample of beer. My tongue hangs out every time I think of it. Damn, I could punish a case of Oertel's. I would even stoop so low as to drink Falls City and it wouldn't have to be cold either. I was looking at some German military maps and they even had Louisville on it. It surprised me a little. Ha! Well, I hope you are all well. I'm doing OK myself so take it easy and I'll be seeing you.

As Always,

Norb

The VIII Corps liberated the city of Brest on September 19. Later Norb wrote that of all the destruction he has seen in the French cities (which was a lot), Brest was the worst. Reorganizing after the operations in Brittany, the VIII Corps moved east to join the rest of the Allied forces along the border of Germany.

Louisville. Kentucky, **September 19**, Tuesday, 1:30 pm

Dear Norb,

Well, it's sunshiny for a while and then it looks very gloomy as if it might rain any minute but now it's beautiful. Well, I told you yesterday we received your letter of September 8th. I suppose I heard and read the same demobilization program as you did. I don't think that would change. I thought to myself [*sic*] you might have a little more army life ahead of you. I don't know how they will work out the points do you? It's going to be worked out that way but I think it sounds fair too. We are hoping that you won't be sent to the Pacific. You might and you might not. You and we just have to have patience and see what happens. They claim they are only beginning with Japan. Well, I think it sounds like they have a very, very good start but these "at home strategists" seem to think it won't take so long with Japan.

Well, your Tums will be on their way with this letter. Hope your tummy will straighten out so you won't need them. Are you still on K-rations?

The Life magazine, September 18th, really has a lot in it this week. It shows Dewey when he made his campaign speech here two weeks ago and Kentucky is their honor state this week. Did you think that clipping looked like you in the jeep? How about that rear-view clipping? Let us know about that too, please.

Marge got herself a ridiculous looking hat last night but it's very becoming. I think Breakfast at Sardis's would try it on. I wrote to Bernie S. [*Spoelker*] yesterday. I think I told you we heard from him two weeks ago. He said to give JoAnn a little more '92 because six pounds didn't carry much punch. I told him she weighs fourteen pounds now and it wasn't from '92 (Mom said it was - indirectly, ha ha). Ann bought JoAnn the first pair of shoes, size 0. So Joe came over with them at 10 pm to show 'em to us. She demands and gets attention (smart woman).

Hoping your stomach is in better shape when you get this letter. I suppose if you had warm meals it would be OK. We all want to know if you get any French kisses. Did you get Mom's and Pop's snapshot? Kindly let us know.

Love,

H.R.

Louisville, Kentucky, **September 20,** Wednesday, 10:00 am

Dear Norb:

Well, it's another lovely day. We're listening to Breakfast at Sardis. Your Tums are on their way. One little item made noise but it was a noisemaker before I put it in box so it went thru. I thought perhaps they would refuse it at the Post Office but as it was beyond my control it was OK.

I seen this piece in this morning's paper stating that Gen. Montgomery said it would be over this year with the Nazis. I sure hope that's right because one man on the air said today it might take another year or two, but I think he's all wet, "dripping wet."

Alma called last night. We didn't have anything special to say. Mr. Madden came in last nite about 6:00 pm. From what I seen of him he's looking fine. Cousin Mary Rawert called yesterday. We talked about an hour. Hope you are OK.

Love from,

H.R.

Louisville, Kentucky, **September 21**, Thursday, 12 noon

Dearest Norb,

It is the first Friday of Autumn. According to Baukhage it seems as if there is really some fighting in Germany. Well, it's a beautiful day, warm and sunshiny. Mrs. Orrill just called. Walter told her he's in the 6th Armored Division in Brest. He also sent a clipping that appeared in Stars and Stripes with the 6th Army Division picture in Brest. What Division or Army are you with? You never, never answer that. I got a letter from Bill Hollkamp. His address, rather his APO, has changed. He's OK. He has been promoted to Cpl. I don't think it will be so long before we see him, do you? Can't you send a clipping with an inkling or clue to where you are at or what Army you are with? But if you think it would worry us, well then you're using sounder judgment than I am in asking.

Well, it seems Katsy starts every school year off with singing for her class. The Sister asked if anybody could sing along. Katsy volunteered and sang "Don't Sweetheart Me Babe." Elizabeth said that's all she does is sing, dance and pose before the mirror.

Friday...Well, it's still a beautiful day. I pulled all our "mater" [*tomato*] stocks up yesterday. It was not much on them anymore, so I guess I'll finish cleaning up the yard today as Oct. 13th is R-Day here, "rat day." Everybody is supposed to lay poison that day. I told Mary all of Louisville was going to celebrate her birthday by laying out poison for rats. She got a kick out of that. If you have some time just put a page to Mary with our letter. She sure is an old faithful with mailing your letters and boxes and anything I might add.

Hoping to hear from you Monday. Kindly think to answer if you got Mrs. Russell's card. It seems we always hear from you on Monday. That's why I said Monday. Is there anything you want? Norb, would you like a little chemical stove? Sutcliffe's advertises a little stove for boys across. It said it's to heat Rations on. It's 55¢ and 24 heat pills come with it. I thought the army probably furnishes that. Let us know.

Love,

H.R.

Louisville, Kentucky, **September 25**, Monday, 2 pm, (3 months til Xmas)

Dearest Norb,

Well, to begin with it's a clear, warm, sunshiny day with cool breezes so it's lovely. I'll begin with Saturday. The President spoke for the first time in this campaign and we all listened. He was very good, the funniest I ever heard him. I'm telling you, when he told that story about Fala his pooch, his audience really roared. I'm inclosing it [*below*], read it word for word if you can. I think you'll get a kick out of it.

> *On September 23, 1944, Roosevelt gave his famous "Fala speech" while campaigning in the 1944 presidential election. The 39:30 minute speech was delivered at a campaign dinner in Washington, DC before the International Brotherhood of Teamsters, Chauffeurs, Warehousemen and Helpers of America. In the speech, Roosevelt attacked Republican opponents in Congress and detailed their attacks on him. Late in the speech, Roosevelt addressed Republican charges that he had accidentally left Fala behind on the Aleutian Islands while on tour there and had sent a US Navy destroyer to retrieve him at an exorbitant cost: "These Republican leaders have not been content with attacks on me, or my wife, or on my sons. No, not content with that, they now include my little dog, Fala. [Laughter] Well, of course, I don't resent attacks, and my family doesn't resent attacks but Fala does resent them. [Laughter] You know, Fala is Scotch, and being a Scottie, as soon as he learned that the Republican fiction writers in Congress and out had concocted a story that I'd left him behind on an Aleutian island and had sent a destroyer back to find him - at a cost to the taxpayers of two or three, or eight or 20 million dollars - his Scotch soul was furious. [Laughter] He has not been the same dog since. [Laughter] I am accustomed to hearing malicious falsehoods about myself — such as that old, worm-eaten chestnut that I have represented myself as indispensable. But I think I have a right to resent, to object, to libelous statements about my dog!" [Laughter]; Source: http://en.wikipedia.org/wiki/Fala_ (dog) on ¼6/2011.*

Did I tell you that Carl Williams, Ann's sister Althea's husband, was in an accident? An enormous truck hit the wagon that he and his brother was in. Carl got hurt the worse, 3/4 of his scalp was torn from his head, but there was no fractured skull so he was lucky. It taken 70 clamps to close, or should I say attach, his scalp and he's doing splendid. Eleanor came in yesterday with the five kids and asked if we would we keep them. She had a chance to go to the country with Aline so we were glad to keep them. She wanted to take Norbie. Marge and I both said what for? And we didn't have to coax her to leave him. He's so good natured. She forgot his clothes so he had quite a few borrowed attires on yesterday. First it was a big outing gown of JoAnn's. It struck him to the middle of his leg. He looked like a golden haired angel, like you on the holy picture. Next came Margie's dresses so I put a pink ribbon in his hair. He was so cute. Lip etc. was up here too. Betsy and Jim came later, so Betsy taught Norbie how to make a snoot, stick out his tongue and put up his dukes, but he knew how to use his fist and he didn't look anything like a girl when he turned loose his fists on Betsy. Betsy was to a party. She won another prize. Every party she makes, she brings home a prize. She saved her piece of cake for Mom. I thought that was so sweet.

Johnny bought a coal and wood range. It's white. He said it looks almost like a gas range. It has a hot water tank attachment. It cost nearly $100.00 bucks but he's thrilled with it. They think that they are going to have new burners installed in their gas range so Eleanor can use the bottled gas but that has been out for the duration. But Johnny heard it was released lately.

I just received a letter from Bernard H [*Hollkamp*]. He said he wrote to you and has not received an answer. I suppose you've gotten the letter from me where he said you and him were practically side by side. He said he was moved about 125 miles. He doubts if he'll ever see Paris but perhaps he'll see Sue [*mispronunciation of Sault?*]. Is Sue a French town? I don't recall hearing that name mentioned.

Lip is sending you a big box of candy for Xmas. She asked me to print your name (was I flattered, ha ha). We won't send you any candy because it might get stale but if you ever think of anything you want say so. We are working on another box so I'm raking my "brain" and Johnny got a Ronson lighter. He asked all his customers and he got three offers so one woman had a used Ronson but it wasn't used for years so she took it to Kendrick's Jewelers. Had something new put on it and sold it to Johnny for half price. She said she gave $10 for it. Johnny was so glad to get it, for the one we sent isn't so hot. Perhaps you can pass that on to a GI who hasn't any. That's all for now. We are OK. Hope you are. We didn't get a letter today.
Love,
H.R.

Louisville, Kentucky, **September 26,** 1 pm

Dear Norb,

Well, my letter was returned to me from yesterday [*from censors*]. I suppose the President's words were too heavy. Ha, ha. It's another beautiful day. Mom wants to add her bit too. According to the noon newscast the Arnhem Bridge was recaptured by the Nazis so that will mean goodbye to that bridge. We haven't heard form you yet this week but the week is young, but it's usually on a Monday when we get your letters. It starts the week right.
Love,
Porky

Louisville, Kentucky, **September 26,** 2pm

Dear Norb,

How are you? We are all well and I hope you are also. I am still not as strong as I used to be. I don't believe I will ever be again. That means more work for Hermina. I tire out for every little bit. It's not nice to take it easy and see others work. Maybe if the war was over, most of us - or all of us - will feel better. I know that all the boys of St. Elizabeth's in the service are going to get a gift. They called us up and asked for your address. Have you ever met any boys you know?

Cousin Anna Heitkemper's niece, Sr. Bernice, is teaching Shirley Ann history. Mary Rawert and Francis [*Heitkemper*] was to see us Sunday. Cousin Mary looks a whole lot better since I saw her last. She was sick a long time. General breakdown the doctor said. She can go to church again. That's a whole lot to be thankful for. You feel like you belong to the world again and not shut up.

Sunday Joe took Marge and me to St. Martin's. That was a treat for me. Memories of long ago come to me. I always liked St. Martin's. [*her parents' 1st parish after immigrating*] I will now close and wish you God's blessing. I also bless you at night in spirit with holy water. Pray for us. We are praying for you. XXXX and all my love.
Mother

Louisville, Kentucky, September 27

Dearest Norb,

Well, it's beginning to cloud up a little. It looks like we might have some rain but we sure did have "glamorous" weather. Lip and the three girls were up. They were really cute. Betsy is learning how to crochet. Her teacher is showing her and it won't take long, that needle was really swinging. Sr. Bertrilla is principal at St. E's. Betsy was talking to her and asked her if she knew her uncle Norbert Rawert. She said do you spell that R-A WERT. Betsy said yes. She said I know him. I taught him here at St. E. She asked how you were and what kind of work you do. Betsy said you do "army work." Well, she said Betsy should tell you hello for her the next time she writes.

Milt likes his Brother [*Christian Brothers*] very much. He told the boys he has never failed a boy yet. Milt liked his idea very much. Very much. Sr. Bernice (Anne Heitkemper's niece) is Shirley's history teacher. She liked her.

I heard on the Air yesterday that the troops in the European Theater were putting on their winter overcoats as the weather is getting cold. If there is anything in the way of warmth you want, say so. Sweater, red flannels, or just anything. In the morning paper it stated the BBC [*British Broadcasting Channel*] banned the song "I'm Dreaming of Christmas With You." It also stated that they think the war will be carried thru the winter but I did read a piece in last week's paper that Gen. "Ike" said it could end this year. They blacked out the news from the European fighting yesterday. We haven't heard from you in ten days. That's three days too long.

I see where Ed Zipperle, Sr. has been chosen as a delegate to the War Dad's Convention to be held in Omaha, Nebraska. He works hard for that. I think Pop has a half-way notion to "join up." They visit out here at St. Michael's and do things to help the soldiers or rather Service-Men. Tony Oberhausuen is doing fine.

Did you get the papers Lip send you, a miniature newspaper form Stewarts? You never mention it. Are you still on dry rations? Would you want one of those Ration-Stoves I wrote you last week about? They come with heat pills. They have them at Sutcliff's for 55¢, pocket size. I thought perhaps the army would give you that. Now you won't have to rake your brain about a Xmas gift this year. If it's convenient just have a picture made that would please us you know, as we didn't see your "snoot" for quite a while. Let us see how you look in France or ??? Did you get Mom's and Pop's snapshot? We are OK. Hope you are too.

Love and God Bless You,

Porky

Louisville, Kentucky, **September 27**

Hi ya Toots, I mean <u>Bootsie</u>,

I've been home by my lonesome every night for quite a while. Lee is painting at night at Kroger food stores and Dewey goes out every night that God sends. I believe in the last 1 ½ years he has been home about four nights. But living back here, I guess he'd just rather be out. I don't blame him. He's only young once. I baked two custard pies for supper. Wish you were here to help us eat them. Lee seen Alma one night as he was going to work. She and another girl were going to the show. She said Hi Shorty. He really has been working very hard. Hope and pray he continues to do so.

How's the French girls? The way the paper reads, mostly all are good to the American boys. There's no one could be too good to our own boys. It sure is raining here tonight. I guess it will turn cooler. The weather has been grand though. Fishing wasn't worth a damn this year, for I really did try hard & you know me. Well, I just can't think of a thing to write any more. I feel sorta hazy, can't concentrate. Now, ain't that not natural for me. For now I'll say so long & hope we'll be seeing you soon.

As ever, Your Fishing sister, hunting brother-in-law, strutting nephew, ha ha,

Joey, Lee, Dewey

Louisville, Kentucky, **September 28,** Thursday 10:45 am

Dearest Norb,

Well, it really came down yesterday afternoon for a little while, but we needed rain two ways - if it rained we would get the furnace fixed and also we just needed rain. We are having the furnace fixed today. We had several light fires this season.

Well, it seemed everybody was sending you a fruitcake. We bought another one to send so we just kept it. Otherwise you would be full of fruitcake, I'm sure. It seemed everybody was so optimistic about the war, now everybody is let down since the loss of the Air-Borne [*sic*] Division in Arnhem. That's tough indeed but there might be more living than is thought at the present.

We were talking about how grand it was of the pastor of the church, where Carl [*Williams*] attends, to announce from the pulpit Sunday that Carl's tobacco has not been cut and asked the men to volunteer to cut the tobacco that day. He said don't let the Sunday work worry you or give that as an excuse. So Eleanor said after church services were over, here comes Fr. Dudine and thirty men to cut the tobacco and by 2:30 they were through. Althea [*Smith*] went to the hospital to tell Carl, and he cried like a baby. The Friday before Fr. Dudine rounded up the 4 H Club boys and they wormed the tobacco. Eleanor said he worked right with them.

Is there anything in the way of woolen you might need? Socks, mittens or stepins [*sic*]. Let us know. Hope you are OK as we all are. Sassy Mary says Hello.
Love,
Hermina

Louisville, Kentucky, **September 30,** Saturday, 11 am
Dear Norb,

Well, the sun is beginning to shine now but it's cool. I'm going to build a fire. This week has been old clothes collection week for the poor in Europe. It's just through the Catholic churches, that I know of. Maybe you'll get to see some of our old clothes. I know you would recognize Pop's longies. Did you ever get the little papers Lip has been sending you? It's a CJ in miniature put out by Stewarts. Well, yesterday was the last ones to be printed as the paper shortage is that acute.

A 16-story hotel is planned for Louisville after the war. It will be past 4ᵗʰ Street. It will contain 1,000 air conditioned rooms. I got a letter from Bern H [*Hollkamp*]. He sure seemed down in the dumps to me. Marge got a letter from Thelma Saunders yesterday. They're OK. Milt is expecting to ship out anytime. Well, I'm out of news I think. Fourth Street is going to get 25 new streetcars after Jan 1, 1945. I believe Portland and Shelby Streets will get some too. They will be particularly noiseless, they claim.
Love,
Porky

Louisville, Kentucky, **October 1,** Sunday
Dearest Norb,

Well, it's another lovely day. I can't imagine it's the first of October. Do you remember you once wrote Patton should have said 45 days to Paris and 45 days to Berlin? Well, that time would be up, but they were to Paris in 45 days. Personally, I don't think the war will end the latter part of the year. Eisenhower said it could end this year. I think he would know more than Churchill about that. Churchill was the cause of this wave of optimism that affected the American people only to be knocked down by the great loss at Arnhem but I don't blame him for that alone. Everything did look rosy. They claim in another month we should know a lot more, so we'll have to hope and pray that it will end this year. They claim the war with the Japs will last anther 1 ½ years. The military experts should have said X days plus 1 ½ years. The military prefers X Day to VE Day as we have been using. They claim X means they don't know when it will end. Nuff said.

Mrs. Madden's brother, Louis Rich, that lived in the old place is Missing in Action in France. His wife got the message Friday. We haven't heard from you for two weeks. It was written September 8th, so we are anxiously awaiting news from you. Would you like any hard mett sausage salami or perhaps a fried chicken, canned like they do in the country? Or clothing, sweets, or anything you can think of? How about vitamins? Did you ever hear the Mr. And Mrs. Henry Ford hour? It's old-folk music and really beautiful. Mom & Pop said that's the kind they danced to. We get it every Saturday from 7 to 7:30. Pop had his bath drawn already but he heard the program coming on so the bath was deferred for a half-hour. They play the quadrille, lances, even an Irish jig. I hope you can hear it. Mom's feet get itchy when she hears it. Hoping this letter finds you OK as we are.

Love from your little Sis,

Porky

Louisville, Kentucky, **October 2**, Monday, 11:10 am

Dearest Norb,

Well, it's another beautiful day. We just finished washing. I was talking to Mrs. Lee (over the fence). I told her the "Can You Top This" program said he calls these women 'Monday Morning Kaltenborns' [*A.K. Kaltenborn was an American commentator*]. I thought that was very funny. I'm going to Johnson's. I might pick up a little dope there so I won't close this letter.

Continued, 3:00 pm:

Well, the plasterers did finally come this afternoon. They are knocking plaster to beat all heck. I'm glad they came but we certainly wouldn't have been sorry if the tenants [*at 1137 Mulberry Street*] would have moved. But they don't break up anything so I guess we should be glad of that. I was at Johnson's. Mr. Johnson just got a box of cigars, German made, from Larny last Friday. I think he said he didn't know enough about them to tell the difference. One man said they were milder and another friend said they were stronger. He sent some kind of emblem and collar and some French money.

Clarence is due home on a furlough sometime this week. Earl just went back this week. He found a cottage there so his wife and baby went back with him. Another Xmas box is on its way. It's got Johnny's gift to you in there and also Joey's three bucks worth, ha, ha. We are going to get up another box and I suppose that will be all we can send you. That's everything we can rake our brains as to what to send, but if there is anything you can rake your "little' brains and think you might want, just say so my dear and we'll try to get it there.

It's been two weeks today since we heard from you. That letter was written September 18th so we are keeping "two" eyes on the mailman. JoAnn gained 14 oz.'s this past week.

She's very, very cute, weighs 15 lbs. 2 oz. She's like a Lucky [*Lucky Strike cigarette*], so round, so firm, so fully packed, so quick and easy on the eyes. Since Dick Fischer left WHAS, Gabriel Heatter substitutes in his place in Pop's eyes. So he got Pop to thinking about using Kremel, so Joe and Ann gave him his Kremel. As he doesn't use it, I put some on his hair for him and then Mom said, "Gee Pop you sure smell sweet." Well, then Walter Winchell came on. Mom said, "Pop, don't you want some Jerkins [*Jergen's*] lotion too?" He said no, he didn't think so, but his hair used to be oily and now their dry. Herm's afraid of getting bald, I believe. We did get a good laugh on him.

I hope you all are having as beautiful weather as we are. I never seen a more beautiful day. It's heavenly. They announced that Dover, England was liberated. I suppose that will popularize "The White Cliffs of Dover." From all indications it seems Russia will help out with Japan after X Day. Hoping you are well and that we hear from your real, real soon, so get your "little," but intelligent, brains working on what you would like to have, so I'll close with love from all. Affectionately yours, your sis,
Hermie

On October 4, while still part of the US Ninth Army, the VIII Corps took over the front in the Ardennes along the Our River and the Schnee Eifel. Because this area of the front was so quiet the Corps was used as an orientation and rest area for new US divisions and divisions that had taken heavy casualties while fighting in the Huertgen Forest. This mission continued until December 16 when the Germans attacked the VIII Corps with over 20 divisions in what became known as the Ardennes Offensive. By that time Norb had been removed from the battlefield and placed in hospital with a "nervous disorder" condition.

The Huertgen Forest (deeply wooded, rough terrain) is located along the border between Belgium and Germany in the southwest corner of the German federal state of North Rhine-Westphalia. From September 19, 1944 until February 10, 1945, this area was the scene of a bloody, drawn out battle which took place over three months during a very cold winter. In 1998 HBO made a film about the Battle of the Huertgen Forest, When Trumpets Fade.

Louisville, Kentucky. **October 4,** Wednesday, 4:30 pm

Dear Norb,

Well, I was just about ready to sit down with "pen in hand" and tell you it was two and a half weeks since we heard from you when the mailman handed me a letter from you. The last letter was written the 8th. This one was written the 12th. This one was very short but unbelievably sweet. We were beginning to feel uneasy. Mom shed a few tears of gladness. Between the time you wrote the letter and the time we received it, the war has taken on a different outlook although it looks better again. Everything was looking so favorably for us when that setback of the English troops at Arnhem was flashed. It seemed everybody's feathers dropped but people were really feeling very optimistic. It put a damper on all optimism, believe me, but I still think this war will go into 1945. Gen. "Ike" said it could end this year. I believe he knows. Clarence Johnson rolled in this morning. Bernie Werner was Killed in Acton. They got word Monday nite.

It's another beautiful day. The plasterer has the undercoat on and the chimney's tore down and back up, so will finish with the skin coat tomorrow. I know they will be glad. Well, I see Al Smith passed away this morning at 6:20 am. He certainly has a big write up in tonite's paper. He deserves it.

Pop is still using Kremel. I told Pop he and JoAnn had a lot in common, a toothless smile and an "oiled" scalp. To be continued.

Continued, 8:00 pm

Well, Gabriel Heatter is on. His news is very encouraging. He is elaborating upon Alfred E. Smith. It sure is swell to hear so much good about anybody. His family certainly can be proud. Well, Lip is here. Betsy is going to mail this. I suppose we will hear from you soon, as I think this letter was delayed. You can't write too often, you know. We are OK. Hope you are well.
Love,
Hermina

In the October 4 letter to home, it is the first time Norb mentions he is "somewhere in Belgium." In 2012 my husband and I took a memorial car tour of the area that Norb travelled during the war, stopping at all the cities he named in the letter below: Valogne, St. Lô, Lessay, areas near La Haye-du-Puits, St. Sauveur, Paris, Versailles and others that he travelled through on the push through France to Germany. On meeting French people at the American Cemetery and other sites as we drove around we got a feeling of the great appreciation that the French have towards the American sacrifice. It was an awe-inspiring trip which brought these letters to life for me.

Norb doesn't say much in his letters home for several reasons. For one he can't discuss the war or location or the censors delete it and while they are on the move through the countryside in the heat of battle he doesn't really have time. He also does not want to concern his family. He does mention on October 6 that he needs some extra heavy wool socks that give some insight to the conditions. By this time his morale was very low.

The letters from here on take a long time to be censored and posted probably due to the war situation and troop movement. There are large gaps of time from one letter to another and it is heard in the letters.

Somewhere in Belgium, **October 4**

Dear Mom & All,

Here's a couple of lines to let you know that all is well except the weather. It's been raining off and on for the last four days. Today it sleeted a little bit. Things are pretty muddy.

Yeah, Breast [*Brest*] was quite a place to see. I seen all the rest nearly. La Hague de Parts [*La Haye-du-Puits*], Velone [*Valogne*], St. Lô, Lessay [*Basse-Normandie region of France*], St. Sauveur, but Breast [*Brest*] was the worst of all. I don't think that there was a five foot square anywhere that didn't show shell marks.

Paris, ah! Paris, how I would like to spend about a week there. It's really a place. I know that just from passing through. Versailles is quite a place also. I have had some of the best beer I have drank since I've left the states today. It really was good beer.

I guess you can forget about that Xmas dinner. I don't think I'll be there but you never can tell. Hoping you are all well and everything. I'm doing alright except for a slight cold. Well, here's mud in your eye & I'll be seeing you. How about a carton of cigarettes? I'm just about out.

As Always,

Norb

Louisville, Kentucky, **October 5**, Thursday

Dear Brother,

How's everything? We are well. It's raining tonight and it's 8:30 o'clock. Hermina made some grape jelly and peach preserves. Do you want some? Just please let us know and it will be in the return mail. I am wondering where you will get your Christmas packages. They are not so large. Well, anyway I wish you could be home by that time. Junior Hubbuch came in today. He looks good. Hermina ordered some Red Stomach drops and they came today. Do you need some? We had some hunk [*sp*] stake [*steak*] for supper and did we have a pulling party. And corn on the cob, cucumbers and potatoes with jackets.

Hermina is calling Alma & she is at church so she will call back. Norb, a prayer for you I guess. Alma has been lucky about her eye. She went to Dr. Baker & he said no operation. Ain't that swell? I have not seen her for a long time. Mamma is lying on the couch asleep. You should hear her puff. Do you remember? Pop is at St. Brigid's Bingo. Hermina is barefooted & I just washed my golden locks so they won't dry fast for it's raining and sort of damp. It has been warm the last couple of days. Indian summer I guess.

[*The following pages were missing*]

[*Marge*]

Louisville, Kentucky, **October 6,** Friday, 7:15 am

Dear Norb,

Well, it's one of the earliest hello's I've ever written to you. It rained nearly all day yesterday and looks like we might get more rain today, but it's warm. I wish it would get cooler and dryer. We could sit on the porch in the early part of evening this week. Moody got us a bushel of pears so that means more preserves. I put up a peck of peaches in jam yesterday and a basket of grapes so we now have some jelly on hand. Would you like some? Will say tooda loo & love.

Hermina

Belgium, **October 6** [*censor's stamp was Nov 9*]

Dear Mom & all,

Here's a short letter to let you know that I'm OK but have been suffering from a slight case of low morale - ha, ha - yeah, that is it! I read the demobilization program. I'll look more like a Civil War vet by the time I get out of the Army. The sun stuck its nose out today for a change and it was good to see it.

These Belgians make some pretty good beer. Tell Pop I'd put it up on the side of Oertel's any day. Belgium is the most modern place I have seen since I have left the States. It's a beautiful country. Very nice homes and stores also. It is not damaged very much due to the fact the Germans had to move out so fast.

I hope you're all feeling OK, especially you Katie. I can't say I ever remember of receiving a picture unless it's still on its way. Well, I'd better close for now and go get some chow. Oh, yeah, you might send me a couple pairs of extra heavy wool socks if you can get your hands on them.

I'll be seeing you.

Norb

Louisville, Kentucky, **October 9**, Monday

Dear Norb,

Well, the day is cool and cloudy. The Dumbarton Oaks meeting is made public today. I heard some of it over the air, but so far I didn't read it. Do you think I'll be able to understand it? It's good to think that a meeting like that took place. Here's hoping that in 25 years we won't be at it again [*but in 1950, just six years later we began to get involved in the Vietnam War, and the rest is history, so to speak.*]. Churchill is meeting Stalin in Russia. St. Louis Cardinals were the winner in the World Series which ended today. Louisville Colonels are playing in the little World Series.

I was to see your friend Abe today. I had to give him the history of Marge's shoes. He always lets you know how well he understands shoes. Wendell Willkie surely is getting his share of "publicity." You know it seems strange that a person has to die to get bouquets. It seems you could get the buds anyhow.

The first frost of the season is predicted for tonite in the wide open spaces. It's 45° at this time. Mrs. Russell gave us a mess of surprise lettuce.

It was really swell. The lettuce dropped the seeds from spring. He put in late turnips so naturally he had to turn over the ground. Now they have beautiful lettuce and turnips right together. I sure enjoyed it. Smack, smack.

The war news seems very good for us in Europe. JoAnn is really getting cute, she's plump like Katsy was. Marge and Pop are chewing the fat and downing Oertel's. Mom is retired and I'm going to be in a short while. Good nite.
Porky

Continued, Tuesday Noon

The thermometer registered 33°. It was a nippy morn. JoAnn is going to look at the Birdie for the first time. Ann's taking her to Beckman's. Margie and Elizabeth are up here and Margie is putting the questions to me. Louisville Colonels won the World Series. Well, it seems Margie is hungry. So am I so I guess I'll put on the bacon.
Love and write whenever you can,
Porky

Norb's mom was seriously ill but no one wanted to worry Norb about it since he had enough worries fighting the war. But in the following letter his sister Elizabeth told him the seriousness of her illness. By all indications, Norb did not get the letters or information of his mom's condition until January 1945, a few days before she died. He was upset that the family did not contact the Red Cross rather than sending him personal letters that were often lost or held up never to be seen for months - if at all.

834 Mulberry Street, Louisville, Kentucky, **October 10**

Dear Norb,

Well, how is everything? I hope OK. I was up at Mamma's today and she sure don't look good. I don't know if Hermina tells you or not. I know Mamma don't want to worry you, but she is sick. She is in bed most all of the time and is real weak. Please don't tell or ask anything in your letter. I ~~feel~~ thought you would want to know.

You wrote me in your letter that you would want to stay with your outfit. Do you think you could get out of the Army about your heart disability? If you could, I believe I would. Now, I don't understand anything at all, but going by what you said. But truthfully, I don't think Mamma will be able to fight many more of these spells. It makes her weaker and weaker. Don't worry about her too much. She is getting everything she wants and needs. Write me and let me know. Don't ever mention I told you this because they wouldn't want you to know.

Well, we are actually getting our garage finished at last. It looks real nice. We are all well at home. It was a frost last night and Nan cut all her flowers and Katsy is taking them back to sister and she can't wait till morning so Sister will think a lot of her. I don't know much news of anything. Papa and Marge just left. They went to see Fr. Rueff. I guess you know he died. He really must of had a lot of friends even if he was like <u>Silent Henry</u>.

I'm going up home tomorrow to peel pears. Papa has to have pear preserves. Moody got some for him and it has to be made tomorrow. It's going on 11 o'clock and I will have to close (Moody saw Clarence Johnson, looks real good and windy as ever) for tonight, so write when you can and don't mention I told you anything.

With Love,

Lip [*Norb's sister Elizabeth*]

Louisville, Kentucky, **October 11**, Wednesday

Dear Norb,

Well, it's a gloomy cool day, a little 'winterish.' The leaves are beginning to fall. Fr. Rueff was buried this morning. It was his request that the church not be decorated in black. A floral design hung at the rectory. The children had school just the same, but there was no school today as the children went to church for the services. That was his request. It sounds just like him, plain and ordinary.

Lip and Margie are up again. Lip has our basement "rented" every Tuesday now until spring. The old sister really has to drape the lines with all sizes [*Lip used the large basement at 1344 Texas Street to wash and hang her laundry in the winter when she couldn't hang clothes on the outside line at her home*]. Margie informed me she likes our high-chair better than hers because hers has a "porch" [*tray*] in front. I thought that was so cute. Katsy and her class just passed. She was thrilled. Lip slipped her a little more money. She is going to a party at St. Theresa. The Sisters were taking them there. They looked so cute but the boys had the biggest grins and the most out of line. We are preserving a bushel of pears. Lip gave a hand at peeling them. We wasn't sorry. It smells good too.

According to the latest news the city of Aachen is under bombardment. It started at noon today.

Friday is R [*Rat*] Day here in Louisville. So far, the Air-Raid Warden wasn't here to pass out poisoned kisses. I said to Lip we haven't got our kisses yet. Margie said I can make kisses so she made gobs of X for you and I can't find them. Betsy was calling off your address. She said APO (window #) 308. Lip laughed so hard. She said, "Well Mother, that's the way we make windows [#] when we draw doll houses." We are hoping for a letter from you. The last we received was written September 18th. Well, I was out of news to begin with. Hope you are OK.

Love,

Hermina

Louisville, Kentucky, **October 12**, Sunday

Dear Norb:

Well, Moody left to go hunting at 5 o'clock and ain't home yet. Maybe he is dragging a deer or elephant home. It is almost 7 o'clock. I hope he never got shot in the ***.

I went to the Shelby show with Margie, Katsy and Betsy. I never saw and heard so much noise in all my life. It was so hot and stinky I had to leave, otherwise I think they would had to get the reviving squad for me. The picture was good. It was "Lassie Come Home." The kids hollered and screamed. They sure got a kick out of it.

We lost our dog. It was poisoned and had to send it away. Every time I get one house broke it gets sick and dies. I don't want any more of them.

Katsy is writing a composition about our home and has to tell what we have in it and Betsy don't like some of our furniture and she said we'll just lie a little to make it sound better. I don't blame her at all.

Milton is taking up biology and he had to cut grasshoppers in two and he discovered he cut up a female grasshopper. He liked it a whole lot. The rest of the kids are all OK, all going to school, and the fightingest bunch you ever saw. Even Margie can start them.

Well, Moody just came in - the champion hunter - two rabbits all day long. The weather is warm and we need a good heavy frost at least this is what he said. I guess it's a good excuse. Saw where you are in Belgium. I wanted to answer you. I feel it is better to know if anything would happen it wouldn't come like a shock. She [*Mom*] talks and knows everyone so she is stronger than you think she is. Her rosary goes all day long. Sometimes she can't get her prayers together. Don't worry. Everything turns out for the best. I hope you are OK like we are. I'll have to close now and go up home so I'll say goodnite and goodbye.

With Love,

Lip and all

Louisville, Kentucky, **October 13**, Friday

Dearest Norb,

Well, it's gloomy, drizzly weather. We got eleven quarts of pear preserves and would you like some? If so, say so. Who could ask for more? Yesterday Mrs. Mary Tobe Moorkamp and her cousin Mrs. Griffin called in the afternoon. They divided their time between us and Mary. So Alma came for supper last night. We knew she was coming and about 5:45 pm and in comes John etc. So we really had eight guests for supper. And after supper Joe, Ann and JoAnn came. Joe didn't stay long as he was going to a stag at Jim Doerr's. So I say, who could ask for more? I sure kidded Alma. She brought us two pictures of herself to keep until you come back. I told her we couldn't really thank her enough for bringing them on the night before Rat Day in Louisville. We all got a kick out of that. Ann got JoAnn's proofs. They are very good of her, I think.

According to the noon newscast, the Allies are nearly in the center of Aachen. Are you still on Maneuvers? The last letter we received was written Sept. 18th.

Mom is taking an afternoon snooze. Eleanor is eagerly awaiting the arrival of her new stove (did I surprise you?). On October 15th the priority is lifted. I do think she will enjoy it. The kids were all very cute and I'm enclosing a lock of Norbert's hair that was cut last night at 11:30 pm especially for you. Mrs. Russell got her new fur-coat yesterday. It's very pretty. It's black seal.

We all came to the conclusion that Alma is getting prettier. She sure looks good and had on a cute black dress with a floral waist. Alma is 'filled out' better. You once said she wasn't filled out very much. You can't say that now. [*Alma was 19*]. That's about all I know at the present time. Write when you can.

Love,

Hermina

Louisville, Kentucky, **October 14**, Saturday, 5:30

Dear Norb:

We just received your letter of October 4th. Was really very glad to hear. You certainly have traveled some. Did you see action in all those places? We are very curious to know that. I feel like you have with Paris and Versailles excepted. Your request? Well, you might have looked for a needle in a haystack - all the places around home are without cigarettes. Joe hasn't had a cigarette since last Tuesday. He's been coming over with his pipe but I didn't realize the shortage was so acute until I started to inquire. I went to Bobby Lee's and he gave me a carton of Raleigh's. They were given to him. He doesn't smoke. I thought that was mighty nice, mighty nice. Will you say thank you in your next letter or when you receive them so I can show it to him? Mrs. Lee is doing fine.

The St. X band [*Norb worked his way through St X by playing clarinet in the band*] has new green suits. They are really snappy looking. They are solid green with gold braid over the shoulder and a gold stripe down the trousers. The hat is a white top and black peak and a white belt finishes the suit. They are really classy looking.

It's really a lovely day but was very cold this morning. But Pop is sitting on the front porch. It's heavenly (the weather and Pop too, ha ha). Pop said a main from the Louisville Railway Co. was measuring up. They wanted to put buses on Texas so there "might" be a change in transportation when you get home but it will probably be some time after V in E Day.

I heard when it was cold over there that it's really cold or stays that way. It's not like Kentucky weather. Joe was out with Clarence Johnson last night. Now when he feels his oats JoAnn gets the attention. My, such baby-talk - you've never heard it before. Ann had the baby's picture taken and got the proofs tonite. Joe wants one of every one of the four

proofs. Will sign off until tomorrow. Goodnite dear brother. Love (and personally, I think you're not in France anymore as you failed to put France on your letter.)
[*Hermina*]

Continued Sunday, **October 15**

Well, it's another beautiful day. We sure had open house. Mrs. Hoffman from Gray Street, Catherine & Marie were here to see us. We surely was shocked. You don't remember them. They were at the cemetery and thought they would stop by. They didn't know we lived in this place so they went on Mulberry Street [*their old house next door at 1137, one level rented to Joe and Ann*]. They asked to see Mrs. Rawert. Ann said, "'I am Mrs. Rawert," and they looked dumbfounded. Ann never knew no Hoffman. So Joe came in - Mrs. Hoffman told us as soon as she seen Joe she knew she was in the right place because Joe looked just like Mom. So Joe walked with them [*next door*] They don't remember you, only as a baby, but according to the family picture they said you look like your Papa. I said you ain't lying. Well, if I continue I'll pay double postage on this letter.

Joe just came in with a pack of Chesterfields [*cigarettes*] He said Jim went after them and "rationed" them out, one pack to a customer. He said that way all could get some. Goodnite and shove your pen around.

Continued, Monday, **October 16**

I'm still at it. It's another lovely day. I must congratulate you on the arrival of a future sister-in-law. Alma called this morning and told us the good news. Hasn't Mrs. Pierce got an edge on Mom now?

Mrs. Hertel just got a supply of cigarettes. He left [*sic*] me have 5 packs for you, but as the Xmas season for sending gifts ends today, I'll need a request. I got off the carton of Raleigh's from Bob Lee yesterday, so your request is being sent to Brown & Williamson. They will send out four cartons, so we'll need another request. Please do not fail to send it as we have some cough drops for you too. We are all OK. Is there a fog in the holler? There hasn't been any here for a long time ha, ha.

I thought you would get a kick out of the way Norb Wafzig described the fall of Brest. He said Mom you know Mrs. Crash on Goss Ave. Well, they fell. Nuff said. Don't fail to put your pen on maneuvers. Hope you are OK. Do you need anything? How about shoes, socks, stepins [*sic*]. The news is very good today.
Love,
H.R.

Louisville, Kentucky, **October 17**, Tuesday, Johnny's Birthday
Dear Norb,

Well, it's another lovely day in Kentucky. I can't think up much to write that's news. I could have done Lip a dirty trick. Moody brought up the laundry and set it on the outside basement steps [*facing the alley way*]. A rag-man came thru and called "Missus do you want to sell them rags?" Lip said if I would have gotten the price she wouldn't have cared. Well, I don't have any more news, perhaps by tonite I can pick some up.

Wednesday, October 18, 3 pm

It's a grand day. It's so warm a coat isn't necessary. Well, I guess I'll call this a letter. It's no news - only it's a letter. We're OK. Hope you are too.
Love and hope you're OK.
Hermina

Louisville, Kentucky, October 20, Friday, 8:30 pm

Dear Norb,

It was another beautiful day but I thought we were going to have some rain but didn't. But tonite it's getting a lot cooler. The past two mornings has [*sic*] been very foggy so Pop is really looking for rain. The news was exceptionally good today. Aachen fell and the Philippines were invaded and three beach heads established. That was a lot of good news in one day.

Marge and Pop are just downing some Oertel's. He got a lot for his money so he's happy. Mom said I should tell you she would be writing you in a few days. Mom was feeling bad the past two weeks and has been in bed the past week. She coughed so terrible. Dr. Stites prescribed some cough medicine. Seem to help until Sunday nite when it loosened up and Mom really brought up the mucous. She ran a temperature Friday, Saturday and Sunday but it was checked after she coughed up the mucous. I asked Dr. Stites to come Monday. He did. He said since Mom had no fever he didn't want her to take all that medicine so he gave her a prescription to give her some appetite. You know when Mom goes to bed she hardly ever eats anything. Her cough is a lot better. She ate a little more than usual today and sat up some this evening so I really do think Mom is improving especially since yesterday. Dr. Stites said it was all in the bronchial tubes and that coughing spell Sunday really helped her out. He told her she didn't realize what she went thru this past year and he thought she did remarkably well at her age [*almost 71*]. We think so, too, but Mom thinks she ought to do the things she did before she was operated on. She sure looks 100% better than she did last week at this time.

I bet you were (or will be shocked at the clipping I'm inclosing). Joey was going home from work Wednesday nite and was crossing at Shelby and Broadway. She said she seen the wheels of a truck coming. It knocked her down. Marge stopped in to see her. Her middle finger was stiff and her left arm was swollen but today the swelling is almost gone. They taken her to the General Hospital but she was home by 7 o'clock. I think she was lucky at that, but it did sure scare her. But she never lost consciousness. Dewey and Lee went to the hospital immediately. Now for the funny part. Joey had a bag of groceries which scattered out and a bundle of kindling which was strewed all over. She said that those men at Shelby & Broadway tried to pick it up. We all had a good laugh at that.

Milt came up today with a chance book from St. X. It's on a $250 war bond. A turkey is given away every hour. Mrs. Russell is going to Horse Cave over the week-end. It will be the first time to see Lavada's baby. It's as old as Joe's and "Great Aunt Mary" is anxious. Jr Received our Christmas gift already. Well, that's about all I know tonite. Only Mrs. Orrill got a letter from Walter, the first in a month, so she feels better and is happy.

Love,

Hermina

The following letter was written on October 22, 1944 but the last postmark on it was February 1, 1945. It had many different postmarks on it as it was sent from place to place to find Norb's latest location. So Norb didn't see it until he was home and out of the Army.

Louisville, Kentucky, **October 22**, Sunday, 5:30 pm

Dear Norb,

Well, it's a beautiful day. I have never seen such a beautiful fall. It's lovely. I am happy to say Mom is feeling some better. She's laying on the divan in the living-room. She just finished eating some ice-cream. We are listening to the Great Gildersleeve [*radio comedy*]. We sure get a kick out of them.

Joey was here today and she looks better than I expected to see her. Her arm is black and blue but the swelling is practically gone. Her finger is better too. Mrs. Russell went to Horse Cave yesterday and was coming home today. She just called form Horse Cave saying she couldn't get on the bus and the 8:30 pm bus is always crowded. Marge, Lip and Margie are at church. Jimmy is serving.

Marge said I should save a little space for her. She wants to scribble a little. So I'll sign off with hoping you are well. The sick and the "injured" are doing fine. Mom is anxious for pumpernickel as the pumpernickel baker is still in the Navy. I was wondering if you wasn't close enough to the land of sauerkraut and pumpernickel to send home a loaf of it as a souvenir. Ha, ha. Well, I'll say too-da-loo til tomorrow. We haven't heard form you last week, the last letter we received was October 4th.

Love,

Porky

Continued, Monday, **October 23**

Well, I saved space but Marge didn't get to write. We had company last night. "Emmy," was here, Joe and Ann and JoAnn and it was like a Stengel meeting - all talking at once. Mom is feeling better. She ate a little more today than usually. We are OK. It's so pretty out.

I really don't have any more news. Mom said she would write as soon as she's able to push a pen around. Mom said you should pray for her so she get her strength back in a big hurry.
Love and Cheerio,
Hermina

In the following letter, Norb says he is in a hotel for a "rest" and that it is the first time he has slept on a real mattress since he left the US (nine months ago). He had been sent there for recuperation as was often the case during the war when troops had seen war face to face and were having trouble dealing with it in bouts of PTSD, or as it was called in those days, shell shock" or "nervous disorder in combat." Whenever possible troops were sent away from the battle front to recuperate before they sent them back out again to fight again. He never talked about it after the war and he also didn't mention it much during the war. But his niece Shirley Muth who was close to Norb said when he came back he was a changed man. When she asked her mom why he was not the same as he used to be - not so funny or joking- she told her the war did it to him. A few days later on October 27 or 28 Norb was flown to the American Red Cross Hospital in England.

Somewhere in Belgium, **October 23**

[Five-page typed letter, all in capital letters]

Dear Mom & all:

Well, the weather is beginning [*sic*] to get a little cool but it's not cold as yet. It rains nearly every day, at least it has for the last week and a half.

I'm pretty cozy at present but I don't know how long it's going to last. I am living in a hotel and sleeping on a mattress between clean white sheets. Believe it or not, it's the first time I've slept on a mattress since I left the United States. It was so soft at first I couldn't get used to it but I'm doing alright now, only it's hard as hell to roll out at 6:30 am. I don't know how long this rest will last but it can't last too long to suit me.

I wish I had learned to speak more German because it would come in handy right now. Although most of the people in Belgium speak French, you find the greater majority in Luxembourg speak German, or the next thing to German anyway. I can catch just a few words of it. I've been listening to a German propaganda program every now and then, and it's really funny. The girl on this program whom we call Axis Sally tries to get you homesick as hell, but the way she goes about it it's more like listening to Fred Allen or someone. You should hear some of the propaganda they put out. Just the day before yesterday they had the whole American fleet sunk.

I've been reading where cigarettes are getting hard to buy back in the United States. Well, they're getting pretty hard to buy here also. We got one pack today for a week's ration. If it wouldn't have been for Park and Tilford sending that carton every month I'd be out by now but, as it is, I still have a few packs left. I had a bunch of German cigarettes but they're not fit to smoke. They must be all Turkish tobacco. I gave them to some Frenchman.

Tell Joe and Ann I received the picture and thought it was very good of JoAnn. As I told you before the beer over here is very good but the alcohol content is very low. It must be about 1 percent but it tastes like beer anyway. It's better than the English, mild and bitter.

Well, I don't know when the war is going to end. Your guess is as good as mine but I don't think it will be much longer now if we have a mild fall and winter. I think Adolph is getting his painting and papering tools cleaned up so he can use them again.

Enclosed you will find a money order for fifty bucks. Do with it as you see fit. Tell Lip I received a letter from her today and one from Marge yesterday. Hermina is considered a regular so I fail to acknowledge them. Tell Mary I said hello. Of all the things to dream, I drempt [*sic*] she was ice skating the other night. Luckily she didn't break the ice.

I see where Gen. Mc'A has gone back to work again. That was <u>damn</u> good news. I hope they clean both messes up at the same time, because frankly, I've done all the traveling I care to do for the next 50 years, and then some.

There are some beautiful things in Europe (women included) but I prefer the Bluegrass. There is some fellow we ran into the other day, about ten miles from here, who was from Chicago. He stayed over here after the last war was over. He runs a little café. The outfit he fought with in the last war is over here again in this one, not far from here. I think he ran into them. I can't imagine what enticed him to stay over here for twenty five years. He showed us his discharge papers, $1,600 in bonds, and he also received his soldier's bonus.

Well, I don't think it will be long before I turn in and make all the use of this bed I can while I have the chance, because that ground is going to get awful hard again, so I'll say goodnight for now, hoping all are well and taking their carter's little liver pills regularly. I remain

As Always,

Norb

The following letter - like most of the ones remaining in the collection after this date - was received after Norb was already back in the US. The last date, of many dates stamped on the envelope, was February 1, 1945.

Louisville, Kentucky, **October 24**

Hi Norb,

Tomorrow I have to go to a doctor and be examined. You know on account of bringing suit or whatever, or if I have any disabilities. Well, here is hoping I get something out of this, for it really was a fright.

Mom ain't so well, Norb. Don't know if they will tell you or not, but I think you should know. She don't eat enough to keep a chippy alive. I bet she don't weigh but maybe 100. I am telling you this confidentially. She told me Sunday she hopes the Lord won't let her lay around and have to be waited on. But I told her I had to be waited on so often. I also told her I felt the same as she does, that I had rather been dead, only no one would believe me then. Maybe if she could just eat she would get better, so write to her as often as you can. I get the blues so bad when I go up there that I can't sleep that night and I'm sick the next day. I was up there Sunday for about 6 hours. I'm sending a clipping out of the Sunday paper. Don't that remind you of the time you and Lee went hunting? Well, I must get supper and you will be hearing from me again.

With love,

Joey, Lee, Dewey

Louisville, Kentucky, **October 25**
[*last postmarked on February 1, 1945*]

Dear Norb,

Well, it's another beautiful day. There has been quite a few fogs but as far as rain, it's clear and sunshiny and not too cool, but the weatherman said rain. Ann is here washing her chenille bedspread. I told Mom she ought to put up a sign at the back basement window - "Four days a week open to be rented" - as a laundry. JoAnn is really having a big time kicking and talking and laughing to her heart's content. She's so cute this morning. Mom said she feels somewhat stronger this morning. You can even tell it in her voice.

Mary said I should tell you hello. We haven't heard from you since October 4th that is when it was written. Joey is doing fine. Her arm is black and blue, Marge said, but it doesn't bother her. She was in at Hubbuch's yesterday to see Marge. They had a big kick out of one of Joey's neighbors who stopped her and told her she heard a kindling truck hit her. You know Joey had a sack of kindling with her.

Hoping to hear from you soon,

Hermina

Louisville, Kentucky, **October 26**

Dear Norb,

Well, it's another beautiful day. Mom is feeling stronger today she said and wants to sit up in a rocker. Joey is here and feeling OK. You'd never know there was anything wrong with her. Margie and Lip were up last night and Margie really has been saying some very cute things. We were eating supper when they came in and Margie said to Marge, "Maah, are you going to eat all those potatoes?" Maah said yeh she thought so Margie said, "Well Maah if you eat all those potatoes, you'll be as fat as Meenie and the soldier boys won't like you." She sure found out young, didn't she?

Miss Emma is here cleaning out her wardrobe. I don't know if she is going to sun anything or not, ha ha. We haven't heard from you last week or this.

Hermina

Louisville, Kentucky, **October 29**

Dear Brother,

We are wondering where you are and how you are. Mom's a bit better tonight. She listened to the news at 8 o'clock. Sure sounds good. We think we will get a letter from you tomorrow. You know it's the best tonic for mother (our dear mother).

Emma was here last week and she talked about her dear mother and Freddie was gone so many years. I was wishing for a record to send you of her talk. Did you get any of our boxes as yet? I sent you a carton of cigarettes from Brown & Williamson. It's the only ones who could get it. Tony went down and got some for me. They sent directly from the factory. Four cartons are all I could get, but can get more if you write again. I must take your request to the factory before I can get the cigarettes. Joe, Johnny, Ann and the baby are gone to Lebanon to see Althea and Carl. Carl is doing fine. Alma called this morning and said Larney wrote her and at the top of his letter he said "Somewhere" so I guess he don't know where he is and he said to tell Mom he would take care of her baby [*Norb*].

Norb, I am wondering about the election. Who is going to make it? Now Frank Nunn sings "The World is Singing," "The World is Waiting for the Sunshine." Do you get to hear the radio? Pop just came in from Huelsman's and he said Joe ain't got a bottle of beer in the house. But Pop took the glass container. Now Frank sings "My Rosary." Mom sure prays many a rosary for her baby.

Well, Lip was up .today. And Margie. I believe she looks more like you every day and she lisps a little, without any ('92). Say, what do you drink now? I often wonder. We are still busy at work. I guess I'll go to Knox this week. I never got a vacation this year. Pop is drinking the brew all by his self so I guess I'll help him a little bit. I guess you know that Joey got slapped by a truck. A neighbor said a kindling truck hit her, and did we laugh. She had a shopping bag of wood to take home. She is doing OK. She was at home to see Mom one day this week. I'll say god bless you Norb and pray for us. Good luck. Is there anything I can do for you?

Marge

Louisville, Kentucky, **October 31**, "Halloween," 8:00 am

Dearest Norb,

Well, I want to begin with how beautiful the weather is, but how thankful we all were to hear from you. Your letter was written on October 6. So you are in Belgium? Well, I feel like you're in a good country but there's a lot of fighting going on in Antwerp isn't it?

Gabriel Heatter [*an American radio commentator whose World War II-era sign-on was "There's good news tonight"*] is now on and announced that Admiral Nimitz announced that 2,594 Jap airplanes were sunk in the past two months. Our losses were around 300 airplanes.

Mr. Zipperle called me today. Zip is in Belgium. So is Larney Johnson. She told me you spied Zip when you two met here several months ago in France. We were wondering who spied who first. I'd rather we thought you did. So you have beer to come up to, if not surpass, Oertel's. Well, we are really glad to hear that. Do you know the name of the beer? Or is that a $64,000 question?

Jr is on his way too. His wife went to visit him a few days before they pulled out. You know her people come from Belgium? According to tonite's headlines Churchill thinks the war might last til spring 1945, but I still stick with Eisenhower. He said it could end in 1944 and I think he would know as well as anybody.

So you still think that French women are the most beautiful? What about these beautiful Kentucky belles? I don't think they're so few or far between either. Well, of all the places you've been! And when you come home and tell your story, we'll all copy your fashion and sit and listen with our 'big mouths' open.

Alma called. She got your letter. So did Lip and Joe. Alma got a letter from Larny last Friday. He told her to tell Mom that he could take care of her baby. That's sweet, isn't it?

Lip is up here. She said the Sky Pilot came through and you were having your books checked [*receiving the Sacraments*]. Mom was glad to hear that and believe me, she never forgets you. Your letter was a big morale booster here too. I told mom I almost felt like writing "Dear Diary" as we never get an answer. But it seems so many people were waiting for a letter about as long as we were - so we heard today - the Johnsons' and Zipperles' kid too.

This is a swell one on Mary. Pop got up at 3:10 am this morning - "Oertel's," ha ha. He turned on the hall light. I awoke from that. And he and Mom were talking. Mary could see the light. She gets up thinking it was 5:00 am. So she had to go in the basement. I heard the patter of her feet, so I said to Mom I bet Mary's getting ready for church. In a few minutes down comes Mary fully dressed at 3:20 am for 5:30 mass. I sure razzed her today about it. She said she thought she would hear that a plenty. So Mom, Pop, Mary and I had a good belly laugh at 3:30 am. She said if we hadn't stopped her she sure would have been on her way because she really thought Pop was getting ready for work.

Now about the socks. We will send you several pair readymade. I called at least six places and Stewarts was the only place who has them so we will send them on. I also ordered some yarn to have two pairs knitted. Ann's mother can knit so Ann will ask her if she can do it right away. Ann said maybe she couldn't knit good enough. I said I didn't know good knitting and neither could you find a mistake. So when you receive this letter you should also send another request as we had to use the first one you know.

It was warm today. We had windows and doors wide open this afternoon. I bet that sounds funny to you. Betsy just came in from a party. It was 6 to 9. She had to bring a "boyfriend" so she asked a neighbor boy. Moody got them. Betsy won two little bracelets.
Love from all,
Hermina

As noted in the following letter to Norb from his cousin, Norb was attached to the US 8th Army at this time.

Somewhere in Germany, **October 31**

Hello Norb,

How is everything with you? We were in Belgium a few days ago. Norb, we were billeted about 4 blocks away from C Company of your battalion. I was talking to one of the fellows. He said you were about 20 miles from there. I got in that afternoon and wrote a letter to you but the next morning I had to stop the letter. We pulled out that day.

Norb, I wouldn't be surprised though, that within a week or two I'll be seeing your outfit again. We're just helping out up here. By rights we're supposed to be with the 8th, the same as you are.

Norb, did you see Nancy, France? [*Nancy was freed from Nazi Germany by the US Third Army in September 1944, during the Lorraine Campaign of WW II at the Battle of Nancy.*] That is a pretty large town. We had a parlor issued to us there. I spent a whole day there. I had a swell time. Plenty cognac, wine and beer.

Have you heard from home lately? I haven't for two weeks. I guess they're moving around has a lot to do with it, don't you think? How are all the folks at home? Well, Norb, if you don't hear from me within a week, please drop me a few lines, will you? So long. I hope I'll run into you soon. Good luck. I don't like Germany one bit.

A friend,

Bernie

[PFC Bernard Hollkamp, 35707865, Co. A, 86th Cmd. Bat.MT1, APO 403 USA]

Louisville, Kentucky, **November 4**, Saturday 9:30 am

Dear Norb,

Well, it's a gloomy day in Louisville. The weather has been beautiful up to this time. It rained for a while during the night but we really need rain and it looks like we are going to get it. We haven't heard from you since October 6th [*a month*] so we are really anxious to hear from you. Pop is glad you're getting the good beer in Belgium. Tomorrow is Cemetery Day at St. Michaels's cemetery so we are expecting Johnny etc. in, as he said Thursday night he was going to stop in. So we might have a houseful before the day is over.

Mom's appetite is oodles better and you know that's a swell sign. She sat up for several days now, a little while in the afternoon, so we are all happy to say Katie is feeling better. I'm going to close hoping you are OK. I'll write more tomorrow "I hope." I have to make the bread for my Pappy.

Love,

H.R.

Louisville, Kentucky, **November 4**, 9 pm

Dear Norb,

Well, it turned out to be another beautiful day in Kaintuck. It rained for a while early this morning but it's really getting cooler now. Mrs. Clephas was here to see us today. Charlie is still in India (this pen could do better) [*a reference to the smudges on the stationery caused from a fountain pen she was using.*]

Katsy's birthday is either today or tomorrow. She'll be 8 years old. I was listening to our next president tonight F.D.R. You know Tuesday is Election Day.

Do you get as much beer as you like? Can you buy that beer always? Or is it like it is here, weaker in the camps? Nosey for a non-beer drinker, huh?

Joey was here today. She never received a letter from you but Joe, Johnny and Elizabeth did. We are anxious for another letter as it will be a month since you last wrote October 6th. We received that letter last Tuesday.

I seen in today's paper where the Yanks were driven back about six blocks in Aachen but I still feel like we might be thru with the man in Europe this year. Well, I am going to say goodnite. Pop just came in with a can of beer, so goodnite.
H.R.

Louisville, Kentucky, **November 5**, Sunday, 5:30 pm

[*Dear Norb,*]

Well, it was a good crowd at the cemetery today: Marge and Lip and Johnny were on the late side getting there but they got there just the same. Katsy's birthday was yesterday. She made up a party at 5 pm. All the guests were asked and the party was 7:00-9:00 pm. Seven little girls attended. They all had a really good time. Pop's in his glory. He's playing pinochle with Joe and John. I was blaming this funny scribbling on the pen. Well, my hands were chapped and I put some Vaseline on them and some of it got on the paper so the ink couldn't penetrate.

Continued, Monday noon, **November 6**

This is a wonderful pen. Writes like a brush. We haven't heard from you as yet but we are living in hopes. Tomorrow is the big day. We vote at 1007 Ash Street. It's a wonderful day. Our old house looks good. The second story is finished, the bright red roof and the white house with the sun shining on it looks good. Well, I'll close. I'm going to Schieman's, Johnson's and Hertel's. And then I'll have my bills paid and something to eat again. Ha, ha, ha.
Love,
Hermina

The next letter from Norb is written in an American Red Cross Hospital in England where he was taken after "nervous disorder" (according to his discharge paper) in Belgium. The mailing address was US Army Hospital, Plant 4131, APO #316-A, C/O P.M. New York, NY. In his letter to his family on November 7, he said he was in the hospital for a "nerve condition." All of his stomach problems he constantly took Tums for were probably related to his nerves. He tried to play it down to his family. Norb was always a kind and gentle man much affected by the war. My sister Dolores (Dee Dee) said she remembered that dad had gone to a psychiatric facility and that Mom wouldn't admit it.

From the time Norb was taken off the battlefield (sometime after October 6) until after he came home in January 1945, he did not receive all the correspondence that was sent to him. He had frequent transfers to different hospitals and the mail could not keep up with these address changes. He did not know the serious condition of his mother's health. The family did not go through the Red Cross to contact him. In a letter date December 3 he stated that he that he received 33 old letters all at once.

American Red Cross Hospital, England, **November 5**

Dear Mom and All,

Well, I suppose you're a little surprised to see England in the heading of this letter. It's a short story. I had a little trouble with my ticker so I decided now is the time to do something about it. I don't believe in putting off anything if you can get it fixed up. I wouldn't even bother telling you because it's nothing serious, but I understand the government sends you a notice so I thought I better write and explain before you do any unnecessary worrying.

You get a complete physical checkup, and I do mean complete. It's really a Mayo's Brothers on a small scale. I'm not sick or anything like that. In fact, I feel pretty damn good.

It's raining outside tonight but that's nothing new for England I never thought I would be walking around on the King's soil again, but I am.

I suppose it will be months before I receive any of those Xmas packages but don't leave that bother you because we get everything we need right here. The chow is good also. It's good to get off those K-Rations for a while.

I had my mug put on a film but the negative is still in Belgium but I wrote my buddy for it, so when I get it I'll send you a picture. I had a bunch of other stuff, a German helmet and leggings and canteen, bayonet, etc., but I decided to leave it behind because I couldn't lug it all with me. [And that was probably the fate of the family correspondence from January through September 1944 also]. Tell Mary hello. My address is US Army Hospital, Plant 4131, APO# 316-A, C/O P.M, NY, NY. Well, take it easy and I'll be doing the same. Hoping all are well. I remain,

As Always,

Norb

Alma's large family moved around a lot. It was a family joke that they moved so often to avoid paying for the rent. At this time Alma was living at 211 N. Clifton, Louisville and Norb sent the following letter to her there.

England, **November 5**

Dearest Alma,

Here's just a couple of lines to let you know I'm OK and thinking about you. Everything is going fine. It's raining outside tonight but that's nothing new for England. I really never thought I would see this place again.

I had a bunch of stuff I wanted to send but I left them all in Belgium. When you go to the hospital you take along just enough to wear and toilet articles [*the reason so many family letters are missing from the collection*]. I also had my picture taken there. I wrote to Frenchie last night and told him to send it to me, so as soon as I get it, I'll send it to you. I can't guarantee you good results. It won't be a picture, it will be the negative.

I have no idea how long I'll be here but I hope it's not very long because I never did go in for hospitals. How's everything in Louisville honey? About the same? I hope it ain't too long before I can find out for myself. I believe I've read enough books to fill the Shelby Library.

Well, darling take it easy, because that's what I'm doing and I guess I'll be doing it for a little while yet. Here's so long for now. Be good or else be careful and I'll be seeing you. I remain,
As always,
Loving you,
Norb

England, **November 6**

Dear Mom and all,

Well, since I've got a lot of time on my hands I should catch up a little on my correspondence. I'm a little behind (don't take that word "behind" the wrong way. It rained again today but not for a change. England is truly all wet. But I'm pretty cozy. Everything is going along smoothly. I'm feeling pretty good. In fact I could do some real damage to a keg of Oertel's. If there's anything wrong with you these people should find it. They put you through your paces alright. They check everything from your teeth to your toenails. Well, this ain't much of a letter but there's not much that's new so I'll say take it easy. I'll be seeing you.
As Always, only a little more cozy,
Norb

England, **November 7**

Dear Joey, Lee and Dewey]

Here's just a couple of lines to say hello. I been in a hospital for a week and a half now [*since around October 29*] and I'm getting a complete physical examination, and do I mean complete. We flew from Paris to England and I've been in England about a week. I think I'll be pulling out again for France before long. I'm dreaming of a white Christmas in Berlin.

I sure hope to God this war don't last much longer - it gets on your nerves after a while - I don't think it will. Well, this ain't much of a letter but it's all for now. So long and good luck,
As Always,
Norb

In the following letter Norb tells his family that all of his medical test results were good. He mentions that it was probably "a bad nerve condition," or shellshock, as they called it in WW II. It must have been a pretty bad 'nerve condition' to have kept him in hospitals until his discharge on April 20, 1945. The discharge paper states his disability is "nervous disorder in combat."

US Army Hospital Plant 4131, APO 316-A, England, **November 7**
Dear Mom and All,
    Well, here's just a couple lines to let you know that all is well including myself. The Doctor even told me so. I've been X-rayed, fluoroscoped, a metabolism test, an electrocardiograph, etc., and all results were good. That was damn good news to me also. I guess I just had a bad nerve condition. He wants to put me in limited service for a couple months. I guess that would be about 50 miles from the front but I had much rather join my old outfit since I've been with the fellows so long. I wouldn't mind a job in Paris though. That is the only way I'd want limited service.
    I guess today was a big day back in the States [*Election Day*]. It got a lot cooler here lately. I don't suppose it will be too long before I head back to France but it may be a couple of weeks yet. I don't mind the rest at all. Well, that's about all I know for now so I'll close, hoping all are well. Tell Mary hello.
As Always,
Norb

Louisville, Kentucky, **November 7**, Tuesday, 11:30 am
Dear Norb:
    I suppose the contents of this letter will surprise you. When Mrs. Russell heard you were in Belgium she wrote to Junior's in-laws in Detroit, so she received this letter I'm inclosing with the addresses. At one time, it was a long time that she didn't hear from her people. I don't know how long ago that was, but I do see in the letter where they have heard from her people through Polish and Canadian soldiers. If you can go visit them or hear something about them I know Mrs. Claeys will appreciate it very much but if you can't well she'll have to be satisfied hearing from the Polish and Canadian soldiers. If they are anything like Mrs. Claeys I know you'll be very welcome indeed. I have just placed my stamp under the rooster and I seem your name posted as one of the absentee voters, so I know you performed your duty as a citizen. Out of 19 absentee ballots thirteen have been received.
    Mom is sorry she couldn't get there [*to vote*] because she feels like everybody should that

can, but Dr. Stites told her not to get up for a week yet. He didn't want her to rush things. Mom is doing lots better.

Love,

H.R.

England, **November 8**

Dear Mom and all,

Well, England had its first snow of the season, but it never stuck. It snowed off and on for a couple of hours. Well, I still have no idea how long I'll be hanging around but after you get out of the hospital they send you to a rehabilitation center. That's where they're supposed to build you up from. I'll be glad to see my outfit again but most of all what I want to see is that Statue of Liberty. That will be the day I'm going to buy a zoot suit with red and green stripes the first thing. Well, there's not much more I can tell you for now except that I'm OK and hope you're the same. Tell Mary hello X.

I remain, as always,

Norb

England [*V-Mail*], **November 13**, Monday night

Dear Mom and All,

Well, I'm not accustomed to writing V-Mail but since I don't have a nickel in my pocket, and I won't until pay day, I thought V-Mail would suffice. Well, I'm OK and hope you are all the same. I still take a pill every now and then but that's about all. The rest of the time I just lay around. I'll get lazy as hell if this keeps up for very long. These hospitals are not good for your constitution. Well, there's nothing new I know for the present so take it easy and I'll be seeing you.

As Always,

Norb

In the following letter Hermina mentions that they haven't received any letters from Norb since October 6 so they are not aware that he has been hospitalized in England. The letter was originally postmarked on November 15. There were four subsequent postmarks to forward the letter to the US to Camp Edwards, Massachusetts and then to Camp Atterbury, Indiana. The last postmark was February 16, 1945, three months after it was first written and sent!

Louisville, Kentucky, **November 15**, Wednesday, 1:50 pm

Dearest Norb,

Well, we still haven't heard from you since October 6th. No news, good news. I called the Post Office. I thought perhaps they could tell me if the mail was held up from the European Theater. The woman told me she hasn't heard from her son since August and that one employee there received three letters yesterday, so it must be held up in some sections. Mrs. Orrill received 4 letters from Walter on Monday.

Mom had the best appetite yesterday that she has had in a month. Elizabeth Toby sent a fried Spring chicken and all that goes with it for Mom and it hit the spot. I should say, spots. I suppose as by this time Mom should have had a few empty places in her stomach but she ate a good breakfast and lunch yesterday then too. She's commencing to get a little cranky and you know that's a good sign.

I wrote to Thelma Saunders about getting a loaf of Pumpernickel for me last week and it came yesterday. It was Rye bread - she realized it wasn't what I wanted. I got a letter from her saying you call it Pumpernickel Rye - but her boss thought he knew what Mom wanted. I thought that was very sweet of her. When the parcel post man delivered it yesterday, the box was soaking wet. I got real tickled - he said, "It says on here handle with care." "Well," he said, "We soaked it" But it didn't go through. I said that it was supposed to be Pumpernickel. He said it isn't heavy enough for that. He said there were two families on his territory [route] that get Pumpernickel thru Cincinnati, so he is going to watch for the address for me and give it to me. There really are some nice people in the world.

Well, your box will be on its way with the socks Tony's wife made. They really are good looking. She sat up until 2:00 am yesterday morning to finish them. She says she knows you can make use of them. I am going to get you several thank you cards as Wilhelmina Heitkemper sent us a carton of cigarettes for you which I thought was very nice. I was at Hertel's this morning. Every place showed empty on his cigarette machine. Well, I am going to close. Hoping you are well and we will hear from you soon.
Love from all,
Hermina

England [*V-Mail*], **November 15**
Dear Mom and All,

Here's just a few lines to let you know that everything is going OK. It was a swell day today. The sun was out nearly all day. I suppose it will rain like hell tomorrow. I haven't received that picture I was telling you about but when I do I will forward the negative unless I can find a place to have them developed here. I'm still sweating out a pay day. I think we get a partial pay the 20th.
As Always,
Norb

Louisville, Kentucky [*V-Mail*], **November 15**
Dear Norb,

Just came up home and Mom is so much better you couldn't believe it. She ate better and was cutting up with Moody [*Muth*]. She sure will be getting up and about if she keeps on. Thought I'd let you know, you'd want to hear. It's getting so cold the rabbits sure will be

hopping. I wrote a letter a few days ago. Don't think I'm losing my mind writing this often but Mom surprised me. Heard Larny Johnson is in Luxembourg. Well, I guess I better close. Saw your knitted socks. They look warm. Hope you get them OK.
Love,
Lip [*Elizabeth*] and All

England, **November 16**

Dear Mom and All,

Well, a million days a million dollars. I hope I'm never rich. Everything is going along OK. I expect to be pulling out of here in the next couple of days. I'll just go next door for a couple weeks to a place they call rehabilitation. That's where you get exercise and drill to build you back up again. I haven't lost much weight. I weigh about 158 with pajamas on.

It was pretty cold last night and today. There was also a fog in the hollow. <u>Ha</u>. There's not much more I know for tonight so I'll sign off for now. So I'll be seeing you.
As Always,
Norb

The following letter was also being considered by Walter Cronkite for his "World War II Letters" book that was later sold to a different publisher who decided to omit Norb's letter.

England, **November 17**

Dear Mom and all,

The news just came over the radio that the new drive is well under way and that the Yanks were well inside Germany, with the Germans burning the towns as the Yanks advance. Well, that's good news anyway. Ma[*y*]be the people won't fall in line with Himmler the way they did with Hitler. Here's hoping they don't anyway.

It's raining outside tonight but it's very cozy in here and with the radio playing makes it all the better. You know a radio is a big morale booster. At least it is for me. You can pass a lot of time with a radio.

I go to the "board" Monday and leave them decide what to do with me. I'm afraid, but this is just a hunch, that they're going to have me carrying piss pots around a hospital or something to that effect. I know my "doc" wants to put me on limited service for a couple of months, but I'm no medic and I have no intention of being one. But we'll just have to wait and see. You know a soldier has some rights, but believe me, they're damn few. But I think if I press it hard enough I might be able to get back with my old outfit. I don't think I would like the Medical Corps. But as they say, that won't be for me to decide.

Well, with the rain tapping on the roof and the lights about ready to go out I think I'll hit the hay. It should be a good night for sleeping. I'll say so-long for now, hoping you are all well, because I feel as fit as a fiddle right now. I'll be seeing you. Tell Mary I said Hello.
As Always,
Norb

US Army Hospital, Plant 4131, England, **November 18**

Dear Mom and all,

Well, it's Saturday night and there's not much that's new around here. The mail still hasn't come through since 20 October. I think they're holding it up to get the packages to the front. Well, that's really more necessary. I hope you all are OK. I'm getting plenty to eat and too much sleep. Well, here's so long for now.

As always,

Norb

On November 18, the Rawert family finally learned that Norb was in the hospital. In the following letter from his sister Josephine (Joey) she encouraged Norb to date other girls and to go have fun. She said she only knew one girl who was faithful to her soldier while he was gone, and she didn't mention Norb's girlfriend Alma. When Alma later saw this letter she was upset with Joey that she would encourage Norb to go out with someone else while away and insinuating that Alma wasn't faithful to him. They never got along well after that.

Louisville, Kentucky. **November 18**

Hi Honey,

Rec'd your V-Mail yesterday. Glad to hear from you, so very glad. Maybe dear they will send you home. I hope the good Lord protects you and may the ones who examine you be guided by Him alone, for He knows what is best for all of us. If all of us would put more trust in Him we would and could save ourselves a lot of grief. I know with Mom being sick, sometimes I get the blues so bad - then again I feel, well, she has lived a long and good life and God knows what is best for us all. But she sure has looked a lot better yesterday and her appetite is so much better. So don't worry and think of yourself and have some enjoyment if you can. If you can go to any dances or have fun, I sure would do it. They nearly all do. The only girl I know of that wouldn't go out with anyone else is Doris Wright [*or Knight*]. The boy she loves is in the Navy and has been gone 10 months and she hasn't been out with anyone else. She said she can't enjoy no one else's company. She loves him and will wait till he comes back. I am positive of that and she is just 20 years old. She is one in a million. I just hope he does the same but I doubt it. Really she should be in young people's company, but that is love.

I guess Lee will go hunting tomorrow. He really is working. I haven't been back to work yet. It's a month today since I was hit by that truck. I am really scared now to cross a street. Well, honey, I'll be dreaming of a white Xmas for you over here. May my dreams come true! Well, I'll be seeing you soon I hope and until then have a good time and think of yourself first. If you don't find time to write to me dear, I'll understand but try and get some enjoyment. It's good for the nerves and rest is good for the heart. Bye bye and good luck.

Be seeing you,

Joey, Lee, Dewey

Louisville, Kentucky, **November 18**

[*Dear Norb,*]

We sure were glad to get your letter. We were so worried about it. I hope your heart shows improvement soon. I am feeling lots better, things don't go so quick when you get my age. [*Within two months his mother would be dead.*] Pray for us. We are praying for you always. I had a Mass said for you and the Poor Souls.

Love,

Mother

England, **November 19**, Sunday night

Dear Mom and All,

It's Sunday night and all is well. About all I do is eat and sleep. Really a life of leisure. I did go on a tour today to some old cathedral that was built in the 11th century. It's something to pass the time away anyway. I thought I'd be able to grab a few beers but the pubs closed just as we neared our destination.

There's nothing new that I know of. The weather is still the same. I can't think of nothing more to write about except I might be pulling out of here next week. I hope so anyway. Here's so long for now and I'll be seeing you.

As Always,

Norb

England [*V-Mail*], **November 20**

Dear Mom and All,

It's been a rainy day here in England and it's still raining tonight. I expect to be in England a little while yet. I would like you to do me a favor and wire me $50 as I have not been paid for October and I won't be paid for November and I'm broke now. I can get a pass every now and then but I can't get far if I'm broke. Send it by wire so it can get here faster. I'm feeling OK and hope you are all the same. As every day is about the same there's not much that's new so I'll say so long for now. Tell Mary hello.

As Always,

Norb

England [*V-Mail*], **November 21**

Dear Mom and All

Good evenin' folks. How' you all? I am OK myself. I went to a USO show they had here at the hospital. It was pretty good. Something to pass the time away anyway. I guess you're a little surprised at the mail you've been receiving. I'm actually getting the writer's cramp but since there's not much to do I usually write a couple a day to a few people. I guess you

receive them in bunches don't you? Well, I'm out of paper so I'll say so long from the King's Sail and a happy Thanksgiving.
As Always,
Norb

Louisville, Kentucky, **November 22,** Wednesday morning
My Dear Norbert,

How are you today? All of us folks back here sure were mighty glad yesterday when that letter came from you. Did your ears burn? They should have, 'cause it was Buzz Buzz, Buzz and it was all "Have you heard from Norb? And how is he?" You sure have friends in Old KY. Joey wasn't at work yesterday so Marge and I came by and told her they had a letter from you. Do you think maybe they will send you home? We all have our fingers crossed. Jimmy [*Junior Russell*] is in the Pacific. Was on his way to Pearl Harbor and goodness only knows where else the last I heard from him. The Old Man [*Russell*] celebrates just like he used to. Last night he got mad at the tomato catsup bottle and threw it down on the kitchen floor with all force and honey I just wish you could peep in and see my kitchen now! It is really decorated in red from floor to ceiling. Guess he thought he was decorating for Christmas. Well, anyhow I'm hurrying to get out of here and go to work before he gets up, for I'm sure leaving the job of cleaning it up for him. But I sure would love to hear you laugh if you could see it.

Always know my prayers and very best wishes are both with you Norb. I'll always pray for your safe and soon return to the ones you love and the ones who all love you.
Mrs. Mary Russell

England [*V-Mail*], **November 23**
Dear Mom and all,

Well, today is Thanksgiving Day. We had a very good dinner. Turkey, mashed potatoes, dressing, cranberry sauce, asparagus and the trimmings. I went to church this morning and got my books straight with the Sky Pilot, and seen a football game this afternoon. By the way, how did St. X finish up this year?

I might be here for a little while yet, don't know exactly how long it will be. Everything seems to be going OK everywhere. I hope it don't last much longer. Well, I'll say goodnight on a full stomach. I'll be seeing you.
As Always,
Norb

It is unknown when the following letter actually reached Norb. He probably received it after being discharged. It was initially postmarked November 23 from Louisville. It was then forwarded and stamped at the Army hospital in England then Nashville, TN on

February 7, 1945. It was also stamped at Camp Edwards, Massachusetts. He still had not learned of the seriousness of his mom's condition.

Louisville, Kentucky, **November 23**, Thanksgiving Day, 10:30 am

Hello Norby,

Reckon you'll be able to read my writing. I'm not much with a pen, can't even give myself 1/4 of a pat on the back with a pencil. Enclosed you will find a clipping about Bernard Spoelker. Guess Horse [*Hermina*] will beat me to it.

Norb, yesterday Mom looked awful bad to me. She looks so weak, all she does is pray the rosary but the Dr. wants her to get up 2 times a day if only for 5 minutes. I'll bet in another 4 months she won't be here at the rate she is going now. Now listen Norb, you take care of yourself. Mom is getting all the attention Hermina can give her. If you do get to come home just don't be too shocked what she looks like. Dewey was up there and he couldn't get over it. She got so skinny or thin but she still says what she thinks and they have to pray the rosary every night. I just don't think she ought to force or try to dominate about church or prayer. I know I pray with more devotion and like to go to church more now than when I was home. I guess because I do so with my own free will, but mom thinks she is doing what is right. Her daddy must have been a house of God on two legs - every night he used to read about the lives of saints while they sewed, so that's why she can't help it.

Lee can't get any 12-gauge shells. Listen Norb, maybe the Army will discharge you with a heart ailment. You got to have rest. There is nothing else that will take the place of it. No smoking or drinking and no worry or fright. I feel better now than I have for a long time, but the least little argument at home and my heart starts to race like mad. I bet the pneumonia you had when you were a baby left you with some sort of heart ailment. That hard breathing, I had it when I was a baby. I know rheumatic fever, what it done it to me. So, Norb, whatever God wills. I guess we have no choice so I'd just get all the rest I could and don't worry about mom too much.

I have a chicken to bake now. I have to go to court on Tuesday. I haven't been back to work yet. So I'll write and let you know the outcome, so for this time I'll say so long and hope you are enjoying a turkey dinner and until I see you, you be a good boy.
Bye bye with love,
Joey, Lee and Dewey

Louisville, Kentucky, **November 23**, Thursday, 5 pm

Dear Norb,

Well, it's getting a lot colder. It was a damp chilly day. It drizzled several times today. It really looks like snow. Manual and Male tied today, 7 to 7. The Stadium was packed, Don Hill said. You wonder how it could be, with so many boys in the service, but cars were lined to Goss Avenue.

Well, we really have a lot to be thankful for if we just stop and think. We had a nice, fat hen. It was good, with all the trimmin's to go with it, and mincemeat pie for dessert. Shirley went out to the game but Milt thought $1.50 was too much for him so he didn't go. Lip, etc. went to Rudy's right after the game. Jim wanted to get an early start so he takes the bus out. They really do go for those wide open spaces.

I really don't have much news. You know Agnes Threedouble's [*neighbor*] husband's stationed at a hospital in England. I'm going to inquire. Perhaps you might see somebody from Louisville yet. Are you bedfast? What kind of treatments are they giving you? We feel like you are given every attention. Marge is putting new seat covers on the kitchen chairs. They really look good. Joe is papering Madden's two upstairs bedrooms and hall. Is there anything we can send you? I suppose you had your share of turkey today. Hoping you are feeling lots better.

Love and best wishes from all,
Hermina

England, **November 24**

Dear Mom and All,

Well, there's not much that's new tonight. Everything is OK. It's still wet in England. According to the papers everything is going good on the weather front. That's damn good news. I don't see how the Germans can hold out much longer. I guess I will spend a merry Xmas in England. Just so they got some Scotch and bitter, and I'll make it a merry Xmas if it is or not.

I suppose you have received that letter where I asked you to send $50 by wire. I thought I had better put it in two letters so you would be sure to find out. I'm dead broke now and this hospital don't pay off in full. Well, I'm out of news for now since I haven't received any mail for a month now so I'll say so long for now. Tell Mary I said hello.
As Always,
Norb

Somewhere in Belgium, **November 24**, Friday night

Hello Noby,

I got your letter this noon and was sure glad to hear from you. I thought you had forgotten us - you hadn't written to us. So you're back in old England. How do you like it or don't you get a chance to go out? Everything is going just fine over here, Norb. We are still in the same place. I guess this is where we will fight the rest of the war. I let the boys read your letter and they were glad to hear that you were in England. I told Warner what you said and he swore like hell. He's still in love with her. He's going to Brussels to see her this weekend. We had a pretty good Thanksgiving dinner, plenty of turkey.

As for Jackson, he got drunk one night and told the colonel what he thought of him so now he is a Pvt. But he sure got a load off his mind. I now hold the T4 [Tech 4] that Jackson lost. Bacon says to hurry and get back here - there's still a war to win. About your shoes Nob, Red says he has them packed and has been waiting for your address so they can send them to you. What do you mean by King's Soil, Rawert, I'd like to know.

Write soon Cozy.

Frenchie

[*Sgt. Ray Hemingway, HQ Co. 59ᵗʰ Signal Btn., APO #308 NY, NY*]

England, **November 26**, Sunday night

[*written on American Red Cross stationery*]

Dear Mom and All,

Well, I thought I'd write a couple of lines letting you know that all is well except that I am eating too damn much and not getting enough exercise but of course that will come later, ha, ha. Soon enough anyway, I guess. It's raining again tonight. That's something that never fails. The weather man has an easy job over here. All he has to do is predict rain for the next day and he's bound to be right.

I see where Gen. Ike is investigating this cigarette business. Well, I hope he gets it straightened out because that's something the boys over here really need, and need bad, and you smoke twice the amount you already would because of the strain. We have a radio in the ward now. It's a morale booster but morale is fairly high now.

I went to the show this afternoon and seen a picture that I seen back in the States about four years ago but it was a good picture and I didn't mind seeing it the second time.

Well, I hope we have some pretty good weather next week. I might put in for a 48-hour pass. I think the "doc" will give me one. I want to catch up on some of my beer drinking although this English beer is rather hard to take. I also have to polish up on my English accent. Like hell! Well, I'll be saying so long for now hoping you are all well. I'll be seeing you.

As Always,

Norb

The following letter from Hermina was addressed to 'US Army Hospital, Plant 4131, APO 316-A, c/o Postmaster, New York, NY.' As so many others, it was routed all over and didn't reach Norb until probably March 1945. On February 7, 1945 it was stamped in Nashville Tennessee. The last postmark was stamped "February 11, 1945 HOSPITAL." It also was stamped at Camp Edwards, Massachusetts.

Louisville, Kentucky, **November 26**, Sunday, 3:00 pm

Dear Norb,

Well, it's a damp, not too cold day. We received eight letters from you this week. It was a little like Christmas with the Santa Claus a little under the weather. We surely were glad to get the letters, especially the one where you said you were doing OK. Even the doctor told you so. You said the X-rays and fluoroscope, metabolism test and electro-cardiogram tests all were very good. I suppose by this time you are at the Rehabilitation Center next door. I hope you'll soon be with the 59th Signal Battalion as you seem to want that the most. I feel that the wear and tear of the past year probably got your nerves sometimes and your ticker just needed a little rest.

You say you weigh 158 in pajamas. Well, I don't think that's so bad considering what you have been through this past year and they claim those K-Rations don't put any fat on you. I suppose that must be true. How big is your waistline? Ha, ha. About 30 inches I would say, possibly 29.

I just got a card from Bernard Hollkamp. A Christmas card. It was a French card. It's very pretty and looks like a handmade one. He said he isn't in France anymore. He didn't think it was so pretty but I did.

Lip and all the girls are here. Betsy crocheted a little piece all by herself. It's very nice. She's a smart kid. We sure did enjoy all those letters. I hope you are getting some of ours by this time. We would like to send you something but we have no request. Your letters have been reaching us in 7 to 8 days but the Air Mail have been a lot slower. To show you, yesterday we got your Air Mail written November 8 and two V-Letters written November 15th and 16th.

We had the 'paperhanger' here Friday so we have a nice, clean looking kitchen and the back bedroom is papered too. The bedroom is really beautiful. It's $1.25 a roll but it looks it. We sure would like it better than that salmon pink paper that was in there (I suppose you call it Salmon-pink). This is green and white striped with leaves running through. I told Joe he's getting swifter all the time. The kitchen is a marble design with red the most prominent color [*I still remember it*].

Well, it won't be long until Christmas will it? Perhaps by that time you will be back with your Company. We had rabbit for dinner. They were very good. At the present time Katsy and Betsy are entertaining with a song. Pop said Shirley really looks like Margie, don't she? I couldn't say no.

Mom said I should tell you she was a good girl and will write you a lot the next time. Marge said they are really busy. She got Ann to ask her mother to do some sewing at home [*for Hubbuch's*]. She is too. Well, I'm just about out of this so-called news so I'll sign off. Hoping you are doing OK and that you'll be with the 59th soon.
Best wishes, love from all,
Hermina

Louisville, Kentucky, **November 27**

Dear Norbert,

I am sorry to hear that you are sick but I hope that you will soon be well again and be out of the hospital. Well, Norbert I heard that you dreamed that I went ice skating. Well, I don't think that it will happen because I never was good on ice and I know I won't be anymore. Now ice and snow are my worst enemies. If they come I will have to fight them but I won't know how. I hope that you will soon be home to show me how to fight the snow and ice. Well, I hope that you are getting along alright and be well and happy and will soon be home to stay.

Yours truly and best regards and money XXXX

Mary [*Hollenkamp*]

The following letter from Norb's sister Marge was postmarked from Louisville on December 1 and after being rerouted to several locations, it was last stamped in Nashville, Tennessee on February 17, 1945, almost 3 months after it had been written. Norb later was furious when he learned that his mother was gravely ill and he was not contacted by the Red Cross. Had he known his mother was gravely ill, he would have tried to come home sooner, instead of arriving just days before her death.

Louisville, Kentucky, **November 28**, Wednesday, 12:25 pm

Dear Norb:

Well, we can't say we don't hear from you because we certainly have been hearing very regular. It seems your V-letters all reach us so much quicker than the Air-Mail letters. We received your Air-letters of November saying your case comes before the board. You say they might make a Pot-toter out of you. Well, for your sake I hope they don't. I hope they put you back in the old outfit but it's best for you to be limited service. Well, it might be hard to accept but you have to think of the future. You know this war isn't going to last forever and the way you take care of yourself now might mean the difference in the years to come, although I hope you'll spend Christmas with the old outfit.

So you are waiting for your mail, too. Well, I hope by this time you have received some letters. I think you can understand how the mail is held up better than we can and I know how we felt when it wasn't coming thru there for a few weeks. Mrs. Russell heard from Jr - he was still on ship. I was at Johnson's, Hertel's and Schieman's. Everything looks about the same.

You said in your letter from Belgium you received a letter from Marge and Lip. I was considered a 'regular' so you don't acknowledge mine. Well, I often wondered how I was considered. Well, I see we won't have any tree lights for Christmas trees. There hasn't been any bulbs made since 1941 and the supply is exhausted.

Mom said she thinks it's better for you to be in the hospital than in the battle at the present time. [*She was so right. Norb's unit participated in the Battle of the Bulge in the Ardennes, Belgium, Luxembourg from 16 December to 25 January. There were 89,000*

casualties, of which 19,00 were killed in Action]. We are anxious to know what the Board decided on. Glad to know you are feeling so good.
Love from All,
Hermina

England [*V-Mail*], **November 28**
Dear Mom and All:
    There's not much that's new tonight. It's raining again but that's not new. Irene Manning is going to be here in person tomorrow so I suppose I'll take a walk over to the show and see what goes on. No mail has come through yet so I can't answer any questions. I suppose it's just about due to come through though. Well, I hope you are all OK. I suppose I'll spend Xmas in England with the King. I remain,
As Always,
Norb

Louisville, Kentucky, **November 29**, Wednesday, 9:40 pm
Dear Norb,
    We received your two letters today, the one requesting fifty dollars by wire. Well, I suppose you will be surprised to receive it by Air-mail. I called Western Union. They said they could send it so Joe and I and Pop went down to Western Union tonite. They informed me then that APO 316-A couldn't be sent by wire so they told me to go to the Post Office but the money order window closes at 6:00 pm so we were out of luck both places. When I called Western Union they told me this money would have to be sent at our own risk, so we really intended to send just half by wire and half by money. The Red Cross told me not to send it by wire, but by money order as they haven't been having very satisfactory results lately. So here's hoping you get it.
    I suppose you'll visit London when you receive this. Didn't you say that you wanted to visit London? I suppose you'll see what damage the robots have done. Have you been sent to the Rehabilitation Center as yet? You said you didn't want to be a Pot-Toter. Well, I think one pot-toter in the family would be really handy. Ann thought so, too.
Goodnite form all,
Hermina

Continued, Thursday:
Dear Norb:
    I called the Red Cross again asking why we couldn't wire you some money. She said there were some restricted areas so I did the best I could and we're sorry you have to wait so long but you can see we done our best. I know you can borrow money from the Red Cross

for an emergency. Could you get some money from them now? I am enclosing the money order for $50.

Love and Best Wishers,

Hermina

Louisville, Kentucky, **November 30**

Dearest Brother,

Just how are you? Tell me all about yourself, as I am anxious to know. Well, I guess it's no need of me telling you, but you are constantly on my mind, or should I say our minds. Everybody comes home to read you letters and their faces light up to read them so you know how sorry we are that you are broke. Well, Hermina sent a money order today or November 30 so I wonder when you will get it. I was wishing you would of asked for something and I would of sent you some along in the box. Of course it would of been at my own risk. Norb, won't the Red Cross borrow you some? Bernard Hollkamp sent Hermina a V-Mail letter today and he must of heard something of you. He met someone that must have known you and he said when did we hear from you and if we knew how you are. I do think it's real sweet of him. He is in Belgium. Bernard says he gets a letter from Omar and they are expecting William home for Christmas. He was real happy over it. I think he deserves the break. Oberhausen is still at Nicholas General Hospital.

Norb, do you think they would send you back to the States if you would just ask them to? How did you take sick, Norb? Oh, I would like to know. If you could come back, try to anyway. I think you could rest better and so would we. Your mail means the world to me. One of your V-Mails went to a lady named Ish [*sp*] Martin on Tyler Lane. He is in the Medics. That's her husband [*arrow pointing to Martin*].

Boy, oh boy, it is cold here today and the cars [*streetcars*] run as last year. When one comes in about 20 minutes you are lucky and then comes another. Mrs. Russell and I got cold standing at Shelby and Chestnut this evening. We are busy as usual at work. I put in 68 hours this week. Buying war bonds. Well, that's correct isn't it? The drive is on now. Well, I think we should all try to buy as many as possible. Mrs. Abell, that's Mrs. Burk's mother, works with me. Mrs. Abell was telling me about Burke. Her grandson left about two weeks ago and is in Kansas in the Cavalry and he was so glad he was. Just 18 and he just loves to be with the horses. Were you close to that place when you were in Missouri?

Just now the 10 o'clock news is on and it's good. I'm glad you have the radio to listen to. I was wishing you had the little radio. We have it on the ice box in the kitchen and it sounds good there. I suppose because it is up high. Norb, did you get any of your Xmas boxes? Write for something and I will be glad to send it. You have four pairs of socks on the way. Mrs. Smith and Tony's wife, Mrs. Hoffman, each knitted two pairs and Tony's anxious to know when you get them. She was so anxious for you to get them. She sat up until 2 o'clock and finished them Tony said, so if you can ever get a card send him one of just mention it in our letter so I can tell him, or better, I will let him read it. I was so very surprised for her to do it. I wanted to pay him and he said if you want to favor a person, you don't want no pay so I thought it was kind of her.

I am sending work to Mrs. Smith now. We are so very busy and she finished her first bunch of drapes yesterday. Hermina would like to do them but she is kept busy about the house and momma cannot do much. Joey is back to work again since Monday. The Chief [*Lee*] don't want her to work and he's not worked for a week or longer [*since it's hunting season*]. Dewey [*Joey's stepson*] is just the same and he really enjoyed the letter you sent to him some time ago. He joined the National Guards and Joey says his leg hurts when they do drill. I don't think he should of joined up, but he was anxious to get into the Navy and you know he could never take it. His pal the Kerren boy got in the Navy and Dewey misses him.

Well, now Lip and all the Muths are OK. Katsy got 50 cents for singing at Rudy's on Thanksgiving Day. They like to hear her and she don't care how many are around. She loves to sing and when Betsy sings with her she also pronounces the words like Katsy and it's funny. They had a show in the basement last Sunday and you should of seen it. It was really good. Now John and family are OK. I made a coat smaller for Peggy and Sunday they came in and Peggy said 'Aunt Marge you crocked [*sp*] this coat didn't you?' She has a cute coat – a red one - for that Irishman [*Alma*]. It was $16.00 for the coat and leggings and two bucks for her hat but she looks nice in it and that baby [*Norbie*] is a doll. He is starting to talk. I let him look at your picture and he kissed you with a lot of spit on the glass, so you really get a juicy smacker. His hair are golden ringlets. Mom Smith [*John's mother-in-law*] said JoAnn looks just like Jackie so I don't know. You can judge for yourself because they sent you another picture of her. Joe really is a proud Paw. It's the only baby that can pull his tie and we all have to watch it and she also is an alarm clock.

Now, I had a bottle of Oertel's '92 and Pop was telling me all about Adler's [Adler Piano where Pop crafted piano cabinets] and how some guy wanted him to go to the country and now he said it's 10 after 11 and he's going to bed. Thursday night and it was Bingo. He also had a wedding this morning [*at St. Brigid's*]. Now, just now, comes Mary and it's damn cold but Mary thinks it's getting warmer. It looks like when I start to write I can't stop - like Fr. Dudine with his sermons. Anyway I'll say so long. Hope to see you real soon. May God bless you and say a prayer for us as always.
Your loving Sis,
Marge

England, **December 3**, Sunday Noon

Dear Mom and All,

Well, I just got back from church about an hour ago and decided to write a couple of letters before going to chow. I received thirty three letters yesterday. It was all old mail but still very good reading material. I have not as yet received any of the packages but I'm not needing anything now anyway.

It's been a nasty morning and I suppose the afternoon will be the same way, I don't know just how long I'll be hanging around here. Couldn't say for sure. Well, I'll say so long for now. I'm feeling OK and hope you are all the same. Tell Mary hello.

As Always,

Norb

England [*V-Mail*], **December 4**

Dear Mom and All,

There's not much that's new. Only the weather was nice today. That's a rare thing in England and I'm sure the King was pleased. Amos and Andy are on the radio now. First time I've heard them for a long time. Their program is a little different now. Well, I'm feeling pretty good and hope you are doing OK. I'm going to hit the hay for now so I'll be seeing you. Tell Mary hello!

As Always,

Norb

England [*V-Mail*], **December 5**

Dear Mom and all,

Well, here is a couple of lines to let you know that all is well and I'm pulling out of here tomorrow. I don't know where I'm going but I'm going. The stay here must have done me good because when I came in the hospital I weighed 159 and now I'm back to 174. But laying around gets you very soft. I haven't done anything for 41 days now and believe me, I'm glad to get out of here. I will drop you a line as soon as I get where I'm going, so don't be worried if you don't hear from me for a while because I might be busy. I'll say so long for now.

As Always,

Norb

England [*V-Mail*], **December 6**

Dear Mom and All,

Well, as you can see I never left here today as I thought I would. I'll most likely leave tomorrow and I'll be glad. Laying around here doing nothing is one of the best ways of going nuts that I can think of. I'd probably be in England for Xmas, although I'd rather spend Xmas in France. It's raining out again tonight. I was reading in the paper where Gen. Marshall said the war will end by Dec. 7. I hope he's right. That's tomorrow. I'll say so long for now and I'll be seeing you.

As Always.

Norb

One of the sad things that happened to me during the writing and researching for this book, was that one of Norb's friends and coworker from Park & Tilford, Tommy Bratten, a Sgt. in the US Army's 29th Infantry Division, was killed in action on Omaha Beach in the D Day Normandy Invasion on June 6. He is buried in the Normandy American Cemetery. He was married to Lizabeth and had a young son. At the time of the letter below, Hermina mentioned that Tommy's wife had still not heard from him after six months. I felt like I had lost a friend when I found the write up of his death on the internet.

Louisville, Kentucky, **December 6**, Wednesday

Dear Norb,

Well, it's six months today since the Invasion of France. I thought then by this time the war in Europe would be over, but I thought wrong, so I guess we'll have to set up the end of the war six months again. Perhaps by Easter it will be over with in Europe. Here's hoping it's before that time.

We haven't heard from you since Monday. The last letter was written Thanksgiving so we naturally are wondering if it's possible you could be traveling again.

Betty Bratten called today. She still has hopes that Tommy might show up as a German Prisoner of War. Of course you can't tell, but that's six months ago today. I feel like in this time he would have showed up unless he was critically wounded.

I just got a letter from Bernard Hollkamp today. I also got one last week from him. In today's letter it was written November 25th. He was in Germany. He said they really had a good Thanksgiving dinner, turkey and a good meal.

Betty Bratten said you got the picture of Tommy Jr she sent you. She also read the very nice letter you wrote her. She said she was going to write to you regular, as she can't write to Tommy. Do you think Alma will object? Ha, ha.

Well, I really don't know any more to write about so take good care of your ticker.
Love and best wishes from all,
Hermina

Louisville, Kentucky [*V-Mail*], **December 7**

Dear Norb,

Well, it's three years today since Pearl Harbor. Time sure flies. We received your letter of Nov 28th this morning as your V-letters come so much quicker. I thought I would write one as you said you still haven't heard from anybody. It's a damp rainy day today. So you think you'll spend Christmas in England? Are you at the Rehabilitation Center? I thought perhaps you would keep the same address. So you are going to see Irene Manning. You have been getting in plenty of shows haven't you? Perhaps I better wish you a Merry Christmas.
Hermina

Louisville, Kentucky [*V-Mail*], **December 8**

Dear Norb,

Feast of the Immaculate Conception. We haven't heard from you today which is unusual but in your V-Letter yesterday you said you thought you would be in England at Christmas time. I hope some of your boxes come through but most of all I hope your mail has come through by this time. We are having a beautiful sunshiny day and we sure appreciate it. I can't tell you how St. X came out but I'll ask Milton to give you the dope.

I think I'll change my mind about the Christmas tree. Mom said she wanted a tree even if there weren't any lights on it. Perhaps I better wish you a Merry Christmas now. And keep up the writing.

Love,

Hermina

England, **December 9,** Saturday night

Dearest Alma,

Well, I'm still here yet, honey, but from what I can gather I'll be pulling out Monday morning. I hope that's right this time. I think it is. I don't know anything that's...[*page torn & words are missing*]...all, everything...OK. The sun's even out today.

I haven't received any mail as yet. It must be held up somewhere. I should be getting return mail now because I been in the hospital for 44 days now and believe me honey that's a long time to spend in a hospital. I don't know where I'm going from here. I haven't the slightest idea but I should find out before long. I might even beat this letter back to the USA.

Well, darling I'm going to crawl back in bed again and I'll be seeing you, loving you

As Always,

Norb

A Christmas card from Alma with a Genie on front:

Louisville, Kentucky, **December 10**

"Hi There! If I owned Aladdin's Lamp; do you know what I would do? I'd rub it, quicker than a wink – and there I'd be with you! We'd share our Christmas happiness and laugh and be so gay, because my thoughts are with you every single day! Merry Christmas!" *Alma wrote on the card*: "To let you know again I'll be thinking of you. Every single day and always. My love, Alma"

Norb had changed hospitals once again as noted on his V-Mail return address of US Army Hospital, Plan t#4166, APO 508, c/o Postmaster New York, NY. His mail moved around so much it mostly didn't catch up with him until months later when he was back in the USA.

From the tone of Norb's V-Mails which sound almost perfunctory, and the short notes rather than letters, it appears that his morale is very low.

England [*V-Mail*], **December 11**

Dear Mom and All,

There's not much that's new except that I've changed hospitals again as you will notice by my address. I'm feeling OK. It didn't rain today for a change. I don't know when I will move from here as yet. I'll leave you know as soon as possible. I'll close for now as there's nothing new. Hoping you're all OK. I remain,
As Always,
Norb

Louisville, Kentucky, **December 11**, Monday

Dear Norb,

I have just finished writing you an Air Mail Letter. As I said in the letter we are laying under about a three inch blanket of snow and it is snowing as I am writing this. It won't be long until Christmas and you expect to spend it in England. Are you doing anything such as carrying pots or any work at the hospital? I suppose by now you know we couldn't wire you the money you asked for but had to send it by money order, Air Mail. Hoping you keep on writing.
Love and best wishes from all,
Hermina

Louisville, Kentucky [*V-Mail*], **December 13**

Dear Norb:

We're having sunshine and snow flurries today. It's rather cold out. Our thermometer registers 21° on the back porch. We haven't received any mail from you since Monday when we received four letters and the Stars and Stripes paper. Well it won't be long until Christmas. Margie is really thrilled over Christmas. Lip said she got her a "wooden iron" with a little cord and wooden plug. I thought that was funny. Dr. Sites was to see Mom. I also explained your condition. He said he thought your condition was functional and not serious.
Love and best wishes,
Hermina

Louisville, Kentucky, **December 16,** 11:25 am (Joe's Birthday)

Dear Norb:

Well, it's a clear, cold sunshiny morning. The thermometer registers 23° on the back porch. I have been wanting to write you but I have been busy. I suppose you received the letter I wrote to you Wednesday. As I'm writing this Mom is sitting up in the Living Room.

She just finished her second breakfast. She feels as good as she has been feeling this week. Her cough seems to be checked some and Dr. Sites told her to sit more, as sitting up seems to clock a cough. I called Fr. Bancroft the other day and told him what Dr. Sites said. He came right over and yesterday morning he heard her confession. She went to Communion and was anointed for death. He told her what Dr. Sites had said - that she could have a hemorrhage anytime. Mom took it swell. She told me a few weeks ago that she expected to go that way. I kidded her and asked her what was the matter with her "stroke?" Dr. Bancroft said she had a strong pulse. He said she could go in a hemorrhage but she could also last a good while yet. Pop took it very hard when she told him what the priest had said and that she was anointed but, as every one of us, he got over the first shock. Then, too, we expected the same thing last year so one can never tell.

Mom looks better today than she has in a week. She still loves her coffee. Mom gets what she wants as well as all the attention everyone can give her so she is getting everything that's possible and we surely are glad to think she likes to change to so many beds. At night it's her bed, during the day it's the back bedroom and the big chair in the Living Room as well as the couch.

Dr. Sites is out of town for a few days, everybody thought we should try to get you home as I called the Red Cross the day before. It's necessary for you to show our letter or cable to the commanding officer [*but Norb was not receiving any communications from anyone for over a month*], so I called Dr. Wynn and asked him if he would talk to the Red Cross as he knows Mom's condition as well as Dr. Sites. Dr. Wynn said he would be glad to so I called the Red Cross and gave them the information they wanted. They told me the chances are slim. I said we were willing to take that chance. We would have to cable you at any other time as this is a restricted time. No one is allowed to send cables overseas during the holiday season. I suppose they couldn't handle all of them so the Red Cross is sending the cable instead.

Norb, I don't know anything else. I could tell you that I thought you would like to know. I called Hensle's Thursday morning and told her to tell Alma. She called Alma and Alma came right out in the afternoon. Every one of us appreciated that.

William Hollkamp is on his way home as Lou said she is getting his mail back and that's a very good sign. He's supposed to be home by Christmas. Joseph Oberhauser is supposed to be home tonight. Well, I suppose I better close. Hoping you are feeling OK. Johnny told us you weigh 174 pounds now. That sounds very good.

Norb, if you have any time I wish you could write a few lines to Cousin Mary Hollenkamp and Mrs. Russell. They are our standbys. Cousin Mary Rawert, too. She comes when she can but she can't any more as she has to take things slow too. Norb, if I confused you about what you are supposed to do, well, I think you will know and it will be the Red Cross cable that you will have to show to the commanding officer. Hope I got it straight.
Love and best wishes from all,
Hermina

Louisville, Kentucky [*V-Mail*], **December 18,** Monday

Dear Norb,

"NOON." Will write more tonight. We received your V-letter written December 4th. Glad to know you are feeling fine. Since yesterday afternoon Mom has been feeling some better, was even kidding us and giving wise answers so that makes us all feel better. Jimmy is doing fine with his broken arm. He's gone to school today. Mary Rawert Hunn, your cousin on Logan Street, gave birth to a nearly 8 pound boy yesterday. I think he will be called "Willie Jr." Today is just a week from Christmas. I can't imagine that. I will close hoping you're OK and I'm happy to say Mom is feeling some better and is going to sit up in the living room.
Love from All,
Hermina

Louisville, Kentucky [*V-Mail*], **December 18**, 4:20 pm

Dear Norb,

Catching up on my writing. I wrote you at noon and I want to get this one off with it. Mom is still feeling better and doesn't cough near so much. Elizabeth told me she didn't tell you about Jimmy's broken arm. Last Wednesday, December 13, a boy bigger than Jim kept pestering him. He warned him if he hurt him he'd have to pay the Dr.'s bill. Well, that did no good so they were wrestling. He threw Jim down and broke his arm in two places but Jim's doing fine. Dr. Woods, a bone specialist, set it at St. Joseph Infirmary. Betsy does my shopping. I gave her carfare and she went to Smith's to get my order. It's a damp day. It snows and melts right away.
Love,
H.R.

Louisville, Kentucky [*V-Mail*], **December 20**, Wednesday

Letter No. 1

Dear Norb,

Well, it's a beautiful day but a little windy. Since Monday Mom has been feeling a good deal better, I'm happy to say. I know you'll be glad to know. I want to try and write you a V-Letter every day but I failed to write yesterday. Jimmy is doing fine with his broken arm. He looks like he's gaining weight. I guess that's because he can't get out there and play as hard as he's used to.

Lou. Hollkamp is here. She said I should tell you Merry Xmas. She was sending you a card. I never got to write any cards this year but I know you'll understand. I'm going to write another V-Letter while I'm at it.
Love from all,
H.R.

Louisville, Kentucky [*V-Mail*], **December 20**, Wednesday

Letter No. 2

Dear Norb,

Well, it's still a beautiful day. Ha, ha. St. Briget's [*Brigid's*] had closing of Forty Hour prayer yesterday. Pop seen Fr. Van Bogart up there Monday night. He asked about you and that we should tell you he asked about you. He never forgets does he?

Norbert Hollkamp is in San Francisco. Lou got his clothes a little after Thanksgiving. He still has his last examination to go through, I think Lou said. Mrs. Russell got your letter. That "Dear Mary and Dude" tickled them. Betsy got our Christmas tree yesterday. It's small but a nice shape. She's anxious to help trim it. Hoping you have a nice Christmas. Love and best wishes from all,
Hermina

Louisville, Kentucky, **December 22**, Friday

Dear Norb,

We received your V-letter saying you were moved to another hospital. Is that close to where you were? I thought you were going to be moved to a rehabilitation center. I suppose your move will delay your boxes reaching you again. Here's hoping you soon get some of them.

The war news certainly has been bad. I sure think of all those we know who are in that area but in the last war Germany threw everything in there when they were about at the end of everything. So according to the news and papers this might be the last time Germany can show any strength. Here's hoping it is.

It's a beautiful but cold day. Mom is sitting on the couch sleeping. She's blowing [*snoring*] right now. Mom felt better this week than last week. We're all set for Christmas but for putting up the tree and crib and Betsy wants to help do that. They sure get a kick out of doing that.

We have never received your war bond for October but due to your being moved, thought that probably had something to do with it. Kindly let us know about that as I will write to Chicago and inquire about it. But I really think it's due to your being moved.

The kids had a chicken dinner at school yesterday and ice cream and cake for dessert. Betsy said it was good. She got tickled at Mr. Schlegel. Santa Claus introduced him as Herman Schlegel [*maintenance man*], the boy who has been in the sixth grade for four years. Betsy said he rolled his trousers up to below his knees. I said to Pop, "How would you like to act like that?" He said, "I wouldn't." Betsy said she spent over $3.00 for Xmas presents. I sure do get tickled to hear how they buy, but it's very cute - everybody is thought of. For Milton she has a comic book. I really thought that was something. For Marge she has a 10¢ bottle of Fitch's Shampoo. She buys what she thinks you like. I sure do think Betsy is cute. She sure uses good judgment. You know Jimmy has been getting up some lady's coal across the street from them. He makes 60¢ a week for doing that so when he broke his arm Betsy took over. When pay day came she gave Betsy the money saying "Here's your brother's money" so Betsy gives it to Jim. But it was divided up. She sure is unselfish. Betsy has been staying with me after school this week. She's very good company. Jimmy's arm is doing fine. The Dr. said in about three weeks they would X-ray it and then they might put on a lighter weight cast but Jimmy looks swell.

I suppose all the night work for the Christmas rush will be over with for this year. Marge didn't think she would have to work tonite. I sure will be glad. Mrs. Kiefer has been helping me clean every Friday. That helps out a lot so she gave me another day which was last Wednesday and we got the house tip-top.

I told you Joe Oberhausen was coming from India. They are expecting him next month but it's Tony Oberhausen who came home. He walks with a brace and a cane I am told.

Well, I suppose for Christmas we'll have the same as Thanksgiving, have a nice baking hen instead of turkey. Mixed nuts were 50¢ at Schieman's seven weeks ago. I tried to get a fountain pen for Marge, for a gift to Maurice. The KY Pen Shop never had a pen for between $4 and $40 so the pen gift was out. We just got your two V-letters from December 5th and 6th this afternoon saying you were going to leave the hospital you are at. And this morning we got your V-letters giving your new address. I also got a V-letter from Bernard H. He said he hasn't 'seen the 59th for some time now. You know he is in Germany. Bernard Spoelker's picture was in the paper the other night. After being told, you could tell it was him. He looks a little thinner.
Merry Xmas and Love and Best Wishes form all,
Hermina

Louisville, Kentucky [*V-Mail*], **December 22**

Dear Norb,

We received your V-Letter saying you were moved to another hospital but I see you are still in England. How do you like your new location? Did you get our money order for $50 you requested about three weeks ago? We haven't heard if you did or not but I suppose we couldn't hear from that yet. I didn't give it time enough. It's a beautiful day. Mom is sitting on the couch in the living room and is feeling pretty good. I got the table up [*for the home made nativity crib that Poppy made*]. Betsy is coming to help me trim the tree. Happy New Year!
Love and Best Wishes from all,
Hermina

Louisville, Kentucky [*V-Mail*], **December 25**

Dear Norb,

It's Christmas Eve, 9:35 pm. Naturally we all thought of you again today especially tonite and was wondering if you have received any gifts, or if you have gotten any boxes by this time. The war news sounded a lot more encouraging tonight. Mom did real good today. She spent most of the afternoon and evening in the living room which made all feel good. Alma came very early this morning. She sent Mom a pot of waxed begonias. They are very pretty. She remembered us all. Joey stayed all night. Lee and Dewey went to the country. Will write more in an Air Mail letter. Let us know how you spent Christmas. Hope you are OK. Love and best wishes,

H.R.

The following letter is the last letter saved in the collection.

Louisville, Kentucky, **December 28**, Thursday

Dear Norb,

I'm inclosing a picture of yesterday's weather scene. It sure was a honey. Marge was an hour late and Alma called. She said it was nearly eleven o'clock by the time she got to work. Perhaps Alma was on one of the buses. I believe she takes the Walnut bus. It was really colder today than yesterday, especially yesterday afternoon.

Mom has been feeling better this week. Every afternoon and every evening she spent in the living room changing about from couch to big chair. She ate better today too, but she hasn't a good appetite but she gets a quart or more of milk every day and most of the time half of that is cream, considering Mom don't do anything different, I think what she eats is sufficient.

We haven't heard from you since last Friday. We are wondering if it could be possible that you might get to come home. The V- letter was written December 11. The war news sounds better today. Here's hoping it continues that way.

Joe Shaugnessy, Lill Steinmetz's Cousin Lizzie's boy, was reported missing in action in September, in France, I think. He's one of the twins. Day before yesterday "Cousin Lizzie" got word from him that he's a German war prisoner. Lill said she was happy to think he was among the living.

As you can see this pen doesn't do too good. Hoping this finds you well and that the New Year will bring peace and happiness.

Norb, I don't have time to write as I used to so I have to use your words, no news, good news and I'll write when I can. It keeps one busy firing up the furnace these cold days. Marge wrote yesterday. She's busy tonite working button holes in Vernon's coat. Saturday the whole gang from the store goes to White Clouds for there [*sic*] Christmas party. Love from all,

Hermina

Epilogue

Victory in Europe did not come until May 8, 1945. WW II did not end until September 2, 1945. Many lives were lost. Norb was fortunate to have come home alive but he suffered the effects of the war for the rest of his life.

Norb was transferred from an Army Hospital in England to Wakeman General and Convalescent Hospital at Camp Atterbury in Indiana sometime before January 1945. Somehow, word finally reached him that his mother was mortally ill. He arrived home in Louisville just before his mother's death on January 6, 1945. In my heart, I know that she was holding on just so that she could see her dear son one last time.

When Norb got out of the army, he tried his hand at various trades. He had a difficult time keeping jobs. He said he was not cut out for them. For a time he worked for Donaldson's Bakery and the US Post office. Later in life, he succeeded as a life insurance sales representative at Lincoln Income Life Insurance Company in Louisville where he often received bonuses, such as turkeys or trips to Key West, for being the top salesman.

On June 22, 1946, he married his longtime girlfriend Alma Lee Pierce and nine months later their first child, Carol (me) was born on March 22, 1947 at St. Joseph's Infirmary. Later they had two more children, Dolores and Norbert, Jr.

Throughout his life, Norb had difficulty with PTSD affects such as depression and health issues. When he was taken from the battlefield in Belgium, he wrote that he had trouble with his "ticker" or heart. I learned later that this was called "soldier's heart" during the American Civil War. I wish I had taken the time to talk to him on those many nights he sat on the front porch pondering the sky and stars. Nevertheless, no one could have a better or kinder man for a dad. I wrote his story to pay tribute to all he gave me.

Norb carried the poem "Don't Quit" in his wallet throughout the war and the rest of his life until September 1984 when, on the death of my son, he passed it onto me along with his big, thick 1945 History of WW II book that held my interest as a child. He knew the poem always had a special meaning to me. When I was young, he paid me 25 cents per stanza to memorize it. He passed the poem on to me at that difficult time knowing that I would need to revisit the words as he did. The yellowed and taped paper will always be a treasure to me.

In 2012, my husband Harold and I took a memorial trip through Normandy and France to retrace my dad's footsteps in WW II. In his letters, he had mentioned some of the cities he traveled through on the march to liberate France and onto Germany: "Yeah, Breast [Brest] was quite a place to see. I seen all the rest nearly. La Hague de Parts [La Haye-du-Puits], Velone [Valogne], St. Lô, Lessay [Basse-Normandie region of France], St. Sauveur, but Breast [Brest] was the worst of all. I don't think that there was a five foot square anywhere that didn't show shell marks. Paris, ah! Paris, how I would like to spend about a week there.

It's really a place. I know that just from passing through. Versailles is quite a place also. I have had some of the best beer I have drank since I've left the states today. It really was good beer."

We drove through all the cities except for Brest. Everywhere we went you could see memorials to the war. It was so awe inspiring to be able to be where my dad was although under much different circumstances. This trip really made the letters come alive for me and made me really appreciate his personal sacrifice to this country and the world. And the local people we met in the Netherlands and France appreciated America's great sacrifice.

It is without question that Norb thought about his many comrades-in-arms with whom he served on the front lines in the European Theater; more specifically in the front lines of Belgium where in the fall and early winter of 1944 he and his fellow soldiers dug in and formed a long, thin line facing Germany and his ancestral enemy. After Norb left his unit for medical reasons, he was moved to the rear in Belgium and then flown out through Paris to a Red Cross Hospital in London. It was in England during recovery and rehabilitation that Norb learned of the German attack on the Allies and the Battle of the Bulge. His Corps Headquarters was located in Bastogne and the Corps and troops were spread along a very thin line. Bastogne was a target of the advancing German Army and they overran most of the Corps positions. Many of them were killed, wounded or captured. Those that survived would live with the horrors of war. No doubt Norb knew many of these men and he would always wonder what happened to his comrades as he arrived back home. He would live with his own thoughts and questions over the next 42 years that he lived. Many of those thoughts consumed him as he sat on the front porch steps of his home on Nachand Lane under the stars with a bottle of '92, thinking and wondering about his past in WW II. Many of these thoughts and memories reflected in behavior observed and not fully understood by his family. I did not understand until I wrote *As Always, Norb.*

After many years of chronic illnesses Norb died at age 67 on April 27, 1988 and was buried with honors at the Zachery Taylor National Cemetery five days later on May 2. He is now at rest in Zachary Taylor National Cemetery surrounded by his fellow veterans and members of the greatest generation, and his wife Alma their grandson Ryan Trainer. He is at peace at last.

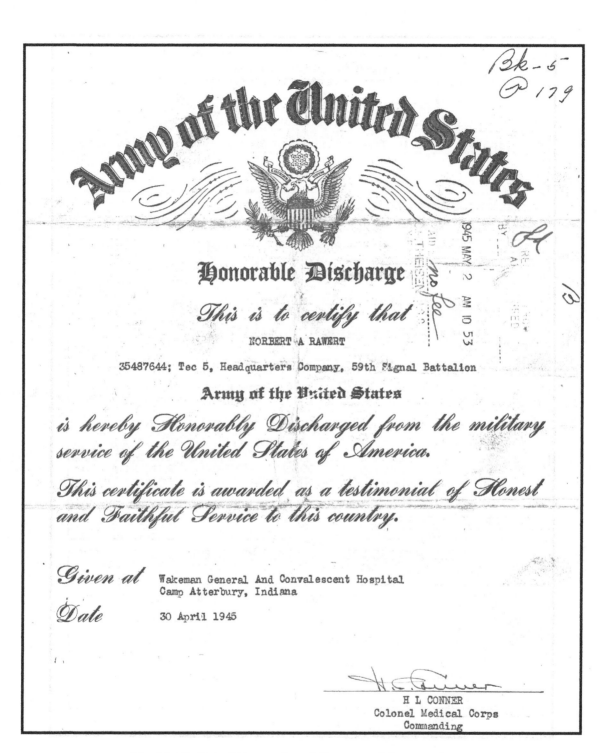

Army of the United States

Honorable Discharge

This is to certify that

NORBERT A RAWERT

35487644; Tec 5, Headquarters Company, 59th Signal Battalion

Army of the United States

is hereby Honorably Discharged from the military service of the United States of America.

This certificate is awarded as a testimonial of Honest and Faithful Service to this country.

Given at Wakeman General And Convalescent Hospital
Camp Atterbury, Indiana

Date 30 April 1945

H L CONNER
Colonel Medical Corps
Commanding

**Norb's Enlisted Record and Report of Separation –
Honorable Discharge**, Form WD AGO 53-55. Side A.

ENLISTED RECORD AND REPORT OF SEPARATION
HONORABLE DISCHARGE

13k-5
P180

1. LAST NAME - FIRST NAME - MIDDLE INITIAL	2. ARMY SERIAL NO.	3. GRADE	4. ARM OR SERVICE	5. COMPONENT
Rawert Norbert A	35487644	T/5	Signal C	AUS

6. ORGANIZATION	7. DATE OF SEPARATION	8. PLACE OF SEPARATION
Hq Company, 59th Signal Battalion	30 Apr 1945	Wakeman Gen and Conv Hosp Camp Atterbury, Indiana

9. PERMANENT ADDRESS FOR MAILING PURPOSES	10. DATE OF BIRTH	11. PLACE OF BIRTH
1344 Texas Ave, Louisville, Kentucky	17 Aug 1920	Louisville, Kentucky

12. ADDRESS FROM WHICH EMPLOYMENT WILL BE SOUGHT	13. COLOR EYES	14. COLOR HAIR	15. HEIGHT	16. WEIGHT	17. NO. DEPEND.
See 9	Blue	Brown	5' 8"	156 LBS.	0

18. RACE		19. MARITAL STATUS			20. U.S. CITIZEN		21. CIVILIAN OCCUPATION AND NO.
WHITE	NEGRO OTHER (specify)	SINGLE	MARRIED	OTHER (specify)	YES	NO	Warehouseman
X			X				

MILITARY HISTORY

22. DATE OF INDUCTION	23. DATE OF ENLISTMENT	24. DATE OF ENTRY INTO ACTIVE SERVICE	25. PLACE OF ENTRY INTO SERVICE
4 Aug 1942	18 Aug 1942		Louisville, Kentucky

26. REGISTERED	27. LOCAL S.S. BOARD NO.	28. COUNTY AND STATE	29. HOME ADDRESS AT TIME OF ENTRY INTO SERVICE
SELECTIVE SERVICE DATA YES X NO	71	Jefferson Co, Kentucky	1344 Texas Ave, Louisville, Ky.

30. MILITARY OCCUPATIONAL SPECIALTY AND NO.	31. MILITARY QUALIFICATION AND DATE (i.e., infantry, aviation and marksmanship badges, etc.)
Auto Clerk--Parts, 348	Carbine (Marksman) 10 Nov 1942 ** M-1 Rifle (Sharpshooter) 9 Sep 1942

32. BATTLES AND CAMPAIGNS

France, One Battle Star; Belguim, One Battle Star

33. DECORATIONS AND CITATIONS

European African Middle Eastern Theatre Ribbon, Good Conduct Medal

34. WOUNDS RECEIVED IN ACTION

None

35.	LATEST IMMUNIZATION DATES			36.	SERVICE OUTSIDE CONTINENTAL U.S. AND RETURN		
SMALLPOX	TYPHOID	TETANUS	OTHER (specify)	DATE OF DEPARTURE	DESTINATION	DATE OF ARRIVAL
28 Aug 43	11 Sep 43	7 Mar 44	Typhus 14 Feb 44	29 Jan 1944	European Theatre	6 Feb 1944
				15 Dec 1944	United States	27 Dec 1944

37. TOTAL LENGTH OF SERVICE						38. HIGHEST GRADE HELD
CONTINENTAL SERVICE			FOREIGN SERVICE			
YEARS	MONTHS	DAYS	YEARS	MONTHS	DAYS	
1	9	27	0	11	0	Tec 5

FOR CONVENIENCE, A CERTIFICATE OF ELIGIBILITY NO. 1178 296 HAS BEEN ISSUED BY THE VETERANS ADMINISTRATION TO BE USED FOR THE FUTURE REQUEST OF ANY BOUNTY OR INSURANCE BENEFIT UNDER TITLE III OF THE SERVICE...EN'S READ-JUSTMENT ACT OF 1944, AS AMENDED, THAT MAY BE AVAILABLE TO THE PERSON TO WHOM THIS SEPARATION ORDER WAS ISSUED

39. PRIOR SERVICE

None

40. REASON AND AUTHORITY FOR SEPARATION
Certificate of Disability for Discharge AR 615-361 And 1st Ind Headquarters Wakeman General And Convalescent Hospital, Camp Atterbury, Indiana*

41. SERVICE SCHOOLS ATTENDED	42. EDUCATION (Years)		
	Grammar	High School	College
Bell Telephone, Kansas City, Missouri	8	4	0

PAY DATA

43. LONGEVITY FOR PAY PURPOSES			44. MUSTERING OUT PAY		45. SOLDIER DEPOSITS	46. TRAVEL PAY	47. TOTAL AMOUNT, NAME OF DISBURSING OFFICER
YEARS	MONTHS	DAYS	TOTAL	THIS PAYMENT			
2	8	27	$ 300	$ 100	–	$ 4.20	$235.90 R C MURNANE Capt FD

INSURANCE NOTICE

IMPORTANT IF PREMIUM IS NOT PAID WHEN DUE OR WITHIN THIRTY-ONE DAYS THEREAFTER, INSURANCE WILL LAPSE. MAKE CHECKS OR MONEY ORDERS PAYABLE TO THE TREASURER OF THE U. S. AND FORWARD TO COLLECTIONS SUBDIVISION, VETERANS ADMINISTRATION, WASHINGTON 25, D. C.

48. KIND OF INSURANCE			49. HOW PAID		50. Effective Date of Allot-ment Discontinuance	51. Date of Next Premium Due (One month after 50)	52. PREMIUM DUE EACH MONTH	53. INTENTION OF VETERAN TO		
Nat. Serv.	U.S. Govt.	None	Allotment	Direct to V. A.				Continue	Continue Only	Discontinue
X			X		30 Apr 1945	31 May 1945	3.30	X	$	

54.		55. REMARKS (This space for completion of above items or entry of other items specified in W. D. Directives)
	RIGHT THUMB PRINT	**M-1, 903, (Marksman) 26 Sep 43 *Dated 27 Apr 1945 No time lost under AW 107 ERC from 4 Aug 1942 to 18 Aug 1942 Lapel Button Issued

56. SIGNATURE OF PERSON BEING SEPARATED	57. PERSONNEL OFFICER (Type name, grade and organization - signature)
Norbert A Rawert	O J Thornburg O J THORNBURG, 2nd Lt MAC, Ass't Chief Pnts Pers Br

WD AGO FORM 53-55
1 November 1944

This form supersedes all previous editions of WD AGO Forms 53 and 55 for enlisted persons entitled to an Honorable Discharge, which will not be used after receipt of this revision.

Norb's Enlisted Record and Report of Separation – Honorable Discharge, Form WD AGO 53-55. Side B.

FILE No. C- 4 893 682

A-3

AWARD OF DISABILITY COMPENSATION OR PENSION

(SERVICE CONNECTED)

Veterans Administration
Branch of Central Office
Fifth Service Command
8 East Chestnut Street
Columbus, 15, Ohio.

May 5, 1945.

YOU ARE REQUESTED TO SIGN THE ATTACHED
SIGNATURE CARD WITH YOUR NAME.

" Norbert A. Rawert "

ON THE LINE INDICATED BY THE BLACK ARROW
AND RETURN SAME TO VETERANS ADMINISTRATION.

LEXINGTON, KY.

To:
Mr. Norbert A. Rawert
1344 Texas Ave.
Louisville, Ky.

In accordance with the provisions of __Public No. 2, 73rd Congress, as amended__

you are hereby notified that as a __T/S Hq. Co. 59th Sig. Bn.__ who was discharged

from the __military__ service of the United States on the __30th__ day of __April__,

19 __45__, you are awarded __a service connected pension__ in the amount of $ __57.50__

from __May 1,__ , 19 __45__, on account of disability resulting from the following condi-

tions held to have been incurred or aggravated during your __World War II Service:__
(War or regular service)

__nervous disability (in combat)__

The monthly payments pursuant to this award will continue during the period in which you

are __50%__ disabled subject to the general conditions mentioned on the reverse side of this communication to which your attention is directed. Upon the happening of any of the contingencies mentioned the Veterans Administration should be notified promptly.

It has been determined that service connection is not shown for the following conditions ____

__None.__

If you are dissatisfied with the findings of the Veterans Administration or the amount of this award
it is your privilege to enter an appeal therefrom within 1 year from the date of this communication. Such
appeal should be submitted to this office for certification to the Board of Veterans' Appeals, Washington
25, D. C. VETERANS ADMINISTRATION, LEXINGTON, KY.

If you should change your present address the Veterans Administration must be immediately notified.
VETERANS ADMINISTRATION, LEXINGTON, KY.

All future communications with reference to this case should be addressed to XXXXXXXX and must bear
the file number C - 4 893 682 as well as your full name and complete rank and organization.

ATTENTION IS INVITED TO THE ENCLOSED NOTICES
PERTAINING TO VOCATIONAL REHABILITATION AND
HOSPITAL TREATMENT.

E. W. HICKS
Manager.

Veterans Administration.

Norb's Award of Disability or Pension Form

DON'T QUIT!

When things go wrong, as they sometimes will,
     When the road you're trudging seems all up-hill,
When funds are low and debts are high,
     And you want to smile but you have to sigh,
When care is pressing you down a bit,
     Rest if you must, but "Don't You Quit!"

Life is queer with its twists and turns,
     As every one of us sometimes learns,
And many a failure turns about,
     When he might have won had he stuck it out.
Don't give up, though the pace seems slow,
     You may succeed with another blow.
Often the goal is nearer than
     It seems to a faint and faltering man.

Often the struggler has to give up,
     When he might have captured the victor's cup.
And he learned too late, when the night slipped down,
     How close he was to the golden crown.
Success is failure turned inside out,
     The silver tint of the clouds of doubt,
And you can never tell how close you are,
     It may be near when it seems afar.
So stick to the fight when you're hardest hit,
     It's when things seem worst that you mustn't quit.

Norb carried the *Don't Quit* poem
in his wallet from 1942-1984

Norbert A. Rawert's final resting
place at Zachery Taylor National
Cemetery, Louisville, Kentucky

Carol at Normandy American Cemetery, Omaha
Beach, Colleville-sur-Mer, France, March 2012

Harold Trainer at Normandy American
Cemetery, Omaha Beach, Colleville-
sur-Mer, France, March 2012

Bibliography

Atkinson, Rick. The Guns of Last Light: The War in Western Europe, 1944-1945. Vol. 3, Liberation Trilogy. New York: Henry Holt and Company, LLC, 2013.

Buell, Hal, ed. World War II, A Complete Photographic History. New York: Black Dog and Leventhal publishers, Inc. 2002.

Carroll, Andrew. Behind the Lines. New York: Scribner, 2005.

Carroll, Andrew. War Letters: Extraordinary Correspondence from American Wars. New York: Scribner, 2001.

Cizewski, Leanord H., http://www.ibiblio.org/cizewski/signalcorps/normsigunits.html.

http://militaryhistory.about.com/od/worldwarii/p/World-War-Ii-Operation-Cobra-Breakout-From-Normandy.htm. Operation Cobra, Breakout From Normandy

King, Larry. Love Stories of World War II. New York: Crown Publishers, 2001.

Middleton, Maj. Gen. Troy H. Headquarters VIII Corps, Report After Action Against Enemy, July 20, 1944, http://www.90thdivisionassoc.org/afteractionreports/PDF/VIII%20AAR%2006-44.pdf

Middleton, Maj. Gen. Troy H. Headquarters. VIII Corps, Report After Action Against Enemy, August 11, 1944.

Murphy, Edward F. Heroes of WW II, 2nd ed. New York: Ballantine Books, 1992.

Raynor, George and Dixie Harris. The Signal Corps: The Outcome," Washington, DC, US Government Printing Office, p 125.

Wallesch, Shayne E. and Wendy J. Hochnadel. 1944 World War II Troop Ship Crossings, http://ww2troopships.com/crossings/1944.htm.

Ward, Geoffrey C. The War, An Intimate History 1941-45. New York: Alfred A. Knoph, 2007.

Wikipedia Free Encyclopedia. RMS Aquitania. https://en.wikipedia.org/wiki/RMS_Aquitania.

Zortman, Earl. "59th Signal Battalion In World War II," Voice of the Arctic, July 2004, 2-6.

Index

Abell family 454

Able family 410

Adams family 129

Adler Piano Company 1, 455

Air Raid 284, 304, 359, 426

Alberts, Renee 356

Allen family 216

Allgeirs' Field 63

All Wool and a Yard Wide Democratic Club 42, 77, 94, 306

American Red Cross 119, 301, 377

Amshoff family 33, 170, 191

Andrew Jackson Hotel, Nashville. TN 353

Army Air Show 63

Ash Street 438

Atherton, Dr. 46, 64, 189, 326

Axe, Mr. or "Old Man Axe" (vegetable cart man) 36

Bader, Rose 325

Baker, Dr. 233

Bancroft, Dr. 460

Bancroft family 334

Battle of Normandy vii

Battle of the Bulge 15

Becker family 136

Beckman's Photography 425

Beeker, Johnny 275

Belgium/Belgians xii, 15, 207, 398, 411, 424, 435, 437, 439, 441, 454

Bernice, Sr. (Anna Heitkemper's niece) 417

Bertrilla, Sr. (Principal at St. E) 417

Besendorf family 294

Besendorf's Dry Goods 249, 294

Bierbaum family 49, 50

Blight, La Vada Thompson 97

Bliler family 69, 215

Blue River Inn (White Clouds, IN) 165, 376

Bodner family 20, 43, 109, 325

Boman-Summers 89

Bosse Funeral Home 120, 204

Bowe family 77

Bowe, Gertie (married Meyer) 45, 137, 177

Bowman Field 160, 177, 305

Bratten family 129, 358, 359, 457

Breitenstein 74

Brooks, Richard (radio host) 149

Bruce, Dr. 205

Bryant 318

Burke Family 454

Burke, Mr. (of Park & Tilford) 119, 124

Burmeister, Danny 46

Burnett Avenue 2

Busath's Candy Store 152

Butler family 33, 56, 65, 67, 257, 407

Caldwell Street
    #1029 80

Camp Atterbury, Indiana xii

Camp Crowder, Missouri 24

Camp Taylor 281

Carter, Dewey 33, 186, 247, 277, 303, 305, 335, 412, 455

Carter, Josephine or "Joey" (wife of Lee Carter) 430

Carter, Lee & Joey (Rawert) family 104, 292, 335, 418

Carter, Lee or "Wahoo" 1, 48, 144, 223, 239, 240, 276

Censoring of letters 416

Chandler, Gov. "Happy" 119

Churchill Downs 108, 110, 290, 292, 297, 328

Churchill, Winston 261, 264, 408, 419

Claeys family (Belgium) 441

Clarksdale's (TV and radio repair, Shelby
    St,) 336
Clay Street 64, 264
Clephas family 44, 45, 47, 438
Courier Journal 31, 45, 105, 132, 160, 419
Cream Top Dairy 242
Cronkite, Walter 240, 444
Curtiss-Wright Company 214, 237, 261
Darrlin, Roy 93
Davis, Dorothy 209
D Day 7
Deaconess Hospital 298
Dillmann family 84, 95
Doerr family 119, 194, 427
Donaldson's Bakery 55, 59, 112, 121, 133, 152,
    174, 226, 240, 330
draft board 341, 347, 407
Dreckman, Fr. 97
Dudine, Fr. (St. E) 68, 87, 117, 119, 150, 161,
    268, 419, 455
Durkee 203
Eagan, Fr. 50
Effkemann 3
Effkemann, Alfons xiii, 3
Effkemann, Josef xiii, 17
Elick, Min 61, 149, 150, 151
Ellison Avenue 227
England/English 245, 320, 321, 385, 395
Ernst, Cliff (Hubbuch's employee) 93
Ever, Herb 65, 178
Fahringer 75
Falls City beer 207, 350
Farry, Carl 64
Fehr's beer 193
Fischer's meat packing company 177
Flechler family 246
Fort Harrison, Indiana 7
France
    Ardennes 13
    Ardennes Forest 15
    Avranches xii, 402
    Brest xii, 15, 402, 412, 414, 423
    Breton 402

    Carentan 14
    Cherbourg 14, 398
    Coutances xii, 398
    Granville xii
    La Haye-du-Puits 14, 423
    le Plessis-Mont-Castre Forest 14
    Lessay 423
    Mont-Castre hills 14
    Nancy 437
    Normandy xiii, 13, 400, 403
    Paris 423
    Rennes 402
    Saint-Malo 402
    St. Lô 14, 398
    St. Sauveur 423
    Valogne 423
France/French 399, 408
Friebert family 195, 202
Frisch family 91
Galings family 151
Gamelhoft 84
Geher's 73
Gehrig, Ray 41
Geppert family 175, 189
Germany xii
    Ahaus xiii, 3, 18, 412
    Wessum xii, 3
Germany/Germans 15, 201, 206, 224, 328,
    330, 372, 393, 398, 399, 402, 412, 424,
    432, 437, 444, 462, 464
    Aachen 428
Gettlefinger, Dr. 106, 258, 288, 371
Gillespie, Mary 333
Girsman (coal man) 187
Goeing, H. J. (Shirley Muth's adopted
    soldier) 317
Goetta (German meat & oat sausage) 140,
    232, 247
Gold, Mrs. Emmy 30
Gorman 209
Goss Avenue 91, 123, 223
Grants 5 & 10¢ Drugstore 244
Griffin family 213, 427

Grimm, Miss Emma 30, 108, 128, 147, 267, 283, 356
Hacker, Fred 26
Halring family 150
Harmann family 281, 339
Harmon family 352
Harpring family (neighbors) 52
Harstern family 293
Hautledge, Fr. (Holy Trinity Church) 263
Heatter, Gabriel 328, 342, 421, 422, 435
Heichelbeck 75
Heim family 240
Heintz family 202, 227, 236
Heitkemper, Anna D. (Alabama) 74, 236, 301, 308, 325, 334
Heitkemper family 3, 117, 328, 334
Heitkemper, Frances 60, 175
Heitkemper. George (Laverne's husband) 166
Heitkemper, Laverne 129, 139, 140, 296, 346
Heitkemper, Wilhelmina 443
Heitzman family 84, 95, 118, 183
Hellman family 52, 72, 94, 114, 115, 117, 245, 308
Hellman, Red 19, 150, 184, 210
Hensle, Robert & Antoinette (Spoelker) family 129, 142, 291, 357
Herbig family 84, 91, 104, 109, 146, 202
Hertel family 84, 189
Hertel Pharmacy (1138 Goss Ave.) 38, 45, 62, 63, 73, 88, 118, 123, 125, 192, 217, 298, 347, 371
Hibbit 333, 336
Hildebrand family 297
Hitler 327, 329, 389
Hoering family 242
Hoffman family 302, 429, 454
Hollenkamp, Cousin Mary 78
Hollenkamp family 50, 67, 85, 109, 111, 112, 120, 131, 363
Hollkamp, Bernard 45
Hollkamp, Cousin Mary 19, 232, 243
Hollkamp family 53, 66, 67, 140, 160, 166, 171, 205, 228, 236, 238, 248, 250, 271, 272,

295, 306, 308, 322, 323, 328, 331, 334, 338, 359, 361, 414, 416, 419, 437, 451, 462, 463
Holy Trinity Catholic Church & School 352
Horne (lawyer) 89, 90, 91, 108
Horn family 335
Howard Hotel, Kansas City, MO 85
Hub, Anna 49
Hubbard family 202, 217
Hubbuch family 31, 36, 46, 55, 57, 71, 76, 77, 85, 89, 90, 102, 116, 147, 154, 159, 211, 276, 311, 312, 315, 347, 423
Hubbuch's 2, 32, 54, 77, 127, 145, 165, 188, 196, 202, 223, 242, 257
Hudson, Dr. 303, 304
Huelsman's Tavern 2, 26, 63, 131, 142, 163, 202, 321
Hunley, Jim 69
Hunn family 356, 461
Huntley family 36
Israel, Jerry 102, 325
Italy/Italians 306, 307, 312, 320, 324, 326, 328
Janes family 194
John Sabel Interiors 2
Johnson, Clarence 52
Johnson family 72, 85, 88, 108, 112, 118, 123, 126, 132, 144, 146, 160, 177, 193, 204, 238, 269, 279, 280, 281, 283, 314, 322, 326, 339, 344, 356, 396, 420, 426, 435, 444
Johnson, Larny 93
Johnson's 327, 364, 420
Jones family 346
Kaiser family 210, 324, 329, 337
Kamber family 227
Kapfhammer's 180
Kegabein family 46, 59, 258
Keller family 303, 322, 326, 327
Kendrick's 359
Kentucky Derby 394
Kentucky Hotel 361
Kentucky Pen Shop 169, 463
Kentucky Street 202
Kerren family 455

Kiefer family 463

Killed In Action 342, 422

Kinzer, Rose (married Earl Johnson) 283

Kipperick 176

Klapeke, Charles 209

Klarer, Rudy 160

Kleiner family 238

Kleiner, Lill Klein 55, 99, 339

Klein family 308, 340

Knue, Fr. (St. E) 47, 236, 239, 263, 347, 395

Koebel family 208

Kosair Picnic 310

Kremer, Fred 43

Krumplemann family 111, 196

Kunz's 46, 180

Lander, Chester (Hubbuch's employee) 308, 347

Lauyan family 192

Lavada 63, 431

Lee family 112, 168, 170, 178, 186, 192, 219, 243, 407, 420

Lenahan, Pat 160

Lester, Mr. (Hubbuch's employee) 85

Levy Brothers Department Store 269

Liken, Dr. 343

Logsdon, Anna Marie (m. Francis State) 34

Louisville Times 31

Lubbers' 113, 303

Lydia Street 102, 325

Ma Beha laundry & dry cleaning company 141

Madden family 20, 34, 37, 38, 42, 69, 262, 298, 330, 409, 420

Maier family 329

Male vs Manual games 364

Maloney, Fr. (St. Brigid) 289, 290

Manual Stadium 61, 116

Marchell, Fr. 41

Martin, Johnny (Hubbuch's employee) 111

Mattingly, Eudora 305

Melcom family 123

Messmer family 336

Meyer, Charles 48

Meyer family 77, 137, 177, 362

Middleton, Maj. Gen. Troy H. xi, 14

Miller, Jimmie 160

Miller, Mildred 187

Milton Avenue 208

Missing In Action 29, 303, 352, 420, 464

Moorcamp family 213

Moorkamp family 427

Mud Daubers Negro football team 119

Muerr family 36

Mulberry Street 300, 320
    #834 1, 425
    #1137 1, 341, 420, 438

Murr, Cletus 38, 39, 43, 57, 211

Murr family 83, 119, 209

Muth, Betsy 1, 31, 37, 38, 132, 140, 147, 204, 205, 243, 261, 267, 274, 301, 319, 324, 335, 339, 363, 409, 415, 417, 426, 436, 451, 455, 461, 462

Muth, Catherine or "Katsy" 1, 36, 39, 41, 42, 52, 65, 82, 93, 100, 119, 140, 165, 190, 192, 204, 215, 240, 243, 258, 261, 265, 304, 317, 319, 330, 338, 345, 352, 409, 414, 426, 438, 455

Muth, Elizabeth or Lip (Rawert) 1, 4, 88, 138, 144, 213, 250, 258, 263, 273, 426, 427

Muth, James or "Jimmy" 1, 38, 61, 78, 83, 87, 96, 100, 106, 112, 126, 127, 164, 212, 223, 250, 292, 300, 305, 336, 409, 461, 463

Muth, Leo J. & Elizabeth family 162, 186, 192, 196, 246, 295

Muth, Leo J. or "Moody" 1, 24, 71, 87, 141, 243, 358, 427

Muth, Margaret or "Margie" 1, 30, 117, 136, 147, 186, 197, 200, 205, 212, 218, 246, 268, 271, 288, 291, 297, 323, 344, 346, 360, 425, 426, 434, 435, 459

Muth, Milton 1, 62, 82, 84, 86, 87, 119, 147, 159, 165, 166, 227, 228, 250, 251, 259, 268, 269, 273, 275, 276, 299, 301, 303, 305, 306, 315, 318, 319, 322, 323, 325, 330, 337, 354, 360, 367, 409, 410, 417, 431

Muth, Rudy & Bell family 2, 89, 117, 138, 175, 197, 198, 250, 251, 279, 350, 352

Muth's Candy Store 2, 28, 112, 113, 152, 304, 305

Muth, Shirley 1, 2, 20, 24, 27, 28, 30, 32, 35, 36, 41, 49, 53, 61, 62, 64, 65, 67, 73, 82, 107, 108, 147, 151, 165, 183, 185, 197, 199, 204, 234, 240, 244, 258, 293, 298, 304, 305, 335, 338, 341, 358, 367, 409, 417

Nattermann family 308

Nazi 123

Nazis 338, 413, 416

Neblett, Dr. 122

Nervous disorders. *See* PTSD; *See* PTSD

Netherlands

    Battle of Achen 430, 438

    Battle of Arnhem 419, 422

Neuner family 29, 36, 128

Nichols General Hospital 328

Niemann family 180, 204, 233, 248, 272, 294

Nienhaus, Josefa 18

Nieters, Fr. 287

Noel, Bro. (St. X) 319, 326

Nord, Fr. (St. E) 277

Normandy Invasion 13, 17, 398

Nottermann family 151

Nunn family 197, 225, 299, 334, 338

Nunn, Howard 189

Oberhausen family 60, 246, 268, 406, 417, 454, 463

Oertel's '92 2, 33, 65, 176, 241, 247, 262, 412

Operation Cobra xii, 14, 15, 402, 411

Operation Market Garden 15

Operation Overlord 7

Orrill family (neighbor) 85, 100, 266, 272, 279, 290, 358, 363, 414, 431

Palmer, Mr. (English teacher) 57

Pannas (German scrapple) 91, 247

Paris 423

Park and Tilford Distillery 2, 7, 25, 81, 83, 95, 132, 137, 139, 192, 231, 381, 432

Patton, Lt. Gen. George S. xii, 8, 365, 400, 402

Paul family 48, 94, 177, 187, 227, 237, 288, 304

peace 25, 36, 320

Peek, Rev. 208

Peter-Burghout 178

Pierce, Agnes Mitchell (Alma's mom) 90, 121, 429

Pierce, Alma vii, xii, 4, 9, 19, 20, 22, 25, 26, 27, 28, 29, 30, 31, 32, 33, 34, 35, 36, 37, 43, 44, 45, 46, 47, 48, 49, 50, 52, 53, 54, 55, 56, 58, 60, 61, 62, 63, 64, 65, 67, 70, 71, 74, 79, 80, 85, 86, 87, 88, 89, 90, 93, 95, 97, 98, 101, 103, 106, 108, 110, 111, 112, 113, 114, 115, 118, 119, 120, 121, 122, 123, 124, 125, 126, 127, 128, 129, 130, 133, 134, 136, 137, 138, 140, 142, 144, 145, 146, 147, 148, 149, 154, 155, 156, 159, 160, 161, 162, 163, 164, 166, 167, 168, 169, 170, 171, 174, 175, 177, 180, 181, 182, 183, 185, 186, 187, 189, 190, 191, 194, 196, 200, 201, 202, 207, 209, 210, 212, 214, 215, 216, 217, 218, 220, 221, 222, 226, 228, 229, 230, 231, 233, 235, 241, 242, 243, 249, 250, 251, 254, 256, 258, 273, 278, 279, 283, 290, 291, 293, 294, 297, 298, 299, 302, 304, 306, 307, 309, 310, 312, 316, 332, 333, 343, 353, 354, 356, 357, 358, 359, 362, 363, 372, 373, 374, 376, 380, 381, 388, 396, 397, 403, 404, 405, 409, 414, 418, 423, 427, 428, 429, 435, 436, 439, 440, 445, 457, 458, 460, 464, 465, 466

Plainview Farms Dairy 2, 152, 298

POWs (Prisoners of War) 142, 280, 315, 325, 457, 464

Preston Street 330

PTSD or Post Traumatic Stress Disorder xiii

Raibel 57

rationing 46, 51, 129, 133, 139, 141, 144, 148, 177, 190, 211, 217, 223, 230, 235, 238, 239, 243, 249, 264, 266, 283, 293, 296, 300, 304, 311, 347, 428

Rauch, Fr. 92

Rawert, Ann (Smith) 1, 238, 244, 436

Rawert, Catherine, "Katie" or "Mommy" 1, 44, 50, 56, 89, 102, 120, 130, 132, 138, 153, 164, 168, 185, 191, 195, 215, 216, 219, 228,

242, 259, 260, 262, 266, 268, 269, 274, 292, 296, 303, 348, 353, 360, 364, 365, 366, 381, 388, 401, 425, 427, 430, 433, 445, 448, 460

Rawert, Catherine (1916-1918) 4

Rawert, Cousin Mary 123, 128, 175, 356, 407

Rawert, Eleanor (Smith) 1, 151, 159, 184

Rawert. Elizabeth (daughter of Frank & Elizabeth) 301

Rawert, Frank (Herman's brother) 301, 307

Rawert, Henry 4, 117

Rawert, Henry (son of Frank & Elizabeth) 301

Rawert, Herman or "Poppy" 27, 43, 46, 49, 85, 87, 150, 169, 181, 226, 229, 234, 235, 274, 275, 281, 287, 290, 293, 295, 303, 323, 331, 341, 345, 376, 410, 417, 438

Rawert, Hermina 1, 4, 19, 235, 239, 353

Rawert, Hilary 1, 238, 240, 248, 279, 291, 297, 326, 343, 346, 347

Rawert, JoAnn 397, 413, 420, 425

Rawert, John 1, 4, 152, 184, 235, 242, 298

Rawert, John & Eleanor family 26, 41, 58, 75, 87, 91, 151, 248, 259, 261, 308, 337, 342, 362, 416, 455

Rawert, John or "Jack", 1, 99, 240, 249, 253, 259, 263, 279, 315, 346, 364

Rawert, Joseph & Ann family 19, 34, 57, 68, 73, 75, 189, 204, 264, 288, 389

Rawert, Josephine or "Joey" (wife of Lee Carter) 1, 4, 108, 110, 131, 186, 188, 247, 431, 434, 445, 448

Rawert, Joseph or "Joe" 1, 4, 52, 61, 63, 79, 99, 103, 119, 120, 123, 127, 137, 145, 148, 149, 156, 158, 166, 194, 204, 205, 228, 233, 235, 238, 244, 287, 318

Rawert, Margaret, "Marge" or "Maah" 1, 4, 78, 128, 315, 333, 350, 352, 375, 413

Rawert, Mary (daughter of Frank & Elizabeth) 356

Rawert, Mary (Frank & Elizabeth's daughter) 147

Rawert, Mary or "Cousin Mary" 60

Rawert, Norbert A., Jr. xii

Rawert, Norbert A., Sr. 7, 17, 24, 433

   American Red Cross Hospital (England) 438, 439

   basic training 7, 32

   clerk duties 7, 25, 141, 157, 182

   combat course & maneuvers 351, 372

   combat course/maneuvers 288

   departure from NY, NY to England 7

   disgust with US Army 96, 99, 227, 282

   foxholes and tents 349

   foxholes & tents 244, 270, 344, 345, 350, 351, 401

   health issues 448

   HQ Co. 59th Signal Battalion 356

   inducted into Army 19

   morale in Army 284, 422, 424

   nervous disorder in combat 439

   Private First Class 7

   promo to Corporal 7, 89, 245

   rest in Luxembourg hotel 432

   Sharpshooter award 44

   Somewhere in Belgium 424, 427, 432

   Somewhere in England 385

   Somewhere in France 399

   Somewhere in Normandy 400

   Technical school 28

   telegraph/teletype class 282, 284

   transfer to HQ CO. 59th Signal BN 7

   US Army Hospital 439

   VIII Corps, Co C, La Haye-du-Puits 13

Rawert, Norbert or "Norby" (son of John) 1, 260, 263, 266, 295, 299, 415

Rawert, Peggy 1, 235, 251, 279, 313

Rawert, Vernon 1, 159, 184, 235, 260, 263, 279

Redd 77

Reddick, Katie 178, 187, 271

Reddle family 58, 126, 207, 242

Red Front Store (Goss Ave.) 123, 305

Redle family 286, 317, 341, 365, 387

Redmann family 262

Reem family 149, 179

Rell 59

Renn 310, 311, 316, 325

Res, Mr. (Chuck-de-Chuck) 266

Rhodes family 131, 133, 221, 226

Richardson, Dr. 298

Rich family 420

Rickenbacker, Capt. Eddie 158

Robben family 174, 359

Robmann family 190

Rodmann 61

Roosevelt, Eleanor 307

Roosevelt, Pres. Franklin D. 89, 212, 414

Roth family 359

Rudolph's Candy Company 152

Rueff, Fr. 344, 426

Russell family (Texas St.) 31, 49, 63, 69, 101,
    111, 118, 136, 148, 149, 160, 162, 164, 168,
    189, 197, 199, 206, 207, 210, 216, 243,
    246, 257, 262, 265, 266, 281, 296, 300,
    331, 337, 370, 428, 441

Russia/Russians 192, 213, 320, 321, 354,
    392, 421

Russmann Funeral Home 181

Sabel, John & family 272

Sacraments 1, 27, 42, 56, 106, 114, 127, 132,
    153, 162, 168, 218, 252, 256, 260, 274,
    319, 329, 340, 353, 366

Saint Anthony Hospital 302

Saint Boniface Catholic Church & School) 42

Saint Brigid Catholic Church & School 1, 50,
    90, 181, 196, 213, 287, 376

Saint Elizabeth Catholic Church & School 2,
    61, 64, 86, 137, 143, 146, 236, 268, 279,
    284, 295, 326, 416

Saint Joseph Infirmary 118, 123, 233

Saint Joseph Orphans' Picnic 310

Saint Martin of Tours Catholic Church &
    School 3, 124, 417

Saint Michael Cemetery 117, 279, 437

Saint Theresa Catholic Church & School 112,
    287, 295

Saint Xavier High School 45, 84, 160, 243,
    318, 359, 410, 428

Sandford, Fr. Joseph 221

Saunders, Eileen 37

Saunders family 443

Scally/Skallie 202

Schaefer family 327

Schaldant family 130

Schenkenfelder family 48, 95

Schieman family 149, 178, 209, 294, 393

Schieman's Grocery (Texas St.) 133, 144, 150,
    158, 209, 238, 283, 347, 463

Schlegel family 41, 104, 338

Schlegel (janitor) 97

Schmidt family 26, 27, 33

Schmidt, Fritz 26, 48, 54

Schnitzelburg xi, xii, xiii, xv, xvi, 1, 17, 32, 84,
    89, 95, 123, 130, 193, 216, 293, 372, 380,
    384, 390

Schnurr 410

Scholtz 84

Schott family 242

Schultz 168

Schutz 59, 61

Seb family 242

Sgroi family 143

Shanks 163

Shaughness family 243

Shaugnessy family 332, 464

Sheeran 178

Sheer, Carmel 407

Shelby Street 293

Shepard Place 64

sinking of AC Carrier Courier Wasp 109

Sister Cornila (St. E.) 54

Slattery, Maurice 166, 222, 316, 333

Smith, Fritz 38, 44

Soam, Dr. 46

Sounders, Thelma 419

Southwestern Bell Telephone Company, Kansas
    City, MO 7

Speckner family 202

Spoelker, Antoinette or "Ante" (wife of R.
    Hensle) 67, 88, 129, 133, 198, 224, 226

Spoelker family 86, 142, 198, 233, 234, 235,
    236, 239, 249, 307, 316, 331

Spoelker, Fr. Bernard (cousin) 49, 50, 86, 124, 142, 154, 193, 198, 244, 297, 316, 357, 413, 463

Standard Oil Company 362

State family 107, 238, 243

State, Francis (m. Anna M. Logsdon) 34

Steinmetz, Ann 151

Steinmetz family 95, 186, 253, 277, 337, 411

Stengel family 197, 431

Stevens, Dr. 41

Stevens, Eddie 35

Stevens family 147

Stites, Dr. 46, 88, 90, 202, 204, 268, 296, 303

Stratman, Frank 45, 51

Stuckenborg family 46, 83

Summershein family 322, 327

Sutcliffe's 104, 408, 414, 418

Tanner family 180, 181

Tap's Corner 339

Taps (local tavern) 100

Taystee's 323

Teske 102

Texas Street 79, 83, 320, 428

    #1344 1, 238, 244

Threedouble family (neighbors) 43, 326, 449

Tindall family 43

Toby family 213

Tully, Dr. 178

Twin Lakes 396

US Army

    59th Signal Battalion 13, 350

    After Action Against Enemy Report 398

    First Army xi, 14

    HQ Co. 59th Signal BN xii

    HQ CO Signal BN with Third Army 402

    Ninth Army xii

    Signal Corps 125

    Third Army xii

    VIII Corps xi, 14, 398

    VIII Corps reassigned to Ninth Army 15

    VIII Corps support of Third Army 15

    XII Corps 351

Utah Beach xi

Vetter (maried to T. Harman) 281

Victory Garden 246

Von Haven, Dr. 226, 339

Wachtel family 43, 55

Wachtel, James 38, 44, 47, 53, 72

Wafzig family 83, 91, 93, 119, 123, 175, 322, 327, 429

Wakeman General and Convalescent Hospital xii

war 2, 134, 248, 342, 354, 386, 393, 402, 413, 417, 419, 424, 457

Watkins 304

Weland family 71

Welsh, Aidon 2

Werner family 342, 422

Wessenger-Gaulbert Apartments 41

Wessling family (relatives) 27, 80, 117, 118, 120, 126, 188, 315, 331, 341

WHAS Louisville radio station 99, 105, 308, 391, 421

White Cottage 94, 111, 119, 198, 233, 247

Willenburg family 198, 202

Williams, Althea (Smith) 419

Williams, Carl (Althea Smith's husband) 415

Williams, Dr. 151

Wise family 143

Wise, Randall (Norb's coworker & friend) 2, 7

Wolskerman 1, 3, 4, 5

Woodbine Street 330

World War I xii

World War II xiii, xv

    Censors xvi

Wright family 242

WW II

    Battle of Achen 426

Wynn, Dr. 371

Zink the meat man 201

Zipperle family 26, 30, 33, 42, 88, 119, 122, 125, 127, 128, 136, 189, 253, 320, 334, 337, 339, 370, 407, 417, 435